PATTERNS OF ANARCHY

LEONARD I. KRIMERMAN received his B.A. and his Ph.D. in philosophy at Cornell University, where for two years he was a teaching assistant in moral philosophy. He is presently an assistant professor of philosophy at Louisiana State University in New Orleans. He is a member of the Southern Society for Philosophy and Psychology and the Southwestern Philosophical Society and has written articles which appeared in *The Southern Journal of Philosophy* and *Philosophical Studies*.

LEWIS PERRY received his M.S. in industrial relations and his Ph.D. in history at Cornell University, and he is presently with the Department of History at the State University of New York at Buffalo. Mr. Perry has written for *Industrial and Labor Relations Research* and *International Journal of Social Psychiatry*.

PATTERNS
OF ANARCHY

A COLLECTION OF WRITINGS ON
THE ANARCHIST TRADITION

Edited by
Leonard I. Krimerman
Lewis Perry

ANCHOR BOOKS
DOUBLEDAY & COMPANY, INC., GARDEN CITY, NEW YORK

The Anchor Books edition is the first publication
of PATTERNS OF ANARCHY: A Collection of Writings
on the Anarchist Tradition
Anchor Books edition: 1966
Library of Congress Catalog Card Number 66–12231
Printed in the United States of America

For
Samuel and Mina Krimerman,
Albert and Irene Perry

ACKNOWLEDGMENTS

Our research was furthered by the assistance of two libraries: the Cornell University Library in Ithaca, New York, and the Tamiment Institute Library in New York City.

It would have been impossible to prepare this anthology without the cooperation of the Freedom Press (17a Maxwell Road, London, S.W.6, England) and the Libertarian League (P.O. Box 261, New York 3, N.Y.). Although we had no previous contact with either group, both enthusiastically helped us, especially by sending great quantities of material that would be hard to find in most libraries. Any student of anarchism would be well advised to get in touch with them. We are also indebted to the *Catholic Worker* for the loan of rare and fragile back issues. Mr. Krimerman is grateful for a supporting grant from the American Philosophical Society. The help of Rosemary Stoehr in typing a great deal of the manuscript, with only the distant prospect of payment, has made us more than ever appreciative of anarchist principles.

Our greatest debts are to our wives Ruth and Eleano.

CONTENTS

SECTION VI: THE ANARCHISTS ON EDUCATION

FOREWORD

When arguments among delegates stalled the Pennsylvania constitutional convention for several months in its business of setting up a new government, life in the commonwealth passed uneventfully. Benjamin Franklin is said to have warned the delegates: "Gentlemen, you see that in the anarchy in which we live society manages much as before. Take care, if our disputes last too long, that the people do not come to think that they can very easily do without us."

Franklin spoke in jest, of course, and would have viewed the loss of the services of government as a calamity. The story may even be apocryphal. But it still illustrates a readiness of distinctions between society and the state which by now have come to appear quite fantastic. Few today entertain either hope or fear that government might be abolished as easily as it was called into being. Modern governments conduct mammoth enterprises in space, control power over incredible rates of overkill, and reach throughout the economy as the biggest business. Somehow the historical sources of anarchism—the American Revolution's demonstration that the state is man-made, the French Revolution's assault on rank and privilege, religious strivings toward perfectionism, philosophical scrutiny of absolute liberty—all have fallen beneath the weight of modern government. Occasionally a civil rights worker or a communist is charged with "criminal anarchy," but the words seem as little able to scare as to inspire. Franklin's joke sounds remote or silly.

Perhaps it is strange, then, that the peace movements, the civil rights struggles, and the agitation of students for unshackled education have evinced vague feelings of affinity to anarchism. In addition, disillusionment with special pleading for Russia and China—as well as fresh strains of authoritarianism in newly liberated nations—has raised further interest in left-wing alternatives to Marxism. A spate of books and articles on anarchism suggests that reawakened concern is not restricted to enthusiastic undergraduates. A sluggish bureaucracy has cast suspicion on the state itself. However, increasing interest does not seem to have encouraged serious examination of anarchist doctrines. Rather, there have been wistful gestures toward an appreciation of anarchism as a noble impossibility, fainthearted ponderings of its literature as a source of incidental insights. It is all as if a coherent view of man and society is too chimerical a goal to be pursued rigorously. The best one can hope for is a good turn of phrase here, some handy categories there. Our governments are too complicated, and our societies too chaotic, to permit more than a faltering motion toward generalization.

Some may feel that this anthology goes against the grain, for we are determined to take anarchism seriously. We have become more and more amazed at how many perceptive social theorists have spoken in the anarchist tradition. We have tried to restore anarchism to its rightful place as more than a rejection of politics, indeed as a rewarding full-scale theory of human conduct. Wistful appreciation and incidental insights are not enough. Any position as fruitful as anarchism merits the respect of an effort to arrange its principles and proposals in a way that facilitates appraisal. In fact, durable insights can follow only from an understanding of why men of vastly different temperaments have committed themselves to this position.

We have departed from our original plan of the book in one respect. A projected section on "Historical Rise and Reactions" refused to fall into shape. There are competent histories of anarchism, which we mention elsewhere, and chronological arrays of documentary selections add little to them. (The literature on anarchism by police captains, newspapermen, judges, and chance observers is enormous.) Our selections, on the other hand, do enable sustained examination of patterns of anarchist thought, a subject the histories tend to brush aside. Moreover, such an approach diminishes the temptation to reduce anarchism to a gallery of outlandish stereotypes.

That temptation is common to both those few who can still shrink from anarchism in horror and those whose dispositions are more favorable. In either case, the point that anarchists offer seriously a system of thought is lost. Since most of the stereotypes surely have some validity, they will here be portrayed briefly; then it may be asked what relation they bear to anarchist theories.

First, anarchists have appeared as seditious lunatics, intent on bomb-throwing and tumultuous upheaval. Max Nomad has remembered a Geneva fanatic who proposed demolishing schools to destroy the bourgeois class of the future. Second is the contrasting portrait of the non-violent anarchist saint. British writers praised Prince Kropotkin's disinterested gentleness. Leo Tolstoy chose the life of a peasant rather than risk the mildest exploitation of his fellow men.

A third stereotype is that of the doctrinaire zealot whose inflexibility, though it did not lead to violence, was self-defeating. There were anarchists who criticized the editorial direction of Johann Most in his own newspaper; the anarchist ideal, they claimed, was a "spontaneous newspaper." More poignant is the example of the obscure tailor, F. Bruner, who asked to be heard by a congressional committee investigating the labor problems of the 1870s. His testimony took less than a page to print, for he could only advise the legislators to retire, to abolish the executive and judicial branches too, and to relinquish all political functions to the populace.

There is a fourth portrait; this trait of renouncing power also had its saintly side, which is familiar to those who regard anarchism as noble, however preposterous. Consider the brief statement made by Errico Malatesta upon his return to Italy after the First World War. His reception was described as overwhelming, and many held that his word would ignite the revolution in his homeland. Malatesta responded in an article called *"Grazie, Ma Basta,"* Thank You, But Enough.

> During the agitation that took place for my return, and during these first days since my return to Italy, things have been done and said which offend my modesty and sense of proportion.
>
> The comrades should remember that the hyperbole is a rhetorical figure of speech which should not be abused. They should above all remember that the exaltation of a man is potentially a dangerous thing and morally unhealthy as much for him who is exalted as for those who do the exalting.
>
> And then I am so made that I find hand-clapping and cheering unpleasant, tending to paralyze me rather than encouraging me to work.
>
> I want to be a comrade among comrades, and if I have the misfortune of being older than others it cannot please me to be continually reminded of this by the deference and attentions which the comrades inflict on me.
>
> Do we understand one another?

There are other stereotypes in the gallery, and among them is one that goes almost unnoticed. It is of the anarchist at his desk working to perfect his critique of society's present form of organization and his itinerary for renovation. For this book, this neglected aspect of anarchism is central. The stereotypes mentioned above are important for the questions they raise about anarchist doctrines (Are violence and futility necessary outcomes of anarchist ideas? Are peace and saintliness possible without anarchism?). But vague images of anarchist personalities are not useful substitutes for inspection of the ways in which anarchist thinkers have explained their convictions.

The arrangement of selections in this anthology deserves some explanation. We have, of course, included something from most of the famous exponents of anarchism—Tolstoy, Godwin, Bakunin, Kropotkin, Goldman, Goodman. We have also tried to call attention to some anarchists who merit equal fame—especially the Americans, Josiah Warren, Adin Ballou, Lysander Spooner, Stephen Pearl Andrews, and Benjamin R. Tucker. But we have resisted the obvious method of choosing a major statement by each author and placing it according to doctrine or chronology. Instead we have isolated the chief problems arising in an evaluation of the anarchist position and allowed these problems to shape our selections into intelligible units.

Logically, the task of defining anarchism seemed to come first. The brief section on definitions shows that the desire to abolish government has excited controversy among anarchists over the concepts of liberty and authority. These controversies reappear, and are possibly resolved, in libertarian approaches to problems in subsequent sections: thus they provide many integrating themes for the entire book. The insights in subsequent sections are often produced by the dialogue among various groups denying to one another the right to the name of anarchist.

The second section, containing classical anarchist attacks on socialism, serves several purposes. For one thing, much of the sharpest anarchist writing has been done on this subject; for another, it is helpful to dispose early of the notion that anarchism is only an outpost on the frontiers of socialism. Our third section discloses the philosophical foundations of anarchist doctrines. It turns out that some of the disputes revealed in the section on definitions are truly basic, at the same time that it becomes evident that none of the schools of

anarchism is a mere stance or unreasoned expression of sentiment. All forms of anarchism are carefully grounded in principles of human excellence and social justice.

The next two sections are concerned with the application
of these philosophical principles. The fourth section contains
examples of the main ways in which anarchists have attacked
the evils of established authority. Here again differences
emerge: some emphasize the use of force, some the strait-
jacket of moral conviction, some economic exploitation. But
all have keyed their sense of injustice to a conviction that
government must be eradicated. The fifth section explores
anarchist recommendations of alternatives to government. It
is not given over to utopian visions; we have been surprised
at how seldom anarchism has indulged its fancy in that direction. Most of the section describes specific activities
which anarchists have maintained are pathways to renovating
society.

To permit further inspection of anarchist alternatives, the
sixth section concentrates on writings about education, both
attacks upon prevailing methods and defenses of anarchist
possibilities. On this subject anarchist writers have excelled,
and here the present-day relevance of anarchist ideas seems
unquestionable. We have another motive for the choice of
education; it is a subject that promises to raise grave questions about the soundness of anarchist thought. For example,
how can anarchist education avoid the danger of coercing the
young, especially if the inculcation of correct moral views is
essential to abolishing the state? The section, we believe,
provides materials to face such questions.

Throughout the first six sections we have aimed at letting
the various kinds of anarchists advance the most cogent arguments that they have yet devised. But we have not felt confident, as might anthologists on other subjects, that the reader
will find critical materials easily accessible. Our solution is a
seventh section devoted entirely to objections to anarchism.
Passing over a lot of hysterical reactions, we have tried to
find the most penetrating and reasoned attacks on a wide
range of the problems raised in the preceding sections. (Here
the socialists, among others, get their chance at rebuttal.)

Here then are seven separate approaches to facilitate appraisal of the anarchist position: clarification of its defining
features, observance of its performance in conflict with a set
of adversaries, disclosure of its bedrock standards, attention
to its rigor in indictment, elaboration of its constructive pro-

posals, reflection on its fecundity in dealing at length with a single subject, and testing its ability to withstand a range of criticisms. In the afterword we sketch our own understanding of the anarchist position, seen as a comprehensive alternative on social, economic, and philosophical problems.

A final word about the history of this anthology. Several years ago both editors began to discuss, in deep ignorance, the likelihood that the anarchist position had not been given its due. One of us was analyzing utilitarianism and the notion of liberty; the other was studying the centralization of federal labor policy since the New Deal. Agreed on the likely value of anarchism, we were almost stymied by the paucity of available materials. Slowly the idea of an anthology took hold as we continued to uncover interesting but neglected anarchist writings. Our amazement at the wealth of anarchist literature has been growing ever since. This anthology, we believe, only skims the surface, and we trust it will lead some readers into the materials listed in the bibliography. But even the most resolute reader will meet difficulties. There is a need for new full editions of the best works of Proudhon, Tucker, Kropotkin, and many others, whom the reader can only begin to appreciate here.

PATTERNS OF ANARCHY

SECTION I

Defining Anarchism

The opportunity for anarchist writers to work out all the implications of their doctrines has been repeatedly curtailed by the need to clarify their most elementary beliefs. There are dozens of anarchist tracts with titles like "What is Anarchism?" and still the question may sound futile. Of course anarchism means that government should be destroyed, so why fuss about defining it further? How many different ways can that be said? However barren, the subject has been much discussed because anarchists have struggled against a widespread misconception that their ideas are wholly negative. While much of the strength of this charge has come from its blurriness, it nonetheless has kept anarchist proposals from getting a full hearing.

Here is how Errico Malatesta addressed the problem in his pamphlet "Anarchy":

> Anarchy is a word which comes from the Greek, and signifies, strictly speaking, WITHOUT GOVERNMENT: the state of a people without any constituted authority.
>
> Before such an organization had begun to be considered possible and desirable by a whole class of thinkers, so as to be taken as the aim of a movement . . . the word *anarchy* was used universally in the sense of disorder and confusion, and it is still adopted in that sense by the ignorant and by adversaries interested in distorting the truth. . . .
>
> Nor is this fact without parallel in the history of words. In those epochs and countries where people have considered government by one man (monarchy) necessary, the word *republic* (that is, government of many) has been used precisely like *Anarchy*, to imply disorder and confusion.

To make his meaning clear, Malatesta urged the "abolition of government" but disavowed advocating the "abolition of the state." Some styles of organization should endure or be supplied. Impatient as he was with what he must have

deemed Jesuitical playing with words, Malatesta was hard put
to make it clear that anarchism has a constructive side.

The eleventh edition of the Encyclopædia Britannica assigned the article on "Anarchism" to Peter Kropotkin, the
world's leading anarchist. Kropotkin began: "Anarchism . . .
is the name given to a principle or theory of life and conduct
under which society is conceived without government." Like
Malatesta, he refused to be restricted to a definition of anarchism that was wholly negative, and thus chaotic. In addition,
he defined anarchism as not a movement alone, but also a
theory. If these two points are granted, defining anarchism
ceases to be a barren chore. For it involves identifying principles which have animated a series of popular movements,
both to criticize established institutions and to defend
schemes for constructive change. Surely, we know of no anarchist who has celebrated chaos. Anarchist literature always
argues either that voluntary sources of social order are already
visible or else that when government is abolished new sources
of order will naturally be tapped. Indeed, government itself
is usually blamed for the very chaos which seems to necessitate authority. We are defining a position which has itself
sought the meaning of order and disorder.

Defining anarchism, therefore, brings together criticisms of
existing evils, analyses of government, and programs to re-
generate society. It is also an avenue to clear thinking about
such inescapable concepts as liberty and authority. No movement has attached more weighty significance to these concepts, and no movement has tried them in a hotter crucible.
Viewed in this way, the task of defining anarchism occupies
this entire anthology. The section at hand proceeds from a
general survey of the sources of anarchism to particular inquiries into its compatibility with communism, individualism, syndicalism, Christianity, and liberalism. The selections
raise two general questions. First, is there an anarchist principle of liberty which is inconsistent with principles of authority
lurking in doctrines that have sought combination with anarchism? This question applies to communist-anarchism, for
example, or Catholic anarchism. Second, since anarchism extends beyond mere denunciation of government, how can it
be distinguished from competing theories, faiths, or movements? Here we must consider especially philosophical
liberalism.

At the very least, this section records the diversity of expression that a supposedly negative doctrine has let loose.

That is, it provides materials to interpret the squabbles that have set anarchists against one another. For some readers, this will feed a taste for irony. We would insist, however, that one cheats himself if he tries only to catalogue anarchists. There is some danger of drawing lines more hard and fast than they actually are and ignoring the agreement that gives substance to anarchism. Further, so simple an endeavor loses sight of a more intriguing question: what issues meant so much as to cause these rebels to erect a forum for debate within their own movement?

1   The Sources and Varieties of Anarchism

Historians have not yet told us all they might about the sources of inspiration for anarchism. James Joll's recent history, *The Anarchists*, makes a stab at the problem: "Although the anarchist movement is a phenomenon of the past century and a half, it represents a type of revolt that can be found far earlier. The anarchists themselves are proud of this ancestry, and lay claims to many a forerunner who would have been surprised to find himself in their company." But a lead review in the *Times Literary Supplement* questioned whether we know that the forerunners would have been surprised and not delighted. The question is important because tight definition of anarchism as a modern political movement involves "the disadvantage that in these terms one gets the impression that anarchism came from nowhere and has gone nowhere." The reviewer recommended that "current anarchist literature" be read in conjunction with the historical account; we have presented many contemporary articles in this anthology fo the same reason. But that still leaves the impression that anarchism came from nowhere. One of the few scholars to face this problem is D. Novak, in the essay reprinted here.

There is a difficult distinction to be made between locating historical sources and making formal definitions; this selection reveals that there may be historical connections between anarchism and other doctrines that in subsequent selections are viewed as formally incompatible with anarchist positions.

Anarchism is one of those concepts about which there generally is deep ignorance or profound misunderstanding. "In the popular mind," says Bertrand Russell, "an Anarchist is a person who throws bombs and commits other outrages, either because he is more or less insane, or because he uses the pretence of extreme political opinions as a cloak for criminal proclivities." Yet in the history of political thought, as well as

"The Place of Anarchism in the History of Political Thought," by D. Novak, from *The Review of Politics* XX:3 (July, 1958), 307–20. Reprinted by permission of *The Review of Politics*.

in the history of social movements, anarchism has played a
role which cannot be overlooked. . . .

The essence of anarchist thought is the emphasis on the
freedom of the individual, leading to the denial and condemnation of any authority which hinders his free and full
development, particularly the State. The rejection of all authority represents the main contribution of anarchism to political thought and distinguishes it from other political and
social theories some of which, for example, liberalism, may
have other features similar to anarchism, and may even start
from the same basis. Bound up with these fundamental ideas
are the theories and criticisms of law and government, of
property, of the whole social and economic system and patterns of behavior prevalent in it, and of the ways and means
suggested or preached as remedies or panaceas for the evils.
Underlying all these thoughts and constantly present in them,
whether explicitly or implicitly, are views of human nature.
It may, then, be suggested that the various anarchist trends
have in common a belief in individual freedom and a denial
of authority, especially in the form of the State. In the development of these fundamental ideas, however, there are
differences among anarchists relating to the questions of government, law, property, social and economic institutions, revolutions, and so on. They also—and this, at first sight, may
seem incongruous—have varying views on human nature. . . .

Some writers on anarchism have attempted to trace anarchist ideas in thinkers and movements of the Western world
from ancient times. One may not accept many claims made
by these writers but, particularly in view of the largely critical
and negative attitude of anarchism to social arrangements,
one must be prepared to encounter anarchist traits in different, and sometimes even contradictory, ideas and systems of
thought. Thus, as in the case of liberalism or socialism, it
can be seen that views akin to anarchism, and sometimes
clearly anarchist, have been formed in the West from the
times of the ancient Greeks to the nineteenth century in both
the secular and religious spheres. . . .

The Stoic ideals of individualism, rationalism, and equality, of the fraternity of men, world citizenship, and cosmo-
politanism . . . remind one of the ideals enunciated by anarchism. Some fundamental tenets of the philosophy of the
founder of Stoicism, Zeno of Citium (336–264 B.C.), bear
such affinity to anarchist communism that he may be called
its forerunner. He proclaimed the supremacy of the moral law

and opposed to Plato's State communism his own ideal of a free community without government. Together with the self-preservation instinct which leads to egoism there is in man, in Zeno's view, the social instinct which makes him join others and co-operate with them for the common good. If men followed their natural instincts, they would live in peace and harmony with their neighbors and there would be no need of coercive institutions. Law courts, police, armies, temples and priests, and even money, would be unnecessary. Men would reach a stateless society of perfect equality and freedom, in which the original attributes of human nature would attain their full expression, so that universal harmony would extend over the whole world.

During the Middle Ages and for several decades following the Reformation the enunciation of ideas attracting the attention of a student of anarchism must be perceived in their broader religious context. During uprisings and rebellions, such as that of 1381 in England, some drastic measures undoubtedly were advocated, but one may be easily mistaken in considering them anarchist.

One of the effects of the Renaissance, and partly also of a reaction to the Reformation in secular matters, was a revival of anti-authoritarian tendencies in the writings of such men as Rabelais, Fénelon and de la Boétie, whose kinship to anarchism has not passed unclaimed. The same can be said about the ideas of the eighteenth century rationalists, above all the French Encyclopedists. Their concepts of rationality, natural law, natural rights, and the freedom of the individual, are not only essential tenets of the liberal doctrine, but also elements which the liberals and anarchists share, although with a different emphasis. In their enthusiasm, however, the French rationalists sometimes voiced clearly anarchist sentiments, as did Diderot, for instance, in his famous remark, "*La nature n'a fait ni serviteurs ni maitres, je ne veux ni donner ni recevoir des lois.*" It must not be forgotten, either, that, no matter what else can be said about Rousseau's romanticism, its idealization of the state of nature and its criticism of organized society in the several *Discourses* suggest its affinity to anarchism. . . .

In common with secular anarchism, religious anarchism attacks and rejects authority exercised by men over men, but it differs from secular anarchism in deriving its conclusions from the Scriptures, as understood and interpreted by the individual or a group of like-minded individuals. To most people,

religious anarchism is associated with the name of Leo Tolstoy, but more or less pronounced anarchist traits can be detected in the ideas and practices of various Christian sects
and groups. . . . Thus the Waldenses and the Albigenses in
the twelfth and thirteenth centuries, some sections of the
Hussites in the early fifteenth century, and the Anabaptists
and the early Quakers in the sixteenth and seventeenth centuries, refused to submit to the commands of the secular
powers when they believed them to violate Christian principles. They condemned war and capital punishment, and refused to obey some laws or to take the oath. Starting from
the affirmation of the equality of men, they proclaimed the
individual's right to interpret the Bible for himself, postu-
lating, explicitly or implicitly, the possibility of the individual's attainment of the "inner light," of seeing things for
himself, which is also assumed in anarchist individualism.
The refusal of some Anabaptists and the early Quakers to
uncover their heads in the presence of kings or magistrates,
as well as the Quaker habit of addressing others as "thou" and
not "you," is another example of this equalitarianism and
individualism. So is also the emphasis on the voluntary basis
of their group life, again evident among the Anabaptists and
the Quakers, expressed in the opposition to the Church (the
designation of the Quaker groups as the Society of Friends
is significant here), and connected with the custom of election of preachers by the congregation or of having no preachers at all. . . .

Among some of the sects, especially when times were
deemed unfavorable, there arose chiliastic views whose vision
of the future bears some resemblance to the anarchist picture of a Stateless society. The millennarians, as Troeltsch
calls them, "looked for the advent of Christ, and for the setting up of the true Kingdom of the 'Saints', without priest
or sacrament, law or oath, king or government, for the kingdom of the complete Christian anarchy of love." Chiliasm
appeared among the Hussites, some of whom strongly believed in the coming of a millennium without kings or other
rulers, without laws, taxes, and other forms of oppression,
when God's law would rule supreme, as well as among the
Anabaptists after the Münster disaster of 1525. It was the
core of the beliefs of the Fifth Monarchy Men in England
in Cromwell's times who, like some anarchist revolutionaries,
expected much destruction to take place before mankind
could be ushered into the millennium. The Fifth Monarchy

Men were naturally targets of much criticism and hostility. . . .

It is clear that modern anarchism has had its intellectual predecessors. It should, however, be pointed out that one may be easily misled into attributing anarchist elements to anti-authoritarian principles which themselves are only parts of a wider philosophy without any deep affinity to anarchism, or which are only fragmentary. Sometimes the anti-authoritarian ideas have been held only vaguely, being based on a belief in a past Golden Age when human nature was not corrupted and everybody lived in happiness and plenty—a belief which was given classic expression by Ovid. Among members of some religious sects this attitude was connected with the belief in the original sinlessness of man and his happy existence in Paradise. Occasionally, when projected into the future, it gave rise to a belief in the millennium which was to come and return to man his lost happiness.

With the publication, in 1793, of William Godwin's *An Enquiry Concerning Political Justice and Its Influence on General Virtue and Happiness*, there began a systematic elaboration and formulation of modern anarchist thought, based upon a comprehensive analysis of the economic, political and social factors, as well as upon scientific, ethical and philosophical thought. This elaboration and presentation was effected, after Godwin, chiefly by Proudhon, Bakunin, Stirner, Tucker, Tolstoy, and Kropotkin. Other anarchist writers, for instance, Elisée Reclus, Errico Malatesta, Jean Grave, Domela Nieuwenhuis, A. Hamon, Max Nettlau, Emma Goldman, Alexander Berkman, and others, draw mainly on their work. Apart from Tolstoy's religious anarchism, the theorists of anarchism adhere mostly to anarcho-communism, and some also to anarcho-syndicalism and anarcho-individualism.

Since the latter part of the last century anarchism has taken predominantly the anarcho-communistic form advocated by Peter Kropotkin (1842–1921), whose ideas are in many respects related to those of William Godwin (1756–1836), Pierre Joseph Proudhon (1809–1865), probably the first man to call himself an anarchist, and Michael Bakunin (1814–1876). The term "anarchist communism" was coined by Peter Kropotkin who first advocated its use at an international anarchist congress in Switzerland in 1880, believing that it conveyed the idea of unity or harmony between individual freedom and a "well-ordered" social life. Anarchist communism views the individual as essentially a social being who can achieve full development only in society, while society can benefit only when its members are free. Individual and social interests are not contradictory but complementary and would attain their natural harmony if authoritarian social institutions, particularly the State, established to create and perpetuate the privileges of some at the expense of others, did not interfere.

Anarcho-syndicalism lays emphasis on the economic as opposed to the political struggle of the working class. It believes that the trade unions, or syndicates, can serve both as leading units in the present-day struggle for the amelioration of the conditions of the workers, and as the bases of a new economic organization of society after a victorious revolution, in which the General Strike is to play the leading part. The anarcho-syndicalists intend to abolish the State and carry on the activities of society through the syndicates, associated by industries and localities. Syndicalism has been an important part of the working class movement in France, especially since the congress in Limoges in 1895, and before the Civil War in Spain in 1936–1939 the anarcho-syndicalist movement was also strong in that country. Anarcho-syndicalism has produced no outstanding theoretician of its own, and its principles are sometimes accepted by anarcho-communists in their approach to the economic problems of society.

The two outstanding representatives of anarchist individualism are Max Stirner (1806–1856) in Germany and Benjamin Tucker (1854–1939) in the United States of America. Stirner developed his views in *Der Einzige und sein Eigentum*, published in Leipzig in 1845. The core of his message was the proclamation of the absolute freedom of the individual. The individual has the right to do whatever he wants, and everything that would curtail his freedom must be fought against. Stirner is not only against the State, the law and private property, but also against many concepts, such as God, country, family, and love, because they claim the individual's allegiance and thus limit his freedom. He did not condemn all ideals as useless, but emphasized that they should be pursued for purely egoistic reasons, for the pleasure and happiness of the individual, and not because they were a duty. He advocated an "association of egoists," which individuals could freely enter to pursue their particular interests, and leave when and as they pleased. Men should undergo an inward change, come to the realization of their own individuality and their own good, and by a violent insurrection overthrow the existing system.

Tucker started with the assumption that every man had the right to oppress other men, provided he had the power to do so. The life of the individual, however, being intimately linked with that of society, it is in the pure self-interest of every individual to grant equal liberty to others. "Mind your own business!" then becomes the moral law of the anarchist. The State interferes with the freedom of the individual and therefore should be abolished, but property in the products of one's own labor is justified. Tucker also admitted the usefulness of a flexible law, which should be applied by jury, particularly in cases of violation of personal liberty and of contract. He advocated peaceful spreading of the anarchist ideas by the printed and spoken word to convince a sufficient number of people of the advantages of anarchism, which would then be gradually established.

The religious anarchism of Leo Tolstoy (1828–1910) follows from his interpretation of the teachings of Christ. . . . Tolstoy emphasizes that it is the teaching of love which is the "fundamental essence of the soul." Only by substituting the law of man for the law of God do men justify violence, oppression, inequality. By following the law of God, men will love, help and forgive one another, and live in peace and harmony without having any use for government, man-made laws, courts, police, armies, prisons, and private property. While living in a corrupted world, the Christians should support neither the State nor the Church and offer passive resistance to them. Tolstoy believes that simple agricultural life best suits human nature and urges return to such a life. . . .

The affinity of anarchism with liberalism has already been noted in this essay. Like liberalism, anarchism bases its social philosophy on the considerations of the value of the individual in terms of his freedom, happiness and prosperity. The same belief that, if individuals are left to pursue their natural desires, general benefit will be the result, is present in anarchism as in early liberalism. However, while the liberal doctrine has been qualified by the admission that some social authority is necessary to lead the "invisible hand" and see to it that the "natural" laws are not tampered with, anarchism refuses to accept such an admission. It still insists on applying the liberal idea of freedom in both the economic and political fields and it extends the liberal plea for a minimum of government to a complete negation of government: "When Jefferson clothes the basic concept of Liberalism in the words, 'That government is best which governs least,' then Anarchists say with Thoreau: 'That government is best which governs not at all.'" The anarchists deny the necessity of government because of their belief—which most non-anarchists will dismiss as utopian—that the dictates of reason, or the social instincts of human nature, or both, if unhampered by external coercion, will secure free, harmonious social life. Such a life, moreover, will not display the inequalities which the liberals accept as a matter of fact, but will result in conditions of equality, reflected in socialistic or communistic arrangements.

Some writers on the political theory of anarchism, however, while accepting its kinship to liberalism, deny that anarchism is related to socialism either as a closely allied doctrine or as a branch of the general socialist theory, and indeed put anarchism and socialism as antitheses. Such judgment arises out of the conception of anarchism as a doctrine championing the rights of the individual against the rights of society, whereas socialism is conceived as a doctrine emphasizing the rights of society against those of the individual. Although this distinction may seem acceptable at first sight, further considerations upset it. Even the individualist anarchists reach conclusions which bring them close to socialists, and the anarchist communists, as the name implies, by trying to reach a synthesis and harmony of the individual and communal, or social tendencies of human nature, are again necessarily brought close to socialists.

Socialism aims at a new society based on the common ownership of all, or a considerable proportion of, the means of production and distribution, in order to create a state in which every individual will receive from society all he needs for the development of his capacities, and in return will contribute, according to his powers, to the benefit of other members of society. This is also the aim of anarchism, particularly the anarchist communism which is now practically the only anarchist trend. It is often forgotten that the aim of socialism is to secure for man the greatest happiness and freedom compatible with the equal claims of others. This is also the goal of anarchism, and it was one of Kropotkin's merits that he paid much attention to the problem of reconciling the individualistic and social proclivities in man.

Like socialism in general, anarchism is opposed to private

ownership of land and capital. Bertrand Russell actually
stresses their relation in this respect and says that both arose
"from the perception that private capital is a source of tyranny by certain individuals over others." Socialism and anarchism differ in their professed aims. Even in this respect,
however, the differences are not such as to violate their basic
affinity: in its view of the ultimate "withering away" of the
State, Marxian socialism is closer to anarchism than to democratic socialism, while in their advocacy of the means for the
transformation of society some anarchists, like the Marxists,
preach violent revolution, and others, like the democratic
socialists, advocate peaceful means. The advocacy and practice of individual terrorism by some anarchists, in particular
towards the end of the last century, estranged them from the
socialists, but terrorism was not condoned by the anarchist
movement as a whole, and as a phenomenon arising out of
extreme individualism and oppressive social and political conditions it has not been confined to the anarchists alone.

In the last century the anarchists considered themselves
part of the socialist movement and were members of the International Working Men's Association until their split with
the Marxists at the Hague Congress of the International in
1872. According to Kropotkin, they were at first called fed-
eralists, anti-authoritarians and anti-statists, but later their
antagonists began to call them anarchists, using the word in a
derogatory sense to denounce them as people set on causing
disorder and chaos without contemplating the consequences
of their actions. The anarchists themselves came to accept
this designation, insisting at first on the word being written
"an-archist", as Proudhon did in 1840, to denote that the
term did not mean disorder but opposition to power. Gradually the word was accepted in its present form. . . .

The kinship of anarchism with socialism helps to explain
both its relative strength in the second half of the last century
and its decline in the present. Together with other branches
of socialist thought in the last century, anarchism was a protest against the evils of the growing industrial society—poverty, disease, ignorance, oppression—and a reaffirmation of the
humanitarian principles of freedom, equality and justice. At
a time when the State excluded vast numbers of people from
the rights of citizenship, it was not difficult for many to accept
the anarchist criticisms directed against it. However, as the
economic, social and cultural conditions of the people gradu-

ally improved, and as the exercise of political power broadened, it became clear that anarchism misjudged the nature of social forces, in particular the nature and potentialities of political power, and inevitably declined.

Having assumed that the State, since it arose as a means of oppression of many by a few, must always be used for the same purpose, the anarchists denied *a priori* any possibility of changing the nature of the State. This genetic fallacy, as the logicians would call it, led them to argue against other socialists on the question of the State and to minimize or decry improvements gained through political means. Most of those who might otherwise have seen some attraction in the anarchist arguments were led to reject them, and supported the democratic socialists who advocated the necessity of effecting the desired social changes through the machinery of the State. The impact of this situation was reflected even among the West European Marxists who were accepting parliamentary government, rather than revolution, as a means of political struggle. Moreover, since the working class was gaining benefits through the State, it tended to look upon the economic struggle as a supplement to, and not the replacement of, the political struggle, as the anarchists urged it to do, and thus even in the syndicates and trade unions the anarchists were losing their influence. Much of what they said appeared unrealistic and utopian. Acts of individual terrorism, committed by some anarchists, especially towards the end of the last century, expressed their impatience and frustration, born of impotence and inability to face and solve social problems, and alienated even those who might otherwise have been sympathetic.

Historical development has proceeded in a direction different from that expected by the anarchists. The great importance today of what we have come to know as the "welfare State" reflects the profound differences between the present concept of the nature and functions of the State and the *laissez faire* concept. . . . As an uncompromising opponent of the State, and as a champion of small groups and conglomerations—political, economic, cultural, social—anarchism was compatible only with a less complex, and therefore more primitive, economic, political and social structure of society. Consequently, its influence in the industrial countries of the West in the present century has declined to infinitesimal proportions. However, as a libertarian philosophy, anarchism cannot be dismissed as unimportant, particularly in the field of social and political ethics. It is still of intellectual significance, presenting a challenge to our thought and making us re-examine our views.

2 An Individualist Attack: Communists Cannot Be Anarchists

This piece probably makes the handsomest contribution to the discussion in this section. John Henry Mackay maintains, from a nonviolent individualist standpoint, that communist-anarchism is a contradiction in terms. No special problems arise from the excerption of this argument from the middle of a novel. Mackay was more interested in formal disquisition and less in the art of fiction than were other authors of novels about London's anarchists during the same period: Henry James in *The Princess Casamassima* and Joseph Conrad in *The Secret Agent*. But Mackay's acquaintance with London's anarchists was not imaginary.

England was a haven for anarchist fugitives from the Continent in the second half of the nineteenth century and was not terrorized by acts of violence as were other European countries. The rumor that an international conspiracy of assassins was directed from London headquarters was hard to dispel. Historians now give slight credence to the idea that anarchism was susceptible of such tight organization. Yet the actual quality of contacts among anarchists has proved difficult to recapture. For this purpose Mackay's novel ought to be helpful, for in it famous revolutionaries are only thinly disguised. Trupp, in the scene that follows, obviously resembles the German refugee Johann Most, who later became the foremost communist-anarchist in the United States. Auban, the Proudhonian individualist, is harder to identify but may well be Mackay himself. In the novel Auban is certain his ideas will fail to win acceptance. Be that as it may, the issue he raises must be reconsidered in this anthology whenever any program of large-scale cooperation is advocated, for syndicalists as well as communists may have to choose between their anarchism and their constructive designs.

After a pause, and after the glasses had been filled again, Auban, who was sitting between his French visitor and the

The Anarchists: A Picture of Civilization at the Close of the Nineteenth Century, by John Henry Mackay, translated by George Schumm (Boston: Benjamin R. Tucker, 1891), pp. 124-49.

young German of whom the American had said that he was
a poet, bent forward and said in French:—

"Trupp and myself would like to ask you, gentlemen, the
favor of an hour for a discussion of the question: What is
Anarchism? this afternoon. And not, as usual, for a discussion
of some special and sharply defined question, but for a discussion of the fundamental principles of Anarchism itself.
For both of us feel that such an interchange of opinions has
become necessary."

He waited to see if the meeting would assent to his proposition. The conversation had ceased. They nodded to him,
and he continued:—

"'What?'—some of you will ask, 'what?—a discussion on
the fundamental principles of Anarchy? Why, have not these
principles been established long ago and so placed beyond
all doubt?'

"Whereupon I answer, No! Notwithstanding fifty years
have almost passed since the word 'Anarchism'—in opposition
to the view still prevalent that Anarchy is nothing but the
disorder of chaos—was for the first time employed to designate a state of society; notwithstanding that in these fifty
years Anarchism has in all civilized countries of the earth
become a part of contemporary history; notwithstanding it
has already laid the indestructible foundation of its own history; notwithstanding there are thousands of persons today
who call themselves 'Anarchists' (here in Europe from ten to
twenty thousand, and in America probably as many more);
notwithstanding all that, I say that there is but a very small
number of individuals who have thoroughly mastered the idea
of Anarchism.

"I will say right here who these few in my opinion are.
They are the thinkers of Individualism who were consistent
enough to apply its philosophy to society. They are—in the
most intellectual and cultured city of the American continent, in Boston—a few courageous, strong, and thoughtful
men wholly independent of all the current movements of the
age,—in the same city where Anarchism found its first and
till now only organ. They are, finally, scattered in all directions, the disciples of Proudhon, to whom this giant is not
dead, even if Socialism in ridiculous conceit fancies it has
buried him. . . ."

"I believe you may add," said Dr. Hurt, "that there are a few
among the great monopolists of capital who have come to
understand what it is that maintains their enormous fortunes

and enables them to steadily increase, and who have therefore not remained wholly ignorant of their greatest enemy."

"So we, the workingmen, we who have always honored the name despite all persecutions, we are no Anarchists? What?" began Trupp, excitedly.

"In the first place, the question of Anarchism is not the concern of a single class, consequently also not of the laboring class, but it is the concern of every individual who values his personal liberty. But then,"—Auban rose, advanced a little towards the centre, and stretched his thin figure, while he continued in a louder voice,—"but then I say that you—those whom you just had in mind, Otto, when you spoke of the workingmen—are indeed no Anarchists. And in order to prove that, I have asked you to-day to listen to me for a half-hour."

"Speak first," said Trupp, apparently calm. "I will answer you after you are through."

Auban continued.

"I can say that I have always wanted only one thing: liberty. Thus I came to the threshold of so many opinions; thus I also came into the movement of Socialism. Then I withdrew from everything, devoted myself to entirely new investigations, and I feel that I have now arrived at the last result of all study: myself!

"I no longer like to talk to many people. The times are past when the words came readily to me while thoughts were wanting, and I no longer lay claim to this privilege of youth, women, and Communists. But the time has come for firmly and strongly opposing those foolish attempts at uniting principles in theory which are practically as different as day and night.

"We must choose sides: here or there. For the one, and thereby against the other. For or against liberty!

"Better honest enemies than dishonest friends!"

The decided tone of these words made an impression on all present. By the earnestness with which Auban had spoken them every one felt that a crisis was at hand. . . .

Auban began again, and he enunciated each of his well-considered words so slowly that it seemed almost as if he read them or had learned them by heart.

"I maintain," he began, "that a great split has arisen in the social movement of the present day, and that it is perceptibly growing larger from day to day.

"The new idea of Anarchism has separated itself from the old one of Socialism. The professors of the one and the followers of the other are concentrating themselves in two great camps.

"As I have said, we are face to face with the alternative of making a choice one way or the other.

"Let us do this to-day. Let us see what Socialism wants, and let us see what Anarchism wants.

"What does Socialism want? . . .

"Wherever I inquired after its ultimate aims, I received two answers.

"The one was: 'It would be ridiculous to already outline the picture of a future which we are only preparing. We leave its formation to our descendants.'

"The other was less reserved. It changed men into angels, pictured with enviable rapidity an Eden of happiness, peace, and liberty, and called that heaven on earth the 'future society.'

"The first answer was made by the Collectivists, the Social Democrats, the State Communists; the second, by the 'free Communists,' who call themselves Anarchists, and those genuinely Christian dreamers who belong to none of the social parties of the present, but whose number is much larger than is commonly believed. Most religious fanatics and philanthropists, for instance, belong to them.

"In this brief presentation, which will strictly keep inside the limits of reality and deal with men only as they are, have always been, and will always be, I must entirely ignore the last-mentioned classes. For the former of these, the free or revolutionary Communists, would never have received any attention in the social movement—notwithstanding almost every decade of the present century witnessed their rise, growth, and disappearance . . . had they not championed a policy whose occasional application during the past twelve years has made of the name 'Anarchist,' falsely assumed by them, in the minds of the mentally blind (and these still constitute about nine-tenths of all mankind) a synonym for robbers and murderers; and the latter, the philanthropical Utopians—well, there have always been such, and we shall presumably have them with us as long as governments shall create misery and poverty by force. . . .

"Socialism wants the socialization of all the means of production, and the societarian, systematic regulation of production in the interests of the community.

"This socialization and regulation must proceed in accordance with the will of the absolute majority and through the persons of the representatives elected and designated by it.

"So reads the first and most important demand of the Socialists of all countries, so far as they keep within the limits of reality and deal with the given conditions.

"It is of course impossible to treat here in detail:

"First, of the possibility of the realization of these principles, which is indeed conceivable only by the aid of an unexampled terrorism and the most brutal compulsion of the individual, but in which I do not believe; and second, of the consequences, in no manner to be estimated, which an unlimited—even if only temporary—dictatorship of the majority would entail upon the progress of civilization. . . .

"And why should I? I need only point to the present conditions from which we are all suffering: to the privileges, forcibly created and maintained by the State, with which it invests capital in the form of interest, and land in the form of rent, on the one side, and to the useless internecine struggle of the labor dependent on that capital, the struggle in which labor irretrievably devours itself, on the other; I need only point to these abominable conditions, to give all thinking people an idea of how completely null and void must become economic, and consequently all personal, liberty, after these separate monopolies shall have become consolidated in the one, comprehensive, absolute monopoly of the community which is to-day called the State and to-morrow the collectivity.

"I say only so much:—

"The forcible exploitation of the majority by the minority to-day would become a forcible exploitation, no more justifiable, of the minority by the majority to-morrow.

"To-day: Oppression of the weak by the strong. To-morrow: Oppression of the strong by the weak.

"In both cases: Privileged power which does as it pleases.

"The best that Socialism might achieve would consequently constitute only a change of rulers.

"Here I put my second question:—

"What does Anarchism want?

"And starting from what has been said, I answer:—

"Anarchism wants the absence of all government which—even if it abolishes 'class rule'—inevitably separates mankind into the two great classes of exploiters and exploited.

"All government is based on force. But wherever there is force there is injustice.

"Liberty alone is just: the absence of all force and all coercion. Equality of opportunities for all constitutes its basis.

"On this basis of equal opportunities, the free, independent, sovereign individual whose only claim on society is that it shall respect his liberty, and whose only self-given law consists in respecting the liberty of others,—that is the ideal of Anarchy.

"When this individual awakes to life, the knell of the State has sounded: society takes the place of government; voluntary associations for definite purposes, the place of the State; free contract, the place of statute law.

"Free competition, the war of 'all against all,' begins. The artificially created conceptions of strength and weakness must disappear as soon as the way has been cleared and the perception of the first egoism has struggled into light that the happiness of the one is that of the other, and *vice versa.*

"When with the State the privileges maintained by it have become powerless, the individual will be enabled to secure the full product of his labor, and the first demand of Anarchism, the one it has in common with Socialism, will be fulfilled.

"When shall I be enabled to secure the full product of my labor?" Auban interrupted himself, as he caught the questioning glance of the Frenchman, and continued:—

"When I can exchange the product of my labor at its full value, instead of being forced, as at present, to sell my labor below its value, i.e. when I must submit to being robbed of a portion of it by force."

After this explanatory clause, Auban again took up the thread of his address.

"For after the disappearance of force, capital, unable any longer to levy the customary tribute, will find itself compelled to participate in the struggle, i.e. to lend itself out for a consideration which the competition among the banks themselves in the business of furnishing mediums of exchange will force down to the lowest point, just as it will make impossible the accumulation of new capital in the hands of the few.

"The power of increase of capital is the death of labor: the vampire that sucks its blood. When it is abolished, labor is free.

"When the resources of nature shall no longer be obstructed by the violent arrangements of an unnatural government which is a mockery on all common sense, and which under the pretence of the care of the general welfare, purchases the mad luxury of an insignificant minority at the cost of the misery of an entire population, then only shall we see how bountiful she is, our mother. Then will the welfare of the individual in truth have become identical with the welfare of the community, but instead of sacrificing himself to it, he will have subjected it to himself.

"For it is this and nothing else that Anarchism wants: the removal of all artificial obstructions which past centuries have piled up between man and his liberty, between man and his intercourse with his fellow-men, always and everywhere in the forms of Communism, and always and everywhere on the basis of that colossal lie, designed by some in shrewd and yet so stupid self-infatuation, and accepted by others in equally stupid self-abasement: that the individual does not live for himself, but for mankind! . . .

"Trusting in the power of reason, which has begun to clear away the confusion of ideas, I calmly look into the future. Though liberty be ever so distant, it will come. It is the necessity towards which, through the individual, mankind is ever moving.

"For liberty is not a condition of rest; it is a condition of vigilance, just as life is not sleep, but wakefulness from which death only can absolve us.

"But liberty raises its last claim in the name of Anarchism by demanding the sovereignty of the individual. Under this name it will fight its last battle in every individual who revolts against the compulsion of his person by the Socialistic world that is forming to-day. No one can hold aloof from this struggle; each must take a position for or against. . . .

"For the question of liberty is an economic question!"

Auban's words had long ago lost their deliberate judicial tone. He had spoken his last sentences rapidly, with a voice full of emotion. But with his hearers the effect of his words varied with the individual.

No one rose to reply at once.

Then Auban added:—

"I have taken my position in the last two years, and I have told you where I stand. Whether I have made myself clear and whether you have understood me—I do not know. But I do know that my place is outside all current movements. Whom I am seeking and whom I shall find is, the individual; you—and you—and you,—you who in lonely struggles have come to the same perception. We shall find each other, and when we shall have become strong enough, the hour of action will have come for us also. But enough."

He ceased, and stepping back, took his old seat.

Several minutes passed, during which various opinions were exchanged in low voices before Trupp began his reply. During Auban's address he had been sitting bent forward, his chin resting on his hand, and his arm on his knee, and had not allowed a word to escape him.

He spoke tersely and as one convinced of what he says, after he had once more surveyed the audience with his keen eye.

"We have just been told of two different Anarchisms, of which the one, we are assured, is none at all. I know but one; that is Communistic Anarchism, which has grown among workingmen into a party, and which alone is known in 'larger circles,' as we say. It is as old, yes, older than the present century: Babœuf already preached it. Whether a few middle-class liberals have invented a new Anarchism is entirely immaterial to me, and does not interest me any more than any other workingman. As regards Proudhon, to whom comrade Auban again and again refers, he has long ago been disposed of and forgotten even in France, and his place has everywhere been taken by the revolutionary, Communistic Anarchism of the real proletariat.

"If the comrades wish to know what this Anarchism wants, which has risen in opposition to the State Communists, I will gladly tell them in a few words.

"Above all, we do not see in the individual a being separate from society, but we regard him as the product of this very society from which he derives all he is and has. Consequently, he can only return, even if in a different form, what in the first place he received from it.

"For this reason, too, he cannot say: this and that belong to me alone. There can be no private property, but everything that has been and is being produced is social property, to which one has just as much right as another, since each one's share in the production of wealth can in no manner be determined. For this reason we proclaim the liberty to consume, i.e. the right of each to satisfy his wants free and unhindered.

"Consequently we are Communists.

"But, on the other hand, we are also Anarchists. For we want a system of society where each member can fully realize his own 'self,' i.e. his individual talents and abilities, wishes, and needs. Therefore we say: Down with all government! Down with it even in the form of administration. For administration always becomes government. We likewise oppose the whole swindle of the suffrage and declare the leaders who have presumed to place themselves at the head of the workingmen as humbugs.

"As Communists we say:—

"To each according to his needs!

"And as Anarchists:—

"From each according to his powers.

"If Auban says such an ideal is impossible, I answer him that he does not yet know the workingmen, although he might know them, for he has associated with them long enough. The workingmen are not such sordid egoists as the *bourgeois* —after they have had their day of reckoning with them, after the last revolution has been fought, they will very well know how to arrange things.

"I believe that after the expropriation of the exploiters and the confiscation of the bank, they will place everything at the disposal of all. The deserted palaces will quickly enough find occupants, and the well-stocked warehouses soon enough customers. We need not cudgel our brains about that!

"Then when each one shall be sufficiently supplied with food, clothing, and shelter, when the hungry shall be fed and the naked clothed,—for there is enough for all for the present, —they will form groups; will, impelled by the instinct of activity, produce in common and consume according to needs.

"The individual will at best receive more, never less, from society than he has given it. For what should the stronger who produces more than he can consume do with the excess of his labor except give it to the weaker?

"And that is not liberty? They will not ask how much or how little each produces and each consumes; no, each will carry his finished work to the warehouses and take therefor in return what he needs for his support. According to the principle of fraternity—"

Here Trupp was interrupted by a shout of laughter from Dr. Hurt. A general commotion arose. Most of them did not know what to think. Auban was angry.

"To me it is not a matter for mirth, but a matter for tears, doctor, when men rush into their destruction with open eyes," he said.

Trupp rose. Every fibre of his whole solid figure was in a

state of tension. He was not offended, for he did not feel himself attacked, but his idea.

"With people like you we shall indeed make short work!"
he exclaimed.

But Dr. Hurt, who had suddenly also become serious, entirely ignored these words.

"Where do you live?" he asked brusquely. "On the earth
or on the moon? What kind of people do you see? Are you
never going to be sensible?"

And turning away, he again broke out in laughter.

"One must hear such things in order to believe them! Two
thousand years after Christ, after two thousand years of the
saddest experience in the following out of a creed which has
caused all the misery, still the same nonsense, in the same
unchanged form!" he exclaimed.

At one blow the spirit of the gathering had changed. In the
place of calm listeners who were recovering themselves from
their astonishment at this interruption, excited participants
took sides for or against.

Trupp shrugged his shoulders.

The success of his words with the majority had been un-
mistakable. Auban saw it with an uneasy surprise: what he
himself had said had been strange and cold reasoning to
them. They longed for the perfection of happiness—Trupp
offered it to them.

Is it possible? This question came to none.

There is something evil about hope, thought Auban and
Hurt, and their thoughts greeted each other silently in a
glance,—it despises reason, which laboriously indeed and only
gradually, but with unfailing certainty, removes stone after
stone and story after story from the giant structure of illusion. . . .

"I am sorry that you were interrupted, Otto."

But Trupp said quickly:—

"I had said what I had to say."

"Well, so much the better. But shall we not attempt to
bring out our opinions somewhat more in detail? Let us look
more closely at special points."

The calm attention of awhile ago soon returned. But it
was now forced, not natural as before. Several persons took
part in the discussion.

Auban began anew, turned towards Trupp:—

"I will attempt to prove that the philosophies of Communism and of Anarchism are also irreconcilably opposed to each other in their conclusions.

"You want the autonomy of the individual, his sovereignty, and the right of self-determination. You want the free development of his natural stature. You want his liberty. We agree in this demand.

"But you have formed an ideal of a future of happiness which corresponds most nearly to your own inclinations, wishes, habits. By naming it 'the ideal of humanity' you are convinced that every 'real and true man' must be just as happy under it as you. You would fain make your ideal the ideal of all.

"I, on the contrary, want the liberty which will enable each to live according to his ideal. I want to be let alone, I want to be spared from any demands that may be made in the name of 'the ideal of humanity.'

"I think that is a great difference.

"I deny only. You build anew.

"I am purely defensive. But you are aggressive.

"I battle exclusively for my liberty. You battle for what you call the liberty of others.

"Every other word you speak is abolition. That means forcible destruction.

"You talk about the abolition of religion. You want to banish its priests, extirpate its teachings, persecute its followers.

"I trust to the steadily increasing perception which puts knowledge in the place of faith. It is economic dependence that forces most people nowadays into recognizing one of the many still existing churches, and prevents them from leaving them.

"After the chains of labor have fallen, the churches will of themselves become deserted, the teachers of a delusive faith and folly will no longer find listeners, and their priests will be forsaken.

"But I should be the last to approve of the crime against the liberty of individuals which would by force seek to prevent a man from adoring God as the creator, Christ as the saviour, the pope as infallible, and Vitzliputzli as the devil, so long as he did not trouble me with his nonsense and demand tribute from me in the name of his infallible faith."

They laughed: perplexed, amused, irritated, pitying such weakness in dealing with the enemy.

But Auban continued unconcerned, for he was firmly resolved, now he had begun, to say the best that he had to say.

"You want free love, like myself.

"But what do you understand by free love?

"That it is the duty of every woman to yield to the desire of every man, and that no man has the right to withdraw himself from the desire of any woman; that the children resulting from those unions belong to human society, and that this society has the duty of educating them; that the separate family, like the individual, must disappear in the great family of humanity: is it not so?

"I shudder when I think of the possibility that this idea might ever prevail.

"No one hates marriage more than I. But it is only the compulsion of marriage which induces men and women to sell themselves to each other, which affects and obstructs free choice, which makes difficult, and for the most part impossible, a separation, which creates a state of misery from which there is no deliverance except death,—it is only this compulsion of marriage that I loathe. Never should I dare raise an objection to the free union of two people who are brought together for life.

"But just as well as the free union of two persons do I understand the inclination of many people to change in the object of their love; and unions for a night, for a spring time— they must be as free as the marriages for life, which alone are sanctioned by public opinion to-day.

"The commands of morality appear ridiculous to me, and to have arisen from the morbid desires of narrow men for regulating natural relations.

"And finally, you throw overboard private property with the same royal ease and such a superficiality of thought as we find only in Communism.

"You say the State must fall in order that property shall fall, for the State protects it.

"I say the State must fall in order that property may exist, for the State suppresses it.

"It is true you do not respect property: *your own* property you do not respect; otherwise you would not allow it to be taken from you day after day. Expel illegitimate property, i.e. that which is not really property, but alienism. But expel it by becoming proprietors yourselves. That is the only way in which to really 'abolish' it, the only reasonable and just way, and at the same time the way of liberty.

"Down with the State in order that labor may be free, which alone creates property! So I exclaim also.

"When money shall be freed from all forcibly protected privileges—"

But now Trupp's patience was at an end.

"What?" he cried, indignant, "even money is to remain, wretched money which has corrupted, debased, and enslaved us all?"

Auban shrugged his shoulders. He was about to become vexed, but then he laughed.

"Allow me a counter-question. Would it make you indignant to be an employer and employee at the same time? A receiver and a payer of wages, and, as a co-operator, master of the capital instead of as at present only its slave? I think not. What arouses our indignation is only the fact that in consequence of forcible robbery it is possible at present to get something without work."

"But what, according to your opinion, is to determine the value of labor?"

"Its utility in free competition, which will determine its value of itself. All fixing of value by authority is unjust and nonsensical. But I know very well that Communism solves this question, too, without much trouble: it simply lumps everything."

"But free competition prevails to-day!" cried Trupp.

"No; we have the competition of labor, but not in the same way the competition of capital. I repeat: You see the pernicious effects of that one-sided competition and of property forcibly invested with privileges, and you exclaim: 'Down with private property!' You do not see that it is this very property which makes us independent, and you do not see that it is therefore only necessary to remove the obstacles in the way of acquiring it in order to abolish the false relation of masters and servants. Believe me, the organization of free credit, i.e. the possibility of each coming into possession of the means of production—this bloodless, thorough-going and greatest of all revolutions—will be followed by a change of all the conditions of life which no one can adequately picture to himself to-day."

He stopped and saw how coolly his words were received. Only Dr. Hurt sat collected, logically examining word after word, calculating. To the majority a revolution was only a chaos of corpses and ruins, and they shook their heads at Auban's words. Therefore he tried to make his meaning clearer.

"Do you know what effect the abolition of interest, and

thereby of usury, would have? A steady demand for human labor; the equilibration of supply and demand; the reduction of prices to the lowest point, and consequently an enormous increase of consumption; the exact exchange of equivalents, and consequently the most equitable distribution of wealth possible. But as a result of this great economic revolution, the country as well as the individual growing more prosperous daily." . . .

Trupp laughed, indignant and irritated.

"A fine revolution! And you want to make us workingmen believe in these crack-brained fancies? Did I not see you before me, I should think I was listening to a *bourgeois* economist. No, dear friend, the revolution that we shall some day make will reach the goal more quickly than all your economic evolutions! We will make shorter work: come and take back what has been stolen from us by open force and scientific cunning!"

"If only the *bourgeoisie* do not make still shorter work of you!" remarked Dr. Hurt. "*Exempla docent!* That is: Learn from history!"

That was his answer to Trupp's previous threat, which he had apparently neglected.

The excitement produced by these words subsided only gradually. They saw in them a defence of the *bourgeoisie*, and showered replies to them.

The German, who occupied the ground of the New York "Freiheit" and the "Pittsburg Proclamation," and who was a member of the "Communistic Workingmen's Educational Society," now took the floor.

"Nothing has so far been said of the real Anarchism which was in existence before anything was known of the Boston middle-class liberalism advocated by Manchester men fifty years behind their times, or of the eccentric cavilling of the 'Autonomists'"—he aimed at Auban and Trupp—"and which still has the most numerous following. It wants the Communism of free society based on the co-operative organization of production. It does not deny the duty of labor, for it declares: No rights without duties. It demands, moreover, the exchange of equivalent products by the productive associations themselves, without middle-men and profit-takers, and that the communes shall regulate all public affairs by means of free contract. But in a free society, so organized, in which the majority will feel very comfortable, the State will be useless."

"Then you grant the majority the right of establishing its will by force?"

"Yes. The individual must give way before the general welfare, for that is higher."

"That is a position, one of the two which I have described. You are on the road to Socialism."

"A fine position for an Anarchist!" said Trupp. "And what becomes of the liberty of the individual? It is nothing but the centralistic Communism which we have left far behind." The flame of dissension which some time ago had broken up the clubs and led to the founding of a new paper, threatened to blaze forth again. "It is my belief, and I stand by it, that in the coming society each will perform his share of labor voluntarily."

The Frenchman now asked him courteously:—

"But assuming the case that men will not labor voluntarily as you expect, what then becomes of the right to satisfy their wants?"

"They will. Rely on it," was Trupp's answer.

"I think it is better now to rely on it."

"You don't know the workingmen."

"But the workingmen become *bourgeois* as soon as they acquire property, and then they will be the first to oppose the expropriation of their property. You ignore human nature, sir; egoism is the spring of all action. Remove that spring, and the machine of progress will cease to operate. The world would fall into ruins. Civilization would have reached its end. The earth would become a stagnant pool; but that is impossible as long as human beings inhabit it."

"Why do you not take the initiative, and demonstrate the possibility of realizing your theories in practice?" Trupp was further asked.

He evaded this question by asking it himself. It was Auban who at once replied:—

"Because the State has monopolized the circulating medium, and would prevent us by force from furnishing one ourselves. Therefore, our attacks are primarily directed against the State, and only against the State."

The discussion between Auban and Trupp seemed to have come to an end, and threatened to entirely break up. Then Auban made a last attempt to force back upon the ground of reality what vague wishes had raised into the empty spaces of phantasy.

"One last question, Otto," sounded his loud and hard voice,
—"only this one:—

"Would you, in the system of society which you call 'free
Communism,' prevent individuals from exchanging their labor among themselves by means of their own medium of
exchange? And further: Would you prevent them from occupying land for the purpose of personal use?"

Trupp faltered.

Like Auban, everybody was anxious to hear his answer.

Auban's question was not to be escaped. If he answered
"Yes!" he admitted that society had the right of control over
the individual and threw overboard the autonomy of the individual which he had always zealously defended; if, on the
other hand, he answered "No!" he admitted the right of private property which he had just denied so emphatically.

He said, therefore:—

"You view everything with the eyes of the man of to-day.
In the future society, where everything will be at the free
disposal of all, where there can be no trade consequently in
the present sense, every member, I am deeply convinced, will
voluntarily abandon all claim to sole and exclusive occupation
of land."

Auban had again risen. He had become somewhat paler, as
he said:—

"We have never been dishonest towards each other, Otto.
Let us not become so to-day. You know as well as I do that
this answer is an evasion. But I will not let go of you now:
answer my question, and answer it with yes or no, if you wish
me ever again to discuss a question with you."

Trupp was evidently struggling with himself. Then he answered—and it was a look at his comrade who had just attacked him, and against whom he would never have violated
the principle of personal liberty, that impelled him to say:—

"In Anarchy any number of men must have the right of
forming a voluntary association, and so realizing their ideas
in practice. Nor can I understand how any one could justly
be driven from the land and house which he uses and occupies." . . .

"Thus I hold you and will not let go of you!" exclaimed
Auban. "By what you have just said you have placed yourself
in sharp opposition to the fundamental principles of Communism, which you have hitherto championed.

"You have admitted private property, in raw materials and

in land. You have squarely advocated the right to the product of labor. That is Anarchy.

"The phrase—everything belongs to all—has disappeared, destroyed by your own hands.

"A single example only, to avoid all further misunderstanding: I own a piece of land. I capitalize its product.

"The Communist says: That is robbery committed against the common property.

"But the Anarchist Trupp—for the first time now I call him so—says: No. No earthly power has any other right, except that of force, to drive me from my possessions, to lessen the product of my labor by even a penny.

"I close. My purpose is accomplished.

"I have demonstrated what I wished to demonstrate: that there can be no reconciliation between the two great antagonisms in which human society moves, between Individualism and Altruism, between Anarchism and Socialism, between liberty and authority.

"I had claimed that all attempts at uniting the irreconcilable must leave behind the solid ground of reality, and disappear in the clouds of Utopianism, and that every serious man must declare himself: for Socialism, and thereby for force and against liberty, or for Anarchism, and thereby for liberty and against force.

"After Trupp has long sought to evade this alternative, I have compelled him by my last question to explain himself. I might repeat the experiment with each one of you. It is infallible.

"Trupp has decided himself for liberty. He is, indeed,—what I should never have believed,—an Anarchist."

Auban ceased. Trupp added:—

"But we will practically carry out the principles of Communism in Anarchy, and our example will so thoroughly convince you of the possibility of realizing our principles that you will accept them as we do, and voluntarily abandon your private property."

Auban did not say anything in response.

He knew very well that this external conciliation was only a fresh and last attempt on the part of his friend to bridge over the deep chasm that had long ago separated them inwardly, as it separated the new from the old, and assigned them outwardly their respective positions.

"Neither I nor anybody else can save any one from his own doom," . . . he thought to himself. From this time forth he joined in the conversation only when he was directly asked. It grew exceedingly lively.

Never had they remained so long as to-day. It was long past eight o'clock, and still no one thought of leaving except Dr. Hurt and the Frenchman.

When the doctor took leave of Auban, he said in a low voice: "I am not going to come again to your Sundays, dear friend. Anything that is right. But the performances that I am asked to attend must not be too crazy. Your 'comrade' jumped with both feet straight into heaven. That's too high for me."

Saying which he went, and Auban looked after him, smiling. The Frenchman also rose, once more expressing his thanks. But Auban said deprecatingly:—

"We have only driven in the posts and erected the bare scaffolding. But it was impossible to do more to-day."

"You will have a hard battle to fight, which you might make easier for yourself if you would drop that word which frightens away innumerable persons who are otherwise near you, yes, who entirely agree with you."

"The word Anarchy describes precisely what we want. It would be cowardly and imprudent to drop it on account of the weaklings. Whoever is not strong enough to study its true meaning and to understand it, he is not strong enough either to think or to act independently. . . ."

He took Dr. Hurt's vacant seat by the fire, and held his head in his hands. All spoke now, even the Russian. The variously pitched voices struck his ear as from a distance. . . .

From what was being said he heard of Trupp's victory and of his own defeat. . . .

They had forgotten him. While he had been speaking, the cool breath of reason had descended on them. Now it was warm again: the warmth of a future, winterless, paradisean life. And they rivalled each other in the description of that life; their words intoxicated them; they forgot where they were. . . .

Auban continued to hear.

They ridiculed the eternal question of their opponents: who would do the dirty and disagreeable work in the future? There would be enough volunteers for everything, remarked one; and another: There would no longer be any such work to do; machines would be invented for everything.

3 A Communist Retort: Individualism Means Reaction

Lest anyone object that the communist-anarchist position is too crudely parodied in Mackay's novel, we here reprint a communist analysis of the individualist position from a New York anarchist magazine of the 1930s. Ordinarily communist-anarchists have not, like Auban and the individualists, resorted to defining their rivals out of the anarchist camp. Instead, they have concentrated on apparent sources of ineffectuality in individualist programs. But this article illustrates how an argument by definition merges with the attack on futility. That is, do not communists, by insisting that individualists are unwittingly allied with forces of reaction, tacitly identify anarchism with their own concept of progress?

Individualists have not always denied this kind of charge. After he came to the United States, Johann Most initiated a long debate between his German-language paper and Benjamin R. Tucker's *Liberty*. Condemning the resemblance between Tucker's views and those of business advocates of free trade, Most accused Tucker of wanting nothing more than "consistent Manchesterism." "Well, what better can a man who professes Anarchism want than that?" replied Tucker. "Yes, genuine Anarchism is consistent Manchesterism, and Communistic or pseudo-Anarchism is inconsistent Manchesterism."

The struggle of the two factions within the Anarchist movement—the Anarchist-Communist and the Anarchist-Individualist—is viewed by many a comrade as a mere family squabble fanned into the dimensions of a bitter feud by an over-zealous spirit of partisanship. One hears the opinion expressed that given a more tolerant attitude on both sides, a general formula could be found which would unite both wings in a mutual effort on the basis of Anarchist principles.

It is more of a pious wish than a well-grounded opinion, and it generally emanates from those whose approach to the movement is strongly colored by an over-dose of sentimental

"Whither the Libertarian Movement?", by Senex. *Vanguard* I:5 (January, 1933), 6–8.

emotionalism. The differences between these two factions
are not of the kind that can be composed by an ingenious
formula, nor can the latter be brought together by a sudden
change of heart. These differences are based upon diametrically opposite conceptions of the nature of the Anarchist
Ideal, the nature of human individuality, of the actuating
forces of the historical process. They will assert themselves
with an ever increasing force in measure that the Anarchist
movement will be drawn into the great social struggles of the
near future. They will be felt in the programmatic concretiza-
tions of the Anarchist Ideal, in the tactical constructions with
which the Anarchist movement is faced already in a country
like Spain where it has become a great historical force. And
they have already broken up the general line of the libertarian
struggles in two polar directions; one, orientated upon an
emerging form of economic relationships; the other, clinging
to a pattern of economic cooperation that is deeply rooted in
the past and is still the most familiar one to the majority of
mankind. One, giving an altogether new turn to the struggles
for the expansion of human liberty; the other, continuing
the old line of entrenchments built by the militant individual
in the past—the encompassing line of property relationships
within which the individual obtained a certain degree of freedom from the encroachments of the social herd. One is the
direction of the Anarchist-Communist movement, the boldest
champion of the future of humanity, the other, that of the
Anarchist-Individualist which still clings to the outlived institutions of the past.

The Anarchist-Communist views any form of property relationships as incompatible with true social progress and therefore doomed by the latter to total extinction. Whatever
compromises the revolutionary forces of the near future will
have to effect with the principles of property ownership, it
will be but in the nature of a temporary expedient, of a
limited historical usefulness. Communism is inevitable because the nature of human cooperation has been undergoing
the most profound changes. It is becoming more and more of
a subtly integrated kind and the crude measurements of
individual contributions conforms less and less to demands of
elementary justice which must be incorporated in the structure of a new society. Some other principles will have to be
laid at the basis of the latter, and that will be not the exact
apportionment of economic values in accordance with individual contributions, but the principle recognizing the right

of every individual to gratify his elementary needs—the recognition of the worth of the human individual as transcending his value as a producer.

The triumph of this Communist principle will necessitate a radical displacement of the center of gravity of the libertarian struggles. Instead of property as the entrenched group of a militant individuality, the latter will have to weave a protective and insulating system of rights which will be along a more vital axis of individual growth than the right to preempt, speculate, exploit, a system of rights based upon a socialized form of production and consumption and not upon a specious form of individual independence from the economic forces of humanity—an exploded middle-class fiction still swallowed innocently by many an Anarchist-Individualist. . . . That the human individuality is not a definitely given quantity, that it is yet in the process of making, that the encroachments of society cannot be stopped by a system of contrived mechanical adjustments,—all that lies beyond the horizon of our "individualists." They have discovered the secret of an automatically functioning libertarian society— labor property: the fulcrum of Absolute Justice, of Natural Harmony, a static equipoise, free from any dynamic dislocations. Labor property! That is the magic key that will open the gates of the Heavenly Kingdom; a little more calculation, a better system of accountancy—and our troubles will be over. And this is being peddled out as the last achievement of anarchist thought!

Labor property in the twentieth century! Labor property in a modern factory of the type described by Stuart Chase in his "Labor And Machines"—an almost completely automatized factory in which machines do almost all the work, with men reduced to mere overseers of the machines. And the rapidly revolutionizing agriculture with biological science shifting the climatical boundaries, modifying and controlling heredity, with mechanical science working its wonders in the field of cultivation. Who is to be the "labor property" owner in those highly intricate economic processes? The men who repair and watch the automatic machines—an insignificant, ever diminishing number? The highly skilled technical staff which designed this wonderful factory? The scientists who worked out the theoretical aspects of the problems on the basis of which these technical revolutions have been made? Should Dr. Lissenko and his staff, a Soviet scientist whose researches established the possibility of cultivating southern plants in the north, become a part owner of the agricultural production all over the world which is going to be shortly revolutionized as a sequence to his researches, or is it the biological scientists all over the world who contributed theoretically and practically towards the solution of this problem and who will obtain their labor share of ownership? Or must we include also the teachers from the lowest grade to the highest academic chair who train and develop the minds of those scientists, technicians, skilled workingmen? Must they also become part owners of an economic enterprise toward which they contributed so much? Is an advanced pedagogical method of any less economic value than an invention? In other words saying, can we exempt anyone who contributes in a general way towards the economic welfare of mankind from claiming "Labor Property" ownership rights in any economic enterprise of humanity. Can anyone lay his hands upon an integrated product of the labor of millions of men and declare it his own?

These are not questions of such an abstruse nature as to be outside the purview of the average man. Every intelligent man knows of the close web of inter-relationships which exist in the modern economic life, everyone knows of the increasing role of science in production,—and "labor-property rights" in the realm of pure science have not even been asserted by capitalist society.

Pure science is a communist affair and so is our economic life which is becoming more and more of an applied science. Every intelligent man sees it clearly and it is only the recoil from the future, the recoil from the gigantic task of liberalizing the new communist forms of social life that is forcing the individualist to ignore the patent economic sequences of the great economic revolution taking place before our eyes.

4 Syndicalism, the Industrial Expression of Anarchism

George Woodcock has recently written *Anarchism: A History of Libertarian Ideas and Movements*. His comments have special authority, for among his previous works were biographies of Proudhon, Godwin, and Kropotkin; moreover, in the 1940s and 1950s he contributed many thoughtful pamphlets to the anarchist cause. He was particularly concerned with the relevance of anarchism to contemporary economic problems. In this selection, taken from a pamphlet on the railroads, he argues that syndicalism is the logical application of anarchist ideas to industry and technology. For an opposing view, see the selection that follows.

Syndicalism is a method of industrial organisation which goes away from all the traditional conceptions of authority and government, of capitalism and the State. While communism, in abolishing individual capitalism, creates a worse monster in its place in the form of the economic state, syndicalism leaves all the patterns of administration which have in the past resulted only in the oppression and exploitation of man by man, and sets out to build an organisational form based on the natural needs of men rather than on the interests of ruling classes, based not on the dictates of authority, but on the voluntary co-operation of free and equal individuals in satisfying the economic needs of the men who form society.

Syndicalism is the industrial manifestation of anarchism. Anarchism itself is a doctrine which teaches the necessity of a society without government. . . . Anarchism advocates, instead of the governmental coercion of the individual, which exists in the most democratic society that still retains the State, a society based on the free co-operation of individual men and women for the fulfilment of their social and economic needs. Organisation, on a voluntary basis, is necessary

"Railroads and Society," by George Woodcock (London: Freedom Press, 1943), pp. 24–31.

for the operation of the means of production and the desirable public services, but no kind of superior body of authority, with its parliaments, police, bureaucracies, codes of law, taxes, armies and secretive intrigues in internal and foreign politics, has any place or value in a society based on justice and reason. In anarchy a man, once he has fulfilled his contractual economic functions, can live as he will, provided he does not interfere with the freedom of his fellows.

Anarchists believe that the means of production should be the property of society, held in common, and that only by such an arrangement will the restricting influence of private property be removed and the resources of nature and science be used to their full extent for the benefit of humanity. In order that there may be no possibility of such private interests arising, they advocate that, once the means of production have been taken out of the hands of their usurping controllers, they shall be run not by any authority or elite of leaders, but by the people who are themselves concerned in production, i.e. by the workers in each industry.

Syndicalism is, as I have already said, the method by which such control by the workers would be organised. It is, moreover, the method by which the workers under a property society would organise themselves for the attainment of the free classless society.

The syndicate is a form of union which differs from the ordinary trade union in that it aims, not only at the gaining of improvements in wages and conditions under the present system, but also at the overthrow of that system and its replacement by a free society by means of the social revolution based on the economic direct action of the workers. This is not to say that it ignores the day-to-day struggle, but its members recognise that only by a complete destruction of the structure of property and authority can justice and security ever be attained for the workers.

The syndicate differs also from the ordinary trade union in its method of organisation. The ordinary trade union follows the pattern of governmental society in that it has a centralised form, with authority at the centre and a permanent bureaucracy who, like any other bureaucracy, rapidly gain privilege and power and rise into a class with an economic position considerably higher than that of the workers who pay them and whom they are supposed to serve. The syndicate, on the other hand, is based on the organisation of the workers by industry at the place of work. The workers of each factory or depot or farm are an autonomous unit, who govern their own affairs and who make all the decisions as to the work they will do. These units are joined federally in a syndicate which serves to co-ordinate the actions of the workers in each industry. The federal organisation has no authority over the workers in any branch, and cannot impose a veto on action like a trade union executive. It has no permanent bureaucracy, and the few privileged officials are chosen on a short term basis, have no privileges which raise their standard of living above that of the workers, and wield no authority of any kind.

The syndicate, being actually governed from below and being untainted by the idea or the institution of authority, represents more truly than any other type of organisation the will of the workers and the good of society. Its lack of centralisation and bureaucracy, of any kind of privilege or vested interest in the present order of society, give it a flexibility of action and a real solidarity which make it the ideal instrument for canalising and influencing in the right way the spontaneous revolutionary activity of the people.

In the social revolution the syndicates will play their part by organising the economic direct action of the workers. On the railways, for instance, they will lead the workers in the expropriation of the lines, stations and rolling stock, and their use only for the purposes of the revolution and not for those of the dispossessed masters.

After the revolution the syndicates will form the framework on which the first phase of the free society will be built. Anarchists do not make any plans for the free society in its maturity, as they believe in the free and continual growth of social institution, and recognise that any hard-and-fast plan of development will create only a sterile society. Nevertheless they recognise that after the old society has been abolished some kind of social structure should be built immediately to take over the means of production and change the economic basis of society from that of a class society to that most appropriate to a free society. This means of organisation they find in the syndicate.

The organisation of industry, transport and farming under the syndicates will follow exactly the same lines as that of the organisation of the workers in the days before the end of the property society, except that now, instead of organising for struggle, the workers will organise for the construction of the

economic basis necessary for the achievement and maintenance of true freedom and justice.

Each working unit, a factory or a railway yard, will be run
by the workers who actually operate it. There will be no authority, no management, and each worker will be jointly and
equally responsible with the rest for the proper functioning
of the industrial unit in which he works.

It should not be assumed from this that the syndicalist
regards the operation of industry as a simple matter. On the
contrary, he knows from experience its complexity, and regards a bureaucracy divorced from the actual work as being
incapable of operating to its maximum efficiency so involved
an organisation as that of a railway. The workers are the men
who have the knowledge of the actual operating of the railways, and if they were to study the problems of operation
and of the co-ordination of their functions, they would be
able to work the railways far more efficiently than the bureaucrats. The opportunity of gaining this knowledge is, of course,
kept from the ordinary railway workers. (Instead, the companies prefer to work the other way round, by instituting
classes to teach bureaucrats in an academic manner the
elements of train working or signalling, usually with little
success.) In this connection, of course, I am using the word
'worker' in a broad sense, to include technical staff associated
with civil engineering and locomotive construction, and also
the sections of the clerical staff concerned with co-ordinating
train operating, as these are both vitally necessary for the
proper working of the railways and upon their direct co-
operation with their fellow workers, eliminating the bureaucrats, will come a real workers' control of railways. It is
therefore vitally necessary that such men should be brought
into any industrial movement among the railwaymen.

The various units will be joined in federations which will
co-ordinate their work throughout the country and make arrangements between the various sections to ensure that each
industry is property co-ordinated. The industrial federations
or syndicates will in turn be united in a national federation
of industry, which will act as the means of co-ordinating the
activities of the various industries.

The old motives of profit and self-interest will cease to
dominate economic life. Instead, the incentive will be the
good of the members of society, without distinction. In such
circumstances there will be no impediment to the exploitation of the resources of nature and science to the full extent

to which men desire it. Men will decide the standard of life they desire and will work to get it. It is hardly to be supposed that they will be content with what they endure to-day, and the possibility of better circumstances together with man's natural need for work will serve to ensure that the workers, left to themselves, will find the means to operate industry a good deal more efficiently than has been the case under capitalism. . . . The method of hierarchical management would cease. Instead, the functions of administration would be vested in the workers themselves and, wherever it was impossible for the workers all to take part directly in administration, by delegates chosen directly from among the workers, who would administer the functioning of the various services in accordance with the wishes of the workers. These delegates would have no authority, nor would they make any decision on questions of policy. Their job would be merely to co-ordinate the work of the railwaymen, which would be carried out entirely on a voluntary basis.

Such delegates would be in no way superior to their fellow workers, in power, privilege or position. Under anarchism the wages system, one of the prime means by which the rulers coerce the workers, would be abolished, and the workers, giving in labour what was necessary for the carrying on of the functions of society, would in their turn receive the goods which they found necessary for a happy life. No worker would get more than his mate because tradition said that his craft was worth twice as much a week, and there would be no railway directors to live in high luxury while their lower paid employees starved on 6o/- a week or less. Men would get, not according to their worth, for social worth cannot be estimated, but according to their need, which is the only just means of sharing the goods of society.

5 Syndicalism Not a Form of Anarchism

Before the government systematized business unionism in the 1930s, American scholars regularly studied syndicalism and revolutionary unionism. *Revolutionary Syndicalism* by the Purdue economist J. A. Estey is one of the most trenchant of these studies, although today quite overlooked. In section VII we include Estey's full-scale account of the impossibilities of syndicalism. He here contends, in contrast to the views of Woodcock in the preceding selection, that syndicalism is mistakenly called a form of anarchism.

Estey, it should be noted, has in mind the national syndicalist movements of Europe. These movements, while generally influenced by anarchism at their inception, have been vulnerable to refashioning by fascists or communists. Estey's perspective, at any rate, is very different from that of Woodcock and other anarchists, who have defined syndicalism as part of their quest for anarchist modes of action. It seems bizarre to call Proudhon anything less than an anarchist, even though he has inspired non-anarchists. All kinds of anarchists, too, trace their heritage back to Proudhon, and his thought can not easily be construed to mean that groups and associations are more real than individuals. Proudhon remains a tricky subject, to which we return later. (See selections 21, 29.)

To regard Syndicalists as Anarchists . . . would be a mistake, though a mistake commonly made, and countenanced to some extent by utterances of Syndicalists themselves. Syndicalism before 1900 received its greatest inspiration from an Anarchist, Fernand Pelloutier, secretary of the *Fédération des Bourses du travail*. Moreover, the founding of *La Voix du Peuple* in 1900, and the real beginning of the fame of the C.G.T. [*Confédération générale du travail*], were due, largely, to the entrance into that organisation of Anarchists like Émile Pouget, former editor of an Anarchist paper *Père Peinard*, Paul Delesalle, a frequent contributor to the litera-

Revolutionary Syndicalism, by J. A. Estey (London: P. S. King, 1913), pp. 127–32. Reprinted by permission of Marten S. Estey.

ture of Syndicalism, and others of the same stamp. The impression spread abroad by the prominence of such men in the labour organisations has been still further heightened by the anti-military, anti-parliamentary, anti-State campaign, which for the last decade has formed the most dramatic part, perhaps, of Syndicalist propaganda. It is not unnatural to infer that those who wish to destroy the State (in the ordinary sense of the term) are Anarchists, and the enemies of Syndicalism, particularly among Socialists, have not been slow to identify the one with the other.

The identification is fallacious. Undoubtedly all Anarchists desire the abolition of the State, but it is not true that all who desire the abolition of the State are Anarchists. Perhaps it would be better to say that it depends on what is meant by an Anarchist. For there are several distinct varieties. On the one hand, there is the philosophic Anarchist of the type of Stirner, who proposes not only to destroy the existing State, but to remain free, thenceforth, from any form of State, any form of government whatever. Then there is the Anarchist like Proudhon, an essentially social creature, who would abolish the State as we know it, only to set up in its place another, more just, more equitable, with less tyranny and centralisation and coercive machinery in general, but still a State. Finally there is the third type, a variant, in fact, of the first, who so ardently desires the abolition of existing government that he hastens to cause its destruction by the indiscriminative use of violent explosives. Of these three types, the last has nothing to do with Syndicalism. Nobody has accused the Syndicalist of being a revolutionary Anarchist. Of the other two, it is most commonly the first, the intellectual, philosophic Anarchism, with which Syndicalism is apt to be identified.

That this identification is essentially false has been fully demonstrated by M. Edouard Berth in an exceedingly able essay, *Les Nouveaux Aspects du Socialisme*, in which he points out the very considerable difference, nay, the "veritable abyss," which separates the ideal of Anarchism (i.e. philosophic Anarchism) from the ideal of Syndicalism, and shows for what very different reasons Anarchists and Syndicalists advocate the abolition of the State. If Anarchists desire its destruction, it is because they object to a State and to a Government, *as* a State and *as* a Government. It is not hostility to a particular form of government, it is hostility to any form of government. . . . To the philosophic Anarchist the individual is everything, and all that tends to suppress or limit individuality is an evil. He cannot recognise the value of social combinations, or of any form of society, because individuals cannot enter into them without arbitrarily (though mutually) limiting their independence. And it is because he regards the State (or *any* form of government) as a social combination in which individuals are sacrificed on the altar of society, that he desires its abolition. In fact, to the philosophic Anarchist, who believes that men, despite superficial harmony, are by nature isolated and unsocial units, every form of society becomes an absurdity.

Quite opposite is the attitude of the Syndicalist. He agrees with the Anarchist only in his desire to abolish the State. But he opposes the State not because all government is objectionable, but because this particular form of government is suited only to capitalistic society, and is utterly incompatible with the economic society which he proposes to introduce. Far from seeing in association any repression or diminution of individuality, the Syndicalist believes that it increases rather than lessens the powers of individuals; that in solitude there is "impotence, misery, incapacity," in association "power, riches, capacity increased a hundredfold." For Syndicalism is essentially a social philosophy, its method of action a social method. What are the labour organisations but the expression of this social tendency? How can the general strike be carried to success save through the solidarity of the labouring classes, a solidarity socialistic, in the actual sense of the word? In what other way could harmonious production be assured and the future State made realisable, except through the association of the labourers, perpetuated in their unions? Between Anarchism and Syndicalism lies the chasm which separates Individualism from Socialism. In fact, the anti-social nature of Anarchism seems to Syndicalists a subtle form of decadence. The denial of the social idea, the refusal on the part of the individual to collaborate in any collective work, are the signs whereby one may recognise a society in the process of decay. The only possible progress for the modern world is in the extension and elaboration of the principle of association; but Anarchism, from the very nature of its ideas, represents a force which must either retard or prevent that progress.

At the same time, though there doubtless exists a veritable abyss between Syndicalists and philosophic Anarchists, there is some justification for the confusion of terms; for Syndicalists in their opposition to the State are, confessedly, disciples of P. J. Proudhon, and Proudhon was pleased to call himself an Anarchist. Yet it must be remembered that Proudhon took care to define what kind of an Anarchist he was, and that no more ardent exponent of association ever lived. His Anarchism, like that of the Syndicalists, was an Anarchism of *groups*, not an Anarchism of individuals. He desired to abolish the existing State, not in order that individuals should enjoy the pleasures of isolation and conduct themselves according to the divine laws of Nature, but rather that groups of individuals, united for productive purposes, might make those voluntary arrangements between themselves, which, based on mutual convenience, are stronger than all the bonds imposed by law and government. He saw in the group rather than in the individual the true reality, he believed that above the individual being stands the collective being, a being which is no mere adding together of isolated individuals, but something *sui generis*, with a character and functions all its own —and more divine. Throughout the entire body of Proudhon's writings runs this panegyric upon association, stamping him at once not as an Anarchist, but as an ardent Socialist. He desired more freedom in society, he demanded that society should be shaped in a federalistic rather than in a centralised mould, but he was emphatically opposed to any and every system which would destroy society. And certainly the collection of isolated individuals, which would represent Anarchism, is synonymous with the destruction of what is meant by the term society.

The attitude of Proudhon is the attitude of the Syndicalists. In their proposal to destroy the State, they are seeking only to remove a form of political order which has had its use, but which, with the coming change in industry, will become an anachronism, and to set up another political order suited to future production, but equally antagonistic to Capitalism and to Anarchism. . . .

Roughly speaking, the absence of centralisation constitutes the essential feature in which, from a political standpoint, the Syndicalist State would be a novelty. For it appears from Syndicalist writings that many of the functions, which to-day are in the hands of State or Municipality, will not be abolished, but will be transferred to the labour organisations on which Syndicalism is founded. Administrative functions of some sort must be carried on, if solidarity is not to be hopelessly shattered. Moreover, while Syndicalists are as little prophetic in political as in economic matters, it seems that the future unit of government, or rather of administration, is, as would be expected from their fondness for decentralisation, to be found in the Syndicalist equivalent of the Municipality—the *Bourses du travail*. Uniting the producers in every trade and industry in an organisation where all differences are subordinated to the interests of labour in general, already endowed with functions of administration in connexion with the labouring class, the *Bourses du travail*, when the republic of free producers is attained, will become synonymous with the adult population of each local centre. Even now their duties are numerous. They have acquired practice in administration both by directing employment bureaux and by the collection and publication of economic statistics. Through their libraries and courses of instruction they have become educative centres for the labouring class. . . .

Such relations between these local units as might be necessary for the sake of harmony and co-ordination, would be supplied by machinery like the existing Federal Committees of the C.G.T. A central body of the kind, possessing no authoritative or coercive powers, an arrangement for convenience and little more, could involve no irksome restraint. Only thus can be solved the problem of realising Socialism without falling into some insidious form of despotism. The association of men must be furthered if the world is to progress, but it must be achieved by purely voluntary bonds, free from every element of compulsion. If it is to be a living organism and not a mechanism doomed to decay, future society must reconcile the principle of association with the principle of independence. And in the Proudhonian Federalism which they have adopted as the type of their political and economic organisation, Syndicalists believe they will bring about this indispensable reconciliation.

6 Can a Christian Be an Anarchist?

Anarchism has frequently been assailed as the inevitably horrible outcome of atheism. Michael Bakunin's inversion of Voltaire—"If there really were a God it would be necessary to abolish him"—is better remembered than anything else he wrote. Nor has atheism been confined to collectivist circles. Benjamin R. Tucker, the individualist, agreed that self-government was incompatible with the authority of Christ. But the relationship between religion and anarchism is certainly intricate, as we are reminded simply by the recurrence of Christian anarchism. Moreover, religious history has witnessed many sects which might well have avowed with Bakunin: "The urge to destroy is a creative urge."

An ingenious view of the bearing of religion on anarchism was presented by a Catholic historian, James Hogan, when civil war in Spain brought the issue to a head. Hogan loathed anarchism, but still contended that "the ordinary idea of anarchism as the negation of authority fails to convey its full significance." He went still further: "The more intense man's awareness of his greatness and misery, the nearer he is to becoming either saint, poet or anarchist." Anarchism, in short, springs from a basically religious awareness of human exile from clearly envisioned ideals of exaltation and freedom. Nevertheless anarchism remained for Hogan, "in its essence a radical expression of atheism and naturalism," a heresy partaking of the spirit of religion and the substance of atheism. Even Bakunin, Hogan was quick to indicate, was haunted in his youth by the problem of God. Bakunin's account of his conversion, we are told, should be read quite literally: "I sought God in man, in his freedom, and now I seek God in revolution." When such a literal reading yields fascinating comparisons with Tolstoy's conversion to Christian anarchism, it is Hogan's claim that no profound differences exist between violent and non-violent anarchism.

Within anarchist movements, analysis of religious motives has been less metaphysical. Insight into the kind of debate that persists can be gained from the following selection, a chapter out of Ammon Hennacy's *Autobiography of a Catholic Anarchist*. In our section on constructive anarchism, detailed attention is paid to the activities of Hennacy and Dorothy Day, two participants in the debate reproduced here. For present purposes it suffices to observe that both have made the same spiritual journey: from radical progressivism, to a yearning for peace and identification with the poor, to devout Catholic anarchism.

I had not met Dorothy since September 1941 in Milwaukee. I had written letters to her and the *Catholic Worker*. She had come to Albuquerque a few months after I left for Phoenix in 1947. Now I was overjoyed to get a card from her saying that she would be here Dec. 29th. . . .

The leading anarchist of this country happened to be in Phoenix just then, so I asked him if he and his atheistic Italian anarchist friends would like to meet Dorothy. Accordingly we met one evening in an anarchist home. The atheistic anarchists led off by saying that anarchism as defined by Bakunin negates all authority: that of the state and that of God. Therefore for Christian and especially Catholic anarchists to use the name anarchism is unethical. Furthermore it hurts the feelings of Italian anarchists who have felt the lash of the Catholic hierarchy.

Dorothy listened carefully to this reiterated statement and replied that this argument had not been brought to her attention before and deserved careful consideration. She felt that man of his own free will accepted God or rejected God and if a man chose to obey the authority of God and reject the authority of the state it was not unethical to do so. She inferred that we were *born into* a state and could not help it, but accepted God of our own free will. She and Bob Ludlow are converts to the Church.

The atheistic anarchist answer was that it was entirely illogical to use the anarchist conception of freedom to accept the authority of God which denies that freedom. Dorothy felt that the authority of God only made her a better rebel and gave her courage to oppose those who sought to carry over the concept of authority from the supernatural to the natural field where it did not belong. She said that the use of the word anarchism by the CW might shock people; that Peter Maurin, although an anarchist, had generally used the word personalist instead, but she felt that Bob Ludlow and myself used it rightly.

Autobiography of a Catholic Anarchist, by Ammon Hennacy (New York: Catholic Worker Books, 1954), pp. 128–31.

Another anarchist present thought that Ludlow had slipped over the use of the word anarchism on Dorothy. She replied that she stood back of all he said on the subject. This same anarchist repeated the regular argument that religion was opium for the people and that the Catholic Church always stood for the rich against the poor and that the CW was as bad as the history of the church. The anarchist leader felt that if the CW was only called the *Anarchist Worker* instead of the CW it would be the best anarchist paper going. It was the word Catholic that spoiled it. These atheistic anarchists felt that if I had not hid behind the CW I would have been arrested long ago for my tax refusal. Dorothy answered that I had been a Christian Anarchist long before the CW was ever heard of. The anarchist leader said that Tolstoy in his Appeal to Social Reformers denounced the regular anarchists of his time and therefore should not be considered an anarchist.

I replied that I had read that article of Tolstoy's long ago and that Tolstoy was simply decrying the atheism and violence of various types of anarchists, and saying that without pacifism and the Fatherhood of God there could not be an effective anarchistic brotherhood of man. I also quoted from a book, *Tolstoy the Man* by Prof. Stirner, issued by Fleming Revel Co. about 1902. Prof. Stirner visited with Tolstoy and quoted him as saying that he was such an anarchist as Jesus and the Sermon on the Mount had made him; not to be afraid of the word anarchism, for the time would come when people would know its true meaning; that one who had accepted and obeyed the laws of God was thereby divorced from obeying the laws of men and did not need them. Stirner was sort of a Fabian Socialist, and he asked Tolstoy if Socialism was not a step on the way to anarchism. Tolstoy answered that it was not, and that it would end in a terrible dictatorship.

Dorothy mentioned the sacrifice of Jesus on the cross, original sin, etc., emphasizing the fact that rebels who sacrifice for a cause need this supernatural help to remain true. The anarchists misunderstood this idea or else were physically unable to accept the importance of sacrifice, saying that what they wanted was better material conditions and not pie in the sky; that religion made people willing slaves. Under pressure from Dorothy and myself they admitted that a good martyr now and then like the Haymarket men and Sacco and Vanzetti, was a good thing; but they did not like the emphasis upon sacrifice.

I felt that this was the trouble with the present atheistic anarchists: that they were not willing to sacrifice enough. I reviewed my prison history to prove that what changed me from being a Socialist and an atheist was the example of that true rebel Jesus. That thus my sanity had been saved and I had emerged from prison an anarchist. That I was associated with the CW because of its brave stand in publicizing my anti-tax campaign when anarchist and pacifist papers said very little about it. That my idea of God was not an authority whom I obeyed like a monarch but a principle of good as laid down by Jesus in the Sermon on the Mount, which I interpreted in day by day decisions as the forces of the state came in conflict with these ideals. And that in the same manner every person had to make a choice between his conception of good and of evil.

The anarchist leader still felt that religious people had no right to use the word anarchist, although we knew that he as an anarchist could not go to law and prevent it. I replied that the atheistic anarchists were more atheistic than they were anarchistic so he should not be adverse to allowing Christians or Catholic Christians to be at least as religious as they were anarchistic, if not more so. That the atheistic anarchist should be glad that the CW had left the state worship of ecclesiastical authorities and were anarchists. I said that the atheistic anarchists did not realize that it was possible for a Catholic to accept spiritual authority and not—like most Catholics, accept the state and temporal authority; that the atheistic anarchist should be glad that someone was fighting authority in one sphere—and the most difficult sphere at that —where the atheistic anarchist stood no chance of being heard. Dorothy told of losing over half of the CW subscribers because the CW opposed Franco and World War II.

The summary of Bob Ludlow on this subject seems conclusive: "There is an incompatability between anarchism and religion only if the Christian insists on transforming the authoritarian set up of the Church to the temporal field or the anarchist insists in rejecting authority in religion. In both cases it comes from a confusion of the supernatural with the natural."

As two of those present were vegetarians, our Italian hosts gave us all that diet. Despite the excitability of the Italian temperament there was good humor and goodwill present at all times. I felt that a fair summary of the question would be that whenever we of the CW became cowardly because of pressure from the Pope, then it would be time for atheistic anarchists to decry our use of the name anarchism. And that as long as they had no Pope to tell them what to do they ought to assert their native anarchism and come out and be as brave fighters against war and capitalism as were Bakunin, Berkman and Goldman, whom they revere.

7 Is Anarchism Distinct from Liberalism?

No other contemporary anarchist rivals Paul Goodman in imagination and scholarship, and consequently this anthology includes five selections from his writings. He is also one of the few recent anarchists whose works are not altogether relegated to tiny sectarian presses. Goodman has made significant contributions in fields as diverse as city planning, literary criticism, *Gestalt* psychology, and the economics of decentralism; he is now working in linguistics. He is also a poet and best-selling novelist. An important feature of his work is his enjoyment of what many modern writers complain of lacking: a tradition. He regards himself as a creative artist reshaping traditional anarchism.

The piece that follows is a sketch of distinctions between the anarchist tradition and philosophical liberalism. The context needs a little clarification. Richard Lichtman, a professor of philosophy, had taken issue with an effort of Goodman's to evaluate different kinds of pornography and to propose ways of improving the good and rooting out the bad. Lichtman sensed a perilous disregard for freedom: "If his concern had been with freedom he might have maintained that the First Amendment protects freedom of sexual expression as it protects freedom in political or religious communication, and that the proper limits in this area are set by precisely the same standards applicable to other areas of human conviction—whether the material in question constitutes a clear and present danger against crucial values that society has the right to protect by law." This general attack, plus Lichtman's frequent allusions to John Stuart Mill, provoked this reply in which Goodman traced the divergence of anarchism from liberalism. If Goodman is right, the differences go much deeper than disagreement over analyses of pornography. For the anarchists can turn the tables on critics who dismiss their views as wholly negative. Goodman is here dissociating himself and anarchism from positions that seem overly defensive or negative.

I am startled to find that I, a community anarchist who believes that coercive sovereign power is always a poor expedient, not only in cases of censorship but of police actions against any crimes, am read by Mr. Lichtman as asking for the coercive suppression of low-grade pornography, and of wanting to *enforce* sexual reform! Perhaps I take my libertarian position so much for granted that I fail to express it; perhaps Mr. Lichtman does not read closely. It is no matter. Let me make my position clear.

He says, "When Goodman finds himself with a conflict of values, he sacrifices freedom to sexual reform." First, in this area I find no such conflict, and I would even assume that there could not be one, since I am convinced that organism-self-regulation works out best. But second, *if* there were such a conflict, I should, with suffering, affirm *both* horns of the dilemma and try to bull it through, since both freedom and organic health are, to me, absolute goods. Mr. Lichtman further attributes to me the notion that "society has the right to censor" neurotic artifacts like loveless lust; or again, when I speak of "harmful pornography" that we should like to see checked, he concludes that "Mr. Goodman is not so much opposed to censorship as he is opposed to censorship of the wrong kind." By this misreading I am baffled. Surely I make clear at sufficient length, including pages of future-thinking, that we must drop *all* censorship of pornography, to the inevitable extreme of Hollywood and Madison Avenue's cashing in on full sexual scenes; my hope being that this will soon diminish the pornographic atmosphere. Likewise, when I proceed to make a rough rating of useful, indifferent, and damaging pornography and say that "the social question is how to improve the first and eliminate the last," I immediately go on to say, "Police courts and administrative officers, however, and even jury courts and high courts, are hardly the right forum for important and subtle moral debates." Is this not clear? The paragraph ends with my ritual slam at J. Edgar Hoover, saying, "One of the few things that is demonstrable is that ignorant suppression is wrong"; and the burden of my entire argument has been that in this field *all* suppression is ignorant, has unthought-of effects. I say several times, "We must un-do repression."

"Reply" on Pornography and Censorship, by Paul Goodman from *Commentary* XXXII:2 (August, 1961), 159–61. Reprinted by permission of the author.

I need not give other examples. We have here an extraordinary misreading not of occasional sentences but of whole trains of argument. The question then is: How can a liberal reader, not malicious, and importantly in agreement with me, so misread my argument? This brings me to the vital issue that is interesting to discuss. What, these days, does it mean to be "liberal"?

Mr. Lichtman asks what I mean by freedom and what is my justification for the freedom I mean to defend. In my opinion, we must understand freedom in a very positive sense: it is *the condition of initiating activity*. Apart from this pregnant meaning, mere freedom from interference is both trivial and *in fact cannot be substantially protected*. For even while persons feel themselves inviolate in their bodies, their rights, their families, etc., they are effectually hemmed in, imposed on, and their resources for action pre-empted. Soon, formally free, they are powerless and enslaved. (In my opinion we are hastening rapidly into an American fascism-of-the-majority of just this kind; a couple of bad reverses and the brutality of it will appear.) The justification for freedom is that initiation is essential for *any* high-grade human behavior. Only free action has grace and force. Certainly there is a difference between a juridical person with "freedom under law" and a child with freedom to grow in a structure of parental morals and culture; but I do not think that Mr. Lichtman understands that there is a difference between a juridical person and a *man*, growing in his community and in history. Our rights as juridical persons, that make society our own as citizens and give us dignity, must be continually fought for by free growing and initiation; otherwise they are empty. This is why some of us are anarchists; we do not put our faith in princes and constitutions. As anarchists, we affirm the Bill of Rights because it is one of *our* historical achievements, basic to proceeding further. *By* proceeding to further initiation—including free sexual expression—we shall also defend the Bill of Rights. *Unless* we proceed further, we shall degenerate to mere "society," a collection of persons without the community of human beings.

Let us consider the history. I submit that in the heroic age of the liberal philosophy, gradually extending over religion, science, economics, and politics, from the sixteenth through the eighteenth centuries, liberals were saying pretty much what I have been saying. Freedom meant freedom to enterprise, to bear witness, to initiate and govern. It was not for self-protection that liberal rights were wrested from church and crown, but to achieve something. By the time we come to Mill in the middle of the nineteenth century, "liberal" thought has begun to sour a good deal. Consider the clause, "The majority, being satisfied with the ways of mankind as they now are. . . ." It is just this that liberals of the great age would resolutely have refused; the majority would have to learn to be dissatisfied and move. Is it mysterious what has occurred? The bourgeois carriers of freedom, who had once found freedom utilitarian, now no longer were finding it utilitarian; they were not hankering for fundamental changes. Mill clings to the great tradition, but with a genteel pessimism.

By the time we come to Mr. Lichtman, however, the "liberal" tradition has undergone a catastrophe. For now we are in the age of organized affluence, of automatic technology, feudal monopoly, and symbolic democracy; and the universally prevalent ideology is that Nothing Can Be Done. Therefore, naturally, "freedom" no longer has anything to do with ongoing initiation; it has become the protection of cowering individuals. Such freedom leads to fascism.

I fear that this is why Mr. Lichtman misreads me. When I make the simple remark that certain sexual behavior is neurotic or base, that certain literature stinks, and that—by the relevant processes of medicine, education, and wise policy and leadership—we obviously ought to cure it or eliminate it, he at once construes this to mean that people are to be compelled! The thought that the quality of life is improvable, which was the dogma of liberalism, is now felt by the cowering individual as a threat of tyranny! And perhaps strangest of all, when I propose that the best way of diminishing undesirable pornography is to do nothing about it, this is called social engineering! That is why, since the nineteenth century, some of us liberals have chosen to call ourselves anarchists.

SECTION II

Criticizing Socialism

Definition proceeds best, in many instances, by distinction and contrast. Very likely, the essays in this section will help to resolve ambiguities arising out of those that precede. We have a further reason for devoting a good deal of space to anarchist criticisms of various forms of socialism. Quite unabashedly we want to place anarchism in a favorable light, and it is our feeling that this subject has moved anarchists to many of their strongest performances.

Anarchism has historically been in constant conflict with socialism. It would require reckless audacity to try to summarize this conflict in a page or two, but a brief review of some main episodes will show that the conflict has been of great importance to both sides. There was the famous war of the books, Proudhon's *Philosophy of Poverty* (1846) and Marx's *Poverty of Philosophy* (1847). There was organizational rivalry within the First International between Marxists and Bakuninists. In 1872 the Marxists removed the headquarters of the International to New York, in flight from the preponderance of Bakuninists in Europe if not, as their adversaries claimed, from the Revolution itself. There were always local ill-feelings, aroused in Britain, for example, by the anarchist habit of disrupting Fabian campaigns with no-vote propaganda of their own. The Russian Revolution intensified the conflict. The anarchist leader Nestor Makhno contrived to keep a formidable army in control of the Ukraine for several years before time and the Red Army wore him down. Famous anarchists were attracted to the Revolution but, irritatingly enough from a Marxist point of view, they soon gained wide publicity with such registers of disenchantment as Peter Kropotkin's *Letter to the Workers of Western Europe*, Alexander Berkman's *The Bolshevik Myth*, and Emma Goldman's *My Disillusionment in Russia*. The highlight of the conflict in the twentieth century, however, was the Spanish Civil War. There the so-called rehearsal for the war between fascism and democracy was oddly superimposed on the fifth act of a more venerable conflict between socialism and anarchism. The most popular faction in Spain, the anarcho-syndicalists, refused to participate in the beleaguered government; that is, they refused until the war was all but lost and communist ascendancy over socialists and anarchists looked nearly irreversible. Recriminations are still swapped by Marxists and anarchists over their different roles thirty years ago in Spain.

These are only the most famous episodes in a conflict that has endured so long that it cannot be explained solely in terms of recruitment and propaganda by two organized left-wing sects. For one thing, socialism is a movement just as hard to define as anarchism is. In fact, one of the achievements of the anarchists in this section is to throw open to question all easy presuppositions about what, after all, is socialism. Some anarchists attack socialism as an enemy movement; some criticize authoritarian tendencies in a socialist movement with which they identify themselves. Part of the uncertainty as to whether anarchism is a movement within socialism can be attributed to uncertainty as to whether socialism, in the last analysis, is an outgrowth of libertarian tendencies. But the organizational lines, too, are fuzzy.

However, this does not mean that a lasting anarchist position cannot be identified. Moreover, enumeration of some of the chief anarchist arguments against the socialists will help to explain the permanence of the conflict. State enterprise, anarchists have insisted, only magnifies the oppressing and alienating system of remote control from which men already suffer. Theories of historical necessity enslave men to notions of progress which sacrifice human values to the advancement of technology. Theories of revolution are corrupted by their authors' resorting to the means of violence, chicanery, and elitism, which are transferred by the vanguard to the new-made society. Theories of gradualism, on the other hand, allow vain leaders to estrange themselves from followers in whose judgment they rest no faith; and estrangement passes insidiously into misrepresentation and ineffectuality. This is not a complete list, but it is enough to suggest that the anarchist position is quite sharply defined, at least in attacking socialism, and further that the issues anarchists have raised are not just extensions of rigid dogmas. Rather, these issues bear on inescapable choices that arise out of any dedication to the renovation of society.

This last suggestion will be clearer if we consider some of the doubts and misgivings that are already heard about the civil rights movement in the American South, where few socialist or anarchist spokesmen can be found. What price will the Negro pay for the massive assistance of the federal government if he really obtains it? Should the movement be aiming for equality in the enjoyment of a style of life that most of its white participants have already found unsatisfactory? Is non-violence merely a tactical pretense, or is it a means that previsions the kind of society that is sought? Will dealing behind the scenes and stifling spontaneous militancy lead to organized misrepresentation and frustration, then despair and submissiveness? These questions, in one form or another, come from observers who are not anarchists. We would claim, however, that anarchism is an obvious vantage point from which they can be answered consistently. In fact, these four questions correspond to the four anarchist criticisms of socialism just enumerated. Anarchist criticisms of socialism voice one response to the decisions that press upon any movement to effect great social changes.

8   Common Sources and Divergent Principles

In preparing this anthology, one of our greatest delights has been learning of Benjamin R. Tucker. At one time or another we have wanted to include essays by Tucker in nearly every section, for he wrote with gritty lucidity on a vast range of subjects. He wrote only one book, and that only a collection of dozens of articles. To some extent he thereby handicapped those who might try to revive his fame. But the articles show how deadly was his aim at weaknesses in the political positions of his time. Mostly out of a modest income from employment as an engineer, he kept alive his journal *Liberty* from 1881 to 1908. The fairness with which he printed long letters in criticism of his anarchism and the rigor he brought to his replies make *Liberty* still interesting reading. (Two such letters are found in selection 53; two replies in the headnotes of selections 3, 13.) Unhappily, despair following his awkward support of the Allied side in World War I led to more than twenty years of silence before he died in 1939.

Tucker's antagonist in this selection was not a particular letter-writer, but the whole socialist position. Through an intricate but always clear exposition, Tucker maintains that anarchism and socialism share the same starting point but have come to uphold principles that are diametrically opposed.

Almost the only persons who may be said to comprehend even approximately the significance, principles, and purposes of Socialism are the chief leaders of the extreme wings of the Socialistic forces, and perhaps a few of the money kings themselves. It is a subject of which it has lately become quite the fashion for preacher, professor, and penny-a-liner to treat, and, for the most part, woful work they have made with it, exciting the derision and pity of those competent to judge. That those prominent in the intermediate Socialistic divisions do not fully understand what they are about is evident from the positions they occupy. If they did; if they

Instead of a Book, by Benjamin R. Tucker (New York: Benjamin R. Tucker, 1893), pp. 4–14.

were consistent, logical thinkers; if they were what the French call *consequent* men,—their reasoning faculties would long since have driven them to one extreme or the other.

For it is a curious fact that the two extremes of the vast army now under consideration, though united . . . by the common claim that labor shall be put in possession of its own, are more diametrically opposed to each other in their fundamental principles of social action and their methods of reaching the ends aimed at than either is to their common enemy, the existing society. They are based on two principles the history of whose conflict is almost equivalent to the history of the world since man came into it; and all intermediate parties, including that of the upholders of the existing society, are based upon a compromise between them. It is clear, then, that any intelligent, deep-rooted opposition to the prevailing order of things must come from one or the other of these extremes, for anything from any other source, far from being revolutionary in character, could be only in the nature of such superficial modification as would be utterly unable to concentrate upon itself the degree of attention and interest now bestowed upon Modern Socialism.

The two principles referred to are *Authority* and *Liberty*, and the names of the two schools of Socialistic thought which fully and unreservedly represent one or the other of them are, respectively, State Socialism and Anarchism. Whoso knows what these two schools want and how they propose to get it understands the Socialistic movement. For, just as it has been said that there is no half-way house between Rome and Reason, so it may be said that there is no half-way house between State Socialism and Anarchism. There are, in fact, two currents steadily flowing from the centre of the Socialistic forces which are concentrating them on the left and on the right; and, if Socialism is to prevail, it is among the possibilities that, after this movement of separation has been completed and the existing order has been crushed out between the two camps, the ultimate and bitterer conflict will be still to come. In that case all the eight-hour men, all the trades-unionists, all the Knights of Labor, all the land nationalizationists, all the greenbackers, and, in short, all the members of the thousand and one different battalions belonging to the great army of Labor, will have deserted their old posts, and, these being arrayed on the one side and the other, the great battle will begin. What a final victory for the State

Socialists will mean, and what a final victory for Anarchists will mean, it is the purpose of this paper to briefly state.

To do this intelligently, however, I must first describe the ground common to both, the features that make Socialists of each of them.

The economic principles of Modern Socialism are a logical deduction from the principle laid down by Adam Smith in the early chapters of his "Wealth of Nations,"—namely, that labor is the true measure of price. But Adam Smith, after stating this principle most clearly and concisely, immediately abandoned all further consideration of it to devote himself to showing what actually does measure price, and how, therefore, wealth is at present distributed. Since his day nearly all the political economists have followed his example by confining their function to the description of society as it is, in its industrial and commercial phases. Socialism, on the contrary, extends its function to the description of society as it should be, and the discovery of the means of making it what it should be. Half a century or more after Smith enunciated the principle above stated, Socialism picked it up where he had dropped it, and in following it to its logical conclusions, made it the basis of a new economic philosophy.

This seems to have been done independently by three different men, of three different nationalities, in three different languages: Josiah Warren, an American; Pierre J. Proudhon, a Frenchman; Karl Marx, a German Jew. That Warren and Proudhon arrived at their conclusions singly and unaided is certain; but whether Marx was not largely indebted to Proudhon for his economic ideas is questionable. However this may be, Marx's presentation of the ideas was in so many respects peculiarly his own that he is fairly entitled to the credit of originality. That the work of this interesting trio should have been done so nearly simultaneously would seem to indicate that Socialism was in the air, and that the time was ripe and the conditions favorable for the appearance of this new school of thought. So far as priority of time is concerned, the credit seems to belong to Warren, the American,—a fact which should be noted by the stump orators who are so fond of declaiming against Socialism as an imported article. Of the purest revolutionary blood, too, this Warren, for he descends from the Warren who fell at Bunker Hill.

From Smith's principle that labor is the true measure of price—or, as Warren phrased it, that cost is the proper limit of price—these three men made the following deductions:

that the natural wage of labor is its product; that this wage, or product, is the only just source of income (leaving out, of course, gift, inheritance, etc.); that all who derive income from any other source abstract it directly or indirectly from the natural and just wage of labor; that this abstracting process generally takes one of three forms,—interest, rent, and profit; that these three constitute the trinity of usury, and are simply different methods of levying tribute for the use of capital; that, capital being simply stored-up labor which has already received its pay in full, its use ought to be gratuitous, on the principle that labor is the only basis of price; that the lender of capital is entitled to its return intact, and nothing more; that the only reason why the banker, the stockholder, the landlord, the manufacturer, and the merchant are able to exact usury from labor lies in the fact that they are backed by legal privilege, or monopoly; and that the only way to secure labor the enjoyment of its entire product, or natural wage, is to strike down monopoly.

It must not be inferred that either Warren, Proudhon, or Marx used exactly this phraseology, or followed exactly this line of thought, but it indicates definitely enough the fundamental ground taken by all three, and their substantial thought up to the limit to which they went in common. And, lest I may be accused of stating the positions and arguments of these men incorrectly, it may be well to say in advance that I have viewed them broadly, and that, for the purpose of sharp, vivid, and emphatic comparison and contrast, I have taken considerable liberty with their thought by rearranging it in an order, and often in a phraseology, of my own, but, I am satisfied, without, in so doing, misrepresenting them in any essential particular.

It was at this point—the necessity of striking down monopoly—that came the parting of their ways. Here the road forked. They found that they must turn either to the right or to the left,—follow either the path of Authority or the path of Liberty. Marx went one way; Warren and Proudhon the other. Thus were born State Socialism and Anarchism.

First, then, State Socialism, which may be described as *the doctrine that all the affairs of men should be managed by the government, regardless of individual choice.*

Marx, its founder, concluded that the only way to abolish the class monopolies was to centralize and consolidate all industrial and commercial interests, all productive and distributive agencies, in one vast monopoly in the hands of the

State. The government must become banker, manufacturer, farmer, carrier, and merchant, and in these capacities must suffer no competition. Land, tools, and all instruments of production must be wrested from individual hands, and made the property of the collectivity. To the individual can belong only the products to be consumed, not the means of producing them. A man may own his clothes and his food, but not the sewing-machine which makes his shirts or the spade which digs his potatoes. Product and capital are essentially different things; the former belongs to individuals, the latter to society. Society must seize the capital which belongs to it, by the ballot if it can, by revolution if it must. Once in possession of it, it must administer it on the majority principle, through its organ, the State, utilize it in production and distribution, fix all prices by the amount of labor involved, and employ the whole people in its workshops, farms, stores, etc. The nation must be transformed into a vast bureaucracy, and every individual into a State official. Everything must be done on the cost principle, the people having no motive to make a profit out of themselves. Individuals not being allowed to own capital, no one can employ another, or even himself. Every man will be a wage-receiver, and the State the only wage-payer. He who will not work for the State must starve, or, more likely, go to prison. All freedom of trade must disappear. Competition must be utterly wiped out. All industrial and commercial activity must be centred in one vast, enormous, all-inclusive monopoly. The remedy for *monopolies* is *monopoly*.

Such is the economic programme of State Socialism as adopted from Karl Marx. The history of its growth and progress cannot be told here. In this country the parties that uphold it are known as the Socialistic Labor Party, which pretends to follow Karl Marx; the Nationalists, who follow Karl Marx filtered through Edward Bellamy; and the Christian Socialists, who follow Karl Marx filtered through Jesus Christ.

What other applications this principle of Authority, once adopted in the economic sphere, will develop is very evident. It means the absolute control by the majority of all individual conduct. The right of such control is already admitted by the State Socialists, though they maintain that, as a matter of fact, the individual would be allowed a much larger liberty than he now enjoys. But he would only be allowed it; he could not claim it as his own. There would be no foundation of society upon a guaranteed equality of the largest possible liberty. Such liberty as might exist would exist by sufferance

and could be taken away at any moment. Constitutional guarantees would be of no avail. There would be but one article
in the constitution of a State Socialistic country: "The right
of the majority is absolute."

The claim of the State Socialists, however, that this right
would not be exercised in matters pertaining to the individual
in the more intimate and private relations of his life is not
borne out by the history of governments. It has ever been the
tendency of power to add to itself, to enlarge its sphere, to
encroach beyond the limits set for it; and where the habit of
resisting such encroachment is not fostered, and the individual is not taught to be jealous of his rights, individuality
gradually disappears and the government or State becomes
the all-in-all. Control naturally accompanies responsibility.
Under the system of State Socialism, therefore, which holds
the community responsible for the health, wealth, and wisdom of the individual, it is evident that the community,
through its majority expression, will insist more and more on
prescribing the conditions of health, wealth, and wisdom, thus
impairing and finally destroying individual independence and
with it all sense of individual responsibility.

Whatever, then, the State Socialists may claim or disclaim,
their system, if adopted, is doomed to end in a State religion,
to the expense of which all must contribute and at the altar of
which all must kneel; a State school of medicine, by whose
practitioners the sick must invariably be treated; a State system of hygiene, prescribing what all must and must not eat,
drink, wear, and do; a State code of morals, which will not
content itself with punishing crime, but will prohibit what
the majority decide to be vice; a State system of instruction,
which will do away with all private schools, academies, and
colleges; a State nursery, in which all children must be
brought up in common at the public expense; and, finally, a
State family, with an attempt at stirpiculture, or scientific
breeding, in which no man and woman will be allowed to
have children if the State prohibits them and no man and
woman can refuse to have children if the State orders them.
Thus will Authority achieve its acme and Monopoly be carried to its highest power.

Such is the ideal of the logical State Socialist, such the goal
which lies at the end of the road that Karl Marx took. Let us
now follow the fortunes of Warren and Proudhon, who took
the other road,—the road of Liberty.

This brings us to Anarchism, which may be described as

*the doctrine that all the affairs of men should be managed by
individuals or voluntary associations, and that the State
should be abolished.*

When Warren and Proudhon, in prosecuting their search
for justice to labor, came face to face with the obstacle of
class monopolies, they saw that these monopolies rested upon
Authority, and concluded that the thing to be done was, not
to strengthen this Authority and thus make monopoly universal, but to utterly uproot Authority and give full sway to
the opposite principle, Liberty, by making competition, the
antithesis of monopoly, universal. They saw in competition
the great leveller of prices to the labor cost of production. In
this they agreed with the political economists. The query then
naturally presented itself why all prices do not fall to labor
cost; where there is any room for incomes acquired otherwise
than by labor; in a word, why the usurer, the receiver of interest, rent, and profit, exists. The answer was found in the
present one-sidedness of competition. It was discovered that
capital had so manipulated legislation that unlimited competition is allowed in supplying productive labor, thus keeping
wages down to the starvation point, or as near it as practicable; that a great deal of competition is allowed in supplying
distributive labor, or the labor of the mercantile classes, thus
keeping, not the prices of goods, but the merchants' actual
profits on them down to a point somewhat approximating
equitable wages for the merchants' work; but that almost no
competition at all is allowed in supplying capital, upon the
aid of which both productive and distributive labor are dependent for their power of achievement, thus keeping the rate
of interest on money and of house-rent and ground-rent at as
high a point as the necessities of the people will bear.

On discovering this, Warren and Proudhon charged the
political economists with being afraid of their own doctrine.
The Manchester men were accused of being inconsistent.
They believed in liberty to compete with the laborer in order
to reduce his wages, but not in liberty to compete with the
capitalist in order to reduce his usury. *Laissez faire* was very
good sauce for the goose, labor, but very poor sauce for the
gander, capital. But how to correct this inconsistency, how to
serve this gander with this sauce, how to put capital at the
service of business men and laborers at cost, or free of usury,
—that was the problem.

Marx, as we have seen, solved it by declaring capital to be
a different thing from product, and maintaining that it be-

longed to society and should be seized by society and employed for the benefit of all alike. Proudhon scoffed at this distinction between capital and product. He maintained that capital and product are not different kinds of wealth, but simply alternate conditions or functions of the same wealth; that all wealth undergoes an incessant transformation from capital into product and from product back into capital, the process repeating itself interminably; that capital and product are purely social terms; that what is product to one man immediately becomes capital to another, and *vice versa*; that if there were but one person in the world, all wealth would be to him at once capital and product; that the fruit of A's toil is his product, which, when sold to B, becomes B's capital (unless B is an unproductive consumer, in which case it is merely wasted wealth, outside the view of social economy); that a steam-engine is just as much product as a coat, and that a coat is just as much capital as a steam-engine; and that the same laws of equity govern the possession of the one that govern the possession of the other.

For these and other reasons Proudhon and Warren found themselves unable to sanction any such plan as the seizure of capital by society. But, though opposed to socializing the ownership of capital, they aimed nevertheless to socialize its effects by making its use beneficial to all instead of a means of impoverishing the many to enrich the few. And when the light burst in upon them, they saw that this could be done by subjecting capital to the natural law of competition, thus bringing the price of its own use down to cost,—that is, to nothing beyond the expenses incidental to handling and transferring it. So they raised the banner of Absolute Free Trade; free trade at home, as well as with foreign countries; the logical carrying out of the Manchester doctrine; *laissez faire* the universal rule. Under this banner they began their fight upon monopolies, whether the all-inclusive monopoly of the State Socialists, or the various class monopolies that now prevail. . . .

The development of the economic programme which consists in the destruction of these monopolies and the substitution for them of the freest competition led its authors to a perception of the fact that all their thought rested upon a very fundamental principle, the freedom of the individual, his right of sovereignty over himself, his products, and his affairs, and of rebellion against the dictation of external authority. Just as the idea of taking capital away from individuals and giving it to the government started Marx in a path which ends in making the government everything and the individual nothing, so the idea of taking capital away from government-protected monopolies and putting it within easy reach of all individuals started Warren and Proudhon in a path which ends in making the individual everything and the government nothing. If the individual has a right to govern himself, all external government is tyranny. Hence the necessity of abolishing the State. This was the logical conclusion to which Warren and Proudhon were forced, and it became the fundamental article of their political philosophy. It is the doctrine which Proudhon named An-archism, a word derived from the Greek, and meaning, not necessarily absence of order, as is generally supposed, but absence of rule. The Anarchists are simply unterrified Jeffersonian Democrats. They believe that "the best government is that which governs least," and that that which governs least is no government at all.

9 Socialism and Enslaving Economics

Leo Tolstoy nurtured anarchist convictions for much of his life, coming to loathe war and execution, to admire simplicity and responsibility. Besieged by doubt and agony during the completion of *Anna Karenina*, he found peace in conversion to a religion identical with anarchism. His rejection of governmental authority and his faith in the strength of a moral revolution have ever since encouraged believers in non-violence. Mahatma Gandhi found a guiding spirit in Tolstoy, just as he gained intellectual sustenance from Kropotkin.

This selection, written in 1900, discloses a good deal of the sense of injustice that animated Tolstoy. But its greatest significance may lie in his anticipation of a shortcoming which later proved disillusioning in socialist countries: the fact that socialists accepted uncritically so many value judgments implicit in orthodox political economy that they were bound to subvert their professed ideal of egalitarianism. His reasoning is echoed today, incongruously enough, by sociologists who claim that a complex economy, dependent on the division of labor, necessarily leads to differentiation of income and prestige.

The theory that it is God's will that some people should own others satisfied people for a very long time. But that theory, by justifying cruelty, caused such cruelty as evoked resistance, and produced doubts as to the truth of the theory.

So now with the theory that an economic evolution is progressing, guided by inevitable laws, in consequence of which some people must collect capital, and others must labour all their lives to increase those capitals, preparing themselves meanwhile for the promised communalisation of the means of production; this theory, causing some people to be yet more cruel to others, also begins (especially among common people not stupefied by science) to evoke certain doubts.

For instance, you see goods-porters destroying their lives by thirty-seven hours labour, or women in factories, or

The Slavery of Our Times by Leo Tolstoy, translated by Aylmer Maude (New York: Edwin C. Walker, 1900), pp. 33–64.

laundresses, or typesetters, or all those millions of people who live in hard, unnatural conditions of monotonous, stupefying, slavish toil, and you naturally ask, What has brought these people to such a state? And how are they to be delivered from it? And science replies that these people are in this condition because the railway belongs to this company, the silk factory to that gentleman, and all the foundries, factories, typographies, and laundries to capitalists, and that this state of things will come right by work-people forming unions, co-operative societies, strikes, and taking part in government, and more and more swaying the masters and the government till the workers first obtain shorter hours and increased wages, and finally all the means of production will pass into their hands, and then all will be well. Meanwhile, all is going on as it should go, and there is no need to alter anything.

This answer must seem to an unlearned man, and particularly to our Russian folk, very surprising. In the first place, neither in relation to the goods-porters, nor the factory women, nor all the millions of other labourers suffering from heavy, unhealthy, stupefying labour does the possession of the means of production by capitalists explain anything. The agricultural means of production of those men who are now working at the railway have not been seized by capitalists: they have land, and horses, and ploughs, and harrows, and all that is necessary to till the ground; also these women working at the factory are not only not forced to it by being deprived of their implements of production, but, on the contrary, they have (for the most part against the wish of the elder members of their families) left the homes where their work was much wanted, and where they had implements of production.

Millions of work-people in Russia and in other countries are in like case. So that the cause of the miserable position of the workers cannot be found in the seizure of the means of production by capitalists. The cause must lie in that which drives them from the villages. That, in the first place. Secondly, the emancipation of the workers from this state of things (even in that distant future in which science promises them liberty) can be accomplished neither by shortening the hours of labour, nor by increasing wages, nor by the promised communalisation of the means of production.

All that cannot improve their position, for the misery of the labourer's position—alike on the railway, in the silk factory and in every other factory or workshop—consists not in the longer or shorter hours of work (agriculturalists sometimes work eighteen hours a day, and as much as thirty-six hours on end, and consider their lives happy ones), nor does it consist in the low rate of wages, nor in the fact that the railway or the factory is not theirs, but it consists in the fact that they are obliged to work in harmful, unnatural conditions often dangerous and destructive to life, and to live a barrack life in towns—a life full of temptations and immorality—and to do compulsory labour at another's bidding.

Latterly the hours of labour have diminished and the rate of wages has increased; but this diminution of the hours of labour and this increase in wages have not improved the position of the worker, if one takes into account not their more luxurious habits—watches with chains, silk kerchiefs, tobacco, vódka, beef, beer, etc.—but their true welfare—that is, their health and morality, and chiefly their freedom.

At the silk factory with which I am acquainted, twenty years ago the work was chiefly done by men, who worked fourteen hours a day, earned on an average fifteen roubles a month, and sent the money for the most part to their families in the villages. Now nearly all the work is done by women working eleven hours, some of whom earn as much as twenty-five roubles a month (over fifteen roubles on the average), and for the most part not sending it home, but spend all they earn here chiefly on dress, drunkenness and vice. The diminution of the hours of work merely increases the time they spend in the taverns.

The same thing is happening, to a greater or lesser extent, at all the factories and works. Everywhere, notwithstanding the diminution of the hours of labour and the increase of wages, the health of the operatives is worse than that of country workers, the average duration of life is shorter, and morality is sacrificed, as cannot but occur when people are torn from those conditions which most conduce to morality—family life, and free, healthy, varied and intelligible agricultural work.

It is very possibly true that, as some economists assert, with shorter hours of labour, more pay, and improved sanitary conditions in mills and factories, the health of the workers and their morality improve in comparison with the former condition of factory workers. It is possible also that latterly, and in some places, the position of the factory hands is better in external conditions than the position of the country population. But this is so (and only in some places) because the government and society, influenced by the affirmation of science, do all that is possible to improve the position of the factory population at the expense of the country population. . . .

The misery of the position of a factory hand, and in general of a town worker, does not consist in his long hours and small pay, but in the fact that he is deprived of the natural conditions of life in touch with nature, is deprived of freedom, is compelled to compulsory and monotonous toil at another man's will. . . .

If there are workmen, as in England, Belgium, or Germany, who for some generations have lived by factory work, even they live so not at their own free will, but because their fathers, grandfathers and great-grandfathers were, in some way, compelled to exchange the agricultural life which they loved for life which seemed to them hard, in towns and at factories. First, the country people were deprived of their land by violence, says Karl Marx, were evicted and brought to vagabondage, and then, by cruel laws, they were tortured with pincers, with red-hot irons, and were whipped, to make them submit to the condition of being hired labourers. Therefore, the question how to free the workers from their miserable position should, one would think, naturally lead to the question how to remove those causes which have already driven some, and are now driving or threatening to drive, the rest of the peasants from the position which they considered and consider good, and have driven and are driving them to a position which they consider bad.

Economic science, although it indicates in passing the causes that drove the peasants from the villages, does not concern itself with the question how to remove these causes, but directs all its attention to the improvement of the worker's position in the existing factories and works, assuming, as it were, that the worker's position at these factories and workshops is something unalterable, something which must at all costs be maintained for those who are already in the factories, and must absorb those who have not yet left the villages or abandoned agricultural work.

Moreover, economic science is so sure that all the peasants have inevitably to become factory operatives in towns, that though all the sages and all the poets of the world have always placed the ideal of human happiness in the conditions of agricultural work; though all the workers whose habits are unperverted have always preferred, and still prefer, agricultural labour to any other; though factory work is always unhealthy and monotonous, while agriculture is the most healthy and varied; though agricultural work is free—that is, the peasant alternates toil and rest at his own will—while factory work, even if the factory belongs to the workmen, is always enforced, in dependence on the machines; though factory work is derivative, while agricultural work is fundamental, and without it no factory could exist—yet economic science affirms that all the country people not only are not injured by the transition from the country to the town, but themselves desire it and strive towards it. . . .

The cause of this evidently unjust assertion is that those who have formulated, and who are formulating, the laws of science belong to the well-to-do classes, and are so accustomed to the conditions, advantageous for themselves, among which they live, that they do not admit the thought that society could exist under other conditions.

The condition of life to which people of the well-to-do classes are accustomed is that of an abundant production of various articles necessary for their comfort and pleasure, and these things are obtained only thanks to the existence of factories and works organised as at present. And, therefore, discussing the improvement of the workers' position, the men of science belonging to the well-to-do classes always have in view only such improvements as will not do away with the system of factory production and those conveniences of which they avail themselves.

Even the most advanced economists—the Socialists, who demand the complete control of the means of production for the workers—expect production of the same or almost of the same articles as are produced now to continue in the present or in similar factories with the present division of labour.

The difference, as they imagine it, will only be that in the future not they alone, but all men, will make use of such conveniences as they alone now enjoy. They dimly picture to themselves that, with the communalisation of the means of production, they, too—men of science, and in general the ruling classes—will do some work, but chiefly as managers, designers, scientists or artists. To the questions, Who will have to wear a muzzle and make white lead? Who will be stokers, miners, and cesspool cleaners? they are either silent, or foretell that all these things will be so improved that even work at cesspools and underground will afford pleasant occupation. That is how they represent to themselves future economic conditions, both in Utopias such as that of Bellamy and in scientific works.

According to their theories, the workers will all join unions and associations, and cultivate solidarity among themselves by unions, strikes and participation in Parliament till they obtain possession of all the means of production, as well as the land, and then they will be so well fed, so well dressed, and enjoy such amusements on holidays that they will prefer life in town, amid brick buildings and smoking chimneys, to free village life amid plants and domestic animals; and monotonous, bell-regulated machine work to the varied, healthy, and free agricultural labour.

Though this anticipation is as improbable as the anticipation of the theologians about a heaven to be enjoyed hereafter by workmen in compensation for their hard labour here, yet learned and educated people of our society believe this strange teaching, just as formerly wise and learned people believed in a heaven for workmen in the next world.

And learned men and their disciples, people of the well-to-do classes, believe this because they must believe it. This dilemma stands before them: either they must see that all that they make use of in their lives, from railways to lucifer matches and cigarettes, represents labour which costs the lives of their brother men, and that they, not sharing in that toil, but making use of it, are very dishonourable men; or they must believe that all that takes place takes place for the general advantage in accord with unalterable laws of economic science. Therein lies the inner psychological cause, compelling men of science, men wise and educated, but not enlightened, to affirm positively and tenaciously such an obvious untruth as that the labourers, for their own well-being, should leave their happy and healthy life in touch with nature, and go to ruin their bodies and souls in factories and workshops.

But even allowing the assertion (evidently unfounded as it is, and contrary to the facts of human nature) that it is better for people to live in towns and to do compulsory machine work in factories rather than to live in villages and work freely at handicrafts, there remains, in the very ideal itself, to which the men of science tell us the economic revolution is leading, an insoluble contradiction. The ideal is that the workers, having become the masters of all the means of production, are to obtain all the comforts and pleasures now possessed by well-to-do people. They will all be well clothed, and housed, and well nourished, and will all walk on electrically lighted, asphalt streets, and frequent concerts and theatres, and read papers and books, and ride on motor cars, etc. But that everybody may have certain things, the production of those things must be apportioned, and consequently it must be decided how long each workman is to work.

How is that to be decided?

Statistics may show (though very imperfectly) what people require in a society fettered by capital, by competition, and by want. But no statistics can show how much is wanted and what articles are needed to satisfy the demand in a society where the means of production will belong to the society itself—that is, where the people will be free.

The demands in such a society cannot be defined, and they will always infinitely exceed the possibility of satisfying them. Everybody will wish to have all that the richest now possesses, and, therefore, it is quite impossible to define the quantity of goods that such a society will require.

Furthermore, how are people to be induced to work at articles which some consider necessary and others consider unnecessary or even harmful?

If it be found necessary for everybody to work, say six hours a day, in order to satisfy the requirements of the society, who in a free society can compel a man to work those six hours, if he knows that part of the time is spent in producing things he considers unnecessary or even harmful?

It is undeniable that under the present state of things most varied articles are produced with great economy of exertion, thanks to machinery, and thanks especially to the division of labour which has been brought to an extreme nicety and carried to the highest perfection, and that those articles are profitable to the manufacturers, and that we find them convenient and pleasant to use. But the fact that these articles are well made and are produced with little expenditure of strength, that they are profitable to the capitalists and convenient for us, does not prove that free men would, without compulsion, continue to produce them. There is no doubt that Krupp, with the present division of labour, makes admirable cannons very quickly and artfully; N. M. very quickly and artfully produces silk materials; X. Y. and Z. produce toilet scents, powder to preserve the complexion, or glazed packs of cards, and K. produces whiskey of choice flavour, etc.; and no doubt, both for those who want these articles and for the owners of the factories in which they are made it is very advantageous. But cannons and scents and whiskey are wanted by those who wish to obtain control of the Chinese market, or who like to get drunk, or are concerned about their complexions; but there will be some who consider the production of these articles harmful. And there will always be people who consider that besides these articles, exhibitions, academies, beer and beef are unnecessary and even harmful. How are these people to be made to participate in the production of such articles?

But even if a means could be found to get all to agree to produce certain articles (though there is no such means, and can be none, except coercion), who, in a free society, without capitalistic production, competition, and its law of supply and demand, will decide which articles are to have the preference? Which are to be made first, and which after? Are we first to build the Siberian Railway and fortify Port Arthur, and then macadamise the roads in our country districts, or *viceversa*? Which is to come first, electric lighting or irrigation of the fields? And then comes another question, insoluble with free workmen, Which men are to do which work? Evidently all will prefer hay-making or drawing to stoking or cesspool cleaning. How, in apportioning the work, are people to be induced to agree?

No statistics can answer these questions. The solution can be only theoretical; it may be said that there will be people to whom power will be given to regulate all these matters. Some people will decide these questions and others will obey them.

But besides the questions of apportioning and directing production and of selecting work, when the means of production are communalised, there will be another and most important question, as to the degree of division of labour that can be established in a socialistically organised society. The now existing division of labour is conditioned by the necessities of the workers. A worker only agrees to live all his life underground, or to make the one hundredth part of one article all his life, or to move his hands up and down amid the roar of machinery all his life, because he will otherwise not have means to live. But it will only be by compulsion that a workman, owning the means of production and not suffering want, can be induced to accept such stupefying and soul-destroying conditions of labour as those in which people now work. Division of labour is undoubtedly very profitable and natural to people; but if people are free, division of labour is only possible up to a certain very limited extent, which has been far overstepped in our society.

If one peasant occupies himself chiefly with boot-making, and his wife weaves, and another peasant ploughs, and a third is a blacksmith, and they all, having acquired special dexterity in their own work, afterwards exchange what they have produced, such division of labour is advantageous to all, and free people will naturally divide their work in this way. But a division of labour by which a man makes one one-hundredth of an article, or a stoker works in 150° of heat, or is choked with harmful gases, such division of labour is disadvantageous, because though it furthers the production of insignificant articles, it destroys that which is most precious—the life of man. And, therefore, such division of labour as now exists can only exist where there is compulsion. Rodbertus says that communal division of labour unites mankind. That is true, but it is only free division, such as people voluntarily adopt, that unites.

If people decide to make a road, and one digs, another brings stones, a third breaks them, etc., that sort of division of work unites people.

But if, independently of the wishes, and sometimes against the wishes, of the workers, a strategical railway is built, or an Eiffel tower, or stupidities such as fill the Paris Exhibition, and one workman is compelled to obtain iron, another to dig coal, a third to make castings, a fourth to cut down trees, and a fifth to saw them up, without even having the least idea what the things they are making are wanted for, then such division of labour not only does not unite men, but, on the contrary, it divides them.

And, therefore, with communalised implements of production, if people are free, they will only adopt division of labour in so far as the good resulting will outweigh the evils it occasions to the workers. And as each man naturally sees good in extending and diversifying his activities, such division of labour as now exists will evidently be impossible in a free society.

To suppose that with communalised means of production there will be such an abundance of things as is now produced by compulsory division of labour is like supposing that after the emancipation of the serfs the domestic orchestras and theatres, the home-made carpets and laces and the elaborate gardens which depended on serf labour would continue to exist as before. So that the supposition that when the Socialist ideal is realised every one will be free, and will at the same time have at his disposal everything, or almost everything, that is now made use of by the well-to-do classes, involves an obvious self-contradiction.

10 Marx, the Bismarck of Socialism

Michael Bakunin, in common with other Russian anarchists like Kropotkin and Tolstoy, came from the educated class and spent his life in the cause of the peasantry. He has been frequently depicted as an *opéra bouffe* character in European history, his life a comic mixture of aborted uprisings, proligate borrowing, romantic paeans to violence, and anxiety over his impotency. In the same vein, his writings are described as preposterous, chaotic, incomplete. One is left to puzzle at his ability to stalemate Marx in competition for the loyalty of the International and at the endurance of the Bakuninist tradition in the Mediterranean countries.

It is undeniable that Bakunin never found time to finish elaborate writing projects; thus there is no anarchist equivalent to *Capital*. In part, this was because he felt he had less to prove. The ancient village practices of cooperation indicated to him how revolution could build on spontaneous social impulses. Many of his beliefs were more clearly defended later in the works of Kropotkin.

It is probably also true that Bakunin's mind was disorderly. But disorderliness, as measured against the systematic fury that produced Marx's tomes, need not imply that he was imperceptive. To his followers he must have shown many excellences which he did not bother to enshrine in literature. K. J. Kenafick, an Australian scholar, arranged passages from Bakunin's writings on various manifestations of Marxism under the title *Marxism, Freedom and the State*. It is from that book, issued in 1950, that we have taken the following selection.

MARXIST IDEOLOGY

The doctrinaire school of Socialists, or rather of German Authoritarian Communists, was founded a little before 1848, and has rendered, it must be recognised, eminent services to the cause of the proletariat not only in Germany, but in Europe. It is to them that belongs principally the great idea of an "International Workingmen's Association" and also the

Marxism, Freedom and the State by Michael Bakunin, translated by K. J. Kenafick (London: Freedom Press, 1950), pp. 20–61.

initiative for its first realisation. . . . It is therefore a perfectly respectable school, which does not prevent it from displaying a very bad disposition sometimes, and above all from taking for the basis of its theories, a principle which is profoundly true when one considers it in its true light, that is to say, from the relative point of view, but which when envisaged and set down in an absolute manner as the only foundation and first source of all other principles, as is done by this school, becomes completely false. . . .

This principle is the absolute opposite to that recognised by the Idealists of all schools. . . . Whilst the Idealists maintain that ideas dominate and produce facts, the Communists, in agreement besides with scientific Materialism say, on the contrary, that facts give birth to ideas and that these latter are never anything else but the ideal expression of accomplished facts and that among all the facts, economic and material facts, the pre-eminent facts, constitute the essential basis, the principal foundation of which all the other facts, intellectual and moral, political and social, are nothing more than the inevitable derivatives.

We, who are Materialists and Determinists, just as much as Marx himself, we also recognise the inevitable linking of economic and political facts in history. We recognise, indeed, the necessity, the inevitable character of all events that happen, but we do not bow before them indifferently and above all we are very careful about praising them when, by their nature, they show themselves in flagrant opposition to the supreme end of history, to the thoroughly human ideal that is to be found under more or less obvious forms, in the instincts, the aspirations of the people and under all the religious symbols of all epochs, because it is inherent in the human race, the most social of all the races of animals on earth. Thus this ideal, to-day better understood than ever, can be summed up in the words: It is *the triumph of humanity, it is the conquest and accomplishment of the full freedom and full development, material, intellectual and moral, of every individual, by the absolutely free and spontaneous organisation of economic and social solidarity as completely as possible between all human beings living on the earth.*

Everything in history that shows itself conformable to that end, from the human point of view—and we can have no other—is good; all that is contrary to it is bad. We know very well, in any case, that what we call good and bad are always, one and the other, the natural results of natural causes, and that consequently one is as inevitable as the other. But as in what is properly called Nature we recognise many necessities that we are little disposed to bless, for example the necessity of dying of hydrophobia when bitten by a mad dog, in the same way, in that immediate continuation of the life of Nature, called History, we encounter many necessities which we find much more worthy of opprobrium than of benediction and which we believe we should stigmatise with all the energy of which we are capable, in the interest of our social and individual morality, although we recognise that from the moment they have been accomplished, even the most detestable historic facts have that character of inevitability which is found in all the phenomena of Nature as well as those of history.

To make my idea clearer, I shall illustrate it by some examples. When I study the respective social and political conditions in which the Romans and the Greeks came into contact towards the decline of Antiquity, I arrive at the conclusion that the conquest and destruction by the military and civic barbarism of the Romans, of the comparatively high standard of human liberty of Greece was a logical, natural, absolutely inevitable fact. But that does not prevent me at all from taking retrospectively and very firmly, the side of Greece against Rome in that struggle, and I find that the human race gained absolutely nothing by the triumph of the Romans. . . .

Let us pass on to France. After a struggle which lasted a century Catholicism, supported by the State, finally triumphed there over Protestantism. Well, do I not still find in France to-day some politicians or historians of the fatalist school and who, calling themselves Revolutionaries, consider this victory of Catholicism—a bloody and inhuman victory if ever there was one—as a veritable triumph for the Revolution? Catholicism, they maintain, was then the State, democracy, whilst Protestantism represented the revolt of the aristocracy against the State and consequently against democracy. It is with sophisms like that—completely identical besides with the Marxian sophisms, which, also, consider the triumphs of the State as those of Social Democracy—it is with these absurdities, as disgusting as revolting, that the mind and moral sense of the masses is perverted, habituating them to consider their blood-thirsty exploiters, their age-long enemies, their tyrants, the masters and the servants of the State, as the organs, representatives, heroes, devoted servants of their emancipation.

It is a thousand times right to say that Protestantism then, not as Calvinist theology, but as an energetic and armed protest, represented revolt, liberty, humanity, the destruction of the State; whilst Catholicism was public order, authority, divine law, the salvation of the State by the Church and the Church by the State, the condemnation of human society to a boundless and endless slavery. . . .

THE STATE AND MARXISM

Karl Marx, the undisputed chief of the Socialist Party in Germany—a great intellect armed with a profound knowledge, whose entire life, one can say it without flattering, has been devoted exclusively to the greatest cause which exists to-day, the emancipation of labour and of the toilers—Karl Marx who is indisputably also, if not the only, at least one of the principal founders of the International Workingmen's Association, made the development of the Communist idea the object of a serious work. . . . His work on Capital, though unfortunately bristling with formulas and metaphysical subtleties, which render it unapproachable for the great mass of readers, is in the highest degree a scientific or realist work: in the sense that it absolutely excludes any other logic than that of the facts. . . .

Marx is not only a learned Socialist, he is also a very clever politician and an ardent patriot. Like Bismarck, though by somewhat different means, and like many other of his compatriots, Socialists or not, he wants the establishment of a great Germanic State for the glory of the German people and for the happiness and the voluntary, or enforced civilisation of the world.

The policy of Bismarck is that of the present; the policy of Marx, who considers himself at least as his successor, and his continuator, is that of the future. And when I say that Marx considers himself the continuator of Bismarck, I am far from calumniating Marx. If he did not consider himself as such, he would not have permitted Engels, the confidant of all his thoughts, to write that Bismarck serves the cause of Social Revolution. He serves it now in his own way; Marx will serve it later, in another manner. That is the sense in which he will be later, the continuator, as to-day he is the admirer of the policy of Bismarck.

Now let us examine the particular character of Marx's policy, let us ascertain the essential points on which it is to be separated from the Bismarckian policy. The principal point, and, one might say, the only one, is this: Marx is a democrat, an Authoritarian Socialist, and a Republican; Bismarck is an out and out Pomeranian, aristocratic, monarchical Junker. The difference is therefore very great, very serious, and both sides are sincere in this difference. On this point, there is no possible understanding or reconciliation possible between Bismarck and Marx. . . .

Let us see now what unites them. *It is the out and out cult of the State.* I have no need to prove it in the case of Bismarck, the proofs are there. From head to foot he is a State's man and nothing but a State's man. But neither do I believe that I shall have need of too great efforts to prove that it is the same with Marx. He loves government to such a degree that he even wanted to institute one in the International Workingmen's Association; and he worships power so much that he wanted to impose and still means to-day to impose his dictatorship on us. It seems to me that that is sufficient to characterise his personal attitude. But his Socialist and political programme is a very faithful expression of it. The supreme objective of all his efforts, as is proclaimed to us by the fundamental statutes of his party in Germany, is the establishment of the great People's State (Volksstaat).

But whoever says State, necessarily says a particular limited State, doubtless comprising, if it is very large, many different peoples and countries, but excluding still more. For unless he is dreaming of the Universal State, as did Napoleon and the Emperor Charles the Fifth, or as the Papacy dreamed of the Universal Church, Marx, in spite of all the international ambition which devours him to-day, will have, when the hour of the realisation of his dreams has sounded for him—if it ever does sound—he will have to content himself with governing a single State and not several States at once. Consequently, whoever says State says, *a* State, and . . . affirms by that the existence of several States, and whoever says *several* States, immediately says: competition, jealousy, truceless and endless war. The simplest logic as well as all history bear witness to it.

Any State, under pain of perishing and seeing itself devoured by neighbouring States, must tend towards complete power, and having become powerful, it must embark on a career of conquest, so that it shall not be itself conquered; for two powers similar and at the same time foreign to each other could not co-exist without trying to destroy each other. Whoever says conquest, says conquered peoples, enslaved and in bondage, under whatever form or name it may be.

It is in the nature of the State to break the solidarity of the human race and, as it were, to deny humanity. The State cannot preserve itself as such in its integrity and in all its strength except it sets itself up as supreme and absolute be-all and end-all, at least for its own citizens, or to speak more frankly, for its own subjects, not being able to impose itself as such on the citizens of other States unconquered by it. From that there inevitably results a break with human, considered as universal, morality and with universal reason, by the birth of State morality and reasons of State. The principle of political or State morality is very simple. The State, being the supreme objective, everything that is favourable to the development of its power is good; all that is contrary to it, even if it were the most humane thing in the world, is bad. This morality is called *Patriotism*. The International is the negation of patriotism and consequently the negation of the State. If therefore Marx and his friends of the German Socialist Democratic Party should succeed in introducing the State principle into our programme, they would kill the International.

The State, for its own preservation, must necessarily be powerful as regards foreign affairs; but if it is so as regards foreign affairs, it will infallibly be so as regards home affairs. Every State, having to let itself be inspired and directed by some particular morality, conformable to the particular conditions of its existence, by a morality which is a restriction and consequently a negation of human and universal morality, must keep watch that all its subjects, in their thoughts and above all in their acts, are inspired also only by the principles of this patriotic or particular morality, and that they remain deaf to the teachings of pure or universally human morality. From that there results the necessity for a State censorship; too great liberty of thought and opinions being, as Marx considers, very reasonably too from his eminently political point of view, incompatible with that unanimity of adherence demanded by the security of the State. That that in reality is Marx's opinion is sufficiently proved by the attempts which he made to introduce censorship into the International, under plausible pretexts, and covering it with a mask.

But however vigilant this censorship may be, even if the State were to take into its own hands exclusively education and all the instruction of the people, as Mazzini wished to do, and as Marx wishes to do to-day, the State can never be sure that prohibited and dangerous thoughts may not slip in and be smuggled somehow into the consciousness of the population that it governs. Forbidden fruit has such an attraction for men, and the demon of revolt, that eternal enemy of the State, awakens so easily in their hearts when they are not sufficiently stupefied, that neither this education nor this instruction, nor even the censorship, sufficiently guarantee the tranquillity of the State. It must still have a police, devoted agents who watch over and direct, secretly and unobtrusively, the current of the peoples' opinions and passions. We have seen that Marx himself is so convinced of this necessity, that he believed he should fill with his secret agents all the regions of the International and above all, Italy, France, and Spain. Finally, however perfect may be, from the point of view of the preservation of the State, the organisation of education and instruction for the people, of censorship and the police, the State cannot be secure in its existence while it does not have, to defend it against its *enemies at home*, an armed force. The State is government from above downwards of an immense number of men, very different from the point of view of the degree of their culture, the nature of the countries or localities that they inhabit, the occupation they follow, the interests and the aspirations directing them—the State is the government of all these by some or other minority; this minority, even if it were a thousand times elected by universal suffrage and controlled in its acts by popular institutions, unless it were endowed with the omniscience, omnipresence and the omnipotence which the theologians attribute to God, it is impossible that it could know and foresee the needs, or satisfy with an even justice the most legitimate and pressing interests in the world. There will always be discontented people because there will always be some who are sacrificed.

Besides, the State, like the Church, by its very nature is a great sacrificer of living beings. It is an arbitrary being, in whose heart all the positive, living, individual, and local interests of the population meet, clash, destroy each other, become absorbed in that abstraction called the common interest, the *public good*, the *public safety*, and where all real wills cancel each other in that other abstraction which bears the name of the *will of the people*. It results from this, that this so-called will of the people is never anything else than the sacrifice and the negation of all the real wills of the population; just as this so-called public good is nothing else than the sacrifice of their interests. But so that this omnivorous abstraction could impose itself on millions of men, it must be represented and supported by some real being, by some living force or other. Well, this being, this force, has always existed. In the Church it is called the clergy, and in the State—the ruling or governing class.

And, in fact, what do we find throughout history? The State has always been the patrimony of some privileged class or other; a priestly class, an aristocratic class, a bourgeois class, and finally a bureaucratic class, when, all the other classes having become exhausted, the State falls or rises, as you will, to the condition of a machine; but it is absolutely necessary for the salvation of the State that there should be some privileged class or other which is interested in its existence. And it is precisely the united interest of this privileged class which is called Patriotism. . . .

But in the People's State of Marx, there will be, we are told, no privileged class at all. All will be equal, not only from the juridical and political point of view, but from the economic point of view. At least that is what is promised, though I doubt very much, considering the manner in which it is being tackled and the course it is desired to follow, whether that promise could ever be kept. There will therefore be no longer any privileged class, but there will be a government, and, note this well, an extremely complex government, which will not content itself with governing and administering the masses politically, as all governments do to-day, but which will also administer them economically, concentrating in its own hands the production and the just division of wealth, the cultivation of land, the establishment and development of factories, the organisation and direction of commerce, finally the application of capital to production by the only banker, the State. All that will demand an immense knowledge and many "heads overflowing with brains" in this government. It will be the reign of *scientific intelligence*, the most aristocratic, despotic, arrogant and contemptuous of all regimes. There will be a new class, a new hierarchy of real and pretended scientists and scholars, and the world will be divided into a minority ruling in the name of knowledge and an immense ignorant majority. And then, woe betide the mass of ignorant ones!

Such a regime will not fail to arouse very considerable discontent in this mass and in order to keep it in check the enlightened and liberating government of Marx will have need of a not less considerable armed force. For the government must be strong, says Engels, to maintain order among these millions of illiterates whose brutal uprising would be capable of destroying and overthrowing everything, even a government directed by heads overflowing with brains.

You can see quite well that behind all the democratic and socialistic phrases and promises of Marx's programme, there is to be found in his State all that constitutes the true despotic and brutal nature of all States, whatever may be the form of their government and that in the final reckoning, the People's State so strongly commended by Marx, and the aristocratic-monarchic State, maintained with as much cleverness as power by Bismarck, are completely identical by the nature of their objective at home as well as in foreign affairs. In foreign affairs it is the same deployment of military force, that is to say, conquest; and in home affairs it is the same employment of this armed force, the last argument of all threatened political powers against the masses, who, tired of believing, hoping, submitting and obeying always, rise in revolt. . . .

SOCIAL REVOLUTION AND THE STATE

What Bismarck has done for the political and bourgeois world, Marx claims to do to-day (i.e., 1872) for the Socialist world, among the proletariat of Europe; to replace French initiative by German initiative and domination; and as, according to him and his disciples, there is no German thought more advanced than his own, he believed the moment had come to have it triumph theoretically and practically in the International. Such was the only object of the Conference which he called together in September 1871 in London. This Marxian thought is explicitly developed in the famous Manifesto of the refugee German Communists drafted and published in 1848 by Marx and Engels. It is the theory of the emancipation of the proletariat and of the organisation of labour by the State.

Its principal point is the conquest of political power by the working class. One can understand that men as indispensable as Marx and Engels should be the partisans of a programme which, consecrating and approving political power, opens the door to all ambitions. Since there will be political power there will necessarily be subjects, got up in Republican fashion, as citizens, it is true, but who will none the less be subjects, and who as such will be forced to obey—because without obedience, there is no power possible. It will be said in answer to this that they will obey not men but laws which they will have made themselves. To that I shall reply that everybody knows how much, in the countries which are freest and most democratic, but politically governed, the people make the laws, and what their obedience to these laws signifies. Whoever is not deliberately desirous of taking fictions for realities must recognise quite well that, even in such countries, the people really obey not laws which they make themselves, but laws which are made in their name, and that to obey these laws means nothing else to them than to submit to the arbitrary will of some guarding and governing minority or, what amounts to the same thing, to be freely slaves.

There is in this programme another expression which is profoundly antipathetic to us revolutionary Anarchists who frankly want the complete emancipation of the people; the expression to which I refer is the presentation of the proletariat, the whole society of toilers, as a "class" and not as a "mass". Do you know what that means? Neither more nor less than a new aristocracy, that of the workers of the factories and towns, to the exclusion of the millions who constitute the proletariat of the countryside and who in the anticipations of the Social Democrats of Germany will, in effect, become subjects of their great so-called People's State. "Class", "Power", "State", are three inseparable terms, of which each necessary presupposes the two others and which all definitely are to be summed up by the words: *the political subjection and the economic exploitation of the masses.*

The Marxians think that just as in the eighteenth century the bourgeoisie dethroned the nobility, to take its place and to absorb it slowly into its own body, sharing with it the domination and exploitation of the toilers in the towns as well as in the country, so the proletariat of the towns is called on to-day to dethrone the bourgeoisie, to absorb it and to share with it the domination and exploitation of the proletariat of the countryside; this last outcast of history, unless this latter later on revolts and demolishes all classes, denominations, powers, in a word, all States.

To me, however, the flower of the proletariat does not mean, as it does to the Marxians, the upper layer, the most civilised and comfortably off in the working world, that layer of semi-bourgeois workers, which is precisely the class the Marxians want to use to constitute their *fourth governing class*, and which is really capable of forming one if things are not set to rights in the interests of the great mass of the proletariat; for with its relative comfort and semi-bourgeois position, this upper layer of workers is unfortunately only too deeply penetrated with all the political and social prejudices and all the narrow aspirations and pretensions of the bourgeois. It can be truly said that this upper layer is the least socialist, the most individualist in all the proletariat.

By the *flower of the proletariat*, I mean above all, that great mass, those millions of non-civilised, disinherited, wretched and illiterates whom Messrs. Engels and Marx mean to subject to the paternal regime of *a very strong government*, to employ an expression used by Engels in a letter to our friend Cafiero. Without doubt, this will be for their own salvation, as of course all governments, as is well known, have been established solely in the interests of the masses themselves. By the flower of the proletariat I mean precisely that eternal "meat" for governments, that great *rabble of the people* ordinarily designated by Messrs. Marx and Engels by the phrase at once picturesque and contemptuous of "lumpen proletariat", the "riff-raff", that rabble which, being very nearly unpolluted by all bourgeois civilisation carries in its heart, in its aspirations, in all necessities and the miseries of its collective position, all the germs of the Socialism of the future, and which alone is powerful enough to-day to inaugurate the Social Revolution and bring it to triumph.

Though differing from us in this respect also, the Marxians do not reject our programme absolutely. They only reproach us with wanting to hasten, to outstrip, the slow march of history and to ignore the scientific law of successive evolutions. Having had the thoroughly German nerve to proclaim in their works consecrated to the philosophical analysis of the past that the bloody defeat of the insurgent peasants of Germany and the triumph of the despotic States in the sixteenth century constituted a great revolutionary progress, they to-day have the nerve to satisfy themselves with establishing a new despotism to the so-called profit of the town-workers and to the detriment of the toilers in the country.

To support his programme of the conquest of political power, Marx has a very special theory which is, moreover, only a logical consequence of his whole system. The political condition of each country, says he, is always the product and the faithful expressions of its economic situation; to change the former it is only necessary to transform the latter. According to Marx, all the secret of historic evolution is there. He takes no account of other elements in history, such as the quite obvious reaction of political, juridical, and religious institutions on the economic situation. He says, "Poverty produces political slavery, the State," but he does not allow this expression to be turned around, to say "Political slavery, the State, reproduces in its turn, and maintains poverty as a condition of its own existence; so that, in order to destroy poverty, it is necessary to destroy the State!" And, a strange thing in him who forbids his opponents to lay the blame on political slavery, the State, as an active cause of poverty, he commands his friends and disciples of the Social Democratic Party in Germany to consider the conquest of power and of political liberties as the preliminary condition absolutely necessary for economic emancipation.

Yet the sociologists of the school of Marx, men like Engels and Lassalle, object against us that the State is not at all the cause of the poverty of the people, of the degradation and servitude of the masses; but that the wretched condition of the masses, as well as the despotic power of the State are, on the contrary, both the one and the other, the effects of a more general cause, the products of an inevitable phase in the economic development of society, of a phase which, from the point of view of history, constitutes true progress, an immense step towards what *they* call the social revolution. To such a degree, in fact, that Lassalle did not hesitate loudly to proclaim that the defeat of the formidable revolt of the peasants in Germany in the sixteenth century—a deplorable defeat if ever there was one, from which dates the centuries-old slavery of the Germans—and the triumph of the despotic and centralised State which was the necessary consequence of it, constituted a real triumph for this revolution; because the peasants, say the Marxians, are the natural representatives of reaction, whilst the modern military and bureaucratic State—a product and inevitable accompaniment of the social revolution, which, starting from the second half of the sixteenth century commenced the slow, but always progressive transformation of the ancient feudal and land economy into the production of wealth, or, what comes to the same thing, into the exploitation of the labour of the people by capital —this State was an essential condition of this revolution.

One can understand how Engels, driven on by the same logic, in a letter addressed to one of our friends, Carlo Cafiero, was able to say, without the least irony, but on the contrary, very seriously, that Bismarck as well as King Victor Emmanuel II had rendered immense services to the revolution, both of them having created political centralisation in their respective countries. . . .

The social revolution, as the Latin and Slav toilers picture it to themselves, desire it and hope for it, is infinitely broader than that promised them by the German or Marxian programme. It is not for them a question of the emancipation parsimoniously measured out and only realisable at a very distant date, of the working class, but the complete and real emancipation of all the proletariat, not only of some countries but of all nations, civilised and uncivilised—a new civilisation, genuinely of the people, being destined to commence by this act of universal emancipation.

And the first word of this emancipation can be none other than "Liberty", not that political, bourgeois liberty, so much approved and recommended as a preliminary object of conquest by Marx and his adherents, but *the great human liberty*, which, destroying all the dogmatic, metaphysical, political and juridical fetters by which everybody to-day is loaded down, will give to everybody, collectivities as well as individuals, full autonomy in their activities and their development, delivered once and for all from all inspectors, directors and guardians.

The second word of this emancipation is *solidarity*, not Marxian solidarity from above downwards by some government or other, either by ruse or by force, on the masses of the people; not that solidarity of all which is the negation of the liberty of each, and which by that very fact becomes a falsehood, a fiction, having slavery as the reality behind it; but that solidarity which is on the contrary the confirmation and the realisation of every liberty, having its origin not in any political law whatsoever, but in the inherent collective nature of man, in virtue of which no man is free if all the men who surround him and who exercise the least influence, direct or indirect, on his life are not so equally. This truth is to be found magnificently expressed in the Declaration of the Rights of Man drafted by Robespierre, and which proclaims that *the slavery of the least of men is the slavery of all.*

The solidarity which we ask, far from being the result of any artificial or authoritarian organisation whatsoever, can only be the spontaneous product of social life, economic as well as moral; the result of the free federation of common interests, aspirations and tendencies. It has for essential bases, *equality, collective labour*—becoming obligatory for each not by the force of law, but by the force of facts—and collective property; as a directing light, experience—that is to say the practice of the collective life; *knowledge and learning*; and as a final goal the establishment of Humanity, and consequently the ruin of all States.

There is the ideal, not divine, not metaphysical but human and *practical*, which alone corresponds to the modern aspirations of the Latin and Slav peoples. They want complete liberty, complete solidarity, complete equality; in a word, they want only Humanity and they will not be satisfied, even on the score of its being provisional and transitory, with anything less than that. The Marxians will denounce their aspirations as folly; that has been done over a long period, that has not turned them from their goal, and they will never change the magnificence of that goal for the completely bourgeois platitudes of Marxian Socialism.

Their ideal is practical in this sense, that its realisation will be much less difficult than that of the Marxian idea, which, besides the poverty of its objective, presents also the grave inconvenience of being absolutely impracticable. It will not be the first time that clever men, rational and advocates of things practical and possible, will be recognised for Utopians, and that those who are called Utopians to-day will be recognised as practical men to-morrow. The absurdity of the Marxian system consists precisely in the hope that by inordinately narrowing down the Socialist programme so as to make it acceptable to the bourgeois Radicals, it will transform the latter into unwitting and involuntary servants of the social revolution. There is a great error there; all the experience of history demonstrates to us that an alliance concluded between two different parties always turns to the advantage of the more reactionary of the two parties; this alliance necessarily enfeebles the more progressive party, by diminishing and distorting its programme, by destroying its moral strength, its confidence in itself, whilst a reactionary party, when it is guilty of falsehood, is always and more than ever true to itself.

As for me, I do not hesitate to say that all the Marxist flirtations with the Radicalism, whether reformist or revolutionary, of the bourgeois, can have no other result than the demoralisation and disorganisation of the rising power of the proletariat, and consequently a new consolidation of the established power of the bourgeois.

POLITICAL ACTION AND THE WORKERS

In Germany, Socialism is already beginning to be a formidable power, despite restrictive and oppressive laws. The workers' parties are frankly Socialist—in the sense that they want a Socialistic reform of the relations between capital and labour, and that they consider that to obtain this reform, the State must first of all be reformed, and that if it will not suffer itself to be reformed peaceably, it must be reformed by a political revolution. This political revolution, they maintain, must precede the social revolution, but I consider this as a fatal error, as such a revolution would necessarily be a bourgeois revolution and would produce only a bourgeois socialism, that is to say it would lead to a new exploitation, more cunning and hypocritical, but not less oppressive than the present.

This idea of a political revolution preceding a social revolution has opened wide the doors of the Social Democratic Party to all the Radical democrats; who are very little of Socialists. And the leaders of the Party have, against the instincts of the workers themselves, brought it into close association with the bourgeois democrats of the People's Party [the Liberals], which is quite hostile to Socialism, as its Press and politicians demonstrate. The leaders of this People's Party, however, have observed that these anti-Socialist utterances displeased the workers, and they modified their tone for they need the workers' assistance in their political aims, just as it has always been the method of the bourgeoisie to carry out a revolution by means of the all-powerful arm of the people and then filch the profits for themselves. Thus these Popular democrats have now become "Socialists" of a sort. But the "Socialism" does not go beyond the harmless dreams of bourgeois co-operativism.

At a Congress in Eisenach, in August, 1869, there were negotiations between the representatives of the two parties, worker and democrat, and these resulted in a programme which definitely constituted the Social Democratic Labour Party. This programme is a compromise between the Socialist and revolutionary programme of the International as determined by the Congresses of Brussels and Basel, and the programme of bourgeois democracy. This new programme called for a "free People's State", wherein all class domination and all exploitation would be abolished. Political liberty was declared to be the most urgently needed condition for the economic emancipation of the working classes. Consequently the social question was inseparable from the political question. Its solution was possible only in a democratic State. The Party was declared to be associated with the International. Some immediate objectives were set out: manhood suffrage, referenda, free and compulsory education, separation of Church and State, liberty of the Press, State aid to workers' co-operatives.

This programme expresses not the Socialist and revolutionary aspirations of the workers, but the policy of the leaders. There is a direct contradiction between the programme of the International, and the purely national programme set out above, between the Socialist solidarity of Labour and the political patriotism of the National State. Thus the Social Democrats find themselves in the position of being united with their bourgeois compatriots against the workers of a foreign country; and their patriotism has vanquished their Socialism. Slaves themselves of the German Government, they fulminate against the French Government as tyrants. The only difference between Bismarck and Napoleon III was that the one was a successful and the other an unsuccessful scoundrel, one was a scoundrel, and the other a scoundrel and a half.

The German Socialists' idea of a Free State is a contradiction in terms, an unrealisable dream. Socialism implying the destruction of the State, those who support the State must renounce Socialism; must sacrifice the economic emancipation of the masses to the political power of some privileged party—and in this case it will be bourgeois democracy.

The programme of the Social Democrats really implies that they trust the bourgeois democrats to help the workers to achieve a Social revolution, after the workers have helped the bourgeois to achieve a political revolution. The way they have swallowed bourgeois ideas is shown by the list of immediate objectives, which except for the last, comprise the well-known programme of bourgeois democracy. And in fact these immediate objectives have become their real objectives, so that they have lent the Social Democratic Party to become a mere tool in the hands of the bourgeois democrats. . . .

I maintain that if ever the Marxian party, that of so-called Social Democracy, continues to pursue the course of political demands, it will see itself forced to condemn, sooner or later, that of economic demands, the course of strike action, so incompatible are these two courses in reality. . . .

The Social Democrats of Germany . . . advised all the workers so unfortunate as to listen to them, to adopt, as the immediate objective of their association, legal agitation for the preliminary conquest of political rights; they thus subordinate the movement for economic emancipation to the movement first of all exclusively political, and by this obvious reversal of the whole programme of the International, they have filled in at a single stroke the abyss they had opened between proletariat and bourgeoisie. They have done more than that, they have tied the proletariat in tow with the bourgeoisie. For it is evident that all this political movement so boosted by the German Socialists, since it must precede the economic revolution, can only be directed by the bourgeois, or what will be still worse, *by workers transformed into bourgeois by their ambition and vanity*, and, passing in reality over the head of the proletariat, like all its predecessors, this movement will not fail once more to condemn the proletariat to be nothing but a blind instrument inevitably sacrificed in the struggle of the different bourgeois parties between themselves for the conquest of political power, that is to say, for the power and right to dominate the masses and exploit them. To whomsoever doubts it, we should only have to show what is happening in Germany, where the organs of Social Democracy sing hymns of joy on seeing a Congress (at Eisenach) of professors of bourgeois political economy recommending the proletariat of Germany to the high and paternal protection of States and in the parts of Switzerland where the Marxian programme prevails, at Geneva, Zurich, Basel, where the International has descended to the point of being no longer anything more than a sort of electoral box for the profit of the Radical bourgeois. These incontestable facts seem to me to be more eloquent than any words.

They are real and logical in this sense that they are a natural effect of the triumph of Marxian propaganda. And it is for that reason that we fight the Marxian theories to the death, convinced that if they could triumph throughout the International, they would certainly not fail to kill at least its spirit everywhere, as they have already done in very great part in the countries just mentioned.

The instinctive passion of the masses for economic equality is so great that if they could hope to receive it from the hands of despotism, they would indubitably and without much reflection do as they have often done before, and deliver themselves to despotism. Happily, historic experience has been of some service even with the masses. To-day, they are beginning everywhere to understand that no despotism has nor can have, either the will or the power to give them economic equality. The programme of the International is very happily explicit on this question. *The emancipation of the toilers can be the work only of the toilers themselves.*

Is it not astonishing that Marx has believed it possible to graft on this nevertheless so precise declaration, which he probably drafted himself, his *scientific Socialism?* That is to say, the organisation and the government of the new society by Socialistic scientists and professors—the worst of all despotic government!

But thanks to this great beloved "riff-raff" of the common people, who will oppose themselves, urged on by an instinct invincible as well as just, to all the governmentalist fancies of this little working-class minority already properly disciplined and marshalled to become the myrmidons of a new despotism, the *scientific Socialism* of Marx will always remain as a Marxian dream. This new experience, more dismal perhaps than all past experiences, will be spared society, because the proletariat in general, and in all countries is animated to-day by a profound distrust against what is political and against all the politicians in the world, whatever their party colour, all of them having equally deceived, oppressed, exploited—the reddest Republicans just as much as the most absolutist Monarchists.

11 The Revolution Betrayed

The great Revolution came in Russia, thereby damaging the Marxist tenet that industrialization was vital to socialism and supporting the Bakuninist faith in the revolutionary potential of supposedly backward countries. Certainly Marxism underwent revision. But the withering away of the state—the Marxist concession to the anarchist idea—became only more and more remote.

Anarchism now required extensive clarification, for socialist adversaries had taken over a huge nation where their accomplishments could be exhibited to the world. Some anarchists were converted by the new evidence. But the aged Kropotkin declined any connection with the new government of Russia and spread word of his despair in his *Letter to the Workers of Western Europe.*

Probably the best analysis by an anarchist of the failure of the Russian Revolution is Emma Goldman's. A famous agitator for women's rights, birth control, and modern drama as well as anarchism, Emma Goldman was deported from the United States in the Red Scare after World War I. She headed for Russia with great enthusiasm, but was soon appalled, and described her disillusionment in two popular books of the early 1920s. Her comrade, lover, and fellow exile, Alexander Berkman, wrote a similar book but was prevented by his publisher from revealing the anarchist principles that informed his analysis. Fortunately, Emma Goldman's publishers were less antiseptic and allowed this chapter to contaminate *My Further Disillusionment in Russia.*

I

Non-Bolshevik Socialist critics of the Russian failure contend that the Revolution could not have succeeded in Russia because industrial conditions had not reached the necessary climax in that country. They point to Marx, who taught that a social revolution is possible only in countries with a highly developed industrial system and its attendant social antago-

---

My Further Disillusionment in Russia, by Emma Goldman (Garden City: Doubleday, Page, 1924), pp. 144–78.

nisms. They therefore claim that the Russian Revolution could not be a social revolution, and that historically it had to evolve along constitutional, democratic lines, complemented by a growing industry, in order to ripen the country economically for the basic change.

This orthodox Marxian view leaves an important factor out of consideration—a factor perhaps more vital to the possibility and success of a social revolution than even the industrial element. That is the psychology of the masses at a given period. Why is there, for instance, no social revolution in the United States, France, or even in Germany? Surely these countries have reached the industrial development set by Marx as the culminating stage. The truth is that industrial development and sharp social contrasts are of themselves by no means sufficient to give birth to a new society or to call forth a social revolution. The necessary social consciousness, the required mass psychology is missing in such countries as the United States and the others mentioned. That explains why no social revolution has taken place there.

In this regard Russia had the advantage of other more industrialized and "civilized" lands. It is true that Russia was not as advanced industrially as her Western neighbours. But the Russian mass psychology, inspired and intensified by the February Revolution, was ripening at so fast a pace that within a few months the people were ready for such ultra-revolutionary slogans as "All power to the Soviets" and "The land to the peasants, the factories to the workers."

The significance of these slogans should not be underestimated. Expressing in a large degree the instinctive and semiconscious will of the people, they yet signified the complete social, economic, and industrial reorganization of Russia. What country in Europe or America is prepared to interpret such revolutionary mottoes into life? Yet in Russia, in the months of June and July, 1917, these slogans became popular and were enthusiastically and actively taken up, in the form of direct action, by the bulk of the industrial and agrarian population of more than 150 millions. That was sufficient proof of the "ripeness" of the Russian people for the social revolution.

As to economic "preparedness" in the Marxian sense, it must not be forgotten that Russia is preeminently an agrarian country. Marx's dictum presupposes the industrialization of the peasant and farmer population in every highly developed society, as a step toward social fitness for revolution.

But events in Russia, in 1917, demonstrated that revolution does not await this process of industrialization and—what is more important—cannot be made to wait. The Russian peasants began to expropriate the landlords and the workers took possession of the factories without taking cognizance of Marxian dicta. This popular action, by virtue of its own logic, ushered in the social revolution in Russia, upsetting all Marxian calculations. The psychology of the Slav proved stronger than social-democratic theories.

That psychology involved the passionate yearning for liberty nurtured by a century of revolutionary agitation among all classes of society. The Russian people had fortunately remained politically unsophisticated and untouched by the corruption and confusion created among the proletariat of other countries by "democratic" liberty and self-government. The Russian remained, in this sense, natural and simple, unfamiliar with the subtleties of politics, of parliamentary trickery, and legal makeshifts. On the other hand, his primitive sense of justice and right was strong and vital, without the disintegrating finesse of pseudo-civilization. He knew what he wanted and he did not wait for "historic inevitability" to bring it to him: he employed direct action. The Revolution to him was a fact of life, not a mere theory for discussion.

Thus the social revolution took place in Russia in spite of the industrial backwardness of the country. But to make the Revolution was not enough. It was necessary for it to advance and broaden, to develop into economic and social reconstruction. That phase of the Revolution necessitated fullest play of personal initiative and collective effort. The development and success of the Revolution depended on the broadest exercise of the creative genius of the people, on the cooperation of the intellectual and manual proletariat. Common interest is the *leit motif* of all revolutionary endeavour, especially on its constructive side. This spirit of mutual purpose and solidarity swept Russia with a mighty wave in the first days of the October-November Revolution. Inherent in that enthusiasm were forces that could have moved mountains if intelligently guided by exclusive consideration for the well-being of the whole people. The medium for such effective guidance was on hand: the labour organizations and the cooperatives with which Russia was covered as with a network of bridges combining the city with the country; the Soviets which sprang into being responsive to the needs of the Russian people; and, finally, the intelligentsia whose traditions for a century expressed heroic devotion to the cause of Russia's emancipation.

But such a development was by no means within the programme of the Bolsheviki. For several months following October they suffered the popular forces to manifest themselves, the people carrying the Revolution into ever-widening channels. But as soon as the Communist Party felt itself sufficiently strong in the government saddle, it began to limit the scope of popular activity. All the succeeding acts of the Bolsheviki, all their following policies, changes of policies, their compromises and retreats, their methods of suppression and persecution, their terrorism and extermination of all other political views—all were but the *means to an end*: the retaining of the State power in the hands of the Communist Party. Indeed, the Bolsheviki themselves (in Russia) made no secret of it. The Communist Party, they contended, is the advance guard of the proletariat, and the dictatorship must rest in its hands. Alas, the Bolsheviki reckoned without their host—without the peasantry, whom neither the *razvyortska*, the Tcheka, nor the wholesale shooting could persuade to support the Bolshevik regime. The peasantry became the rock upon which the best-laid plans and schemes of Lenin were wrecked. But Lenin, a nimble acrobat, was skilled in performing within the narrowest margin. The new economic policy was introduced just in time to ward off the disaster which was slowly but surely overtaking the whole Communist edifice.

II

The "new economic policy" came as a surprise and a shock to most Communists. They saw in it a reversal of everything that their Party had been proclaiming—a reversal of Communism itself. In protest some of the oldest members of the Party, men who had faced danger and persecution under the old regime while Lenin and Trotsky lived abroad in safety, left the Communist Party embittered and disappointed. The leaders then declared a lockout. They ordered the clearing of the Party ranks of all "doubtful" elements. Everybody suspected of an independent attitude and those who did not accept the new economic policy as the last word in revolutionary wisdom were expelled. Among them were Communists who for years had rendered most devoted service. Some of them, hurt to the quick by the unjust and brutal procedure, and shaken to their depths by the collapse of what they held most high, even resorted to suicide. But the smooth sailing of Lenin's new gospel had to be assured, the gospel of the sanctity of private property and the freedom of cut-throat competition erected upon the ruins of four years of revolution.

However, Communist indignation over the new economic policy merely indicated the confusion of mind on the part of Lenin's opponents. What else but mental confusion could approve of the numerous acrobatic political stunts of Lenin and yet grow indignant at the final somersault, its logical culmination? The trouble with the devout Communists was that they clung to the Immaculate Conception of the Communist State which by the aid of the Revolution was to redeem the world. But most of the leading Communists never entertained such a delusion. Least of all Lenin.

During my first interview I received the impression that he was a shrewd politician who knew exactly what he was about and that he would stop at nothing to achieve his ends. After hearing him speak on several occasions and reading his works I became convinced that Lenin had very little concern in the Revolution and that Communism to him was a very remote thing. The centralized political State was Lenin's deity, to which everything else was to be sacrificed. Someone said that Lenin would sacrifice the Revolution to save Russia. Lenin's policies, however, have proven that he was willing to sacrifice both the Revolution and the country; or at least part of the latter, in order to realize his political scheme with what was left of Russia.

Lenin was the most pliable politician in history. He could be an ultra-revolutionary, a compromiser and conservative at the same time. When like a mighty wave the cry swept over Russia, "All power to the Soviets!" Lenin swam with the tide. When the peasants took possession of the land and the workers of the factories, Lenin not only approved of those direct methods but went further. He issued the famous motto, "Rob the robbers," a slogan which served to confuse the minds of the people and caused untold injury to revolutionary idealism. Never before did any real revolutionist interpret social expropriation as the transfer of wealth from one set of individuals to another. Yet that was exactly what Lenin's slogan meant. The indiscriminate and irresponsible raids, the accumulation of the wealth of the former bourgeoisie by the new Soviet bureaucracy, the chicanery practised toward those whose only crime was their former status, were all the results of Lenin's "Rob the robbers" policy. The whole subsequent history of the Revolution is a kaleidoscope of Lenin's compromises and betrayal of his own slogans.

Bolshevik acts and methods since the October days may seem to contradict the new economic policy. But in reality they are links in the chain which was to forge the all-powerful, centralized Government with State Capitalism as its economic expression. Lenin possessed clarity of vision and an iron will. He knew how to make his comrades in Russia and outside of it believe that his scheme was true Socialism and his methods the revolution. No wonder that Lenin felt such contempt for his flock, which he never hesitated to fling into their faces. "Only fools can believe that Communism is possible in Russia now," was Lenin's reply to the opponents of the new economic policy.

As a matter of fact, Lenin was right. True Communism was never attempted in Russia, unless one considers thirty-three categories of pay, different food rations, privileges to some and indifference to the great mass as Communism.

In the early period of the Revolution it was comparatively easy for the Communist Party to possess itself of power. All the revolutionary elements, carried away by the ultra-revolutionary promises of the Bolsheviki, helped the latter to power. Once in possession of the State the Communists began their process of elimination. All the political parties and groups which refused to submit to the new dictatorship had to go. First the Anarchists and Left Social Revolutionists, then the Mensheviki and other opponents from the Right, and finally everybody who dared aspire to an opinion of his own. Similar was the fate of all independent organizations. They were either subordinated to the needs of the new State or destroyed altogether, as were the Soviets, the trade unions and the cooperatives—three great factors for the realization of the hopes of the Revolution.

The Soviets first manifested themselves in the revolution of 1905. They played an important part during that brief but significant period. Though the revolution was crushed, the Soviet idea remained rooted in the minds and hearts of the Russian masses. At the first dawn which illuminated Russia in February, 1917, the Soviets revived again and came into bloom in a very short time. To the people the Soviets by no means represented a curtailment of the spirit of the Revolution. On the contrary, the Revolution was to find its highest, freest practical expression through the Soviets. That was

why the Soviets so spontaneously and rapidly spread throughout Russia. The Bolsheviki realized the significance of the
popular trend and joined the cry. But once in control of the
Government the Communists saw that the Soviets threatened
the supremacy of the State. At the same time they could not
destroy them arbitrarily without undermining their own prestige at home and abroad as the sponsors of the Soviet system.
They began to shear them gradually of their powers and finally to subordinate them to their own needs.

The Russian trade unions were much more amenable to
emasculation. Numerically and in point of revolutionary fibre
they were still in their childhood. By declaring adherence to
the trade unions obligatory the Russian labour organizations
gained in physical stature, but mentally they remained in the
infant stage. The Communist State became the wet nurse of
the trade unions. In return, the organizations served as the
flunkeys of the State. "A school for Communism," said Lenin
in the famous controversy on the functions of the trade unions. Quite right. But an antiquated school where the spirit
of the child is fettered and crushed. Nowhere in the world are
labour organizations as subservient to the will and the dictates of the State as they are in Bolshevik Russia.

The fate of the cooperatives is too well known to require
elucidation. The cooperatives were the most essential link between the city and the country. Their value to the Revolution
as a popular and successful medium of exchange and distribution and to the reconstruction of Russia was incalculable. The
Bolsheviki transformed them into cogs of the Government
machine and thereby destroyed their usefulness and efficiency.

III

It is now clear why the Russian Revolution, as conducted
by the Communist Party, was a failure. The political power of
the Party, organized and centralized in the State, sought to
maintain itself by all means at hand. The central authorities
attempted to force the activities of the people into forms corresponding with the purposes of the Party. The sole aim of
the latter was to strengthen the State and monopolize all
economical, political, and social activities—even all cultural
manifestations. The Revolution had an entirely different object, and in its very character it was the negation of authority
and centralization. It strove to open ever-larger fields for proletarian expression and to multiply the phases of individual
and collective effort. The aims and tendencies of the Revolu-

tion were diametrically opposed to those of the ruling political party.

Just as diametrically opposed were the *methods* of the Revolution and of the State. Those of the former were inspired by the spirit of the Revolution itself: that is to say, by emancipation from all oppressive and limiting forces; in short, *by libertarian principles*. The methods of the State, on the contrary—of the Bolshevik State as of every government—were based on *coercion*, which in the course of things necessarily developed into systematic violence, oppression, and terrorism. Thus two opposing tendencies struggled for supremacy: the Bolshevik State against the Revolution. That struggle was a life-and-death struggle. The two tendencies, contradictory in aims and methods, could not work harmoniously: the triumph of the State meant the defeat of the Revolution.

It would be an error to assume that the failure of the Revolution was due entirely to the character of the Bolsheviki. Fundamentally, it was the result of the principles and methods of Bolshevism. It was the authoritarian spirit and principles of the State which stifled the libertarian and liberating aspirations. Were any other political party in control of the government in Russia the result would have been essentially the same. It is not so much the Bolsheviki who killed the Russian Revolution as the Bolshevik idea. It was Marxism, however modified; in short, fanatical governmentalism. Only this understanding of the underlying forces that crushed the Revolution can present the true lesson of that world-stirring event. The Russian Revolution reflects on a small scale the century-old struggle of the libertarian principle against the authoritarian. For what is progress if not the more general acceptance of the principles of liberty as against those of coercion? The Russian Revolution was a libertarian step defeated by the Bolshevik State, by the temporary victory of the reactionary, the governmental idea.

That victory was due to a number of causes. . . . The main cause, however, was not the industrial backwardness of Russia, as claimed by many writers on the subject. That cause was cultural which, though giving the Russian people certain advantages over their more sophisticated neighbours, also had some fatal disadvantages. The Russian was "culturally backward" in the sense of being unspoiled by political and parliamentary corruption. On the other hand, that very condition involved inexperience in the political game and a naive faith in the miraculous power of the party that talked the loudest and made the most promises. This faith in the power of government served to enslave the Russian people to the Communist Party even before the great masses realized that the yoke had been put around their necks.

The libertarian principle was strong in the initial days of the Revolution, the need for free expression all-absorbing. But when the first wave of enthusiasm receded into the ebb of everyday prosaic life, a firm conviction was needed to keep the fires of liberty burning. There was only a comparative handful in the great vastness of Russia to keep those fires lit —the Anarchists, whose number was small and whose efforts, absolutely suppressed under the Tsar, had had no time to bear fruit. The Russian people, to some extent instinctive Anarchists, were yet too unfamiliar with true libertarian principles and methods to apply them effectively to life. Most of the Russian Anarchists themselves were unfortunately still in the meshes of limited group activities and of individualistic endeavour as against the more important social and collective efforts. The Anarchists, the future unbiased historian will admit, have played a very important role in the Russian Revolution—a role far more significant and fruitful than their comparatively small number would have led one to expect. Yet honesty and sincerity compel me to state that their work would have been of infinitely greater practical value had they been better organized and equipped to guide the released energies of the people toward the reorganization of life on a libertarian foundation.

But the failure of the Anarchists in the Russian Revolution—in the sense just indicated—does by no means argue the defeat of the libertarian idea. On the contrary, the Russian Revolution has demonstrated beyond doubt that the State idea, State Socialism, in all its manifestations (economic, political, social, educational) is entirely and hopelessly bankrupt. Never before in all history has authority, government, the State, proved so inherently static, reactionary, and even counter-revolutionary in effect. In short, the very antithesis of revolution.

It remains true, as it has through all progress, that only the libertarian spirit and method can bring man a step further in his eternal striving for the better, finer, and freer life. Applied to the great social upheavals known as revolutions, this tendency is as potent as in the ordinary evolutionary process. The authoritarian method has been a failure all through history and now it has again failed in the Russian

Revolution. So far human ingenuity has discovered no other principle except the libertarian, for man has indeed uttered the highest wisdom when he said that liberty is the mother of order, not its daughter. All political tenets and parties notwithstanding, no revolution can be truly and permanently successful unless it puts its emphatic veto upon all tyranny and centralization, and determinedly strives to make the revolution a real revaluation of all economic, social, and cultural values. Not mere substitution of one political party for another in the control of the Government, not the masking of autocracy by proletarian slogans, not the dictatorship of a new class over an old one, not political scene shifting of any kind, but the complete reversal of all these authoritarian principles will alone serve the revolution.

In the economic field this transformation must be in the hands of the industrial masses: the latter have the choice between an industrial State and anarcho-syndicalism. In the case of the former the menace to the constructive development of the new social structure would be as great as from the political State. It would become a dead weight upon the growth of the new forms of life. For that very reason syndicalism (or industrialism) alone is not, as its exponents claim, sufficient unto itself. It is only when the libertarian spirit permeates the economic organizations of the workers that the manifold creative energies of the people can manifest themselves, and the revolution be safeguarded and defended. Only free initiative and popular participation in the affairs of the revolution can prevent the terrible blunders committed in Russia. For instance, with fuel only a hundred versts [about sixty-six miles] from Petrograd there would have been no necessity for that city to suffer from cold had the workers' economic organizations of Petrograd been free to exercise their initiative for the common good. The peasants of the Ukraina would not have been hampered in the cultivation of their land had they had access to the farm implements stacked up in the warehouses of Kharkov and other industrial centres awaiting orders from Moscow for their distribution. These are characteristic examples of Bolshevik governmentalism and centralization, which should serve as a warning to the workers of Europe and America of the destructive effects of Statism.

The industrial power of the masses, expressed through their libertarian associations—Anarcho-syndicalism—is alone able to organize successfully the economic life and carry on production. On the other hand, the cooperatives, working in harmony with the industrial bodies, serve as the distributing and exchange media between city and country, and at the same time link in fraternal bond the industrial and agrarian masses. A common tie of mutual service and aid is created which is the strongest bulwark of the revolution—far more effective than compulsory labour, the Red Army, or terrorism. In that way alone can revolution act as a leaven to quicken the development of new social forms and inspire the masses to greater achievements.

But libertarian industrial organizations and the cooperatives are not the only media in the interplay of the complex phases of social life. There are the cultural forces which, though closely related to the economic activities, have yet their own functions to perform. In Russia the Communist State became the sole arbiter of all the needs of the social body. The result . . . was complete cultural stagnation and the paralysis of all creative endeavour. If such a debacle is to be avoided in the future, the cultural forces, while remaining rooted in the economic soil, must yet retain independent scope and freedom of expression. Not adherence to the dominant political party but devotion to the revolution, knowledge, ability, and—above all—the creative impulse should be the criterion of fitness for cultural work. In Russia this was made impossible almost from the beginning of the October Revolution, by the violent separation of the intelligentsia and the masses. It is true that the original offender in this case was the intelligentsia, especially the technical intelligentsia, which in Russia tenaciously clung—as it does in other countries—to the coat-tails of the bourgeoisie. This element, unable to comprehend the significance of revolutionary events, strove to stem the tide by wholesale sabotage. But in Russia there was also another kind of intelligentsia—one with a glorious revolutionary past of a hundred years. That part of the intelligentsia kept faith with the people, though it could not unreservedly accept the new dictatorship. The fatal error of the Bolsheviki was that they made no distinction between the two elements. They met sabotage with wholesale terror against the intelligentsia as a class, and inaugurated a campaign of hatred more intensive than the persecution of the bourgeoisie itself—a method which created an abyss between the intelligentsia and the proletariat and reared a barrier against constructive work.

Lenin was the first to realize that criminal blunder. He pointed out that it was a grave error to lead the workers to believe that they could build up the industries and engage in cultural work without the aid and cooperation of the intelligentsia. The proletariat had neither the knowledge nor the training for the task, and the intelligentsia had to be restored in the direction of the industrial life. But the recognition of one error never safeguarded Lenin and his Party from immediately committing another. The technical intelligentsia was called back on terms which added disintegration to the antagonism against the regime.

While the workers continued to starve, engineers, industrial experts, and technicians received high salaries, special privileges, and the best rations. They became the pampered employees of the State and the new slave drivers of the masses. The latter, fed for years on the fallacious teachings that muscle alone is necessary for a successful revolution and that only physical labour is productive, and incited by the campaign of hatred which stamped every intellectual a counter-revolutionist and speculator, could not make peace with those they had been taught to scorn and distrust.

Unfortunately Russia is not the only country where this proletarian attitude against the intelligentsia prevails. Everywhere political demagogues play upon the ignorance of the masses, teach them that education and culture are bourgeois prejudices, that the workers can do without them, and that they alone are able to rebuild society. The Russian Revolution has made it very clear that both brain and muscle are indispensable to the work of social regeneration. Intellectual and physical labour are as closely related in the social body as brain and hand in the human organism. One cannot function without the other.

It is true that most intellectuals consider themselves a class apart from and superior to the workers, but social conditions everywhere are fast demolishing the high pedestal of the intelligentsia. They are made to see that they, too, are proletarians, even more dependent upon the economic master than the manual worker. Unlike the physical proletarian, who can pick up his tools and tramp the world in search of a change from a galling situation, the intellectual proletarians have their roots more firmly in their particular social environment and cannot so easily change their occupation or mode of living. It is therefore of utmost importance to bring home to the workers the rapid proletarization of the intellectuals and the common tie thus created between them. If the Western world is to profit by the lessons of Russia, the demagogic flattery of the masses and blind antagonism toward the intelligentsia must cease. That does not mean, however, that the toilers should depend entirely upon the intellectual element. On the contrary, the masses must begin right now to prepare and equip themselves for the great task the revolution will put upon them. They should acquire the knowledge and technical skill necessary for managing and directing the intricate mechanism of the industrial and social structure of their respective countries. But even at best the workers will need the cooperation of the professional and cultural elements. Similarly the latter must realize that their true interests are identical with those of the masses. Once the two social forces learn to blend into one harmonious whole, the tragic aspects of the Russian Revolution would to a great extent be eliminated. No one would be shot because he "once acquired an education." The scientist, the engineer, the specialist, the investigator, the educator, and the creative artist, as well as the carpenter, machinist, and the rest, are all part and parcel of the collective force which is to shape the revolution into the great architect of the new social edifice. Not hatred, but unity; not antagonism, but fellowship; not shooting, but sympathy—that is the lesson of the great Russian debacle for the intelligentsia as well as the workers. All must learn the value of mutual aid and libertarian cooperation. Yet each must be able to remain independent in his own sphere and in harmony with the best he can yield to society. Only in that way will productive labour and educational and cultural endeavour express themselves in ever newer and richer forms. That is to me the all-embracing and vital moral taught by the Russian Revolution.

IV

In the previous pages I have tried to point out why Bolshevik principles, methods, and tactics failed, and that similar principles and methods applied in any other country, even of the highest industrial development, must also fail. I have further shown that it is not only Bolshevism that failed, but Marxism itself. That is to say, the STATE IDEA, the *authoritarian principle,* has been proven bankrupt by the experience of the Russian Revolution. If I were to sum up my whole argument in one sentence I should say: The inherent tendency of the State is to concentrate, to narrow, and monopolize all social activities; the nature of revolution is, on the contrary, to grow, to broaden, and disseminate itself in ever-wider circles. In other words, the State is institutional and static; revolution is fluent, dynamic. These two tendencies are incompatible and mutually destructive. The State idea killed the Russian Revolution and it must have the same result in all other revolutions, unless the *libertarian idea prevail*.

Yet I go much further. It is not only Bolshevism, Marxism, and Governmentalism which are fatal to revolution as well as to all vital human progress. The main cause of the defeat of the Russian Revolution lies much deeper. It is to be found in the whole Socialist conception of revolution itself.

The dominant, almost general, idea of revolution—particularly the Socialist idea—is that revolution is a violent change of social conditions through which one social class, the working class, becomes dominant over another class, the capitalist class. It is the conception of a purely physical change, and as such it involves only political scene shifting and institutional rearrangements. Bourgeois dictatorship is replaced by the "dictatorship of the proletariat"—or by that of its "advance guard," the Communist Party; Lenin takes the seat of the Romanovs, the Imperial Cabinet is rechristened Soviet of People's Commissars, Trotsky is appointed Minister of War, and a labourer becomes the Military Governor General of Moscow. That is, in essence, the Bolshevik conception of revolution, as translated into actual practice. And with a few minor alterations it is also the idea of revolution held by all other Socialist parties.

This conception is inherently and fatally false. Revolution is indeed a violent process. But if it is to result only in a change of dictatorship, in a shifting of names and political personalities, then it is hardly worth while. It is surely not worth all the struggle and sacrifice, the stupendous loss in human life and cultural values that result from every revolution. If such a revolution were even to bring greater social well being (which has not been the case in Russia) then it would also not be worth the terrific price paid: mere improvement can be brought about without bloody revolution. It is not palliatives or reforms that are the real aim and purpose of revolution, as I conceive it.

In my opinion—a thousandfold strengthened by the Russian experience—the great mission of revolution, of the SOCIAL REVOLUTION, is a *fundamental transvaluation of values*. A transvaluation not only of social, but also of human values. The latter are even preeminent, for they are the basis of all social values. Our institutions and conditions rest upon deep-seated ideas. To change those conditions and at the same time leave the underlying ideas and values intact means only a superficial transformation, one that cannot be permanent or bring real betterment. It is a change of form only, not of substance, as so tragically proven by Russia.

It is at once the great failure and the great tragedy of the Russian Revolution that it attempted (in the leadership of the ruling political party) to change only institutions and conditions while ignoring entirely the human and social values involved in the Revolution. Worse yet, in its mad passion for power, the Communist State even sought to strengthen and deepen the very ideas and conceptions which the Revolution had come to destroy. It supported and encouraged all the worst antisocial qualities and systematically destroyed the already awakened conception of the new revolutionary values. The sense of justice and equality, the love of liberty and of human brotherhood—these fundamentals of the real regeneration of society—the Communist State suppressed to the point of extermination. Man's instinctive sense of equity was branded as weak sentimentality; human dignity and liberty became a bourgeois superstition; the sanctity of life, which is the very essence of social reconstruction, was condemned as unrevolutionary, almost counter-revolutionary. This fearful perversion of fundamental values bore within itself the seed of destruction. With the conception that the Revolution was only a means of securing political power, it was inevitable that all revolutionary values should be subordinated to the needs of the Socialist State; indeed, exploited to further the security of the newly acquired governmental power. "Reasons of State," masked as the "interests of the Revolution and of the People," became the sole criterion of action, even of feeling. Violence, the tragic inevitability of revolutionary upheavals, became an established custom, a habit, and was presently enthroned as the most powerful and "ideal" institution. Did not Zinoviev himself canonize Dzerzhinsky, the head of the bloody Tcheka, as the "saint of the Revolution"? Were not the greatest public honours paid by the State to Uritsky, the founder and sadistic chief of the Petrograd Tcheka?

This perversion of the ethical values soon crystallized into the all-dominating slogan of the Communist Party: THE END JUSTIFIES ALL MEANS. Similarly in the past the Inquisition and the Jesuits adopted this motto and subordinated to it all morality. It avenged itself upon the Jesuits as it did upon the

Russian Revolution. In the wake of this slogan followed lying, deceit, hypocrisy and treachery, murder, open and secret. It should be of utmost interest to students of social psychology that two movements as widely separated in time and ideas as Jesuitism and Bolshevism *reached exactly similar results* in the evolution of the principle that the end justifies all means. The historic parallel, almost entirely ignored so far, contains a most important lesson for all coming revolutions and for the whole future of mankind.

There is no greater fallacy than the belief that aims and purposes are one thing, while methods and tactics are another. This conception is a potent menace to social regeneration. All human experience teaches that methods and means cannot be separated from the ultimate aim. The means employed become, through individual habit and social practice, part and parcel of the final purpose; they influence it, modify it, and presently the aims and means become identical. From the day of my arrival in Russia I felt it, at first vaguely, then ever more consciously and clearly. The great and inspiring aims of the Revolution became so clouded with and obscured by the methods used by the ruling political power that it was hard to distinguish what was temporary means and what final purpose. Psychologically and socially the means necessarily influence and alter the aims. The whole history of man is continuous proof of the maxim that to divest one's methods of ethical concepts means to sink into the depths of utter demoralization. In that lies the real tragedy of the Bolshevik philosophy as applied to the Russian Revolution. May this lesson not be in vain.

No revolution can ever succeed as a factor of liberation unless the MEANS used to further it be identical in spirit and tendency with the PURPOSES to be achieved. Revolution is the negation of the existing, a violent protest against man's inhumanity to man with all the thousand and one slaveries it involves. It is the destroyer of dominant values upon which a complex system of injustice, oppression, and wrong has been built up by ignorance and brutality. It is the herald of NEW VALUES, ushering in a transformation of the basic relations of man to man, and of man to society. It is not a mere reformer, patching up some social evils; not a mere changer of forms and institutions; not only a re-distributor of social well-being. It is all that, yet more, much more. It is, first and foremost, the TRANSVALUATOR, the bearer of *new* values. It is the great TEACHER of the NEW ETHICS, inspiring man with a new concept of life and its manifestations in social relationships. It is the mental and spiritual regenerator.

Its first ethical precept is the identity of means used and aims sought. The ultimate end of all revolutionary social change is to establish the sanctity of human life, the dignity of man, the right of every human being to liberty and well-being. Unless this be the essential aim of revolution, violent social changes would have no justification. For *external* social alterations can be, and have been, accomplished by the normal processes of evolution. Revolution, on the contrary, signifies not mere *external* change, but *internal*, basic, fundamental change. That internal change of concepts and ideas, permeating ever-larger social strata, finally culminates in the violent upheaval known as revolution. Shall that climax reverse the process of transvaluation, turn against it, betray it? That is what happened in Russia. On the contrary, the revolution itself must quicken and further the process of which it is the cumulative expression; its main mission is to inspire it, to carry it to greater heights, give it fullest scope for expression. Only thus is revolution true to itself.

Applied in practice it means that the period of the actual revolution, the so-called transitory stage, must be the introduction, the prelude to the new social conditions. It is the threshold to the NEW LIFE, the new HOUSE OF MAN AND HUMANITY. As such it must be of the spirit of the new life, harmonious with the construction of the new edifice.

To-day is the parent of to-morrow. The present casts its shadow far into the future. That is the law of life, individual and social. Revolution that divests itself of ethical values thereby lays the foundation of injustice, deceit, and oppression for the future society. The *means* used to *prepare* the future become its *cornerstone*. Witness the tragic condition of Russia. The methods of State centralization have paralysed individual initiative and effort; the tyranny of the dictatorship has cowed the people into slavish submission and all but extinguished the fires of liberty; organized terrorism has depraved and brutalized the masses and stifled every idealistic aspiration; institutionalized murder has cheapened human life, and all sense of the dignity of man and the value of life has been eliminated; coercion at every step has made effort bitter, labour a punishment, has turned the whole of existence into a scheme of mutual deceit, and has revived the lowest and most brutal instincts of man. A sorry heritage to begin a new life of freedom and brotherhood.

It cannot be sufficiently emphasized that revolution is in vain unless inspired by its ultimate ideal. Revolutionary methods must be in tune with revolutionary aims. The means used to further the revolution must harmonize with its purposes. In short, the ethical values which the revolution is to establish in the new society must be *initiated* with the revolutionary activities of the so-called transitional period. The latter can serve as a real and dependable bridge to the better life only if built of the same material as the life to be achieved. Revolution is the mirror of the coming day; it is the child that is to be the Man of To-morrow.

12 What Modern Socialism Tries to Learn from Anarchism

No doubt, many socialists want the state to wither away. Indeed, there was no shortage of libertarian sentiments among nineteenth-century socialists, a fact too easily forgotten in the wake of Stalinism. Benjamin R. Tucker recognized this fact when he traced socialism and anarchism to the same sources, although he added that a wrong view of the role of the state would force the socialists to forsake their professed goal of *liberating* mankind. For Tucker, the principle of liberty was tightly bound to the goal of ending exploitation. Tolstoy pursued a different, in some ways more searching course of criticism. That socialists failed to renounce state authority was not bad enough; they also overlooked subjugating tendencies characteristic of a modern economy. There would be no equality to compensate for regimentation. Tolstoy refused to identify even the sources of his beliefs with socialism. Bakunin, of course, competed with Marx for leadership in the International Workingmen's Association. Therefore he never questioned their common pursuit of an ideal that he would not have called socialism perhaps, but the revolution. His many followers in the International bear witness to pervading libertarian sentiments. Bakunin did not voice Tolstoy's passion for renunciation of immoral tendencies in modern economic systems, but the two Russians shared love for the peasantry, whom Marx disdained, and faith in their capacity to develop by themselves the type of society in which they would be free. Bakunin had at least as much in common with Tucker. He prophesied on the basis of Marxist utterances that the Marxists' theory of revolution would head them toward either parliamentary misrepresentation or elitist tyranny, predicting what Tucker also stated to be the irresistible consequence of the principle of authority in socialism. Finally, Emma Goldman's analysis of the New Economic Policy sounded like the substantiation of Tolstoy's direst misgivings. Her distinction of anarchism from Bolshevism in terms of their attitudes toward means-and-ends may be taken as a valuable reformulation of the diametrically opposed principles that Tucker had scrutinized. Her emphasis on the spontaneous libertarian spirit that was available throughout Russia seemed to vindicate Bakunin's confidence in revolution. Reviewing the four previous selections, by an individualist, a Christian, a collectivist, and a communist, we find it impossible to isolate a single basic criticism common to all and yet inaccurate to call the criticisms unrelated. Different kinds of socialist opponents have provoked varying attacks, in the process teaching the anarchists much about their own principles.

Perhaps the anarchists may now be allowed to teach the socialists. That is the intent of the following British editorial, which considers evidence of recent interest in anarchism on the part of socialists who are fond of freedom. It sketches anarchist proposals for the 1960s for the benefit of truly democratic socialists, taking it for granted that the principle of authority is not irrevocably a part of socialism.

Question: I know that you are not a member of the Labour Party, or even an orthodox Socialist. But when you call yourself an anarchist, are you not drawing on the anarchist tradition *within the Labour movement* rather than associating yourself with anything like a formal Anarchist position?

Do you not, therefore, feel some kind of allegiance to the Labour movement? It is not just that other people think it important. Surely it is important for you too. You can hardly draw upon an anarchist tradition in the Conservative Party.

Answer: I agree about that. I am somebody who comes very much from a Labour background: from South Wales, from a family that has always voted Labour and has known what Tory rule can be like. And yet I often find myself out of sympathy with the Labour movement. My sympathies are with the people not from the formal anarchist movement—I think it is a fair comment that the leading anarchist in this country should be a knight and that the formal anarchist movement in this country is totally useless and an absolute disaster for any kind of serious anarchist thinking—but I have a sort of sympathy with what are called the 'emotional anarchists'—people like students, intellectuals, unattached people.

These questions and answers are taken from a long interview under the title "Direct Action?" published in the March–April *New Left Review*. The questions were asked by Stuart

"Moving With the Times . . . But Not in Step," *Anarchy* 3 (May, 1961), pp. 65–72.

Hall and Paddy Whannel, and answered by Alan Lovell, a regular *Peace News* writer and a member of the Committee of 100. Although some good points are made, the interview as a whole is not particularly interesting. . . . What is interesting for us is the view of anarchism held by Lovell and his interlocutors.

Three conceptions of anarchism emerge from the interview—emotional anarchism, formal anarchism, and the anarchist tradition within the labour movement. (There also emerges an alleged "leading anarchist", but how many of Lovell's anarchist acquaintances in the Committee of 100 or in DAC or CND [British Peace Groups] regard Sir Herbert Read in this light?). Lest we should have here the beginning of yet another anarchist myth, it is worth while examining these categories.

Is there really a difference between the "formal anarchist movement" and the "anarchist tradition within the Labour movement"? Presumably, like ourselves, Lovell's questioners regard the Labour *movement* as something wider than the Labour Party, but if we do, where but in the Labour movement are the anarchists to be located? Where else, historically, would we place Proudhon, Bakunin, Kropotkin, Malatesta, Landauer, or the Russian, Spanish, French, Bulgarian or Latin-American anarchists? Was it not in commemoration of the Chicago anarchists of 1887 that the modern celebration of May Day as a labour festival began? Were Sacco and Vanzetti, Berkman and Emma Goldman, Durand or Durrutti, outside the Labour movement?

In this country, the "father of anarchism" William Godwin, was the intellectual father of such precursors of socialism as Francis Place, Robert Owen, Thomas Hodgskin, and you have only to read the history of the First International or the life of William Morris to see the extent to which the anarchists were, in the late nineteenth century, an integral part of the Labour movement.

The anarchists haven't changed, but the Labour movement, strait-jacketed into *one* concept of socialism, the Marxist one abroad, the Fabian one here, has changed—to its cost. For us, the most interesting characteristic of the trend we call the New Left today, is the way in which some of its adherents have been groping towards an anarchist approach, taking their cue from some older socialist thinkers like Arthur Lewis, with his declaration that

"Contrary to popular belief, Socialism is not committed either by its history or by its philosophy to the glorification of the State or to the extension of its powers. On the contrary, the links of Socialism are with liberalism and with anarchism, with their emphasis on individual freedom . . ."

or like G. D. H. Cole with his rediscovery towards the end of his life of the relevance of such thinkers as Bakunin and Kropotkin, and his re-affirmation of his early guild socialist principles. . . .

Similarly Charles Taylor, examining the quality of life in contemporary Britain in ULR 5 [*Universities and Left Review*], demands "viable smaller societies, on a face-to-face scale" and "the extension of the individual's power over the collective forces which shape his life", and E. P. Thompson (who has come a long way in the last five years), writes in NLR 6 [*New Left Review*], that

"we can only find out how to break through our present political conventions, and help people to think of socialism as something done *by* people and not *for* people or *to* people, by pressing in new ways *on the ground*. One socialist youth club of a quite new kind, in East London, or Liverpool or Leeds; one determined municipal council, probing the possibility of new kinds of municipal ownership in the face of Government opposition; one tenants' association with a new dynamic, pioneering on its own account new patterns of social welfare—play-centres, nursery facilities, community services for and by the women—involving people in the discussion and solution of problems of town planning, racial intercourse, leisure facilities; one pit, factory, or sector of nationalised industry where new forms of workers' control can actually be forced on management . . ."

Here he is talking what is very like our own language. Yet among the writers of the New Left there are also strange inconsistencies and hangovers from orthodox socialism and Marxism. Some of its ablest thinkers have learned nothing from the history of socialism in our time. Raymond Williams . . . puts the formula thus:

"What is the alternative to capitalism? Socialism. What is a socialist culture? State control."

Such a mountain of analysis: such a political mouse! The New Left *needs* the lessons which it can draw from the anarchist approach; the question is whether it is capable of learning them.

The editor of NLR 6, discussing the Campaign for Nuclear Disarmament, writes of *"the anarchist case, which I believe to be a felt but unarticulated strand in CND politics, and which is weak largely because it has not been put. In any event, that anarchism and libertarianism has been a most fertile element in the Campaign . . ."* But the anarchist case has been *put*, for anyone who cared to read it. The point is that it does not appear to have been *taken*, and if the anarchist strand is weak, it is precisely because of the lack of what Lovell calls "serious anarchist thinking".

Like him we have a sympathy with the people he calls emotional anarchists—"people like students, intellectuals, unattached people", the people who have, as he suggested elsewhere in his interview, "an emotional bias towards anarchism, but it is very much of an emotional bias and completely unthought-out". We wish they *would* start thinking it out. We want in fact that serious anarchist thinking which the emotional anarchists aren't doing, and which, in his odd way, he thinks would be disastrous in the "formal anarchists", the people who actually call themselves anarchists, and who know the word's meaning, its history and its literature. . . .

Today it is not possible to speak with the confident revolutionary optimism of our predecessors. The experiences of our own century have given us a healthy suspicion of rhetoric and of universal panaceas. We have seen too many and we know too much.

What are we to say here in Britain in the second half of the twentieth century? We are a tiny minority of disaffected citizens in the centre of a disappearing empire whose economic structure is still geared to an obsolete role, an appendage to one of the two contending military and economic power blocs. What is the task of the anarchists in such a society? Can we draw up, not a programme, but simply a list of those fields where anarchist activity is useful and in which, according to personal predilection or opportunity, we can promote our ideas?

WAR AND PEACE

One of the characteristics of governments is their maintenance of what Martin Buber calls the "latent external crisis", the fear of an external enemy, by which they maintain their ascendency over their own subjects. This has in our day become the major activity of governments and their biggest field of expenditure and effort, reaching the stage where they propose to decimate each others' populations at the touch of a button. War is the trade of governments, and obviously the anarchists support, in common with other factions of the left, all anti-war activities, but they can hardly be expected to see anything but illusions in calls for summit conferences or in the signing of petitions. The petitions go to the wrong address; they should be addressed not to governments but to people.

We have to build up a disobedient and unreliable public, widening and deepening the impulses which find expression in the three prongs of the nuclear disarmament movement. War is not the result of the H-bomb. The H-bomb is the logical outcome of the pursuit of war, which in turn is only possible because governments are able to harness their obedient subjects to it. But there are deeper causes; not merely the clash of ideologies, the division of the world into have and have-nots, but the dissatisfactions and frustrations which evidently make the idea of war acceptable for millions of people. . . . We have to uncover the dulled and muffled nerve of moral and social responsibility which will make it intolerable.

THE PERSON AND THE FAMILY

The mass of mankind, Thoreau observed tartly, lead lives of quiet desperation. Is this why we tolerate war—as an exciting break in meaningless routine? And yet who but ourselves has decreed the situation in which work is drained of meaning and purpose except as a source of income or status, marriage and the family a trap, leisure a desperate attempt to stave off boredom? Look around you at the domestic resentments, the glum faces emerging from factory and office into the tedium of the rush-hour journey home, the frantic consumption at the behest of the hidden persuaders. How desperately we need to find different ways of life which will liberate instead of imprisoning the individual. And how we need the anarchists to experiment with new ways of living, a new assertion of individual values, more dignity and more satisfaction in daily life.

WORK AND INDUSTRY

At one time, forty years ago, there was a strong syndicalist stream in the trade union movement, calling for workers' control of industry. It died away, as the industrial workers pinned their faith on the Labour Party's programme of nationalisation and concentrated on winning a bigger slice of the capitalist cake. One of the most formidable tasks before us is the re-kindling of the urge for responsibility and autonomy in industry: to put workers' control back on the agenda. . . .

CRIME AND PUNISHMENT

To anarchist thinkers from Godwin onward, crime has been not the manifestation of individual wickedness, but a symptom of material or mental poverty and deprivation. From Kropotkin with his study of *Organised Vengeance Called Justice* and his dictum that prisons are the universities of crime, to Alex Comfort's modern study of political delinquency, the anarchists have opposed the system of retributive justice which creates more criminals than it cures, and have sought the identification and avoidance of the *causes* of crime. A wealth of evidence has been accumulated, even officially, which supports this view and there is here an immense field for anarchist effort in changing the social climate and public attitudes.

EDUCATION

There have been in this century great changes in educational theory and practice, which represent a partial and incomplete, if unacknowledged victory for ideas which are libertarian in origin. We are however, now in a period when the more sophisticated educational theorists are almost joining hands with those who never got that far, in reacting against the alleged influences of the advocates of freedom in education. Social pressures and parental 'status-anxiety', are already impinging on those partial advances . . . The anarchist movement, which has included some very astute educational thinkers, needs urgently to re-define and re-assert ideas, and to counter the counter-revolution in educational thought, pointing out that the trouble with 'child-centred' education is not that it has gone too far, but that it has not gone far enough, and in fact, in many schools, has not even begun.

DECENTRALISATION AND AUTONOMY

The modern state is infinitely more centralised and ubiquitous than that of the time of the classical anarchists. It has also adopted or usurped many of the functions which are those of *society*, and which Kropotkin, for instance, in his *Mutual Aid*, listed as evidence of the innate sociality of man which makes the imposition from above of state organisation unnecessary. In social organisation and in industry, and consequently in the distribution of population, centralisation has been the great characteristic of modern life, and one which militates against the possibility of anything like an anarchist society. The tendency itself is, however, one which changes in means of communication and in sources of motive power have already rendered obsolete, and there is a great deal of sociological data to demonstrate its undesirability in human terms. The anarchists and those who think like them on this issue, have to change the centralising habit of mind for one which seeks decentralisation and devolution, pressing for more and more local autonomy in all aspects of life.

THE WORLD OUTSIDE

Nothing stands still. The great monolith of the Soviet empire is by no means as monolithic as it was. A generation has grown up which is bored and dissatisfied with the chanting of Marxist slogans and which is equally unimpressed by the "free enterprise" of the West. The workers' councils which sprang up in Poland and Hungary in the revolutionary period of 1956, Tito's fears that his officially-sponsored version of syndicalism from above might get out of hand and turn into the real thing, the "silent pressures from below" in the Soviet Union itself, indicate how tendencies which have more in common with anarchism than with orthodox socialism are ready to spring into life where we least expect them. The trends in India represented by the *Gramdan* movement as the successor to Vinoba Bhave's *Bhoodan*, and by Jayaprakash Narayan's advocacy of "village democracy", the moral example of Danilo Dolci's activities in Sicily, all such movements suggest a possible role for the anarchist, outside and independent of the struggle for power which canalises the activities of so many socially conscious people into sterile political posturing.

A DIFFERENT KIND OF SOCIALISM

In the New Left, and among the people who have been roused into activity by the nuclear disarmament campaign, there is interest and concern for all these fields of activity. But as long as they ruefully give their support to the Labour Party as a lesser evil, or devote their energy to trying to influence its policies, they are simply evading the need to work out the implications and explore the possibilities of a different *kind* of socialism: the means of effecting social change without recourse to the conquest of the coercive machinery of the state.

In 1962 the Harvard historian H. Stuart Hughes ran for the Senate as a peace candidate. He was criticized by some parts of the American left for declaring his socialistic and atheistic convictions, which were thought an irresponsible embarrassment to the simple issue of peace. Paul Goodman's anarchist critique of the campaign, in contrast, called into question the concept of political power and the effectiveness of the ballot for social change.

Repudiation of the ballot has long made anarchists anathema to the socialists and incomprehensible to much of the public. Anarchists, however, have considered their case against the ballot easy to make plain. Here is a version by Benjamin R. Tucker:

> Now, what is the ballot? It is neither more nor less than a paper representative of the bayonet, the billy, and the bullet. It is a labor-saving device for ascertaining on which side force lies and bowing to the inevitable. The voice of the majority saves bloodshed, but it is no less the arbitrament of force than is the decree of the most absolute of despots backed by the most powerful of armies. . . . Reason devoted to politics fights for its own dethronement. The moment the minority becomes the majority, it ceases to reason and persuade, and begins to command and enforce and punish.

Another anarchist might emphasize that the ballot confers a semblance of legitimacy on remote control over problems that can more competently be handled on a community basis without voting. And all would agree that huge vote returns are no sensitive index to what really matters to individual persons.

Underlying the stubbornness of anarchists concerning the ballot is the belief expressed by Emma Goldman in her attack on Bolshevism: "There is no greater fallacy than the belief that aims and purposes are one thing, while methods and tactics are another." In response to the reluctant decision of Spanish anarcho-syndicalists to support the anti-fascist government, Emma Goldman was uncompromising.

> First, the question as to whether the abstention from participation in elections is for Anarchists a matter of principle? I certainly think it is. . . . After all, participation in election means

the transfer of one's will and decisions to another, which is contrary to the fundamental principles of Anarchism.

Secondly, since Anarchists do not believe in the Jesuitic formulas of the Bolsheviki that the end justifies the means it is but logical for Anarchists not to consider political participation as a "simple question of tactics." Such tactics are not only incompatible with Anarchist thought and principles, but they also injure the stand of Anarchism as the one and only truly revolutionary social philosophy.

Not all anarchists have felt that this rule is unexceptionable. The editor of the anarchist magazine *Vanguard* attached this comment to Emma Goldman's article: "If there is any criticism to be leveled in [the anarcho-syndicalists'] direction, it should be based upon an analysis of the concrete situation with which they were faced and not abstract principles. Anti-electionism is not a dogma, but a revolutionary tactic the effectiveness of which may occasionally be qualified by unusual conditions and factors."

In evaluating the Hughes campaign Paul Goodman's remarks show how the anarchist attack on socialism can be turned into a fresh examination of the entire social system. In the first selection in this anthology, D. Novak accounts for the demise of anarchism as due to the "genetic fallacy" in assuming that government was limited to the form in which it originated. Goodman may prove that anarchism is no less flexible than government and thus that it is Novak, after all, who commits his own fallacy.

1

The spirited candidacy of Stuart Hughes for Senator—like an actualization of Leo Szilard's courageous plan to finance and organize a national party for peace—makes it useful to review the ambiguities involved in this kind of politics.

"War is the health of the State"—modern history teaches no other lesson, whether we think of the weird personal, fanatic, and dynastic wars of the sixteenth and seventeenth centuries or the economic and geo-political wars of recent generations. The sovereign national States have lived and grown by preparing for war and waging war; and as the Pow-

" 'Getting Into Power,' " from *People or Personnel*, by Paul Goodman (New York: Random House, Inc., 1965), pp. 175–89. © Copyright 1963, 1964, 1965 by Paul Goodman. Reprinted by permission of Random House, Inc.

ers have aggrandized themselves, they have become more crashingly destructive. I do not mean that men have not used also simpler social organizations, feudal, tribal, free city, in order to kill one another *en masse*, but centralized sovereign power, radiating from baroque capitals, has proved to be the ideal executive of murderous will. In our own nation at present, it would be impossible to describe the economy without regarding war-making as a crucial factor; the foreign relations of the United States are carried on entirely in terms of bellicose power-blocs, and either to expand "influence" or to hang onto it; and to mention my own field where I can speak at first hand, our primary education and heavily State-subsidized higher education have become regimented to apprentice-training for war, more directly if less sickeningly than the psychological national regimentation endemic in French and German schooling. (The Russians go in for both the technological and psychological aspects.)

This solidifying of national sovereign bellicosity is at present all the more irrational, and of course all the more necessary if the sovereigns are to maintain themselves, since the cultural, technological, economic, and communications relations of the world are now overwhelmingly supra-national. (What a pity that, partly to combat colonialism and partly out of the emulative stupidity and cupidity of their Western-trained leaders, peoples of Africa and Asia are adopting the same fatal and outmoded style.)

The only possible pacifist conclusion from these facts is the anarchist one, to get rid of the sovereignties and to diminish, among people, the motivations of power and grandiosity. This means, regionally, to decentralize or centralize directly in terms of life-functions, empirically examined. My own bias is to decentralize and localize wherever it is feasible, because this makes for alternatives and more vivid and intimate life. It multiplies initiative. And it is safer. On the basis of this weakening of the Powers, and of the substitution of function for power, it would be possible also to organize the world community, as by the functional agencies of the United Nations, UNICEF, WHO, somewhat UNESCO; and to provide *ad hoc* cooperation like the Geo-physical Year, exploring space, or feeding the Chinese.

Rigidly applied, this logic would seem to make pacifist State politics absurd. It is not in the nature of sovereign power to decree itself out of existence. (Thus, it is absurd for picketers of the White House to petition Mr. Kennedy as the President, rather than to sermonize him as a man or lecture him as a boy.) Also, such politics confuses the basic issue, that *pacifism is necessarily revolutionary*. A moment's recollection of the defection of the French and German socialist deputies from their pacifism in 1914 will show that this confusion is not trivial. Nevertheless, the attitude of the General Strike for Peace is as follows: in November we shall urge people actively and explicitly to refuse to vote, to strike against voting, except for candidates who are unambiguously committed to immediate action to relax the Cold War, for instance Stuart Hughes or Robert Kastenmeier. Our reasoning is that, in our increasingly monolithic society and economy, any anti-war activity is likely to exert a revolutionary influence willy-nilly. And secondly, as Professor Hughes himself has said, the machinery of an electoral campaign *can* be a powerful means of education, especially by compelling mention of what the mass-media ordinarily refuse to mention. We wish to cooperate with pacifist activity of *every* kind, whether SANE, Quaker, Third Party politics, or Committee for Nonviolent Action, because although "objectively" we are in a revolutionary situation in that the Powers-that-be are certainly bent on destroying themselves and everything else, nevertheless people do not take this seriously and there is an almost total lack of practical will to make the necessary reorganization of society. To say it grimly, unlike 1914, people do not even have political representatives to betray them.

Personally, what I enjoy about Professor Hughes' campaign is that often, when the students were out getting signatures to put him on the ballot, people would say, "Do you mean he is *neither* a Democrat *nor* a Republican? Then give me the pen!" (It is said by people from Massachusetts, that this response is peculiarly appropriate to the ordinary local politics of Massachusetts; but I take this as local boasting.) In the deadly routine that the Americans have sunk into, the mere possibility of an *alternative* is a glorious thing. Especially if there is the framework of a permanent organization. Also such a campaign must be a remarkable experience for Hughes himself, to confront many people who do not at all have the same assumptions. And it gives some concrete activity to his phalanx, the New England professors of the Council of Correspondence. The students of Brandeis, Harvard, etc. are also busy with it; but on them this *kind* of political involvement might be, in my opinion, more ambiguous, and that is why I am writing this essay.

2

For let me turn to an issue much deeper and more fateful for pacifism than these questions of strategy and tactics. This is the assumption, now appallingly unanimous among the ordinary electorate, professional politicians, most radicals, and even political scientists who should know better, that politics is essentially a matter of "getting into power," and then "deciding," directing, controlling, coercing, the activities of society. The model seems to be taken from corporations with top-management, and there is something prestigious about being a "decision-maker." (Even C. Wright Mills was mesmerized by this image; but, as I tried to show recently in *Commentary*, in such a set-up less and less of human value is really decided by any responsible person, though plenty of disvalue is ground out by the set-up itself.) It is taken for granted that a man wants "power" of this kind, and it is quite acceptable for people like Joseph Kennedy and his sons to work toward it, even though this is directly contrary to the political ideal that the office and its duties seek the man rather than the man the office. It is axiomatic that a party's primary purpose is to get into power, although this was not the original idea of "factions," in Madison's sense, which were functional though divisive interest groups. More dangerously still, it is taken for granted that a nation wants to be a Great Power, and maintain itself so at any cost, even though this may be disadvantageous to its culture and most of its citizens.

And following the popular Leviathan like a jolly-boat, the political-sociologists devote their researches to the analysis and simulation of power struggles, as if this were their only possible subject; and as advisers, they take part in the power struggles, rather than helping to solve problems. Unfortunately, the thinking of Hughes and Szilard seems to share some of this assumption about the paramountcy of "getting into power"—just as David Riesman is always hounding people who are in "power." And, frankly, when I question such a universal consensus, I wonder if I am on the right planet. Nevertheless, these persons are deluded. They are taking a base and impractical, and indeed neurotic, state of affairs as if it were right and inevitable. The state of affairs is impractical because, finally, no good can come of it; though of course, since it *is* the state of affairs, it must be transiently coped with and changed. Unless we remember much more clearly than we seem to, what this "power" is, our behavior in the madhouse cannot be prudent and therapeutic. So with chagrin I find myself forced to review elementary political theory and history.

Living functions, biological, psychosociological, or social, have very little to do with abstract, preconceived "power" that manages and coerces from outside the specific functions themselves. Indeed, it is a commonplace that abstract power —in the form of "will power," "training," "discipline," "bureaucracy," "reform schooling," "scientific management," etc. —uniformly *thwarts* normal functioning and debases the persons involved. (It has a natural use, in emergencies, when not high-grade but minimal low-grade behavior is required.) Normal activities do not need extrinsic motivations, they have their own intrinsic energies and ends-in-view; and decisions are continually made by the ongoing functions themselves, adjusting to the environment and one another.

We may then define the subject of normal politics. It is the constitutional relations of functional interests and interest groups in the community in which they transact. This is the bread and butter of ancient political theory and obviously has nothing to do with sovereignty or even power—for the ancients the existence of power implies unconstitutionality, tyranny. But even modern authors who move in a theory of "sovereignty," like Spinoza, Locke, Adam Smith, Jefferson, or Madison, understand that the commonwealth is strongest when the functional interests can seek their own level and there is the weakest exercise of "power." For instance, Spinoza tries to play power like a fish, Jefferson to de-energize it, Madison to balance it out, Smith to make it an umpire.

Let us now quickly sketch the meaning of the recent transcendent importance of "power" and "getting into power," as if otherwise communities could not function.

First, and least important, there is the innocuous, nonviolent, and rather natural development of a kind of abstract power in an indigenous (non-invaded) society. The functions of civilization include production, trade and travel, the bringing up of the young in the mores; also subtle but essential polarities like experimentation and stability; also irrational and superstitious fantasies like exacting revenge for crime and protecting the taboos. Different interests in the whole will continually conflict, as individuals or as interest groups; yet, since all require the commonwealth, there is also a strong functional interest in adjudication and peace, in harmonizing social invention or at least compromise. It is plausible that in the interests of armistice and adjudication, there should arise a kind of abstract institution above the conflicts, to settle them or to obviate them by plans and laws; this would certainly be power. (This derivation is plausible but I doubt that it is historical, for in fact it is just this kind of thing that lively primitive communities accomplish by quick intuition, tone of voice, exchange of a glance, and suddenly there is unanimity, to the anthropologist's astonishment.) Much more likely, and we know historically, abstract power is invented in simple societies in emergencies of danger, of enemy attack or divine wrath. But such "dictatorship" is *ad hoc* and surprisingly lapses. Surprisingly, considering that power corrupts; yet it makes psychological sense, for emergency is a negative function, to meet a threat to the pre-conditions of the interesting functions of life; once the danger is past, the "power" has no energy of function, no foreground interest, to maintain it. To give a very late example: it seemed remarkable to the Europeans, but not to the Americans, that Washington, like Cincinnatus, went home to his farm; and even the Continental Congress languished. There were no conditions for "power."

(Indeed—and this is why I have chosen the example—in the last decades of the eighteenth century, in many respects the Americans lived in a kind of peaceful community anarchy, spiced by mutinies that were hardly punished. The Constitution, as Richard Lee pointed out, was foisted on them by trickery, the work of very special interest groups; it would have been quite sufficient simply to amend the Articles.)

Altogether different from this idyl is the universal history of most of the world, civilized or barbarian. Everywhere is invasion, conquest, and domination, involving for the victors the necessity to keep and exercise power, and for the others the necessity to strive for power, in order to escape suffering and exploitation. This too is entirely functional. The conqueror is originally a pirate; he and his band do not share in the commonwealth, they have interests apart from the community preyed on. Subsequently, however, piracy becomes government, the process of getting people to perform by extrinsic motivations, of penalty and blackmail, and later bribery and training. But it is only the semblance of a commonwealth, for activity is not voluntary. Necessarily, such directed and extrinsically motivated performance is not so strong, efficient, spontaneous, inventive, well-structured, or lovely as the normal functioning of a free community of interests. Very soon society becomes lifeless. The means of community action, initiative, decision, have been preempted by the powerful. But the slaveholders, exploiters, and governors share in that same society and are themselves vitiated. Yet they never learn to get down off the people's back and relinquish their power. So some are holding on to an increasingly empty power; others are striving to achieve it; and most are sunk in resignation. Inevitably, as people become stupider and more careless, administration increases in size and power; and conversely. By and large, the cultures that we study in the melancholy pages of history are pathetic mixtures, with the ingredients often still discernible: There is a certain amount of normal function surviving or reviving—bread is baked, arts and sciences are pursued by a few, etc.; mostly we see the abortions of lively social functioning saddled, exploited, prevented, perverted, drained dry, paternalized by an imposed system of power and management that preempts the means and makes decisions *ab extra*. And the damnable thing is that, of course, everybody believes that except in this pattern nothing could possibly be accomplished: if there were no marriage license and no tax, none could properly mate and no children be born and raised; if there were no tolls there would be no bridges; if there were no university charters, there would be no higher learning; if there were no usury and no Iron Law of Wages, there would be no capital; if there were no markup of drug prices, there would be no scientific research. Once a society has this style of thought, that every activity requires licensing, underwriting, deciding by abstract power, it becomes inevitably desirable for an ambitious man to seek power and for a vigorous nation to try to be a Great Power. The more some have the power drive, the more it seems to be necessary to the others to compete, or submit, just in order to survive. (And importantly they are right.) Many are ruthless and most live in fear.

Even so, this is not the final development of the belief in "power." For that occurs when to get into power, to be prestigious and in a position to make decisions, is taken to be the social good itself, apart from any functions that it is thought to make possible. The pattern of dominance-and-submission has then been internalized and, by its clinch, fills up the whole of experience. If a man is not continually proving his potency, his mastery of others and of himself, he becomes prey to a panic of being defeated and victimized. Every vital function must therefore be used as a means of proving or it is felt as a symptom of weakness. Simply to enjoy, produce, learn, give or take, love or be angry (rather than cool), is to be vulnerable. This is different, and has different consequences, from the previous merely external domination and submission. A people that has life but thwarted functions will rebel when it can, against feudal dues, clogs to trade, suppression of thought and speech, taxation without representation, insulting privilege, the Iron Law of Wages, colonialism. But our people do not rebel against poisoning, genetic deformation, imminent total destruction.

Rather, people aspire to be top-managers no matter what the goods or services produced. One is a promoter, period; or a celebrity, period. The Gross National Product must increase without consideration of the standard of life. There is no natural limit, so the only security is in deterrence. The environment is rife with projected enemies. There is a huddling together and conforming to avoid the vulnerability of any idiosyncrasy, at the same time as each one has to be one-up among his identical similars. Next, there is excitement in identifying with the "really" powerful, the leaders, the Great Nations, the decision-makers, dramatized on the front page. But these leaders, of course, feel equally powerless in the face of the Great Events. For it is characteristic of the syndrome that as soon as there is occasion for any practical activity, toward happiness, value, spirit, or even simple safety, everyone suffers from the feeling of utter powerlessness; the internalized submissiveness now has its innings. Modern technology is too complex; there is a population explosion; the computer will work out the proper war game for us; they've got your number, don't stick your neck out; "fallout is a physical fact of our nuclear age, it can be faced like any other fact" (*Manual of Civil Defense*); "I'm strong, I can take sex or leave it" (eighteen-year-old third-offender for felonious assault). In brief, the underside of the psychology of power is that Nothing Can Be Done; and the resolution of the stalemate is to explode. This is the Cold War.

I have frequently explored this psychology of proving, resignation, and catastrophic explosion (Wilhelm Reich's "primary masochism"), and I shall not pursue it again. It is filling the void of vital function by identifying with the agent

that has frustrated it; with, subsequently, a strongly defended
conceit, but panic when any occasion calls for initiative, originality, or even animal response. Here I have simply tried to
relate this psychology to the uncritical unanimous acceptance
of the idea of "getting into power in order to . . ." or just
"getting into power" as an end in itself. There is a vicious
circle, for (except in emergencies) the very exercise of abstract power, managing and coercing, itself tends to stand in
the way and alienate, to thwart function and diminish energy, and so to increase the psychology of power. But of
course the consequence of the process is to put us in fact in a
continual emergency, so power creates its own need. I have
tried to show how, historically, the psychology has been ex-
acerbated by the miserable system of extrinsic motivation by
incentives and punishments (including profits, wages, unemployment), reducing people to low-grade organisms no different from Professor Skinner's pigeons; whereas normal function is intrinsically motivated toward specific ends-in-view,
and leads to growth in inventiveness and freedom. Where
people are not directly in feelingful contact with what is to
be done, nothing is done well and on time; they are always
behind and the emergency becomes chronic. Even with good
intentions, a few managers do not have enough *mind* for the
needs of society—not even if their computers gallop through
the calculations like lightning. I conclude that the consensus
of recent political scientists that political theory is essentially
the study of power-maneuvers, is itself a neurotic ideology.
Normal politics has to do with the relations of specific functions in a community; and *such a study would often result in
practical political inventions that would solve problems*—it
would not merely predict elections and solve nothing, or
play war games and destroy mankind.

Let me sum up these remarks in one homely and not newsy
proposition: Throughout the world, it is bad domestic politics
that creates the deadly international politics. Conversely,
pacifism is revolutionary: we will not have peace unless there
is a profound change in social structure, including getting rid
of national sovereign power.

3

After this pedantic excursion, let me return, for a paragraph,
to Professor Hughes. He does not have the psychology that
Nothing Can Be Done, for he is doing something with immense energy. Indeed, his most valuable service, in my

opinion, is to show that even in the framework of routine politics, there is a possible alternative mode of proceeding. (Adlai Stevenson, by contrast, never seemed to believe this.) Also, he obviously has no wish to "get into power" except precisely to stop the arms race and relax the Cold War. His campaign is primarily educational; and even if he were elected, I think, he would not feel that he has "power" but a splendid public forum. (This is the line of Kastenmeier and the Liberal Project Congressmen.)

Yet we cannot overlook the deep contradiction between peace and "getting into power" at all. With the strong background support of the unusually courageous New England professors, the hard work of politically renascent youth, and the total disgust of many of the electorate in the face of our insane policies, Professor Hughes has been able to by-pass the demoralizing and stupefying demands of the political clubhouse, or the emasculating horse's-ass-making requirements of rising to an important nomination through respectable channels. Nevertheless, the program with which he now appears before the electorate—I presume he means it sincerely—is inadequate to the needs of the situation. In foreign affairs, it is the kind of compromising that has no future. As a domestic program it is valueless, as if he had not put his mind to this as immediately important; yet it is just in this, in my view, that he could shake and begin to revive our people. And suppose he (or Szilard's candidates) were elected: he could hardly take a Constitutional oath to proceed to ring down the flag. Of course he has no such purpose, but nothing less will serve.

Concretely, our system of government at present comprises the military-industrial complex, the secret para-military agencies, the scientific war corporations, the blimps, the horse's asses, the police, the administrative bureaucracy, the career diplomats, the lobbies, the corporations that contribute party funds, the under-writers and real-estate promoters that batten on Urban Renewal, the official press and the official opposition press, the sounding-off and jockeying for the next election, the National Unity, etc., etc. All this machine is grinding along by the momentum of the power and profit motives and style long since built into it; it *cannot* make decisions of a kind radically different than it does. Even if an excellent man happens to be elected to office, he will find that it is no longer a possible instrument for social change on any major issues of war and peace or the way of life of

the Americans. Indeed, as the members of the Liberal Project
have complained, office does not give even a good public
forum, for the press does not report inconvenient speeches.

So we must look, finally, not to this kind of politics, but to
direct functioning in what concerns us closely, in order to
dispel the mesmerism of abstract power altogether. This has,
of course, been the thinking of radical pacifism. The civil
disobedience of the Committee for Nonviolent Action is the
direct expression of each person's conscience of what it is
impossible for him to live with. The studied withdrawal and
boycotting advocated by the General Strike for Peace is a
direct countering of the social drift toward catastrophe that
occurs just because we cooperate with it. (The same holds
for refusal in what is one's "private" important business, like
the Women's Strike against poisoned milk or young men's
refusing the draft.) Best of all, in principle, is the policy that
Dave Dellinger espouses and tries to live by, to live com-
munally and without authority, to work usefully and feel
friendly, and so *positively to replace an area of power with
peaceful functioning.* (Interestingly, even a critical and pur-
gative group like *The Realist* is coming around to this point
of view—with a hard row to hoe among urban poor people.)
Similar is to work in foreign lands as a citizen of humanity,
trying to avoid the Power blocs and their aims, e.g. the
Friends Service. The merit of all these activities is that they
produce a different kind of human relations and look to a
different quality of life. This is a global and perhaps impos-
sibly difficult task. But think. There is no history of mankind
without these wars, which now have come to the maximum:
can we have any hope except in a different kind of human
relations?

It will be said that there is no time. Yes, probably. But let
me cite a remark of Tocqueville. In his last work, *L'Ancien
Regime,* he notes "with terror," as he says, how throughout
the eighteenth century writer after writer and expert after
expert pointed out that this and that detail of the Old
Regime was unviable and could not possibly survive; added
up, they proved that the entire Old Regime was doomed and
must soon collapse; and yet *there was not a single man who
foretold that there would be a mighty revolution.*

SECTION III

Philosophical Foundations

This section occupies a pivotal position in the anthology. Looking backward, we can see it as a contribution to the major aims of sections I and II. Furthermore, this section is indispensable to all those that follow, for the philosophical conclusions which are advanced and defended here become in turn the stated or assumed premises on which the anarchist builds.

More specifically the philosophical excerpts that follow have two aims. First, to establish principles by which one can determine the sort of life men ought to live and the sort of society that is morally imperative or intrinsically desirable (worth pursuing for itself and not merely as a means). And second, to analyze the meaning which is or ought to be carried by the key concepts in practical or moral judgments, for example, "rights," "equity," "authority," "coercion," and "human nature." Understood in this light, the theories that follow constitute approaches to the perennial problems of ethical and political philosophy.

Of course, our six libertarian philosophers sometimes contradict one another. And, though an absence of conflict might well unnerve any anarchist, the differences are not always trivial. Still, there are important areas of consensus, one of which calls for immediate comment.

Thomas Hobbes, in Chapter XXI of *Leviathan*, defines liberty as the absence of external impediments. Many philosophers have regarded this conception of liberty as a fundamental moral standard and the most precious of human values. But Hobbes's view would not have been acceptable to any of the anarchist thinkers whose writings are presented below. For what they submit as most worth securing goes beyond the clearing away of obstacles and restrictions. Their standard of what is ultimately desirable, and of what society should preserve, resides in a more constructive ideal which they alternatively designate as "the sovereignty of the individual" (Andrews), "personality" (Berdyaev), "independent judgment" (Godwin), "self-ownership" (Stirner), and so on. Correct or not, this unanimous rejection of the Hobbesian notion of freedom for a more positive chief good provides a unifying theme in anarchist thought.

14 Non-Resistance: A Basis for Christian Anarchism

Christian anarchism, based on the injunction of non-resistance to evil, has been commonly traced to the later writings of Leo Tolstoy. But Tolstoy should not be regarded as a Christian innovator. For one thing, he followed a long history of small Protestant sects that viewed political authority as a deterrent to the expression of the millennial perfection of man. In fact, whenever religious groups had discarded the idea that humanity was by nature sinful, the usefulness of government had fallen under suspicion. Tolstoy, thus, comes late in the tradition of radical insistence that no intermediary was needed between man and God. His major religious work, *The Kingdom of God Is Within You*, was an attempt to systematically justify this tradition and its case against the State.

Tolstoy cannot even be regarded as an innovator in the systematic formulation of Christian anarchism. One of his important predecessors was Adin Ballou, who expounded the case for Christian anarchism not only in the lecture reprinted below and in his major work *Practical Christian Socialism* (1854), but in his capacities as editor of such pacifist and abolitionist journals as *The Non-resistant and Practical Christian* (1845–1849) and as minister to the exemplary Hopedale Community in Massachusetts. Tolstoy more completely details the State's record of violence and inhumanity and displays the full Biblical evidence that Christianity and all forms of human government are incompatible. But no Christian anarchist has ever equalled the clarity and rigor with which Ballou sets forth his position.

Ballou unequivocally rejects a standing article of faith among political philosophers: that is, that there is always *an* obligation to obey "the law of the land" or "the government," even though certain considerations can occasionally defeat this obligation. He marshals a set of ingenious arguments to show that government is "a mere cipher," with "no rightful claim to the allegiance of man."

A natural question here concerns the relevance of Ballou's position for non-believers. The answer seems to be that the libertarian conclusions he maintains do not essentially depend on the Christian appeals with which they are sometimes decorated. How this is so may be gathered from the evidence supplied by Ballou's concept of "divine government," from his case against allegiance to human authority, and from the ways in which he defends Christ's manner of handling those who would do us evil.

But Ballou's principles, for all that has been said, are not free of difficulties. For example, given his strictures against human government, how can he decide which of two conflicting—and therefore human—applications of the canon of non-resistance is correct? Further, Ballou, like Tolstoy, disclaimed the title of "anarchist." This he justified on the ground of being "no antagonist to human government." But the power of non-resistance that he upholds can redirect, thwart—antagonize—political pontiffs.

What is human government? It is the will of man—whether of one, few, many or all, in a state or nation—exercising absolute authority over man, by means of cunning and physical force. This *will* may be ascertained, declared and executed, with or without written constitutions and laws, regularly or irregularly, in moderation or in violence; still it is alike human government under all forms and administrations. . . .

What is the divine government? It is the infallible will of God prescribing the duty of moral agents, and claiming their primary undivided allegiance, as indispensable to the enjoyment of pure and endless happiness. . . . [I]t is denominated 'the kingdom and reign of Christ.' The kingdom of Christ is the kingdom of God; for what is Christ's is God's. The Father dwelleth in the Son, and without Him the Son can do nothing. In this kingdom the all perfect God is sole King, Lawgiver, and Judge. He divides his authority with no *creature*; he is absolute Sovereign; he claims the whole heart, mind, and strength. . . .

From this it appears that human government, properly so called, can in no case be either superior to, or coequal with, the divine. Can this conclusion be avoided? There are three, and but three cases, in which *human* government may dispute supremacy with the *divine*. 1. When God requires *one* thing and man requires the *contrary*. In this case, whom ought we to obey? All christians must answer, with the faithful apostles of old, 'We ought to obey God rather than men.' But must we disobey parents, patriarchs, priests, kings, nobles, presi-

---

Remarks at the First Annual Meeting of the Non-Resistance Society, by Adin Ballou in Boston, Massachusetts, September 25, 1839, passim. (*Non-Resistance and Government*)

dents, governors, generals, legislatures, constitutions, armies, mobs, *all* rather than disobey God? We MUST; and then patiently endure the penal consequences. Then surely human government is nothing against the government of God. 2. Human government and divine government sometimes agree in prescribing the same duty; i.e. God and man both require the same thing. In *this* case ought not the reverence of *human* authority to constitute at least a *part* of the motive for doing right. We will see. Did man originate this duty? No. Did he first declare it? No. Has he added one *iota* of *obligation* to it? No. *God* originated it, first declared it, and made it in the highest possible degree obligatory. Human government has merely borrowed it, re-echoed, and interwoven it with the tissue of *its* own enactments. . . . Man has *adopted* it, and incorporated it with his own devices, but he has added nothing to its rightfulness or force. Here again *human* government is virtually *nothing*. It has not even a claim of *joint reverence* with that of the *divine*. 3. Human legislators enact many laws for the relief, convenience, and general welfare of mankind, which are demonstrably *right* and *salutary*, but which God never *expressly* authorized in detail. In this case has not human authority a *primary* claim to our reverence? Let us see. What is the motive from which a true christian will perform these requirements of *man*? Must he not first be convinced that they are in perfect harmony with the great law of love to God and man—that they agree with what the divine Lawgiver has *expressly* required? Doubtless. Well, when fully convinced of *this*, what are they to him but mere amplifications of the heavenly law—new applications of its plain principles—more minute details of acknowledged general duty? What, therefore, is demonstrably *right*, he will feel bound to approve and scrupulously practice, not for *human* government's sake, but for *righteousness' sake*—or, in other words, for the divine government's sake. This must be his great motive; for no other would be a *holy* motive. It is one thing to *discover* new items of duty—new applications of moral obligation—and another to *create* them. Man may *discover* and point out new details—circumstantial peculiarities of duty —but he cannot *create principles*, nor originate moral obligation. The infinite Father has preoccupied this whole field. What then if the Legislature discover a new item of duty, arising out of a new combination of circumstances, and enact a good law for the observance of that duty, with pains and penalties annexed; or what if a Convention like this discover the existence of such an item of duty, and affirm it in the form of a solemn resolution; the duty once made plain, no matter how, would not the truly good man be under precisely the same obligation to perform it? And if the Legislature should afterwards without cause repeal such *law*, and enact a bad one in its stead; or if this Convention should *not* affirm the existence of the duty before declared, would not the enlightened christian be under precisely the same obligation *still*? None of these supposed circumstances ought to weigh a feather upon the conscience. The sense of obligation must look directly to the Great Source of moral perfection, and the grand controlling motive of a holy heart in the performance of every duty must be, *God requires it—it is right—it is best*. We must perform all our duties as unto God, and not unto man.

The conclusion is therefore, unavoidable, that the *will* of *man* (human government) whether in one, a thousand, or many millions, has no intrinsic authority—no moral supremacy—and no rightful claim to the allegiance of man. It has no original, inherent authority whatsoever over the conscience. What then becomes of *human* government, as contradistinguished from the divine government? Is it not a mere cypher? When it *opposes* God's government it is *nothing*; when it *agrees* with his government it is *nothing*; and when it *discovers* a new item of duty—a new application of the general law of God—it is *nothing*.

We now arrive at the third inquiry, . . . viz. What is the object of non-resistants with respect to human government? Is it their object to *purify* it, to *reform* it? No; for our principles forbid us to take any part in the management of its machinery. We can neither fight for it, legislate in it, hold its offices, vote at its elections, nor act any political part within its pale. To *purify*, to *reform* it—if such were our object—we must actively participate in its management. Moreover, if human government, properly so called, is what I have shown it to be, there can be no such thing as *purifying* it. Where there is nothing but *dross*, there is nothing to refine. Separate from what is commonly considered human government all that it has *borrowed*, or *stolen* from the *divine*, and what remains? What is there in the mere *human* worth purifying—capable of purification? Nothing. Again; is it our object to *subvert* human government—to overthrow it—to turn it upside down? By no means. We utterly disclaim any such object. We are no Jacobins, Revolutionists, Anarchists; though

often *slanderously so denominated*. And here I must be permitted to make some explanations, demanded by the public
misapprehension of our real position and general movement.
It seems to be taken for granted, that we have started a
crusade to force the practice of non-resistance upon nations,
states, bodies politic and all existing organizations of human
society; which is considered tantamount to an attempt for
the violent *subversion* of human government. This is a very
great mistake. We are not so insane as to imagine any such
result practicable in the nature of things. We put our enter-
prize on purely christian grounds, and depend for success
wholly on the use of christian means. We have nothing to do
with nations, states, and bodies politic, merely *as such*; for
they have neither souls nor consciences. We address ourselves
to *individuals*, who have both soul and conscience, and expect
to affect organized masses of men only through their individual members. And as to any kind of force, other than that
of truth and love sustained by a consistent example, as
non-resistants, we utterly *eschew* it, with respect to all moral
agents, collectively and individually. . . .

What then is the object of non-resistants with respect to
human governments—if it is neither to *purify* nor *subvert*
them? The resolution [of this convention] declares that it is
to *supersede* them. To supersede them with *what?* With the
kingdom of Christ. *How?* By the spiritual regeneration
of their individual subjects—by implanting in their minds higher
principles of feeling and action—by giving them *heavenly* instead of *earthly motives*. And now, to understand this process
of superseding, let us consider the nature of Christ's kingdom.
It is not an outward, temporal kingdom, like those of this
world. It is spiritual, moral, eternal. When the Jews demanded information about the coming of this kingdom,
ignorantly expecting it to appear with unparalleled external
majesty, pomp, and circumstance, Jesus replied: 'The kingdom of God cometh not with observation; neither shall men
say, lo here, or lo there; for behold, the kingdom of God is
within you.' . . . Of this kingdom the apostle truly says—it
'is not meat and drink; but righteousness, and peace, and joy
in the Holy Ghost.' The fruit of its spirit, he further says—
'is love, joy, peace, long-suffering, gentleness, goodness, faith,
meekness, temperance.' 'Now they that are Christ's have
crucified the flesh with its affections and lusts.' Having learned
to renounce carnal weapons of defence, worldly honors, political preferments, and a vain dependence on the operations

of human government for the cure of moral disorders, they cease to avenge themselves on evil doers, either on their own responsibility as individuals, or on that of the State through its penal laws. They deem it their duty to forgive, not punish —to yield unto wrath and suffer wrong, without recompensing evil for evil—referring their cause always unto Him who hath said, 'Vengeance is mine; I will repay,'—and thus obeying Christ in his injunction, to love enemies; bless them that curse, do good to them that hate, and pray for the despiteful and persecuting.

This is the doctrine and practice which non-resistants *profess* to have embraced, and according to the tenor of which they propose to *supersede* all human government with the *divine*. This is the real object of their present movement. They cease to take any active part in the affairs of human government. They cease to put their trust in the wisdom of man for guidance, or in the arm of flesh for protection. Yet they stand not in the attitude of *antagonists* to human government; nor can they allow themselves to be mistaken for anarchists, nor be considered as willing to give any just cause of offence to the 'powers that be.' Neither can they enter into any quarrel with professedly good men, who feel called to no higher mission than that of *reigning* or *serving* in the kingdoms of this world. But we hear a voice from above, saying—'What is that to thee? follow thou me.' And we deem it our privilege, through whatever of reproach or suffering we may be called, to show unto all good men whose reliance is even *secondarily* upon human government for the conversion of the world, *'a more excellent way.'* . . .

But the cry salutes our ears from the open mouths even of professing christians.—'Non-resistance is *impracticable* in the present state of the world; you must wait till the millennium.' I answer; 'to him that believeth all things are possible.' Let the power of love and forbearance be faithfully exemplified, and it will remove mountains. And as to the millennium, what is it? Is it a state of things to come about like the seasons, by the revolution of the planets? Is it to be the result of some arbitrary mechanical process? or of a mere chemical agency? Is it to be the effect of *physical* or of *moral* causes? Alas! how many are expecting the millennium to come 'with observation;' just as the Jews of old were expecting the kingdom of God; not knowing that this millennium and kingdom, must be *within* men, before it can ever be *around* them. Let us have the spirit of the millennium, and do the works of the millennium. Then will the millennium have already come; and then will it speedily embosom the whole earth. What is this cry of *impracticability*, but a cry of rebellion against the living God? . . . In Christ *He* annuls the temporary ordinances of *revenge*, and commands forbearance —non-resistance to the physical violence of man, even of the most injurious. Hear his 'Revised Statutes,'—'Ye have heard that it hath been said, An eye for an eye, and a tooth for a tooth: but I say unto you, that ye resist not evil; but whosoever shall smite thee on thy right cheek, turn to him the other also. And if any man will sue thee at the law, and take away thy coat, let him have thy cloak also.' Now is it impracticable to obey this holy commandment? Is not God the best judge of what is practicable? Who has a right to question the expediency or practicability of what the Infinite Father through his Son has enjoined? And let us be careful not to narrow down the meaning of this commandment. It is much more comprehensive than most expositors have been willing to allow. It forbids not merely all personal, individual, self-assumed right of retaliation, but all revenge *at law*—all procuring of punishment to our injurers in the way of *legal prosecution* and *judicial sentence*. . . . Here then is an end to controversy, with all who mean to be wholly Christ's; they *must* be *non-resistants.* . . .

But all this passes for nothing with many, who exclaim— 'What are you going to do with the wolves and tigers of human kind? Are you going to give them full range for their prey? Will you invite the thief, the robber, the burglar, the murderer—to come and carry off your property, ravish away your treasures, spoil your house, butcher your wife and children, and shed your own heart's blood? Will you be such a *fool*, such an enemy to yourself, your family and society? Will you encourage all manner of rapine and bloodshed, by assurances that you will never resist, nor even prosecute the basest ruffians?' What a terrible appeal is this? how full of frightful images, and horrid anticipations of evil, from the practice of non-resistance. But if I am a christian, will such appeals move me? Am I a christian, and do I doubt that God will protect me and mine against all the thieves, robbers and murderers in the world, while I conscientiously do my duty? . . .

I have a right to expect, and I do confidently expect, that in practising the sublime virtue of non-resistance for the kingdom of heaven's sake, God will keep all that I commit to him in perfect safety, even here on earth, as long as it is for my good to be exempted from loss and suffering. I do firmly believe that in acting out these principles steadily and consistently, I shall continue longer uninjured, longer in the enjoyment of life, longer safe from the depredations, assaults and murderous violence of wicked men, than with all the swords, guns, pistols, dirks, peace officers, sheriffs, judges, prisons and gallows of the world. If this is the faith of a fool, then am I willing to be accounted a fool, till time shall test the merits of my position. It may not prove to be such great folly after all. 'Well,' says the objector, 'I should like to know how you would manage matters, if the ruffian should actually break into your house with settled intent to rob and murder; would you shrink back coward like, and see your wife and children slaughtered before your eyes?' I cannot tell how I might act in such a dreadful emergency—how weak and frail I should prove. But I can tell how I *ought* to act—how I should wish to act. If a firm, consistent non-resistant, I should prove myself no *coward*; for it requires the noblest courage, the highest fortitude, to be a true non-resistant. If what I ought to be, I should be calm, and unruffled by the alarm at my door. I should meet my wretched fellow-man with a spirit, an air, a salutation, a deportment, so Christ-like, so little expected, so confounding, so morally irresistible, that in all probability his weapons of violence and death would fall harmless to his side. I would say—'friend, why comest thou hither? surely not to injure those who wish thee nothing but good? This house is one of peace and friendship to all mankind. If thou art cold, warm thyself at our fire; if hungry, refresh thyself at our table; if thou art weary, sleep in our bed; if thou art destitute, poor, and needy, freely take of our goods. Come, let us be friends, that God may keep us all from evil and bless us with his protection.' What would be the effect of such treatment as this? Would it not completely overcome the feelings of the invader, so as either to make him retreat inoffensively out of the house, or at least forbear all mediated violence? Would it not be incomparably safer than to rush to the shattered door, half distracted with alarm, grasping some deadly weapon and bearing it aloft, looking fiery wrath, and mad defiance at the enemy? How soon would follow the moral encounter, and how extremely uncertain the issue? The moment I appeared in such an attitude (just the thing expected), would not ruffian coolness and well trained muscular force be almost sure to seal the fate of myself and family? But in acting the non-resistant part, should I not be likely, in nine cases out of ten, to escape with perfect safety? ('Yes,' said a brother, 'in *ninety-nine* cases out of a hundred.') Yea, and perhaps nine hundred and ninety-nine out of a thousand. . . . 'Nay,—but we are in duty bound to love our neighbor—to seek the peace and welfare of society—to do our part towards protecting the innocent and helpless against the ravages of merciless wolves—to maintain wholesome penal restraints.' Answer. We think we are seeking this great end more effectually, as non-resistants, than we could do by becoming informers, prosecutors, jailers or hangmen. 'An *ounce* of *prevention* is worth more than a *pound* of *curative*.' . . .

'But we want the best men in office, the best laws and the best administration of government. Will you be recreant to your trust as citizens? Will you withhold your votes from the side and cause of right? Will you leave knaves and villains to govern the world?' Answer. We expect to do as much towards keeping the world in order by a straight-forward, consistent, exemplary practice of our principles, nay *more*, than by *voting, office-holding, legislating*, or punishing criminals. A truly good man wields an influence on our ground great and salutary wherever he is known. It is not by the poor test of *numbers* that righteousness can gain its deserved respect in the world. It is not by getting into places of worldly power and emolument, that christians are to promote human welfare. It is not by fighting with carnal weapons, and wielding the instruments of legal vengeance, that they can hope to strengthen the bonds of moral restraint. Majorities often decree folly and iniquity. *Power* oftener corrupts its possessor, than benefits the powerless. The real power which restrains the world is *moral power*, acting silently and unostentatiously within and upon the soul. He, therefore, who has the fewest outward ensigns of authority, will, if wise and holy, contribute most to the good order of mankind. Besides, even unprincipled men in office are compelled to bow to a strong public sentiment, superinduced by the efforts of good men in private life. They are not wanting in vanity to be *esteemed* the friends of virtue, and from this motive generally conform their laws and proceedings more or less to a *right* general opinion. If we can do any thing towards promoting a sound morality, as we hope to do, we shall make our influence felt without envy, not only in the lowest depths of society, but in the high places of political power. . . . Every true non-resistant will be a great conservator of *public* as well as *private* morals. Away then with the intrigues and tricks of political ambition, the petty squabbles of partizans and office-holders, the hollow bluster of demagogues, and the capricious admiration of a tickled multitude. Let us obey God, declare the truth, walk in love, and *deserve* the gratitude of the world, though we never *receive* it.

'But should non-resistants ever become the great majority in any community, pray how would they get on with public affairs. There must be highways, and bridges, and school houses, and education, and alms-houses, and hospitals.' Very well; nothing easier than for communities of *christian non-resistants* to get along with all these matters. Suppose them to meet, in those days, from time to time within each town, or more general community, *voluntarily*, just as we are here assembled. Suppose them all anxious to *know* their duty, and ready to *do* it, as soon as clearly pointed out. Then of course the wisest will speak to attentive ears and upright minds. They will propose measures, discuss them in friendship, and come to a conclusion in favor of the *best*—without wounding personal vanity, or breeding a quarrel with each other's self-ishness. The law of love and the counsels of wisdom will prevail without strife, and all be eager to contribute their full share of expense and effort to the object. Instead of the leading *few* striving, as *now*, who shall be *first* and greatest, the strife will then be, who shall have the least *authority*. And among the mass, instead of the strife, as now, who shall bear the lightest burden, the only strife will be—who shall do *most* for the promotion of every good work. Happy days, whenever they arrive! If there shall be any *poor* in those days, or any *insane*, or any *unlettered*, or unaccommodated travellers, they will soon be abundantly provided for, without the aid of physical force, pains or penalties. God hasten that blessed era of love and peace, and grant success to all our well directed efforts in his holy cause. Thus finally may all human governments be *superseded* by the *divine* government, and the kingdoms of this world be swallowed up in the one all-glorious kingdom of our Lord Jesus Christ.

The life of Nicholas Berdyaev parallels in many ways that of Tolstoy. Both were born into the Russian aristocracy; both developed a deep distrust for the strategies and certain fundamental aims of Marxism (and for this were alike denounced as reactionaries in their native land); both came to Christianity late in life and only after much spiritual anguish and travail; and both construed religion as a non-institutional, revolutionary, and liberating force and launched unsparing libertarian critiques of "Christendom."

Like the non-resistant anarchists, Berdyaev frames his philosophical position by means of Christian concepts like the Second Coming and the Divinity of Christ. But there are notable differences, among which is Berdyaev's capacity to extend a thought which for Ballou—and Tolstoy—had remained an undeveloped suggestion. For example, all three arrive at the important anarchist contention that master and slave, ruler and ruled, are blood brothers, progeny of the same spiritual affliction. But it is left to Berdyaev to introduce an illuminating conceptual framework, including such notions as "personality," "objectivization," and "existential time," to explain forcefully this contention and its implications.

In addition, there appear to be genuine points of disagreement. One of these concerns the nature of the Kingdom of God. Both Berdyaev and the non-resistors regard this Kingdom as an existential condition or personal *summum bonum* and not as a social regime with geographical and temporal coordinates. But the *summum bonum* vividly depicted by Berdyaev is by no means identical with that affirmed by Tolstoy or Ballou. For Berdyaev, it is creative autonomy, rather than non-resisting love, that constitutes the true inner kingdom. Perhaps there is no need for an anarchist to choose between these two seemingly incompatible positions: but this too is a claim which requires extensive discussion and defense.

The selections reprinted below have been taken from Berdyaev's *Slavery and Freedom* and their dominant aim is to identify and trace the implications of his concept of "personality." There are two ways in which his unorthodox and uncondensable point of view may be placed within more familiar philosophical terrain. First of all, it seems plain that Berdyaev had no fear of what is called the "Naturalistic Fallacy." On the contrary, he was convinced that only through existential inquiry into man's capacities and activities, that is, into *what man is,* could light be thrown on what is morally binding or intrinsically valuable, and thus, on *what men ought to seek.* Secondly, and in justification of Berdyaev's implicit contempt for the supposed fallacy of deriving "ought-statements" from "statements of fact," it should be noted that in stressing personality as man's essential feature, Berdyaev draws very close to a distinction made in recent philosophy between "activity" and "behavior." (See here, for example, Alburey Castell's *The Self in Philosophy*; A. I. Melden's *Free Action*; and R. S. Peters' *The Concept of Motivation.*) Not all of what is involved in Berdyaev's notion of "personality" can be translated by means of this contemporary distinction. But some of it surely can be: that men are persons, in Berdyaev's sense, entails that their conduct is in many cases a form of activity in that it must be explained by reference to their intentions, decisions, beliefs, and aspirations and not by reference to external forces beyond their control. Again: with certain qualifications of detail, Berdyaev's concept of personality is entirely congruent with—and may well provide a firm basis for—William Dray's contention that explanation in history is and should be centered upon a "rational" rather than a causal model. (See here Dray's *Laws and Explanations in History*, *The Philosophy of History*, and his contribution to Patrick Gardiner's *Theories of History.*)

PERSONALITY

The entire world is nothing in comparison with human personality, with the unique person of a man, with his unique fate. . . . Man, the only man known to biology and sociology, man as a natural being and a social being, is the offspring of the world and of the processes which take place in the world. But personality, man as a person, is not a child of the world, he is of another origin. And this it is that makes man a riddle. Personality is a break through, a breaking in upon this world; it is the introduction of something new. Personality is not nature, it does not belong to the objective hierarchy of na-

Slavery and Freedom, by Nicholas Berdyaev, translated by R. M. French (London: Geoffrey Bles Ltd., 1943, and New York: Charles Scribner's Sons, 1944), pp. 20–49, 59–69, 250–68. Copyright 1944 Charles Scribner's Sons. Reprinted by permission of Geoffrey Bles Ltd. and Charles Scribner's Sons. Subheads supplied in part by the editors.

ture, as a subordinate part of it. . . . Man is a personality
not by nature but by spirit. By nature he is only an individual. Personality is not a monad entering into a hierarchy of
monads and subordinate to it. Personality is a microcosm, a
complete universe. It is personality alone that can bring together a universal content and be a potential universe in an
individual form. That universal content is not to be attained
by any other reality in the world of nature or of history. Such
other realities are always characterized as parts. Personality
is not a part and cannot be a part in relation to any kind of
whole, not even to an immense whole, or to the entire world.
This is the essential principle of personality, and its mystery.
To whatever extent empirical man enters as a part into any
sort of natural or social whole, it is not as a personality that
he does so, and his personality is left outside this subordination of the part to the whole. . . .

Personality is indestructible. Personality creates itself and
exists by its own destiny finding the source of its strength in
an existence which surpasses it. Personality is potentially the
universal, but quite certainly a distinct, unrepeatable, irre-
placeable being with a unique form. Personality is the
exception, not the rule. The secret of the existence of personality lies in its absolute irreplaceability, its happening but
once, its uniqueness, its incomparableness. . . . In human
personality there is much that is generic, belonging to the
human race, much which belongs to history, tradition, society, class, family, much that is hereditary and imitative, much
that is 'common'. But it is precisely this which is not 'personal' in personality. That which is 'personal' is original,
connected with the primary fountain head, authentic. Personality must perform its self-existent, original, creative acts,
and this alone makes it personality and constitutes its unique
value. Personality must be the exception, no law at all is
applicable to it. . . . Personality in man is the triumph over
the determination of the social group. Personality is not a
substance but an act, a creative act. . . .

Personality is not an object among other objects and not a
thing among other things. It is a subject among subjects
and the turning of it into an object or a thing means death.
The object is always evil, only the subject can be good. It
might be said that society and nature provide the material for
the formation of personality. But personality is emancipation
from dependence upon nature, from dependence upon society and the state. . . . Personality determines itself from

within, outside the whole object world, and only determination from within and arising out of freedom, is personality. . . . Objectivization is impersonality, the ejection of man into the world of determinism. . . . The worth of man is the personality within him. Human worth consists solely in personality. Human worth is liberation from slavery, liberation also from the servile understanding of religious life and of the relation between man and God. God is the guarantee of the freedom of personality from the enslaving power of nature and society, of the Kingdom of Caesar and of the object world. This takes place in the realm of the spirit and not in the realm of the object world. And no categories of the object world can be transferred to these inward existential relations. Nothing in the object world is an authentic existential centre.

Personality as an existential centre, presupposes capacity to feel suffering and joy. Nothing in the object world, nation or state or society, or social institution, or church, possesses this capacity. They speak of the sufferings of the masses of the people in an allegorical sense. No communities in the object world can be recognized as personality. Collective realities are real values, but not real personalities, their existentiality refers to the realities of personalities. . . .

The worth of man, that is to say personality, and again that is to say freedom, presupposes acquiescence in pain, and the capacity to bear pain. The degradation of my people or my faith causes pain in me, but not in the people and not the religious community, which do not possess an existential centre, and consequently are devoid of capacity to feel pain. Capacity to experience pain is inherent in every living creature, above all in man, but it is in animals also, and perhaps in another way in plants as well, but not in collective realities nor in ideal values. This question is of first importance, it is by it that the ethics of personalism are defined. Man, human personality is the supreme value, not the community, not collective realities which belong to the object world, such as society, nation, state, civilization, church. That is the personalist scale of values. . . .

The relation between man and God is not a causal relation, it is not the relation between the particular and the common, nor between means and end, nor between slave and master. . . . God does not exist as an objective reality found to be necessary by me, as the objectivization of a universal idea. He exists as an existential contact and meeting, as the process of transcension, and in that meeting God is personality. . . .

The theological doctrine that God created man for His own glory and praise is degrading to man, and degrading to God also. It is a striking fact that any doctrine which is degrading to man also degrades God. The relation of personality to personality, even the most exalted personality of God, cannot be a relation of means and end, all personality is an end in itself. The relation of means and end exists only in the world of objectivization, i.e., the world of the ejection of existence into the external. . . . But human personality is not a means to any suprapersonal value as its end, it is not an instrument of the divine power. When suprapersonal values turn human personality into a means to an end, it shows that man has fallen into idolatry. Personality is a paradox to rational thought; paradoxically it juxtaposes the personal and the suprapersonal, the finite and the infinite, the abiding and the changing, freedom and fate. . . .

Outside personality there is no absolute unity and totality in the world, to which personality would be subordinate: outside personality everything is partial, even the world itself is partial. Everything objectivized, everything which is an object can be partial only. Such is the whole objectivized world, and the whole of objectivized society with its objectivized bodies. This objectivized world is distinguished by a solidity which is able to threaten to crush personality, but it is not distinguished by wholeness nor by totality. An existential centre, and a suffering destiny are to be found in subjectivity, not in objectivity. But all the higher hierarchical ranks to which they subordinate personality belong to the world of objectivization. Objectivization is always antipersonalistic, hostile to personality and signifies the estrangement of personality. And everything which is existential in the objectivized ranks of the world, in the nation, in mankind, in the cosmos, etc. belongs to the inward being of personality and is not subordinate to any hierarchical centre. The cosmos, mankind, nation, etc., are to be found in human personality as in an individualized universe or microcosm, and their falling away from it, their ejection into external reality among objects, is the result of the fall of man, of his subordination to impersonal reality, exteriorization, and alienation. . . .

The psychical life of man contains an active creative principle which synthetizes personality; it is the activity of the spirit in man, which penetrates not only the life of the soul but also the bodily life. The spirit creates the form of personality and the character of man. Without the synthetizing activity of the spirit, personality becomes dissociated; man falls into parts, the spirit loses its integrality, its capacity for active reactions. The freedom of personality is certainly not its right; that is a superficial view. Freedom of personality is a duty, it is a fulfilment of vocation, the realization of the divine idea of man, an answer to the divine call. Man ought to be free, he dare not be a slave, because he ought to be a man. Such is the will of God. Man likes being a slave and puts forward a claim to slavery as a right, a claim which changes its form from time to time. It is precisely slavery to which man lays claim as a right. Freedom ought not to be a declaration of the rights of man; it ought to be a declaration of man's obligations, of the duty of man to be a personality, to display the strength of the character of personality. One ought not to refuse personality. One can refuse life and sometimes one ought to refuse it, but not personality, not the dignity of man, not the freedom to which that dignity is linked.

Personality is bound up with the consciousness of vocation. Every man ought to be conscious of that vocation, which is independent of the extent of his gifts. It is a vocation in an individually unrepeatable form to give an answer to the call of God and to put one's gifts to creative use. Personality which is conscious of itself listens to the inward voice and obeys that only. It is not submissive to outward voices. The greatest among men have always listened exclusively to the inward voice and have refused to conform so far as the world is concerned. Personality is connected also with asceticism and presupposes asceticism, that is to say spiritual exercise, the concentration of inward strength, the making of choice, the refusal to acquiesce in a mingling with impersonal forces, both within man and in the surrounding world. . . . Asceticism is by no means submission and obedience. It is personality's refusal of submission and obedience, it is the fulfilment of its vocation, its answer to the call of God. Personality in its essence is not submissive and obedient. It is resistance, an unbroken creative act. . . .

Personality is shaped by the clash with evil in itself and in its environment. . . . Complete insensitiveness to sin, to guilt, and to evil, is commonly also insensitiveness to personality, it is the dissolution of personality in the common, cosmic and social. . . . No man can be an incarnation and personification of evil, the evil in him is always partial. For this reason, there cannot be a final judgment upon anybody. This lays down limits also to the very principle of punishment. A man may commit a crime, but the man as a whole personality cannot be a criminal; he must not be treated as an incarnation of crime; he remains a personality, in him is the image of God. And the personality which has committed a crime does not belong as a whole and finally to the state and society. A personality is a citizen of the Kingdom of God and not of the kingdom of Caesar; the judgment and condemnation of the kingdom of Caesar in relation to it are partial, nor are they final. For this reason personalism is decisively and radically opposed to the death penalty.

Personality in man cannot be socialized. The socialization of man is only partial and does not extend to the depth of personality, to its conscience, to its relation to the source of life. Socialization which is extended to the depth of existence, to spiritual life, is the triumph of *das Mann*, and of social routine. It is the tyranny of the average and common over the personally individual. Therefore, the principle of personality ought to stand as a principle of social organization, one which will not permit the socialization of the inward existence of man.

MASTER, SLAVE AND FREE MAN

It is well to repeat constantly that man is a being who is full of contradictions and that he is in a state of conflict with himself. Man seeks freedom. There is within him an immense drive towards freedom, and yet not only does he easily fall into slavery, but he even loves slavery. Man is a king and a slave. In the *Phänomenologie des Geistes*, Hegel gives expression to some remarkable thoughts on the subject of master and slave, about *Herrschaft* and *Knechtschaft*. He is not there discussing the social categories of master and slave, but something deeper. It is the problem of the structure of consciousness. There are three conditions of man, three structures of consciousness, and they may be distinguished under the names of 'master', 'slave' and 'free man'. Master and slave are correlatives. Neither of them can exist without the other. The free man, however, exists in himself; he has his own quality within him, without correlation to anything placed in antithesis to him. The master is an existing consciousness for himself, but that consciousness is derived through some other, it is through the slave that he exists for himself. If the consciousness of a master is consciousness of

the existence of some other for him, then the consciousness
of the slave is the existence of himself for the other. The
consciousness of the free man, on the other hand, is consciousness of the existence of each one for himself, but with
a free outgoing from himself to the other and to all. . . .
Prometheus was a free man and a liberator; whereas a dictator is a slave and an enslaver; the will to power is always a
servile will. Christ was a free man, the freest of the sons of
men. He was free from the world; He was bound only by
love. Christ spoke as one having authority but He did not
have the will to authority, and He was not a master. Caesar,
the hero of imperialism, is a slave; he is the slave of the
world, the slave of the will to power, the slave of the human
masses, without whom he cannot realize his will to power.
The master knows only the height to which his slaves raise
him. Caesar knows only the height to which the masses raise
him. But the slaves, and the masses, also overthrow all masters and all Caesars. Freedom is freedom not only from the
masters but from the slaves also. The master is determined
from without; the master is not a personality, just as the
slave is not a personality. Only the free man is a personality
and he is that even if the whole world should wish to enslave
him. . . .

The psychology of the dictator, who is essentially a *par-
venu,* is a perversion of man. He is the slave of his own en-
slavements. He is, in the most profound sense, the antithesis
of Prometheus the liberator. The leader of the crowd is in
the same state of servitude as the crowd; he has no existence
outside the crowd, outside slavery, over which he plays the
master. He is entirely ejected into the external. . . .

That will to power, the imperialistic will is opposed to
the dignity and freedom of man is absolutely clear. . . . But
the actual problem of force, and one's attitude towards it,
are very complex and difficult. When men revolt against violence, they commonly have in view forms of violence which
are crude and leap to the eyes. They beat men, put them in
prison, kill them. But human life is full of unnoticed, more
refined forms of violence. Psychological violence plays a still
greater rôle in life than physical. Man is deprived of his
freedom and is made a slave not only as the result of physical
violence. . . . A system of upbringing may completely deprive a man of his freedom and incapacitate him for freedom
of judgment. . . . Crystallized, hardened public opinion becomes violence upon man. Man can be a slave to public

opinion, a slave to custom, to morals, to judgments and opinions which are imposed by society. It is difficult to over-estimate the violence which is perpetrated by the press in our time. The average man of our day holds the opinions and forms the judgments of the newspaper which he reads every morning: it exercises psychological compulsion upon him. And in view of the falsehood and venality of the press, the effects are very terrible as seen in the enslavement of man and his deprivation of freedom of conscience and judgment. . . .

It is a very interesting fact that psychologically the easiest thing of all to accept as freedom is the absence of movement, the habitual condition. In movement there is already a certain exercise of force upon the surrounding world, upon material environment and upon other people. Movement is change, and it does not ask for the acquiescence of the world in this altered position, which is an effect of that change caused by the movement. Such an acceptance of rest as the absence of force; and of movement, change, as force, has conservative results in social life. Habitual, time-hardened slavery may not appear to be a form of violence, while a movement which is directed to the abolition of slavery may appear to be violence. The social reformation of society is accepted as violence by those to whom a certain habitual social order has presented itself as freedom, even though it may be terribly unjust and wrong. All reforms in the position of the working classes call forth from the side of the bourgeois classes, shouts about the violation of freedom and the use of force. Such are the paradoxes of freedom in social life. Slavery lies in wait for man on all sides. The fight for freedom presupposes resistance and without resistance its pathos is enfeebled. Freedom which has been established by an habitual way of living, passes over into an unnoticed enslavement of men; this is freedom which has become objectivized, whereas all the while freedom is the realm of the subject. . . .

Men pitted either reason or nature against the authoritarian and hierarchical order in European history. Reason or nature rebelled against authority, but the freedom of man was not attained in this way. Man remains subjected to impersonal reason, to a sovereign society or simply to natural necessity. To the authoritarian consciousness or to the authoritarian order of life must be opposed, not reason, and not nature, and not a sovereign society, but spirit, that is to say, freedom, the spiritual principle in man, which organizes his personality and is independent of objectivized nature and the objectivized logical world. This presupposes a change of direction in the conflict against the slavery of man, that is to say it presupposes the personalistic transvaluation of values in the defence of which this book is written. The inward existential universalism of personality must be opposed to the outward objectivized universalism which is ever more and more creating new forms of slavery. Everything which is not personal, everything alienated into the sphere of the 'common', is the seduction and slavery of man. The free man is a self-governing being not a governed being; nor is it the self-government of a society and a people, but the self-government of a man who has become a personality. The self-government of a society, and of a people is still the government of slaves. . . .

Fear can be a more exalted condition than heedless submersion in everyday things. But fear, fear of all sorts, is all the same a form of human slavery. . . . Murder is committed not only by gangsters; murder is committed in an organized way and upon a colossal scale by the state, by those who are in possession of power, or by those who have only just seized it. And, mark, in all these murders, the horror of death shews itself dulled and blunted, even almost entirely absent, although the horror of the death ought to be doubled—as being horror of death in general, and horror of the death which is the result of murder having been committed as well. Capital punishment is ceasing to be taken as murder, so is death in war, and especially, it is ceasing to be taken as a death which arouses horror. And this is a consequence of the objectivization of human existence.

In the objectivized world, all values are perverted. Man instead of being a resuscitator, a conqueror of death, has become a murderer, a sower of death. And he kills, in order to create a life in which there will be less fear. Man kills from fear; at the root of every murder, whether committed by an individual person or by the state, lies fear and slavery. Fear and slavery always have fateful results. If man were to succeed in triumphing over slavish fear, he would cease to murder. From fear of death man sows death, as a result of feeling a slave, he desires to dominate. Domination is always constrained to kill. The state is always subject to fear and therefore it is constrained to kill. It has no desire to wrestle against death. Men in authority are very much like gangsters.

AN ANARCHIST THEORY OF TIME AND A
PERSONALIST ESCHATOLOGY

Creativeness is liberation from slavery. Man is free when he finds himself in a state of creative activity. Creativeness leads to ecstasy of the moment. The products of creativeness are within time, but the creative act itself lies outside time. Thus also every heroic act leads outside time. . . .

In the spiritual liberation of man there is movement in the direction of freedom, truth and love. Freedom cannot be vain and lead to no result. 'Ye shall know the truth and the truth shall make you free'. But the knowledge of truth presupposes freedom. Knowledge of truth which is not free, is not only valueless, it is also impossible. But freedom also presupposes the existence of truth, of meaning, of God. Truth and meaning liberate, and again liberation leads to truth, and meaning. Freedom must be loving and love must be free. It is only the gathering together of freedom, truth and love which realizes personality, free and creative personality. The exclusive affirmation of one of these principles only always introduces distortion, and injures human personality. Each one of the principles can in and by itself be a source of seduction and slavery. . . .

Human consciousness is subject to a variety of illusions in understanding the relation between this world in which man feels himself to be in a state of servitude, and the other world in which he awaits his liberation. Man is the point of intersection of two worlds. One of the illusions consists in interpreting the difference between the two worlds as a difference of substance. In actual fact it is a difference in mode of existence. Man passes from slavery to freedom, from a state of disintegration to a condition of completeness, from impersonality to personality, from passivity to creativeness, that is to say he passes over to spirituality. This world is the world of objectivization, of determinism, of alienation, of hostility, of law. While the other world is the world of spirituality, of freedom, love, kinship.

Another illusion of consciousness lies in this that the relations between the two worlds are understood as absolute objectivized transcendence. In this case the transition from one world to the other is passively awaited and the activity of man

PHILOSOPHICAL FOUNDATIONS

has no part to play. In actual fact the other world, the world of spirituality, the Kingdom of God, is not only awaited, it is constructed also by the creativeness of man, it is the creative transfiguration of a world which is exposed to the malady of objectivization. It is spiritual revolution. That other world cannot be established by human strength only, but also it cannot be established without the creative activity of man. This brings me to the problem of eschatology, to the problem of the end of history, and it means the liberation of man from his slavery to history. . . .

The problem of time occupies a position at the centre of present day philosophy. It is enough to name Bergson and Heidegger. This problem has a special significance for a philosophy of the existential type. The philosophy of history is to a considerable extent the philosophy of time. History is linked with time. To speak of time, is not always to speak of one and the same thing. Time has a variety of meanings and it is needful to make distinctions. There are three times: cosmic time, historical time, and existential time, and every man lives in these three forms of time. Cosmic time is symbolized by the circle. It is connected with the motion of the earth round the sun, with the reckoning of days, months, and years, with the calendar and the clock. This is a circular movement in which a return is constantly taking place, morning comes and evening, spring and autumn. This is nature's time, and as natural beings we live in this time. . . .

But man is a being who lives in several dimensions of time, in several spheres of existence. Man is not only a cosmic natural being, subject to cosmic time which moves in cycles. Man is also a historical being. Historical life is actuality of another order than nature. History, of course, is subject to cosmic time also, it knows reckoning by years and centuries, but it knows also its own historical time. Historical time comes into being through movement and change of another sort than that which occurs in the cosmic cycle. Historical time is symbolized not by the circle but by the straight line stretching out forwards. The special property of historical time is precisely this stretching out towards what is coming, this reaching forward to determine. In what is coming it waits for the disclosure of a meaning. Historical time brings novelty with it; in it that which was not becomes that which was. . . .

In addition to cosmic time and historical time, which are objectivized and subordinate to number, though in different ways, there is also existential time, profound time. Existential time must not be thought of in complete isolation from cosmic and historical time, it is a break-through of one time into the other. . . . Existential time may be best symbolized not by the circle nor by the line but by the point. That is precisely what is meant by saying that existential time can least of all be symbolized by extension. This is inward time, not exteriorized in extension, not objectivized. It is the time of the world of subjectivity, not objectivity. It is not computed mathematically, it is not summed up nor divided into parts. The infinity of existential time is a qualitative infinity, not a quantitative. A moment of existential time is not subject to number, it is not a fractional part of time in a sequence of moments of objectivized time. A moment of existential time is an emergence into eternity. . . . Every man knows from his own inward experience that he is a participant in several of his own moments of eternity. The protraction of existential time has nothing in common with the protraction of objectivized time, cosmic or historical. This protraction depends upon the intensity of experience within human existence. Minutes which are short from the objective point of view may be lived through as an infinity, and an infinity in opposite directions, in the direction of suffering and in the direction of joy and triumphant rapture. Every state of ecstasy leads out from the computation of objectivized mathematical time and leads into existential qualitative infinity. One moment may be eternity, another moment may be an evil and repellent endlessness. The fact that those who are happy do not keep a watchful eye upon the clock, indicates an emergence from mathematical time, a forgetfulness of clocks and calendars. The greater part of men's life is unhappy and is, therefore, chained to mathematical time. . . .

Every creative act is performed in existential time and is merely projected in historical time. The creative impulse and ecstasy is outside objectivized and mathematical time, it does not take place on a flat surface, on the level of the mediocrity of our life, it happens vertically, not horizontally. But the result of the creative act is exteriorized in the time stream of history. The existential breaks through in the historical and the historical in return acts upon the existential. Everything significant and great in history, everything authentically new is a break-through in the existential plane, in creative subjectivity. The emergence of every notable man in history is a phenomenon of that kind. . . . The end of history is an event of existential time. And at the same time we must not think of this event as being outside history. The end of history, which is accomplished in existential time, happens both 'in the next world' and 'in this world'. The end of history cannot be objectivized, and that is what makes it difficult to understand and explain. . . .

There are two ways of understanding apocalypse, a passive way and an active. In the history of Christian consciousness the former way has always been predominant. There has been a passive foreboding of and a passive waiting for the end of the world; it is determined exclusively by God, judgment upon the world is divine judgment only. On the other view, the end of the world is actively, creatively prepared by man; it depends upon the activity of man also, that is to say it will be a result of divine-human work. Passive waiting for the end is accompanied by the feeling of terror. On the other hand the active preparation of the end is conflict and may be accompanied by the feeling of triumph. The apocalyptic consciousness may be conservative and reactionary and such it frequently has been; and it may be revolutionary and creative, and that is what it ought to be. . . . The conservative apocalyptic consciousness has a feeling of horror when faced by the ruin of things which present themselves as historical sanctities. The revolutionary apocalyptic consciousness actively and creatively turns to the realization of human personality and to the society which is linked with the principle of personality. An active relation to the end of history presupposes a more or less prolonged period of change in the structure of consciousness, a spiritual and social revolution even in historical time, which cannot be brought about by human efforts only, but also cannot be achieved without human effort or by passive waiting. The outpouring of the Spirit, which changes the world, is the activity of the spirit in man himself. . . . Active eschatology is the justification of the creative power of man. Man is liberated from the sway of the objectivization which had enslaved him. And then the problem of the end of history will present itself in a new aspect. The end of history is the victory of existential time over historical time, of creative subjectivity over objectivization, of personality over the universal-common, of existential society over objectivized society. . . .

The creative power of man as it changes the structure of consciousness, can be not only a consolidation of this world, not only a culture, but also a liberation of the world, and the end of history, that is to say, the establishment of the Kingdom of God, not as a symbolic but as a real kingdom. The Kingdom of God denotes not only redemption from sin and a return to original purity, but the creation of a new world. Every authentic creative act of man enters into it, every real act of liberation. It is not only the other world, it is this world transfigured. It is the liberation of nature from captivity, it is the liberation of the animal world also, for which man is answerable. And it begins now, at this moment. The attainment of spirituality, the will to truth and right, to liberation, is already the beginning of the other world. And with it there is no estrangement between the creative act and the creative product; the creative product is to be found, so to speak, in the creative act itself; it is not exteriorized; the very creative power itself is incarnation. . . .

The slavery of man is his Fall, his sin. This Fall has its own structure of consciousness, it is conquered not only by repentance and redemption from sin, but by the activity of all the creative powers of man. When man does that to which he is called, then only will the Second Coming of Christ take place, and then there will be a new heaven and a new earth and the kingdom of freedom will come.

16 The Anarchism of *Der Einzige*

In 1848, Johann Kaspar Schmidt, writing under the assumed name of Max Stirner, published his one great philosophical work *Der Einzige und sein Eigentum* (*The Ego and His Own*). Karl Marx saw this work as the culmination of German idealism and was convinced that it stood in irretrievable contradiction to his own view that "the nature of individuals . . . depends on the material conditions determining their production." As a result, he devoted hundreds of pages in *The German Ideology* to refuting Stirner (see selection 56 below). Some four decades later, *Der Einzige und sein Eigentum* was briefly revived by the group of Boston radicals led by Benjamin R. Tucker. But today Stirner's name has virtually disappeared from philosophical literature and discussion; recent editions of *The German Ideology* no longer include those sections containing Marx's attack on him. And though a new edition of Stirner's book was printed in 1963 by the Libertarian Press, he has but a tiny audience among those concerned with proposing and initiating anarchist programs.

This neglect is certainly unfortunate and ill-deserved. Much of it can be blamed on Stirner's uncompromising style. On first reading, *The Ego and His Own* strikes one as nothing more than a medley of fragmentary insights, with little argument and almost no continuity, development, or structure. "But," wrote Professor Victor Basch in his comprehensive study *L'Individualism Anarchiste: Max Stirner*, "if you read this book several times; if, after having penetrated the intimacy of each of its parts, you traverse it as a whole, gradually the fragments weld themselves together, and Stirner's thought is revealed in all its unity, in all its force, and in all its depth."

But what conclusions does Stirner affirm? What are his basic tenets? These questions are misdirected. If we attempted an answer, we would be caught in the contradiction that what is wholly individual and autonomous can be understood by means of categories which are not the product of its own unique activity and which presuppose that its most essential features are those it shares with other, repeatable phenomena. Stirner's Unique One *owns* himself. But to apply to a person language used in accordance with socially designed conventions which have never been under his control is to assume that that person does *not* own his behavior. Those who submit to the games we play with words may properly be characterized by ordinary discourse. But where shall we find words to describe those who, like Stirner's *Einzige*, regard such games as "spooks" from which one must be liberated?

> The system-makers and system-builders thus far cannot get it out of their heads that any discourse about the nature of an ego must turn upon the common characteristics of egos. . . . They ask, What is the principle of the self-conscious egoist—the *Einzige?* To this perplexity, Stirner says: Change the question; put "who?" instead of "what?" and an answer can then be given by naming him.

These are the apposite words of J. L. Walker, the American exponent of Stirner's philosophy, taken from Walker's introduction to *Der Einzige und sein Eigentum.*

It is occasionally held that some forms of government can be used to disintegrate or diminish the need for any government. If this is so, it may also be possible to use language to bring us to the point where conventional categories can be laid aside or have been divested of their capacity to obstruct the free spirit. Here then is an expression (undoubtedly oversimple) of the idea central to Stirner's philosophizing:

> There is only one end which is worth pursuing for itself: the power to resist and repudiate all hopes, desires, ideals, interests, principles and loyalties, and to choose fresh goals at will—transforming and transcending them as one sees fit. Only upon achieving this "end," can one claim to own oneself. For those who view other goals as intrinsically desirable are the possessions of, and controlled by, things external to themselves.

This approach to *Der Einzige* has at least two important corollaries. In the first place, it permits an intelligent answer to the question of whether Stirner is an egoist. The answer of course is: "Yes —in his sense." And Stirner's sense does *not* involve the prescription that men should strive for personal happiness or glory or to realize their human powers. On the contrary, Stirner sets forth the injunction: "Become your own." We can identify this "view" as Libertarian Egoism, and thus distinguish it from forms of egoism, such as those based on obtaining pleasure, which recommend goals that may well come to own the agents who quest after them.

Secondly, does not Stirner's Libertarian Egoism afford a possible, and largely ignored, approach to the philosophical problem of free will? Can the dispute as to whether men should ever be considered free agents, responsible for their actions, be settled without deciding whether men can come to possess their aims, beliefs, and activities? Stirner would probably have argued that where men act from interests or convictions they do not own we are faced with actions for which they are not accountable. And if this is correct, we may be forced to admit that the lack of self-ownership is a neglected way of defeating or reducing the claim that a given act is voluntary: philosophers may have to rethink the framework inside of which discussions of free will have very often been restricted. In brief, Stirner's view implies a set of fresh philosophical issues. Is ownership, in Stirner's sense, a necessary condition of responsibility? If a man does not own the acts he performs, can these be counted as voluntary actions or are they simply responses to factors over which he has no control? Can one be held to account for conduct which stems from beliefs and goals, or ideals and interests, of which one is not the owner?

SELF-OWNERSHIP AND ITS ENEMIES

I have no need to take up each thing that wants to throw its cause on us and show that it is occupied only with itself, not with us, only with its good, not with ours. . . . Do truth, freedom, humanity, justice, desire anything else than that you grow enthusiastic and serve them?

They all have an admirable time of it when they receive zealous homage. Just observe the nation that is defended by devoted patriots. The patriots fall in bloody battle or in the fight with hunger and want; what does the nation care for that? By the manure of their corpses the nation comes to "its bloom!" The individuals have died "for the great cause of the nation," and the nation sends some words of thanks after them and—has the profit of it. I call that a paying kind of egoism. . . . And will you not learn by these brilliant examples that the egoist gets on best? I for my part take a lesson from them, and propose, instead of further unselfishly serving those great egoists, rather to be the egoist myself.

God and mankind have concerned themselves for nothing, for nothing but themselves. Let me then likewise concern myself for *myself*, who am equally with God the nothing of all others, who am my all, who am the only one. . . . Away, then, with every concern that is not altogether my concern! You think at least the "good cause" must be my concern? What's good, what's bad? Why, I myself am my

---

The Ego and His Own, by Max Stirner (Johann Kaspar Schmidt), translated by Steven T. Byington (New York: Libertarian Press, 1962), passim. Subheads provided by the editors.

concern, and I am neither good nor bad. Neither has meaning for me.

The divine is God's concern; the human, man's. My concern is neither the divine nor the human, not the true, good, just, free, etc., but solely what is *mine*, and it is not a general one, but is—unique, as I am unique.

Nothing is more to me than myself! . . . Where does unselfishness begin? Right where an end ceases to be *our* end and our *property*, which we, as owners, can dispose of at pleasure; where it becomes a fixed end or a—fixed idea; where it begins to inspire, enthuse, fanaticize us; in short, where it passes into our *stubbornness* and becomes our—master. One is not unselfish so long as he retains the end in his power; one becomes so only at that "Here I stand, I cannot do otherwise," the fundamental maxim of all the possessed; one becomes so in the case of a *sacred* end, through the corresponding sacred zeal.

I am not unselfish so long as the end remains my *own*, and I, instead of giving myself up to be the blind means of its fulfillment, leave it always an open question. My zeal need not on that account be slacker than the most fanatical, but at the same time I remain toward it frostily cold, unbelieving, and its most irreconcilable enemy; I remain its *judge*, because I am its owner. . . .

Christianity has aimed to deliver us from a life determined by nature, from the appetites as actuating us, and so has meant that man should not let himself be determined by his appetites. This does not involve the idea that *he* was not to have appetites, but that the appetites were not to have him, that they were not to become *fixed*, uncontrollable, indissoluble. Now, could not what Christianity (religion) contrived against the appetites be applied by us to its own precept that *mind* (thought, conceptions, ideas, faith) must determine us; could we not ask that neither should mind, or the conception, the idea, be allowed to determine us, to become fixed and inviolable or "sacred"? Then it would end in the *dissolution of mind*, the dissolution of all thoughts, of all conceptions. As we there had to say, "We are indeed to have appetites, but the appetites are not to have us," so we should now say, "We are indeed to have *mind*, but mind is not to have us." If the latter seems lacking in sense, think of the fact that with so many a man a thought becomes a "maxim," whereby he himself is made prisoner to it, so that it is not he that has the maxim, but rather it that has him. . . .

Before the sacred, people lose all sense of power and all confidence; they occupy a *powerless* and *humble* attitude toward it. And yet no thing is sacred of itself, but by my *declaring it sacred*, by my declaration, my judgment, my bending the knee; in short, by my—conscience. . . . For little children, just as for animals, nothing sacred exists, because, in order to make room for this conception, one must already have progressed so far in understanding that he can make distinctions like "good and bad," "warranted and unwarranted"; only at such a level of reflection or intelligence—the proper standpoint of religion—can unnatural (that is, brought into existence by thinking) *reverence*, "sacred dread," step into the place of natural fear. To this sacred dread belongs holding something outside oneself far mightier, greater, better warranted, better; the attitude in which one acknowledges the might of something alien—not merely feels it, then, but expressly acknowledges it, admits it, yields, surrenders, lets himself be tied (devotion, humility, servility, submission). . . . The man is now no longer employed in creating, but in *learning* (knowing, investigating), occupied with a fixed *object*, losing himself in its depths, without return to himself. The relation to this object is that of knowing, fathoming, basing, not that of *dissolution* (abrogation). "Man is to be religious," that is settled; therefore people busy themselves only with the question how this is to be attained, what is the right meaning of religiousness, etc. Quite otherwise when one makes the axiom itself doubtful and calls it in question, even though it should go to smash. . . .

Moral influence takes its start where humiliation begins; yes, it is nothing else than this humiliation itself, the breaking and bending of the temper down to humility. . . . if I say to a child, "You will go hungry if you will not eat what is put on the table," this is not moral influence. But, if I say to it, "You will pray, honor your parents, respect the crucifix, speak the truth, for this belongs to man and is man's calling," or even "this is God's will," then moral influence is complete; then a man is to bend before the *calling* of man, be tractable, become humble, give up his will for an alien one which is set up as rule and law; he is to *abase* himself before something *higher*: self-abasement. . . .

"But, for heaven's sake, if one is to give children no good instruction, why, then they will run straight into the jaws of sin, and become good-for-nothing hoodlums!" Gently, you prophets of evil. Good-for-nothing in your sense they certainly will become; but your sense happens to be a very good-for-nothing sense. The impudent lads will no longer let anything be whined and chattered into them by you, and will have no sympathy for all the follies for which you have been raving and driveling since the memory of man began; they will abolish the law of inheritance; they will not be willing to *inherit* your stupidities as you inherited them from your fathers; they destroy *inherited sin.* If you command them, "Bend before the Most High," they will answer: "If he wants to bend us, let him come himself and do it; we, at least, will not bend of our own accord." And, if you threaten them with his wrath and his punishment, they will take it like being threatened with the bogieman. . . .

ARE FREEDOM AND SELF-OWNERSHIP IDENTICAL?

What do you want to become free from, then? From your hardtack and your straw bed? Then throw them away!—But that seems not to serve you: you want rather to have the freedom to enjoy delicious foods and downy beds. . . . How, therefore, do you mean to come to the enjoyment of those foods and bed? Evidently not otherwise than in making them your property!

If you think it over rightly, you do not want the freedom to have all these fine things, for with this freedom you still do not have them; you want really to have them, to call them *yours* and possess them as *your property.* . . .

What a difference between freedom and ownness! . . . I am free from what I am rid of, owner of what I have in my power or what I control. My own I am at all times and under all circumstances, if I know how to have myself and do not throw myself away on others. To be free is something that I cannot truly will, because I cannot make it, cannot create it: I can only wish it and—aspire toward it, for it remains an ideal, a spook. The fetters of reality cut the sharpest welts in my flesh every moment. But my own I remain. Given up as serf to a master, I think only of myself and my advantage; his blows strike me indeed, I am not free from them; but I endure them only for my benefit, perhaps in order to deceive him and make him secure by the semblance of patience, or, again, not to draw worse upon myself by contumacy. But, as I keep my eye on myself and my selfishness, I take by the forelock the first good opportunity to trample the slaveholder into dust. That I then become free from him and his whip is only the consequence of my ante-

cedent egoism. Here one perhaps says I was "free" even in
the condition of slavery—to wit, "intrinsically" or "inwardly."
But "intrinsically free" is not "really free," and "inwardly" is
not "outwardly." I was own, on the other hand, my own,
altogether, inwardly and outwardly. . . .

"Ah, but there is nothing better than freedom!"

What have you then when you have freedom— . . . complete freedom? Then you are rid of everything that embar-
rasses you, everything, and there is probably nothing that does
not once in your life embarrass you and cause you inconvenience. And for whose sake, then, did you want to be rid of
it? Doubtless for your sake, because it is in your way! But, if
something were not inconvenient to you; if, on the contrary,
it were quite to your mind (such as the gently but irresistibly
commanding look of your loved one)—then you would not
want to be rid of it and free from it. Why not? For your sake
again! So you take yourselves as measure and judge over all.
. . . For whose sake do you care about God's and the other
commandments? You surely do not suppose that this is done
merely out of complaisance toward God? No, you are doing
it—*for your sake* again.— Here too, therefore, you are the main
thing, and each must say to himself, *I* am everything to myself and I do everything *on my account*. If it ever became
clear to you that God, the commandments, and so on, only
harm you, that they reduce and ruin you, to a certainty you
would throw them from you just as the Christians once condemned Apollo or Minerva or heathen morality. They did
indeed put in the place of these Christ and afterward Mary,
as well as a Christian morality; but they did this for the sake
of *their* souls' welfare too, therefore out of egoism or ownness.

And it was by this egoism, this ownness, that they got *rid*
of the old world of gods and became *free* from it. Ownness
created a new freedom; for ownness is the creator of everything, as genius (a definite ownness), which is always
originality, has for a long time already been looked upon as
the creator of new productions that have a place in the history
of the world.

If your efforts are ever to make "freedom" the issue, then
exhaust freedom's demands. Who is it that is to become free?
You, I, we. Free from what? From everything that is not you,
not I, not we. I, therefore, am the kernel that is to be delivered from all wrappings and—freed from all cramping
shells. What is left when I have been freed from everything
that is not I? Only I; nothing but I. But freedom has nothing

to offer to this I himself. As to what is now to happen further after I have become free, freedom is silent—as our governments, when the prisoner's time is up, merely let him go, thrusting him out into abandonment.

Now why, if freedom is striven after for love of the I after all—why not choose the I himself as beginning, middle, and end? Am I not worth more than freedom? Is it not that I make myself free, am not I the first? Even unfree, even laid in a thousand fetters, I yet am; and I am not, like freedom, extant only in the future and in hopes, but even as the most abject of slaves I am—present.

Think that over well, and decide whether you will place on your banner the dream of "freedom" or the resolution of "egoism," of "ownness." "Freedom" awakens your *rage* against everything that is not you; "egoism" calls you to *joy* over yourselves, to self-enjoyment; "freedom" is and remains a *longing*, a romantic plaint, a Christian hope for unearthliness and futurity; "ownness" is a reality, which *of itself* removes just so much unfreedom as by barring your own way hinders you. What does not disturb you, you will not want to renounce; and, if it begins to disturb you, why, you know that "you must obey yourselves rather than men!" . . .

I know that my freedom is diminished even by my not being able to carry out my will on another object, be this other something without will, like a rock, or something with will, like a government, an individual; I deny my ownness when—in presence of another—I give myself up, give way, desist, submit; therefore by *loyalty, submission*. For it is one thing when I give up my previous course because it does not lead to the goal, and therefore turn out of a wrong road; it is another when I yield myself a prisoner. I get around a rock that stands in my way, till I have powder enough to blast it; I get around the laws of a people, till I have gathered strength to overthrow them. . . .

My freedom becomes complete only when it is my—*might*; but by this I cease to be a merely free man, and become an own man. Why is the freedom of the peoples a "hollow word"? Because the peoples have no might! . . . Might is a fine thing, and useful for many purposes; for "one goes further with a handful of might than with a bagful of right." You long for freedom? You fools! If you took might, freedom would come of itself. See, he who has might "stands above the law." How does this prospect taste to you, you "law-abiding" people? But you have no taste!

The cry for "freedom" rings loudly all around. But is it felt and known what a donated or chartered freedom must mean? It is not recognized in the full amplitude of the word that all freedom is essentially—self-liberation—that I can have only so much freedom as I procure for myself by my ownness. Of what use is it to sheep that no one abridges their freedom of speech? They stick to bleating. Give one who is inwardly a Mohammedan, a Jew, or a Christian, permission to speak what he likes: he will yet utter only narrow-minded stuff. . . . If they nevertheless give you freedom, they are simply knaves who give more than they have. For then they give you nothing of their own, but stolen wares: they give you your own freedom, the freedom that you must take for yourselves; and they *give* it to you only that you may not take it and call the thieves and cheats to an account to boot. In their slyness they know well that given (chartered) freedom is no freedom, since only the freedom one *takes* for himself, therefore the egoist's freedom, rides with full sails. Donated freedom strikes its sails as soon as there comes a storm—or calm; it requires always a—gentle and moderate breeze. . . .

OWNNESS, THE STATE, AND THE UNION OF EGOISTS

But what concept is the highest to the State? Doubtless that of being a really human society, a society in which every one who is really a man . . . can obtain admission as a member. . . . If the State must count on our humanity, it is the same if one says it must count on our *morality*. Seeing Man in each other, and acting as men toward each other, is called moral behavior. . . . Morality is incompatible with egoism, because the former does not allow validity to *me*, but only to the Man in me. But, if the State is a *society of men*, not a union of egos each of whom has only himself before his eyes, then it cannot last without morality, and must insist on morality.

Therefore we two, the State and I, are enemies. I, the egoist, have not at heart the welfare of this "human society," I sacrifice nothing to it, I only utilize it; but to be able to utilize it completely I transform it rather into my property and my creature; that is, I annihilate it, and form in its place the *Union of Egoists*. . . .

Right is the *spirit of society*. If society has a *will*, this will is simply right: society exists only through right. But, as it endures only exercising a *sovereignty* over individuals, right is its SOVEREIGN WILL. . . . All existing right is—*foreign*

law. . . . The social reformers preach to us a *"law of society."*
There the individual becomes society's slave, and is in the
right only when society makes him out in the right, when he
lives according to society's statutes and so is—*loyal.* . . .

In consideration of right the question is always asked,
"What or who gives me the right to it?" Answer: God, love,
reason, nature, humanity, etc. No, only *your might, your*
power gives you the right (your reason, therefore, may give
it to you). . . . Children have no right to the condition of
majority because they are not of age, because they are children. Peoples that let themselves be kept in nonage have no
rights to the condition of majority; if they ceased to be in
nonage, then only would they have the right to be of age.
This means nothing else than "What you have the *power* to
be you have the *right* to." I derive all right and warrant from
me; I am entitled to everything that I have in my power. I
am entitled to overthrow Zeus, Jehovah, God, if I can; if I
cannot, then these gods will always remain in the right and
in power as against me. . . . The only thing I am not entitled to is what I do not do with a free cheer, that is, what
I do not entitle myself to.

I decide whether it is the right thing in me; there is no
right outside me. If it is right for me, it is right. Possibly
this may not suffice to make it right for the rest; that is their
care, not mine: let them defend themselves. And if for the
whole world something were not right, but it were right for
me, that is, I wanted it, then I would ask nothing about the
whole world. So every one does who knows how to value himself, every one in the degree that he is an egoist; for might
goes before right, and that—with perfect right. . . .

People are at pains to distinguish law from arbitrary orders,
from an ordinance: the former comes from a duly entitled
authority. But a law over human action (ethical law, State
law, etc.) is always a declaration of will, and so an order. . . .
States last only so long as there is a ruling will and this ruling
will is looked upon as tantamount to the own will. The
lord's will is—law. What do your laws amount to if no one
obeys them? What your orders, if nobody lets himself be
ordered? The State cannot forbear the claim to determine
the individual's will, to speculate and count on this. For the
State it is indispensable that nobody have an own will; if
one had, the State would have to exclude (lock up, banish,
etc.) this one; if all had, they would do away with the State.
The State is not thinkable without lordship and servitude

(subjection); for the State must will to be the lord of all that it embraces, and this will is called the "will of the State." . . .

Every State is a *despotism*, be the despot one or many, or (as one is likely to imagine about a republic) if all be lords, that is, despotize one over another. For this is the case when the law given at any time, the expressed volition of (it may be) a popular assembly, is thenceforth to be law for the individual, to which obedience is due from him or toward which he has the duty of obedience. If one were even to conceive the case that every individual in the people had expressed the same will, and hereby a complete "collective will" had come into being, the matter would still remain the same. Would I not be bound to-day and henceforth to my will of yesterday? My will would in this case be *frozen*. Wretched *stability!* My creature—to wit, a particular expression of will—would have become my commander. But I in my will, I the creator, should be hindered in my flow and my dissolution. Because I was a fool yesterday I must remain such my life long. So in the State-life I am at best—I must just as well say, at worst—a bondman of myself. Because I was a willer yesterday, I am today without will: yesterday voluntary, today involuntary.

How change it? Only by recognizing no *duty*, not *binding* myself nor letting myself be bound. If I have no duty, then I know no law either. . . .

We are accustomed to classify States according to the different ways in which "the supreme might" is distributed. If an individual has it—monarchy; if all have it—democracy; etc. Supreme might then! Might against whom? Against the individual and his "self-will." The State practices "violence," the individual must not do so. The State's behavior is violence, and it calls its violence "law"; that of the individual, "crime." Crime, then—so the individual's violence is called; and only by crime does he overcome the State's violence when he thinks that the State is not above him, but he is above the State. . . .

Solely from the principle that all *right* and all *authority* belong to the *collectivity of the people* do all forms of government arise. For none of them lacks this appeal to the collectivity, and the despot, as well as the president or any aristocracy, acts and commands "in the name of the State." They are in possession of the "authority of the State," and it is perfectly indifferent whether, were this possible, the people as a *collectivity* (all individuals) exercise this State-*authority*, or whether it is only the representatives of this collectivity, be there many of them as in aristocracies or one as in monarchies. Always the collectivity is above the individual, and has a power which is called *legitimate*, which is law.

Over against the sacredness of the State, the individual is only a vessel of dishonor. . . . Society would have every one come to his right indeed, but yet only to that which is sanctioned by society, to the society-right, not really to *his* right. But I give or take to myself the right out of my own plenitude of power, and against every superior power I am the most impenitent criminal. Owner and creator of my right, I recognize no other source of right than—me, neither God nor the State nor nature nor even man himself with his "eternal rights of man," neither divine nor human right.

Right "in and for itself." Without relation to me, therefore! "Absolute right." Separated from me, therefore! A thing that exists in and for itself! An absolute! An eternal right, like an eternal truth!

According to the liberal way of thinking, right is to be obligatory for me because it is thus established by human reason, against which my reason is "unreason." Formerly people inveighed in the name of divine reason against weak human reason; now, in the name of strong human reason, against egoistic reason, which is rejected as "unreason." And yet none is real but this very "unreason." Neither divine nor human reason, but only your and my reason existing at any given time, is real, as and because you and I are real. . . .

I do not demand any right, therefore I need not recognize any either. What I can get by force I get by force, and what I do not get by force I have no right to, nor do I give myself airs or consolation, with my imprescriptible right.

With absolute right, right itself passes away; the dominion of the "concept of right" is canceled at the same time. For it is not to be forgotten that hitherto concepts, ideas, or principles ruled us, and that among these rulers the concept of right, or of justice, played one of the most important parts.

Entitled or unentitled—that does not concern me, if I am only *powerful*, I am of myself *empowered*, and need no other empowering or entitling.

Right—is a wheel in the head, put there by a spook; power —that am I myself, I am the powerful one and owner of power. Right is above me, is absolute, and exists in one higher, as whose grace it flows to me: right is a gift of grace from the judge; power and might exist only in me the power-ful and mighty. . . .

What is called a State is a tissue and plexus of dependence and adherence; it is a *belonging together*, a holding together, in which those who are placed together fit themselves to each other, or, in short, mutually depend on each other: it is the *order* of this *dependence*. . . . The fight of the world to-day is, as it is said, directed against the "established." Yet people are wont to misunderstand this as if it were only that what is now established was to be exchanged for another, a better, established system. But war might rather be declared against establishment itself, the State, not a particular State. . . .

The State always has the sole purpose to limit, tame, sub-ordinate, the individual—to make him subject to some gener-ality or other; it lasts only so long as the individual is not all in all, and it is only the clearly-marked restriction of me, my limitation, my slavery. Never does a State aim to bring in the free activity of individuals, but always that which is bound to the purpose of the State. Through the State nothing in common comes to pass either, as little as one can call a piece of cloth the common work of all the individual parts of a machine; it is rather the work of the whole machine as a unit, *machine work*. In the same style everything is done by the *State machine* too; for it moves the clockwork of the individual minds, none of which follow their own impulse. The State seeks to hinder every free activity by its censorship, its supervision, its police, and holds this hindering to be its duty, because it is in truth a duty of self-preservation. The State wants to make something out of man, therefore there live in it only *made* men; every one who wants to be his own self is its opponent and is nothing. . . . Can State and peo-ple still be reformed and bettered now? As little as the nobility, the clergy, the church, etc.: they can be abrogated, annihilated, done away with, not reformed. Can I change a piece of nonsense into sense by reforming it, or must I drop it outright?

Henceforth what is to be done is no longer about the *State* (the form of the State, etc.), but about me. With this all questions about the prince's power, the constitution, and so on, sink into their true abyss and their true nothingness. I, this nothing, shall put forth my *creations* from myself. . . .

If the State is sacred, there must be censorship. The political liberals admit the former and dispute the inference. But in any case they concede repressive measures to it, for

—they stick to this, that State is more than the individual and exercises a justified revenge, called punishment.

Punishment has a meaning only when it is to afford expiation for the injuring of a *sacred* thing. . . . Curative means or healing is only the reverse side of punishment, the theory of cure runs parallel with the theory of punishment; if the latter sees in an action a sin against right, the former takes it for a sin of the man against himself, as a decadence from his health. But the correct thing is that I regard it either as an action that suits me or as one that does not suit me, as hostile or friendly to me, that I treat it as my property, which I cherish or demolish. "Crime" or "disease" are not either of them an egoistic view of the matter, a judgment starting from me, but starting from another—to wit, whether it injures right, general right, or the health partly of the individual (the sick one), partly of the generality (society). "Crime" is treated inexorably, "disease" with "loving gentleness, compassion," and the like.

Punishment follows crime. If crime falls because the sacred vanishes, punishment must not less be drawn into its fall; for it too has significance only over against something sacred. Ecclesiastical punishments have been abolished. Why? Because how one behaves toward the "holy God" is his own affair. But, as this one punishment, ecclesiastical punishment, has fallen, so all punishments must fall. As sin against the so-called God is a man's own affair, so is that against every kind of the so-called sacred. . . . The criminal code has continued existence only through the sacred, and perishes of itself if punishment is given up. Now they want to create everywhere a new penal law, without indulging in a misgiving about punishment itself. But it is exactly punishment that must make room for satisfaction, which, again, cannot aim at satisfying right or justice, but at procuring *us* a satisfactory outcome. If one does to us what we *will not put up with*, we break power and bring our own to bear: we satisfy ourselves on him, and do not fall into the folly of wanting to satisfy right (the spook). . . .

Property is the expression for *unlimited dominion* over somewhat (thing, beast, man) which "I can judge and dispose of as seems good to me." . . . Under the dominion of the State there is no property of mine. . . . The State, I mean to say, cannot intend that anybody should for his own sake have property or actually be rich, nay, even well-to-do; it can acknowledge nothing, yield nothing, grant nothing to me as me.

The State cannot check pauperism, because the poverty of possession is a poverty of me. . . . It binds the possessions of property to *conditions*—as it binds everything to them, as in marriage, allowing validity only to the marriage sanctioned by it, and wresting this out of my power. But property is *my* property only when I hold it *unconditionally*: only I, an *unconditional* ego, have property, enter a relation of love, carry on free trade. . . . For the State's understanding, what befalls me as ego is something accidental, my wealth as well as my impoverishment. But, if I with all that is mine am an accident in the State's eyes, this proves that it cannot comprehend *me*: I go beyond its concepts, or, its understanding is too limited to comprehend me. Therefore it cannot do anything for me either.

Pauperism is the *valuelessness of me,* the phenomenon that I cannot realize value from myself. For this reason State and pauperism are one and the same. The State does not let me come to my value, and continues in existence only through my valuelessness: it is forever intent on getting benefit from me, exploiting me, turning me to account, using me up. . . . Pauperism can be removed only when I as ego realize value from myself, when I give my own self value, and make my price myself. I must rise in revolt to rise in the world. . . .

What then is *my* property? Nothing but what is in my power! To what property am I entitled? To every property to which I—*empower* myself. I give myself the right of property in taking property to myself, or giving myself the proprietor's power. . . . Let me then withdraw the might that I have conceded to others out of ignorance regarding the strength of my own might! Let me say to myself, what my might reaches to is my property; and let me claim as property everything that I feel myself strong enough to attain, and let me extend my actual property as far as *I* entitle, that is, empower, myself to take. . . .

All attempts to enact rational laws about property have put out from the bay of love into a desolate sea of regulations. Even Socialism and Communism cannot be excepted from this. Every one is to be provided with adequate means, for which it is little to the point whether one socialistically finds them still in a personal property, or communistically draws them from the community of goods. The individual's mind in this remains the same; it remains a mind of dependence. The distributing *board of equity* lets me have only what the sense of equity, its loving care for all, prescribes.

For me, the individual, there lies no less of a check in *collective wealth* than in that of *individual others;* neither that is mine, nor this: whether the wealth belongs to the collectivity, which confers part of it on me, or to individual possessors, is for me the same constraint, as I cannot decide about either of the two. On the contrary, Communism, by the abolition of all personal property, only presses me back still more into dependence on another, to wit, on the generality or collectivity. . . .

Egoism takes another way to root out the non-possessing rabble. It does not say: Wait for what the board of equity will—bestow on you in the name of the collectivity . . . but: Take hold, and take what you require! With this the war of all against all is declared. I alone decide what I will have. . . .

That a society (such as the society of the State) diminishes my liberty offends me little. . . . But ownness I will not have taken from me. And ownness is precisely what every society has designs on, precisely what is to succumb to its power. . . .

There is a difference whether my liberty or my ownness is limited by a society. If the former only is the case, it is a coalition, an agreement, a union; but, if ruin is threatened to ownness, it is a power of itself, a power *above me,* a thing unattainable by me, which I can indeed admire, adore, reverence, respect, but cannot subdue and consume, and that for the reason that I am resigned. It exists by my resignation, my self-renunciation, my spiritlessness, called—HUMILITY. My humility makes its courage, my submissiveness gives it its dominion.

But in reference to *liberty,* State and union are subject to no essential difference. The latter can just as little come into existence, or continue in existence, without liberty's being limited in all sorts of ways, as the State is compatible with unmeasured liberty. Limitation of liberty is inevitable everywhere, for one cannot get rid of everything; one cannot fly like a bird merely because one would like to fly so, for one does not get free from his own weight. . . . The union will assuredly offer a greater measure of liberty, as well as (and especially because by it one escapes all the coercion peculiar to State and society life) admit of being considered as "a new liberty"; but nevertheless it will still contain enough of unfreedom and involuntariness. For its object is not this—liberty (which on the contrary it sacrifices to ownness), but only ownness. Referred to this, the difference between State and union is great enough. The former is an enemy and murderer of ownness, the latter a son and co-worker of it . . . the State is the lord of my spirit, who demands faith and prescribes to me articles of faith, the creed of legality; it exerts moral influence, dominates my spirit, drives away my ego to put itself in its place as "my true ego"—in short, the State is *sacred*, and as against me, the individual man, it is the true man, the spirit, the ghost; but the union is my own creation, my creature, not sacred, not a spiritual power above my spirit, as little as any association of whatever sort. As I am not willing to be a slave of my maxims, but lay them bare to my continual criticism without *any warrant*, and admit no bail at all for their persistence, so still less do I obligate myself to the union for my future and pledge my soul to it, as is said to be done with the devil, and is really the case with the State and all spiritual authority. . . .

For me no one is a person to be respected, not even the fellow-man, but solely, like other beings, an object in which I take an interest or else do not, an interesting or uninteresting object, a usable or unusable person.

And, if I can use him, I doubtless come to an understanding and make myself at one with him, in order, by the agreement, to strengthen my power, and by combined force to accomplish more than individual force could effect. In this combination I see nothing whatever but a multiplication of my force, and I retain it only so long as it is my multiplied force. But thus it is a—union.

Neither a natural ligature nor a spiritual one holds the union together, and it is not a natural, not a spiritual league. It is not brought about by one *blood*, not by one *faith* (spirit). In a natural league—like a family, a tribe, a nation, yes, mankind—the individuals have only the value of *specimens* of the same species or genus; in a spiritual league—like a commune, a church—the individual signifies only a *member* of the same spirit; what you are in both cases as a unique person must be—suppressed. Only in the union can you assert yourself as unique, because the union does not possess you, but you possess it or make it of use to you. . . .

You bring into a union [of egoists] your whole power, your competence, and *make yourself count*; in a society you are *employed*, with your working power; in the former you live egoistically, in the latter humanly, that is, religiously, as a "member in the body of this Lord"; to a society you owe what you have, and are in duty bound to it, are—possessed by "social duties"; a union you utilize, and give it up undutifully and unfaithfully when you see no way to use it further. If a society is more than you, then it is more to you than yourself; a union is only your instrument, or the sword with which you sharpen and increase your natural force; the union exists for you and through you, the society conversely lays claim to you for itself and exists even without you; in short, the society is *sacred*, the union your *own*; the society consumes you, you consume the union. . . .

Revolution and insurrection must not be looked upon as synonymous. The former consists in an overturning of conditions, of the established condition or status, the State or society, and is accordingly a *political* or *social* act; the latter has indeed for its unavoidable consequence a transformation of circumstances, yet does not start from it but from men's discontent with themselves, is not an armed rising, but a rising of individuals, a getting up, without regard to the arrangements that spring from it. The Revolution aimed at new *arrangements*; insurrection leads us no longer to *let* ourselves be arranged, but to arrange ourselves, and sets no glittering hopes on "institutions." It is not a fight against the established, since, if it prospers, the established collapses of itself; it is only a working forth of me out of the established. If I leave the established, it is dead and passes into decay. Now, as my object is not the overthrow of an established order by my elevation above it, my purpose and deed are not a political or social but (as directed toward myself and my ownness alone) an *egoistic* purpose and deed.

Der Einzige ON THOUGHT, LANGUAGE, AND TRUTH

If thoughts are free, I am their slave; I have no power over them, and am dominated by them. But I want to have the thought, want to be full of thoughts, but at the same time I want to be thoughtless, and, instead of freedom of thought, I preserve for myself thoughtlessness. . . . And really I have thoughts only as *man*; as I, I am at the same time *thoughtless*. He who cannot get rid of a thought is so far *only* man, is a thrall of *language*, this human institution, this treasury of *human* thoughts. Language or "the word" tyrannizes hardest over us, because it brings up against us a whole army of *fixed ideas*. Just observe yourself in the act of reflection, right now, and you will find how you make progress only by becoming thoughtless and speechless every moment. You are not thoughtless and speechless merely in (say) sleep, but even in the deepest reflection; yes, precisely then most so. And only by this thoughtlessness, this unrecognized "freedom of thought" or freedom from the thought, are you your own. Only from it do you arrive at putting language to use as your *property*.

If thinking is not *my* thinking, it is merely a spun-out thought; it is slave work, or the work of a "servant obeying at the word." For not a thought, but I, am the beginning for my thinking, and therefore I am its goal too, even as its whole course is only a course of my self-enjoyment; for absolute or free thinking, on the other hand, thinking itself is the beginning, and it plagues itself with propounding this beginning as the extremest "abstraction" (such as being). . . .

Presuppose means nothing else than put a *thought* in front, or think something before everything else and think the rest from the starting-point of this that has *been thought*, measure and criticize it by this. In other words, this is as much as to say that thinking is to begin with something already thought. . . .

Before my thinking, there is—I. From this it follows that my thinking is not preceded by a *thought*, or that my thinking is without a "presupposition." For the presupposition which I am for my thinking is not one *made by thinking*, not one *thought* of, but it is posited thinking itself, it is the *owner* of the thought, and proves only that thinking is nothing more than—*property*, that an "independent" thinking, a "thinking spirit," does not exist at all.

This reversal of the usual way of regarding things might so resemble an empty playing with abstractions that even those against whom it is directed would acquiesce in the harmless aspect I give it, if practical consequences were not connected with it.

To bring these into a concise expression, the assertion now made is that man is not the measure of all things, but I am this measure. . . .

I will answer Pilate's question, What is truth? . . . As long as you believe in the truth, you do not believe in yourself, and you are a—*servant*, a—*religious man*. You alone are the truth, or rather, you are more than the truth, which is nothing at all before you. . . . For all free criticism a thought was the criterion; for own criticism I am, I the unspeakable, and so not the merely thought-of; for what is merely thought of is always speakable, because word and thought coincide.

That is true which is mine, untrue that whose own I am; true, as in the union; untrue, the State and society. "Free and true" criticism takes care for the consistent dominion of a thought, an idea, a spirit; "own" criticism, for nothing but my *self-enjoyment*. But in this the latter is in fact—and we will not spare it this "ignominy"!—like the bestial criticism of instinct. I, like the criticizing beast, am concerned only for myself, not "for the cause." I am the criterion of truth, but I am not an idea, but more than idea, that is, unutterable. . . .

They say of God, "Names name thee not." That holds good of me: no *concept* expresses me, nothing that is designated as my essence exhausts me; they are only names. Likewise they say of God that he is perfect and has no calling to strive after perfection. That too holds good of me alone.

I am *owner* of my might, and I am so when I know myself as *unique*. In the *unique one* the owner himself returns into his creative nothing, of which he is born. Every higher essence above me, be it God, be it man, weakens the feeling of my uniqueness, and pales only before the sun of this consciousness. If I concern myself for myself, the unique one, then my concern rests on its transitory, mortal creator, who consumes himself, and I may say:

All things are nothing to me.

In 1792, a year before the publication of William Godwin's *An Enquiry Concerning Political Justice and Its Influence on Morals and Happiness*, the British sentenced Thomas Paine to death for publishing *The Rights of Man*. *Political Justice* is a far more radical work than Paine's—and a better reply to Edmund Burke's *Reflections on the Revolution in France*. Nonetheless, the historical reaction against the French Revolution and those who supported any part of it left Godwin unmolested. Moreover, his chief work enjoyed an initial reception unique among philosophical treatises for its vigor and enthusiasm. Of this reception, William Hazlitt wrote:

> No work in our time gave such a blow to the philosophical mind of the country as the celebrated *Enquiry Concerning Political Justice*. Tom Paine was considered for a time as a Tom Fool to him, Paley an old woman, Edmund Burke a flashy sophist. Truth, moral truth, it was supposed, had here taken up its abode. . . .

It should be mentioned that *Political Justice* provides what has remained the classic libertarian analysis of the concept of "authority," a concept political philosophers in general have said little about. In addition, one of the book's chief aims is to substantiate the conclusion that ". . . the grand moral evils that exist in the world, the calamities by which we are so grievously oppressed, are to be traced to political institutions as their source." This conclusion, which Godwin bequeathed to anarchism, rests primarily on the following argument:

1   Knowledge can be obtained only by those who possess the capacity for independent judgment.
2   By corrupting man's understanding with prejudices like patriotism and compelling him to rely on the dictates of "authorities," government presents the most extensive and most frequent threat to the development of independent judgment.
3   The only source of crime, vice, and injustice is a lack of knowledge on the part of the agent.
4   Hence, government constitutes the most extensive and most frequent source of crime, vice, and injustice.

Two points concerning this argument deserve comment. First, it confronts us with the contention that the moral and legal evils which are so often trotted out in defense of the perpetuation of political institutions are in fact the product of those very institutions. Proof of this contention would in one stroke reduce a great many of the arguments against anarchism to absurdity.

But Godwin's argument is noteworthy in a second way: it supplies an *epistemological* premise to establish his moral conclusion. This appeal to the concept of knowledge (to its internal relation to independent judgment) and to the sources of human ignorance and error, most clearly distinguishes Godwin from other anarchist thinkers.

THE RIGHT OF INDEPENDENT JUDGMENT

Every man has a certain sphere of discretion, which he has a right to expect shall not be infringed by his neighbors. This right flows from the very nature of man. First, all men are fallible: no man can be justified in setting up his judgment as a standard for others. We have no infallible judge of controversies; each man in his own apprehension is right in his decisions; and we can find no satisfactory mode of adjusting their jarring pretensions. If every one be desirous of imposing his sense upon others, it will at last come to be a controversy, not of reason, but of force. Secondly, even if we had an infallible criterion, nothing would be gained, unless it were by all men recognized as such. If I were secured against the possibility of mistake, mischief and not good would accrue, from imposing my infallible truths upon my neighbor, and requiring his submission independently of any conviction I could produce in his understanding. Man is a being who can never be an object of just approbation, any further than he is independent. He must consult his own reason, draw his own conclusions and conscientiously conform himself to his ideas of propriety. Without this, he will be neither active, nor considerate, nor resolute, nor generous.

For these two reasons it is necessary, that every man should

An Enquiry Concerning Political Justice and Its Influence on Morals and Happiness, by William Godwin, 2 vols. (London, 1798). Facsimile of 3rd ed., with Notes and Introduction by F. E. L. Priestly (Toronto: The University of Toronto Press, 1946), passim. Subheads provided in part by the editors.

stand by himself, and rest upon his own understanding. For that purpose each must have his sphere of discretion. No man must encroach upon my province, nor I upon his. He may advise me, moderately and without pertinaciousness, but he must not expect to dictate to me. He may censure me freely and without reserve; but he should remember that I am to act by my deliberation and not his. . . . I ought to exercise my talents for the benefit of others; but that exercise must be the fruit of my own conviction; no man must attempt to press me into the service. I ought to appropriate such part of the fruits of the earth as by any accident comes into my possession, and is not necessary to my benefit, to the use of others; but they must obtain it from me by argument and expostulation, not by violence. It is in this principle that what is commonly called the right of property is founded. Whatever then comes into my possession, without violence to any other man, or to the institutions of society, is my property. This property, it appears by the principles already laid down, I have no right to dispose of at my caprice; every shilling of it is appropriated by the laws of morality; but no man can be justified, in ordinary cases at least, in forcibly extorting it from me. When the laws of morality shall be clearly understood, their excellence universally apprehended, and themselves seen to be coincident with each man's private advantage, the idea of property in this sense will remain, but no man will have the least desire, for purposes of ostentation or luxury, to possess more than his neighbors. . . .

The most essential of those rights which constitute the peculiar sphere appropriate to each individual, and the right upon which every other depends as its basis, is the right of private judgment. It will therefore be of use to say something distinctly on this head.

To a rational being there can be but one rule of conduct, justice, and one mode of ascertaining that rule, the exercise of his understanding.

If in any instance I am made the mechanical instrument of absolute violence, in that instance I fall under a pure state of external slavery. If on the other hand, not being under the influence of absolute compulsion, I am wholly prompted by something that is frequently called by that name, and act from the hope of reward or the fear of punishment, the subjection I suffer is doubtless less aggravated, but the effect upon my moral habits may be in a still higher degree injurious. . . .

"I have deeply reflected," suppose, "upon the nature of virtue, and am convinced that a certain proceeding is incumbent on me. But the hangman, supported by an act of parliament, assures me I am mistaken." If I yield my opinion to his *dictum*, my action becomes modified, and my character also. An influence like this, is inconsistent with all generous magnanimity of spirit, all ardent impartiality in the discovery of truth and all inflexible perseverance in its assertion. Countries, exposed to the perpetual interference of decrees, instead of arguments, exhibit within their boundaries the mere phantoms of men. We can never judge from an observation of their inhabitants, what men would be if they knew of no appeal from the tribunal of conscience and if, whatever they thought, they dared to speak and dared to act. . . .

If there be any truth more unquestionable than the rest, it is, that every man is bound to the exertion of his faculties in the discovery of right, and to the carrying into effect all the right with which he is acquainted. It may be granted that an infallible standard, if it could be discovered, would be considerably beneficial. But this infallible standard itself would be of little use in human affairs unless it had the property of reasoning as well as deciding, of enlightening the mind as well as constraining the body. If a man be in some cases obliged to prefer his own judgment, he is in all cases obliged to consult that judgment before he can determine whether the matter in question be of the sort provided for or no. So that from this reasoning it ultimately appears, that the conviction of a man's individual understanding is the only legitimate principle imposing on him the duty of adopting any species of conduct.

Such are the genuine principles of human society. Such would be the unconstrained condition of its members in a state where every individual within the society, and every neighbor without, was capable of listening with sobriety to the dictates of reason.

DOES GOVERNMENT REST ON A SOCIAL CONTRACT?

Government . . . being first supposed necessary for the welfare of mankind, the most important principle that can be imagined relative to its structure seems to be this: that as government is a transaction in the name and for the benefit of the whole, every member of the community ought to have some share in the selection of its measures. The arguments in support of this proposition are various.

First, it has already appeared that there is no satisfactory criterion marking out any man or set of men to preside over the rest.

Secondly, all men are partakers of the common faculty, reason; and may be supposed to have some communication with the common instructor, truth. It would be wrong in an affair of such momentous concern that any chance for additional wisdom should be rejected. . . . Thirdly, government is a contrivance instituted for the security of individuals; and it seems both reasonable that each man should have a share in providing for his own security, and probable that partiality and cabal will by this means be most effectually excluded.

Lastly, to give each man a voice in the public concerns comes nearest to that fundamental purpose of which we should never lose sight, the uncontrolled exercise of private judgment. Each man will thus be inspired with a consciousness of his own importance, and the slavish feelings that shrink up the soul in the presence of an imagined superior will be unknown. . . .

It may perhaps be imagined by some persons that the doctrine here delivered, of the justice of proceeding in common concerns by a common deliberation, is nearly coincident with that which affirms a lawful government to derive its authority from a social contract. Let us consider what is the true difference between them: and this seems principally to lie in the following particular.

The principle of a social contract is an engagement to which a man is bound by honor, fidelity or consistency to adhere. According to the principle here laid down, he is bound to nothing. He joins in the common deliberation because he foresees that some authority will be exercised and because this is the best chance that offers itself for approximating the exercise of that authority to the dictates of his own understanding. But when the deliberation is over, he finds himself as much disengaged as ever. If he conform to the mandate of authority, it is either because he individually approves it, or from a principle of prudence because he foresees that a greater mass of evil will result from his disobedience, than of good. . . .

Upon what foundation can political authority with the greatest propriety rest? One of the most popular theories, relative to the foundation of political authority, we have seen to be that of an original contract, affirming . . . that, in obeying a government regularly constituted, we did nothing more than perform our engagements.

The reasonings in support of this hypothesis are obvious. Suppose a number of persons living in any neighborhood should perceive that great common benefit would accrue from building a bridge, sinking a canal or making a highway. The simplest mode for them to adopt, is, to consult together and raise the money necessary for effecting this desirable purpose, by each man assessing himself according to his ability and contributing his quota to a common fund. Now it is plain that, in this case, each pays his assessment (supposing the payment to be voluntary) in consideration of the previous agreement; his contribution would be of no avail, however desirable was the object to be effected, had he not reason to depend upon the rest of the neighborhood, that they would pay theirs. "But government," say the advocates of an original contract, "when regularly instituted, is precisely such a provision as the one here stated for building a bridge or making a road; it is a consultation and settlement among the different members of a community as to the regulations most conducive to the benefit of the whole. It is upon this principle that taxes are paid, and that the force of the community is drawn out in such proportions as are necessary to repress the external or internal disturbers of its tranquillity. The ground therefore upon which each man contributes his share of effort or property, is, that he may perform his contract and discharge that for which he has engaged as a member of the community."

The refutation of this hypothesis has been anticipated in the preceding chapters. —Government can with no propriety be compared to the construction of a bridge or a canal, a matter of mere convenience and refinement. It is supposed to be of the most irresistible necessity; it is indisputably an affair of hardship and restraint. It constitutes other men the arbitrators of my actions, and the ultimate disposers of my destiny. —Almost every member of every community that has existed on the face of the earth might reasonably say, "I know of no such contract as you describe; I never entered into any such engagement; I never promised to obey; it must therefore be an iniquitous imposition to call upon me to do something, under pretense of a promise I never made." —The reason a man lives under any particular government is partly necessity; he cannot easily avoid living under some government, and it is often scarcely in his power to abandon the country in which he was born; it is also partly a choice of evils; no man can be said, in this case, to enjoy that freedom which is essential to the forming a contract unless it could be shown that he had a power of instituting, somewhere, a government adapted to his own conceptions. —Government in reality, as has abundantly appeared, is a question of force, and not of consent.

THE PERNICIOUS TENDENCY OF GOVERNMENT

Reverence nothing but wisdom and skill: government may be vested in the fittest persons; then they are entitled to reverence because they are wise, and not because they are governors; and it may be vested in the worst. . . . Be upon your guard against confounding things so totally unconnected with each other as a purely political obedience, and respect. Government is nothing but regulated force; force is its appropriate claim upon your attention. It is the business of individuals to persuade; the tendency of concentrated strength, is only to give consistency and permanence to an influence more compendious than persuasion.

All this will be made somewhat clearer if we reflect upon the proper correlative of obedience, authority. . . .

The first kind of authority then, is the authority of reason. . . . The second species of authority is that which depends for its validity upon the confidence of him with whom it prevails, and is where, not having myself acquired such information as to enable me to form a judicious opinion, I yield a greater or less degree of deference to the known sentiment and decision of another. . . . Authority in the last of the three senses alluded to is where a man, in issuing his precept, does not deliver that which may be neglected with impunity; but his requisition is attended with a sanction, and the violation of it will be followed with a penalty. This is the species of authority which properly connects itself with the idea of government. It is a violation of political justice, to confound the authority which depends upon force, with the authority which arises from reverence and esteem; the modification of my conduct which might be due in the case of a wild beast, with the modification which is due to superior wisdom. . . .

The consequence which has flowed from confounding them, has been, a greater debasement of the human character, than could easily have followed upon direct and unqualified slavery. . . . Where I make the voluntary surrender of my understanding, and commit my conscience to another man's keeping, the consequence is clear. I then become the most mischievous and pernicious of animals. I annihilate my individuality as a man. . . . I can have no conscious integrity, for I do not understand my own principles and have never brought them to the test of examination. I am the ready tool of injustice, cruelty and profligacy; and, if at any time I am not employed in their purposes, it is the result of accident, not of my own precaution and honesty. . . .

One of the lessons most assiduously inculcated upon mankind in all ages and countries is that of reverence to our superiors. If by this maxim be intended our superiors in wisdom, it may be admitted, but with some qualification. But, if it imply our superiors in station only, nothing can be more contrary to reason and justice. Is it not enough that they have usurped certain advantages over us to which they can show no equitable claim; and must we also humble our courage, and renounce our independence, in their presence? Why reverence a man because he happens to be born to certain privileges; or because a concurrence of circumstances . . . has procured him a share in the legislative or executive government of our country? Let him content himself with the obedience which is the result of force; for to that only is he entitled.

Reverence to our superiors in wisdom is to be admitted, but with considerable limitations. I am bound, as has already appeared, to repose certain functions, such as that of building my house, or educating my child, in the hands of him by whom those functions will most properly be discharged. It may be right that I should act under the person to whom I have thus given my suffrage, in cases where I have reason to be persuaded of his skill, and cannot be expected to acquire the necessary skill myself. But in those cases of general justice which are equally within the province of every human understanding, I am a deserter from the requisitions of duty if I do not assiduously exert my faculties, or if I be found to act contrary to the conclusions they would dictate, from deference to the opinions of another. . . .

The mind of one man is essentially distinct from the mind of another. If each do not preserve his individuality, the judgment of all will be feeble and the progress of our common understanding inexpressibly retarded. . . . Nothing can be more necessary for the general benefit than that we should divest ourselves, as soon as the proper period arrives, of the shackles of infancy; that human life should not be one eternal childhood; but that men should judge for themselves, unfettered by the prejudices of education or the institutions of their country.

To a government, therefore, that talked to us of deference to political authority, and honor to be rendered to our superiors, our answer should be: "It is yours, to shackle the body and restrain our external actions; that is a restraint we understand. Announce your penalties, and we will make our election of submission or suffering. But do not seek to enslave our minds. Exhibit your force in its plainest form, for that is your province; but seek not to inveigle and mislead us. Obedience and external submission is all you are entitled to claim; you can have no right to extort our deference and command us not to see, and disapprove of, your errors."

A corollary which flows from these principles is deserving of our attention. Confidence is in all cases the offspring of ignorance. It must therefore continually decline in relation, as was above stated, to "those cases of general justice which are equally within the province of every human understanding," in proportion as wisdom and virtue shall increase. But the questions that belong to the department of government, are questions of general justice. The conduct of an enlightened and virtuous man can only be conformable to the regulations of government, so far as those regulations are accidentally coincident with his private judgment, or as he acts with prudent and judicious submission to the necessity of the case. He will not act from confidence; for he has himself examined, as it was his duty to do, the merits of the action; and he has not failed to detect the imposture, that would persuade us there is a mystery in government, which uninitiated mortals must not presume to penetrate. Now it is sufficiently known that the empire of government is built in opinion; nor is it enough for this purpose that we refuse to contribute to overturn it by violence; the opinion must go to the extent of prompting us to actual support. No government can subsist in a nation, the individuals of which shall merely abstain from tumultuous resistance, while in their genuine sentiments they censure and despise its institution. In other words, government cannot proceed but upon confidence, as confidence on the other hand cannot exist without ignorance. The true supporters of government are the weak and uninformed, and not the wise. In proportion as weakness and ignorance shall diminish, the basis of government will also decay. This however is an event which ought not to be contemplated with alarm. A catastrophe of this description would be the true euthanasia of government. If the annihilation of blind confidence and implicit opinion can at any time be effected, there will necessarily succeed in their place, an unforced concurrence of all in promoting the general welfare. . . . We shall do well to remember this characteristic of government and apply it as the universal touchstone of the institution itself. As in the commencement of the present Book we found government indebted for its existence to the errors and perverseness of a few, so it now appears, that it can not otherwise be perpetuated than by the infantine and uninstructed confidence of the many. . . .

What should we think of an act of parliament appointing some individual president of the court of criticism, and judge in the last resort of the literary merit of dramatic compositions? Is there any solid reason why we should expect better things from authority usurping the examination of moral or political excellence?

Nothing can be more unreasonable than the attempt to retain men in one common opinion by the dictate of authority. The opinion thus obtruded upon the minds of the public is not their real opinion; it is only a project by which they are rendered incapable of forming an opinion. Whenever government assumes to deliver us from the trouble of thinking for ourselves, the only consequences it produces are torpor and imbecility. . . .

We shall be still more completely aware of the pernicious tendency of positive institutions if we proceed explicitly to contrast the nature of mind and the nature of government. One of the most unquestionable characteristics of the human mind has appeared to be its progressive nature. Now, on the other hand, it is the express tendency of positive institution to retain that with which it is conversant forever in the same state. Is then the perfectability of understanding an attribute of trivial importance? Can we recollect with coldness and indifference the advantages with which this quality seems pregnant to the latest posterity? And how are these advantages to be secured? By incessant industry, by a curiosity never to be disheartened or fatigued, by a spirit of enquiry to which a philanthropic mind will allow no pause. The circumstance most indispensibly necessary is that we should never stand still, that every thing most interesting to the general welfare, wholly delivered from restraint, should be in a state of change, moderate and as it were imperceptible, but continual.

Is there any thing that can look with a more malignant aspect upon the general welfare than an institution tending to give permanence to certain systems and opinions? Such institutions are two ways pernicious; first, which is most material, because they render the future advances of mind inexpressibly tedious and operose; secondly, because by violently confining the stream of reflection and holding it for a time in an unnatural state, they compel it at last to rush forward with impetuosity, and thus occasion calamities which, were it free from restraint, would be found extremely foreign to its nature. . . .

The just conclusion from the above reasonings is nothing more than a confirmation, with some difference in the mode of application, of the fundamental principle, that government is little capable of affording benefit of the first importance to mankind. It is calculated to induce us to lament, not the apathy and indifference, but the unauspicious activity of government. It incites us to look for the moral improvement of the species, not in the multiplying of regulations, but in their repeal. It teaches us that truth and virtue, like commerce, will then flourish most, when least subjected to the mistaken guardianship of authority and laws.

The contemporary American philosopher John Rawls once wrote that "Only a few persons have rejected punishment entirely, which is rather surprising when one considers all that can be said against it." Godwin was one of the few (as was Stirner—in his own way), and he remains a principal source of philosophical arguments on this issue.

CAN PUNISHMENT BE JUSTIFIED?

The subject of punishment is perhaps the most fundamental in the science of politics. Men associated for the sake of mutual protection and benefit. . . . It has appeared that the action of society, in conferring rewards, and superintending opinion, is of pernicious effect. Hence it follows that government, or the action of society in its corporate capacity, can scarcely be of any utility, except so far as it is requisite for the suppression of force by force; for the prevention of the hostile attack of one member of the society, upon the person or property of another, which prevention is usually called by the name of criminal justice, or punishment. . . .

Punishment is also often used to signify, the voluntary infliction of evil upon a vicious being, not merely because the public advantage demands it, but because there is apprehended to be a certain fitness and propriety in the nature of things, that render suffering, abstractedly from the benefit to result, the suitable concomitant of vice. . . .

[I]t appears, whether we enter philosophically into the principle of human actions, or merely analyze the ideas of rectitude and justice which have the universal consent of mankind, that, in the refined and absolute sense in which that term has frequently been employed, there is no such thing as desert; in other words, that it cannot be just that we should inflict suffering on any man, except as it tends to good. Hence it follows also that punishment, in the last of the senses enumerated . . . by no means accords with any sound principles of reasoning. It is right that I should inflict suffering, in every case where it can be clearly shown that such infliction will produce an overbalance of good. But this infliction bears no reference to the mere innocence or guilt of the person upon whom it is made. An innocent man is the proper subject of it, if it tend to good. A guilty man is the proper subject of it under no other point of view. To punish him, upon any hypothesis, for what is past and irrecoverable, and for the consideration of that only, must be ranked among the most pernicious exhibitions of an untutored barbarism. Every man upon whom discipline is employed, is to be considered as to the purpose of this discipline as innocent. The only sense of the word punishment, that can be supposed to be compatible with the principles of the present work, is that of pain inflicted on a person convicted of past injurious action, for the purpose of preventing future mischief. . . .

Let us proceed to consider the three principal ends that punishment proposes to itself, restraint, reformation, and example. Under each of these heads, the argument on the affirmative side must be allowed to be cogent, not irresistible. Under each of them considerations will occur, that will oblige us to doubt universally of the propriety of punishment. . . .

For restraint. Restraint from what? "From some future injury which it is to be feared he will commit." This is the very argument which has been employed to justify the most execrable tyrannies. By what reasonings have the inquisition, the employment of spies, and the various kinds of public censure directed against opinion, been vindicated? By recollecting that there is an intimate connection between men's opinions and their conduct; that immoral sentiments lead, by a very probable consequence, to immoral actions. There is not more reason, in many cases at least, to apprehend that the man who has once committed robbery, will commit it again, than the man who has dissipated his property at the gaming-table or who is accustomed to profess that, upon any emergency, he will not scruple to have recourse to this expedient. Nothing can be more obvious than that, whatever precautions may be allowable with respect to the future, justice will reluctantly class among these precautions a violence to be committed on my neighbour. Nor is it oftener unjust, than it is superfluous. Why not arm myself with vigilance and energy, instead of locking up every man whom my imagination may bid me fear, that I may spend my days in undisturbed inactivity? If communities, instead of aspiring, as they have hitherto done, to embrace a vast territory, and glut their vanity with ideas of empire, were contented with a small district, with a proviso of confederation in cases of necessity, every individual would then live under the public eye; and the disapprobation of his neighbours, a species of coercion, not derived from the caprice of men, but from the system of the universe, would inevitably oblige him, either to reform, or to emigrate. —The sum of the argument under this head is, that all punishment for the sake of restraint, is punishment upon suspicion, a species of punishment, the most abhorrent to reason, and arbitrary in its application, that can be devised.

The second object which punishment may be imagined to propose to itself, is reformation. We have already seen various objections that may be offered to it in this point of view. Coercion cannot convince, cannot conciliate, but on the contrary alienates the mind of him against whom it is employed. Coercion has nothing in common with reason, and therefore can have no proper tendency to the cultivation of virtue. It is true that reason is nothing more than a collation and comparison of various emotions and feelings; but they must be the feelings originally appropriate to the question, not those which an arbitrary will, stimulated by the possession of power, may annex to it. Reason is omnipotent: if my conduct be wrong, a very simple statement, flowing from a clear and comprehensive view, will make it appear to be such; nor is it probable that there is any perverseness that would persist in vice, in the face of all the recommendations with which virtue might be invested, and all the beauty in which it might be displayed.

But to this it may be answered, "that this view of the subject may indeed be abstractedly true, but that it is not true relative to the present imperfection of human faculties. The grand requisite for the reformation and improvement of the human species, seems to consist in the rousing of the mind. It is for this reason that the school of adversity, has so often been considered as the school of virtue. In an even course of easy and prosperous circumstances, the faculties sleep. But, when great and urgent occasion is presented, it should seem that the mind rises to the level of the occasion. Difficulties awaken vigour and engender strength; and it will frequently happen that, the more you check and oppress me, the more will my faculties swell, till they burst all the obstacles of oppression."

The opinion of the excellence of adversity, is built upon a very obvious mistake. If we will divest ourselves of paradox and singularity, we shall perceive that adversity is a bad thing, but that there is something else that is worse. Mind can neither exist, nor be improved, without the reception of ideas. It will improve more in a calamitous, than a torpid state. A man will sometimes be found wiser at the end of his career, who has been treated with severity, than with neglect. But, because severity is one way of generating thought, it does not follow that it is the best.

It has already been shown that coercion, absolutely considered, is injustice. Can injustice be the best mode of disseminating principles of equity and reason? Oppression, exercised to a certain extent, is the most ruinous of all things. What is it but this, that has habituated mankind to so much ignorance and vice for so many thousand years? Is it probable that that which has been thus terrible in its consequences, should, under any variation of circumstances, be made a source of eminent good? All coercion sours the mind. He that suffers it, is practically persuaded of the want of a philanthropy sufficiently enlarged, in those with whom he has intercourse. He feels that justice prevails only with great limitations, and that he cannot depend upon being treated with justice. The lesson which coercion reads to him is, "Submit to force, and abjure reason. Be not directed by the convictions of your understanding, but by the basest part of your nature, the fear of personal pain, and a compulsory awe of the injustice of others." It was thus Elizabeth of England and Frederic of Prussia were educated in the school of adversity. The way in which they profited by this discipline, was by finding resources in their own minds, enabling them to regard, with an unconquered spirit, the violence employed against them.

Can this be the best mode of forming men to virtue? If it be, perhaps it is further requisite, that the coercion we use should be flagrantly unjust, since the improvement seems to lie, not in submission, but resistance.

But it is certain that truth is adequate to excite the mind, without the aid of adversity. By truth is here understood a just view of all the attractions of industry, knowledge and benevolence. If I apprehend the value of any pursuit, shall I not engage in it? If I apprehend it clearly, shall I not engage in it zealously? If you would awaken my mind in the most effectual manner, speak to the genuine and honourable feelings of my nature. For that which you would recommend to me, impregnate your mind with its evidence, and speak from the clearness of your view, and the fulness of conviction. Were we accustomed to an education, in which truth was never neglected from indolence, or told in a way treacherous to its excellence, in which the preceptor subjected himself to the perpetual discipline of finding the way to communicate it with brevity and force, but without prejudice and acrimony, it cannot be believed, but that such an education, would be more effectual for the improvement of the mind, than all the modes of angry or benevolent coercion that ever were devised.

The last object which punishment proposes, is example. Had legislators confined their views to reformation and restraint, their exertions of power, though mistaken, would still have borne the stamp of humanity. But, the moment vengeance presented itself as a stimulus on the one side, or the exhibition of a terrible example on the other, no barbarity was thought too great. Ingenious cruelty was busied to find new means of torturing the victim, or of rendering the spectacle impressive and horrible.

It has long since been observed, that this system of policy constantly fails of its purpose. Further refinements in barbarity, produce a certain impression, so long as they are new; but this impression soon vanishes, and the whole scope of a gloomy invention is exhausted in vain. The reason of this phenomenon, is that, whatever may be the force with which novelty strikes the imagination, the inherent nature of the situation speedily recurs, and asserts its indestructible empire. We feel the emergencies to which we are exposed, and we feel, or think we feel, the dictates of reason inciting us to their relief. Whatever ideas we form in opposition to the mandates of law, we draw, with sincerity, though it may be with some mixture of mistake, from the essential conditions of our existence. We compare them with the despotism which society exercises in its corporate capacity; and, the more frequent is our comparison, the greater are our murmurs and indignation against the injustice to which we are exposed. But indignation is not a sentiment that conciliates; barbarity possesses none of the attributes of persuasion. It may terrify; but it cannot produce in us candour and docility. Thus ulcerated with injustice, our distresses, our temptations, and all the eloquence of feeling present themselves again and again. Is it any wonder they should prove victorious?

Punishment for example, is liable to all the objections which are urged against punishment for restraint or reformation, and to certain other objections peculiar to itself. It is employed against a person not now in the commission of offence, and of whom we can only suspect that he ever will offend. It supersedes argument, reason and conviction, and requires us to think such a species of conduct our duty, because such is the good pleasure of our superiors, and because, as we are taught by the example in question, they will make us rue our stubbornness if we think otherwise. In addition to this it is to be remembered that, when I am made to suffer as an example to others, I am myself treated with supercilious neglect, as if I were totally incapable of feeling and morality. If you inflict pain upon me, you are either just or unjust. If you be just, it should seem necessary that there should be something in me that makes me the fit subject of pain, either absolute desert, which is absurd, or mischief I may be expected to perpetrate, or lastly, a tendency in what you do, to produce my reformation. If any of these be the reason why the suffering I undergo is just, then example is out of the question: it may be an incidental consequence of the procedure, but it forms no part of its principle. It must surely be a very artificial and injudicious scheme for guiding the sentiments of mankind, to fix upon an individual as a subject of torture or death, respecting whom this treatment has no direct fitness, merely that we may bid others look on, and derive instruction from his misery. This argument will derive additional force from the reasonings of the following chapter.

OF THE APPLICATION OF PUNISHMENT

A further consideration, calculated to show not only the absurdity of punishment for example, but the iniquity of punishment in general, is that delinquency and punishment are in all cases incommensurable. No standard of delinquency ever has been or ever can be discovered. No two crimes were ever alike; and therefore the reducing them, explicitly or implicitly, to general classes, which the very idea of example implies, is absurd. Nor is it less absurd to attempt to proportion the degree of suffering to the degree of delinquency, when the latter can never be discovered. Let us endeavor to clear the truth of these propositions.

Man, like every other machine the operations of which can be made the object of our senses, may, in a certain sense be affirmed to consist of two parts, the external and the internal. The form which his actions assume is one thing; the principle from which they flow is another. With the former it is possible we should be acquainted; respecting the latter there is no species of evidence that can adequately inform us. Shall we proportion the degree of suffering to the former or the latter, to the injury sustained by the community, or to the quantity of ill intention conceived by the offender? . . .

It is true that we may, in many instances, be tolerably informed respecting external actions, and that there will at first sight appear to be no great difficulty in reducing them to general rules. Murder, according to this system, suppose, will be the exertion of any species of action affecting my neighbor so as that the consequences terminate in death. The difficulties of the magistrate are much abridged upon this principle, though they are by no means annihilated. It is well known how many subtle disquisitions, ludicrous or tragical according to the temper with which we view them, have been introduced to determine in each particular instance whether the action were or were not the real occasion of the death. It never can be demonstratively ascertained.

But dismissing this difficulty, how complicated is the iniquity of treating all instances alike, in which one man has occasioned the death of another? Shall we abolish the imperfect distinctions which the most odious tyrannies have hitherto thought themselves compelled to admit between chance-medley, manslaughter and malice prepense? Shall we inflict on the man who, in endeavoring to save the life of a drowning fellow creature, oversets a boat and occasions the death of a second, the same suffering as on him who, from gloomy and vicious habits, is incited to the murder of his benefactor? In reality, the injury sustained by the community is by no means the same in these two cases; the injury sustained by the community is to be measured by the antisocial dispositions of the offender; and if that were the right view of the

subject, by the encouragement afforded to similar dispositions from his impunity. But this leads us at once from the
external action to the unlimited consideration of the intention
of the actor. The iniquity of the written laws of society is of
precisely the same nature, though not of so atrocious a degree,
in the confusion they actually introduce between various intentions, as if this confusion were unlimited. One man shall
commit murder to remove a troublesome observer of his depraved dispositions, who will otherwise counteract and expose
him to the world. A second, because he cannot bear the in-
genuous sincerity with which he is told of his vices. A third,
from his intolerable envy of superior merit. A fourth, because he knows that his adversary meditates an act pregnant
with extensive mischief, and perceives no other mode by
which its perpetration can be prevented. A fifth, in defense
of his father's life or his daughter's chastity. Each of these
men, except perhaps the last, may act either from momentary
impulse or from any of the infinite shades and degrees of
deliberation. Would you award one individual punishment to
all these varieties of action? Can a system that levels these
inequalities and confounds these differences be productive of
good? That we may render men beneficent towards each other,
shall we subvert the very nature of right and wrong? Or is
not this system, from whatever pretenses introduced, calculated in the most powerful manner to produce general injury?
Can there be a more flagrant injury than to inscribe, as we
do in effect, upon our courts of judgment, "This is the Hall
of Justice, in which the principles of right and wrong are daily
and systematically slighted, and offenses of a thousand different magnitudes are confounded together by the insolent
supineness of the legislator and the unfeeling selfishness of
those who have engrossed the produce of the general labor to
their particular emolument!"

But suppose, secondly, that we were to take the intention
of the offender, and the future injury to be apprehended, as
the standard of infliction. This would no doubt be a considerable improvement. This would be the true mode of reconciling punishment and justice if, for reasons already assigned, they were not in their own nature incompatible. It is
earnestly to be desired that this mode of administering retribution should be seriously attempted. It is to be hoped that
men will one day attempt to establish an accurate criterion,
and not go on forever, as they have hitherto done, with a
sovereign contempt of equity and reason. This attempt would

lead, by a very obvious process, to the abolition of all punishment.

It would immediately lead to the abolition of all criminal law. An enlightened and reasonable judicature would have recourse, in order to decide upon the cause before them, to no code but the code of reason. They would feel the absurdity of other men's teaching them what they should think, and pretending to understand the case before it happened, better than they who had all the circumstances under their inspection. They would feel the absurdity of bringing every offense to be compared with a certain number of measures previously invented and compelling it to agree with one of them. . . .

The great advantage that would result from men's determining to govern themselves, in the suffering to be inflicted, by the motives of the offender and the future injury to be apprehended, would consist in their being taught how vain and presumptuous it is in them to attempt to wield the rod of retribution. Who is it that, in his sober reason, will pretend to assign the motives that influenced me in any article of my conduct, and upon them to found a grave, perhaps a capital, penalty against me? The attempt would be iniquitous and absurd, even though the individual who was to judge me had made the longest observation of my character and been most intimately acquainted with the series of my actions. How often does a man deceive himself in the motives of his conduct, and assign to one principle what in reality proceeded from another? Can we expect that a mere spectator should form a judgment sufficiently correct, when he who has all the sources of information in his hands is nevertheless mistaken? Is it not to this hour a dispute among philosophers whether I be capable of doing good to my neighbor for his own sake? . . . Meanwhile the individuals whose office it is to judge of this inscrutable mystery are possessed of no previous knowledge, utter strangers to the person accused, and collecting their only materials from the information of two or three ignorant and prejudiced witnesses. . . .

But this is not all. The motive, when ascertained, is a subordinate part of the question. The point upon which only society can equitably animadvert, if it had any jurisdiction in the case, is a point, if possible, still more inscrutable than that of which we have been treating. A legal inquisition into the minds of men, considered by itself, all rational enquirers have agreed to condemn. What we want to ascertain is not the intention of the offender but the chance of his offending again. For this purpose we reasonably inquire first into his intention. But when we have found this our task is but begun. This is one of our materials to enable us to calculate the probability of his repeating his offense or being imitated by others. Was this an habitual state of his mind, or was it a crisis in his history likely to remain an unique? What effect has experience produced on him; or what likelihood is there that the uneasiness and suffering that attend the perpetration of eminent wrong may have worked a salutary change in his mind? Will he hereafter be placed in circumstances that shall impel him to the same enormity? Precaution is in its own nature a step in a high degree precarious. Precaution that consists in inflicting injury on another will at all times be odious to an equitable mind. Meanwhile, be it observed that all which has been said upon the uncertainty of crime tends to aggravate the injustice of punishment for the sake of example. Since the crime upon which I animadvert in one man can never be the same as the crime of another, it is as if I should award a grievous penalty against persons with one eye to prevent any man in the future from putting out his eyes by design. . . .

SOCIETY WITHOUT POLITICAL AUTHORITY

The only principle which can be substituted in the room of law is that of reason exercising an uncontrolled jurisdiction upon the circumstances of the case. To this principle no objection can arise on the score of wisdom. It is not to be supposed that there are not men now existing whose intellectual accomplishments rise to the level of law. . . . But if men can be found among us whose wisdom is equal to the wisdom of law, it will scarcely be maintained that the truths they have to communicate will be the worse for having no authority but that which they derive from the reasons that support them. . . .

Whatever inconveniences may arise from the passions of men, the introduction of fixed laws cannot be the genuine remedy. Let us consider what would be the operation and progressive state of these passions, provided men were trusted to the guidance of their own discretion. Such is the discipline that a reasonable state of society employs with respect to man in his individual capacity: why should it not be equally valid with respect to men acting in a collective capacity? Inexperience and zeal would prompt me to restrain my neighbor whenever he is acting wrong and, by penalties and inconveniences designedly interposed, to cure him of his errors. But reason evinces the folly of this proceeding, and teaches me that, if he be not accustomed to depend upon the energies of intellect, he will never rise to the dignity of a rational being. As long as a man is held in the trammels of obedience and habituated to look to some foreign guidance for the direction of his conduct, his understanding and the vigor of his mind will sleep. Do I desire to raise him to the energy of which he is capable? I must teach him to feel himself, to bow to no authority, to examine the principles he entertains, and render to his mind the reason of his conduct.

The habits which are thus salutary to the individual will be equally salutary in the transactions of communities. Men are weak at present because they have always been told they are weak and must not be trusted with themselves. Take them out of their shackles, bid them inquire, reason and judge, and you will soon find them very different beings. Tell them that they have passions, are occasionally hasty, intemperate and injurious, but they must be trusted with themselves. Tell them that the mountains of parchment in which they have been hitherto entrenched are fit only to impose upon ages of superstition and ignorance; that henceforth we will have no dependence but upon their spontaneous justice; that, if their passions be gigantic, they must rise with gigantic energy to subdue them; that, if their decrees be iniquitous, the iniquity shall be all their own. The effect of this disposition of things will soon be visible; mind will rise to the level of its situation; juries and umpires will be penetrated with the magnitude of the trust reposed in them. . . .

The juridical decisions that were made immediately after the abolition of law would differ little from those during its empire. They would be the decisions of prejudice and habit. But habit, having lost the center about which it revolved, would diminish in the regularity of its operations. Those to whom the arbitration of any question was entrusted would frequently recollect that the whole case was committed to their deliberation, and they could not fail occasionally to examine themselves respecting the reason of those principles which had hitherto passed uncontroverted. Their understandings would grow enlarged in proportion as they felt the importance of their trust and the unbounded freedom of their investigation. Here then would commence an auspicious order of things, of which no understanding of man at present in existence can foretell the result, the dethronement of implicit faith and the inauguration of reason and justice. . . .

Man is not originally vicious. He would not refuse to listen to, or be convinced by, the expostulations that are addressed to him, had he not been accustomed to regard them as hypocritical and to conceive that while his neighbor, his parent and his political governor pretended to be actuated by a pure regard to his interest or pleasure, they were in reality, at the expense of his, promoting their own. Such are the fatal defects of mysteriousness and complexity. Simplify the social system . . . render the plain dictates of justice level to every capacity; remove the necessity of implicit faith; and we may expect the whole species to become virtuous and reasonable. It might then be sufficient for juries to recommend a certain mode of adjusting controversies without assuming the prerogative of dictating that adjustment. It might then be sufficient to invite offenders to forsake their errors. If their expostulations proved, in a few instances, ineffectual, the evils arising out of this circumstance would be of less importance than those which proceed from the perpetual violation of the exercise of private judgment. . . . The reader has probably anticipated the ultimate conclusion from these remarks. If juries might at length cease to decide, and be contented to invite, if force might gradually be withdrawn and reason trusted alone, shall we not one day find that juries themselves, and every other species of public institution, may be laid aside as unnecessary? . . . With what delight must every well-informed friend of mankind look forward to the auspicious period, the dissolution of political government, of that brute engine which has been the only perennial cause of the vices of mankind, and which, as has abundantly appeared in the progress of the present work, has mischiefs of various sorts incorporated with its substance, and not otherwise removable than by its utter annihilation.

Stephen Pearl Andrews, the son of a New England clergyman, was
a man of exceptional and varied gifts. Besides being a successful lawyer and distinguished orator, he was the master of thirty-two languages, and a pioneer in the comparative study of language. His
Discoveries in Chinese and Primary Synopsis of Universology were
attempts to "found etymology upon a new science—the Philosophical and Historical Evolution of Human Thought, *which has under-
laid and inspired the development of human language . . ."*

The great liberal causes of nineteenth-century America found in
Andrews an eloquent and fearless champion. In 1843 he was openly
and persistently advocating the demise of racial slavery; consequently,
both the home and the law practice he had established in Houston
were destroyed. Undaunted, Andrews rallied British financial support for a plan to free the state of Texas by purchasing all of its
slaves. But the war with Mexico irreparably quashed the project.

In 1853 Andrews entered the lists against another typical American form of oppression—the dictation of private morals. Arguing in
the *Tribune* against such notables as Henry James, Sr. and Horace
Greeley, Andrews maintained that sexual behavior and family life
should be liberated from all forms of social, political, and ecclesiastical authority and transformed into domains of personal initiative and
private responsibility. And this principle applied as much to women—
for whom generations of princes, priests, and parents had established
a fixed and subservient status—as to men. Appealing to "the sovereignty of the individual," Andrews insisted on "complete emancipation and self-ownership" for *both* sexes.

Here we are brought to the heart of Andrews' individualist anarchism, a position which he intentionally set forth as a development and justification of Josiah Warren's views (see selection 28).
From Warren, Andrews inherited a whole set of axioms, chief among
which were (a) the Sovereignty of the Individual and (b) the principle that Cost is the equitable limit of Price. As Warren himself insisted, it would be difficult to improve upon Andrews' exposition of
these principles. Nonetheless, a word of caution about the first may
be of some use.

For neither Warren nor Andrews was individual sovereignty to be
interpreted as providing men, *under present conditions*, with a moral

carte blanche. They both work from a model of the good society—an applied model in Warren's case—in which men's lives are disentangled and disconnected, where every agent is independent of his fellows and in which no one is compelled to suffer consequences for actions he did not perform. And it is *only* in such a society, they would contend, that the moral principle of individual sovereignty is fully binding, i.e. that each man should be the final judge of what is right and wrong, just and unjust, desirable and undesirable. In societies where disconnection has *not* been achieved, there are moral limits inside which right conscience must restrict itself: these concern the welfare of those whose interests have been involuntarily interfused with one's own.

Nonetheless, our most pressing obligation is to shape new circumstances so that human dependency, and the coercive institutions which produce it and are parasitic upon it can be brought to an absolute minimum.

Andrews and Warren recommend the establishment of communities from which the treacherous and unjustifiable conditions which underlie our present political and moral customs have been eliminated —thus permitting such customs to be replaced by the sovereign individual.

THE SOVEREIGNTY OF THE INDIVIDUAL

The doctrine of the Sovereignty of the Individual—in one sense itself a principle—grows out of the still more fundamental principle of "INDIVIDUALITY," which pervades universal nature. Individuality is positively the most fundamental and universal principle which the finite mind seems capable of discovering, and the best image of the Infinite. There are no two objects in the universe which are precisely alike. Each has its own constitution and peculiarities, which distinguish it from every other. Infinite diversity is the universal law. . . . This diversity reigns throughout every kingdom of nature, and mocks at all human attempts to make laws, or constitutions, or regulations, or governmental institutions of any sort, which shall work justly and harmoniously amidst the unforeseen contingencies of the future. . . .

In proportion as an object is more complex, it embodies a greater number of elements, and each element has its own individualities, or diversities, in every new combination into which it enters. Consequently these diversities are multiplied into each other, in the infinite augmentation of geo-

---

The Science of Society, by Stephen Pearl Andrews (New York: Fowler & Wells, 1852), passim. Subheads provided in part by the editors.

metrical progression. Man, standing, then, at the head of the created universe, is consequently the most complex creature in existence—every individual man or woman being a little world in him- or herself, an image or reflection of God, an epitome of the Infinite. Hence the individualities of such a being are utterly immeasurable, and every attempt to adjust the capacities, the adaptations, the wants or the responsibilities of another human being, except in the very broadest generalities, is unqualifiedly futile and hopeless. Hence every ecclesiastical, governmental or social institution which is based on the idea of demanding conformity or likeness in any thing, has ever been, and ever will be, frustrated by the operation of this subtile, all-pervading principle of Individuality. . . . This indestructible and all-pervading Individuality furnishes, itself, the law, and the only true law, of order and harmony. Governments have hitherto been established, and have apologized for the unseemly fact of their existence, from the necessity of establishing and maintaining order; but order has never yet been maintained . . . for the precise reason that the organic, essential and indestructible natures of the objects which it was attempted to reduce to order have always been constricted and infringed by every such attempt. Just in proportion as the effort is less and less made to reduce man to order, just in that proportion they become more orderly. . . .

Individuality is the essential law of order. This is true throughout the universe. When every individual particle of matter obeys the law of its own attraction, and comes into that precise position, and moves in that precise direction, which its own inherent individualities demand, the harmony of the spheres is evolved. By that means only natural classification, natural order, natural organization, natural harmony and agreement are attained. Every scheme or arrangement which is based upon the principle of thwarting the inherent affinities of the individual monads which compose any system or organism is essentially vicious, and the organization is false—a mere bundle of revolutionary and antagonistic atoms. . . .

In all events, and at all hazards, this Individuality of every member of the human family must be recognized and indulged, because first, as we have seen, it is infinite, and cannot be measured or prescribed for; then, because it is inherent, and cannot be conquered; and, finally, because it is the essential element of order, and cannot, consequently, be infringed without engendering infinite confusion, such as has hitherto universally reigned, in the administration of human affairs. If, now, Individuality is a universal law which must be obeyed if we would have order and harmony in any sphere, and, consequently, if we would have a true constitution of human government, then the absolute Sovereignty of the Individual necessarily results. The monads or atoms of which human society is composed are the individual men and women in it. They must be so disposed of, as we have seen, in order that society may be harmonic, that the destiny of each shall be controlled by his or her own individualities of taste, conscience, intellect, capacities and will. But man is a being endowed with consciousness. He, and no one else, knows the determining force of his own attractions. No one else can therefore decide for him, and hence Individuality can only become the law of human action by securing to each individual the sovereign determination of his own judgment and of his own conduct, in all things, with no right reserved either of punishment or censure on the part of anybody else, whomsoever; and this is what is meant by the Sovereignty of the Individual, limited only by the ever-accompanying condition, resulting from the equal Sovereignty of all others, that the onerous consequences of his actions be assumed by himself. . . .

It would, perhaps, be injudicious to conclude this exhibit of the doctrine of the Individual Sovereignty, without a more formal statement of the scientific limit upon the exercise of that Sovereignty which the principle itself supplies. If the principle were predicated of one Individual alone, the assertion of his Sovereignty, or, in other words, of his absolute right to do as he pleases, or to pursue his own happiness in his own way, would be confessedly to invest him with the attributes of despotism over others. But the doctrine which I have endeavored to set forth is not that. It is the assertion of the concurrent Sovereignty of all men, and of all women. . . . This concurrence of Sovereignty necessarily and appropriately limits the Sovereignty of each. Each is Sovereign only within his own dominions, because he cannot extend the exercise of his Sovereignty beyond those limits without trenching upon, and interfering with, the prerogatives of others, whose Sovereignty the doctrine equally affirms. What, then, constitutes the boundaries of one's own dominions? . . . The limitation is this: every Individual is the rightful Sovereign over his own conduct in all things, whenever, and just so far as, the consequences of his conduct can be assumed by himself; or, rather, inasmuch as no one objects to assuming agreeable consequences, whenever, and as far as, this is true of the disagreeable consequences. For disagreeable consequences, endurance, or burden of all sorts, the term "Cost" is elected as a scientific technicality. Hence the exact formula of the doctrine, with its inherent limitation, may be stated thus: *"The Sovereignty of the Individual, to be exercised at his own cost."* . . .

It results from this analysis that, wherever such circumstances exist that a person cannot exercise his own Individuality and Sovereignty without throwing the "cost," or burden, of his actions upon others, the principle has so far to be compromised. Such circumstances arise out of connected or amalgamated interests, and the sole remedy is disconnection. The exercise of Sovereignty is the exercise of the deciding power. Whoever has to bear the cost should have the deciding power in every case. If one has to bear the cost of another's conduct, and just so far as he has to do so, he should have the deciding power over the conduct of the other. Hence dependence and close connections of interest demand continual concessions and compromises. Hence, too, close connection and mutual dependence is the legitimate and scientific root of Despotism, as disconnection or Individualization of interests is the root of freedom and emancipation.

If the close combination, which demands the surrender of our will to another, is one instituted by nature, as in the case of the mother and the infant, then the relation is a true one, notwithstanding. The surrender is based upon the fact that the child is not yet strictly an Individual. The unfolding of its Individuality is gradual, and its growing development is precisely marked, by the increase of its ability to assume the consequences of its own acts. If the close combination of interests is artificial or forced, then the parties exist toward each other in false relations, and to false relations no true principle can apply. Consequently, in such relations, the Sovereignty of the Individual must be abandoned. The law of such relations is collision and conflict, to escape which, while remaining in the relations there is no other means but mutual concessions and surrenders of the selfhood. Hence, inasmuch as the interests of mankind have never yet been scientifically individualized by the operations of an equitable commerce, and the limits of encroachment never scientifically defined, the axioms of morality, and even the provisions of positive legislation, have been doubtless appropriate adaptations to the ages of false social relations to which they have been applied, as the cataplasm or the sinapism may be for disordered conditions of the human system. We must not, however, reason, in either case, from that temporary adaptation in a state of disease to the healthy condition of society or the Individual. Much that is relatively good is only good as a necessity growing out of evil. The greater good is the removal of the evil altogether. The almshouse and the foundling hospital may be necessary and laudable charities, but they can only be regarded by the enlightened philanthropist as the stinking apothecary's salve, or the dead flies, applied to the bruises and sores of the body politic. Admitted temporary necessities, they are offensive to the nostrils of good taste. The same reflection is applicable to every species of charity. The oppressed classes do not want charity, but justice, and with simple justice the necessity for charity will disappear or be reduced to a minimum. So in the matter before us. The disposition to forego one's own pleasures to secure the happiness of others is a positive virtue in all those close connections of interest which render such a sacrifice necessary, and inasmuch as such have hitherto always been the circumstances of the Individual in society, this abnegation of selfhood is the highest virtue which the world has hitherto conceived. But these close connections of interest are themselves wrong, for the very reason that they demand this sacrifice and surrender of what ought to be enjoyed and developed to the highest extent. The truest and the highest virtue, in the true relations of men, will be the fullest unfolding of all the Individualities of each, and the truest relations of men are those which permit that unfolding of the Individualities of each, not only without collision or injury to any, but with mutual advantage to all.

THE COST PRINCIPLE

The question of the proper, legitimate and just reward of labor, and other kindred questions, are becoming confessedly of immense importance to the welfare of mankind. They demand radical, thorough and scientific investigation. Political Economy, which has held its position for the last half century as one of the accredited sciences, is found in our day to have but a partial and imperfect application to matters really involved in the production and distribution of wealth. Its failure is in the fact that it treats wealth as if it

PHILOSOPHICAL FOUNDATIONS 213

were an abstract thing having interests of its own, apart from
the well-being of the laborers who produce it. In other words,
human beings, their interests and happiness, are regarded by
Political Economy in no other point of view than as mere
instruments in the production or service of this abstract
Wealth. It does not inquire in what manner and upon what
principles the accumulation and dispensation of wealth
should be conducted in order to eventuate in the greatest
amount of human comfort and happiness, and the most complete development of the individual man and woman. It
simply concerns itself with the manner in which, and the
principles in accordance with which, men and women *are
now* employed, in producing and exchanging wealth. It is as
if the whole purposes, arrangements and order of a vast pal-
ace were viewed as mere appendages to the kitchen, or contrivances for the convenience of the servants, instead of view-
ing both kitchen and servants as subordinate parts of the
system of life, gaiety, luxury and happiness which should appropriately inhabit the edifice, according to the design of its
projectors. . . .

It has been the function of writers and preachers upon
Morals, hitherto, to inculcate the duty of submitting to the
exigencies of false social relations. The Science of Society
teaches, on the other hand, the rectification of those relations themselves. So long as men find themselves embarrassed
by complicated connections of interest, so that the consequences of their acts inevitably devolve upon others, the
highest virtue consists in mutual concessions and abnegation
of selfhood. Hence the necessity for Ethics, in that stage of
progress, to enforce the reluctant sacrifice, by stringent appeals to the conscience. The truest condition of society, however, is that in which each individual is enabled and constrained to assume, to the greatest extent possible, the *Cost*
or disagreeable consequences of his own acts. That condition
of society can only arise from a general disintegration of interests,—from rendering the interests of all as completely individual as their persons. The Science of Society teaches the
means of that individualization of interests, coupled, however, with cooperation. Hence it graduates the individual, so
to speak, out of the sphere of Ethics into that of Personality—out of the sphere of duty or submission to the wants
of others, into the sphere of integral development and
freedom. . . .

According to Mr. Josiah Warren, the following is THE PROBLEM TO BE SOLVED in all its several branches:

1 "The proper, legitimate and just reward of labor."

2 "Security of person and property."

3 "The greatest practicable amount of freedom to each individual."

4 "Economy in the production and uses of wealth."

5 "To open the way to each individual for the possession of land and all other natural wealth."

6 "To make the interests of all to cooperate with and assist each other, instead of clashing with and counteracting each other."

7 "To withdraw the elements of discord, of war, of distrust and repulsion, and to establish a prevailing spirit of peace, order and social sympathy."

And according to him, also, the following PRINCIPLES are the means of the solution:

I "INDIVIDUALITY."

II "THE SOVEREIGNTY OF EACH INDIVIDUAL."

III "COST THE LIMIT OF PRICE."

IV "A CIRCULATING MEDIUM, FOUNDED ON THE COST OF LABOR."

V "ADAPTATION OF THE SUPPLY TO THE DEMAND." . . .

It is especially appropriate that something should be shown which will bridge over the seeming gap between so metaphysical a statement as that of the Sovereignty of the Individual, as set forth in the preceding number, and the merely commercial consideration of an appropriate limit of price. . . . What is to be the consequence of this general individualization of interests? Such is, to a very great extent, the order of the actual condition of ownership and administration in our existing society, which is, nevertheless, replete with social evils. Indeed, hitherto those evils have been attributed, by Social Reformers, to the prevalent individualization of interests among men, more than to any other cause. Hence they have made war upon it, and proposed combined or amalgamated interests, or extensive partnership arrangements, as the only possible means of securing attractive industry, and cooperation, and economy in the production and uses of wealth. We now assert that, in order to secure what is more important than all else, the possibility of the free exercise of Individual Sovereignty, an indispensable condition is a still greater amount than now exists of Individuality, or disconnection in the property relations of men. We affirm that nearly all that there is good in existing society results from that element. What then follows? Do we abandon the high aims of Socialists in other respects? Is all thought of cooperation and the economies surrendered by us? Clearly they are, unless some new and hitherto undiscovered element is brought in. To go back from the present field of effort of the Social Reformers to so much of Individuality as can exist in the present order of society, and stop at that alone, is evidently to return to the present social disorder, in which it is sufficiently demonstrated by experience that the exercise of the Sovereignty of the Individual—the point we aim to secure—is itself just as impossible as the other conditions desired. But why is it impossible? For the reason that Individuality of interests, upon which that exercise rests, is itself only partially possible in a social state in which there is a general denial of equity in the distribution of wealth—equity being what the *Cost Principle* alone can supply. If the woman, or the youth under age, is denied the means of acquiring an independent subsistence, by the fact that they receive less than equivalents for their industry, they are necessarily thrown into a state of dependence upon others. The exercise of their own Sovereignty, then, is obviously an impossibility for them. . . . By refusing equity in the distribution of wealth; by reducing the earnings of women, and youths, and hired men, and slaves below equivalents; by thus grasping power over others . . . the members of community are brought into the relation of oppressors and oppressed, and both together and alike involved in a common destiny of mutual restrictions, espionage, suspicions, heartburnings, open destructive collisions and secret hostility, and each is thereby shorn of the possibility of exercising his prerogative of sovereign control over his own actions. . . .

The sole basis upon which the exercise of that Sovereignty can rest is Equity—the rendering to each of that which is his. *The Cost Principle furnishes the law of that rendering.* That, and that alone, administers Equity. Hence it places all in a condition of independence. It dissolves the relation of protectors and protected by rendering protection unnecessary. It takes away the necessity resulting from dependence for combinations of interest and government, and hence for mutual responsibility for, and interference with, each other's deportment, by devolving the *Cost*, or disagreeable effects, of the conduct of each upon himself—submitting him to the government of natural consequences—the only legitimate government. In fine, the *Cost Principle* in operation renders possible, harmless and purely beneficent the universal exercise of Individual Sovereignty.

Hence it follows that the *Cost Principle* underlies *Individuality*, or the disconnection of interests, in the same manner as *Individuality* itself underlies and sustains the *Sovereignty of the Individual*. . . . Without Equity as a basis on which to rest, the Sovereignty of the Individual is true still as an abstract principle, but wholly incapable of realization. The Individual Sovereign is so *de jure*, but not *de facto*. He is a Sovereign without dominions, treated as a pretender, and his claims ridiculed by the actual incumbent. . . .

Simple Equity is this, that *so much of* YOUR *labor as I take and apply to* MY *benefit, so much of* MY *labor ought I to give you to be applied to* YOUR *benefit; and, consequently, if I take a product of your labor instead of the labor itself, and pay you in a product of my labor, the commodity which I give you ought to be one in which there is* JUST AS MUCH LABOR *as there is in the product which I receive.*

The same idea may be differently presented in this manner. It is Equity that *every individual should sustain just as much of the common burden of life as has to be sustained* BY ANYBODY *on his account.* . . . If I exchange my labor against yours, the first measure that suggests itself for the relative amount of labor performed by each is the length of time that each is employed. If all pursuits were equally laborious, or, in other words, if all labor were equally repugnant or toilsome—if it *cost* equal amounts of human suffering or endurance for each hour of time employed in every different pursuit, then it would be exact Equity to exchange one hour of labor for one other hour of labor. . . . Such, however, is not the case. Some kinds of labor are exceedingly repugnant, while others are less so, and others still more pleasing and attractive. . . .

It follows, therefore, in order to arrive at a satisfactory measure of Equity, and the adoption of a scientific system of commerce: 1. That some method must be devised for comparing the relative repugnance of different kinds of labor. 2. That, in making the comparison, *each individual* must make his or her own estimate of the repugnance to him or her of the labor which he or she performs. . . .

*The amount of burden involved in rendering a given amount of labor, or a given commodity, is technically denominated the "*COST*" of that labor or commodity, and the* *labor or commodity which is received in return for that which is rendered is denominated the "*PRICE*" of it.* Hence, inasmuch as it is simple Equity that these two should be the *equivalents* of each other, or exactly equal in the amount of burden imposed, the scientific *formula* is that "COST IS THE LIMIT (OR SCIENTIFIC MEASURE) OF PRICE." . . .

The first grand consequence resulting from the simple principle of Equity—Cost the Limit of Price—is, as already intimated, that *whatever we possess which has cost* NO *human labor, which has imposed no burden in its production, which has* COST *nothing, although it is susceptible of being property, is, nevertheless, not a rightful subject of* PRICE. All property of this kind, whether it is equally open to the enjoyment of all mankind—the property of the race, like air and water—or whether it attaches more particularly to some Individual, like genius or skill, is denominated NATURAL WEALTH. The formula relating to this subject is, then that NATURAL WEALTH BEARS NO PRICE—that is, that it cannot, of itself, be made the subject of price upon any equitable grounds whatsoever. . . .

Take an illustration as between nations. A small but industrious and civilized people inhabit a country lying between the dominions of a powerful empire on one side, and hordes of treacherous savages on the other, who threaten to invade and lay waste the country. The feeble nation applies to the powerful one to extend a degree of protection over them. . . . Assume that the cost of the aid thus rendered is equal to one million of dollars per annum, and that by estimate it saves the whole property of the weaker nation from destruction, the income upon which amounts to a hundred million of dollars. What tribute in the nature of payment shall the weaker nation render to the stronger? According to one rule, it will be an amount equal to the expenditure by the stronger. According to the other, it will be an amount equal to the benefit incurred—namely, a yearly tribute equal to the whole products of the land. Is it not clear which is the humanitary, courteous or civilized basis of the transaction and which the barbarous one? According to the latter, the choice of the people whose safety is endangered lies between two sets of savages, each of whom will rob them equally of all they possess. Is it not clear, then, that the humanitary basis of remuneration is not measured by the extent of the benefit conferred—*the Value*—but by the extent of the burden assumed—*the Cost?* . . .

It results, then, that the natural and necessary effect of *the*

Cost Principle is to limit the relative power and advantage of the intellectually strong over the intellectually weak in the same manner as Law, Morality, Religion, Machinery and the other appliances of civilization have already, in civilized countries, partially limited the power and neutralized the advantage of the physically strong over the physically weak. . . .

The second grand result from the principle of Equity— Cost the Limit of Price—is that *the value of labor or of a commodity has nothing whatever to do legitimately with fixing the* PRICE *of the labor or commodity.* . . . There is certainly nothing more reasonable, according to existing ideas, than that "*a thing ought to bring what it is worth.*" . . . There is no statement upon any subject upon which mankind would more generally concur, and yet that statement covers a fallacy which lies at the basis of the prevalent system of *exploitation* or civilized cannibalism. . . .

"What a thing is worth" is another expression for the Value of a commodity or labor. The *Value* of a commodity or labor is *the degree of benefit which it confers upon the person who receives it, or to whose use it is applied.* The Cost of it is, on the other hand, as already explained, *the degree of burden which the production of the commodity or the performance of the labor imposed upon the person who produced or performed it.* They are therefore by no means the same. No two things can possibly be more distinct. The burden or cost may be very great and the benefit or value very little, or *vice versa.* In the case of an exchange or transfer of an article from one person to another, the Cost relates to the party who makes the transfer, the burden of the production falling on him, and the Value to the party to whom the transfer is made, the article going to his benefit. It is the same if the object exchanged is labor directly. It follows, therefore, that to say that "a thing should bring what it is worth," which is the same as to say that *its price should be measured by its value,* is quite the opposite of affirming that it should bring *as much as it cost the producer to produce it.* Hence, both rules cannot be true, for they conflict with and destroy each other. But we have already seen that it is exactly equitable that Cost be adopted as the universal limit of price—in other words, that as much burden shall be assumed by each party to the exchange as is imposed upon the opposite party. Consequently the accepted axiom of trade that "a thing should bring what it is worth" proves, when tested by simply balancing the scales of Equity, to be not only erroneous, but, so to speak, the antipodes of the true principle. . . .

The principal among the higher results growing directly out of the operations of the Cost Principle may be generalized under the heads of: 1. Attractive Industry. 2. Cooperation instead of Antagonism. . . . The main features of Attractive Industry are . . . that each individual have, at all times, the choice of his own pursuits, with the opportunity to vary them *ad libitum*. This last, the opportunity to vary one's industry, results from the fact that all avenues are equally open to all by the extinction of speculation, and the adoption of cost as the limit of price, whereby it becomes the interest of all that each should perfect himself in various occupations, thereby discovering those at which he can be most effective, and avoiding the liability to be employed at those for which he has no attraction or capacity. . . .

In the next place, as these two properties—namely, a marked attraction and eminent ability for a particular kind of labor—accompany each other, it follows that the best talent is procured at the lowest instead of the highest price. . . . In other words, contrary to what is now the case, the man or woman who can do the *most work* of any given kind *in a given time* and *do it best*, will work at the *cheapest rate*, so that, both on account of *the more and better work* and of the *less price*, he or she will have the advantage in bidding for his or her favorite occupation, *competition* intervening to bring down the average of price to the lowest point for every article, *but with none but beneficial results to anyone*, as will be presently more distinctly shown. . . . The point to be shown now is, that under the operation of the COST PRINCIPLE, excellence of performance—the point competed for, whether by individuals or machinery—enures equally to the benefit of all, and hence that competition, rightly directed, and working under the true law of price, is cooperative and not antagonistic. . . .

Suppose, then, that in such a village A is an extraordinary adept with the axe. He can chop three cords of wood a day. C and D are the next in facility at this labor to A, and can chop two cords and a half a day. Now, under the operation of this principle, as showed previously, if they are employed at all in chopping, they will all be paid at the same rate per hour. If there *is* any difference, it will *probably* be that A, along with this superior ability, will have an extraordinary fondness for the kind of labor as compared with other kinds, or, what is the same thing, he will have less repugnance for it, and that he will, if thoroughly imbued with the principle, place his labor at a less price than the established average price for wood-chopping. The consequence will be that the services of A will be first called into requisition for all the wood-chopping in the village, so long as there is not more than he can or is willing to do. It will only be when the quantity of labor is greater than he can or will perform that the services of C and D will be required. . . . The point now, to be illustrated, is that it is the whole village that is benefited by the superior excellence of A, and then of B and C, etc., in this business and not those individuals alone. While A can chop all the wood for the village, the price of wood-chopping is less . . . than when the inferior grades of talent have to be brought in; because he does more work in the hour, and is paid no more in any event, and perhaps less for it. Consequently, again, the cost, and hence the price of cooking, and hence again of board, is all less to every consumer. So of heating rooms. So of the blacksmith's work, the shoemaker's work, and, in fine, of every article of consumption produced in the village; because the manufacturers of all these articles, while engaged in the manufacture, consume wood, which wood has to be chopped, and the cost of which enters into the cost of their products; and inasmuch as these products are again sold at cost, it follows that the price of every article manufactured and consumed is reduced by the superior excellence of A as a wood-chopper. In this general advantage, A is merely a common participant with the other inhabitants; but then, in turn, the same principle is operating to place each of those others in that occupation in which he excels, and their excellence in each of these occupations, respectively, is operating in the same manner to reduce the price of every other article which A, as well as others, has to purchase. Hence it follows that the very competition which crowds a man out of one occupation and fills it with another, on account of his superior performance, turns just as much to the benefit of the man who is put out of his place, as it does to that of the man who is installed in it. . . . Hence it follows that under the operation of the COST PRINCIPLE competition is rendered cooperative. . . .

Let us look a little more specifically into this operation of the principle, as relates to the rent of lands and houses. . . . The rent of lands is *nothing*, provided they are maintained in as good a condition, in all respects, as that in which they were when received by him who hires them. If the owner maintains them in that condition, manuring them, fencing them, etc., then the rent is the equivalent of the cost of doing so. If the hirer puts the lands in a better condition than they were in when he received them, the price is due from the owner and renter of the lands to him, inverting the present order of payment, and is measured by the cost of such augmentation of value. So, if the owner sells the lands, it will be remembered that the price is the cost of the successive augmentations of value upon the soil since the land was in its natural state, and which still remain with it. Hence it follows that not only is all speculation in land extinguished, but along with it all temptation to monopolize the soil. . . .

As relates to the hiring of houses and structures of all sorts, the operation of the principle is the same. The rent is a mere equivalent of cost to the wear and tear of the premises. If the tenant keeps them in thorough repair, so that there is no depreciation of value, the rent is zero. If, on the other hand, the deterioration is suffered to go on, the annual amount of that deterioration, as averaged upon the term which the property may last, is the annual rent. . . . It follows that the more permanent the structure the less the rent, so that buildings capable of defying the inroads of time—stone structures and the like, for example—will command no rent at all. . . . Hence, again, the tendency of this operation of the principle is to force the capitalist to build indestructible edifices, and, finally, to house the whole population free of rent. Is that consummation to be deplored? . . .

THE COST PRINCIPLE AND THE WAGE-SYSTEM

We come, finally, to the consideration of the much-abused "Wages System." . . . It is not all men who are made for designers, contrivers and directors. That is perhaps one of the most exact generalizations of mankind into classes by which they are divided into Originators, Organizers and Executors. . . . *Naturally* each is content with the performance of his own function, according to his organization. The few only will desire to lead; the mass of mankind will prefer to follow, so soon as an equality of rewards renders it alike honorable either to follow or to lead.

It is, then, a natural relation that one man should employ another to aid him in actualizing his design; that he who has a design to execute should adjoin to himself the labor of him who has none, or no other one than that of securing the means of his own subsistence in circumstances of personal comfort. For that purpose—the execution of the design—they two enter into a combination, while *in interest* they are still individual and distinct,—the interest of one being in his design, and that of the other in the wages he is to earn. But every combined movement demands an individual lead. . . . Hence, it is proper and right that one man should hire another, and, if he hires him, it is proper and right that he should remunerate him for his labor, and such remuneration is *wages*. Hence, it follows that the "Wages System" is essentially proper and right. It is right that one man employ another, it is right that he pay him wages and it is right that he direct him absolutely, arbitrarily, if you will, in the performance of his labor. . . . It is not in any, nor in all of these features combined, that the wrong of our present system is to be sought for and found. *It is in the simple failure to do Equity.* It is not that men are employed and paid, but that they are *not* paid *justly*, and that no measure of Justice or Equity *has ever heretofore been known among men.*

When all avenues are alike open to you and me, there is no hardship in the fact that I, having no genius for great enterprises, or preferring to avoid the responsible charge of them, choose freely to labor under your direction for the execution of your designs. It is a great hardship, however, if I am first forced into that position by a system of labor and wealth which leaves me no election, and then robbed, by the operation of the same system, of one half or two thirds of my earnings, for your benefit. In the large establishment, such as we are now contemplating, conducted on the Cost Principle, the proprietor will realize no more in the form of pecuniary results from the undertaking than the humblest laborer employed by him, unless he works harder, *and not so much if he does not work so hard*—taking into account all the elements of labor or repugnance, both physical and mental. . . .

In conclusion, it will strike the judicious reader that the Cost Principle . . . marks the line with precision between what is right and what is wrong in the present system, and between what is right and what is wrong in all the proposed systems of Social Reform . . . that it combines, in fine, the simplicity of fundamental truth in its primary statement with that minuteness of application to the most ramified details which entitle it to the appellation of a Universal Principle.

The excerpts that follow have been taken from Kropotkin's pamphlets, and they develop and defend the view outlined by Senex in selection 3 above. For Kropotkin, the justification for this view is primarily an empirical task, to be carried out by close and comprehensive observation of such facts as might be gathered by a biologist or anthropologist. Human culture manifests an evolving pattern and direction, which it is the function of the anarchist philosopher to record, much as celestial motions and patterns are recorded by the astronomer. And when this is accomplished, so Kropotkin maintains, it will be clear that anarchist communism is the conclusion toward which all the data of biology, anthropology, and history are directed. (For an extensive elaboration of this thesis, his major scientific work, *Mutual Aid: A Factor in Evolution*, should be consulted.) During his life Kropotkin was almost as renowned for his scientific achievements as for his anarchist activities: he wrote over eighty articles for the eleventh edition of the Encyclopædia Britannica.

In Kropotkin's view, the phrase "scientific anarchism" is a redundancy. In the pamphlet "Anarchism: Its Philosophy and Its Ideal," he argued that anarchism is in harmony with, and the moral expression of, a theoretical principle which has come to be essential for all the sciences, be they physical, biological, or social. That is, no longer are individual phenomena and their relations explained as the regulated outcome of vast centralizing forces or universal laws. On the contrary, the model for scientific explanation which now prevails is a thoroughly *decentralized* one. Consider astronomy, for example:

> After having fixed all their attention on the sun and the large planets, astronomers are beginning to study now the infinitely small ones that people the universe. . . . It is to these infinitely tiny bodies that astronomers today look for an explanation of our solar system, the movements which animate its parts, and the harmony of their whole. Yet another step, and soon universal gravitation itself will be but the result of all the disordered and incoherent movements of these infinitely small bodies—of oscillations of atoms that manifest themselves in all possible directions. Thus the center, the origin of force, formerly transferred from the earth to the sun, now turns out to be scattered and disseminated.

Or for that matter, biology:

> And when a physiologist speaks now of the life of a plant or of
> an animal, he sees an agglomeration, a colony of millions of sep-
> arate individuals rather than a personality, one and indivisible.
> . . . More than that: in each micro-scopic cell, the physiologist
> discovers today a world of autonomous organisms, each of
> which lives its own life, looks for well-being for itself and attains
> it by grouping and associating with others. In short, each indi-
> vidual is a cosmos of cells, each cell is a cosmos of infinitely
> small ones. . . . A whole revolution is thus produced in the
> philosophy of life.

Kropotkin's emphatic insistence on scientific observation aligns
him with such later anarchist thinkers as Paul Goodman, Sir Herbert
Read, and Alex Comfort, who draw heavily on the findings of *Gestalt*
psychology and psychoanalysis. And it serves to distinguish his position not so much from individualist anarchism, as from those libertarians like Godwin and Ballou who relied on *a priori* conceptions of
what is desirable or what is just in human affairs. For Kropotkin's
ultimate appeal, as a scientific anarchist, is not to what ought to be,
but to what is or what is steadily evolving.

Last, it should not be missed that Kropotkin stands the common
notion of Darwin's theory of evolution on its head, transforming the
"survival of the fittest" doctrine into a contention which supports the
feasibility of anarchism. "We can prove," he avowed, ". . . how in
the animal world and human world the law of mutual aid with the
courage and initiative which follow from it secures victory to the
species most capable of practicing it."

ANARCHIST COMMUNISM: ITS BASIS AND ITS PRINCIPLES

Anarchism, the no-government system of socialism, has a
double origin. It is an outgrowth of the two great movements
of thought in the economic and the political fields which
characterize the nineteenth century, and especially its second
part. In common with all socialists, the anarchists hold that
the private ownership of land, capital, and machinery has
had its time; that it is condemned to disappear; and that all
requisites for production must, and will, become the common
property of society, and be managed in common by the pro-

Revolutionary Pamphlets, Peter Kropotkin, edited by Roger Baldwin
(New York: Vanguard Press, 1927), pp. 46–67, 93–113, 137–41.
Subheads provided in part by the editors.

ducers of wealth. And in common with the most advanced representatives of political radicalism, they maintain that the ideal of the political organization of society is a condition of things where the functions of government are reduced to a minimum, and the individual recovers his full liberty of initiative and action for satisfying, by means of free groups and federations—freely constituted—all the infinitely varied needs of the human being. . . .

As to the method followed by the anarchist thinker, it entirely differs from that followed by the utopists. The anarchist thinker does not resort to metaphysical conceptions (like "natural rights," the "duties of the State," and so on) to establish what are, in his opinion, the best conditions for realizing the greatest happiness of humanity. He follows, on the contrary, the course traced by the modern philosophy of evolution. . . . [H]e merely considers society as an aggregation of organisms trying to find out the best ways of combining the wants of the individual with those of cooperation for the welfare of the species. He studies society and tries to discover its *tendencies*, past and present, its growing needs, intellectual and economic, and in his ideal he merely points out in which direction evolution goes. He distinguishes between the real wants and tendencies of human aggregations and the accidents (want of knowledge, migrations, wars, conquests) which have prevented these tendencies from being satisfied. And he concludes that the two most prominent, although often unconscious, tendencies throughout our history have been: first, a tendency towards integrating labor for the production of all riches in common, so as finally to render it impossible to discriminate the part of the common production due to the separate individual; and second, a tendency towards the fullest freedom of the individual in the prosecution of all aims, beneficial both for himself and for society at large. The ideal of the anarchist is thus a mere summing-up of what he considers to be the next phase of evolution. It is no longer a matter of faith; it is a matter of scientific discussion. . . .

Anarchists recognize the justice of both the just-mentioned tendencies towards economic and political freedom, and see in them two different manifestations of the very same need of equality which constitutes the very essence of all struggles mentioned by history. Therefore, in common with all socialists, the anarchist says to the political reformer: "No substantial reform in the sense of political equality and no limitation of the powers of government can be made as long as society is divided into two hostile camps, and the laborer remains, economically speaking, a slave to his employer." But to the state socialist we say also: "You cannot modify the existing conditions of property without deeply modifying at the same time the political organization. You must limit the powers of government and renounce parliamentary rule. To each new economic phase of life corresponds a new political phase. Absolute monarchy corresponded to the system of serfdom. Representative government corresponds to capital-rule. Both, however, are class-rule. But in a society where the distinction between capitalist and laborer has disappeared, there is no need of such a government; it would be an anachronism, a nuisance. Free workers would require a free organization, and this cannot have any other basis than free agreement and free cooperation, without sacrificing the autonomy of the individual to the all-pervading interference of the State. The no-capitalist system implies the no-government system."

Meaning thus the emancipation of man from the oppressive powers of capitalism and government as well, the system of anarchism becomes a synthesis of the two powerful currents of thought which characterize our century.

In arriving at these conclusions anarchism proves to be in accordance with the conclusions arrived at by the philosophy of evolution. By bringing to light the plasticity of organization, the philosophy of evolution has shown the admirable adaptability of organisms to their conditions of life, and the ensuing development of such faculties as render more complete both the adaptations of the aggregates to their surroundings and those of each of the constituent parts of the aggregate to the needs of free cooperation. . . . [I]t has enforced thus the opinion already expressed by social moralists as to the perfectibility of human nature. It has shown us that, in the long run of the struggle for existence, "the fittest" will prove to be those who combine intellectual knowledge with the knowledge necessary for the production of wealth, and not those who are now the richest because they, or their ancestors, have been momentarily the strongest.

By showing that the "struggle for existence" must be conceived not merely in its restricted sense of a struggle between individuals for the means of subsistence but in its wider sense of adaptation of all individuals of the species to the best conditions for the survival of the species, as well as for the greatest possible sum of life and happiness for each and all, it has permitted us to deduce the laws of moral science from the social needs and habits of mankind. It has shown us the infinitesimal part played by positive law in moral evolution, and the immense part played by the natural growth of altruistic feelings, which develop as soon as the conditions of life favor their growth. It has thus enforced the opinion of social reformers as to the necessity of modifying the conditions of life for improving man, instead of trying to improve human nature by moral teachings while life works in an opposite direction. Finally, by studying human society from the biological point of view, it has come to the conclusions arrived by anarchists from the study of history and present tendencies as to further progress being in the line of socialization of wealth and integrated labor combined with the fullest possible freedom of the individual. . . .

The means of production and of satisfaction of all needs of society, having been created by the common efforts of all, must be at the disposal of all. The private appropriation of requisites for production is neither just nor beneficial. . . . The present wage-system has grown up from the appropriation of the necessaries for production by the few; it was a necessary condition for the growth of the present capitalist production; and it cannot outlive it, even if an attempt be made to pay to the worker the full value of his produce, and hours-of-labor-checks be substituted for money. Common possession of the necessaries for production implies the common enjoyment of the fruits of the common production; and we consider that an equitable organization of society can only arise when every wage-system is abandoned, and when everybody, contributing for the common well-being to the full extent of his capacities, shall enjoy also from the common stock of society to the fullest possible extent of his needs.

We maintain, moreover, not only that communism is a desirable state of society, but that the growing tendency of modern society is precisely towards communism—free communism. . . . Museums, free libraries, and free public schools; parks and pleasure grounds; paved and lighted streets, free for everybody's use; water supplied to private dwellings, with a growing tendency towards disregarding the exact amount of it used by the individual; . . . all these are tokens showing in what direction further progress is to be expected.

It is in the direction of putting the wants of the individual *above* the valuation of the services he has rendered, or might render, to society; in considering society as a whole, so intimately connected together that a service rendered to any individual is a service rendered to the whole society. The librarian of the British Museum does not ask the reader what have been his previous services to society, he simply gives him the books he requires; and for a uniform fee, a scientific society leaves its gardens and museums at the free disposal of each member. The crew of a lifeboat do not ask whether the men of a distressed ship are entitled to be rescued at a risk of life; and the Prisoners' Aid Society does not inquire what a released prisoner is worth. Here are men in need of a service; they are *fellow* men, and no further rights are required. . . .

By taking for our watchword anarchy in its sense of no-government, we intend to express a pronounced tendency of human society. . . . We already foresee a state of society where the liberty of the individual will be limited by no laws, no bond—by nothing else but his own social habits and the necessity, which everyone feels, of finding cooperation, support, sympathy among his neighbors. . . . One of the noblest achievements of our century is undoubtedly the Lifeboat Association. Since its first humble start, it has saved no less than thirty-two thousand human lives. It makes appeal to the noblest instincts of man; its activity is entirely dependent upon devotion to the common cause, while its internal organization is entirely based upon the independence of the local committees. The Hospitals Association and hundreds of like organizations, operating on a large scale and covering each a wide field, may also be mentioned under this head. . . . At the same time, hundreds of societies are constituted every day for the satisfaction of some of the infinitely varied needs of civilized man. We have societies for . . . gymnastics, for shorthand-writing, for the study of a separate author, for games and all kinds of sports, for forwarding the science of maintaining life, and for favoring the art of destroying it; philosophical and industrial, artistic and anti-artistic; for serious work and for mere amusement—in short, there is not a single direction in which men exercise their faculties without combining together for the accomplishment of some common aim. Every day new societies are formed, while every year the old ones aggregate together into larger units, federate across the national frontiers, and cooperate in some common work.

The most striking feature of these numberless free growths is that they continually encroach on what was formerly the domain of the State or the Municipality. A householder in a Swiss village on the banks of Lake Leman belongs now to at least a dozen different societies which supply him with what is considered elsewhere as a function of the municipal government. Free federation of independent communes for temporary or permanent purposes lies at the very bottom of Swiss life, and to these federations many a part of Switzerland is indebted for its roads and fountains, its rich vineyards, well-kept forests, and meadows which the foreigner admires. . . .

These facts—so numerous and so customary that we pass by without even noticing them—are in our opinion one of the most prominent features of the second half of the nineteenth century. The just-mentioned organisms grew up so naturally, they so rapidly extended and so easily aggregated together, they are such unavoidable outgrowths of the multiplication of needs of the civilized man, and they so well replace State-interference, that we must recognize in them a growing factor of our life. Modern progress is really towards the free aggregation of free individuals so as to supplant government in all those functions which formerly were entrusted to it, and which it mostly performed so badly.

ON HUMAN NATURE AND THE ALLEGED NECESSITY
OF THE STATE

Anarchism, when it works to destroy authority in all its aspects, when it demands the abrogation of laws and the abolition of the mechanism that serves to impose them, when it refuses all hierarchical organization and preaches free agreement, at the same time strives to maintain and enlarge the precious kernel of social customs without which no human or animal society can exist. Only instead of demanding that those social customs should be maintained through the authority of a few, it demands it from the continued action of all.

Communist customs and institutions are of absolute necessity for society, not only to solve economic difficulties, but also to maintain and develop social customs that bring men in contact with one another. They must be looked to for establishing such relations between men that the interest of each should be the interest of all; and this alone can unite men instead of dividing them. . . .

In fact, all that was an element of progress in the past or an instrument of moral and intellectual improvement of the human race is due *to the practice of mutual aid*, to the customs that recognized the equality of men and brought them to ally, to unite, to associate for the purpose of producing and consuming, to unite for purposes of defense, to federate and to recognize no other judges in fighting out their differences than the arbitrators they took from their own midst.

Each time these institutions, issued from popular genius, when it had reconquered its liberty for a moment,—each time these institutions developed in a new direction, the moral level of society, its material well-being, its liberty, its intellectual progress, and the affirmation of individual originality made a step in advance. And, on the contrary, each time that in the course of history, whether following upon a foreign conquest, or whether by developing authoritarian prejudices, men become more and more divided into governors and governed, exploiters and exploited, the moral level fell, the well-being of the masses decreased in order to insure riches to a few, and the spirit of the age declined.

History teaches us this, and from this lesson we have learned to have confidence in free communist institutions to raise the moral level of societies, debased by the practice of authority.

Today we live side by side without knowing one another. We come together at meetings on an election day: we listen to the lying or fanciful professions of faith of a candidate, and we return home. The State has the care of all questions of public interest; the State alone has the function of seeing that we do not harm the interests of our neighbor, and, if it fails in this, of punishing us in order to repair the evil.

Our neighbor may die of hunger or murder his children,—it is no business of ours; it is the business of the policeman. You hardly know one another, nothing unites you, everything tends to alienate you from one another, and finding no better way, you ask the Almighty (formerly it was a God, now it is the State) to do all that lies within his power to stop antisocial passions from reaching their highest climax.

In a communist society such estrangement, such confidence in an outside force, could not exist. Communist organizations cannot be left to be constructed by legislative bodies called parliaments, municipal or communal councils. It must be the work of all, a natural growth, a product of the constructive genius of the great mass. Communism cannot be imposed from above; it could not live even for a few months if the constant and daily cooperation of all did not uphold it. It must be free.

It cannot exist without creating a continual contact between all for the thousands and thousands of common transactions; it cannot exist without creating local life, independent in the smallest unities—the block of houses, the street, the district, the commune. . . .

. . . [T]hese remarks contain our answer to those who affirm that communism and anarchism cannot go together. They are, you see, a necessary complement to one another. The most powerful development of individuality, of individual originality—as one of our comrades has so well said,—can only be produced when the first needs of food and shelter are satisfied; when the struggle for existence against the forces of nature has been simplified; when man's time is no longer taken up entirely by the meaner side of daily subsistence,—then only, his intelligence, his artistic taste, his inventive spirit, his genius, can develop freely and ever strive to greater achievements.

Communism is the best basis for individual development and freedom; not that individualism which drives man to the war of each against all—this is the only one known up till now,—but that which represents the full expansion of man's faculties, the superior development of what is original in him, the greatest fruitfulness of intelligence, feeling and will.

Such being our ideal, what does it matter to us that it cannot be realized at once!

MORALITY AND ANARCHISM

The idea of good and evil exists within humanity itself. Man, whatever degree of intellectual development he may have attained, . . . considers as good that which is useful to the society wherein he lives, and as evil that which is hurtful to it.

But whence comes this conception, often so vague that it can scarcely be distinguished from a feeling? There are millions and millions of human beings who have never reflected about the human race. They know for the most part only the clan or family, rarely the nation, still more rarely mankind. How can it be that they should consider what is useful for the human race as good, or even attain a feeling of solidarity with their clan, in spite of all their narrow, selfish interests?

This fact has greatly occupied thinkers at all times, and it continues to occupy them still. . . . But let us remark in passing that though the explanations of the fact may vary, the fact itself remains none the less incontestable. And should our explanation not be the true one, or should it be incomplete, the fact with its consequences to humanity will still remain. . . .

In a fine work, *The Theory of Moral Sentiment,* . . . Adam Smith has laid his finger on the true origin of the moral sentiment. He does not seek it in mystic religious feelings; he finds it simply in the feeling of sympathy.

You see a man beat a child. You know that the beaten child suffers. Your imagination causes you yourself to suffer the pain inflicted upon the child; or perhaps its tears, its little suffering face tell you. And if you are not a coward, you rush at the brute who is beating it and rescue it from him.

This example by itself explains almost all the moral sentiments. The more powerful your imagination, the better you can picture to yourself what any being feels when it is made to suffer, and the more intense and delicate will your moral sense be. The more you are drawn to put yourself in the place of the other person, the more you feel the pain inflicted upon him, the insult offered him, the injustice of which he is a victim, the more will you be urged to act so that you may prevent the pain, insult, or injustice. And the more you are accustomed by circumstances, by those surrounding you, or by the intensity of your own thought and your own imagination, to *act* as your thought and imagination urge, the more will the moral sentiment grow in you, the more will it become habitual. . . . Adam Smith's only mistake was not to have understood that this same feeling of sympathy in its habitual stage exists among animals as well as among men.

The feeling of solidarity is the leading characteristic of all animals living in society. The eagle devours the sparrow, the wolf devours the marmot. But the eagles and the wolves respectively aid each other in hunting, the sparrow and the marmot unite among themselves against the beasts and birds of prey so effectually that only the very clumsy ones are caught. In all animal societies solidarity is a natural law of far greater importance than that struggle for existence, the virtue of which is sung by the ruling classes in every strain that may best serve to stultify us.

When we study the animal world and try to explain to ourselves that struggle for existence maintained by each living being against adverse circumstances and against its enemies, we realize that the more the principles of solidarity and equality are developed in an animal society and have become habitual to it, the more chance has it of surviving and coming triumphantly out of the struggle against hardships and foes. The more thoroughly each member of the society feels his solidarity with each other member of the society, the more completely are developed in all of them those two qualities which are the main factors of all progress: courage on the one hand, and on the other, free individual initiative. And on the contrary, the more any animal society or little group of animals loses this feeling of solidarity—which may chance as the result of exceptional scarcity or else of exceptional plenty—the more do the two other factors of progress, courage and individual initiative, diminish. . . . We can prove with a wealth of examples how in the animal and human worlds the law of mutual aid is the law of progress, and how mutual aid with the courage and individual initiative which follow from it secures victory to the species most capable of practising it.

Now let us imagine this feeling of solidarity acting during the millions of ages which have succeeded one another since the first beginnings of animal life appeared upon the globe. Let us imagine how this feeling little by little became a habit, and was transmitted by heredity from the simplest microscopic organism to its descendants—insects, birds, reptiles, mammals, man—and we shall comprehend the origin of the moral sentiment, which is a necessity to the animal, like food or the organ for digesting it. . . .

Thus by an unprejudiced observation of the animal kingdom, we reach the conclusion that wherever society exists at all, this principle may be found: *Treat others as you would like them to treat you under similar circumstances.*

And when we study closely the evolution of the animal world, we discover that the aforesaid principle, translated by the one word *Solidarity*, has played an infinitely larger part in the development of the animal kingdom than all the adaptations that have resulted from a struggle between individuals to acquire personal advantages. . . . This is the reason why practical solidarity never ceases; not even during the worst periods of history. Even when temporary circumstances of domination, servitude, exploitation cause the principle to be disowned, it still lives deep in the thoughts of the many, ready to bring about a strong recoil against evil institutions, a revolution. If it were otherwise society would perish. . . .

It is the whole evolution of the animal kingdom speaking in us. . . . Even if we wished to get rid of it we could not. It would be easier for a man to accustom himself to walk on all fours than to get rid of the moral sentiment. It is anterior in animal evolution to the upright posture of man.

The moral sense is a natural faculty in us like the sense of smell or of touch. . . .

Besides this principle of treating others as one wishes to be treated oneself, what is it but the very same principle as equality, the fundamental principle of anarchism? . . . We do not wish to be ruled. And by this very fact, do we not declare that we ourselves wish to rule nobody? . . . We do not wish to have the fruits of our labor stolen from us. And by that very fact, do we not declare that we respect the fruits of others' labor? . . .

Equality in mutual relations with the solidarity arising from it, this is the most powerful weapon of the animal world in the struggle for existence. . . .

By proclaiming ourselves anarchists, we proclaim before-hand that we disavow any way of treating others in which we should not like them to treat us; that we will no longer tolerate the inequality that has allowed some among us to use their strength, their cunning or their ability after a fashion in which it would annoy us to have such qualities used against ourselves. Equality in all things, the synonym of equity, this is anarchism in very deed. It is not only against the abstract trinity of law, religion, and authority that we declare war. By becoming anarchists we declare war against all this wave of deceit, cunning, exploitation, depravity, vice—in a word, in-equality—which they have poured into all our hearts. We declare war against their way of acting, against their way of thinking. The governed, the deceived, the exploited, the prostitute, wound above all else our sense of equality. It is in the name of equality that we are determined to have no more prostituted, exploited, deceived and governed men and women. . . .

It must have been obvious that in all we have hitherto said, we have not attempted to enjoin anything. We have simply set forth the manner in which things happen in the animal world and amongst mankind.

Formerly, the church threatened men with hell to moralize them, and she succeeded in demoralizing them instead. The judge threatens with imprisonment, flogging, the gallows, in the name of those social principles he has filched from society. . . . But we are not afraid to forego judges and their sentences. We forego sanctions of all kinds, even obligations to morality. We are not afraid to say: "Do what you will; act as you will"; because we are persuaded that the great majority of mankind, in proportion to their degree of enlightenment and the completeness with which they free themselves from existing fetters, will behave and act always in a direction useful to society just as we are persuaded beforehand that a child will one day walk on its two feet and not on all fours, simply because it is born of parents belonging to the genus *homo*.

All we can do is give advice. And again while giving it we add: "This advice will be valueless if your own experience and observation do not lead you to recognize that it is worth following." . . .

In our daily life we do already give free scope to our feelings of sympathy or antipathy; we are doing so every moment. We all love moral strength, we all despise moral weakness and cowardice. . . . This alone is enough to keep the conception of good and ill at a certain level and to communicate it one to another. It will be still more efficient when there is no longer judge or priest in society, when moral principles have lost their obligatory character and are considered merely as relations between equals. . . .

The principle of equality sums up the teachings of moralists. But it also contains something more. This something more is respect for the individual. By proclaiming our morality of equality, or anarchism, we refuse to assume a right which moralists have always taken upon themselves to claim, that of mutilating the individual in the name of some ideal. We do not recognize this right at all, for ourselves or anyone else.

We recognize the full and complete liberty of the individual; we desire for him plenitude of existence, the free development of all his faculties. We wish to impose nothing upon him; thus returning to the principle which Fourier placed in opposition to religious morality when he said: "Leave men absolutely free. Do not mutilate them as religions have done enough and to spare. Do not fear even their passions. In a free society these are not dangerous."

Provided that you yourself do not abdicate your freedom; provided that you yourself do not allow others to enslave you; and provided that to the violent and antisocial passions of this or that person you oppose your equally vigorous social passions, then you have nothing to fear from liberty. . . .

And yet if societies knew only this principle of equality; if each man practised merely the equity of a trader, taking care all day long not to give others anything more than he was receiving from them, society would die of it. The very principle of equality itself would disappear from our relations. For, if it is to be maintained, something grander, more lovely, more vigorous than mere equity must perpetually find a place in life.

And this greater than justice is here.

Until now humanity has never been without large natures overflowing with tenderness, with intelligence, with good-will, and using their feeling, their intellect, their active force in the service of the human race without asking anything in return.

This fertility of mind, of feeling or of good-will takes all possible forms. . . . It is in the inventor who lives from day to day forgetting even his food, scarcely touching the bread with which perhaps some woman devoted to him feeds him like a child, while he follows out the intention he thinks destined to change the face of the world. It is in the ardent revolutionist to whom the joys of art, of science, even of family life, seem bitter, so long as they cannot be shared by all, and who works despite misery and persecution for the regeneration of the world. . . . It is in the man who is revolted at the sight of a wrong without waiting to ask what will be its result to himself, and when all backs are bent stands up to unmask the iniquity and brand the exploiter, the petty despot of a factory or great tyrant of an empire. . . .

Such men and women as these make true morality, the only morality worthy the name. All the rest is merely equality in relations. Without their courage, their devotion, humanity would remain besotted in the mire of petty calculations. It is such men and women as these who prepare the morality of the future, that which will come when our children have ceased to reckon, and have grown up to the idea that the best use for all energy, courage and love is to expend it where the need of such a force is most strongly felt. . . . The moral sentiment of duty which each man has felt in his life . . . the unconsciously anarchist Guyau says, "is nothing but a superabundance of life, which demands to be exercised, to give itself; at the same time, it is the consciousness of a power." . . .

Power to act is duty to act. And all this moral "obligation" of which so much has been said or written is reduced to the conception: the condition of the maintenance of life is its expansion.

"The plant cannot prevent itself from flowering. Sometimes to flower means to die. Never mind, the sap mounts all the same," concludes the young anarchist philosopher.

It is the same with the human being when he is full of force and energy. Force accumulates to him. He expands his life. He gives without calculation, otherwise he could not live. If he must die like the flower when it blooms, never mind. The sap rises, if sap there be.

Be strong. Overflow with emotional and intellectual energy, and you will spread your intelligence, your love, your energy of action broadcast among others! This is what all moral teaching comes to. . . . That which mankind admires in a truly moral man is his energy, the exuberance of life which urges him to give his intelligence, his feeling, his action, asking nothing in return. . . .

A higher morality has begun to be wrought out.

What this morality will be we have sought to formulate, taking as our basis the study of man and animal.

We have seen the kind of morality which is even now shaping itself in the ideas of the masses and of the thinkers. This morality will issue no commands. It will refuse once and for all to model individuals according to an abstract idea, as it will refuse to mutilate them by religion, law or government. It will leave to the individual man full and perfect liberty. It . . . will say to man: "If you are not conscious of strength within you, if your energies are only just sufficient to maintain a colorless, monotonous life, without strong impressions, without deep joys, but also without deep sorrows, well then, keep to the simple principles of a just equality. . . . But if you feel within you the strength of youth, if you wish to live, if you wish to enjoy a perfect, full and overflowing life—that is, know the highest pleasure which a living being can desire—be strong, be great, be vigorous in all you do.

"Sow life around you. . . . Struggle! To struggle is to live, and the fiercer the struggle the intenser the life. Then you will have lived; and a few hours of such life are worth years spent vegetating.

"Struggle so that all may live this rich, overflowing life. And be sure that in this struggle you find a joy greater than anything else can give."

This is all that the science of morality can tell you. Yours is the choice. . . .

SECTION IV

Anarchism on the Attack:
What Is Wrong with Society as It Is?

This section strives to understand the anarchist critique of established authority. We have already referred, in the first section, to the difficulties under which anarchism has labored because of popular misconceptions that it is exclusively negative. In the fifth section we shall take pains to show the variety of constructive proposals anarchism has engendered. It is clear that a lot of the work of anarchism should be spent in attacking coercive institutions. This is an obligation the anarchists themselves have chosen, for at the heart of their commitment is the concern to liberate society from the dictation of principles of authority. This concern yields two divergent manners of attack. For some anarchists, government authorizes the domination of society by bad institutions and principles while preventing the ascendance of good ones; for others, government and bad institutions are major symptoms of the corruption of society by bad principles.

The divergence should not be exaggerated. We cannot overlook the agreement of all anarchists that their conceptions of good and evil—as developed in the preceding section on philosophical foundations—oblige them to attack institutionalized authority. In this way they differ strikingly from conservative reformers whose sense of injustice is overridden by a concern to salvage institutions. They differ also from radicals who assert that something is fundamentally wrong with things as they are but argue only for the elimination of a set of institutions at fault—slavery, liquor, war, the wage system, private property. For the anarchist, institutional authority in all its forms must fall before libertarian principles: the revolution must be exhaustive. The criticisms we have selected show a rare measure of agreement among anarchists. They all maintain that government can be identified with the chief social evil. Again, there are differences on the question of what constitutes government, authority, or coercion. Government will be found a complex, subtle term. But there is a common stand of opposition to the control of persons by persons. If what all the adherents to a position agree to defines that position fairly, then a definition of anarchism can be sighted here.

A thoughtful reader may here conclude that anarchism must, after all, be defined negatively, as opposition to forms of government. To some extent the meaning of anarchism may hinge on the meaning of government. But the word "negative" need not be used in derogation, for we can look for constructive uses in a negative position. In opposing government, anarchists develop a constructive viewpoint on what it means for one man to govern another. They cannot stop with a simple sense of government and their definitions may well prove useful to someone who is undecided about the value of government. In addition, if the meaning of anarchism depends on the meaning of government, the nature of government can hardly change without a corresponding adjustment in the nature of anarchism.

The organization of this section can be clarified briefly. We have separated three lines of attack that anarchists have adopted. First, they have stressed that government is not voluntary, that it rests on force. Second, they have pointed out ways in which men may be governed by their own moral systems. Third, they have criticized government as a façade for economic exploitation. This separation is mainly for convenience in analysis: probably every anarchist adopts all three lines of attack, with variations only in the particulars of a bill of indictment. The section closes with two studies of the same general subject, criminology, which present contrasting views of government: as a source of evil and as a symptom of evil. It also suggests the capacity of anarchism to remain effectively critical as government has changed.

Anarchist strategy for attacking government might well begin with proving that government cannot rest on the consent of the governed. If it did rest on consent, the anarchist might say, it would have to be called anarchy, not government. If the tie between government and consent is severed, then specific criticisms of governmental practices cannot be dismissed lightly as accidental abuses. Each abuse must be added to the record of the tyranny of irresponsible power.

There is no shortage of evidence that could be used to separate government from consent. It is a nice fiction to pretend that the governed think in terms of consent at all, let alone to pretend that consent is actually sought. Few persons have a chance to select their nationality. There is little recourse for those who begrudge their consent to government policies. The right of government to enforce obedience or suppress revolts is seldom questioned. When governments are overthrown, even by popular revolution, it is far from clear that consent is thereby bestowed on a new government. Instead, it might be said that government relies on the apathy and disorganization of the governed, which is interrupted once in a while by governmental folly.

Such common-sense propositions provide anarchists with abundant material out of which to fashion an argument, but they have not often done so. (But see selection 17.) To those living under autocracy and monarchy the question of consent looked academic and absurd; it became important only against a background of representative government.

Lysander Spooner and other American individualists were certain that government and consent are incompatible. The selection that follows may at first seem eccentric, although it presents a clear analysis of government by consent. Lysander Spooner's route to anarchism was unusual. As a lawyer, he firmly believed in many of the bywords of the founding fathers: government should rest on the consent of the governed; the right of revolution is inalienable; no generation can bind a subsequent generation; personal enterprise is more honest and efficient than governmental enterprise; trial by jury discovers justice more accurately than centralized statute. In his early writings, including a famous treatise on the unconstitutionality of slavery, there was some tension between literal construction of the Constitution and arguments undermining the validity of constitutional law. Finally, the Civil War and Reconstruction drove him to realize that his strict principles could not be reconciled with the conduct of government. Native American principles, it might be said, led him to a consistent anarchism. Spooner's career is a reminder that the anarchist case against government does not have to be pieced together after conversion to the cause. For most of his life he was associated with no anarchist movement.

The question of treason is distinct from that of slavery; and is the same that it would have been, if free States, instead of slave States, had seceded.

On the part of the North, the war was carried on, not to liberate the slaves, but by a government that had always perverted and violated the Constitution, to keep the slaves in bondage; and was still willing to do so, if the slaveholders could be thereby induced to stay in the Union.

The principle, on which the war was waged by the North, was simply this: That men may rightfully be compelled to submit to, and support, a government that they do not want; and that resistance, on their part, makes them traitors and criminals.

No principle, that is possible to be named, can be more self-evidently false than this; or more self-evidently fatal to all political freedom. Yet it triumphed in the field, and is now assumed to be established. If it be really established, the number of slaves, instead of having been diminished by the war, has been greatly increased; for a man, thus subjected to a government that he does not want, is a slave. And there is no difference, in principle—but only in degree—between political and chattel slavery. The former, no less than the latter, denies a man's ownership of himself and the products of his labor; and asserts that other men may own him, and dispose of him and his property, for their uses, and at their pleasure.

Previous to the war, there were some grounds for saying that—in theory, at least, if not in practice—our government was a free one; that it rested on consent. But nothing of that

No Treason, by Lysander Spooner (Boston: The Author, 1867).

kind can be said now, if the principle on which the war was carried on by the North, is irrevocably established.

If that principle be *not* the principle of the Constitution, the fact should be known. If it *be* the principle of the Constitution, the Constitution itself should be at once overthrown. . . .

The North has thus virtually said to the world: It was all very well to prate of consent, so long as the objects to be accomplished were to liberate ourselves from our connexion with England, and also to coax a scattered and jealous people into a great national union; but now that those purposes have been accomplished, and the power of the North has become consolidated, it is sufficient for us—as for all governments—simply to say: *Our power is our right.* . . .

. . . Majorities, *as such*, afford no guarantees for justice. They are men of the same nature as minorities. They have the same passions for fame, power, and money, as minorities; and are liable and likely to be equally—perhaps more than equally, because more boldly—rapacious, tyrannical and unprincipled, if intrusted with power. There is no more reason, then, why a man should either sustain, or submit to, the rule of a majority, than of a minority. Majorities and minorities cannot rightfully be taken at all into account in deciding questions of justice. And all talk about them, in matters of government, is mere absurdity. Men are dunces for uniting to sustain any government, or any laws, *except those in which they are all agreed.* And nothing but force and fraud compel men to sustain any other. To say that majorities, as such, have a right to rule minorities, is equivalent to saying that minorities have, and ought to have, no rights, except such as majorities please to allow them.

. . . It is not improbable that many or most of the worst of governments—although established by force, and by a few, in the first place—come, in time, to be supported by a majority. But if they do, this majority is composed, in large part, of the most ignorant, superstitious, timid, dependent, servile, and corrupt portions of the people; of those who have been over-awed by the power, intelligence, wealth, and arrogance; of those who have been deceived by the frauds; and of those who have been corrupted by the inducements, of the few who really constitute the government. Such majorities very likely, could be found in half, perhaps in nine-tenths, of all the countries on the globe. What do they prove? Nothing but the tyranny and corruption of the very governments that have reduced so large portions of the people to their present ignorance, servility, degradation, and corruption; an ignorance, servility, degradation, and corruption that are best illustrated in the simple fact that they *do* sustain the governments that have so oppressed, degraded, and corrupted them. They do nothing towards proving that the governments themselves are legitimate; or that they ought to be sustained, or even endured, by those who understand their true character. The mere fact, therefore, that a government chances to be sustained by a majority, of itself proves nothing that is necessary to be proved, in order to know whether such government should be sustained, or not. . . .

But to say that the consent of either the strongest party, or the most numerous party, *in a nation*, is a sufficient justification for the establishment or maintenance of a government that shall control the whole nation, does not obviate the difficulty. The question still remains, how comes such a thing as "a nation" to exist? How do many millions of men, scattered over an extensive territory—each gifted by nature with individual freedom; required by the law of nature to call no man, or body of men, his masters; authorized by that law to seek his own happiness in his own way, to do what he will with himself and his property, so long as he does not trespass upon the equal liberty of others; authorized also, by that law, to defend his own rights, and redress his own wrongs; and to go to the assistance and defence of any of his fellow men who may be suffering any kind of injustice—how do many millions of such men *come to be a nation*, in the first place? How is it that each of them comes to be stripped of all his natural, God-given rights, and to be incorporated, compressed, compacted, and consolidated into a mass with other men, whom he never saw; with whom he has no contract; and towards many of whom he has no sentiments but fear, hatred, or contempt? How does he become subjected to the control of men like himself, who, by nature, had no authority over him; but who command him to do this, and forbid him to do that, as if they were his sovereigns, and he their subject; and as if their wills and their interests were the only standards of his duties and his rights; and who compel him to submission under peril of confiscation, imprisonment, and death?

Clearly all this is the work of force, or fraud or both. . . .

The question, then, returns, What is implied in a government's resting on consent?

Manifestly this one thing (to say nothing of others) is necessarily implied in the idea of a government's resting on consent, viz: *the separate, individual consent of every man who is required to contribute, either by taxation or personal service, to the support of the government.* All this, or nothing, is necessarily implied, because one man's consent is just as necessary as any other man's. If, for example, A claims that his consent is necessary to the establishment or maintenance of government, he thereby necessarily admits that B's and every other man's are equally necessary; because B's and every other man's rights are just as good as his own. On the other hand, if he denies that B's or any other particular man's consent is necessary, he thereby necessarily admits that neither his own, nor any other man's is necessary; and that government need not be founded on consent at all.

There is, therefore, no alternative but to say, either that the separate, individual consent of every man, *who is required to aid, in any way, in supporting the government,* is necessary, or that the consent of no one is necessary.

Clearly this individual consent is indispensable to the idea of treason; for if a man has never consented or agreed to support a government, he breaks no faith in refusing to support it. And if he makes war upon it, he does so as an open enemy, and not as a traitor—that is, as a betrayer, or treacherous friend.

All this, or nothing, was necessarily implied in the Declaration made in 1776. If the necessity for consent, then announced, was a sound principle in favor of three millions of men, it was an equally sound one in favor of three men, or of one man. If the principle was a sound one in behalf of men living on a separate continent, it was an equally sound one in behalf of a man living on a separate farm, or in a separate house.

Moreover, it was only as separate individuals, each acting for himself, and not as members of organized governments, that the three millions declared their consent to be necessary to their support of a government; and, at the same time, declared their dissent to the support of the British Crown. The governments then existing in the Colonies, had no constitutional power, *as governments,* to declare the separation between England and America. On the contrary, those governments, *as governments,* were organized under charters from, and acknowledged allegiance to, the British Crown. Of course the British king never made it one of the chartered or constitutional powers of those governments, *as governments*, to absolve the people from their allegiance to himself. So far, therefore, as the Colonial Legislatures acted as revolutionists, they acted only as so many individual revolutionists, and not as constitutional legislatures. And their representatives at Philadelphia, who first declared Independence, were, in the eye of the constitutional law of that day, simply a committee of Revolutionists, and in no sense constitutional authorities, or the representatives of constitutional authorities.

It was also, in the eye of the law, only as separate individuals, each acting for himself, and exercising simply his natural rights as an individual, that the people at large *assented to, and ratified the Declaration.*

It was also only as so many individuals, each acting for himself, and exercising simply his natural rights, that they revolutionized the *constitutional character* of their local governments, (so as to exclude the idea of allegiance to Great Britain); changing their forms only as and when their convenience dictated.

The whole Revolution, therefore, as a Revolution, was declared and accomplished by the people, acting separately as individuals, and exercising each his natural rights, and not by their governments in the exercise of their constitutional powers.

It was, therefore, as individuals, and only as individuals, each acting for himself alone, that they declared that their consent—that is, their individual consent, for each one could consent only for himself—was necessary to the creation or perpetuity of any government that they could rightfully be called on to support.

In the same way each declared, for himself, that his own will, pleasure, and discretion were the only authorities he had any occasion to consult, in determining whether he would any longer support the government under which he had always lived. And if this action of each individual were valid and rightful when he had so many other individuals to keep him company, it would have been, in the view of natural justice and right, equally valid and rightful, if he had taken the same step alone. He had the same natural right to take up arms alone to defend his own property against a single tax-gatherer, that he had to take up arms in company with three millions of others, to defend the property of all against an army of tax-gatherers.

Thus the whole Revolution turned upon, asserted, and, in

theory, established, the right of each and every man, at his discretion, to release himself from the support of the government under which he had lived. And this principle was asserted, not as a right peculiar to themselves, or to that time, or as applicable only to the government then existing; but as a universal right of all men, at all times, and under all circumstances. . . .

Furthermore, those who originally agreed to the Constitution, could thereby bind nobody that should come after them. They could contract for nobody but themselves. They had no more natural right or power to make political contracts, binding upon succeeding generations, than they had to make marriage or business contracts binding upon them.

Still further. Even those who actually voted for the adoption of the Constitution, did not pledge their faith *for any specific time;* since no specific time was named, in the Constitution, during which the association should continue. It was, therefore, merely an association during pleasure; even as between the original parties to it. Still less, if possible, has it been any thing more than a merely voluntary association, during pleasure, between the succeeding generations, who have never gone through, as their fathers did, with so much even as any outward formality of adopting it, or of pledging their faith to support it. Such portions of them as pleased, and as the States permitted to vote, have only done enough, by voting and paying taxes, (and unlawfully and tyrannically extorting taxes from others,) to keep the government in operation for the time being. And this, in the view of the Constitution, they have done voluntarily, and because it was for their interest, or pleasure, and not because they were under any pledge or obligation to do it. Any one man, or any number of men, have had a perfect right, at any time, to refuse his or their further support; and nobody could rightfully object to his or their withdrawal.

There is no escape from these conclusions, if we say that the adoption of the Constitution was the act of the people, as individuals, and not of the States, as States. On the other hand, if we say that the adoption was the act of the States, as States, it necessarily follows that they had the right to secede at pleasure, inasmuch as they engaged for no specific time.

The consent, therefore, that has been given, whether by individuals, or by the States, has been, at most, only a consent for the time being; not an engagement for the future. In truth, in the case of individuals, their actual voting is not to be taken as proof of consent, *even for the time being.* On the contrary, it is to be considered that, without his consent having ever been asked, a man finds himself environed by a government that he cannot resist; a government that forces him to pay money, render service, and forego the exercise of many of his natural rights, under peril of weighty punishments. He sees, too, that other men practise this tyranny over him by the use of the ballot. He sees further that, if he will but use the ballot himself, he has some chance of relieving himself from this tyranny of others, by subjecting them to his own. In short, he finds himself, without his consent, so situated that, if he use the ballot, he may become a master; if he does not use it, he must become a slave. And he has no other alternative than these two. In self-defence, he attempts the former. His case is analogous to that of a man who has been forced into battle, where he must either kill others, or be killed himself. Because, to save his own life in battle, a man attempts to take the lives of his opponents, it is not to be inferred that the battle is one of his own choosing. Neither in contests with the ballot—which is a mere substitute for a bullet—because, as his only chance of self-preservation, a man uses a ballot, is it to be inferred that the contest is one into which he voluntarily entered; that he voluntarily set up all his own natural rights, as a stake against those of others, to be lost or won by the mere power of numbers. On the contrary, it is to be considered that, in an exigency, into which he had been forced by others, and in which no other means of self-defence offered, he, as a matter of necessity, used the only one that was left to him.

Doubtless the most miserable of men, under the most oppressive government in the world, if allowed the ballot, would use it, if they could see any chance of thereby ameliorating their condition. But it would not therefore be a legitimate inference that the government itself, that crushes them, was one which they had voluntarily set up, or ever consented to.

Therefore a man's voting under the Constitution of the United States, is not to be taken as evidence that he ever freely assented to the Constitution, *even for the time being.* Consequently we have no proof that any very large portion, even of the actual voters of the United States, ever really and voluntarily consented to the Constitution, *even for the time being.* Nor can we ever have such proof, until every man is left perfectly free to consent, or not, without thereby subjecting himself or his property to injury or trespass from others. . . .

One essential of a free government is that it rest wholly on voluntary support. And one certain proof that a government is not free, is that it coerces more or less persons to support it, against their will. All governments, the worst on earth, and the most tyrannical on earth, are free governments to that portion of the people who voluntarily support them. And all governments—though the best on earth in other respects—are nevertheless tyrannies to that portion of the people—whether few or many—who are compelled to support them against their will. A government is like a church, or any other institution, in these respects. There is no other criterion whatever, by which to determine whether a government is a free one, or not, than the single one of its depending, or not depending, solely on voluntary support.

No middle ground is possible on this subject. Either "taxation without consent is robbery," or it is not. If it is *not*, then any number of men, who choose, may at any time associate; call themselves a government; assume absolute authority over all weaker than themselves; plunder them at will; and kill them if they resist. If, on the other hand, "taxation without consent *is* robbery," it necessarily follows that every man who has not consented to be taxed, has the same natural right to defend his property against a tax-gatherer, that he has to defend it against a highwayman.

Benjamin R. Tucker begins where Spooner left off. If government
does not rest on consent, he reasoned, then it must rest on force.
And if force cannot be checked by the withdrawal of individual consent, then it becomes a Frankenstein, an uncontrollable machine.
Much as Spooner believed in consent, Tucker believed in the social
contract and found it compatible only with anarchism.

We already have paid tribute to Tucker's rigor and lucidity, but
this essay shows him in some difficulty. First, it is questionable
whether the distinction between invasion and defense is anywhere
near as simple as Tucker maintains. The position he took in support
of the allies was tortuous, and socialists ridiculed him when he attempted to reconcile anarchist views with conscription. Secondly,
Tucker in this essay identifies his position with both Proudhon and
Stirner. But Stirner dismissed Proudhon as just another rulebound
moralist (see selection 22), and might have leveled the same charge
against Tucker, in view of his affectionate talk about contracts and
social laws. It is possible that the two difficulties are related, in that
identification with the necessities of a group may produce an elastic
definition of defense that stretches into invasive forms of government.

Presumably the honor which you have done me in inviting
me to address you to-day upon "The Relation of the State to
the Individual" is due principally to the fact that circumstances have combined to make me somewhat conspicuous
as an exponent of the theory of Modern Anarchism,—a theory which is coming to be more and more regarded as one of
the few that are tenable as a basis of political and social life.
In its name, then, I shall speak to you in discussing this question, which either underlies or closely touches almost every
practical problem that confronts this generation. The future
of the tariff, of taxation, of finance, of property, of woman, of

Instead of a Book, by Benjamin R. Tucker (New York: Benjamin
R. Tucker, 1893), pp. 21–29.

marriage, of the family, of the suffrage, of education, of invention, of literature, of science, of the arts, of personal habits, of private character, of ethics, of religion, will be determined by the conclusion at which mankind shall arrive as to whether and how far the individual owes allegiance to the State.

Anarchism, in dealing with this subject, has found it necessary, first of all, to define its terms. Popular conceptions of the terminology of politics are incompatible with the rigorous exactness required in scientific investigation. . . . Take the term "State," for instance, with which we are especially concerned to-day. It is a word that is on every lip. But how many of those who use it have any idea of what they mean by it? And, of the few who have, how various are their conceptions! We designate by the term "State" institutions that embody absolutism in its extreme form and institutions that temper it with more or less liberality. We apply the word alike to institutions that do nothing but aggress and to institutions that, besides aggressing, to some extent protect and defend. But which is the State's essential function, aggression or defence, few seem to know or care. . . . Brought face to face with these diverse views, the Anarchists, whose mission in the world is the abolition of aggression and all the evils that result therefrom, perceived that, to be understood, they must attach some definite and avowed significance to the terms which they are obliged to employ, and especially to the words "State" and "government." Seeking, then, the elements common to all the institutions to which the name "State" has been applied, they have found them two in number: first, aggression; second, the assumption of sole authority over a given area and all within it, exercised generally for the double purpose of more complete oppression of its subjects and extension of its boundaries. That this second element is common to all States, I think, will not be denied,—at least, I am not aware that any State has ever tolerated a rival State within its borders; and it seems plain that any State which should do so would thereby cease to be a State and to be considered as such by any. The exercise of authority over the same area by two States is a contradiction. That the first element, aggression, has been and is common to all States will probably be less generally admitted. Nevertheless, I shall not attempt to reenforce here the conclusion of Spencer, which is gaining wider acceptance daily,—that the State had its origin in aggression, and has continued as an aggressive institution from its birth. Defence was an afterthought, prompted by necessity; and its introduction as a State function, though effected doubtless with a view to the strengthening of the State, was really and in principle the initiation of the State's destruction. Its growth in importance is but an evidence of the tendency of progress toward the abolition of the State. Taking this view of the matter, the Anarchists contend that defence is not an essential of the State, but that aggression is. Now what is aggression? Aggression is simply another name for government. Aggression, invasion, government, are interconvertible terms. The essence of government is control, or the attempt to control. He who attempts to control another is a governor, an aggressor, an invader; and the nature of such invasion is not changed, whether it is made by one man upon another man, after the manner of the ordinary criminal, or by one man upon all other men, after the manner of an absolute monarch, or by all other men upon one man, after the manner of a modern democracy. On the other hand, he who resists another's attempt to control is not an aggressor, an invader, a governor, but simply a defender, a protector; and the nature of such resistance is not changed whether it be offered by one man to another man, as when one repels a criminal's onslaught, or by one man to all other men, as when one declines to obey an oppressive law, or by all other men to one man, as when a subject people rises against a despot, or as when the members of a community voluntarily unite to restrain a criminal. This distinction between invasion and resistance, between government and defence, is vital. Without it there can be no valid philosophy of politics. Upon this distinction and the other considerations just outlined, the Anarchists frame the desired definitions. This, then, is the Anarchistic definition of government: the subjection of the non-invasive individual to an external will. And this is the Anarchistic definition of the State: the embodiment of the principle of invasion in an individual, or a band of individuals, assuming to act as representatives or masters of the entire people within a given area. As to the meaning of the remaining term in the subject under discussion, the word "individual," I think there is little difficulty. Putting aside the subtleties in which certain metaphysicians have indulged, one may use this word without danger of being misunderstood. Whether the definitions thus arrived at prove generally acceptable or not is a matter of minor consequence. I submit that they are reached scientifically, and serve the purpose of a clear conveyance of thought. The Anarchists, having by their adoption taken due care to be explicit, are entitled to have their ideas judged in the light of these definitions.

Now comes the question proper: What relations should exist between the State and the individual? The general method of determining these is to apply some theory of ethics involving a basis of moral obligation. In this method the Anarchists have no confidence. The idea of moral obligation, of inherent rights and duties, they totally discard. They look upon all obligations, not as moral, but as social, and even then not really as obligations except as these have been consciously and voluntarily assumed. If a man makes an agreement with men, the latter may combine to hold him to his agreement; but, in the absence of such agreement, no man, so far as the Anarchists are aware, has made any agreement with God or with any other power of any order whatsoever. The Anarchists are not only utilitarians, but egoists in the farthest and fullest sense. So far as inherent right is concerned, might is its only measure. . . . Those who desire a greater familiarity with this particular phase of the subject should read a profound German work, *"Der Einzige und sein Eigenthum,"* written years ago by a comparatively unknown author, Dr. Caspar Schmidt, whose *nom de plume* was Max Stirner. Read only by a few scholars, the book is buried in obscurity, but is destined to a resurrection that perhaps will mark an epoch.

If this, then, were a question of right, it would be, according to the Anarchists, purely a question of strength. But, fortunately, it is not a question of right: it is a question of expediency, of knowledge, of science,—the science of living together, the science of society. The history of humanity has been largely one long and gradual discovery of the fact that the individual is the gainer by society exactly in proportion as society is free, and of the law that the condition of a permanent and harmonious society is the greatest amount of individual liberty compatible with equality of liberty. The average man of each new generation has said to himself more clearly and consciously than his predecessor: "My neighbor is not my enemy, but my friend, and I am his, if we would but mutually recognize the fact. We help each other to a better, fuller, happier living; and this service might be greatly increased if we would cease to restrict, hamper, and oppress each other. Why can we not agree to let each live his own life, neither of us transgressing the limit that separates our individualities?" It is by this reasoning that mankind is approaching the real social contract, which is not, as Rousseau thought, the origin of society, but rather the outcome of a long social experience, the fruit of its follies and disasters. It is obvious that this contract, this social law, developed to its perfection, excludes all aggression, all violation of equality of liberty, all invasion of every kind. Considering this contract in connection with the Anarchistic definition of the State as the embodiment of the principle of invasion, we see that the State is antagonistic to society; and, society being essential to individual life and development, the conclusion leaps to the eyes that the relation of the State to the individual and of the individual to the State must be one of hostility, enduring till the State shall perish.

"But," it will be asked of the Anarchists at this point in the argument, "what shall be done with those individuals who undoubtedly will persist in violating the social law by invading their neighbors?" The Anarchists answer that the abolition of the State will leave in existence a defensive association, resting no longer on a compulsory but on a voluntary basis, which will restrain invaders by any means that may prove necessary. "But that is what we have now," is the rejoinder. "You really want, then, only a change of name?" Not so fast, please. Can it be soberly pretended for a moment that the State, even as it exists here in America, is purely a defensive institution? Surely not, save by those who see of the State only its most palpable manifestation,—the policeman on the street-corner. And one would not have to watch him very closely to see the error of this claim. Why, the very first act of the State, the compulsory assessment and collection of taxes, is itself an aggression, a violation of equal liberty, and, as such, vitiates every subsequent act, even those acts which would be purely defensive if paid for out of a treasury filled by voluntary contributions. How is it possible to sanction, under the law of equal liberty, the confiscation of a man's earnings to pay for protection which he has not sought and does not desire? And if this is an outrage, what name shall we give to such confiscation when the victim is given, instead of bread, a stone, instead of protection, oppression? To force a man to pay for the violation of his own liberty is indeed an addition of insult to injury. But that is exactly what the State is doing. Read the "Congressional Record"; follow the proceedings of the State legislatures; examine our statute-books; test each act separately by the law of equal liberty,—you will find that a good nine-tenths of existing legislation serves, not to enforce that fundamental social law, but either to prescribe the individual's personal habits, or, worse still, to create and sustain commercial, industrial, financial, and proprietary monopolies which deprive labor of a large part of the reward that it would receive in a perfectly free market. "To be governed," says Proudhon, "is to be watched, inspected, spied, directed, law-ridden, regulated, penned up, indoctrinated, preached at, checked, appraised, sized, censured, commanded, by beings who have neither title nor knowledge nor virtue. To be governed is to have every operation, every transaction, every movement noted, registered, counted, rated, stamped, measured, numbered, assessed, licensed, refused, authorized, indorsed, admonished, prevented, reformed, redressed, corrected. To be governed is, under pretext of public utility and in the name of the general interest, to be laid under contribution, drilled, fleeced, exploited, monopolized, extorted from, exhausted, hoaxed, robbed; then, upon the slightest resistance, at the first word of complaint, to be repressed, fined, vilified, annoyed, hunted down, pulled about, beaten, disarmed, bound, imprisoned, shot, mitrailleused, judged, condemned, banished, sacrificed, sold, betrayed, and, to crown all, ridiculed, derided, outraged, dishonored." And I am sure I do not need to point out to you the existing laws that correspond to and justify nearly every count in Proudhon's long indictment. How thoughtless, then, to assert that the existing political order is of a purely defensive character instead of the aggressive State which the Anarchists aim to abolish!

This leads to another consideration that bears powerfully upon the problem of the invasive individual, who is such a bugbear to the opponents of Anarchism. Is it not such treatment as has just been described that is largely responsible for his existence? I have heard or read somewhere of an inscription written for a certain charitable institution:

"This hospital a pious person built,
But first he made the poor wherewith to fill't."

And so, it seems to me, it is with our prisons. They are filled with criminals which our virtuous State has made what they are by its iniquitous laws, its grinding monopolies, and the horrible social conditions that result from them. We enact many laws that manufacture criminals, and then a few that punish them. Is it too much to expect that the new social conditions which must follow the abolition of all interference with the production and distribution of wealth will in the end so change the habits and propensities of men that our jails and prisons, our policemen and our soldiers,—in a word, our whole machinery and outfit of defence,—will be superfluous? That, at least, is the Anarchists' belief. . . .

A half-hour is a very short time in which to discuss the relation of the State to the individual, and I must ask your pardon for the brevity of my dealing with a succession of considerations each of which needs an entire essay for its development. If I have outlined the argument intelligibly, I have accomplished all that I expected. But, in the hope of impressing the idea of the true social contract more vividly upon your minds, in conclusion I shall take the liberty of reading another page from Proudhon, to whom I am indebted for most of what I know, or think I know, upon this subject. Contrasting authority with free contract, he says, in his "General Idea of the Revolution of the Nineteenth Century":—

"Of the distance that separates these two *regimes*, we may judge by the difference in their styles.

"One of the most solemn moments in the evolution of the principle of authority is that of the promulgation of the Decalogue. The voice of the angel commands the People, prostrate at the foot of Sinai:

"Thou shalt worship the Eternal, and only the Eternal.

"Thou shalt swear only by him.

"Thou shalt keep his holidays, and thou shalt pay his tithes.

"Thou shalt honor thy father and thy mother.

"Thou shalt not kill.

"Thou shalt not steal.

"Thou shalt not commit adultery.

"Thou shalt not bear false witness.

"Thou shalt not covet or calumniate.

"For the Eternal ordains it, and it is the Eternal who has made you what you are. The Eternal is alone sovereign, alone wise, alone worthy; the Eternal punishes and rewards. It is in the power of the Eternal to render you happy or unhappy at his will.

"All legislations have adopted this style; all, speaking to man, employ the sovereign formula. The Hebrew commands in the future, the Latin in the imperative, the Greek in the infinitive. The moderns do not otherwise. The tribune of the parliament-house is a Sinai as infallible and as terrible as that of Moses; whatever the law may be, from whatever lips it may come, it is sacred once it has been proclaimed by that prophetic trumpet, which with us is the majority.

"Thou shalt not assemble.

"Thou shalt not print.

"Thou shalt not read.

"Thou shalt respect thy representatives and thy officials, which the hazard of the ballot or the good pleasure of the State shall have given you.

"Thou shalt obey the laws which they in their wisdom shall have made.

"Thou shalt pay thy taxes faithfully.

"And thou shalt love the Government, thy Lord and thy God, with all thy heart and with all thy soul and with all thy mind, because the Government knows better than thou what thou art, what thou art worth, what is good for thee, and because it has the power to chastise those who disobey its commandments, as well as to reward unto the fourth generation those who make themselves agreeable to it.

"With the Revolution it is quite different.

"The search for first causes and for final causes is eliminated from economic science as from the natural sciences.

"The idea of Progress replaces, in philosophy, that of the Absolute.

"Revolution succeeds Revelation.

"Reason, assisted by Experience, discloses to man the laws of Nature and Society; then it says to him:—

"These laws are those of necessity itself. No man has made them; no man imposes them upon you. They have been gradually discovered, and I exist only to bear testimony to them.

"If you observe them, you will be just and good.

"If you violate them, you will be unjust and wicked.

"I offer you no other motive.

"Already, among your fellows, several have recognized that justice is better, for each and for all, than iniquity; and they have agreed with each other to mutually keep faith and right, —that is, to respect the rules of transaction which the nature of things indicates to them as alone capable of assuring them, in the largest measure, well-being, security, peace.

"Do you wish to adhere to their compact, to form a part of their society?

"Do you promise to respect the honor, the liberty, and the goods of your brothers?

"Do you promise never to appropriate, either by violence,

or by fraud, or by usury, or by speculation, the product or
the possession of another?

"Do you promise never to lie and deceive, either in justice,
or in business, or in any of your transactions?

"You are free to accept or to refuse.

"If you refuse, you become a part of the society of savages.
Outside of the communion of the human race, you become
an object of suspicion. Nothing protects you. At the slightest
insult, the first comer may lift his hand against you without
incurring any other accusation than that of cruelty needlessly
practised upon a brute.

"On the contrary, if you swear to the compact, you become
a part of the society of free men. All your brothers enter into
an engagement with you. Promise you fidelity, friendship,
aid, service, exchange. In case of infraction, on their part or
on yours, through negligence, passion, or malice, you are responsible to each other for the damage as well as the scandal
and the insecurity of which you have been the cause: this
responsibility may extend, according to the gravity of the
perjury or the repetitions of the offence, even to excommuni-
cation and to death.

"The law is clear, the sanction still more so. Three articles,
which make but one,—that is the whole social contract. Instead of making oath to God and his prince, the citizen
swears upon his conscience, before his brothers, and before
Humanity. Between these two oaths there is the same difference as between slavery and liberty, faith and science,
courts and justice, usury and labor, government and economy,
non-existence and being, God and man."

This chapter from Max Stirner's *The Ego and His Own* turns the tables on Protestantism, supposedly liberated from Catholicism, and humanism, supposedly liberated from Protestantism. Stirner argues that moralists deceive themselves into thinking they are free, when they have really surrendered to *idées fixes* in their heads. They are still not their own men. If the argument can be accepted, it will make those in preceding selections more convincing, for it provides original ways of identifying appearances of consent that cannot count as real as well as forms of invasion that do not parade naked force.

To some extent all anarchists will accept Stirner's arguments, discounting apparent signs of consent and stressing the subtlety of coercion. But it is an open question whether many would follow him to his extreme position. Stirner might well have rejected many of the criticisms presented in this section as dependent on moral standards which impede self-ownership.

Man, your head is haunted; you have wheels in your head! You imagine great things, and depict to yourself a whole world of gods that has an existence for you, a spirit-realm to which you suppose yourself to be called, an ideal that beckons to you. You have a fixed idea!

Do not think that I am jesting or speaking figuratively when I regard those persons who cling to the Higher, and (because the vast majority belongs under this head) almost the whole world of men, as veritable fools, fools in a madhouse. What is it, then, that is called a "fixed idea"? An idea that has subjected the man to itself. When you recognize, with regard to such a fixed idea, that it is a folly, you shut its slave up in an asylum. And is the truth of the faith, say, which we are not to doubt; the majesty of the people, which we are not to strike at (he who does is guilty of—lese-majesty); virtue, against which the censor is not to let a word pass, that moral-

The Ego and His Own, by Max Stirner, translated by Steven T. Byington (New York: Libertarian Book Club, 1963), pp. 43–58.

ity may be kept pure;—are these not "fixed ideas"? Is not all the stupid chatter of most of our newspapers the babble of fools who suffer from the fixed idea of morality, legality, Christianity, and so forth, and only seem to go about free because the madhouse in which they walk takes in so broad a space? Touch the fixed idea of such a fool, and you will at once have to guard your back against the lunatic's stealthy malice. For these great lunatics are like the little so-called lunatics in this point too—that they assail by stealth him who touches their fixed idea. They first steal his weapon, steal free speech from him, and then they fall upon him with their nails. Every day now lays bare the cowardice and vindictiveness of these maniacs, and the stupid populace hurrahs for their crazy measures. One must read the journals of this period, and must hear the Philistines talk, to get the horrible conviction that one is shut up in a house with fools. "Thou shalt not call thy brother a fool; if thou dost—etc." But I do not fear the curse, and I say, my brothers are arch-fools. Whether a poor fool of the insane asylum is possessed by the fancy that he is God the Father, Emperor of Japan, the Holy Spirit, or whatnot, or whether a citizen in comfortable circumstances conceives that it is his mission to be a good Christian, a faithful Protestant, a loyal citizen, a virtuous man—both these are one and the same "fixed idea." He who has never tried and dared not to be a good Christian, a faithful Protestant, a virtuous man, and the like, is *possessed* and prepossessed by faith, virtuousness, etc. Just as the schoolmen philosophized only *inside* the belief of the church; as Pope Benedict XIV wrote fat books *inside* the papist superstition, without ever throwing a doubt upon this belief; as authors fill whole folios on the State without calling in question the fixed idea of the State itself; as our newspapers are crammed with politics because they are conjured into the fancy that man was created to be a *zoon politicon*—so also subjects vegetate in subjection, virtuous people in virtue, liberals in humanity, without ever putting to these fixed ideas of theirs the searching knife of criticism. Undislodgeable, like a madman's delusion, those thoughts stand on a firm footing, and he who doubts them—lays hands on the *sacred!* Yes, the "fixed idea," that is the truly sacred! . . .

Take notice how a "moral man" behaves, who today often thinks he is through with God and throws off Christianity as a bygone thing. If you ask him whether he has ever doubted that the copulation of brother and sister is incest, that monogamy is the truth of marriage, that filial piety is a sacred duty, then a moral shudder will come over him at the conception of one's being allowed to touch his sister as wife also. And whence this shudder? Because he *believes* in those moral commandments. This moral *faith* is deeply rooted in his breast. Much as he rages against the *pious* Christians, he himself has nevertheless as thoroughly remained a Christian —to wit, a *moral* Christian. In the form of morality Christianity holds him a prisoner, and a prisoner under *faith*. Monogamy is to be something sacred, and he who may live in bigamy is punished as a *criminal*; he who commits incest suffers as a *criminal*. Those who are always crying that religion is not to be regarded in the State, and the Jew is to be a citizen equally with the Christian, show themselves in accord with this. Is not this of incest and monogamy a *dogma of faith*? Touch it, and you will learn by experience how this moral man is a *hero of faith* too, not less than Krummacher, not less than Philip II. These fight for the faith of the Church, he for the faith of the State, or the moral laws of the State; for articles of faith, both condemn him who acts otherwise than *their faith* will allow. The brand of "crime" is stamped upon him, and he may languish in reformatories, in jails. Moral faith is as fanatical as religious faith! . . .

Piety has for a century received so many blows, and had to hear its superhuman essence reviled as an "inhuman" one so often, that one cannot feel tempted to draw the sword against it again. And yet it has almost always been only moral opponents that have appeared in the arena, to assail the supreme essence in favor of—another supreme essence. So Proudhon, unabashed, says: "Man is destined to live without religion, but the moral law is eternal and absolute. Who would dare to-day to attack morality?" Moral people skimmed off the best fat from religion, ate it themselves, and are now having a tough job to get rid of the resulting scrofula. If, therefore, we point out that religion has not by any means been hurt in its inmost part so long as people reproach it only with its superhuman essence, and that it takes its final appeal to the "spirit" alone (for God is spirit), then we have sufficiently indicated its final accord with morality, and can leave its stubborn conflict with the latter lying behind us. It is a question of a supreme essence with both, and whether this is a superhuman or a human one can make (since it is in any case an essence over me, a super-mine one, so to speak) but little difference to me. In the end the relation to the human essence, or to "Man," as soon as ever it has shed the snakeskin of the old religion, will yet wear a religious snakeskin again.

So Feuerbach instructs us that, "if one only *inverts* speculative philosophy, always makes the predicate the subject, and so makes the subject the object and principle, one has the undraped truth, pure and clean." Herewith, to be sure, we lost the narrow religious standpoint, lost the *God*, who from this standpoint is subject; but we take in exchange for it the other side of the religious standpoint, the *moral* standpoint. Thus we no longer say "God is love," but "Love is divine." If we further put in place of the predicate "divine" the equivalent "sacred," then, as far as concerns the sense, all the old comes back again. According to this, love is to be the *good* in man, his divineness, that which does him honor, his true *humanity* (it "makes him Man for the first time," makes for the first time a man out of him). So then it would be more accurately worded thus: Love is what is *human* in man, and what is inhuman is the loveless egoist. But precisely all that which Christianity and with it speculative philosophy (i.e., theology) offers as the good, the absolute, is to self-ownership simply not the good (or, what means the same, it is *only the good*). Consequently, by the transformation of the predicate into the subject, the Christian *essence* (and it is the predicate that contains the essence, you know) would only be fixed yet more oppressively. God and the divine would entwine themselves all the more inextricably with me. To expel God from his heaven and to rob him of his *"transcendence"* cannot yet support a claim of complete victory, if therein he is only chased into the human breast and gifted with indelible *immanence*. Now they say, "The divine is the truly human!"

The same people who oppose Christianity as the basis of the State, who oppose the so-called Christian State, do not tire of repeating that morality is "the fundamental pillar of social life and of the State." As if the dominion of morality were not a complete dominion of the sacred, a "hierarchy."

So we may here mention by the way that rationalist movement which, after theologians had long insisted that only faith was capable of grasping religious truths, that only to believers did God reveal himself, and that therefore only the heart, the feelings, the believing fancy was religious, broke out with the assertion that the "natural understanding," human reason, was also capable of discerning God. What does that mean but that the reason laid claim to be the same visionary as the fancy? . . . It had to come to this—that the *whole* man with all his faculties was found to be *religious*; heart and affections, understanding and reason, feeling, knowledge, and will—in short, everything in man—appeared religious. Hegel has shown that even philosophy is religious. And what is not called religion to-day? The "religion of love," the "religion of freedom," "political religion"—in short, every enthusiasm. So it is, too, in fact.

To this day we use the Romance word "religion," which expresses the concept of a condition of being *bound*. To be sure, *we* remain bound, so far as religion takes possession of our inward parts; but is the mind also bound? On the contrary, that is free, is sole lord, is not our mind, but absolute. Therefore the correct affirmative translation of the word religion would be "*freedom of mind*"! In whomsoever the mind is free, he is religious in just the same way as he in whom the senses have free course is called a sensual man. The mind binds the former, the desires the latter. Religion, therefore, is boundness or *religio* with reference to me—I am bound; it is freedom with reference to the mind—the mind is free, or has freedom of mind. Many know from experience how hard it is on *us* when the desires run away with us, free and unbridled; but that the free mind, splendid intellectuality, enthusiasm for intellectual interests, or however this jewel may in the most various phrase be named, brings us into yet more grievous straits than even the wildest impropriety, people will not perceive; nor can they perceive it without being consciously egoists. . . .

Morality could not come into opposition with piety till after the time when in general the boisterous hate of everything that looked like an "order" (decrees, commandments, etc.) spoke out in revolt, and the personal "absolute lord" was scoffed at and persecuted; consequently it could arrive at independence only through liberalism, whose first form acquired significance in the world's history as "citizenship," and weakened the specifically religious powers. . . . For, when morality not merely goes alongside of piety, but stands on feet of its own, then its principle lies no longer in the divine commandments, but in the law of reason, from which the commandments, so far as they are still to remain valid, must first await justification for their validity. In the law of reason man determines himself out of himself, for "Man" is rational, and out of the "essence of Man" those laws follow of necessity. Piety and morality part company in this—that the former makes God the lawgiver, the latter Man. . . .

Why do certain *opposition parties* fail to flourish? Solely for the reason that they refuse to forsake the path of morality or legality. Hence the measureless hypocrisy of devotion, love, etc., from whose repulsiveness one may daily get the most thorough nausea at this rotten and hypocritical relation of a "lawful opposition."—In the *moral* relation of love and fidelity a divided or opposed will cannot have place; the beautiful relation is disturbed if the one wills this and the other the reverse. But now, according to the practice hitherto and the old prejudice of the opposition, the moral relation is to be preserved above all. What is then left to the opposition? Perhaps the will to have a liberty, if the beloved one sees fit to deny it? Not a bit! It may not *will* to have the freedom, it can only *wish* for it, "petition" for it, lisp a "Please, please!" What would come of it, if the opposition really *willed*, willed with the full energy of the will? No, it must renounce *will* in order to live to *love*, renounce liberty—for love of morality. It may never "claim as a right" what it is permitted only to "beg as a favor." Love, devotion, etc., demand with undeviating definiteness that there be only one will to which the others devote themselves, which they serve, follow, love. Whether this will is regarded as reasonable or as unreasonable, in both cases one acts morally when one follows it, and immorally when one breaks away from it. The will that commands the censorship seems to many unreasonable; but he who in a land of censorship evades the censoring of his book acts immorally, and he who submits it to the censorship acts morally. If some one let his moral judgment go, and set up a secret press, one would have to call him immoral, and imprudent in the bargain if he let himself be caught; but will such a man lay claim to a value in the eyes of the "moral"? Perhaps!—That is, if he fancied he was serving a "higher morality."

The web of the hypocrisy of to-day hangs on the frontiers of two domains, between which our time swings back and forth, attaching its fine threads of deception and self-deception. No longer vigorous enough to serve *morality* without doubt or weakening, not yet reckless enough to live wholly to egoism, it trembles now toward the one and now toward the other in the spider-web of hypocrisy, and, crippled by the curse of *halfness*, catches only miserable, stupid flies. If one has once dared to make a "free" motion, immediately one waters it again with assurances of love, and—*shams resignation*; if, on the other side, they have had the face to reject the free motion with *moral* appeals to confidence, immediately the moral courage also sinks, and they assure one how they hear the free words with special pleasure; they—*sham approval*. In short, people would like to have the one, but not go without the other; they would like to have a *free* will, but not for their lives lack the *moral will*. . . .

A Nero is a "bad" man only in the eyes of the "good"; in mine he is nothing but a *possessed* man, as are the good too. The good see in him an arch-villain, and relegate him to hell. Why did nothing hinder him in his arbitrary course? Why did people put up with so much? Do you suppose the tame Romans, who let all their will be bound by such a tyrant, were a hair the better? In old Rome they would have put him to death instantly, would never have been his slaves. But the contemporary "good" among the Romans opposed to him only moral demands, not their *will*; they sighed that their emperor did not do homage to morality, like them; they themselves remained "moral subjects," till at last one found courage to give up "moral, obedient subjection." And then the same "good Romans" who, as "obedient subjects," had borne all the ignominy of having no will, hurrahed over the nefarious, immoral act of the rebel. Where then in the "good" was the courage for the *revolution*, that courage which they now praised, after another had mustered it up? The good could not have this courage, for a revolution, and an insurrection into the bargain, is always something "immoral," which one can resolve upon only when one ceases to be "good" and becomes either "bad" or—neither of the two. Nero was no viler than his time, in which one could only be one of the two, good or bad. . . .

"But surely one cannot put a rascal and an honest man on the same level!" Now, no human being does that oftener than you judges of morals; yes, still more than that, you imprison as a criminal an honest man who speaks openly against the existing constitution, against the hallowed institutions, and you entrust portfolios and still more important things to a crafty rascal. So *in praxi* you have nothing to reproach me with. "But in theory!" Now there I do put both on the same level, as two opposite poles—to wit, both on the level of the moral law. Both have meaning only in the "moral world, just as in the pre-Christian time a Jew who kept the law and one who broke it had meaning and significance only in respect to the Jewish law; before Jesus Christ, on the contrary, the Pharisee was no more than the "sinner and publican." So before self-ownership the moral Pharisee amounts to as much as the immoral sinner.

Nero became very inconvenient by his possessedness. But a self-owning man would not sillily oppose to him the "sacred," and whine if the tyrant does not regard the sacred; he would oppose to him his will. How often the sacredness of the inalienable rights of man has been held up to their foes, and some liberty or other shown and demonstrated to be a "sacred right of man!" Those who do that deserve to be laughed out of court—as they actually are—were it not that in truth they do, even though unconsciously, take the road that leads to the goal. They have a presentiment that, if only the majority is once won for that liberty, it will also will the liberty, and will then take what it *will* have. The sacredness of the liberty, and all possible proofs of this sacredness, will never procure it; lamenting and petitioning only shows beggars. . . .

What now follows from this for the judgment of the moral man? This: that he throws the egoist into the only class of men that he knows besides moral men, into that of the— immoral. He cannot do otherwise; he must find the egoist immoral in everything in which the egoist disregards morality. If he did not find him so, then he would already have become an apostate from morality without confessing it to himself, he would already no longer be a truly moral man. One should not let himself be led astray by such phenomena, which at the present day are certainly no longer to be classed as rare, but should reflect that he who yields any point of morality can as little be counted among the truly moral as Lessing was a pious Christian when, in the well-known parable, he compared the Christian religion, as well as the Mohammedan and Jewish, to a "counterfeit ring." Often people are already further than they venture to confess to themselves. For Socrates, because in culture he stood on the level of morality, it would have been an immorality if he had been willing to follow Crito's seductive incitement and escape from the dungeon; to remain was the only moral thing. But it was solely because Socrates was—a moral man. The "unprincipled, sacrilegious" men of the Revolution, on the contrary, had sworn fidelity to Louis XVI, and decreed his deposition, yes, his death; but the act was an immoral one, at which moral persons will be horrified to all eternity.

Yet all this applies, more or less, only to "civic morality," on which the freer look down with contempt. For it (like civism, its native ground, in general) is still too little removed and free from the religious heaven not to transplant the latter's laws without criticism or further consideration to its domain instead of producing independent doctrines of its own. Morality cuts a quite different figure when it arrives at the consciousness of its dignity, and raises its principle, the essence of man, or "Man," to be the only regulative power. Those who have worked their way through to such a decided consciousness break entirely with religion, whose God no longer finds any place alongside their "Man," and, as they . . . themselves scuttle the ship of State, so too they crumble away that "morality" which flourishes only in the State, and logically have no right to use even its name any further. For what this "critical" party calls morality is very positively distinguished from the so-called "civic or political morality," and must appear to the citizen like an "insensate and unbridled liberty." But at bottom it has only the advantage of the "purity of the principle," which, freed from its defilement with the religious, has now reached universal power in its clarified definiteness as "humanity."

Therefore one should not wonder that the name "morality" is retained along with others, like freedom, benevolence, self-consciousness, and is only garnished now and then with the addition, a "free" morality—just as, though the civic State is abused, yet the State is to arise again as a "free State," or, if not even so, yet as a "free society."

Because this morality completed into humanity has fully settled its accounts with the religion out of which it historically came forth, nothing hinders it from becoming a religion on its own account. For a distinction prevails between religion and morality only so long as our dealings with the world of men are regulated and hallowed by our relation to a superhuman being, or so long as our doing is a doing "for God's sake." If, on the other hand, it comes to the point that "man is to man the supreme being," then that distinction vanishes, and morality, being removed from its subordinate position, is completed into—religion. For then the higher being who had hitherto been subordinated to the highest, Man, has ascended to absolute height, and we are related to him as one is related to the highest being, religiously. Morality and piety are now as synonymous as in the beginning of Christianity, and it is only because the supreme being has come to be a different one that a holy walk is no longer called a "holy" one, but a "human" one. If morality has conquered, then a complete —*change of masters* has taken place.

Tucker's decision to identify his views with those of Stirner caused a schism in individualist anarchism in America. John Beverley Robinson was one of the Stirnerites who stayed on Tucker's side. Like Tucker, he was also a follower of Proudhon. In 1916 Robinson published *The Economics of Liberty*, from which this selection is taken, as an explanation of Proudhon's economic system. The book summarized the critique of economic control that individualist anarchists had been making in America for half a century. (The split over egoism was doubly unfortunate in view of the broad areas on which both sides agreed.) The selection makes it easy to understand why many anarchists had backgrounds in the movements for a single tax on land values, free trade, expansion of credit, and trust-busting. Indeed, one might say that Proudhon put in rational order for the anarchists almost all the ideas of economic protest of the Gilded Age.

Robinson started by using complicated graphs to develop a definition of "privilege" that resembles Marx's notion of "surplus value." (In selection 8 Tucker traced both anarchist and socialist theories back to Adam Smith and the labor theory of value.) "Conceive that in the typical community," Robinson stated, "a certain number of the members, ceasing themselves to produce, were empowered to take from each of the remaining members a portion of his product." Such is "the operation of privilege in general—abstract privilege—the power of one to command the services of another without compensation." This operation prevents "the free action of industry and the substantial equality of fortunes." Supposing a community of 100 persons of whom 10 ceased to produce and yet were privileged to take 20 per cent of the product, Robinson tried to show how privilege expands: "This will leave 90 producers, and the total product will be 90. Of this, by the hypothesis, the non-producers are to receive 20 per cent, which is 18; the rest, 72, remaining for the producers. Thus, although the total product has been reduced only 10 per cent, the share of the producers has been cut down 28 per cent." Each of the privileged class now receives "a portion in excess of that received by any of the producers." With this excess, the privileged are able "to support a certain additional number of the producers as personal servitors," and thus the circle of the privileged expands, since these servitors "become at once a part of the privileged class by virtue of their new allegiance." They may be judges, legislators, priests, soldiers, policemen. Robinson then worked out a more elaborate model to show the combined operation of expanding privilege and increasing productivity. While for a time increased productivity may mask the deprivations of privilege, the expanding nature of privilege will eventually prove catastrophic unless some other countervailing force interferes. Although "the producers now enjoy many comforts and luxuries which formerly they could not obtain," still "when it is argued that they should therefore demand nothing more this demonstration confounds the conclusion." Great prosperity, Robinson was arguing in 1916, may immediately precede universal crisis.

So much for privilege in the abstract. Robinson then, in the pages which we reprint, examined specific institutions of privilege. In each case he seeks out the economic consequences of the ability of one man to command another.

LAND OWNERSHIP

In a commercial society there are two general divisions of activity, production and exchange.

Corresponding to these there are two forms of privilege by which all industry is controlled; land ownership, which controls production, and the money privilege, which controls exchange. Our business now is with the first of these, namely, the privilege of land ownership.

The word land, in its economic sense, is used in a far wider significance than in its usual colloquial meaning. Land, in the economic sense, means all natural opportunities for labor to exert itself. . . .

Rent is the part of the product taken by the land owners from the producers for permitting the producers to go to work. . . .

The land owner gives nothing whatever, but permission to you to live and work on his land. He does not give his product in exchange for yours. He did not produce the land. He obtained a title at law to it; that is, a privilege to keep everybody off his land until they paid him his price. He is well called the lord of the land—the landlord!

The Economics of Liberty, by John Beverley Robinson (Minneapolis: Herman Kuehn, 1916), pp. 67–103.

Even if the merchant has bought his warehouse outright, so that he pays no rent directly, he still pays rent indirectly, through the purchase price paid to the previous owner.

Directly or indirectly everybody must pay rent to the owners of the soil. Either in the form of annual or monthly payments, or in the form of a price paid for purchase, everybody must pay for a place to live upon and a place to work upon.

But, you will say, men must be secure in the possession of the products of their labor; and how can they be secure unless they own their land?

There are two kinds of land ownership, proprietorship or property, by which the owner is absolute lord of the land, to use it or to hold it out of use, as it may please him; and possession, by which he is secure in the tenure of land which he uses and occupies, but has no claim upon it at all if he ceases to use it. He cannot hold it out of use, and prevent others from using it. For the secure possession of his crops or buildings or other products, he needs nothing but the possession of the land which he uses.

For instance, in the mining regions, vast areas of mining land are held out of use by the mining companies, which own all the land about. How long, do you think, would these terrible strikes in Colorado and Michigan and West Virginia have lasted, if the miners had been free to go to work and open up new mines on the unused land? Not an hour! Not a minute!

All that is necessary to do away with Rent is to do away with absolute property in land; to make all land that is not in use free to anybody to enter upon it and use it.

Nor will any temporizing measure short of this suffice. Great as were the services of Henry George in familiarizing people with the destructive nature of our present system of land tenure, his single tax scheme cannot be regarded as a remedy.

For the reason that, if rent must be paid, it is no particular relief to pay it to the government in the form of a tax, rather than to pay it to an individual in the form of rent.

If the coal miners of West Virginia were free to go to work and open up new mines on any unused land, it would immediately relieve the situation; but if they first had to pay a government tax, almost equal to the rental value, they would be as badly off as ever; the land would be as inaccessible as ever.

No, the only real remedy is a change of heart, through which land using will be recognized as proper and legitimate, but land holding will be regarded as robbery and piracy. . . .

Both government and law exist, as any lawyer can tell you, to protect property, that is, proprietorship in land among other forms of property. Without force, that is, government, proprietorship in land would cease; and, on the other hand, without proprietorship there would be no function for force government, and it would lapse into a more perfect form of social organization.

A free association would uphold the producer in the possession of land for use; and all efforts to restore the land to the people must include, as a necessary condition, the extinction of the governmental form of organization and the erection of free society.

THE MONEY PRIVILEGE

Sometimes, instead of purchasing a commodity out and out, people want to buy only the use of it, for a longer or shorter period. The price paid for such temporary use is commonly called hire. . . .

In precisely the same way money is often hired, and the hire paid for the use of it is called Interest.

In the past, when gold and silver were the only money, the hire of gold and silver was on the same footing as that of any other commodity. Large sums were paid for the use of money, because the available amount of gold and silver was far less than was needed to carry on the commercial transactions of the times. . . .

Modern money is an entirely different affair. Modern money is almost altogether credit money. Gold is used to a certain extent; but the great bulk of the money in use is not gold but promissory notes, called bank notes—paper money, in short. . . .

The business of a bank is to lend money; which amounts, nowadays, to lending credit. All the credit notes—the ordinary bank notes—in circulation were originally borrowed from some bank.

"You are living on borrowed money," says a man to his friend. "Not at all; this money in my pocket is my own; it is not borrowed," answers his friend. "You may not have borrowed it," is the reply, "but somebody originally borrowed it, without doubt."

And with perfect truth, for there is no way to obtain bank

notes but from a bank, and the bank does not give them away, but lends them. In this way, the charge that the bank makes for the use of its notes—the interest—is a continual and universal tax upon all the members of the community.

Not an old woman that buys a paper of pins, without yielding a part of the price to the banks as interest! . . .

. . . [T]here are various laws of the different States and of the United States, arbitrarily prohibiting the manufacture and loan of current notes by anybody but a lawfully organized bank; with penalties ranging from fine to imprisonment. By the Federal law the fine takes the form of a ten per cent tax upon the notes circulated, which acts as a complete prohibition.

Were it not for these restrictive and prohibitory laws which support the money privilege or banking monopoly, it would be easy to start competitive banks; and, with free competition, the charge for money lent would be brought down to a minimum, as in other kinds of lending business.

A livery stable keeper, for instance, must charge enough to pay for feed, care, cleaning and all incidental expenses, and for the replacement of his horses and vehicles as they wear out; and in addition his personal income or wages.

Under free conditions, the same would occur in banking.

If people were as free to establish banks and lend currency as they are now to establish livery stables and lend horses, competition among banks would reduce the rate of interest to the minimum necessary to cover expenses and to give them who were employed in the business an equitable wage. . . .

All that part of the product which is now taken by Interest would belong to the producer. Capital, however capital may be defined, would practically cease to exist as an income producing fund, for the simple reason that if money, wherewith to buy capital, could be obtained for one-half of one per cent, capital itself could command no higher price.

If the laws restricting the issue of currency were done away with, such a state of affairs would easily be brought about by voluntary associations.

Banks could and would be established, not, as now, by a handful of stockholders for their own profit, but by associations of business men for their convenience and advantage. These men would pledge their assets to support the credit of the bank, and would accept the current notes of the bank in exchange for their own notes, paying only the trifling percentage required to defray the cost of carrying on the bank.

Anybody outside the association could obtain a loan by pledging his possessions to the amount of the loan, plus an allowance for deterioration, according to the nature of the commodity pledged, plus an allowance for risk.

The notes of the bank would be redeemable, not in gold, but in any valuable commodity. Gold would no longer be the basis of the circulating paper currency; but all commodities would be available as a basis, that is, as security.

Thus, financial crises would be impossible.

At present, financial crises occur, chiefly because the paper currency is redeemable in gold only. There is never enough gold to redeem all the currency in circulation. Accordingly, when the supply of gold runs short, the security behind the notes is diminished, the loaning of notes is restricted or suspended, and the panic follows.

Paper currency has hitherto been regarded with suspicion, as insecure. Whenever any measures are proposed looking toward the relief of the people by increasing the volume of the present governmentally controlled currency, the newspapers enlarge upon the dangers of an inflated paper currency.

And with justice, as long as the redemption of the currency is possible with only a single commodity—gold.

But it is only under this condition that a paper currency is insecure. When not only gold but all commodities are available for the redemption of the paper currency, its volume is limited only by the value of all the wealth of the country, and it can never become insecure up to this limit. . . .

Just which commodity shall be so used, depends chiefly upon its comparative invariability in value. Hitherto gold has been used, ostensibly upon the ground that it varied less in value than any other commodity, although really, age-long custom has had a powerful influence upon the choice of gold. . . .

What the standard will be under free conditions it is impossible to predict. Experiment and experience are needed to decide the matter. It is not impossible that more than one standard or measure may be used; a statement that seems an absurdity on the face of it; yet the desirability and feasibility of a multiple standard, even under present conditions, is warmly defended by the well-known economist, Irving Fisher.

If such a multiple standard is feasible now, it would become much more so under free conditions, when speculative fluctuations would be largely eliminated, and all values would tend toward a stable and normal relation.

All business men will realize the impetus to exchange, and indirectly to production, that such a change in the money system would give. . . .

A convulsion would undoubtedly occur, if the change were sudden and general. But with the gradual establishment of free banks, each one compelled to maintain its credit in order to do business at all, no convulsion could occur.

Gradually such free banks would associate, in order to support each other's credit, and, in the end, they would displace the present banks and inaugurate the new system, without any serious disturbance.

Nothing prevents the establishment of free banks but the governmental restrictions already recounted. There is little prospect that these restrictions will be relaxed, because in all nations, the bankers are the real power behind the government, and compel the maintenance of the restrictions that give them their devouring monopoly.

Such partial experiments as have been possible in the past, have proved abundantly successful.

The Massachusetts Land Bank, during Colonial times, prospered, and brought prosperity to the community, until it was forcibly suppressed by special act of Parliament.

The People's Bank, founded by Proudhon in the latter days of the French Revolution, flourished and grew, until it was forcibly suppressed by Bonaparte.

TAXATION

Third in our enumeration, although primary in its nature, among the methods of obtaining a portion of the products of the community, without taking part in production, the oldest and simplest is taking what is desired by force.

This, when done by the upper classes, is called taxation.

In the monarchical military organizations of the past, the character of this privilege is easily seen. The tax was levied in the name of the king or war leader, to whom the natural subservience of human nature spontaneously rendered submission.

It was the king's army, the king's people, the king's taxes; and he who questioned the propriety of the royal prerogative of taking from his people without return or accounting, was reckoned, and felt himself to be, a criminal, guilty of the highest crime of disloyalty.

Such is still the attitude of the generality. To evade the customs tax, to "swear off" the income tax, is still felt by most people to be the immoral avoidance of a just claim, even though they permit themselves to be guilty of these delinquencies.

Although the form of society has been much modified, the industrial having begun to supplant the military, the nature of taxation remains the same. It is still the taking of other people's possessions without their agreement, even if with their tacit consent; that is to say, no opportunity is offered by which the payment may be withheld, on the ground that the services offered in return are not worth the amount demanded, or are not wanted at all as would be done in ordinary mercantile transactions.

It is often said by reformers that government should be conducted upon business principles. This is impossible, because business rests upon doing its work well in return for what is freely given in payment; whereas government demands and takes its income, whether its work is well done or not, and whether it is wanted or not.

The distinction is ineffaceable.

The officials of a governmental organization, whether autocratic, constitutional or democratic, are in the position of those of a corporation of which the chief expenses are the salaries of the officials and employees, and the income is obtained by forcible levies.

It is impossible that an income so obtained should be expended as carefully and economically, and as much in the interest of those who pay it, as if it had to be obtained by offering a fair equivalent to taxpayers, and convincing them that the proposed bargain was to their advantage, leaving them free to accept or decline at their pleasure.

For this reason denunciation of governmental corruption is entirely futile, indeed, laughable to them who have once clearly comprehended the true state of affairs.

The functions fulfilled by government today are chiefly of a commercial character, yet the service given is remunerated, not by bargain and sale, but by forcible levy. It is inevitable that officials should use this force-collected income to secure their own continuance in office by conferring valuable privileges upon their supporters, who, in turn, use every effort to strengthen the government.

The fact of this co-operation is well known. Everybody knows that behind each political party stands a group of rich men, and that their influence over the votes which are to elect the officials is given in return for the continuance of the privileges by which their wealth has been created.

This power of taking money from the individual without his consent, is the fundamental privilege upon which all the others are based, and by which they are licensed. It stands upon no logical ground, but is the royal prerogative—the will of the prince—in the language of former days.

It will perhaps be thought that a tax imposed by a representative assembly loses the character of a forcible levy, and becomes practically a mercantile transaction. Brief consideration will show that this is not the case. Although the severity of taxation by an autocrat is much mitigated by constitutionalism, the principle remains the same. Taxes are no longer imposed by leasing the collection to a pacha or proconsul, and letting him plunder unchecked. Modern governments have learned the importance of keeping the goose in good health, that it may lay more golden eggs.

But the vote is useless against taxation. Whichever party wins, taxes go on, and must go on. It is not possible to vote for a representative who will oppose taxation, for it is from taxation that he gets his bread and butter.

The essence of economic exchange is the freedom of both parties to withhold consent to a bargain. Even if it could be shown that the equivalent given were fully equal to the assessment levied, it would still lack the freedom of choice of the individual to permit it to be ranked as a commercial transaction. . . .

Great as is this forced deduction from the products of the workers, the damage inflicted by taxation indirectly is still greater. First must be placed that cause by taxes upon imports. These restrict freedom of exchange in two ways; by limiting or preventing trade between the nations which impose them, and by fostering monopolies among producers.

When nations give up the last remnants of the military state of the past and become fully commercialized, these tariffs will be abolished, and production and exchange incalculably stimulated.

LIBERTY

We have seen that privilege, in its various forms, is the engine by which industry is deprived of a large part of its product; and that, in order to permit the producer to retain his whole product, it is necessary that privilege should be abolished.

When privilege is abolished, and the worker retains all that he produces, then will come the powerful trend toward equality of material reward for labor that will produce substantial financial and social equality, instead of the mere political equality that now exists.

To bring about equality, it is unnecessary to use any artificial means for the distribution of products: it is only necessary to give free play to the natural forces that govern production and exchange.

And with equality will come fraternity: no longer the rich trampling on the poor; no longer prosperity for one, only at the price of impoverishment for the other; no longer the petty social strife for precedence.

Distinction and honor will be awarded to personal merit; as, even now, we honor an Agassiz, a Darwin, a Tolstoi and a Curie—names that will survive when all the famous financiers of the day are forgotten, or pilloried with those of buccaneers and assassins.

When the fathers of the American Republic had abolished titles of nobility, with primogeniture and entail, by which the land was given to the few; when they had established the rule of the majority and representative assemblies; they thought that they had abolished privilege.

The event shows that they had not. Democracy has had its day; and has proved its total inability to abolish or even to control privilege. On the contrary, in this democratic country, privilege grows and overruns all limits, grasping everything in sight, ignoring all claims of reason and humanity, far beyond anything it has attempted under the old monarchical systems of Europe. . . .

We are urged to be "good citizens," to take part in ward primaries, to vote at elections. It is impossible. Even at the elections of private clubs, as long as all runs smoothly, hardly one in ten of the members votes. If the management is not satisfactory, resignations pour in. But from the governmental club there is no possibility of resigning: we are forced to pay our dues, whether we like it or not.

Apart from such comparatively petty practical difficulties, the fundamental theoretical difficulty remains, that government, in all its forms, is based upon privilege—the privilege of taxation—and therefore cannot abolish privilege.

Even if we grant that all reforms are accomplished, that government has successfully overthrown the land privilege and the money privilege, we shall find that, in overthrowing these, we have but fortified the governmental privilege.

No governmental system of currency reform has ever been proposed that did not involve the monopoly of money by the government itself.

No scheme of land reform, not even the single tax proposition, can be carried out, without some plan for seizing abandoned land and again renting it; which means that government would become the supreme landlord.

Privilege can never overthrow privilege.

We are compelled, therefore, to discard all governmental, that is to say, compulsory, modes of organization, in our search for some way of abolishing privilege.

Privilege, by its very nature, means restriction. A privilege to do certain things cannot be granted to one, without prohibiting or restricting others from doing the same thing. What we seek to do away with, therefore, is not privilege directly, but the restriction upon action of some, that results in privilege to others.

You cannot grant to one man the privilege of holding land out of use, without prohibiting others from using the land so held. You cannot grant to one man the privilege of offering current promissory notes, without prohibiting others from a similar act.

We are in search, then, of a system of social organization that shall prevent any one from restricting the acts of others; that shall insure to all freedom of individual action and freedom of contract with others, so that nothing shall be prohibited between individuals to which both parties consent.

24 Labor: A New Monopoly?

John Beverley Robinson conceived it possible for a countervailing force to save the economy from catastrophes threatened by expanding privilege. But it does not follow, as it might appear, that this is precisely what trade unions have done and that anarchists now should be content with the economic system. Anarchists would be more likely to say that the new unions in America are a new form of privilege, protected by the government in precisely the way Robinson described with regard to older monopolies. Robinson's general concept of privilege can be detected in the following article on American unionism, written for the New York anarchist magazine *Why?* in 1947. Privilege both deprives workers economically and conflicts with their liberty.

Although the author of this article, Frank Lanham, speaks of anarchist types of unionism, it should be noted that there is real disagreement among anarchists on this subject. To be sure, many anarchists favor syndicalism as a properly libertarian form of workers' organization and thus might agree with Lanham (see selections 4, 32, 36, 54). But any anarchist who, like Tolstoy, disapproves of the existing division of labor would have trouble understanding as anarchistic an organization that gets along with the existing industrial setup, particularly a labor movement, like the one Lanham designs, that seeks immediate economic returns. The egoist or sovereign individual, to whom the very principle of a *union* suggests invasion and loss of self-ownership, would also raise doubts about unionism.

Unionism is a ticklish subject. Union members have a natural suspicion of "honest" discussions of unionism, because they know this has often been the disguise for reactionary, NAM propaganda. But I think that such blind faith and fear of facts is worse than the danger of providing information to the enemies of the workers. The facts of unionism have to be faced.

"Two Kinds of Unionism: Some Basic Ideas," by Frank Lanham from *Why?* V:2 (April, 1947), 10–12.

At the same time I want to make it clear that anarchists are not in sympathy with those who scoff at the objectives of unionism and dismiss the whole subject with glib references to Petrillo and Lewis.

My purpose here is to try to set forth some fundamental ideas of unionism in what I believe to be anarchist terms.

The kind of unionism prevalent in America today is what might be called "official unionism." That is, the union officials run the organization, make all the major decisions and sometimes all the minor ones too. All the members do is join the union, pay dues, obey the contract and working rules, and go on or off strike as the union officials order. This is the very extreme case, but most American unions are pretty much of this pattern.

What official unionism means is that workers hire the services of union officials by paying dues and initiation fees, much as they might hire a lawyer to represent them in court.

The idea of the union as a set of officials who "represent" the workers is well established by the laws of the nation as well as by the union constitution. The worker is not supposed to take part in the business of looking after his economic interests. It is expected that he will vote in an NLRB election to accept the services of certain accredited representatives of labor unions, who will deal with his employers and look out for his economic interests. Contracts are between the union and the boss, not between the workers and the boss.

The well known effect of official-controlled unionism is that unions often do not represent the interests of their members. This is obvious in wildcat strikes, when workers have to take action in defiance of the union officials. But the clash between union members and officials exists all the time. In most cases, union officials make policies and contracts that the membership does not actually want, but to which it submits rather than resist the boss, the union and the government all at once. The most notorious instances occurred during the war, when many unions kept workers from acting against the wage-freeze.

The clash between the union members and their "representatives" is a very natural thing, but it is much misunderstood. Actually it comes down to this: By electing or accepting professional union officials, workers have created a new social and economic class. The class of union officials is a small one, but it is definitely separate from any other class. The officials are neither workers nor employers: they are simply union officials.

Their economic interests are different from those of both workers and employers. They are directly concerned with neither high wages nor high profits; in the conflict between workers and employers, they are literally neutral. Their concern is with high salaries for themselves, with high dues, with increased membership. Occasionally, in the rare case of a Lewis, they see their job as a means to political power. Usually they have the so-called bureaucratic mind—that is, they want to hang on to what they have, to maintain a moderate standard of well-to-do-ness.

Sometimes a union official retains a sentimental interest in his membership, as a hangover from the days when he worked for a living. But this is a rare thing.

When we understand the unique economic position of the union leader, we can understand the behavior of the British Labor Party, which is based on the British trade union officials. Bevin and Attlee have risen to parliamentary leadership because they control the membership of the British trade unions. But their government policies show no special concern for the workers, but rather for a "national interest," which they, as neither workers nor employers, can see more clearly than either of those groups.

How much the official type of union represents the needs and desires of the membership depends on how much is in it for the union official. The miners gain from the fact that Lewis wants economic victories to promote his prestige, while the average AF of L official wants only to keep what he has and does not go out of his way to win higher wages.

Officials are necessarily concerned with the possibility that their members will revolt. Workers may leave the union, or even join another union, if the officials never get them anything. The degree to which unions do get things for the members depends a good deal on how soon the union official can expect to have rebellion on his hands.

In other words, the unions of the official type gain for the workers only enough to keep them submissive: they do not try to get what the workers *actually* want and need.

If this were the only possible kind of unionism, the subject would hardly be worth discussing. But it is not.

. . . I anticipate objections that what I shall say is idealistic and utopian; I admit it; but I intend to show that the idea is pertinent and is necessary to understand what exists and is possible.

The anarchist idea of unionism is that the workers *are* the union. The union is not a structure, not a set of officials, not an International, but the workers themselves who have joined together to increase their economic power, to increase their ability to win economic concessions from the employers.

An anarchist union need not even be formally organized, in the sense of having a permanent organization, name, headquarters, officials, or dues. Some of these things may be useful at times, but they are not necessary in order for there to be a union. . . .

I granted that this type of organization is "impractical" and "idealistic." Why is it so? Not because it cannot function. As long as the basic unit of organization is small enough, such so-called "pure democracy" is workable. But the fact is that it does not exist in unions today. It is not developing; the reverse is the case. Why?

Because workers don't want it (if they did, they would be anarchist, and then there would be no need for anything so moderate as unions). Because the union officials and bosses and government officials don't want it.

People today lean to the delegation of responsibility—which means—let somebody else do it. Most workers would sooner hire someone else to do their thinking for them. The anarchist way means a lot of brain-work and time and responsibility.

There are always a few union men who are only too glad to accept this responsibility for the rest, and become officials, for the money and power and prestige that is in it.

The bosses like this, because they would sooner deal with someone with the economic interests of the union official than with workers who have the anti-boss interests of workers.

The government likes official unionism because the government is dominated by the bosses and because the government, too, would sooner deal with union officials than with workers.

The foregoing criticism of union structure must not be taken as condemnation of unions. Even some of the very worst unions are far better than no union at all. Even in the most official-controlled union, the officials must still consider the workers more than an open-shop employer has to. . . .

. . . Wages are raised, hours are shortened, both are standardized to end discrimination; health and safety conditions are improved; and the union usually protects the worker against arbitrary discharge. The worker has some degree of security, he has some degree of self-respect, he can talk back to the boss and not lose his job.

Unions differ, but almost all of them are an advance over non-union conditions. These differences are not confined to wage-rates; the differences are vital. . . .

But if there is this fundamental difference between non-unionism and official unionism, there is a vast difference between official unionism and workers' unionism. There is a vast difference between the unionism of the IWW, the MESA, and even the auto workers, and the unionism of the steel workers and miners and garment workers and many more.

It is the difference between a union which gets for the workers only what is necessary to keep them from rebelling, and a union which expresses the workers' needs, and is their means of getting these.

Free unionism is more than a nice idea. Freedom is good, but it is also practical: the man to whom you delegate responsibility for your affairs does not have your interests, and will promote your interests only to the extent it will promote his. You are safe only if you look out for your own interests.

Since I admitted the idealistic nature of free workers' unions, some may wonder why I am still harping on them. The reason is this: unions vary in all degrees, from the absolutely official-controlled to the worker-controlled. The closer they are to being run by their members, the better they are for the members. Thus, more and more control of a union by the workers is a useful objective. As workers gain more control, or prevent the officials from seizing more control, they enable themselves to get better conditions for themselves.

These conditions count. Economics is by no means everything, but when we consider how much of the ordinary person's life is taken up with earning a living, and how much the rest of his and his family's life is influenced by what happens on his job, then we cannot dismiss unionism and action for economic objectives as trivial. A better society cannot be our sole interest.

25 Oppression and the Rise of Welfarism

This selection complements the previous discussion of the trade unions in up-dating anarchist criticisms of government. It emphasizes regulation and its partner emphasized economic loss: these two objects of criticism were both subsumed under Robinson's general definition of privilege. The selection is from *Ethics and American Unionism*, published in 1958 by the Libertarian League. Sam Weiner, its author, has written on the American labor movement for libertarian periodicals for over thirty years.

The Great Depression of the early thirties marked the collapse of the system of "private enterprise." It also sparked the spontaneous uprising of the workers which culminated in the sit-down strikes of 1936–37. The whole system of human exploitation was threatened. The political State saved itself, and all that was essential to capitalism by doing what "private enterprise" could not do. Concessions were made to the workers, farmers and middle-class groups and the private capitalists were deprived of some of their power.

In regulating the relations between the classes, the State increased its own power and the foundations of state capitalist "welfarism" were laid. The State could not have done this alone; it had to overcome the resistance of old-line capitalism and hence needed the cooperation of a mass labor movement in order to control the restless masses. The government of Franklin Delano Roosevelt enacted "favorable" labor legislation and gave the "progressive" labor leaders a chance to fill their treasuries with the dues and assessments of the newly organized workers.

At first the labor fakers of the craft unions would not cooperate. They resisted change because they shared the economic and social ideas of private enterprise capitalism. On

Ethics and American Unionism, by Sam Weiner (New York: The Libertarian League, 1958), pp. 11–13. Reprinted by permission of the author.

the other hand, the conservative unions could not undertake
an effective program of organizing the unorganized because
of their antiquated organic structure and the jurisdictional
problems it created. A split took place and the CIO was born.

Time is a great healer and twenty years blurred the differences between the rival factions. The CIO was now firmly
established and the conservative unionists had adjusted themselves to the fact that "welfarism" was here to stay. They
must learn to live with it, and those who could not would be
eliminated. Both cliques of labor mis-leaders came to see the
advantages and the need of peaceful co-existence. There were,
after all, no fundamental differences between them. The CIO
admitted craft unions and the AFL would accept dues from
industrial unions. They were as two thieves who had long
fought over the loot and who finally worked out a settlement.
The united AFL-CIO is the result. Rival capitalists will also
form a trust when it pays them to do so. Greed and jurisdictional conflict may divide them but enlightened self-interest
draws them together. Wolves may hunt either alone or in
packs according to circumstances. The "ethics" of expediency
are flexible.

The character and function of the North American unions
have changed greatly. A State-regulated economy needs a
State-regulated labor movement. The government will help
the unions so long as the leaders can assure the smooth co-
operation of a docile labor force. The "Welfare State" has
come to assume ever greater social functions and has inter-
vened on an ever-greater scale in the control of economic and
social life. It regulates, and shows an increasing tendency to
dominate the whole field of social security, business, labor,
crop and price supports, public power, housing, etc.

This process was expanded and accelerated by World War
II, the Korean war, "defense" spending, foreign aid programs,
and the prosecution of the "cold war." The bureaucratic administrative apparatus kept pace with the expansion of governmental power. Individual liberty and local initiative have
diminished as the State domination of society has increased.
The individual has had less and less to say about his own life
and interests as the Government prescribes, to an ever greater
degree, the conditions under which he must live. This process continues inexorably, regardless of the political party in
power.

A similar development has been going on in the labor organizations. As the unions have increased in membership,

as they have converted themselves into job trusts and gone into the field of welfare, they have established a similar system within their own domain. The administrative machinery has grown in proportion. The labor bureaucracy—by itself or jointly with the employers—controls an estimated 35 *billion* dollars in welfare funds, which it uses to reinforce its positions and render the membership ever more dependent upon them.

The dictatorship of the leaders over the workers has been further increased by the vicious practice of industry-wide "collective bargaining" on a national scale, long-term contracts and the power to discipline dissidents among the members.

Just as the citizen's rights are curtailed by the growing power of the bureaucracy of the State, so the workers' rights are curtailed by the ever greater usurpation of power by the labor bureaucracy. Subjected to the triple exploitation and suppression by the employers, the State and the union bureaucracy, the worker has ever less to say about his wages and his working conditions. Instead of fighting for shorter hours and to wrest better conditions of life for himself and his family, he is forced to seek more "overtime". Or else he sends his wife out to work . . . or both.

The merger of the AFL and the CIO was an attempt to better fit the union structure to the needs of state capitalist "welfarism," which requires a maximum centralization of control over the working class. A military commander cannot tolerate jurisdictional disputes between sections of the armed forces. The army must be firmly disciplined. It must obey as a unit. A regimented labor movement is a civilian army and jurisdictional disputes cannot be tolerated.

The State drives towards complete control of society. This is inherent in its nature and especially so in such a period as the present. State capitalist "Welfarism" is exploitation streamlined. AFL-CIO unionism is business unionism streamlined. The groundwork is being prepared for a future totalitarian society in the United States and the AFL-CIO already plays the role of "labor front" in the embryonic set-up. When the process is completed, as it will be if not stopped by working class resistance on a massive scale, the unions will end up by being as impotent as are the unions in Russia. During the whole period of the struggle against Fascism and "Communism," the basic features common to both of them have been or are being adapted for our own country.

26 Law, the Supporter of Crime

This tract by Kropotkin presents a classic anarchist critique of law and authority. Kropotkin often wrote about criminals and prisons, partly because two terms in jail deeply impressed him with the injustice of the penal system and partly because anarchism must defeat the assertion that government is needed to protect the public from malefactors. It should not be overlooked that his argument does not depend on the belief in unequivocal human goodness that too many critics have attributed to anarchists, and to Kropotkin particularly.

"When ignorance reigns in society and disorder in the minds of men, laws are multiplied, legislation is expected to do everything, and each fresh law being a fresh miscalculation, men are continually led to demand from it what can proceed only from themselves, from their own education and their own morality." It is no revolutionist who says this, not even a reformer. It is the jurist, Dalloy, author of the collection of French law known as *Repertoire de la Legislation*. And yet, though these lines were written by a man who was himself a maker and admirer of law, they perfectly represent the abnormal condition of our society.

In existing States a fresh law is looked upon as a remedy for evil. Instead of themselves altering what is bad, people begin by demanding a *law* to alter it. If the road between two villages is impassable, the peasant says:—"There should be a law about parish roads." If a park-keeper takes advantage of the want of spirit in those who follow him with servile observance and insults one of them, the insulted man says, "There should be a law to enjoin more politeness upon park-keepers." If there is stagnation in agriculture or commerce, the husbandman, cattle-breeder, or corn speculator argues,

"Law and Authority," by Peter Kropotkin from *Kropotkin's Revolutionary Pamphlets*, edited by Roger Baldwin (New York: Vanguard Press, 1927), pp. 195–218.

"It is protective legislation that we require." Down to the old clothesman there is not one who does not demand a law to protect his own little trade. If the employer lowers wages or increases the hours of labor, the politician in embryo exclaims, "We must have a law to put all that to rights." In short, a law everywhere and for everything! A law about fashions, a law about mad dogs, a law about virtue, a law to put a stop to all the vices and all the evils which result from human indolence and cowardice.

We are so perverted by an education which from infancy seeks to kill in us the spirit of revolt, and to develop that of submission to authority; we are so perverted by this existence under the ferrule of a law, which regulates every event in life—our birth, our education, our development, our love, our friendship—that, if this state of things continues, we shall lose all initiative, all habit of thinking for ourselves. Our society seems no longer able to understand that it is possible to exist otherwise than under the reign of law, elaborated by a representative government and administered by a handful of rulers. And even when it has gone so far as to emancipate itself from the thralldom, its first care has been to reconstitute it immediately. "The Year I of Liberty" has never lasted more than a day, for after proclaiming it men put themselves the very next morning under the yoke of law and authority. . . .

The millions of laws which exist for the regulation of humanity appear upon investigation to be divided into three principal categories: protection of property, protection of persons, protection of government. And by analyzing each of these three categories, we arrive at the same logical and necessary conclusion: *the uselessness and hurtfulness of law.*

Socialists know what is meant by protection of property. Laws on property are not made to guarantee either to the individual or to society the enjoyment of the produce of their own labor. On the contrary, they are made to rob the producer of a part of what he has created, and to secure to certain other people that portion of the produce which they have stolen either from the producer or from society as a whole. When, for example, the law establishes Mr. So-and-So's right to a house, it is not establishing his right to a cottage he has built for himself, or to a house he has erected with the help of some of his friends. In that case no one would have disputed his right. On the contrary, the law is establishing his right to a house which is *not* the product of his labor; first of all because he has had it built for him by others to whom he has not paid the full value of their work, and next because that house represents a social value which he could not have produced for himself. The law is establishing his right to what belongs to everybody in general and to nobody in particular. The same house built in the midst of Siberia would not have the value it possesses in a large town, and, as we know, that value arises from the labor of something like fifty generations of men who have built the town, beautified it, supplied it with water and gas, fine promenades, colleges, theatres, shops, railways and roads leading in all directions. Thus, by recognizing the right of Mr. So-and-So to a particular house in Paris, London or Rouen, the law is unjustly appropriating to him a certain portion of the produce of the labor of mankind in general. And it is precisely because this appropriation and all other forms of property bearing the same character are a crying injustice, that a whole arsenal of laws and a whole army of soldiers, policemen and judges are needed to maintain it against the good sense and just feeling inherent in humanity.

Half our laws,—the civil code in each country,—serves no other purpose than to maintain this appropriation, this monopoly for the benefit of certain individuals against the whole of mankind. Three-fourths of the causes decided by the tribunals are nothing but quarrels between monopolists—two robbers disputing over their booty. And a great many of our criminal laws have the same object in view, their end being to keep the workman in a subordinate position towards his employer, and thus afford security for exploitation.

As for guaranteeing the product of his labor to the producer, there are no laws which even attempt such a thing. It is so simple and natural, so much a part of the manners and customs of mankind, that law has not given it so much as a thought. Open brigandage, sword in hand, is no feature of our age. Neither does one workman ever come and dispute the produce of his labor with another. If they have a misunderstanding they settle it by calling in a third person, without having recourse to law. The only person who exacts from another what that other has produced, is the proprietor, who comes in and deducts the lion's share. As for humanity in general, it everywhere respects the right of each to what he has created, without the interposition of any special laws.

As all the laws about property which make up thick volumes of codes and are the delight of our lawyers have no other object than to protect the unjust appropriation of human labor by certain monopolists, there is no reason for their existence, and, on the day of the revolution, social revolutionists are thoroughly determined to put an end to them. Indeed, a bonfire might be made with perfect justice of all laws bearing upon the so-called "rights of property," all title-deeds, all registers, in a word, of all that is in any way connected with an institution which will soon be looked upon as a blot in the history of humanity, as humiliating as the slavery and serfdom of past ages.

The remarks just made upon laws concerning property are quite as applicable to the second category of laws; those for the maintenance of government, i.e., constitutional law.

It again is a complete arsenal of laws, decrees, ordinances, orders in council, and what not, all serving to protect the diverse forms of representative government, delegated or usurped, beneath which humanity is writhing. We know very well—anarchists have often enough pointed out in their perpetual criticism of the various forms of government—that the mission of all governments, monarchical, constitutional, or republican, is to protect and maintain by force the privileges of the classes in possession, the aristocracy, clergy and traders. A good third of our laws—and each country possesses some tens of thousands of them—the fundamental laws on taxes, excise duties, the organization of ministerial departments and their offices, of the army, the police, the church, etc., have no other end than to maintain, patch up, and develop the administrative machine. And this machine in its turn serves almost entirely to protect the privileges of the possessing classes. Analyze all these laws, observe them in action day by day, and you will discover that not one is worth preserving.

About such laws there can be no two opinions. Not only anarchists, but more or less revolutionary radicals also, are agreed that the only use to be made of laws concerning the organization of government is to fling them into the fire.

The third category of law still remains to be considered; that relating to the protection of the person and the detection and prevention of "crime." This is the most important because most prejudices attach to it; because, if law enjoys a certain amount of consideration, it is in consequence of the belief that this species of law is absolutely indispensable to the maintenance of security in our societies. These are laws developed from the nucleus of customs useful to human communities, which have been turned to account by rulers to sanctify their own domination. The authority of the chiefs of tribes, of rich families in towns, and of the king, depended upon their judicial functions, and even down to the present day, whenever the necessity of government is spoken of, its function as supreme judge is the thing implied. "Without a government men would tear one another to pieces," argues the village orator. "The ultimate end of all government is to secure twelve honest jurymen to every accused person," said Burke.

Well, in spite of all the prejudices existing on this subject, it is quite time that anarchists should boldly declare this category of laws as useless and injurious as the preceding ones.

First of all, as to so-called "crimes"—assaults upon persons— it is well known that two-thirds, and often as many as three-fourths, of such "crimes" are instigated by the desire to obtain possession of someone's wealth. This immense class of so-called "crimes and misdemeanors" will disappear on the day on which private property ceases to exist. "But," it will be said, "there will always be brutes who will attempt the lives of their fellow citizens, who will lay their hands to a knife in every quarrel, and revenge the slightest offense by murder, if there are no laws to restrain and punishments to withhold them." This refrain is repeated every time the right of society *to punish* is called in question.

Yet there is one fact concerning this head which at the present time is thoroughly established; the severity of punishment does not diminish the amount of crime. Hang, and, if you like, quarter murderers, and the number of murders will not decrease by one. On the other hand, abolish the penalty of death, and there will not be one murder more; there will be fewer. Statistics prove it. But if the harvest is good, and bread cheap, and the weather fine, the number of murders immediately decreases. This again is proved by statistics. The amount of crime always augments and diminishes in proportion to the price of provisions and the state of the weather. Not that all murderers are actuated by hunger. That is not the case. But when the harvest is good, and provisions are at an obtainable price, and when the sun shines, men, lighter-hearted and less miserable than usual, do not give way to gloomy passions, do not from trivial motives plunge a knife into the bosom of a fellow creature.

Moreover, it is also a well known fact that the fear of

punishment has never stopped a single murderer. He who kills his neighbor from revenge or misery does not reason much about consequences; and there have been few murderers who were not firmly convinced that they should escape prosecution.

Without speaking of a society in which a man will receive a better education, in which the development of all his faculties, and the possibility of exercising them, will procure him so many enjoyments that he will not seek to poison them by remorse—even in our society, even with those sad products of misery whom we see today in the public houses of great cities—on the day when no punishment is inflicted upon murderers, the number of murders will not be augmented by a single case. And it is extremely probable that it will be, on the contrary, diminished by all those cases which are due at present to habitual criminals, who have been brutalized in prisons.

We are continually being told of the benefits conferred by law, and the beneficial effect of penalties, but have the speakers ever attempted to strike a balance between the benefits attributed to laws and penalties, and the degrading effect of these penalties upon humanity? Only calculate all the evil passions awakened in mankind by the atrocious punishments formerly inflicted in our streets! Man is the cruelest animal upon earth. And who has pampered and developed the cruel instincts unknown, even among monkeys, if it is not the king, the judge, and the priests, armed with law, who caused flesh to be torn off in strips, boiling pitch to be poured into wounds, limbs to be dislocated, bones to be crushed, men to be sawn asunder to maintain their authority? Only estimate the torrent of depravity let loose in human society by the "informing" which is countenanced by judges, and paid in hard cash by governments, under pretext of assisting in the discovery of "crime." Only go into the jails and study what man becomes when he is deprived of freedom and shut up with other depraved beings, steeped in the vice and corruption which oozes from the very walls of our existing prisons. Only remember that the more these prisons are reformed, the more detestable they become. Our model modern penitentiaries are a hundredfold more abominable than the dungeons of the middle ages. Finally, consider what corruption, what depravity of mind is kept up among men by the idea of obedience, the very essence of law; of chastisement; of authority having the right to punish, to judge irrespective of our conscience and the esteem of our friends; of the necessity for executioners, jailers, and informers—in a word, by all the attributes of law and authority. Consider all this and you will assuredly agree with us in saying that a law inflicting penalties is an abomination which should cease to exist.

Peoples without political organization, and therefore less depraved than ourselves, have perfectly understood that the man who is called "criminal" is simply unfortunate; that the remedy is not to flog him, to chain him up, or to kill him on the scaffold or in prison, but to help him by the most brotherly care, by treatment based on equality, by the usages of life among honest men. In the next revolution we hope that this cry will go forth:

"Burn the guillotines; demolish the prisons; drive away the judges, policemen and informers—the impurest race upon the face of the earth; treat as a brother the man who has been led by passion to do ill to his fellow; above all, take from the ignoble products of middle-class idleness the possibility of displaying their vices in attractive colors; and be sure that but few crimes will mar our society."

The main supports of crime are idleness, law and authority; laws about property, laws about government, laws about penalties and misdemeanors; and authority, which takes upon itself to manufacture these laws and to apply them.

No more laws! No more judges! Liberty, equality, and practical human sympathy are the only effectual barriers we can oppose to the anti-social instincts of certain among us.

27 Power Attracts Delinquents: A Contemporary Study

In the preceding selections, government has been successively criticized as authority that is not consented to, as administration that is not contracted for, as moral power that is not self-imposed, as coercion that plunders individuals, as representation lacking identity of interests with the people it represents, as regulation under the pretense of welfare, and as policing that instigates criminality. Together these lines of attack comprise the standard case against government. None of them will be discarded by anarchism as out of date. They are not tied to some notion of government that was laid to rest with monarchy. They can easily be aimed at twentieth-century parliamentarianism, the welfare state, totalitarianism.

But some might doubt that the persistent flexibility of a nineteenth-century doctrine is very surprising. They might maintain that the same can be said for other doctrines, such as liberalism or socialism. To this the anarchist could reply that anarchism, unlike its competitors, has developed consistent principles and has not scrapped embarrassing ones or inserted convenient substitutes. At this point the objector might retort that anarchism has rescued its consistency by ignoring modern scholarship. The anarchist might ridicule this objection, for he is not always impressed by the modern educational system. (See selection 46.) But he could also argue that modern erudition is relevant to the anarchist critique of society and, moreover, that the libertarian position has already pointed the modern scholar toward fruitful areas of research. It is in order to determine the bearings of modern scholarship on the anarchist critique of government that we conclude this section with portions of Alex Comfort's *Authority and Delinquency in the Modern State*.

Alex Comfort is a poet, novelist, and biologist. His writings in social science, all following a cross-disciplinary approach, include *Sex and Society* and *Darwin and the Naked Lady*. He has been Lecturer in Physiology at the London Hospital and Nuffield Research Fellow in the biology of senescence at University College, London. Comfort resembles Kropotkin in putting empirical science in the service of anarchism, but there is an interesting difference in their outlooks. To Kropotkin, government appeared to bring about criminal behavior; to Comfort, it appears a haven for social delinquents.

INTRODUCTION

The attempt to establish criminology as a distinct branch of knowledge encounters immediate difficulties. Anti-social conduct and delinquency, in the sense of action and attitude prejudicial to the welfare of others, are psychiatric entities: crime, on the other hand, is an arbitrary conception embracing both aggressive delinquency, such as murder or rape, and actions whose importance is predominantly administrative, such as the purchase of alcohol after closing time. Since the scope of crime depends directly upon legislation, it may be altered at any time to embrace any pattern of behaviour. Under modern conditions it is quite possible for the criminal psychiatrist to be confronted with the task of reforming an individual whose conflict with society arises from a high rather than a low development of sociality. Refusal to participate in the persecution of a racial minority, or in the military destruction of civilian populations, have recently figured as crimes in civilized Western societies. Under these conditions the independent tradition of the psychiatrist must lead him to decide at what point the psychopathy of the individual exceeds that of society, which he should attempt to fortify, and by what standards. More important perhaps is the growing awareness that, great as is the nuisance-value of the criminal in urban society, the centralized pattern of government is to-day dependent for its continued function upon a supply of individuals whose personalities and attitudes in no way differ from those of admitted psychopathic delinquents. Society, so far from penalizing anti-social behaviour *per se*, selects the forms, often indistinguishable, which it will punish, and the forms which it must foster by virtue of its pattern. The egocentric psychopath who swindles in the financial field is punishable—if his activities are political, he enjoys immunity and esteem, and may take part in the determination of laws.

In spite, therefore, of the extent and seriousness of delinquency as a social problem, its most serious aspect for humanity to-day is the prevalence of delinquent action by

Authority and Delinquency in the Modern State, by Alex Comfort (London: Routledge & Kegan Paul Ltd., 1950), pp. ix–xi, 13–18, 78–85. Reprinted by permission of Routledge & Kegan Paul Ltd.

persons immune from censure, and by established governments. The importation of science into the study of crime
is an irreversible step, and its outcome can be only the suppression of science itself or the radical remodelling of our
ideas of government and the regulation of behaviour. . . .

The object of this study is to relate the elements in the
behaviour of modern governments which lead to the international equivalent of crime to those with which we are already partly familiar in individuals. Society has throughout
its history treated crime as something hostile to itself, to be
abolished by punishment or prevention. At the same time it
has arbitrarily delimited the conduct which is criminal, while
depending to a greater or lesser extent on the presence within
itself of potential delinquents. No society based on centralized power has been able to dispense with large groups of
people whose make-up is in no way different from that of
punishable delinquents—it has abolished private, but tolerated public, executioners, for example. . . . While some
such toleration has always been present, its study to-day gains
urgency from the alarming growth of delinquent acts by
states and by organs of power during the last fifty years.

THE FORMS OF TOLERATED DELINQUENCY

Tolerated delinquents appear in centralized cultures at two
distinct levels. They may enter and control the machinery of
legislative and political power, as policy-makers and rulers.
They may also be found, and tend in general to be more
numerous, in the machinery of enforcement which intervenes
between the policy-maker and the citizen. We owe our present recognition of the presence and the role of these tolerated
delinquents, and of their capacity for mischief, to the rise of
totalitarian states, but the reappearance of delinquency and
military tyranny as socially accepted policies in civilized
states has led, and must lead, to a scrutiny of similar mechanisms within the social democracies.

Social democracy was devised, in so far as it arose as a consciously determined system, to limit the possible abuse of
power by delegates. The powers of the delegates themselves
were created by public discontent with irresponsible government. In terms of liberal theory, therefore, social democracy
should contain extensive safeguards against the capture of
authority by delinquent individuals or groups. The Constitution of the United States was framed with this object deliberately in view. The safeguards provided by constitutions and

by theories of government, however, leave out of account the far greater effects upon society of economic and social forces which the theorists were in no position to foresee. Democracy is exposed to the hazards which other societies have faced, from the ambition of energetic and unscrupulous individuals, and from the over-concentration of power, but it carries risks of its own. The range of aspirants to political power in a monarchy is limited to the circle of military leaders and the nobility, who might hope for success as usurpers: the wider the qualification for office, the greater the competition. Democratic societies, especially in their centralized form, offer the prospect of entry into public affairs to many aggressive personalities whose ambitions might otherwise be limited to local affairs. The actual control, moreover, which the delegate rulers exercise over the life of ordinary citizens, is more effective and thorough than that which older monarchs could contemplate, and the fact of delegacy limits to some extent the resistance of the public to such control. With the growth of urban society, and the extension of the range and scope of administration, the policy-makers have acquired resources of force and persuasion which meet with very little organized resistance, except in times of economic slump or widespread poverty.

At the same time, the concentration of populations and of political functions in cities has led to a gradual increase in the size and extent of the machinery of enforcement. These organizations gradually acquire an autonomous function, which may be free from the control of the policy-makers and of the public alike. The urban police have played a considerable part in the conflicts surrounding political parties, and in the setting-up of dictatorships. It may be recalled that the Roman Constitution imposed special and deliberate checks on the use of the army for domestic enforcement by the distinction which it drew between *imperium domi* and *imperium militiae*, military commanders being normally divested of authority within the city limits. The unique sequence of psychopathic emperors who figure in later Roman history owed their power in almost every case to independent action by the enforcement units of the army (the Imperial bodyguard), who were often recruited from, or supported by, foreign mercenaries. In this case the executive was physically and literally an out-group, foreign to the mores and attitudes of Roman society. The breakdown of this system followed upon the appearance in the executive of aspirants powerful and ambitious enough to dismember between them the central authority.

Meanwhile the liberal theory of Western democracies has exercised little or no influence over the pattern of their biological growth. Centralization has produced major changes, many of them detrimental, in the status of the family and in the security of the individual, which have not been neutralized by technical advances. Halliday has drawn attention to the growing importance of culturally inherent anxiety in such societies. The historical evidence drawn from the fate of older city-cultures which have outrun their biological foundations is far from reassuring. An increasing tendency for fear, insecurity, and an orientation towards war to become permanent features of such cultures can be identified in our own. Mumford has already presented an alarmingly realistic picture of the processes of disintegration in urban aggregates —under these conditions, psychopathic processes and attitudes become pandemic: guilt and its projections in military aggression may become even more prominent in democratic and traditionally pacific cultures than in others which have fewer scruples. The effects of the atomic bomb upon the modern American conscience have been more marked than those of military defeat upon the German. The liberal safeguards in modern social democracy are increasingly forced to contend with factors which never entered the heads of their inventors. The totalitarianisms which modern liberals denounce, and upon which they frequently project their own guilt and insecurity, are the end-product of similar processes in cultures whose resistance has been lowered by tradition or circumstance.

In the aristocratic oligarchies, the personnel of government was recruited by inheritance within the ruling caste, and received occasional accessions from below through intermarriage and the appearance of new and self-made noblemen. Government was one function among many which this class discharged. In centralized democracies, government is an occupation, and one which generally excludes other forms of activity. It must therefore compete with other occupations of equal dignity and status for the personnel which it requires. The leadership of a modern political party offers neither economic nor intellectual incentives which are superior to those provided by technology, the professions, or the higher administrative grades of the Civil Services—its appeal to a given individual is likely to depend chiefly upon the power of modifying the lives of others which it confers. The machinery of enforcement, the police and the prison services, has in the past maintained its recruitment because of the degree of personal security associated with government employment. The police and the army were for many years the only pensionable and established occupations to which working men could readily find an entry. This is no longer the case. The increase of social security and the rise in industrial living standards have largely nullified their appeal. By comparison with other employments, the enforcement services offer poor remuneration and a severer discipline. Here, as in the legislature, deliberate choice is likely to play an increasing part in recruitment. There is, therefore, in centralized societies, a tendency for the personnel of these occupations to be drawn increasingly from those whose main preoccupation is a desire for authority, for powers of control and of direction over others. In the case of would-be politicians, these impulses may spring from a highly developed political and social sense; they may equally well spring from maladjustment and a deep-seated impulse toward self-assertion and dominance. In social democracies there is interposed between the individual who desires office, and the office which he desires, the mechanism of election and of the party system, involving the need to induce large electorates of varying intelligence to support the candidate at the polls. In such a process, integrity and altruism may be at a disadvantage beside astuteness and single-minded ambition. Moreover, while altruism and social idealism may find ready outlets in other fields, such as scientific research, medicine, religion, or social service, all of which carry a satisfactory intellectual social prestige, the centralization of power attracts inevitably towards the administrative centre those for whom power is an end in itself. The desire for success through riches or success through fame and esteem are more adequately catered for in other spheres of society, and though political power may be approached by these other routes it remains the predominant attribute of government in modern urban cultures.

Considerations of this kind may be held to constitute a risk rather than a fact in the psychology of English politics at the present time. The number of ambitious and unscrupulous men in any contemporary parliament is probably no higher than in previous periods when a different background existed. Other factors, however, beside those of party politics may at any time intervene to bring into office, through elec-

toral channels, psychopathic persons or groups who will exhibit delinquent behaviour, either as a long-sought aim, as the
focus and expression of pent-up public anxiety and frustration, or through the deteriorating influence which wide
power, isolation, and crisis may exert over unstable individuals. The standards of British Members of Parliament, and
of the public, underwent recognizable change during the
inter-war depression, and during the second World War.
Against such changes, and against the stress imposed by modern government upon initially social individuals, institutional safeguards are not likely to prove effective.

Moreover, whatever we may consider to be the normal
standard of private integrity, and however fully this standard is upheld by English politicians, a distinct division exists
between private qualities and public policy. It is characteristic of political psychopathy to-day that grossly delinquent public policies may coexist with good private adjustment. The suggestion that those who order public frauds,
massacres or deportations must necessarily be criminal or sadistic in their private relationships has no support in theory
or in observation. Where actions are recognizably psychopathic, the normality of their perpetrators in other fields is
not more relevant than the superficial adjustment which
criminals frequently display outside their specific behaviour
disorder. It seems clear that the intense strain and the other
incidentals of modern political office have an observable effect in evoking delinquent conduct in persons who would
probably not otherwise exhibit it. It is arguable whether Hitler would have been actively delinquent had he failed to secure office, in spite of his manifestly abnormal make-up.

In discussing these phenomena in their contemporary context, reference may be made to history, but obvious reasons
prevent the publication of case-histories or estimates of living persons. The long-range diagnosis of mental abnormality,
in a person who is known only through his reported utterances, is in any case to be discouraged. But we can hardly fail
to see the relevance of psychiatric classification to the political scene of the last twenty years. The fact that abnormal
persons exist, and acquire power, within the political system
is not in itself a condemnation of the system. The same applies to other fields of activity. The important judgments
upon which we must base our estimate of the modern state
are, first, whether it attracts psychopaths selectively; second,
whether the impulse to power is itself a manifestation of de-

linquency, in some or all of those who display it; and third, whether institutional patterns increase and foster abnormal emphases in the state-holders. . . .

SOCIOLOGY OF POWER

It is not here possible to deal at all fully with the comparative sociology of power.

The appearance of organized government in primitive societies has been related to the rise of hunting as a group activity, and to the appearance of private property. It is almost certainly related to the development of organized war. A more interesting observation is the parallel appearance of organized government and of antisocial patterns of behaviour. This can be interpreted in two ways—if the state is the community's attempt to safeguard itself against social disorder and disintegration, its rise can be regarded as a response to new stresses, and to the breakdown of older and simpler forms of individual adjustment. It is also possible, however, that the stress factors which produced the supply of delinquents provided the supply of power-seekers. . . . No close parallel can yet be drawn between the picture of the rise of government which we derive from social anthropology, and that of the origins of the desire for power which we derive from psychoanalysis. It seems likely that at the point in any culture when it ceases to be capable of absorbing its own abnormal members, the demand for coercion appears hand in hand with the emergence of individuals who desire to coerce.

There is a good deal of evidence that in cultures where the main task resembles that of science, to maintain life and society in the face of external difficulties, competition for power accounts for an extremely small part of the total energy of individuals. Cohesion of this kind in the face of an external threat occurs in our own society. The desire for approval and love is also demonstrably a fundamental part of the make-up of individuals. It plays a large part in determining deliberate attempts to secure status. The limits which determine its expression are based on the self-appointed task of the culture concerned, as embodied in its standards. The warrior is a figure of admiration to warlike tribes, and the proficient thief to communities of thieves. On an entirely superficial assessment of motives, many forms of delinquency are roundabout means of securing the type of approval which the individual desires; where society, or the individual's own attitude, deny it, money may buy, or position enforce it. The psychoanalytical explanation of society begins by drawing attention to the fact that it is in the approval or disapproval of our parents that we first experience this basic desire. Freud's main contribution to the theory of society was in showing the interaction between this desire and the equally fundamental sexual development of the individual. Throughout life the two are parallel, and the distinction is even less clear cut in childhood, when sexuality is not tied to the specific pattern of adult reproductive behaviour. In most human societies, as in some higher animals, the father tends to occupy a special position as the source of parental approval, the administrator of rewards and punishments, and an alternate source of pleasure and frustration. He is alternately admired as a model of strength, wisdom and success, and resented as an object of jealousy and a barrier to the child's sexual and non-sexual ambitions. So far as we can guess, the earliest form of social hierarchy may well have been a family of families based on the dynamic position of fatherhood.

The striking differences between 'power-centred' and 'life-centred' cultures are closely analogous to the differences between power-seeking and life-seeking individuals. Almost all the existing evidence suggests that the psychoanalytical view of such differences, which attributes them to identification with one or other parent, has widespread value in interpreting cultural as well as individual behaviour. In the most typical instances, the 'patriform' society, based upon jealousy of the father, concentrates its prohibitions upon sex and disobedience to authority, the 'matriform' against offences which threaten the food supply. Both civilized and primitive societies are fairly easily divisible between these two types— among modern political groups classical 'patriform' societies occasionally appear, in which death or castration are typical punishments, and the status of women is lowered. Nazi Germany was one such example. With the growth of centralization, however, it is possibly more accurate to describe modern societies as effecting a division between 'patriform' individuals, who gravitate into government and enforcement, and 'matriform' individuals who enter fields where co-operation, production, and creation are more important than command, prohibition and coercion. There is, it seems, a good deal of evidence, both from sociology and individual psychiatry, for the view that modern government may select a particular and a maladjusted section of the community when it recruits its members.

How much sexual content we find in these infantile attitudes will depend to some extent on our definition of sexuality. The attempt to express all dynamic psychology in terms of the Oedipus situation is probably an over-simplification, and leaves us with the need to explain why the existence of incestuous impulses is so strongly repudiated by the child. It is, however, demonstrably true that social standards are derived directly from parental example, and that the 'conscience' is formed, in content at least, by these standards coupled to the desire to win approval. Independent social sense does not emerge fully until early adolescence, by which time the child's attitude towards its fellows is already largely fixed in terms of its attitude towards the father. The desire for power appears to be, in many cases, an attempt to establish the kind of status which the father held, and which the child admired or envied. The desire to obey is almost an equal component of the political pattern, and this in turn can be regarded as a carry-over into adult life of a yearning for the security of the nursery with its external standards.

Aggression, another component of adult delinquency, is by no means an abnormal or necessarily an undesirable element. Humanity maintains itself by an aggressive attitude toward its environment—interpersonal aggression is at root a desire to recognize and to be recognized; to avoid being ignored or isolated. To this extent at least 'hate is the precursor of love'. Sadism in its Freudian sense is almost certainly a primary mammalian impulse, in which elements of aggression, the seeking for dynamic relationships, and a desire for pursuit and capture or for strong skin stimulation during mating combine. The type of sadism which features in the discussion of political and military atrocities is an outgrowth of this: the desire to inflict suffering as a means to, or a substitute for, normal sexual and socio-sexual relationships.

Freud regarded sadism, in its more general sense, as a primary impulse which is converted into masochism, the desire to suffer or to submit, only where it provokes a reaction of guilt in the subject. West . . . in his study of aggression in society points to some of the difficulties of this view: a desire to suffer is probably more fundamental to the individual than Freud himself suspected. Freud certainly recognized the 'willingness to suffer pain on the circuitous route to pleasure' which contributes to many of the more complicated patterns of conduct that confound simple theories of human social history as a pursuit of happiness.

From all this we can identify the components of the desire for power as:

(1) simple patterns of dominance;

(2) self-identification with the coercive father, and a desire to imitate his status;

(3) power as a sexual substitute, or as a form of compensation for failure to secure status and affection elsewhere;

(4) the attitude of societies which offer political power as a legitimate and approved activity.

These carry their own converse in the desire for obedience:

(1) as an acceptance of the dominance of others;

(2) as a perpetuation of childhood behaviour, and the desire for security of status through submission;

(3) as a means of reconciling sadism with the disapproval and resistance which it evokes;

(4) as a positive duty, inculcated by tradition.

Any attempt to apply rigid ideas of 'normality' to these patterns runs into immediate difficulties, whether the normal implies prevalence or desirability. Dominance patterns are apparently inseparable from all types of relationship among men and animals, and political authority only accounts for some of them. Identification with the father is also in essence a normal pattern—moral deficiency in various forms seems to be associated with an absence of home security, and it looks as if abnormal and harmful emphases only occur when the element of coercion and force in the father-image is unduly prominent: the identification in this case may take the form of rebellion or of an overmastering desire to inflict on others the type of authority which the father imposes. To this extent coercive 'patriform' societies perpetuate their structure through coercive family relationships. The association of power and pain-inflicting behaviour with sexuality is undoubtedly a neurosis in its social manifestations, if we define a neurosis as the fixed repetition of inappropriate behaviour in response to conflict, and it is one which the withholding of sexual outlets in our own society appears to propagate. The emphasis in centralized society which plays the most important part in producing militant political tyrannies is probably the desire for a continuance of the external, parental, conscience into adult life. The strain of dependence on individual judgment, and the lack of status which the adult feels in centralized, asocial life are prominent causes of the unlimited and masochistic obedience which Fascism demands, and democracy may occasionally obtain. Obedience in modern societies is more often a hideous vice than a Christian virtue.

What is striking about these elements in social behaviour is that the better the individual adjustment, the more easily they are absorbed in ordinary patterns of living, and the less incentive remains to make them a basis for an overmastering impulse to regulate the behaviour of others. The closest connection between power and abnormality is in the essentially uncreative and unproductive nature of the impulse to regulate by prohibition. This impulse is almost always the expression of a failing, rather than a successful, adaptation. We try to prohibit those things which inspire guilty, resentful, or jealous feelings: prohibition is a substitute for participation. The prohibition of indecency is a standby of those for whom sexual experience is a source of guilt and distaste: the prohibition of wealth may represent the reaction of the man who has been deprived of its benefits and insulted by its possessors. To some extent the prohibition of delinquency is the reaction of those who have a deep-rooted community of desire with the delinquent. Like Dr. Johnson, they are forging their own handcuffs.

The modern conception of 'human nature' in psychiatry, in so far as it is united and articulate, has been well stated by Fleming.

> The problem of the educator is not so much that of 'training' towards spontaneous kindliness, initiative, honesty or emotional sincerity as of permitting opportunities for these attributes to reveal themselves. The child, the adolescent or the adult is not merely a 'savage' or a 'beast' whose anti-social impulses towards self-assertion, cruelty, or greed require to be restrained; but a human being—social in nature ('a son of God')—who is capable of evil as well as good but who can find satisfaction only in the 'good'. In an atmosphere of frustration, aggression, discouragement and neglect he will appear aggressive, cruel, anti-social and inhibited; but removal of such influences will result in the revelation of a new creature.
>
> Abundant evidence on these lines has been collected in the last twenty years from experiments in the situational treatment of problem children, and (more recently) from observation of the re-education of Nazified youth and the rehabilitation of neurotic prisoners of war. Human beings are social. They need to give affection, to exercise responsibility, and to attain insight; and in the

absence of imposed frustrations and the presence of the complementary affection, trust and patient encouragement of friendly and receptive groups, they have been observed to blossom into social virtues whose flowering appeared impossible under other sorts of husbandry. [*Adolescence*, p. 210]

The violence of the contrast between this view and the idea of government as a weight placed upon the lid of human delinquent impulses to keep it down is not softened by the close connection between the administrative encouragement of large centralized aggregates and the denial of precisely those conditions of social and personal development which this modern body of experience advocates. Centralized society fails to provide these conditions either for the rulers or the ruled, and the reactions of both combine to threaten its violent collapse. Politics against this background is seen less as a delinquent activity of power-drunk individuals—the stereotype which appeals to the revolutionary when he is out of office—than as an activity which is unprofitable in itself, since its presuppositions contradict its purposes. Almost all its remedies aggravate the type of behaviour they profess to eliminate. The addictive elements in political office, which Acton recognized, might well make scientific sociology unwilling to give more than a guarded support to measures of decentralization which involve the election of individuals to office. It prefers to deal directly with the individual, through education and the setting up of experimental communities which fulfil the requirements laid down by scientific study.

SECTION V

Constructive Anarchism:
Alternative Communities and Programs

The readings in this section have been divided into four sets. Each of the first three treats an historic form of anarchism: individualist anarchism, communist anarchism, and syndicalism. Here the theoretical principles of section III are further illuminated by the way they are used to shape the direction of concrete libertarian activity. The final set of readings contains the constructive proposals of four contemporary anarchists. These proposals do not spring from any one element within the anarchist fold; rather, each constitutes a synthesis of diverse libertarian points of view.

There is no greater unity among anarchists concerning programs and communities than there is concerning definitions or fundamental principles. Many of the syndicalist strategies set forth by Rudolf Rocker are simply incompatible with the pacifist convictions of such religious anarchists as Dorothy Day and Ammon Hennacy. Furthermore, there are sharp distinctions among those who emphasize a program of individual regeneration, those who rely on small-group experiments designed to function within a non-anarchist social structure, and those with all-inclusive plans for social revolution.

There are other differences, some fundamental, others peripheral. But important patterns of resemblance can also be traced. All our selections at least tacitly affirm what has been called the unity of ends and means: the strategies involved in preparing for the long-range goals of anarchism must themselves express anarchist principles. Because of this affirmation, anarchists resist proposals to gain control over the existing structures of authority for the alleged purpose of eliminating those structures. More important, they maintain that instruments and tactics—general strikes, adventure playgrounds, citizen banks—must themselves be anarchist societies in miniature. The rank-and-file worker must develop and keep control over his own decentralized organizations; the pupil must be trusted to determine his own curriculum. In this way, tactics and instruments become ends in themselves. Nothing less will allow us to develop agents who do not need to be regulated by, or to submit others to, "the world-wide system of States in which a man [is] hounded from one baroque jurisdiction to another baroque jurisdiction, and . . . [has] no asylum or even exile."

28 The Pattern of Life in an Individualist Anarchist Community

> . . . a remarkable American, Mr. Warren, had framed a System of Society, on the foundation of "the Sovereignty of the Individual," had obtained a number of followers, and had actually commenced the formation of a Village Community (whether it now exists I know not), which, though bearing a superficial resemblance to some of the projects of Socialists, is diametrically opposite to them in principle, since it recognizes no authority in Society over the individual, except to enforce equal freedom of development for all individualities. . . . I borrowed from the Warrenites their phrase, the sovereignty of the individual. . . .
>
> John Stuart Mill, *Autobiography*

Josiah Warren, Mill's "remarkable American," would be a rich and fascinating subject for a comprehensive biography. Born a member of the famous New England Warrens, he was a music teacher, theorist, and concertmaster; he invented and manufactured lamps and printing presses; he trained youths in practical skills by means of libertarian methods that were highly original and much relied on by non-anarchists (see his recommendation of kibbutzim-like Infant Schools at the end of this selection). He was the editor and printer of the first anarchist periodical (*The Peaceful Revolutionist*, Cincinnati, 1833); he wrote penetrating analyses of the failure of Robert Owen's American socialist venture, New Harmony; and he inspired several lively communal experiments which tested, improved, and disseminated libertarian concepts. (These experiments ranged from a "Time Store," which sold farm and household goods on the cost principle in Cincinnati around 1827, to the Long Island settlement "Modern Times," which ran from 1850 until the Civil War wrecked its economy.)

As if these achievements were not enough for one life, Warren labored in several books toward a rigorous exposition of the theoretical foundations of individualist anarchism. In these books, doctrines later reworked with lucidity and power by Andrews, Spooner, and Tucker were first systematically set forth.

The selection which follows is taken from Warren's *Equitable Commerce*. It details a full-scale libertarian community (like Warren's "Equity Villages" in Ohio or "Modern Times") and the means of its implementation.

THE APPLICATION

Elements of New Society

The first step to be taken by any number of persons in these practical movements appears to be, that each individual or head of a family, should consider his or her present *wants*, and what he can give in exchange, with a view to have them recorded in a book kept for that purpose. . . . We will now suppose that the wants of twenty individuals are recorded in one column of a book, and what they can supply in another column; and in another, the price per hour which each demands for his or her labor. These become the fundamental data for operations.

Every one wishing to take some part in practical operations, now has before him in this report of wants, the business to be done. It will immediately be seen that land is indispensible, and must be had before any other step can be taken to advantage. Some one seeing this want, after consulting the wishes or demands of the co-operators, proceeds *on his individual* estimate of this demand, at his own risk, and at his own cost, to purchase or otherwise procure land to commence upon, lays it out in lots to suit the demand, and sells them to the co-operators at the ultimate *cost* (including contingent expenses of money and labor in buying and selling). The difference in the price of a house lot thus bought and sold, compared with its price when sold for its *value*, will be found sufficient to make the difference between every one having a home upon the earth, instead of one half of men and women being homeless.

We will now suppose the lots purchased and paid for by each one who is to occupy them. They will *want* to consult continually together, in order to co-operate with each other's movements; this will require or *demand* a place for meetings. As soon as this want is apparent, then is the time for some one to estimate this want, and take it on himself *individually* to provide a room, and see himself remunerated according to cost, which cannot fail to be satisfactory to all in proportion as they are convinced that *cost* is the limit of his demands;

Equitable Commerce, by Josiah Warren (New Harmony, Ind., 1846), pp. 80–96.

which he can always prove by keeping an account of expenses and receipts, open at all times to the most public inspection. . . .

When business commences, the estimates of prices must commence, and the circulating medium will be wanted. For instance, if the keeper of the room for meetings has expended a hundred hours of his labor in keeping it in order, etc., and if there are twenty who have regularly or substantially received the benefits of it, then five hours' equivalent labor is due from each.

This calls for the circulating medium, and he may receive from the carpenter, the blacksmith, the shoemaker, the tailoress, the washerwoman, etc., their labor notes, promising a certain number of hours of their definite kinds of labor. The keeper of the room is now equipped with a circulating medium with which he can procure the services of either of the persons *at a price which is agreed and settled on beforehand*, which will obviate all disturbance in relation to prices—he holds a currency whose product to him will not be less at the "report of scarcity," nor "rise at 12 o'clock." From year to year, he can get a certain DEFINITE QUANTITY OF LABOR FOR THE LABOR HE PERFORMED, which cannot be said, nor made to be true, with regard to any money the world has ever known.

An extraordinary feature presents itself in this stage of the operations of Equitable Commerce. When the washerwoman comes to set her price according to the cost or hardness of the labor compared with others, it is found that its price exceeds that of the ordinary labor of men! Of course, the washerwoman must have more per hour than the vender of houselots or the inventor of pills! To deny this, is to deny the very foundation of the whole superstructure! We must admit the claims of the hardest labor to the highest reward, or we deny our own rights, extinguish the little light we have obtained, and throw every thing back into confusion. What is the obstacle to the honest admission and free action of this principle? What would be the ultimate result of carrying it thoroughly out, and giving to every one what equity demands? It would result in surrounding every one with an abundance, with peace, liberty, harmony, and security, and reduce the labor of each to two or three hours per day. . . .

The larger the purchases of lumber, provisions, etc., at once, the cheaper will the prices be to each receiver upon the cost principle, and these economies, together with the social sympathies, will offer the natural inducements for an associated movement. But there is great danger that even these inducements will urge many into such movements prematurely—we cannot be too cautious NOT TO RUN BEFORE THE DEMAND. Let no one move to an Equity Village, till he has thoroughly consulted the *demand* for his labor at that place, and satisfied himself individually, that he can sustain himself *individually*. . . . Previously to any movement upon a new locality, it will probably be perceived, that a boarding-house would be necessary to accommodate the few pioneers until they could build for themselves. Instead of making this the business of the whole association, some one *Individual* perceiving this *want*, can make it his business to provide one adapted to the demand, by ascertaining how many persons are likely to require it, and what style of living they prefer. If these persons are satisfied that *cost* will be honestly made the limit of the price of their accommodations, then every one will be interested in reducing this cost, by lending such articles of furniture as he can spare, by communicating any thing that will enable the keeper to purchase to advantage, and to transport provisions and materials, and to get up the establishment with as little cost as possible; but during all these operations every one's interest will be distinctly *individual*. The future keeper of the house has the deciding power individually in every thing relative to it, and each boarder makes his contract with the keeper; but as no combination takes place, no vote of any majority is called upon until the boarders become so closely connected that each individual cannot exercise his individual taste when all cannot be gratified, then it is, and not till then, that the will of the majority is the best practicable resort of the keeper but he must not surrender his individual prerogative of management, even in this case, or all will be confusion.

When this calls for too great a sacrifice from any one, the remedy will be found only in *disconnection* from that boarding-house, and a resort to another more congenial to his taste, or to private accommodations. In such case, there being no combination to consult, none but the one person is put to inconvenience; no other persons are disturbed. In this boarding-house, if the keeper of it keeps an account of all his expenditures of money and labor, open at all times to the inspection of his boarders, and divides the cost among them, he cannot be charged with penurious management for his own profit, nor can any of the ordinary dissatisfaction from this cause disturb the general harmony. This arrangement is imperfect, inasmuch as there is more or less of united interests involved in it. The perfect form (excepting in the principle of fixing prices), is found in the eating-houses in the cities, where any individual can go at any time, and get any particular fare that suits his individual demands. He gratifies his own tastes at his own individual cost, and is not involved in expenses for others, and therefore there is no collision between any parties. . . .

It will now be found necessary to ascertain the amount of labor required in the production of all those things which we expect to exchange. This naturally suggests itself to each one in his own business, and if all bring in their estimates, either at public meetings, or have them hung up in the public room, they become the necessary data for each individual to act upon. It is this open, daylight, free comparison of prices, which naturally regulates them; while land, and all trades, arts, and sciences, will be thrown open to every one, so that he or she can immediately abandon an unpaid labor, which will preserve them from being ground by competition below equivalents.

If A sets his estimate of the making of a certain kind of coat at 50 hours, and B sets his at 30 hours, the price per hour, and the known qualities of workmanship being the same in both, it is evident that A could get no business while B could supply the demand. It is evident that A has not given an honest estimate, or, that he is in the wrong position for the general economy; but he can immediately consult the report of the demand, and select some other business for which he may be better adapted. If he concludes to make shoes, his next step is to get instruction in this branch—he refers to the column of *supplies*, and ascertains the name and price per hour of the shoemakers—he goes to one of them, makes his arrangement for instruction, then provides himself with a room and tools, sends for his instructor, pays him according to the time employed, and becomes a shoemaker. Is this thought impracticable? The new shoemaker, having paid his instructor for his labor, has the proceeds of it, together with his own, at his own disposal, and if these be sold for equivalents, he will find his new apprenticeship *quite self-sustaining*.

The same course will have to be pursued with regard to all trades and professions—the supply must be adapted to the demand; which demand should be continually made known at a particular place, by each one who wants any thing, while those who want employment will know where to apply for it, and what they can get in exchange; and if one is not already qualified to supply some portion of the demand, he will be obliged to qualify himself, or fall back upon the land, and supply all his own wants, and be deprived of the advantages of division and exchange, or he must manufacture some article that will sell abroad.

We have now progressed far into practical operations without any combination or unity of interests. Every interest and every responsibility being kept strictly individual, no legislation has been necessary. There has been no demand for artificial organization. There being no public business to manage, no government has been necessary, and therefore NO SURRENDER OF THE NATURAL LIBERTY HAS BEEN REQUIRED.

Now, let us imagine one small item of *united* interests, and trace its consequences. We will suppose that A and B get a horse in partnership, to transport their baggage to the new location. The horse is taken sick—A proposes a medicine, which B thinks would be fatal; neither party has the power to lay down his own opinion and take up that of the other. These are parts of the individualities of each, which are perfectly natural, and, therefore, uncontrollable. A brings arguments and facts to sustain his opinion; B does the same, still they differ, and the horse is growing worse. What is to be done? One dislikes to proceed contrary to the views of the other, and both remain inactive for the same reason. There is no deciding power, and the horse is growing worse; what can they do but call a third party to act in behalf of both? To this third party both commit the management of the horse, and surrender their right of decision—this third party is *government*. This government cannot possibly decide both ways, and either A or B, or both remain fearful and dissatisfied. The disturbance now extends itself to the third party, producing a social disease in addition to that of the horse. This is in the wrong direction. We must take another course —retrace our steps—*look into causes*, and we shall find the wrong in the *unity* of interests. DISUNITE these—let A own the horse *individually*; then, if he is sick, A has the deciding power, listens to such council as he judges useful, and then proceeds to treat the horse. If the horse dies, A takes on himself the *cost* of his own decisions and acts, and the social harmony remains undisturbed. TO BE PERFECTLY HARMONIOUS, ALL INTERESTS MUST BE PERFECTLY INDIVIDUAL. . . .

Again; let any laws, rules, regulations, constitutions, or any other articles of association be drawn out by the most acute minds, and be adopted by the whole. As soon as action commences, it will be found that the compact entered into becomes *differently* interpreted. We have no power to interpret language alike; *but we have agreed to agree.* New circumstances now occur, *different* from those contemplated in the compact. New expedients are to be resorted to—language is the only medium of communication, and this is variously interpreted—two or more interpretations of the same language neutralize each other—an opinion expressed, is misunderstood, and requires correction—the correction contains words subject to a greater or less extent of meaning than the speaker intended—these require qualification. The qualification is variously understood, and requires explanation—the explanations require qualifications to infinity. Different opinions and expedients are now offered—all of which partake of the same elements of confusion—counter opinions rise up on all sides—new expedients are proposed, all subject to various interpretations and appreciations, all requiring explanations and qualifications, and these, in their turn, demand qualifications and explanations. Different estimates are formed of the best *expedients*, but there is no *liberty* to *differ*; all must conform to the articles of compact or organization, the meaning of which can never be determined. Opinions, arguments, expedients, interests, hopes, fears, persons, and personalities, all mingle in one astounding confusion. All order is destroyed—all harmony has changed to discord. What is the origin of all this? It is the different interpretations of the same language, and the difference in the occasions of its applications, where there is not liberty to differ. A deepseated, unseen, indestructible, inalienable *individuality*, ever active, unconquered, and unconquerable, is always directly at war with every demand for uniformity or conformity of thoughts and feelings. We ask again, what is to be done? As we cannot divest ourselves or events of natural individualities, there is but one remedy —this is, to AVOID ALL NECESSITY FOR ARTIFICIAL ORGANIZATIONS; which necessity is founded in UNITED INTERESTS. . . .

A still more subtle, and more serious invasion of the rights of property, the natural liberty, and social harmony, is constantly at work in the form of *indefinite obligations*. If A lend B a hammer, it may be of great value to B, but no price is set upon it; this is considered a neighborly accommodation, and common morality says, "neighbors should accommodate each other." The next day A applies to B for the loan of his favorite horse. B wishes to train his horse in a particular manner, and knows that he cannot do this, if different people use him—besides, he wants to use him, or he wants him to rest, and no compensation is offered by A as an inducement. He evidently makes the request on the ground that "neighbors should accommodate each other;" and on this ground B loses all proper control over his horse; and, on the same principle, over every thing that he possesses which is not for sale; so that, by this means, his proper control over his own becomes almost annihilated. The cause is *indefiniteness* in our obligations. The remedy is *definiteness* in our obligations. Let every transaction be an individual one, resting on its own merits, and not mixed up or *united* with another. If A lends B a hammer, and he thinks the cost of doing so is worthy of notice, let B pay it at once, or give a representative of an equivalent; if it is unworthy of notice, it should be entirely disregarded, and never mixed up with its *value*, nor referred to in future transactions.

It is only by thus *individualizing* of our transactions and their elements, that each citizen can enjoy the legitimate control over his own person, time, or property. It is only by this means that we can distinguish a disinterested present, or act of benevolence and sympathy, from one prompted by a mercenary design. If we present a rose to a friend, it is understood to be an expression of sympathy—a simple act of moral commerce, and the receiver feels free from any obligation to make any other return than an expression of the natural feeling which immediately results therefrom; but if one should give half of his property to another, the receiver could not feel equally free from future indefinite obligations. Why? Perhaps, not that the property was any more *valuable* to the receiver than the rose, but, that it *cost* more.

A delicate regard to the rightful liberty of every one, and the necessity of self-preservation, would seem to admonish us to make *cost* the limit of gratuitous favors, while those of immense *value*, which *cost* nothing, can be given and received without hesitation or reluctance, and will purify our moral commerce from any mixture with the mercenary or selfish taint, and carry it to the very highest state of perfection.

We will suppose our practical operations so far progressed upon our new premises, as to require the establishment of a store. No one has money enough to stock one, and the sovereignty of each over his own at all times, seems to forbid borrowing of each other, or one becoming security for another. The most harmonious mode will be found to be for the store-keeper to borrow money *outside* of these operations until borrowing is unnecessary. The next best resort, though not perfectly harmonious, but which may not be seriously disturbing, is for the store-keeper to borrow very small sums from the co-operators, giving them notes for the same, *payable on demand*, so that if any one, for any cause, wishes to withdraw his investment, he can do so, at any time, without words. The store-keeper then proceeds, like ordinary store-keepers, to purchase on his own responsibility and risk, whatever he thinks is in demand, but he observes the time that he employs in purchasing, and on his return opens an account against the store for his labor and contingent expenses —placing the labor in one column and the money in another. He then considers what percentage will probably pay these and all other contingencies of the business, decides on this, and lets it be as publicly known as possible; preserving, however, his liberty to change it when he thinks necessary. We will suppose this to be six per cent in money and fifteen minutes labor on each dollar's worth of goods, for expenses of traveling, purchasing, insurance, losses, drayage, etc., and all the labor of keeping the store, except that of dealing out the goods. When he places them upon the shelves for sale, he marks them with these additions to prime cost, and places them in such a manner that customers can examine them, and know at once their prices, without taking up the time and attention of the keeper; but when the keeper deals out the goods he charges this item of his labor in each individual case, according to the time employed, which is measured by a clock. This arrangement sweeps away at once all the higgling and chaffering about prices, so disgusting in the present system, but which is inseparably connected with it. Perhaps when the habits engendered by it shall have been cured, the time of the keeper may be made up by regular installments of each dealer, but, as things are, while one will purchase his supplies in large quantities, another will purchase in small, while one will detain him an hour in higgling another knows better, and it seems necessary that the one should have the natural advantage of his better practice, and the other exercise his bad habits at *his own cost*.

When the keeper receives pay for his goods and his labor, he records those receipts, by a short and easy method, before the eyes of his customers, and this record shows the amount received—say six per cent in money, and a certain per cent in labor. Say ten pounds of wheat on every dollar's worth of goods go to pay expenses, and an account of these expenses being balanced against these receipts, shows whether the keeper receives more or less than an equivalent for his labor —if more, perhaps he will reduce it—if less, he must increase his percentage. He can do this perfectly harmoniously, if the customers are allowed to know the necessity of it, which they can do, if the documents with the bills of purchase are habitually exposed upon the table at the public meetings, or in any other manner made public.

In all these operations the store-keeper acts entirely as an individual; if he wishes for counsel, he will seek it of those whom he thinks most capable of counseling. If he wishes to know the views of the whole on any point, he can obtain them at the public meetings, but, having done so, he does not allow the public voice to rise above his individual prerogative; but paying as much deference to their opinions and wishes as he judges best, he proceeds upon his own individual decision, always at *his own risk*, and all is harmonious.

In a similar manner can manufactures and all other business be conducted. If each individual is *free* to make any investment or to decline it—to invest one sum or another, according to his or her inclination in each case; and if the amount be so small as that the risk do not disturb the peace of its owner, and he is at liberty to withdraw it without words or conditions whenever he may choose, one may use the property of another for the general interest, without much disturbance of the general harmony, provided it be made evident to all, that the means are used for the purposes intended, and on the cost principle. So much of connected interests may not be *perfectly* harmonious; but the occasional discords may admonish us that the principle is wrong; and like those of music, if not too frequent and out of proportion, may serve to set off the general harmony to more advantage.

WORKING OF MACHINERY

If one person have not sufficient surplus means to procure machinery for a certain business, all will have an equal interest in assisting in establishing it, provided that each is satisfied that he will have its products at *cost*; but if there is no limit to their price, then they can have no such co-operating interest. The wear of the machinery and all contingent expenses, together with the labor of attendance, would constitute this *cost*. The owner of the machinery would receive nothing from the mere ownership of it; but as it wore away, he would receive in proportion, till at last, when it was worn out, he would have received back the whole of his original investment, and an equivalent for his labor in lending his capital and receiving it back again. Upon this principle, the benefits of the labor-saving powers of the machinery are equally dispersed through the whole community. No one portion is benefited at the cost of another. If one portion is thrown out of employment by it, the land, and all *arts and trades, and professions being open to them,* so that they are easily and comfortably sustained during a new apprenticeship, they are not only not injured, but benefited by new inventions of which they receive their share of the advantages, while they turn and assist in reducing the labor still to be performed by hand; but (cost being made the limit of price) NOT THEREBY REDUCING ITS REWARD. Those engaged in these pursuits will now have less employment, but having *their share* of the natural wealth of the machinery, they have, in the same proportion, *less demand for employment;* in other words, THE BURTHEN OF THEIR LABOR IS REDUCED IN PROPORTION TO THE INTRODUCTION OF MACHINERY. Thus, *cost* being made the limit of price, solves the great problem of *machinery against labor.* . . .

A proper regard to the Individualities of person's tastes, etc., would suggest that hotels be occupied by such persons as are most agreeable to each other; therefore, children generally, as well as their parents, would be much more comfortable not to be so closely mixed up as they would be in a boarding-house with their parents. The connection is already, even in private families, too close for the comfort of either. *Disconnection* will be found the real movement for the happiness of both; and hotels for children, according to the peculiarities of their wants and pursuits, would follow of course. I have seen Infant Schools, in which one woman attended twenty children not above two years old, and where the children entertained each other; taking most of their burthens on themselves, to infinitely more advantage to themselves than the best mothers could have conferred, and, perhaps, fifteen mothers were thus relieved from the most enslaving portion of their domestic labors. And if such institutions were opened and conducted by individuals upon individual responsibilities (instead of combinations), and upon the cost principle, every mother and father, and every member of every family, would be deeply interested in promoting the convenience and reducing the cost of such establishments, and in taking advan-

tage of them. Instead of the offensive process of legislating
upon the fitness of this or that person for those situations,
which is rendered necessary in a combination, any individual
who thought that he or she could supply the demand, might
make proposals, and the patronage received would decide.
This would be an entirely individual movement, there would
be no use for laws, governments, or legislation, but there
would be co-operating interests. Every mother would be free
to send her child or not, according to her individual estimate
of the proposed keeper, the arrangements, and the conditions; and it would, therefore, be a *peaceful* process; whereas,
if every mother should be required by a government, or laws,
or public opinion, to send her children, without the consent
of her own individual approbation, we might expect what we
always experience in combination—resistance, discord, and defeat. The Individual "is by nature a law unto himself" or herself, and if we ever attain our objects, this is not to be overlooked or disregarded.

Pierre-Joseph Proudhon has already been noted as a seminal thinker
whose influence on the development of anarchism is unrivaled. In
the following essay by Charles A. Dana, Proudhon's major economic
programs—all of which served his key doctrine that we must not aim
to *overthrow* the state but to bring about its "dissolution in the
economic organism"—are integrated with a degree of cohesion that
Proudhon's own writings rarely achieved. Dana, who was Assistant
Secretary of War under Abraham Lincoln, surveys a bit of the philosophical soil in which the programs of Proudhon were rooted, but
more needs to be said. One of Proudhon's most arresting and most
characteristic arguments unfolds along these lines:

1   Labor is the sole source of all economic values and should therefore be used as the basis of the price and wage systems; as a consequence, ownership of capital, currency, and land gives no title to any
form of economic reward or compensation.
2   A just society is grounded on reciprocity (mutuality) in human
relations, the exemplary form of which is direct, contractual exchange of service for service, product for product, labor for labor;
here agreements are arranged which neither bind nor affect those not
party to them and which do not require overseeing or enforcement
by administrators and politicians. Such contracts allow for association
without jeopardizing liberty and independence.
3   Property is an essential safeguard of such values as individuality,
liberty, and just relations when kept within the limits of the two
previous precepts. But it has been corrupted by the collusion between capitalism and the state into forms of legally enforced usury
(rent, profit, interest): the law protects monopolies of capital and
currency, permitting men to increase wealth through mere ownership
of these resources. (This is part of what Proudhon meant by char-
acterizing property as "theft" and as a "contradiction.")
4   Human society is composed of an inexhaustible supply of mutually contradictory elements which defy unification or "synthesis"
and which are justified in following their own natural directions and
in reconciling their conflicts without external regulation or imposed
compromise.
5   These conflicting elements have been aggravated by the perversion of property (step 3) into warring factions bent on mutual

suppression or annihilation. The hostile and explosive opposition between capital and labor, together with its source in corrupted prop-
erty-relations, forms "the social problem."

6 Solving this problem exceeds the capacities of both democracy
and communism. For the latter would violate the labor theory of
value and, in addition, sacrifice one of the opposed elements to an
invented notion of solidarity, thus forgetting that human society will
always be generated from incompatibles between which there can
(and should) be reciprocity but no unity. And the former focuses on
state-centered devices like majority rule and extended suffrage, which
make no contact with the essential economic features of the social
problem and which strengthen one of the major sources of that
problem.

7 Rather, the "solution to the social problem" is to be found in a
revolutionary movement that withdraws support from government
and attaches it to citizen-controlled activities (thus dissolving the
state). These activities would (a) operate through voluntary associations in which individuals or localities could federate or contract
with each other on terms mutually agreed to and where combinations
of units (syndicates) had no title to alter the decisions, interests, or
idiosyncrasies of the smaller units composing them and (b) center
around economic projects that would exchange products and services at costs determined by the labor theory of value, basing currency on productive human effort and not on a monopolizable min-
eral, and furnishing credit and capital without interest and homes
and land without rent—that would, in short, reconstruct the economic organism so as to be free from government-licensed forms of
usury.

8 In this way, property, the major source of the social problem,
would be transformed; no longer a mode of theft but a liberty-pro-
tecting institution of mutuality, it could justifiably be retained. Government would be superfluous, since it has a function only where
contradictions, which are inevitable, are harassed into destructive antagonisms, which are not inevitable but in large part the consequence
of government (or government protected) interference, suppression,
and exploitation. Nor would the new economic organism, as opposed
to the political creature it replaced, have any need to perpetuate itself by keeping control over or enforcing order upon the contradictory
elements in society. A social order would gradually take shape, fulfilling and extending the revolutionary ideals of 1789—which for
Proudhon were most completely expressed by steps 1–4 above.

To gain a sense of Proudhon's importance for anarchism, the
reader might compare the proposals made in the rest of this section
with this eight-step argument. Even the communist and pacifist

anarchists, when it comes to concrete programs and modes of organization, are deep in Proudhon's debt.

His fundamental principle is the Equality of Functions. All branches of labor are, he maintains, of the same essential value. We quote from the *Création de l'Ordre dans l'Humanité*:

"What is the comparative measure of values? In other terms, what is for every producer the natural price of the thing he desires to sell relatively to that he desires to buy?

"A. Smith replies: 'The price of each thing is the labor requisite for its production. Accordingly two labourers, by reciprocally estimating their labor, may always find the comparative measure of their products, whatever the value of the articles which they propose to exchange.'

"The error of Smith and those who have followed him is to think that economy becomes more and more remote from its abstract principles as civilization advances; instead of which it is the organic development of Society which renders the application of these principles possible. Yes, the price of everything is the labor necessary to produce it; and, since each laborer is individually paid by his own product, the product of one ought also to be able to pay the labor of another; the only difficulty is to find a comparative measure of values. It will not do to say with Smith: This measure might exist in the savage state, but can be found no longer. Rather let us say: Labor can be equitably valued neither in the barbarous state nor during the ascending period of civilization, nor while there exist those whom pride makes lazy, men incapable through hereditary vice, knaves from intemperance of any sort, traders not controlled by the community; but the time will surely arrive."

This does not mean that every laborer should share equally with all others, which is the doctrine of a school of Communists; no man is less liable to the charge of Communism than Proudhon. He proposes no such arbitrary equality. He means that the labor of a shoe-maker, for example, is as valuable in itself as that of a goldsmith, clerk, artist, physician, legislator,

---

"Proudhon and His Bank of the People," by Charles A. Dana from *Proudhon's Solution of the Social Problem*, edited by Henry Cohen (New York: Vanguard Press, 1927), pp. 15–31.

and that only the accidents of a transitional state of society cause one's work to be valued twice or ten times as high as another's, supposing them equal in talent and industry in their respective employments. It is a sign of great imperfection in the social organization, M. Proudhon would say, when a congressman gets eight dollars a day and a carpenter, who may be vastly superior in his profession to the congressman in his, has to put up with ten and six-pence. This principle, it should not be forgotten, does not preclude the action of natural inequalities of capacity and assiduity, but merely gives them a basis of equality, inequality being, as Proudhon holds, the law of nature always based on its opposite. . . .

PROPERTY

We resume our statement of the economical principles of the great French Radical, and, in order to meet the curiosity of our readers, abandon the logical order of their development, and commence with the last and most startling of all his propositions:

"Property, *de facto et de jure*, is contradictory in its nature, and this is the precise ground why it is an actual thing.

"In fact, Property is the right of possession; at the same time it is the right of exclusion.

"Property is the reward of labor; and at the same time the negation of labor.

"Property is the immediate product of society; and the dissolution of society.

"Property is an institution of justice; and PROPERTY IS ROBBERY.

"From all this it follows that property will yet be transformed according to a positive, complete, social, and true idea; whereby, the old institution of property being abolished, it will become equally real and beneficial for all. And the proof of this is, once again, that property is a Contradiction." . . .

None of the writers who have come up to the defence of Property as it is have stated more ably or clearly than he the necessity for the institution as the basis and condition of society; none have more insisted on the service which it has rendered to the progress of the human race. . . . But it is the characteristic of ideas and institutions to pass through a state of contradiction, of affirmation and negation, of positive and negative, so to say; and this law applies to the facts of political economy as well as to others. . . .

To illustrate this universal presence of the law of contradiction, or of opposites: The invention of machinery is an inestimable benefit to the community, including the laboring classes; but, on the other hand, it throws workmen out of employment, renders their existence precarious, makes them wholly dependent upon the owners of the machines, and necessarily results in pauperism. This is clear to the eyes of all who have eyes to open, and the perception of it is the cause of the attempts that laborers make to destroy machines which, they think, will deprive them of work. What does this indicate? That there should be no machinery, or that pauperism is a good of which we cannot have enough? By no means. It indicates that things are in a state of discord or transition; and,—to borrow an illustration from metaphysics,—just as the contradiction between free will and necessity shows that there is a higher philosophical truth and a more universal formula to be arrived at, which will absorb and reconcile the two, so, in the contradiction between the increase of the aggregate well-being by means of machinery and the corresponding increase of misery by the same means, is there both the ground and the assurance of the establishment of some new and comprehensive social principle in which that antagonism will disappear. In other words, society will yet be so arranged that machinery will work for the equal good of all, and not bring slavery and want to any.

Now, the same contradiction must attach to property, and the adage of Proudhon merely states it in the strongest language. Yet those who speak of it omit half the proposition, and that the first half, "Property is an institution of justice," in order to dwell on the negative, "Property is Robbery." But, taking both clauses together, this is no more than to say: While the right of possession is founded in absolute justice, and without it society could not exist, in the present state of unrelated and hostile individual interests Property becomes an irresistible means, combining the elements of fraud and violence, of taking from the producers, or from those into whose hands the chances of the battle have flung them, the products of labor without giving a fair equivalent, and quite as often without giving any equivalent at all. Or, as Proudhon has it, Property is Robbery. . . .

We conclude this subject with a paragraph translated from the *Contradictions Economiques:*

"Thus property is formed as a matter of convention, which differs as much from justice as eclecticism does from truth, or the real value of a thing does from its market price. In the series of variations which it undergoes between the two extremities of injustice,—namely, rude violence and faithless cunning,—the contending parties continually end by some convention. But justice follows upon their agreement and compels the fulfillment of its conditions; the true law continually evolves itself from the sophistical and arbitrary law, and reform is accomplished through the conflict between intelligence and power. This immense movement, which has its starting-point in the obscurity of savage life and its ending on the day when society rises to the synthetic idea of Possession and of Value, and this mass of changes and of overturnings brought about by the social instinct and perpetually seeking their scientific and definite solution, are what I name the religion of property."

Does this "synthetic idea" mean Communism? No, says our author; it means Reciprocity, Association.

LABOR AND CAPITAL

Labor is productive; capital is not.

Labor produces capital and consumes it; capital produces nothing.

The laborer without capital would soon supply his wants by its production, for the earth and its energies are for his use, the sun shines to aid his toil, the air gives vitality to his corn and vines, the rain brings forward the harvest, and nature, which has created the sheep, the cow, and the horse for his service, has a thousand hidden forces to be employed by the inventions of his brain; but capital with no laborers to consume it can only lie useless and rot back into the first elements of matter.

But, you say, the laborer with capital produces more than one without. Therefore capital is productive as the tool and instrument of labor, and I, its owner, am, in strict and absolute justice, entitled to some share of this larger product which the laborer has realized by its aid.

Not so, friend! Your capital has in itself still produced nothing; it has simply enabled the laborer to derive a greater aid from those powers of nature which are free to all men and are ever ready to help industry; it is thus that the product has been increased, and not because your wheat, or wool, or iron, or steel, or the labor heretofore incorporated with them have created anything. Nature and active labor produce; the remains of past labor, called capital, are only capable of being consumed. If the laborer has used anything of yours, let him give you an equivalent therefor; justice demands nothing more.

Perhaps you answer that, if the laborer will not give you more than an equivalent, he shall not have your capital to use, and may see how he will do without it.

That is another matter. We were not speaking of your wishes or of his necessities. It may be better for him to give you an enormous share of his product rather than be deprived of using your surplus; but that has nothing to do with strict justice, and by no means proves that your capital or anybody's else is productive, as we will show you when Labor and Credit and Exchanges—or, in other words, Production, Circulation, and Consumption—are once rightly organized.

Well, if this be so, what then?

Why, interest and rent are not founded in any permanent principle, but merely arise from temporary necessities. By and by men will pay and receive no more of them. . . .

CREDIT

Did space or time permit us to treat the entire subject thoroughly, we should have taken it up under several distinct heads,—namely: capital is essentially unproductive, and therefore rent and interest are robbery; rent and interest violate the law of fraternity, and cannot do otherwise; the natural increase of wealth tends to their diminution and ultimate disappearance, as is evident from history. They may and will be done away with by the organization of mutual credit, and therefore are intrinsically false.

What is credit?

It is a sort of corollary to the exchange of products, or a kind of second stage of that process. A has a bushel of wheat which he does not need and which B needs, but B has nothing at present to give in exchange for it. A lets him have it, and receives his promise to deliver an equivalent at some future time, when he shall have produced it. Such is the operation of credit, which arose soon after the first commencement of exchanges. Presently it assumed a new feature, which may be illustrated thus: B needs A's bushel of wheat and has an article produced by himself, but cannot divide it so as to render an equivalent, or does not wish to dispose of it at present, and accordingly takes the wheat on credit. Thus credit is the giving of one product in consideration of the future return of another yet to be produced, or which is already produced, but not on the spot or in a condition which will allow it to be delivered. The uses and advantages of this operation are well known, and need no explanation.

All credit presupposes labor, and, if labor were to cease, credit would be impossible.

What, then, is the legitimate source of credit? Who ought to control it? And for whose benefit should it most directly be used?

The laboring classes.

But, instead of credit being governed by the producers in a nation, it is always in the hands of the intermediaries, the exchangers and agents of circulation; and, instead of being used to aid the workers, it is generally used to make money, —i.e., to get the greatest possible amount of the products of labor for the least return, and, if possible, for none at all. And it is manifest that, if the working classes could once gain possession of this great instrument, which rightfully belongs to them, they might escape from the necessity of working for others, or, in other words, of giving the larger part of their products for the use of capital; they might become the owners of the tools they use, become emancipated from the domination exercised over them by their agents and public servants, set up for themselves, and enjoy the fruit of their industry.

But how can they gain possession of this instrument?

By the organization of credit, on the principle of reciprocity or mutualism, if we may use a new word.

In such an organization credit is raised to the dignity of a social function, managed by the community; and, as society never speculates upon its members, it will lend its credit, not as our banks do theirs, so as to make seven per cent or more out of the borrowers, but at the actual cost of the transaction. A practical illustration of the above-named principle in a similar matter may be found in the system of mutual insurance.

MONEY

The precious metals have an intrinsic value, which grows out of their uses in the arts, and another value as the representative of other products. It is only in their latter capacity that they are called money. Their use in that capacity is easy to account for. Their compactness and indestructibility naturally led the world to fix on them for such a purpose.

But, as the aggregate of products and of exchanges enlarged, it was found that gold and silver were inadequate for the transaction of business, and the social genius produced the bill of exchange and the bank-note. This was a great invention, whose benefits are not generally understood, whereby commerce and, consequently, both production and consumption were vastly increased, and with them human well-being.

Still, though a new sort of representative was apparently introduced, in reality there was no change. The bill of exchange was and is only a species of shadow, the representation of a representative, gold and silver remaining as the actual medium of circulation.

The difficulties which belong to the use of gold and silver as money are these:

1 They are articles of commerce as well as representatives, whereas a representative of values should have no other character, and be useful for no other purpose.

2 The quantity of gold and silver not being proportioned to the amount of products to be represented and put into circulation, while at the same time the circulation cannot be performed without them, it follows that whoever can get control of the specie of the world can rule the markets with despotic hand, and may work his will upon communities and nation; and also that such a monopoly of the circulating medium can be effected with an ease almost infinitely greater than a monopoly of any other article of general use. And thus specie money, from being a convenient medium of circulation, has become the tyrant of both the production and the consumption of the world.

3 By means of this tyranny labor is kept in subjection; financial speculations, stock-jobbing, and usury are perpetrated; and interest is maintained at a ruinous rate in every country. Destroy it, and a monopoly even more unjust and pernicious than the monopoly of the soil—that other great outrage upon natural justice—is destroyed, and society is relieved of scores of parasites, who go back to useful occupations, since they are no longer able to live upon the industry of others.

The question then arises whether any other basis than gold or silver can be found for the circulation. M. Proudhon says yes.

Gold and silver feed and clothe and shelter no man; they are good to the mass of people merely because they can be exchanged for food and clothing and shelter. If we, then, can discover anything which shall be equally or more portable, equally certain of being everywhere received in exchange for all products, and at the same time safe from being monopolized, we shall accomplish a great good, and the precious metals may be dispensed with except for their original uses. Is such a circulating medium possible in connection with such a system of credit as that of which we have above given the general features? In other words, can Production, Circulation, and Consumption be organized upon the principle of Mutualism, Reciprocity, Solidarity?

M. Proudhon's answer to this question will be found in our article in which we describe the Bank of the People.

A MUTUALIST BANK

We have stated some of the main points of Proudhon's political economy to be:

1 Equality of functions, or of different employments.
2 Non-productivity of capital.
3 Mutualism of credit, or credit at cost.

In his pamphlets and in the earlier numbers of his paper he gives the name of Bank of Exchange to the practical institution by which he proposes to realize the idea of credit at cost, or, as he expresses it, mutual and gratuitous credit. . . . An institution actually carrying it out with success, and loaning money, everywhere current, not at a high rate of interest, but at the actually trifling cost of transacting its business operations and covering contingencies, would afford the most conclusive proof of the non-productivity of capital; that is to say it would prevent rents from rising above the mere cost of keeping the premises rented in repair, and would totally abolish usury and interest; for, if a man can borrow, without interest, the notes of a bank which are of universal currency and perfectly guaranteed, he will not go to his neighbor and ask credit of him with interest, nor hire his land or his house at any more than it may cost to preserve the same in good condition; and thus, rent and interest being abolished, where remains any productivity of capital? People will then not accumulate wealth as they do now in order to lend at interest, that they may enjoy the fruit of others' toil, themselves doing nothing, but the products of labor, no longer hoarded by the few, will be exchanged and enjoyed by the many; and everywhere new wants in the masses will give a new stimulus to productive industry, which will thrive accordingly to an extent of which, in the present state of monopoly, we have no conception, and there will be universal abundance and satis-

faction; and then whoever wishes to enjoy must labor therefore in some useful vocation, as music, literature, or black-
smithing, or carpentry, or some other. And so there will at
last be gained an equilibrium of values, or just relation of
different branches of labor to each other; or, in other words,
the equality of functions will be established, and the trades
of shoemaker, governor, artist, farmer, etc., be equally remunerated, and that not be arbitrary enactment, but by the natural tendency and effect of the laws which rule in political
economy as well as elsewhere. Such are the ideas of Proudhon. Their final expression is the institution of mutual
credit, whose members—and it should include the whole productive part of the community—combine to lend each other
the credit of the institution at cost, just as the members of a
mutual insurance company combine to afford each other at
cost the guaranty of the company against loss of property by
fire or otherwise. The principle is precisely the same in both
cases.

The Bank of Exchange is composed of men engaged in
productive labor, who, feeling the abuses attached to the fiction which makes gold and silver the basis of the circulation,
associate themselves together to restore the real basis,—
namely, consumable products; and, feeling the evils which
result from the monopoly of credit in the hands of the non-
producing class, they determine to abolish the same.

The institution of mutual credit has two phases: the one
is during the time of its formation, before the whole body of
producers is completed. In the former gold and silver are required for partial use; in the latter they are dispensed with.

Let us suppose a community in which are men pursuing all
branches of useful industry—and by the word useful we mean
to include the fine arts with the trades producing articles of
luxury and elegance—whatever beautifies as well as what supports life—farmers, mechanics, manufacturers, housekeepers,
schoolmasters, artists. They form an institution of mutual
credit, or Bank of Exchange; it issues its notes, loaning them
to A, B, and C as they are wanted and as security is given.
Every man in the community belongs to the bank, and is
bound to receive the notes in exchange for whatever he has
to dispose of. They are, in fact, payable at the farm or the
workshop of every one of the members, not in gold and silver, but in consumable products; and indeed they are not
bank-notes, but bills of exchange, drawn, so to say, on every
member of the bank, and bearing the signature of every

other. They are true representatives, since they stand directly for articles of use. And, as the bank is formed by the whole community, not for the especial advantage of any individual or class, but for the mutual benefit of all, of course no interest is exacted on loans, except enough to cover risks and expenses. Thus, while every man is left free to follow his own productive business in his own way, and the principle of individual liberty suffers no diminution, there is a complete reciprocity established throughout.

The point where a true reform of society must commence is the function of exchanges, for that is the point where economic relations converge. By introducing mutualism into exchanges and credit we introduce it everywhere, and labor will assume a new aspect and become truly democratic. . . .

But how shall this bank be established in our present world as it is in Paris, for instance? There are two ways, says Proudhon. The better way is for the government to do it; let it take the Bank of France, repaying its stockholders, and convert it into the Bank of Exchange, the notes being a legal tender as they now are. Let the rate of interest be reduced, but yet kept sufficiently high to meet the expenses of the government, thereby dispensing with the whole business of tax-assessing and tax-gathering; two or three per cent would be enough to do that at the beginning, and thereafter still further reductions might be made; the revenue would then be collected more surely and without its being felt by the payers; all branches of industry now languishing because the gold and silver that formed the basis of the circulation had been withdrawn and hidden through fear of the revolution by those who controlled them would be revived by suitable loans; neither honest labor, nor the State, need then ever again to fall into the clutches of the usurers; and, instead of passing through a period of depression, want of employment and of bread among the working classes, with ruinous experiments of national workshops and insurrections and bloodshed, followed by a powerful reaction against the new institutions of the country, the republic could at once have entered upon a career of active industry, prosperity, peace, and progress. . . .

Well, continues our economist, if you will not allow the State . . . to undertake this reform we must begin at the other end. We must appeal to individuals, and, if possible, bring together a sufficient body to undertake the work. . . .

30 The Pattern of Life under Decentralized Communism

Certain Marxist views have always attracted communist anarchists. Kropotkin himself thought that expropriation was essential for an anarchist revolution. This view was also held by Alexander Berkman who, together with Emma Goldman, labored unsuccessfully to bring anarchism to life in American society. He was imprisoned and finally deported on the ground of representing a threat to American security. In the selection that follows, Berkman applies many of Kropotkin's key principles—such as mutual aid, regional autonomy, and the indeterminancy of economic values—to the tasks of revolution and rebuilding.

Berkman provides a cogent reply to the familiar charge that a communist-anarchist system cannot ensure a sufficient supply of necessary labor. But his reply is not the only one available to a libertarian communist. For example, in *Anarchy and Chaos*, George Woodcock argued (1) that the need for productive, socially useful, and voluntarily organized work is a natural one, the satisfaction of which is integral to human health; (2) that workers today require external incentives only because this natural need is thwarted in the coercive, stifling, and absurd conditions of labor under capitalism; and (3) that "the anarchists therefore believe that the free distribution, without obligation, of goods to satisfy the needs of every man will, by making him economically free, give him a greater incentive to work. . . ." This view is perfectly compatible with Berkman's and could be used to strengthen his case.

In a nutshell, then, the meaning of Communist Anarchism is this: the abolition of government, of coercive authority and all its agencies, and joint ownership—which means free and equal participation in the general work and welfare.

"You said that Anarchy will secure economic equality," remarks your friend. "Does that mean equal pay for all?"

Now and After: The A.B.C. of Anarchist Communism, by Alexander Berkman (London: Freedom Press, 1942; new edition, 1964), pp. 196–97, 273–88.

It does. Or, what amounts to the same, equal participation in the public welfare. Because, as we already know, labor is social. No man can create anything all by himself, by his own efforts. Now, then, if labor is social, it stands to reason that the results of it, the wealth produced, must also be social, belong to the collectivity. No person can therefore justly lay claim to the exclusive ownership of the social wealth. It is to be enjoyed by all alike.

"But why not give each according to the value of his work?" you ask.

Because there is no way by which value can be measured. That is the difference between value and price. Value is what a thing is worth, while price is what it can be sold or bought for in the market. What a thing is worth no one really can tell. . . . Suppose the carpenter worked three hours to make a kitchen chair, while the surgeon took only half an hour to perform an operation that saved your life. If the amount of labor used determines value, then the chair is worth more than your life. Obvious nonsense, of course. Even if you should count in the years of study and practice the surgeon needed to make him capable of performing the operation, how are you going to decide what "an hour of operating" is worth? . . .

The exchange of commodities by means of prices leads to profit making, to taking advantage and exploitation; in short, to some form of capitalism. If you do away with profits, you cannot have any price system, nor any system of wages or payment. That means that exchange must be according to value. But as value is uncertain or not ascertainable, exchange must consequently be free, without "equal" value, since such does not exist. In other words, labor and its products must be exchanged without price, without profits, freely, according to necessity. This logically leads to ownership in common and to joint use. Which is a sensible, just, and equitable system, and is known as Communism. . . .

"Let me get this straight," you remark. "There is to be equal sharing, you say. Then you won't be able to buy anything?"

No, there will be no buying or selling. The revolution abolishes private ownership of the means of production and distribution, and with it goes capitalistic business. Personal possession remains only in the things you use. Thus, your watch is your own, but the watch factory belongs to the people. Land, machinery, and all other public utilities will be collective property, neither to be bought nor sold. Actual use will be considered the only title—not to ownership but to possession. The organization of the coal miners, for example, will be in charge of the coal mines, not as owners but as the operating agency. Similarly will the railroad brotherhoods run the railroads, and so on. Collective possession, co-operatively managed in the interests of the community, will take the place of personal ownership privately conducted for profit.

"But if you can't buy anything, then what's the use of money?" you ask.

None whatever; money becomes useless. You can't get anything for it. When the sources of supply, the land, factories, and products become public property, socialized, you can neither buy nor sell. As money is only a medium for such transactions, it loses its usefulness.

"But how will you exchange things?"

Exchange will be free. The coal miners, for instance, will deliver the coal they mined to the public coal yards for the use of the community. In their turn the miners will receive from the community's warehouses the machinery, tools, and the other commodities they need. That means free exchange without the medium of money and without profit, on the basis of requirement and the supply of hand. . . . With the abolition of capitalism no one will be interested in raising the price of coal or limiting its supply. As much coal will be mined as will be necessary to satisfy the need. Similarly will as much food be raised as the country needs. It will be the *requirements* of the community and the supply obtainable which will determine the amount it is to receive. This applies to coal and food as to all other needs of the people.

"But suppose there is not enough of a certain product to go around. What will you do then?"

Then we'll do what is done even in capitalistic society in time of war and scarcity: the people are rationed, with the difference that in the free community rationing will be managed on principles of equality.

"But suppose the farmer refuses to supply the city with his products unless he gets money?"

The farmer, like any one else, wants money only if he can buy with it the things he needs. He will quickly see that money is useless to him. In Russia during the Revolution you could not get a peasant to sell you a pound of flour for a bagful of money. But he was eager to give you a barrel of the finest grain for an old pair of boots. It is plows, spades, rakes, agricultural machinery, and clothing which the farmer wants, not money. For these he will let you have his wheat, barley, and corn. In other words, the city will exchange with the farm the products each requires, on the basis of need.

It has been suggested by some that exchange during the period of revolutionary reconstruction should be based on some definite standard. It is proposed, for example, that every community issue its own money, as is often done in time of revolution; or that a day's work should be considered the unit of value and so-called labor notes serve as medium of exchange. But neither of these proposals is of practical help. Money issued by communities in revolution would quickly depreciate to the point of no value, since such money would have no secure guarantees behind it, without which money is worth nothing. Similarly labor notes would not represent any definite and measurable value as a means of exchange. What would, for instance, an hour's work of the coal miner be worth? Or fifteen minutes' consultation with the physician? Even if all effort should be considered equal in value and an hour's labor be made the unit, could the house painter's hour of work or the surgeon's operation be equitably measured in terms of wheat?

Common sense will solve this problem on the basis of human equality and the right of every one to life.

"Such a system might work among decent people," your friend objects; "but how about shirkers? Were not the Bolsheviki right in establishing the principle that 'whoever doesn't work, doesn't eat'?"

No, my friend, you are mistaken. . . . It was impractical because it required an army of officials to keep tab on the people who worked or didn't work. It led to incrimination and recrimination and endless disputes about official decisions. So that within a short time the number of those who didn't work was doubled and even trebled by the effort to force people to work and to guard against their dodging or doing bad work. It was the system of compulsory labor which soon proved such a failure that the Bolsheviki were compelled to give it up.

Moreover, the system caused even greater evils in other directions. Its injustice lay in the fact that you cannot break into a person's heart or mind and decide what peculiar physical or mental condition makes it temporarily impossible for him to work. Consider further the precedent you establish by introducing a false principle and thereby rousing the opposition of those who feel it wrong and oppressive and therefore refuse cooperation.

A rational community will find it more practical and beneficial to treat all alike, whether one happens to work at the time or not, rather than create more non-workers to watch those already on hand, or to build prisons for their punishment and support. For if you refuse to feed a man, for whatever cause, you drive him to theft and other crimes—and thus you yourself create the necessity for courts, lawyers, judges, jails, and warders, the upkeep of whom is far more burdensome than to feed the offenders. And these you have to feed, anyhow, even if you put them in prison.

The revolutionary community will depend more on awakening the social consciousness and solidarity of its delinquents than on punishment. It will rely on the example set by its working members, and it will be right in doing so. For the natural attitude of the industrious man to the shirker is such that the latter will find the social atmosphere so unpleasant that he will prefer to work and enjoy the respect and good will of his fellows rather than to be despised in idleness. . . . On the foundations of liberty, justice, and equality, as also on understanding and sympathy, must be built every phase of life in the social revolution. Only so it can endure. This applies to the problems of shelter, food, and the security of your district or city, as well as to the defense of the revolution.

As regards housing and local safety Russia has shown the way in the first months of the October Revolution. House committees, chosen by the tenants, and city federations of such committees, take the problem in hand. They gather statistics of the facilities of a given district and of the number of applicants requiring quarters. The latter are assigned according to personal or family need on the basis of equal rights.

Similar house and district committees have charge of the provisioning of the city. Individual application for rations at the distributing centers is a stupendous waste of time and energy. Equally false is the system, practiced in Russia in the first years of the Revolution, of issuing rations in the institutions of one's employment, in shops, factories, and offices. The better and more efficient way, which at the same time insures more equitable distribution and closes the door to favoritism and misuse, is rationing by houses or streets. The

authorized house or street committee procures at the local
distributing center the provisions, clothing, etc., apportioned
to the number of tenants represented by the committee. . . .
Taking care of the sanitary and kindred needs of street and
district by voluntary committees of house and locality affords
the best results, since such bodies, themselves tenants of the
given district, are personally interested in the health and
safety of their families and friends. . . .

PRODUCTION

It should be clearly understood that *the social revolution
necessitates more intensive production* than under capitalism
in order to supply the needs of the large masses who till
then had lived in penury. This greater production can be
achieved only by the workers having previously prepared
themselves for the new situation. Familiarity with the processes of industry, knowledge of the sources of supply, and
determination to succeed will accomplish the task. The enthusiasm generated by the revolution, the energies liberated,
and the inventiveness stimulated by it must be given full
freedom and scope to find creative channels. . . .

On the other hand, the new situation will greatly simplify
the present very complex problems of industry. For you must
consider that capitalism, because of its competitive character
and contradictory financial and commercial interests, involves
many intricate and perplexing issues which would be entirely
eliminated by the abolition of the conditions of to-day. Questions of wage scales and selling prices; the requirements of
the existing markets and the hunt for new ones; the scarcity
of capital for large operations and the heavy interest to be
paid on it; new investments, the effects of speculation and
monopoly, and a score of related problems which worry the
capitalist and make industry such a difficult and cumbersome
network to-day would all disappear. . . . All this would be
automatically done away with by the socialization of industry
and the termination of the competitive system; and thereby
the problems of production will be immensely lightened. The
knotted complexity of capitalist industry need therefore inspire no undue fear for the future. Those who talk of labor
not being equal to manage "modern" industry fail to take
into account the factors referred to above. . . .

Furthermore it must be considered that the task of increased production would be enormously facilitated by the

addition to the ranks of labor of vast numbers whom the altered economic conditions will liberate for work.

Recent statistics show that in 1920 there were in the United States over 41 million persons of both sexes engaged in gainful occupations out of a total population of over 105 millions. Out of those 41 millions only 26 millions were actually employed in the industries, including transportation and agriculture, the balance of 15 millions consisting mostly of persons engaged in trade, of commercial travelers, advertisers, and various other middlemen of the present system. In other words, 15 million persons would be released for useful work by a revolution in the United States. A similar situation, proportionate to population, would develop in other countries.

The greater production necessitated by the social revolution would therefore have an additional army of many million persons at its disposal. The systematic incorporation of those millions into industry and agriculture, aided by modern scientific methods of organization and production, will go a long way toward helping to solve the problems of supply.

Capitalist production is for profit; more labor is used today to sell things than to produce them. The social revolution reorganizes the industries on the basis of the needs of the populace. Essential needs come first, naturally. Food, clothing, shelter—these are the primal requirements of man. The first step in this direction is the ascertaining of the available supply of provisions and other commodities. The labor associations in every city and community take this work in hand for the purpose of equitable distribution. Workers' committees in every street and district assume charge, cooperating with similar committees in the city and State, and federating their efforts throughout the country by means of general councils of producers and consumers. . . .

With the aid of industrial machinery and by scientific cultivation of the land freed from monopoly the revolution must first of all supply the elemental wants of society. In farming and gardening intensive cultivation and modern methods have made us practically independent of natural soil quality and climate. To a very considerable extent man now makes his own soil and his own climate, thanks to the achievements of chemistry. Exotic fruits can be raised in the north to be supplied to the warm south, as is being done in France. Science is the wizard who enables man to master all difficulties and overcome all obstacles. The future, liberated from the incubus of the profit system and enriched by the work of the millions of non-producers of to-day, holds the greatest welfare for society. That future must be the objective point of the social revolution; its motto: bread and well-being for all. . . .

The revolution must strive to enable every community to sustain itself, to become materially independent. No country should have to rely on outside help or exploit colonies for its support. That is the way of capitalism. The aim of Anarchism, on the contrary, is material independence, not only for the individual, but for every community.

This means gradual decentralization instead of centralization. Even under capitalism we see the decentralization tendency manifest itself in spite of the essentially centralistic character of the present-day industrial system. Countries which were before entirely dependent on foreign manufactures, as Germany in the last quarter of the nineteenth century, later Italy and Japan, and now Hungary, Czechoslovakia, etc., are gradually emancipating themselves industrially, working their own natural resources, building their own factories and mills, and attaining economic independence from other lands. International finance does not welcome this development and tries its utmost to retard its progress, because it is more profitable for the Morgans and Rockefellers to keep such countries as Mexico, China, India, Ireland, or Egypt industrially backward, in order to exploit their natural resources and at the same time be assured of foreign markets for "overproduction" at home. The governments of the great financiers and lords of industry help them secure those foreign natural resources and markets, even at the point of the bayonet. . . . In short, capitalism needs centralization. But a free country needs decentralization, independence not only political but also industrial, economic. . . .

Decentralization will cure society of many evils of the centralized principle. Politically decentralization means freedom; industrially, material independence; socially it implies security and well-being for the small communities; individually it results in manhood and liberty.

Equally important to the social revolution as independence from foreign lands is decentralization within the country itself. Internal decentralization means making the larger regions, even every community so far as possible, self-supporting. In his very illuminating and suggestive work, *Fields, Factories, and Workshops,* Peter Kropotkin has convincingly shown how a city like Paris even, now almost exclusively commercial, could raise enough food in its own environs to support its population abundantly. . . .

When the social revolution begins in any land, its foreign commerce stops: the importation of raw materials and finished products is suspended. The country may even be blockaded by the bourgeois governments, as was the case with Russia. Thus the revolution is compelled to become self-supporting and provide for its own wants. Even various parts of the same country may have to face such an eventuality. They would have to produce what they need within their own area, by their own efforts. Only decentralization could solve this problem. The country would have to reorganize its activities in such a manner as to be able to feed itself. It would have to resort to production on a small scale, to home industry, and to intensive agriculture and horticulture. . . .

The role of industrial decentralization in the revolution is unfortunately too little appreciated. Even in progressive labor ranks there is a dangerous tendency to ignore or minimize its importance. Most people are still in the thraldom of the Marxian dogma that centralization is "more efficient and economical." They close their eyes to the fact that the alleged "economy" is achieved at the cost of the worker's limb and life, that the "efficiency" degrades him to a mere industrial cog, deadens his soul, and kills his body. Furthermore, in a system of centralization the administration of industry becomes constantly merged in fewer hands, producing a powerful bureaucracy of industrial overlords. It would indeed be the sheerest irony if the revolution were to aim at such a result. It would mean the creation of a new master class.

The revolution can accomplish the emancipation of labor only by gradual decentralization, by developing the individual worker into a more conscious and determining factor in the processes of industry, by making him the impulse whence proceeds all industrial and social activity. The deep significance of the social revolution lies in the abolition of the mastery of man over man, putting in its place the management of things. Only thus can be achieved industrial and social freedom.

"Are you sure it would work?" you demand.

I am sure of this: if that will not work, nothing else will. The plan I have outlined is a free communism, a life of voluntary cooperation and equal sharing. There is no other way of securing economic equality which alone is liberty.

In the preceding selection Alexander Berkman argued for industrial
decentralization and economic autonomy, two aims stressed by almost every contribution to this section. But these aims may appear
ludicrous. Does not history, as the Marxists allege, betray a relentless
pattern of increasing centralization? Does not contemporary industry
require that authoritative decisions be turned over to a small group
of leaders and that technology be geographically concentrated in a
few enormous urban centers? For Senex, modern science favors a negative answer to all such questions. It has developed modes of production which only regional decentralization can fully or properly
exploit. And this means that there may yet be ways of restoring our
swollen cities to human proportions—a point Paul Goodman approaches from another perspective in selection 35.

Senex's short piece is remarkably instructive concerning the relations between different forms of anarchism. On one hand, though
ostensibly a defense of anarchism-communism, his model of independent and federated regions appears to have outgrown the quarrels
between communist and individualist anarchists and to sacrifice little
that is central in the proposals of Warren, Proudhon, and Berkman.
But this selection opens up a deep contrast between Tolstoy's con-
demnations of modern industry and those anarchists who, following
Kropotkin, have viewed mechanization as the most fertile soil for
the cultivation of libertarian values, and raises the question of
whether this dispute, also, can be outgrown.

The idea of an integrated and regionally decentralized economy forming one of the theoretical bases of the ideal of the
Anarchist commune has by now advanced beyond the theoretical stage and is forcing itself to the fore of economic ac-
tualities. "What was a bold prophecy on the part of Kropotkin," writes Lewis Mumford in his . . . book *The Culture of
Cities*, "has become a definite movement, as the technical

"Decentralization and Socialism," by Senex in *Vanguard* IV:4
(July, 1938), 8–10.

means of economic regionalism and the social impulses that gave it direction have converged."

And, without detracting [in] the least from the great originality of this book, one might say that the latter has shown the convergence of various streams of modern thought and truly valuable social experimentation upon the focal point of Anarchism-Communism: the ex-territorial commune as the basic cell of a federated society. Mumford uses the term "region" instead of ex-territorial commune, but the connotations of his term are the same. For to Mumford a region is not just a political or geographic unit, but "the basic configuration in human life," and also "a permanent sphere of cultural influences and a center of economic activities." It is "an area large enough to embrace a sufficient range of interests, and small enough to keep the interests in focus and to make them a subject of direct collective concern."

A region thus conceived is something altogether different from the political and administrative divisions which disregard functional boundaries. These divisions are the work of the tyrannous political state whose emergence upon the stage of modern history is viewed by Mumford as a colossal tragedy resulting from the disintegration of the superior social and political pattern of the medieval city. Like Kropotkin, Mumford rejects the pseudo-scientific view of the Marxists which attributes to the State the category of a historic necessity brought about by the nascent forms of modern Capitalism.

To Mumford, the triumph of the tyrannous political State over the medieval commune was no more of a historic necessity than the victory of Fascism, whose role and dynamics, as it is clear to every student of Kropotkin, are similar to the one manifested by the emerging absolutist State. It was the logical end-point of a process of enthropy—a "running down" of collective energy, which, *unlike the reverse process of a creative upswing*, is historically determined in its various phases.

Mumford dedicates a considerable portion of the book to the analysis of the general forms of the medieval commune, which to him, as to every libertarian thinker, represents the greatest approach to the natural function of a city as a specialized organ of social transmission. The breakdown of this normal pattern of communal life was the starting point of the process of social disruption, of crystallization of chaos now reaching its highest in the development of a functionally

perverted city—the megalopolis—and the threatened collapse
of civilization. . . .

Mumford also upholds one of the favorite ideas of Kropotkin and Reclus in respect to the role of social intelligence in
forestalling the threatened collapse of civilization and the
shaping of new forms. Conscious orientation can forestall the
tragic end of the downgrade cycle of civilization and turn it
into the starting point of a new regeneration cycle. . . . This
conscious orientation will be centered not only upon the very
general aims of the socialist ideal such as the collective ownership of land and the means of production, but upon the
evolvement of an integrated form of social life based upon
regional units. And contrary to the opinions of the State socialists, this orientation upon regionalism (the Bakuninites in
the First International called it Communalism) is much more
in consonance with the basic trends of modern technics than
the centralized State economics of the Marxists. The ruraliza-
tion of industry and industrialization of agriculture are assuming the nature of clearly manifested economic tendencies.
. . . With the removal of the present system, economic life
will shape itself in greater obedience to the demands of modern technics which point in the direction of regional decentralization and integration of economic activities on a local
scale. Specialization of industry and gigantic units are a liability under conditions demanding flexibility and ease of
adaptation. And they will become superfluous with the growing mobility of power, its wider distribution from central
energy station. Along with that go other factors favoring decentralization such as the greater application of systematic
knowledge in the exploitation of resources and organization of
work; the growing importance of biological and social sciences;
soil regeneration, selective breeding, intensification of crop
yields through cultivation of plants in specially prepared
tanks, and in general, the raising of agriculture to the status
of a scientific industry leading to the leveling of agricultural
advantages and the fusion of city and rural areas. Those are
technical factors operating at the present, but in sketching the
outlines of the collective society of the near future one should
also take into consideration the incidence of a technic which
is just emerging from its experimental stage: the utilization
of new sources of power such as solar energy; storage of electric energy; special energy crops grown under conditions laid
down by scientific agronomy; the use of television and the
fuller exploitation of the airplane. And it is clear that each

of these factors will contribute to the acceleration of the same tendency toward decentralization and wide distribution of agricultural, industrial and cultural advantages now centered only in certain areas.

Mumford effectively disposes of the stock arguments advanced against the idea of regional decentralization which were held up against Kropotkin by the state socialists of a generation ago. Regionalism, he declares, is not synonymous with autarchy, economic and cultural isolation. Nor does it connote the return to the parochialism and political independence of the medieval cities with their mutual strifes. The region will be the integrated cell but not an independent political unit, a miniature state possessing the attributes of political sovereignty. Inter-regional controls will exist, and for the time being, those controls will be vested in the political state stripped of its power functions and transformed into a "service" state. This is quite in keeping with the realistic trends in libertarian thought which is coming to grapple with the problem of the transitional period in a sober fashion. *For political sovereignty can be attenuated but cannot be conjured out of existence by a revolutionary fiat. . . .*

Inter-regional control does not have to coincide with the boundaries of the national state. It will tend to be world-wide, just as the foreign trade of the region based upon a special sort of currency directly attached to the commodities exchanged and valid only for this specific function. This, together with free migration, lack of definite boundaries between regions, the extra-territorial linkage effected by the associations within the region and tending to be world-wide with the vanishing of the national state,—all that will gradually create the new world culture, permeated with universal values and shot through with the infinite variety of local *motifs* and cultural idioms of the regions.

This is the ideal of the federalist, libertarian socialism as taught by Proudhon, Bakunin and Kropotkin.

Rudolf Rocker was a prolific modern anarchist whose writings encompassed such varied fields as literary criticism and American intellectual history. But his major contribution to anarchism was a classic exposition of anarcho-syndicalism, the crucial portions of which appear below. His account makes it evident that almost all of anarcho-syndicalism can be seen as extending the anarchist-communist position of Berkman and Kropotkin. Both views, it emerges, are committed to the collective ownership of productive forces (worker ownership) and to decentralized modes of operation where decisions originate from "the bottom up" (worker control).

The term "workers' syndicate" meant in France at first merely a trade union organization of producers for the immediate betterment of their economic and social status. But the rise of revolutionary Syndicalism gave this original meaning a much wider and deeper import. Just as the party is, so to speak, the unified organization for definite political effort within the modern constitutional state, and seeks to maintain the bourgeois order in one form or another so, according to the Syndicalist view, the trade union, the syndicate, is the unified organization of labour and has for its purpose the defence of the interests of the producers within existing society and the preparing for and the practical carrying out of the reconstruction of social life after the pattern of Socialism. It has, therefore, a double purpose: 1. As the fighting organization of the workers against the employers to enforce the demands of the workers for the safeguarding and raising of their standard of living; 2. As the school for the intellectual training of the workers to make them acquainted with the technical management of production and economic life in general so that when a revolutionary situation arises they will be capable of taking

Anarcho-Syndicalism, by Rudolf Rocker (Indore, India: Modern Publishers, 1938), pp. 98–154. Subheads provided by the editors.

the socio-economic organism into their own hands and re-making it according to Socialist principle. . . .

Education for Socialism does not mean for them trivial campaign propaganda and so-called "politics of the day," but the effort to make clear to the workers, the intrinsic connections among social problems, by technical instruction and the development of their administrative capacities, to prepare them for their role of re-shapers of economic life, and give them the moral assurance required for the performance of their task. No social body is better fitted for this purpose than the economic fighting organization of the workers; it gives a definite direction to their social activities and toughens their resistance in the immediate struggle for the necessities of life and the defence of their human rights. This direct and unceasing warfare with the supporters of the present system develops at the same time the ethical concepts without which any social transformation is impossible: vital solidarity with their fellows-in-destiny and moral responsibility for their own actions.

Just because the educational work of the Anarcho-Syndicalists is directed toward the development of independent thought and action, they are outspoken opponents of all those centralizing tendencies which are so characteristic of political labour parties. But centralism, that artificial organization from above downward which turns over the affairs of everybody in a lump to a small minority, is always attended by barren official routine; and this crushes individual conviction, kills all personal initiative by lifeless discipline and bureaucratic ossification, and permits no independent action. The organization of Anarcho-Syndicalism is based on the principles of Federalism, on free combination from below upward, putting the right of self-determination of every member above everything else and recognizing only the organic agreement of all on the basis of like interests and common convictions.

It has often been charged against Federalism that it divides the forces and cripples the strength of organized resistance. . . . But here, too, the facts of life have spoken more clearly than any theory. There was no country in the world where the whole labour movement was so completely centralized and the technique of organization developed to such extreme perfection as in Germany before Hitler's accession to power. A powerful bureaucratic apparatus covered the whole country and determined every political and economic expression of the organized workers. In the very last elections the

Social Democratic and Communist parties united over twelve million voters for their candidates. But after Hitler seized power six million organized workers did not raise a finger to avert the catastrophe which had plunged Germany into the abyss, and which in a few months beat their organizations completely to pieces.

But in Spain, where Anarcho-Syndicalism had maintained its hold upon organized labour from the days of the First International, and by untiring libertarian propaganda and sharp fighting had trained it to resistance, it was the powerful C[onferacion] N[acional de] T[rabajadores] which by the boldness of its action frustrated the criminal plans of Franco. . . .

For the state, centralism is the appropriate form of organization, since it aims at the greatest possible uniformity in social life for the maintenance of political and social equilibrium. But for a movement whose very existence depends on prompt action at any favourable moment and on the independent thought and action of its supporters, centralism could but be a curse, by weakening its power of decision and systematically repressing all immediate action. If, for example, as was the case in Germany, every local strike had first to be approved by the Central, which was often hundreds of miles away and was usually not in a position to pass a correct judgment on the local conditions, one cannot wonder that the inertia of the apparatus of organization renders a quick attack quite impossible, and there thus arises a state of affairs where the energetic and intellectually alert groups no longer serve as patterns for the less active, but are condemned by these to inactivity, inevitably bringing the whole movement to stagnation. Organization is, after all, only a means to an end. When it becomes an end in itself, it kills the spirit and the vital initiative of its members and sets up that domination by mediocrity which is the characteristic of all bureaucracies.

Anarcho-Syndicalists are, therefore, of the opinion that trade union organization should be of such a character as to afford workers the possibility of achieving the utmost in their struggle against the employers, and at the same time provide them with a basis from which they will be able in a revolutionary situation to proceed with reshaping of economic and social life.

Their organization is accordingly constructed on the following principles: The workers in each locality join the unions for their respective trades, and these are subject to the veto of no Central but enjoy the entire right of self-determination. The trade unions of a city or a rural district combine in a so-called labour cartel. The labour cartels constitute the centres for local propaganda and education; they weld the workers together as a class and prevent the rise of any narrow-minded factional spirit. In times of local labour trouble they arrange for the solidaric co-operation of the whole body of organized labour in the use of every agency available under the circumstances. All the labour cartels are grouped according to districts and regions to form the National Federation of Labour Cartels, which maintains the permanent connection between the local bodies, arranges for free adjustment of the productive labour of the members of the different organization on co-operative lines, provides for the necessary co-ordination in the work of education, in which the stronger cartels will need to come to aid of the weaker ones, and in general supports the local groups with council and guidance.

Every trade union is, moreover, federatively allied with all the organizations in the same trade throughout the country, and these in turn with all related trades, so that all are combined in general industrial alliances. It is the task of these alliances to arrange for the co-operative action of the local groups, to conduct solidaric strikes where the necessity arises, and to meet all the demands of the day-to-day struggle between capital and labour. Thus the Federation of Labour Cartels and the Federation of Industrial Alliances constitute the two poles about which the whole life of the trade unions revolves.

Such a form of organization not only gives the workers every opportunity for direct action in their struggles for daily bread, it also provides them with the necessary preliminaries for carrying through the reorganization of social life on a Socialist plan by their own strength and without alien intervention, in case of a revolutionary crisis. Anarcho-Syndicalists are convinced that a Socialist economic order cannot be created by the decrees and statutes of a government, but only by the solidaric collaboration of the workers with hand or brain in each special branch of production; that is, through the taking over of the management of all plants by the producers themselves under such form that the separate groups, plants, and branches of industry are independent members of the general economic organism and systematically carry on pro-

duction and the distribution of the products in the interest of
the community on the basis of free mutual agreements.

In such a case the labour cartels would take over the existing social capital in each community, determine the needs
of the inhabitants of their districts, and organize local consumption. Through the agency of the national Federation of
Labour Cartels it would be possible to calculate the total requirements of the country and adjust the work of production
accordingly. On the other hand, it would be the task of the Industrial Alliances to take control of all the instruments of
production, machines, raw materials, means of transportation,
and the like, and to provide the separate producing groups
with what they need. In a word: 1. Organization of the plants
by the producers themselves and direction of the work by
labour councils elected by them. 2. Organization of the total
production of the country by the industrial and agricultural
alliances. 3. Organization of consumption by the Labour
Cartels. . . .

It is the great merit of Libertarian Socialism in Spain,
which now finds expression in the C. N. T. and the
F[edercion] A[narquista] I[berica], that since the days of
the first International it has trained the workers in that spirit
which treasures freedom above all else and regards the intellectual independence of its adherents as the basis of its
existence. The libertarian labour movement in Spain has
never lost itself in the labyrinth of an economic metaphysics
which crippled its intellectual buoyancy by fatalistic conceptions, as was the case in Germany; nor has it unprofitably
wasted its energy in the barren routine tasks of bourgeois
parliaments. Socialism was for it a concern of the people, an
organic growth proceeding from the activity of the masses
themselves and having its basis in their economic organizations.

Therefore the C. N. T. is not simply an alliance of industrial workers like the trade unions in every other country.
It embraces within its ranks also the syndicates of the peasant
and field-workers as well as those of the brain-workers and the
intellectuals. If the Spanish peasants are now fighting shoulder to shoulder with city workers against Fascism, it is the result of the great work of Socialist education which has been
performed by the C. N. T. and its forerunners. . . .

In Catalonia to-day three-fourths of the land is collectivized
and co-operatively cultivated by the peasants' syndicates. In
this each community presents a type by itself and adjusts its

internal affairs in its own way, but settles economic questions through the agency of its Federation. Thus there is preserved the possibility of free enterprise, inciting new ideas and mutual stimulation. One-fourth of the country is in the hands of small peasant proprietors, to whom has been left the free choice between joining the collectives or continuing their family husbandry. . . .

But the workers' syndicates have made their most astounding achievements in the field of industry, since they took into their hands the administration of industrial life as a whole. In Catalonia in the course of a year the railroads were fitted out with a complete modern equipment, and in punctuality the service reached a point that had been hitherto unknown. The same advances were achieved in the entire transport system, in the textile industry, in machine construction, in building, and in the small industries. . . . Above all, they [the Syndicates] have proved *that the workers, even without the capitalist, are able to carry on production and to do it better than a lot of profit-hungry entrepreneurs.* Whatever the outcome of the bloody war in Spain may be, to have given this great demonstration remains the indisputable service of the Spanish Anarcho-Syndicalists, whose heroic example has opened for the Socialist movement new outlooks for the future. . . .

[The workers] must understand that however different the immediate preliminaries for their liberation might be in different countries, the effects of capitalist exploitation are everywhere the same and they must, therefore, give to their efforts the necessary international character.

Above all they must not tie up these efforts with the interests of the national states, as has, unfortunately, happened in most countries hitherto. The world of organized labour must pursue its own ends, as it has its own interests to defend, and these are not identical with those of the state or those of the possessing classes. A collaboration of workers and employers such as was advocated by the Socialist Party and the trade unions in Germany after the World War can only result in the workers being condemned to the role of the poor Lazarus, who must be content to eat the crumbs that fall from the rich man's table. Collaboration is possible only where the ends and, most important of all, the interests are the same. . . . As long as the worker ties up his interests with those of the bourgeoisie of his country instead of with those of his class, he must logically also take in his stride all the results of that relationship. He must stand ready to fight the wars of the possessing classes for the retention and extension of their markets, and to defend any injustice they may perpetrate on other peoples. The Socialist press of Germany was merely being consistent when, at the time of the World War, they urged the annexation of foreign territory. This was merely the inevitable result of the intellectual attitude and the methods which the political labour parties had pursued for a long time before the War. Only when the workers in every country shall come to understand clearly that their interests are everywhere the same, and out of this understanding learn to act together, will the effective basis be laid for the international liberation of the working class. . . .

It, therefore, concerns us to-day to reconstruct the economic life of the peoples from the ground up and build it up anew in the spirit of Socialism. But only the producers themselves are fitted for this task, since they are the only value creating element in society out of which a new future can arise. Theirs must be the task of freeing labour from all the fetters which economic exploitation has fastened on it, of freeing society from all the institutions and procedure of political power, and of opening the way to an alliance of free groups of men and women based on co-operative labour and a planned administration of things in the interest of the community. To prepare the toiling masses in city and country for this great goal and to bind them together as a militant force is the objective of modern Anarcho-Syndicalism, and in this its whole purpose is exhausted.

THE LIBERATION OF LABOR: BY POLITICS OR DIRECT ACTION?

The attitude of Anarcho-Syndicalism toward the political power of the present-day state is exactly the same as it takes toward the system of capitalist exploitation. Its adherents are perfectly clear that the social injustices of that system rest, not on its unavoidable excrescences, but in the capitalist economic order as such. But, while their efforts are directed at abolishing the existing form of capitalist exploitation and replacing it by a Socialist order, they never for a moment forget to work also by every means at their command to lower the rate of profit of the capitalists under existing conditions, and to raise the producer's share of the products of his labour to the highest possible.

Anarcho-Syndicalists pursue the same tactics in their fight

against that political power which finds its expression in the
state. They recognize that the modern state is just the consequence of capitalist economic monopoly, and the class divisions which this has set up in society, and merely serves
the purpose of maintaining this status by every oppressive instrument of political power. But, while they are convinced
that along with the system of exploitation its political protective device, the state, will also disappear, to give place to
the administration of public affairs on the basis of free agreement, they do not at all overlook that the efforts of the
worker within the existing political order must always be directed toward defending all achieved political and social
rights against every attack of reaction, constantly widening
the scope of these rights wherever the opportunity for this
presents itself.

For just as the worker cannot be indifferent to the economic conditions of his life in existing society, so he cannot
remain indifferent to the political structure of his country.
Both in the struggle for his daily bread and for every kind of
propaganda looking toward his social liberation he needs political rights and liberties, and he must fight for these himself in every situation where they are denied him, and must
defend them with all his strength whenever the attempt is
made to wrest them from him. It is, therefore, utterly absurd to assert that the Anarcho-Syndicalists take no interest
in the political struggles of the time. . . .

Of course, if one accepts Lenin's cynical phrase and thinks
of freedom as merely a "bourgeois prejudice," then, to be
sure, political rights and liberties have no value at all for the
workers. . . . But the Anarcho-Syndicalists would be the very
last to mistake the importance of these rights to the workers.
If they, nevertheless, reject any participation in the work of
bourgeois parliaments, it is not because they have no sympathy with political struggles in general, but because they
are firmly convinced that parliamentary activity is for the
workers the very weakest and most hopeless form of the political struggle. For the bourgeois classes the parliamentary
system is without a doubt an appropriate instrument for the
settlement of such conflicts as arise, and for making profitable
collaboration possible. . . . But for the working class the situation is very different. For them the existing economic order
is the source of their economic exploitation, and the organized
power of the state the instrument of their political and social
subjection. Even the freest ballot cannot do away with the

glaring contrast between the possessing and the non-possessing classes in society. It can only serve to impart to a system of social injustice the aspect of legal right and to induce the slave to set the stamp of legality on his own servitude.

But, most important of all, practical experience has shown that the participation of the workers in parliamentary activity cripples their power of resistance and dooms to futility their warfare against the existing system. . . . Anarcho-Syndicalists, then, are not in any way opposed to the political struggle, but in their opinion this struggle, too, must take the form of direct action, in which the instruments of economic power which the working class has at its command are the most effective. . . .

The fact is that, when the Socialist labour parties have wanted to achieve some decisive political reform, they have always found that they could not do so by their own strength and have been obliged to rely wholly on the economic fighting power of the working class. The political general strikes in Belgium, Sweden and Austria for the attainment of universal suffrage are proof of this. And in Russia it was the great general strike of the working people that in 1905 pressed the pen into the tsar's hand for the signing of the constitution. . . . The focal point of the political struggle lies, then, not in the political parties, but in the economic fighting organizations of the workers. It was the recognition of this which impelled the Anarcho-Syndicalists to centre all their activity on the Socialist education of the masses and on the utilization of their economic and social power. Their method is that of direct action in both the economic and the political struggles of the time. That is the only method which has been able to achieve anything at all in every decisive moment in history. And the bourgeoisie in its struggles against absolutism has also made abundant use of this method, and by refusal to pay taxes, by boycott and revolution, has defiantly asserted its position as the dominant class in society. So much the worse if its representatives of to-day have forgotten the story of their fathers and howl bloody murder at the "unlawful methods" of the workers fighting for liberation. As if the law had ever permitted a subject class to shake off its yoke.

By direct action the Anarcho-Syndicalists mean every method of immediate warfare by the workers against their economic and political oppressors. Among these the outstanding are: the strike, in all its gradations from the simple wage-struggle to the general strike; the boycott; sabotage in its countless forms; anti-militarist propaganda; and in peculiarly critical cases, such, for example, as that in Spain to-day, armed resistance of the people for the protection of life and liberty.

Among these fighting techniques the strike, that is, organized refusal to work, is the most used. . . . In its simplest form it is for the workers an indispensable means of raising their standard of living or defending their attained advantages against the concerted measures of the employers. But the strike is for the workers not only a means for the defence of immediate economic interests, it is also a continuous schooling for their powers of resistance. . . . Here we come to the general cultural significance of the labour struggle. The economic alliance of the producers not only affords them a weapon for the enforcement of better living conditions, it becomes for them a practical school, a university of experience, from which they draw instruction and enlightenment in richest measure. The practical experiences and occurrences of the everyday struggles of the workers find an intellectual precipitate in their organizations, deepen their understanding, and broaden their intellectual outlook. . . . One of the most important results of the daily economic struggles is the development of solidarity among the workers, and this has for them a quite different meaning from the political coalition of parties whose following is composed of people of every social class. A feeling of mutual helpfulness, whose strength is constantly being renewed in the daily struggle for the necessities of life, which is constantly making the most extreme demands on the co-operation of men subjected to the same conditions . . . gradually develops into a new sense of right, and becomes the preliminary ethical assumption of every effort at the liberation of an oppressed class.

To cherish and strengthen this natural solidarity of the workers and to give to every strike movement a more profoundly social character, is one of the most important tasks which the Anarcho-Syndicalists have set themselves. For this reason the sympathetic strike is one of their choicest weapons. . . . Through it the economic battle becomes a deliberate action of the workers as a class. The sympathetic strike is the collaboration of related, but also of unrelated, categories of labour, to help the battle of a particular trade to victory by extending the strike to other branches of labour, where this is necessary. In this case the workers are not satisfied with giving financial assistance to their fighting brethren,

but go further, and by crippling entire industries cause a
break in the whole economic life in order to make their demands effective. . . .

Direct action by organized labour finds its strongest expression in the general strike; in the stoppage of work in every
branch of production by the organized resistance of the proletariat, with all the consequences arising from it. It is the
most powerful weapon which the workers have at their command and gives the most comprehensive expression to their
strength as a social factor. . . . The general strike can serve
various purposes. It can be the last stage of a sympathetic
strike, as, for example, the general strike in Barcelona in February, 1902, or that in Bilbao in October, 1903, which enabled the mineworkers to get rid of the hated truck system
and compelled the employers to establish sanitary conditions
in the mines. It can as easily be a means by which organized
labour tries to enforce some general demand, as, for example,
in the attempted general strike in the U. S. A. in 1886, to
compel the granting of the eight-hour day in all industries. . . .

But the general strike can also have political objectives in
view, as, for example, the fight of the Spanish workers in
1904, for the liberation of political prisoners, . . . But in
Spain the widespread strike movement among the workers
and peasants after the Fascist revolt in July, 1936, developed
into a "social general strike" (*huelga general*) and led to
armed resistance, and with this to the abolition of the
capitalist economic order and the reorganization of the economic life by the workers themselves.

The great importance of the general strike lies in this: At
one blow it brings the whole economic system to a standstill
and shakes it to its foundations. Moreover, such an action is
in no wise dependent on the practical preparedness of all the
workers, as all the citizens of a country have never partici-
pated in a political overturn. That the organized workers in
the most important industries quit work is enough to cripple
the entire economic mechanism, which cannot function without the daily provision of coal, electric power, and the raw
materials of every sort. But when the ruling classes are confronted with an energetic, organized working class, schooled
in daily conflict, and are aware of what they have at stake,
they become much more willing to make the necessary concessions, and, above all, they fear to take a course with the
workers which might drive them to extremes. . . .

A general strike . . . leads inevitably to a scattering of the military forces, as in such a situation the important concern is the protection of all important centres of industry and the transport system against the rebellious workers. But this means that military discipline, which is always strongest when soldiers operate in large formations, is relaxed. Where the military in small groups faces a determined people fighting for its freedom, there always exists the possibility that at least a part of the soldiers will reach some inner insight and comprehend that, after all, it is their own parents and brothers at whom they are pointing their weapons. For militarism, also, is primarily a psychologic problem, and its disastrous influence always manifests itself most perilously where the individual is given no chance to think about his dignity as a human being, no chance to see that there are higher tasks in life than lending oneself to the uses of a bloody oppressor of one's own people. . . .

Among the weapons in the Anarcho-Syndicalist armoury, sabotage is the one most feared by the employer and most harshly condemned as "unlawful." . . . Sabotage consists in the workers putting every possible obstacle in the way of the ordinary modes of work. For the most part this occurs when the employers try to avail themselves of a bad economic situation or some other favourable occasion to lower the normal conditions of labour by curtailment of wages or by lengthening of the hours of labour. The term itself is derived from the French word, *sabot*, wooden shoe, and means *to work clumsily as if by sabot blows*. The whole import of sabotage is actually exhausted in the motto, for bad wages, bad work. . . . In fact the policy of *"ca' canny"* (go slow), which, along with the phrase itself, the English workers took over from their Scottish brethren, was the first and most effective form of sabotage. There are to-day in every industry a hundred means by which the workers can seriously disturb production; everywhere under the modern system of division of labour, where often the slightest disturbance in one branch of the work can bring to a standstill the whole process of production. Thus the railway workers in France and Italy by the use of the so-called *grève perlée* (string-of-pearls strike) threw the whole system of transportation into disorder. For this they needed to do nothing more than to adhere to the strict letter of the existing transport laws, and thus make it impossible for any train to arrive at its destination on time. . . . The so-called *sit down strike*, which was transplanted from Europe to

America with such surprising rapidity and consists in the workers remaining in the plant day and night without turning a finger in order to prevent the installing of strike-breakers, belongs in the realm of sabotage. . . .

Another effective form of direct action is the *social strike*, which will, without doubt, in the immediate future play a much larger part. It is concerned less with the immediate interests of the producers than with the protection of the community against the most pernicious outgrowths of the present system. The social strike seeks to force upon the employers a responsibility to the public. Primarily it has in view the protection of the consumers, of whom the workers themselves constitute the great majority. The task of the trade union has heretofore been restricted almost exclusively to the protection of the worker as producer. As long as the employer was observing the hours of labour agreed on and paying the established wage this task was being performed. In other words: *the trade union is interested only in the conditions under which its members work, not in the kind of work they perform.* Theoretically it is, indeed, asserted that the relation between employer and employee is based upon a contract for the accomplishment of a definite purpose. The purpose in this case is social production. But a contract has meaning only when both parties participate equally in the purpose. In reality, however, the worker has to-day no voice in determining production, for this is given over completely to the employer. The consequence is that the worker is debased by doing a thousand things which constantly serve only to injure the whole community for the advantage of the employer. He is compelled to make use of inferior and often actually injurious materials in the fabrication of his products, to erect wretched dwellings, to put up spoiled foodstuffs, and to perpetrate innumerable acts that are planned to cheat the consumer.

To interfere vigorously here, is, in the opinion of the Anarcho-Syndicalists, the great task of the trade unions in the future. An advance in this direction would at the same time enhance the position of the workers in society, and in large measure confirm that position. Various efforts in this field have already been made, as witness, for example, the strike of the building-workers in Barcelona, who refused to use poor material and the wreckage from old buildings in the erection of workers' dwellings (1902), the strikes in the various large restaurants in Paris because the kitchen workers were unwilling to prepare for serving cheap, half-decayed meat (1906).

. . . The resolution of the German armament workers at the congress in Erfurt (1919) to make no more weapons of war and to compel their employers to convert their plants to other uses, belongs also in this category. . . .

As outspoken opponents of all nationalist ambitions, the revolutionary Syndicalists, especially in the Latin countries, have always devoted a very considerable part of their activity to anti-militarist propaganda, seeking to hold the workers in soldiers' coats loyal to their class and to prevent their turning their weapons against their brethren in time of a strike. . . . The Anarcho-Syndicalists know that wars are only waged in the interest of the ruling classes; they believe, therefore, that any means is justifiable that can prevent the organized murder of peoples. In this field also the workers have every means in their hands, if only they possess the desire and the moral strength to use them.

Above all it is necessary to cure the labour movement of its internal ossification and rid it of the empty sloganeering of the political parties, so that it may forge ahead intellectually and develop within itself the creative conditions which must precede the realization of Socialism. The practical attainability of this goal must become for the workers an inner certainty and must ripen into an ethical necessity. The great final goal of Socialism must emerge from all the practical daily struggles, and give them a social character. In the pettiest struggle, born of the needs of the moment, there must be mirrored the great goal of social liberation, and each such struggle must help to smooth the way and strengthen the spirit which transforms the inner longing of its bearers into will and deed.

33 The One-Man Revolution

As an account of day-to-day anarchist activity and its implications,
nothing surpasses Ammon Hennacy's *The Autobiography of a Catholic Anarchist*. In more than one sense, the book bears witness to
Tolstoyan principles: Hennacy regards anarchism as a necessary corollary of pacifism; he advocates rural simplicity and voluntary poverty,
and he insists that the locus of anarchist activities must reside not
in any shuffling or redirection of institutions but in a cleansing of
our own inner feelings and aspirations. But the *Autobiography*'s
great value is that it confronts us, quite inescapably, with the life
of a courageous radical, a life in which uncompromised principles
and acute practical wisdom have been mutually reinforcing.

The excerpt which follows begins with Hennacy's conversion from
militant socialism to anarchist pacifism, an episode which occurred
while he was serving a prison sentence for opposing the "blood tax"
imposed during the First World War. Today, a half century later,
Hennacy's Christian anarchism finds expression in the Catholic
Worker movement: in Salt Lake City, he manages their Joe Hill
"house of hospitality" for the dispossessed.

1

I had passed through the idea of killing myself. This was an
escape, not any solution to life. The remainder of my two
years in solitary must result in a clear-cut plan whereby I
could go forth and be a force in the world. . . . I had called
loudly for the sword and mentally listed those whom I desired to kill when I was free. Was this really the universal
method which should be used? I would read the Sermon on
the Mount again. . . . I spent months making a decision;
there was no sudden change. I had all the time in the world
and no one could talk to me or influence me. I was deciding
this idea for myself. Gradually I came to gain a glimpse of

The Autobiography of a Catholic Anarchist, by Ammon Hennacy
(New York: Catholic Worker Books, 1954), pp. 26–31, 45, 66,
102–3, 164–83. Subsection numbers provided by the editors.

what Jesus meant when he said, "The Kingdom of God is Within You." In my heart now after six months I could love everybody in the world but the warden, but if I did not love him then the Sermon on the Mount meant nothing at all. I really saw this and felt it in my heart but I was too stubborn to admit it in my mind. One day I was walking back and forth in my cell when, in turning, my head hit the wall. Then the thought came to me: "Here I am locked up in a cell. The warden was never locked up in any cell and he never had a chance to know what Jesus meant. Neither did I until yesterday. So I must not blame him. I must love him." Now the whole thing was clear. This Kingdom of God must be in everyone: in the deputy, the warden, in the rat and the pervert—and now I came to know it—in myself. . . . The warden had said that he did not understand political prisoners. He and the deputy, in plain words, did not know any better; they had put on the false face of sternness and tyranny because this was the only method which they knew. It was my job to teach them another method: that of goodwill overcoming their evil intentions, or rather habits. The opposite of the Sermon on the Mount was what the whole world had been practicing, in prison and out of prison; and hate piled on hate had brought hate and revenge. It was plain that this system did not work. . . .

I asked for radical books to read and among other books Tolstoy's *Kingdom of God is Within You* was brought. I felt that it must have been written especially for me, for here was the answer already written out to all the questions that I had tried to figure out for myself in solitary. To change the world by bullets or ballots was a useless procedure. If the workers ever did get a majority of either, they would have the envy and greed in their hearts and would be chained by these as much as by the chains of the master class. And the State which they would like to call a Cooperative Commonwealth would be based on power; the state would not wither away but would grow. Therefore the only revolution worthwhile was the one-man revolution within the heart. Each one could make this by himself and not need to wait on a majority. I had already started this revolution in solitary by becoming a Christian. Now I had completed it by becoming an Anarchist.

2

The basic idea of Socialists, Communists, Anarchists and radicals of all kinds is that there should be a society where each should give according to his ability and receive according to his need—where all should be brothers. . . . Robert Owen, Fourier, and countless radicals have started cooperative colonies which supposedly operated without capitalistic principles, but they all failed for the same reason the Russian Revolution failed—because they based everything on economics and forgot that something more than a lack of capitalistic principles was needed to overcome selfishness and greed . . . In other words, they forgot the teachings of the Sermon on the Mount.

However, for those who are ready there is a basis upon which they can build lives of satisfaction without depending upon politicians or upon a majority believing as they do. Voluntary Poverty and Pacifism is the basis upon which such ideals must be built today. Look about you and wherever your income derives from rent, interest, profit, making munitions, being a part of government, or depends upon the weakness and vices of your fellow men, then gradually remove yourself from this activity. Individually or cooperatively produce most of what you need on the land. It is further necessary to refuse to fight in a war or to support it. And in everyday life, respect and love every man and return good for evil. . . .

Orthodox economists tell us that the farmer who uses a horse and a plow and very little machinery cannot afford to compete in the market with the farmer who uses up-to-date machinery.

It happens that I do not care to own property and have it taken away by the government for nonpayment of taxes, for most of the taxes in my lifetime will go to pay for World War II and to prepare for World War III. One who eats meat can raise a few hogs and chickens in the country and here [Arizona] turkeys do well. For a vegetarian who simplifies his needs, the cash that is needed for certain purposes can be earned as a farm laborer; and most of the food to be consumed can be raised on an acre or two. To raise food for animals and then eat the animals is expensive. Why not raise the grain and eat it yourself?

I am not competing on the market with others any more than I am losing an election when I do not enter the lists of voting. My ideals are above and beyond that nose counting which takes place at the ballot box, and the economic system which myself and other free spirits follow is above and beyond the market place. The B-29's roar over my head hourly. These planes of death exist, as do the market place and the voting booth, but they do not need to be a part of my life if I do not choose to help pay for them or live in fear because of the warmonger's security in these false gods.

3

"How are you going to get people to put up the sword? My son died in Korea. I know you didn't kill him. God bless you!" said an elderly woman as I was picketing the post office in Phoenix, Dec. 18, 1950 in response to Truman's "emergency" declaration. The woman had seen my big sign which read:

> "Put up thy Sword. He that taketh the
> Sword Shall Perish by the Sword." Jesus' words.

On the reverse of this sign was a picture of a pot, colored green, with a sign on it: *capitalist*. Opposite was a red kettle —*Communist*. Underneath was the caption:

> "The Pot Calls the Kettle Black". . . .

My leaflet was as follows:

What's All the Shooting About?

It's about men who put money ahead of God. It's about young men on both sides misled into dying and killing each other.

It's about rationing, inefficiency, dictatorship, inflation, and politicians stealing a little more than usual.

War is what happens when one nation prepares to defend itself against another nation that prepares to defend itself.

World War I and World War II did not end war nor make the world safe for democracy. Neither will this one.

There just isn't any sense to war!

What can we do about it? If the politicians think one person is important enough to become a soldier, a munition maker, a bond buyer, or an income tax payer, then one person is important enough to:

> REFUSE to become a soldier,
> REFUSE to make munitions,
> REFUSE to buy bonds, and to
> REFUSE to pay income taxes.

War does not protect you—it will destroy you!

You cannot overcome Communism with bullets. It

can be overcome by each person doing what he knows in his heart to be right. The way of Jesus, of St. Francis, of Tolstoy, and of Gandhi teaches us to love our enemy, to establish justice, to abolish exploitation, and to rely upon God rather than on politicians and governments.

If you are a Christian why not follow Christ? You might as well die for what you believe as for what you don't believe. If you must fight, fight war itself. Don't be a traitor to humanity! *Wars will cease when men refuse to fight!*

But does the One-Man Revolution work? Of course. The surest way to further invasion, intimidation, and the other accompaniments of authority is by failing to register a strong and unequivocal protest against them. The non-violent resistance of even a single individual, on the other hand, is an obstruction: it generates doubts, it produces difficulties, it inspires mutinies, it *sometimes* modifies official policy. Rarely does it leave its opponents unaltered. To be sure, the most important effects of One-Man Revolutions—the awakening of similar personal insurrections—are constantly ignored: this is a consequence of the popular fallacy, criticized by Karl Popper in the final chapter of *The Open Society and Its Enemies*, that History is nothing but a series of congressional debates, military engagements, political treaties, and other official events. These effects are illustrated by the three cases which follow, the first of which took place in Milwaukee during the thirties, while the latter two occurred during 1949–50 in Phoenix. Throughout the second of these incidents, Hennacy carried a sign which declared:

75%
Of Your Income Tax
Goes for War
And the Bomb.

I Have
Refused to Pay
Income Taxes
For the Last
Seven Years.

It is now *twenty-three* years since he last permitted the government to collect this war-tax. (And he has gladly done without movies, gasoline, alcohol, Greyhounds, and other items on which taxes are gathered.)

4

At that time some Fascist-minded American Legion members were putting out a well printed sheet each week calling upon all patriots to run radicals and pacifists out of the city. My boss knew that this was dangerous but he did not know how to combat it. He asked me to speak at a private meeting at his home to several dozen of the more liberal-minded Legionnaires. They had never met a pacifist nor an anarchist before and we had an exciting evening. I asked them to meet my Communist friend, Fred Basset Blair. They went up in the air at the mention of his name but I kidded them about their timidity until they consented to have him meet with them. I was there also. A Socialist and a Technocrat spoke also and by the time winter was over the true Legionnaires had argued their vigilantes out of the idea and they disbanded.

5

I had a small quantity of leaflets [*Catholic Workers*], and folded tax statements in the back pocket of my levis. I had walked the three sides of this block three other times when I picketed against payment of taxes, so the ground was familiar. Shouts of "Go back to Russia, you Commie" were frequent. One Catholic lady who said she had bought CW's from me at St. Mary's cordially took a slip. When I walked on, a man shouted for me to go back to Russia. The lady turned to him and said "Go back to Russia yourself!"

Those who fast do not stop to eat so I kept on during the noon hour. . . . A crowd gathered around. One man was especially noisy, poking his finger in my face and shouting, "Russia," "the boys in Korea," etc. One big man said that back in his state they took fellows like me and threw them in the river.

"Where do you come from Buddy?" I asked.

"From Ohio, 'long the Ohio River," he replied.

"So do I, and I was acting like a radical there when I was 16 and no one threw me in" I answered quickly. The crowd laughed. Another big fellow said that if I came back tomorrow with my "damn Communist papers" they would take me out in the desert and throw me up against a cactus and I would stick there. In a very quiet voice, but firmly I said:

"You are not really as mean a man as you make out to be."

At this the crowd melted away, although my two interrogators insulted me as I passed by with my sign again. But they could find no one to back them up. Jack had been on the outside of the crowd and a lady told him, not knowing that he was my friend, that I was not a Commie for I picketed here every year. . . .

In the afternoon the leader of those who had reviled me stopped with a friendly smile and apologized, saying that he had been drunk; that now he knew what my ideas were. Each day of my fast now he performed kindly acts to help me and argued with others that I was a fine fellow. . . . The tax man came along and good naturedly said that he had a bid of $5 for my signs from someone who wanted them as a souvenir. (I did not ask him if he was the bidder.) I had given him CW's before and had shown him Dorothy's [Dorothy Day, editor of the *Catholic Worker*] telegram. Now he was friendly and asked about my life, my daughters, my ideas, and said that he understood my opposition to the status quo. . . .

The last day of my picketing was the hottest of all. To tell the truth I became a clock-watcher and drank more water than ever. I met a few surly people now and then, but more and more people took my leaflet. One elderly man took my leaflet and remarked that he and his family were friends of mine, for I had given literature to his wife the day before and he had read my tax statement and leaflet to his congregation of fundamentalists at his little mission west of Phoenix. One man whose employment kept him near to my picketing had muttered patriotic obscenities all the times I had picketed here. Today he was pleasant and wondered how I got by without paying taxes.

6

I saw that Joe [Craigmyle] had given himself up and was placed in the county jail in lieu of $10,000 bail. The paper referred to him as a "draft evader". I wrote to the paper giving these definitions:

"*Evade*—to get away from by artifice; to avoid by dexterity, subterfuge, address or ingenuity."
"*Resist*—to stand against; to withstand; to stop; to obstruct; to strive against."

I asked them why they did not call things by their right names, but of course they did not print it. . . .

The Monday after Christmas Joe was to have his trial for

refusing to register. As the papers tend to hide or distort the witness which he was making against war we thought it would be a good idea if I picketed the Federal Building during his trial. It was drizzling rain that morning and the wind was blowing so that my 2½-ft. by 3-ft. home-made sign took my two hands to keep it steady. It read:

"HONOR TO DRAFT RESISTER BEING SENTENCED TODAY"
"YOUR INCOME TAX FIGHTS THE POOR OF INDONESIA."

Underneath one arm I displayed the current CW. Passersby read the sign to one another and employees in the Federal Building read it from the windows. Half a dozen people stopped and asked questions in a sympathetic manner, some of them youngsters who had never heard of the term Conscientious Objector. To them and to the reporters I gave copies of the CW. . . . The young reporter of the evening paper took half a dozen pictures and questioned me sympathetically about the purpose of my picketing. That night the headline read: "DRAFT RESISTER ADMITS GUILT AS FRIEND PICKETS COURT". Note that Joe was called "resister" instead of "evader." Some of the facts of Joe's history and mine were twisted in the report but the essential quotation as to our purpose was correct. "We are governed by the Sermon on the Mount which tells us to return good for evil. But courts and governments return evil for evil. That's why we would abolish them and let every man be governed by his own conscience."

The *Catholic Worker* bids well to be the most widely circulated of all libertarian newspapers. It was organized in 1933 by Dorothy Day, and—for "a penny (or two) a copy"—has been the intrepid voice of radical Christian pacifism ever since. It has never failed to denounce the militarism on both sides of the Cold War, and has fostered a quietly effective program of direct action. The main outlines of this program, which has clear affinities with both Proudhon and Tolstoy, were conceived during the Depression years by Peter Maurin. Maurin, who helped originate the Catholic Worker movement in New York City, referred to its program as "the Green Revolution." Why he did so and how that revolution took root and developed are described in this selection.

"Lenin said, 'There can be no revolution without a theory of revolution,' so I am trying to give the theory of a green revolution," he [Peter Maurin] said.

He delighted in the title of agitator. . . . He stressed the need of building a new society within the shell of the old— that telling phrase from the preamble to the I.W.W. constitution, "a society in which it is easier for people to be good," he added with a touching simplicity, knowing that when people are good, they are happy. . . .

Peter rejoiced to see men do great things and dream great dreams. He wanted them to stretch out their arms to their brothers, because he knew that the surest way to find God, to find the good, was through one's brothers. Peter wanted this striving to result in a better physical life in which all men would be able to fulfill themselves, develop their capacities for love and worship, expressed in all the arts. He wanted them to be able to produce what was needed in the way of homes, food, clothing, so that there was enough of these ne-

The Long Loneliness, by Dorothy Day (New York: Harper & Row, 1952), pp. 170–73, 185, 195, 220–35, 285–86. Reprinted by permission of Harper & Row.

cessities for everyone. A synthesis of "cult, culture and cultivation," he called it, as he tried to give me the long view,
the vision. . . .

He not only wished to give me a Catholic outline of history—but he also wished to repeat over and over again his
program of action; round-table discussions, houses of hospitality and agronomic universities. We were to popularize this
program for immediate needs, which in itself would be the
seed for a long-range program, a green revolution, by publishing a paper for the man in the street.

What Peter called round-table discussions I was already
familiar enough with as meetings, whether indoors or from
a soapbox. I could see the necessity for them, "for the clarification of thought," as he always said, and I knew that humanly speaking they would always go on. But he wanted more
than supper-table conversations; he wanted to plan meetings
too for the beginnings of a school, to bring the workers and
scholars together.

Since I came from a newspaper family, with my two older
brothers working on newspapers at that time, and my father
still a writer though no longer an editor, I could see the need
for such a paper as Peter described.

But how were we going to start it?

Peter did not pretend to be practical along these lines. "I
enunciate the principles," he declared grandly.

"But where do we get the money?" I asked him, clinging
to the "we," though he was making clear his role as theorist.

"In the history of the saints, capital was raised by prayer.
God sends you what you need when you need it. You will be
able to pay the printer. Just read the lives of the saints."

St. Francis de Sales scattered leaflets like any radical. St.
John of God sold newspapers on the streets. We didn't have
to do things on a big scale, Peter made it clear.

I had been reading the life of Rose Hawthorne not long
before, how she started what has since become a chain of
cancer hospitals in a four-room tenement apartment such as
the one I was living in. Why not start a newspaper in the
same way? I began to look on our kitchen as an editorial office, my brother as an assistant to write heads and to help
with mechanical make-up. Tamar [her daughter, then six
years old] and I could go out to sell papers on the streets! . . .

Peter, the "green" revolutionist, had a long-term program
which called for hospices, or houses of hospitality, where the
works of mercy could be practiced to combat the taking over

by the state of all those services which could be built up by mutual aid; and farming communes to provide land and homes for the unemployed, whom increasing technology was piling up into the millions. In 1933, the unemployed numbered 13,000,000.

The idea of the houses of hospitality caught on quickly enough. The very people that Peter brought in, who made up our staff at first, needed a place to live. Peter was familiar with the old I.W.W. technique of a common flophouse and a pot of mulligan on the stove.

The Green Revolution, as we have seen, includes a substantial measure of community life, which sharply distinguishes its form of religious anarchism from Hennacy's One-Man Revolution. But what can the sort of community sustained by the Catholic Worker group contribute toward resolving the complex problems of an increasingly urbanized society? Dorothy Day's answer follows below; for another point of view, see selection 55.

In the helpless resentment of [those denied work in New York] there was a fury which city authorities were afraid would gather into a flood of wrath, once they were gathered into a mob. So among every group in the public square, at the meetings of the unemployed, there were careful guardians of law and order watching, waiting to pounce on these gray men, the color of the lifeless trees and bushes and soil in the squares in winter, who had in them as yet none of the green of hope, the rising sap of faith.

Both Peter and Steve tried to arouse that hope. Both of them were personalists, both were workers. They did not want mass action, or violence. They were lambs in the simplicity of their program. They wanted to see the grass spring up between the cobbles of the city streets. They wanted to see the workers leave the cities with their wives and children and take to the fields, build themselves homes, where they would have room to breathe, to study, to pray, where there could be work for all.

"There is no unemployment on the land," Peter used to shout, and he would be met by jeers. "What about the migrants, the tenant farmers. They either work like slaves for the bosses, or they rot like the men in Tobacco Road."

"Fire the bosses," Peter used to say.*

---

*Dorothy Day says elsewhere: "Peter and his slogans! 'Fire the bosses' meant 'Call no man master, for all ye are brothers.' "

The trouble was that he never filled in the chasms, the valleys, in his leaping from crag to crag of noble thought.

He wanted men to think for themselves. Voluntary poverty, the doing without radios, cars, television sets, cigarettes, movies, cosmetics, all these luxuries, would enable men to buy the necessities. In a village community there would be work, even work in the gardens for the invalids, the children, the old, the crippled, the men and women who hung around the street corners and the market places, waiting for someone to hire them.

"Personalism and communitarianism," was Peter's cry. . . .

As Peter pointed out, ours was a long-range program, looking for ownership by the workers of the means of production, the abolition of the assembly line, decentralized factories, the restoration of crafts and ownership of property. This meant, of course, an accent on the agrarian and rural aspects of our economy and a changing of emphasis from the city to the land. . . .

Peter was not so much interested in labor as he was in work and community. He felt that as long as men sought jobs and wages, and accepted the assembly line and the material comforts the factory system brought, they would not think in terms of community, except for that which the union brought them. They might be gathered together in time of crisis, during strikes, but would they listen to what he said about the need for ownership and responsibility?

Every talk of Peter's about the social order led to the land. He spoke always as a peasant, but as a practical one. He knew the craving of the human heart for a toehold on the land, for a home of one's own, but he also knew how impossible it was to attain it except through community, through men banding together in farming communes to live to a certain extent in common, work together, own machinery together, start schools together. . . .

Community—that was the social answer to the long loneliness. That was one of the attractions of religious life and why couldn't lay people share in it? Not just the basic community of the family, but also a community of families, with a combination of private and communal property. This could be a farming commune, a continuation of the agronomic university Peter spoke of as a part of the program we were to work for. Peter had vision and we all delighted in these ideas.

"But not a five-year plan," he would say. He did not believe in blueprints or a planned economy. Things grow organically. . . .

Peter did not wish to turn to the government for funds. "He who is a pensioner of the state is a slave of the state," he felt. . . . Peter's plan was that groups should borrow from mutual-aid credit unions in the parish to start what he first liked to call agronomic universities, where the worker could become a scholar and the scholar a worker. Or he wanted people to give the land and money. He always spoke of giving. Those who had land and tools should give. Those who had capital should give. Those who had labor should give that. "Love is an exchange of gifts," St. Ignatius had said. It was in these simple, practical, down-to-earth ways that people could show their love for each other. If the love was not there in the beginning, but only the need, such gifts made love grow. . . .

Peter set much store on labor as a prime requisite for a new order. "Work, not wages." . . . Packed in that one tight little phrase is all the dynamite of revolution. Men wanted work more than they wanted bread, and they wanted to be responsible for their work, which meant ownership.

I know that as this is read, it will be questioned. "This is how people should be, but are they? Give them relief checks and they will sit back and do nothing for the rest of their days. When they do have jobs they see how much they can get away with in giving as little labor as possible for the highest pay they can get." One hears these complaints from householders and even from heads of religious orders. . . . Peter was no dreamer but knew men as they were. That is why he spoke so much of the need for a philosophy of work. Once they had that, once their desires were changed, half the battle was won. To make men desire poverty and hard work, that was the problem. It would take example, and the grace of God, to do it. . . . Peter's Christian philosophy of work was this. God is our creator. God made us in His image and likeness. Therefore we are creators. He gave us a garden to till and cultivate. We become co-creators by our responsible acts, whether in bringing forth children, or producing food, furniture, or clothing. The joy of creativeness should be ours.

But because of the Fall the curse is laid on us of having to earn our bread by the sweat of our brows, in labor. St. Paul said that since the Fall nature itself travaileth and groaneth. So man has to contend with fallen nature in the beasts and in the earth as well as in himself. But when he overcomes the obstacles, he attains again to the joy of creativity. Work is not then all pain and drudgery. . . .

Farms like ours began to dot the country. In Aptos, California, in Cape May, New Jersey, in Upton, Massachusetts, in Avon, Ohio, in South Lyon, Michigan—a dozen sprang up as Catholic Worker associates. Many others consisted of young married groups trying to restore the idea of community.

Some were started and abandoned as too isolated, or because of lack of water, lack of funds, lack of people who knew how to work. Men found out the reasons for cities and relief rolls when they ventured onto the land and sought to do manual labor. How to work in industry so as not to compromise oneself and yet earn a living for a family?

The problem did not really become acute until the family entered in. The family thought Peter's farming commune idea was solely for them. The scholars thought the agronomic university idea was for them. The sick and unemployed thought the Catholic Worker farms in general were for women and children and the helpless. . . . We consoled ourselves that we might not be establishing model communities, but many a family was getting a vacation, many a sick person was nursed back to health, crowds of slum children had the run of the woods and fields for weeks, and groups of students spent happy hours discussing the green revolution. . . .

One of the main difficulties of all these farm ventures is the lack of skills, money and equipment; lack of leadership too is a factor. There could be, I believe, groups of families on the land, surrounding a chapel, disciplined by family life and daily attendance at Mass, all subject to one another, with a division of skills and labor and accepting too the authority of one co-ordinator. . . . If lay communities were given the start, if young families were given an initial subsidy, free and clear, and left to work out their way of life, great things could be done.

At Peter Maurin farm, on Staten Island, we have a three-acre asparagus bed which might eventually bring in enough money to pay the taxes of five hundred dollars a year. Our bakery there could make the place self-sustaining if we did not give away all the bread.

Through the skill of David Mason, former head of the house of hospitality in Philadelphia, proofreader and writer by profession, a "surplus commodity" oven from a battleship was set up in a little outer kitchen in the rear of the farmhouse. We can bake a hundred loaves at a time and several of us have learned to bake. Now we have the satisfaction of feeding our two houses, on Staten Island and Chrystie Street, and the breadline of hundreds of men who come twice a day for meals, with the best of whole-wheat bread, made from whole-grain flour which we buy by the half ton.

What a delightful thing it is to be boldly profligate, to ignore the price of coffee and go on serving the long line of destitute men who come to us, good coffee and the finest of bread.

"Nothing is too good for the poor," our editor Tom Sullivan says, and he likes that aphorism especially when he is helping himself to something extra good.

Tom is the "co-ordinator" of the house of hospitality on Chrystie Street, New York, though we never use that title. He is in charge of the house, and his is a gentle and unobtrusive authority. He has won the respect of the men and their co-operation so that many of them take on jobs in the house and kitchen and keep the work going. . . .

The most significant thing about The Catholic Worker is poverty, some say.

The most significant thing is community, others say. We are not alone any more.

But the final word is love. At times it has been, in the words of Father Zossima, a harsh and dreadful thing, and our very faith in love has been tried through fire.

We cannot love God unless we love each other, and to love we must know each other. We know Him in the breaking of bread, and we know each other in the breaking of bread, and we are not alone any more. Heaven is a banquet and life is a banquet, too, even with a crust, where there is companionship.

We have all known the long loneliness and we have learned that the only solution is love and that love comes with community.

It all happened while we sat there talking, and it is still going on.

Paul Goodman's chief aim in the following selection is to explode several common objections to the libertarian position (some of which are expounded in section VII, below). But he also takes two further directions: first, a continuation of his critique of the centralized style of contemporary society; and second, an account of numerous decentralized activities and programs that work to liberate us from that style.

In a centralized system, the function to be performed is the goal of the organization rather than of any persons (except as they identify with the organization). The persons are personnel. Authority is top-down. Information is gathered from below in the field, is processed to be usable by those above. Decisions are made in headquarters, and policy, schedule and standard procedure are transmitted downward by chain of command. The enterprise as a whole is divided into departments of operation to which personnel are assigned with distinct roles, to give standard performance. This is the system in Mr. Goldwater's department store, in the Federal government and in the State governments, in most elementary and higher education, in the CIO, in hospitals, in neighborhood renewal, in network broadcasting and in the deals that chain-grocers make with farmers. The system was designed for disciplining armies, for bureaucratic record-keeping and tax-collection and for certain kinds of mass-production. It has now pervaded every field.

The principle of decentralism is that people are engaged in the function they perform; the organization is how they co-operate. Authority is delegated away from the top as much as possible and there are many centers of decision and policy-

"On Some Prima-Facie Objections to Decentralism," condensed from *People or Personnel*, by Paul Goodman (New York: Random House, Inc., 1965). © Copyright 1963, 1964, 1965 by Paul Goodman. Reprinted by permission of Random House, Inc.

making. Information is conveyed and discussed in face-to-face contacts between field and headquarters. And each person becomes aware of the whole operation. He works at it in his own way according to his capacities. Groups arrange their own schedules. Historically, this system of voluntary association has yielded most of the values of civilization, but it is thought to be entirely unworkable under modern conditions and the very sound of it is strange. . . .

A Marxist student objects that blurring the division of labor, local option, face-to-face communication and other decentralist positions are relics of a peasant ideology, provincial and illiberal.

In fact, there have always been two strands to decentralist thinking. Some authors, e.g. Lao-tse or Tolstoy, make a conservative peasant critique of centralized court and town as inorganic, verbal and ritualistic. But other authors, e.g. Proudhon or Kropotkin, make a democratic urban critique of centralized bureaucracy and power, including feudal industrial power, as exploiting, inefficient, and discouraging initiative. In our present era of State-socialism, corporate feudalism, regimented schooling, brainwashing mass-communications and urban anomie, both kinds of critique make sense. We need to revive both peasant self-reliance and the democratic power of professional and technical guilds.

Any decentralization that could occur at present would inevitably be post-urban and post-centralist; it could not be provincial. There is no American who has not been formed by national TV, and no region that has not been homogenized by the roads and chain-stores. A model of present-day decentralization is the Israeli *kibbutz*. Some would say that such a voluntary community is fanatical, but no one would deny that it is cosmopolitan and rationalistic; it is post-centralist and post-urban.

Decentralizing has its risks. Suppose that the school system of a Northern city were radically decentralized, given over to the parents and teachers of each school. Without doubt some of the schools would be Birchite and some would be badly neglected. Yet it is hard to imagine that many schools would be worse than the present least-common-denominator. There would certainly be more experimentation. There would be meaningful other choices to move to, *and* it could be arranged that all the schools would exist in a framework of general standards that they would have to achieve or suffer the consequences.

Invariably some student argues that without the intervention of the Federal government the Negroes in the South will never get their civil rights. This may or may not be so; but certainly most progress toward civil rights has come from local action that has embarrassed and put pressure on Washington. And the Negro organizations themselves have been decentrally coordinated; as Dr. King has pointed out, the "leadership" is continually following the localities. But the basic error of this student is to think that the "States Rights" of the segregationists is decentralist (although an authentic regionalism would be decentralist). If each locality indeed had its option, the counties where the Negroes are in a majority would have very different rules! and again, there would be a meaningful choice for other Negroes to move to. . . .

Then a student raises a related objection: Decentralism is for small towns, it cannot work with big dense populations. But this objection has no merit. Decentralism is a kind of social organization; it does not involve geographical isolation, but a particular sociological use of geography.

In important respects, a city of five millions can be decentrally organized as many scores of unique communities in the framework of a busy metropolis.

Usually in modern urban administration, the various municipal functions—school, job-induction, post office, social work, health, police and court for misdemeanors, housing and rent control, election district, etc.—are divided into units only for the administrative convenience of City Hall. The districts do not coincide with one another nor with neighborhoods. A citizen with business or complaint must seek out the district office of each department, or perhaps go to City Hall. And correspondingly, there is no possible forum to discuss the coordination of the various functions except at the very top, with the Mayor or before the Council.

Decentralist organization would rather follow the actuality of living in an urban community, where housing, schooling, shopping, policing, social services, politics are integrally related. Each neighborhood should have a local City Hall. Such *arrondissements* could have considerable autonomy within the municipal administration that controls transit, sanitation, museums, etc., whatever is necessarily or conveniently centralized. Taxes could be collected centrally and much of the take divided among the neighborhoods to be budgeted locally.

For the average citizen, the convergence of all kinds of related businesses in one local center is not only convenient but must lead to more acquaintanceship and involvement. Poor people especially do not know their way around, are stymied by forms to fill out, and have no professional help; they are defeated by fighting City Hall and soon give up. Besides, each neighborhood has interlocking problems peculiar to itself. These can be reasonably confronted by citizens and local officials, but they are lost in the inner politics of central bureaucracies that have quite different axes to grind. A neighborhood should certainly police itself, according to its own mores, and avoid the present police brutality inevitable in trying to impose an unworkable city-wide conformity.

A neighborhood so constituted might learn to decide on its own redevelopment. In programs for urban renewal, the Federal government follows the traditional formula of balancing centralism and decentralism and asks for approval of plans by the local community. Cities therefore set up local "planning boards." But this works out as follows: Occasionally, middle-class residential neighborhoods can organize themselves to prevent any change whatever; poor people are entirely passive to the powers that be; usually, the boards are rubber stamps for City Hall and promoters. The say of a neighborhood in its destiny can be meaningful only if the neighborhood has begun to be conscious of itself as a community. For this, mere "consent" or "participation" is not enough; there must be a measure of real initiating and deciding, grounded in acquaintance and trust.

However, the question is not whether decentralization can work in dense urban populations, but how to make it work, for it is imperative. The increase of urban social disease and urban mental disease is fundamentally due to powerlessness, resignation and withdrawal. People's only way to assert vitality is to develop symptoms. The central authorities try to cope as stern or hygienic caretakers; the citizens respond by becoming "community-dependent"—in jail, in the hospital, on relief; that is, they become chronic patients. With many, this has gone on for two or three generations.

Yet something further needs to be said about big dense populations. In my opinion, there is a limit of urban density and urban sprawl beyond which no form of social organization, centralist or decentralist, can cope. Urban crowding creates a peculiar climate of both too many social relations and a kind of sensory and emotional deprivation. Instead of contact and communication, there is noise and withdrawal.

It is no different than among John Calhoun's over-crowded rodents who become confused and die. E.g. the density of population in Central Harlem, 67,000 persons per square mile, is nearly three times that of New York City as a whole. Even apart from the other unfavorable conditions of the Negroes, such crowding itself is pathological, overstimulating yet culturally impoverishing, destructive of solitude, excessively and brutally policed. . . .

A student hotly objects that decentralism is humanly unrealistic, it "puts too much faith in human nature" by relying on intrinsic motives, like interest in the job and voluntary association. . . . This objection is remarkably off-base. My experience is that most decentralists are crotchety and skeptical and tend rather to follow Aristotle than Rousseau. We must avoid concentration of power precisely because we *are* fallible; *quis custodiet custodes?* Democracy, Aristotle says, is to be preferred because it is the "least evil" form of government, since it divides power among many. I think the student states the moral issue upside down. The moral question is not whether men are "good enough" for a type of social organization, but whether the type of organization is useful to develop the potentialities of intelligence, grace, and freedom in men.

More deeply, the distrust of "human nature", of course, is anxious conformism. One must save face, not make a mistake in any detail; so one clings to an assigned role. But, unfortunately, the bigger the organization, the more face to save. For instance . . . the government Peace Corps is many times as expensive as similar less official operations largely because an errant twenty-year-old well-digger might become an International Incident, so one cannot be too careful in selecting him. Convenience of supervision overrides performance. And the more "objective" the better. If the punch card approves, no one is guilty. To bureaucrats, a fatal hallmark of decentralist enterprises is their variety in procedure and persons; how can one *know*, with a percentage validity, that these methods and persons are *right?* . . .

Finally, the moral objection is stated also the opposite way: decentralizing is impossible, not because people are incapable but because the powers-that-be won't allow it. (This student is an Angry Young Man.) Granting that in some areas decentralization is workable, how could it possibly be brought about? . . . In principle, there are two ways in which an over-centralized system can become more mixed. Either voluntary associations form spontaneously because of pressing needs to which the central system is irrelevant or antipathetic; or the central authority itself chooses, or is forced, to build in decentral parts because its method simply is not working.

Certainly there are major social trends toward spontaneous do-it-yourself associations. We have already noticed the spontaneity, localism, and decentralist federation of the Negro civil-rights movement, as opposed to the more conventional maneuvering of the Urban League and the older NAACP. But this is part of a general spread of para-legal demonstrating, boycotting and show of power that clearly express dissent with formal procedures that are not effective. Nonviolent activism is peculiarly epidemic; it immediately provides something to do rather than being merely balked—a beautiful feature of it, perhaps, is to balk the authorities—yet it does not require forming political parties or organizing private armies. (When the nonviolence is authentic, indeed, its very action is decentralizing; it restores the opposition to being persons rather than personnel. Violence has the contrary effect.) . . .

Consider the following example. In some areas of England it is traditional to work by a Gang or collective contract. (This has been studied by Professor Melman of Columbia University.) A group of workmen agree to complete in a certain period a certain quantity of piece-work, for which they are paid a sum of money divided equally. The capitalist provides the machinery and materials, but *everything else*—work rules, methods, schedule, hiring—is left to group decision. This arrangement has proved feasible in highly skilled work like building and in semi-skilled work on automobile assembly lines. The group may be half a dozen or a couple of thousand. Humanly, the arrangement has extraordinary advantages. Men exchange jobs and acquire many skills; they adjust the schedule to their convenience (or pleasures); they bring in and train apprentices; they invent labor-saving devices, since it is to their own advantage to increase efficiency; they cover for one another when sick or for special vacations. Obviously such a system, so amazingly at variance with our top-down regulation, timeclock discipline, labor union details and competitive spirit, is hard to build into most of our industry. Yet it would suit a lot of it and make a profound difference. Where would it suit? How could it be tailored?

An attempt to build in decentralization is at present occurring in the New York school system. Because of a combination of near-riots in poor neighborhoods, some spectacular run-of-the-mill scandals, and the post-Sputnik spotlight on upgrading, a new and pretty good Board has been appointed. Deciding that the system is over-centralized, these gentlemen have resuscitated twenty-five local districts—averaging forty thousand children each!—and appointed local Boards with rather indefinite powers, to serve as liaison to the neighborhoods. But unlike the case of urban renewal planning boards mentioned above the intention *is* to delegate positive powers; and anyway, the remarkably strong-minded body of people who have been appointed to the local school boards have no intention of being rubber stamps. At present, there is a jockeying for position and power. The local boards are empowered to hold budget hearings and "suggest" allocation of money. What does this mean? Could they suggest to eliminate some of the curriculum and services and substitute others? Some local board members want to decentralize radically, making the field superintendents and the local boards nearly autonomous within the big system, as is reasonable, since the different neighborhoods have different conditions and therefore have different curricular, staff and service needs. . . .

It seems to me as follows. We are in a period of excessive centralization. It is demonstrable that in many functions this style is economically inefficient, technologically unnecessary and humanly damaging. Therefore we ought to adopt a political maxim: to decentralize where, how and how much is expedient. But where, how and how much are empirical questions; they require research and experiment.

In the existing over-centralized climate of opinion, it is just this research and experiment that we are not getting. Among all the departments, agencies and commissions in Washington, I have not heard of one that deals with the organizational style of municipalities, social work, manufacturing, merchandising or education, in terms of their technical and economic efficiency and their effects on persons. Therefore, I urge students who are going on to graduate work to choose their theses in this field.

36 The Organization of Anarchy

Colin Ward is the editor of *Anarchy* magazine (published by Freedom Press), which in recent years has widened the scope of anarchism to consider science fiction, anthropology, and jazz, as well as
such standard topics as decentralized industry, criminology, and education. *Anarchy*, with its sister newspaper *Freedom*, has helped to
spark the current interest in anarchist and syndicalist proposals in
Great Britain.

Ward's essay usefully broaches an issue often considered troublesome for anarchism: What kinds of joint action, if any, are compatible with individual liberty? For a sharply opposing view, see selection 54.

You may think in describing anarchism as a theory of organisation I am propounding a deliberate paradox: "anarchy"
you may consider to be, by definition, the *opposite* of organisation. In fact, however, "anarchy" means the absence of
government, the absence of *authority*. Can there be social
organisation without authority, without government? The anarchists claim that there can be, and they also claim that it
is desirable that there should be. They claim that, at the
basis of our social problems is the principle of government.
It is, after all, governments which prepare for war and wage
war, even though you are obliged to fight in them and pay
for them; the bombs you are worried about are not the bombs
which cartoonists attribute to the anarchists, but the bombs
which governments have perfected, at your expense. It is,
after all, governments which make and enforce the laws
which enable the 'haves' to retain control over social assets
rather than share them with the 'have-nots'. It is, after all,
the principle of authority which ensures that people will work
for someone else for the greater part of their lives, not be-

---

Anarchism as a Theory of Organization, by Colin Ward. Not previously published.

cause they enjoy it or have any control over their work, but because they see it as their only means of livelihood.

I said that it is governments which make wars and prepare for wars, but obviously it is not governments alone—the power of a government, even the most absolute dictatorship, depends on the tacit assent of the governed. Why do people consent to be governed? It isn't only fear: what have millions of people to fear from a small group of politicians? It is because they subscribe to the same values as their governors. Rulers and ruled alike believe in the principle of authority, of hierarchy, of power. These are the characteristics of the *political principle*. The anarchists, who have always distinguished between the state and society, adhere to the *social principle*, which can be seen where-ever men link themselves in an association based on a common need or a common interest. "The State" said the German anarchist Gustav Landauer, "is not something which can be destroyed by a revolution, but is a condition, a certain relationship between human beings, a mode of human behaviour; we destroy it by contracting other relationships, by behaving differently."

Anyone can see that there are at least two kinds of organisation. There is the kind which is forced on you, the kind which is run from above, and there is the kind which is run from below, which can't *force* you to do anything, and which you are free to join or free to leave alone. We could say that the anarchists are people who want to transform all kinds of human organisation into the kind of purely voluntary association where people can pull out and start one of their own if they don't like it. I once, in reviewing that frivolous but useful little book *Parkinson's Law*, attempted to enunciate four principles behind an anarchist theory of organisation: that they should be (1) voluntary, (2) functional, (3) temporary, and (4) small. They should be voluntary for obvious reasons. There is no point in our advocating individual freedom and responsibility if we are going to advocate organisations for which membership is mandatory. They should be functional and temporary precisely because permanence is one of those factors which harden the arteries of an organisation, giving it a vested interest in its own survival, in serving the interests of office-holders rather than its function. They should be small precisely because in small face-to-face groups, the bureaucratising and hierarchical tendencies inherent in organisations have least opportunity to develop.

But it is from this final point that our difficulties arise. If

we take it for granted that a small group can function anarchically, we are still faced with the problem of all those
social functions for which organisation is necessary, but which
require it on a much bigger scale. "Well," we might reply, as
some anarchists have, "if big organisations are necessary,
count us out. We will get by as well as we can without them."
We can say this all right, but if we are propagating anarchism
as a social philosophy we must take into account, and not
evade, social facts. Better to say "Let us find ways in which
the large-scale functions can be broken down into functions
capable of being organised by small functional groups and
then link these groups in a federal manner." The classical
anarchist thinkers, envisaging the future organisation of society, thought in terms of two kinds of social institution: as
the territorial unit, the *commune*, a French word which you
might consider as the equivalent of the word 'parish' or the
Russian word 'soviet' in its original meaning, but which also
has overtones of the ancient village institutions for cultivating the land in common; and the *syndicate*, another French
word from trade union terminology, the syndicate or workers'
council as the unit of industrial organisation. Both were envisaged as small local units which would federate with each
other for the larger affairs of life, while retaining their own
autonomy, the one federating territorially and the other
industrially.

The nearest thing in ordinary political experience, to the
federative principle propounded by Proudhon and Kropotkin
would be the Swiss, rather than the American, federal system.
And without wishing to sing a song of praise for the Swiss
political system, we can see that the 22 independent cantons
of Switzerland are a successful federation. It is a federation
of like units, of small cells, and the cantonal boundaries cut
across linguistic and ethnic boundaries so that, unlike the
many unsuccessful federations, the confederation is not dominated by one or a few powerful units. For the problem of
federation, as Leopold Kohr puts it in *The Breakdown of
Nations*, is one of *division*, not of union. Herbert Luethy
writes of his country's political system:

> Every Sunday, the inhabitants of scores of communes
> go to the polling booths to elect their civil servants, rat-
> ify such and such an item of expenditure, or decide
> whether a road or a school should be built; after settling
> the business of the commune, they deal with cantonal

elections and voting on cantonal issues; lastly . . . come the decisions on federal issues. In some cantons, the sovereign people still meet in Rousseau-like fashion to discuss questions of common interest. It may be thought that this ancient form of assembly is no more than a pious tradition with a certain value as a tourist attraction. If so, it is worth looking at the results of local democracy.

The simplest example is the Swiss railway system, which is the densest network in the world. At great cost and with great trouble, it has been made to serve the needs of the smallest localities and most remote valleys, not as a paying proposition but because such was the will of the people. It is the outcome of fierce political struggles. In the 19th century, the "democratic railway movement" brought the small Swiss communities into conflict with the big towns, which had plans for centralisation . . . And if we compare the Swiss system with the French which, with admirable geometrical regularity, is entirely centred on Paris so that the prosperity or the decline, the life or death of whole regions has depended on the quality of the link with the capital, we see the difference between a centralised state and a federal alliance. The railway map is the easiest to read at a glance, but let us now superimpose on it another showing economic activity and the movement of population. The distribution of industrial activity all over Switzerland, even in the outlying areas, accounts for the strength and stability of the social structure of the country and prevented those horrible 19th century concentrations of industry, with their slums and rootless proletariat.

I quote all this, as I said, not to praise Swiss democracy, but to indicate that the federal principle which is at the heart of anarchist social theory, is worth much more attention than it is given in the textbooks on political science. Even in the context of ordinary political institutions its adoption has a far-reaching effect.

Another anarchist theory of organisation is what we might call the theory of spontaneous order: that given a common need, a collection of people will, by trial and error, by improvisation and experiment, evolve order out of chaos—this order being more durable and more closely related to their needs than any kind of externally imposed order. Kropotkin derived this theory from the observations of the history of human society and of social biology which led to his book *Mutual Aid*, and it has been observed in most revolutionary situations, in the *ad hoc* organisations which spring up after natural catastrophes, or in any activity where there is no existing organisational form or hierarchical authority. This concept was given the name *Social Control* in the book of that title by Edward Allsworth Ross, who cited instances of "frontier" societies where, through unorganised or informal measures, order is effectively maintained without benefit of constituted authority: "Sympathy, sociability, the sense of justice and resentment are competent, under favourable circumstances, to work out by themselves a true, natural order, that is to say, an order without design or art."

An interesting example of the working-out of this theory was the Pioneer Health Centre at Peckham, London, started in the decade before the war by a group of physicians and biologists who wanted to study the nature of health and healthy behaviour instead of studying ill-health like the rest of their profession. They decided that the way to do this was to start a social club whose members joined as families and could use a variety of facilities including a swimming bath, theatre, nursery and cafeteria, in return for a family membership subscription and for agreeing to periodic medical examinations. Advice, but not treatment, was given. In order to be able to draw valid conclusions the Peckham biologists thought it necessary that they should be able to observe human beings who were free—free to act as they wished and to give expression to their desires. So there were no rules and no leaders. "I was the only person with authority," said Dr. Scott Williamson, the founder, "and I used it to stop anyone exerting any authority." For the first eight months there was chaos. "With the first member-families", says one observer, "there arrived a horde of undisciplined children who used the whole building as they might have used one vast London street. Screaming and running like hooligans through all the rooms, breaking equipment and furniture," they made life intolerable for everyone. Scott Williamson, however, "insisted that peace should be restored only by the response of the children to the variety of stimuli that was placed in their way," and, "in less than a year the chaos was reduced to an order in which groups of children could daily be seen swimming, skating, riding bicycles, using the gymnasium or playing some

game, occasionally reading a book in the library . . . the
running and screaming were things of the past."

More dramatic examples of the same kind of phenomenon
are reported by those people who have been brave enough,
or confident enough to institute self-governing non-punitive
communities of delinquents or maladjusted children: August
Aichhorn and Homer Lane are examples. Aichhorn ran that
famous institution in Vienna, described in his book *Wayward Youth*. Homer Lane was the man who, after experiments in America started in Britain a community of juvenile
delinquents, boys and girls, called The Little Commonwealth. Lane used to declare that "Freedom cannot be given.
It is taken by the child in discovery and invention." True to
this principle, remarks Howard Jones, "he refused to impose
upon the children a system of government copied from the
institutions of the adult world. The self-governing structure
of the Little Commonwealth was evolved by the children
themselves, slowly and painfully to satisfy their own needs."

Anarchists believe in *leaderless groups*, and if this phrase
is familiar to you it is because of the paradox that what was
known as the leaderless group technique was adopted in the
British and American armies during the war—as a means of
selecting leaders. The military psychiatrists learned that
leader or follower traits are not exhibited in isolation. They
are, as one of them wrote, "relative to a specific social situation—leadership varied from situation to situation and from
group to group." Or as the anarchist Michael Bakunin put it
a hundred years ago, "I receive and I give—such is human
life. Each directs and is directed in his turn. Therefore there
is no fixed and constant authority, but a continual exchange
of mutual, temporary, and, above all, voluntary authority and
subordination." This point about leadership was well put in
John Comerford's book, *Health the Unknown*, about the
Peckham experiment:

Accustomed as is this age to artificial leadership . . .
it is difficult for it to realise the truth that leaders require no training or appointing, but emerge spontaneously when conditions require them. Studying their
members in the free-for-all of the Peckham Centre, the
observing scientists saw over and over again how one
member instinctively became, and was instinctively but
not officially recognised as, leader to meet the needs of
one particular moment. Such leaders appeared and dis-

appeared as the flux of the Centre required. Because they were not consciously appointed, neither (when they had fulfilled their purpose) were they consciously overthrown. Nor was any particular gratitude shown by members to a leader either at the time of his services or after for services rendered. They followed his guidance just as long as his guidance was helpful and what they wanted. They melted away from him without regrets when some widening of experience beckoned them on to some fresh adventure, which would in turn throw up its spontaneous leader, or when their self-confidence was such that any form of constrained leadership would have been a restraint to them. A society, therefore, if left to itself in suitable circumstances to express itself spontaneously works out its own salvation and achieves a harmony of action which superimposed leadership cannot emulate.

Don't be deceived by the sweet reasonableness of all this. This anarchist concept of leadership is quite revolutionary in its implications as you can see if you look around, for you see everywhere in operation the opposite concept: that of hierarchical, authoritarian, privileged and permanent leadership. There are very few comparative studies available of the effects of these two opposite approaches to the organisation of work. Two of them I will mention later; another, about the organisation of architects' offices was produced in 1962 for the Institute of British Architects under the title *The Architect and His Office*. The team which prepared this report found two different approaches to the design process, which gave rise to different ways of working and methods of organisation. One they categorised as *centralised*, which was characterised by autocratic forms of control, and the other they called *dispersed*, which promoted what they called "an informal atmosphere of free-flowing ideas." This is a very live issue among architects. Mr. W. D. Pile, who in an official capacity helped to sponsor the outstanding success of postwar British architecture, the school-building programme, specifies among the things he looks for in a member of the building team that: "He must have a belief in what I call the non-hierarchical organisation of the work. The work has got to be organised not on the star system, but on the repertory system. The team leader may often be junior to a team member. That will only be accepted if it is commonly accepted that primacy lies with the best idea and not with the senior man." And one of our greatest architects, Walter Gropius, proclaims what he calls the technique of "collaboration among men, which would release the creative instincts of the individual instead of smothering them. The essence of such technique should be to emphasise individual freedom of initiative, instead of authoritarian direction by a boss . . . synchronizing individual effort by a continuous give and take of its members . . ."

This leads us to another corner-stone of anarchist theory, the idea of workers' control of industry. A great many people think that workers' control is an attractive idea, but one which is incapable of realisation (and consequently not worth fighting for) because of the scale and complexity of modern industry. How can we convince them otherwise? Apart from pointing out how changing sources of motive power make the geographical concentration of industry obsolete, and how changing methods of production make the concentration of vast numbers of people unnecessary, perhaps the best method of persuading people that workers' control *is* a feasible proposition in large-scale industry is through pointing to successful examples of what the guild socialists called "encroaching control." They are partial and limited in effect, as they are bound to be, since they operate within the conventional industrial structure, but they do indicate that workers have an organisational capacity on the shop floor, which most people deny that they possess.

Let me illustrate this from two recent instances in modern large-scale industry. The first, the gang system worked in Coventry, was described by an American professor of industrial and management engineering, Seymour Melman, in his book *Decision-Making and Productivity*. He sought, by a detailed comparison of the manufacture of a similar product, the Ferguson tractor, in Detroit and in Coventry, England, "to demonstrate that there are realistic alternatives to managerial rule over production." His account of the operation of the gang system was confirmed by a Coventry engineering worker, Reg Wright, in two articles in *Anarchy*.

Of Standard's tractor factory in the period up to 1956 when it was sold, Melman writes: "In this firm we will show that at the same time: thousands of workers operated virtually without supervision as conventionally understood, and at high productivity; the highest wage in British industry was paid; high quality products were produced at acceptable prices in extensively mechanised plants; the management conducted its affairs at unusually low costs; also, organised workers had a substantial role in production decision-making." From the standpoint of the production workers, "the gang system leads to keeping track of goods instead of keeping track of people." Melman contrasts the "predatory competition" which characterises the managerial decision-making system with the workers' decision-making system in which "The most characteristic feature of the decision-formulating process is that of mutuality in decision-making with final authority residing in the hands of the grouped workers themselves." The gang system as he described it is very like the collective contract system advocated by G. D. H. Cole, who claimed that "The effect would be to link the members of the working group together in a common enterprise under their joint auspices and control, and to emancipate them from an externally imposed discipline in respect of their method of getting the work done."

My second example again derives from a comparative study of different methods of work organisation, made by the Tavistock Institute in the late 1950s, reported in E. L. Trist's *Organisational Choice,* and P. Herbst's *Autonomous Group Functioning.* Its importance can be seen from the opening words of the first of these: "This study concerns a group of miners who came together to evolve a new way of working together, planning the type of change they wanted to put through, and testing it in practice. The new type of work organisation which has come to be known in the industry as composite working, has in recent years emerged spontaneously in a number of different pits in the north-west Durham coal field. Its roots go back to an earlier tradition which had been almost completely displaced in the course of the last century by the introduction of work techniques based on task segmentation, differential status and payment, and extrinsic hierarchical control." The other report notes how the study showed "the ability of quite large primary work groups of 40–50 members to act as self-regulating, self-developing social organisms able to maintain themselves in a steady state of high productivity." The authors describe the system in a way which shows its relation to anarchists thought:

The composite work organisation may be described as one in which the group takes over complete responsibility for the total cycle of operations involved in mining the coal-face. No member of the group has a fixed work-role. Instead, the men deploy themselves, depending on the requirements of the on-going group task. Within the limits of technological and safety requirements they are free to evolve their own way of organising and carrying out their task. They are not subject to any external authority in this respect, nor is there within the group itself any member who takes over a formal directive leadership function. Whereas in conventional long-wall working the coal-getting task is split into four to eight separate work roles, carried out by different teams, each paid at a different rate, in the composite group members are no longer paid directly for any of the tasks carried out. The all-in wage agreement is, instead, based on the negotiated price per ton of coal produced by the team. The income obtained is divided equally among team members.

The works I have been quoting were written for specialists in productivity and industrial organisation, but their lessons are clear for people who are interested in the idea of workers' control. Faced with the objection that even though it can be shown that autonomous groups can organise themselves on a large scale and for complex tasks, it has not been shown that they can successfully co-ordinate, we resort once again to the federative principle. There is nothing outlandish about the idea that large numbers of autonomous industrial units can federate and co-ordinate their activities. If you travel across Europe you go over the lines of a dozen railway systems—capitalist and communist—co-ordinated by freely arrived at agreement between the various undertakings, with no central authority. You can post a letter to anywhere in the world, but there is no world postal authority,—representatives of different postal authorities simply have a congress every five years or so.

There are trends, observable in these occasional experiments in industrial organisation, in new approaches to problems of delinquency and addiction, in education and community organisation, and in the "de-institutionalisation" of hospitals, asylums, childrens' homes and so on, which have much in common with each other, and which run counter to the generally accepted ideas about organisation, authority and government. Cybernetic theory with its emphasis on self-organising systems, and speculation about the ultimate social effects of automation, leads in a similar revolutionary direction. George and Louise Crowley, for example, in their comments on the report of the Ad Hoc Committee on the Triple Revolution, (*Monthly Review*, Nov. 1964) remark that, "We find it no less reasonable to postulate a functioning society without authority than to postulate an orderly universe without a god. Therefore the word *anarchy* is not for us freighted with connotations of disorder, chaos, or confusion. For humane men, living in non-competitive conditions of freedom from toil and of universal affluence, anarchy is simply the appropriate state of society."

In Britain, Professor Richard Titmuss remarks that social ideas may well be as important in the next half-century as technical innovation. I believe that the social ideas of anarchism: autonomous groups, spontaneous order, workers' control, the federative principle, add up to a coherent theory of social organisation which is a valid and realistic alternative to the authoritarian, hierarchical and institutional social philosophy which we see in application all around us. Man will be compelled, Kropotkin declared, "to find new forms of organisation for the social functions which the State fulfils through the bureaucracy" and he insisted that "as long as this is not done nothing will be done." I think we have discovered what these new forms of organisation should be. We have now to make the opportunities for putting them into practice.

The "adventure playground" is a peculiarly fertile concept, a
microcosm of anarchy. It develops and confirms Ward's account, in
the preceding selection, of libertarian organization; it reaffirms the
anarchist thesis of an essential unity between tactics and goals; it re-
calls the important Proudhonian insight that the ideal libertarian
project is not utopian in the sense of attempting to remove all
sources of tension; and it suggests that anarchist ideas are often in-
fluential and even adopted under different designations. Furthermore,
as an anarchist program for the young, it discloses many parallels
between libertarian education and the anarchist's over-all reconstruction of society and thus links this section with the next.

When we call ourselves anarchists, that is, people who advocate the principle of *autonomy* as opposed to *authority* in
every field of personal and social life, we are constantly reminded of the apparent failure of anarchism to exercise any
perceptible influence on the course of political events, and as
a result we tend to overlook the unconscious adoption of
anarchist ideas in a variety of other spheres of life. Some of
these minor anarchies of everyday life provide analogies, some
provide examples, and some, when you describe their operation, sound like veritable parables of anarchy.

All the problems of social life present a choice between
libertarian and authoritarian solutions, and the ultimate
claim we may make for the libertarian approach is that it is
more efficient—it fulfils its function better. The adventure
playground is an arresting example of this living anarchy, one
which is valuable both in itself and as an experimental veri-
fication of a whole social approach. The need to provide children's playgrounds as such is a result of high-density urban
living and fast-moving traffic. The authoritarian solution to
this need is to provide an area of tarmac and some pieces of

"Adventure Playground: A Parable of Anarchy," by Colin Ward in
Anarchy 7 (September, 1961), pp. 193–201.

expensive ironmongery in the form of swings, see-saws and
roundabouts, which provide a certain amount of fun (though
because of their inflexibility children soon tire of them),
but which call for no imaginative or constructive effort on
the child's part and cannot be incorporated in any self-chosen
activity. Swings and roundabouts can only be used in one
way, they cater for no fantasies, for no developing skills, for
no emulation of adult activities, they call for no mental effort
and very little physical effort, and we are giving way to simpler and freer apparatus like climbing frames, log piles, "jun-
gle gyms," commando nets, or to play sculptures—abstract
shapes to clamber through and over, or large constructions in
the form of boats, traction engines, lorries or trains. But even
these provide for a limited age-group and a limited range of
activities, and it is not surprising that children find more
continual interest in the street, the derelict building, the
bombed site or the scrap heap.

For older boys, team-games are the officially approved activity, and as Patrick Geddes wrote before the first world war,
"they are at most granted a cricket pitch, or lent a space between football goals, but otherwise are jealously watched, as
potential savages, who on the least symptom of their natural
activities of wigwam-building, cave-digging, stream-damming
and so on—must be instantly chivvied away, and are lucky
if not handed over to the police."

That there should be anything novel in simply providing
facilities for the spontaneous, unorganized activities of childhood is an indication of how deeply rooted in our social behavior is the urge to control, direct and limit the flow of life.
But when they get the chance, in the country, or where there
are large gardens, woods or bits of waste land, what are children doing? Enclosing space, making caves, tents, dens, from
old bricks, bits of wood and corrugated iron. Finding some
corner which the adult world has passed over and making
it their own. But how can children find this kind of private
world in towns, where, as Agnete Vestereg of the Copenhagen
Junk Playground writes:

> Every bit of land is put to industrial or commercial
> use, where every patch of grass is protected or enclosed,
> where streams and hollows are filled in, cultivated and
> built on?

> But more is done for children now than used to be
> done, it may be objected. Yes, but that is one of the

chief faults—the things are *done*. Town children move about in a world full of the marvels of technical science. They may see and be impressed by things; but they long also to take possession of them, to have them in their hands, to make something themselves, to create and recreate.

The Emdrup playground was begun in 1943 by the Copenhagen Workers' Cooperative Housing Association after their landscape architect, Mr. C. T. Sorensen, who had laid out many orthodox playgrounds, had observed that children seemed to get more pleasure when they stole into the building sites and played with the materials they found there. In spite of a daily average attendance of 200 children at Emdrup, and [the fact] that "difficult" children were specially catered for, it was found that "the noise, screams and fights found in dull playgrounds are absent, for the opportunities are so rich that the children do not need to fight."

The initial success at Copenhagen has led in the years since the war to a widespread diffusion of the idea and its variations, from "Freetown" in Stockholm and "The Yard" at Minneapolis, to the *Skrammellegeplads* or building playgrounds of Denmark and the Robinson Crusoe playgrounds of Switzerland, where children are provided with the raw materials and tools for building what they want and for making gardens and sculpture. . . .

When the Yard was opened at Minneapolis with the aim of giving the children "their own spot of earth and plenty of tools and materials for digging, building and creating as they see fit,"

it was every child for himself. The initial stockpile of secondhand lumber disappeared like ice off a hot stove. Children helped themselves to all they could carry, sawed off long boards when short pieces would have done. Some hoarded tools and supplies in secret caches. Everybody wanted to build the biggest shack in the shortest time. The workmanship was shoddy.

Then came the bust. There wasn't a stick of lumber left. Hi-jacking raids were staged on half-finished shacks. Grumbling and bickering broke out. A few children packed up and left.

But on the second day of the great depression most of the youngsters banded together spontaneously for a salvage drive. Tools and nails came out of hiding. For over a week the youngsters made do with what they had. Rugged individualists who had insisted on building alone invited others to join in—and bring their supplies along. New ideas popped up for joint projects. By the time a fresh supply of lumber arrived a community had been born.

As in Copenhagen the prophesied casualties did not happen. "After a year of operation, injuries consisted of some bandaged thumbs and small cuts and bruises for the entire enrolment of over 200 children. No child has ever used a tool to hit another person."

This question of safety is so often raised when adventure playgrounds are discussed that it is worth citing the experience in this country (where the pernicious notion that whenever accidents happen someone must be sued has actually caused some local authorities to close their orthodox playgrounds—so that the kids can get run over instead). The insurance company was so impressed by the engrossed activity at the Clydesdale Road (Paddington) playground, with its complete lack of hooliganism that it quoted lower rates than for an ordinary playground. . . .

As Lady Allen [of Hurtwood, author of *Play Parks*, an account and recommendation of Swedish adventure playgrounds] says, a good adventure playground "is in continual process of destruction and growth." The splendid variety of activities which came and went at Lollard from vegetable-growing to producing a magazine, plays, operettas, jiving and "beauty sessions" were a measure of its success. As at Emdrup, this playground kept the interest of older children and young people up to the age of twenty, thus enlarging the scope of possible projects. The older boys built and equipped a workshop and eagerly sought to serve the community in which they lived, doing repairs and redecorations for old people in the district, paying for the materials from a fund of their own. These were the same young people who are such a "problem" to their elders. The difference is that between the atmosphere of the irresponsible society, and that which was precariously built at the playground. The place, said the warden, "stands for far more than a mere playground," and the Chairman summed up

This playground is different because it's a place where the children have an infinite choice of opportunities. They can handle basic things—earth, water, plants, timber—and work with real tools; and they have an adult friend, a person they trust and respect. Here every child can develop a healthy sense of self-esteem, because there is always something at which they can excel. The wide age range, from two years to twenty-three, is perhaps unique in any playground. There can be progressive development through rich play opportunities, to a growing sense of responsibility to the playground, to younger children, and finally to others outside the playground. Their willingness to help others is the sign of real maturity which is the object of all who work with young people.

The Grimsby playground, started [in England] in 1955, has a similar story. Its cycle of growth and renewal is annual. At the end of each summer the children saw up their shacks and shanties into firewood which they deliver in fantastic quantities to old age pensioners. When they begin building in the spring, "it's just a hole in the ground—and they crawl into it." Gradually the holes give way to two-storey huts. But

> they never pick up where they left off at the end of the previous summer. It's the same with fires. They begin by lighting them just for fun. Then they cook potatoes and by the end of the summer they're cooking eggs, bacon and beans.

Similarly with the notices above their dens. It begins with nailing up "Keep Out" signs (just as in The Yard at Minneapolis). After this come more personal names like "Bughole Cave" and "Dead Man's Cave," but by the end of the summer they have communal names like "Hospital" or "Estate Agent." There is an ever-changing range of activities "due entirely to the imagination and enterprise of the children themselves . . . at no time are they expected to continue an activity which no longer holds an interest for them . . . Care of tools is the responsibility of the children. At the end of 1958 they were still using the same tools purchased originally in 1955. Not one hammer or spade has been lost, and all repairs have been paid for out of the Nail Fund."

Finally, in case it isn't obvious, why do we claim the adventure playground movement as an experiment in anarchy? Well, let us repeat yet again Kropotkin's definition of an anarchist society as one which seeks the most complete development of individuality combined with the highest development of voluntary association in all its aspects, in all possible degrees, for all imaginable aims; ever changing, ever modified associations which carry in themselves the elements of their durability and constantly assume new forms which answer best to the multiple aspirations of all. A society to which pre-established forms, crystallized by law, are repugnant; which looks for harmony in an ever-changing and fugitive equilibrium between a multitude of varied forces and influences of every kind, following their own course . . .

Every one of these phrases is recognizably a description of the microcosmic society of the successful adventure playground, and it leads us to speculate on the wider applications of the idea which is in essence the old revolutionary notion of "free access to the means of production," in this instance to the means of every kind of creative and recreative activity. We think of course of the Peckham Experiment—a kind of adventure playground for people of all ages, or the kind of variations on work and leisure in freely chosen activity envisaged in Paul and Percival Goodman's *Communitas*. The adventure playground is a free society in miniature, with the same tensions and ever-changing harmonies, the same diversity and spontaneity, the same unforced growth of cooperation and release of individual qualities and communal sense, which lie dormant in a society devoted to competition and acquisitiveness.

SECTION VI

The Anarchists on Education

From William Godwin's *An Account of the Seminary That Will Be Opened on Monday the Fourth Day of August at Epsom in Surrey* (1783) to Paul Goodman's *Compulsory Mis-education* (1964), anarchism has persistently regarded itself as having distinctive and revolutionary implications for education. Indeed, no other movement whatever has assigned to educational principles, concepts, experiments, and practices a more significant place in its writings and activities.

Why have the anarchists evidenced such a powerful concern for both the theoretical and the practical problems of education? It is not solely because anarchism regards education as an indispensable instrument for the eventual realization of some ideal social order, for this way of conceiving education and its value is shared by men of almost all persuasions. Whatever form of community life one wishes to introduce or preserve, one must ensure that new generations acquire both a commitment to its principles and the skills needed to implement its major objectives.

An explanation of the anarchists' stress on education might better be sought in their view that education should ideally function as *the focus of intrinsic value,* that is, as the living center and clearest model of what is ultimately desirable in human relations. In other words, education is not a mere training ground for some future community nor is its foremost aim that of producing a supply of well-trained and dedicated anarchist revolutionaries. On the contrary, education must itself manifest, indeed consist of, libertarian relations and activities. Education does not simply lay the groundwork for subsequent achievements; at its best it constitutes the most complete and most feasible paradigm of those achievements.

Consider the relationship between teacher and pupil. In its most desirable form this relation provides the anarchist with a precise and attainable model of the ideal relation between the ordinary adult citizen and the institutions which guide or direct his life. The teacher's major aim should be to develop the powers, the autonomy, and the personality (in

Berdyaev's sense) of his pupil. Authority and coercion, if he permits himself any at all, should be employed temporarily and solely to eliminate immediate deficiencies (for example, the child's natural ignorance in matters of physical health). Above all, a teacher should strive to encourage his pupils to become men who transcend his own wisdom and accomplishments and are thus fully capable of initiating and executing further steps in their own development by themselves. In short, then, the only forms of coercion, authority, control, interference, and leadership which, for a libertarian, can count as legitimate in the larger community are those that a teacher may rightfully utilize in his endeavor to wean the young away from any further dependence on external regulation. To paraphrase the *Republic*, could it not be said that for an anarchist the good society is merely the educational community writ large?

The following selections have been organized in a way that resembles the over-all arrangement of our anthology. This has been done to convey fully the anarchists' view that educational principles and programs are a direct index to the good society. Thus, the first four selections proffer philosophical reflections concerning the nature and aims of education, while the next two advance a libertarian critique of some fairly common educational practices, and the last five detail educational experiments in which libertarian principles find extensive expression. But these lines of organization do not form exclusive categories. There are forceful presentations of philosophical concepts and standards in such programmatic selections as those by Goodman and Tolstoy. Furthermore, criticisms of abusive or sterile educational approaches and presuppositions are essential to the arguments in almost all of what follows. (See, for example, Sir Herbert Read's comparison of coercive and spontaneous morality and Tony Gibson's objections to progressive education.)

38 Art as the Basis of Libertarian Education

Sir Herbert Read is a renowned contemporary art critic who has also been a prolific writer of short stories, philosophical essays, and programs for education. He ranks with Paul Goodman and Alex Comfort as one of the most famous of living anarchists.

Sir Herbert's anarchism is composed of several interwoven themes, central among which are the following:

1 That freedom is best conceived not as a negative rejection of external restrictions but as a positive self-regulating form of responsible activity.

2 That only by giving primacy of place to art—in his provocative sense of the term—can the aims of libertarian education be achieved.

3 That on the success of libertarian education, on the release of spontaneous, freely initiated forms of self-discipline and self-fulfillment, depends the psychic health of the individual, of his community, and, in today's world, of humanity itself. (Corroboration for this view, Sir Herbert frequently avows, can be found in the writings of such psychologists and philosophers as Jean Piaget, Carl Jung, Trigant Burrow, Martin Buber, Susan Isaacs and Erich Fromm.) In the passages below, these three themes are developed into a compelling account of education and of the need to reconstruct it in accord with anarchist principles.

WHAT IS THE PURPOSE OF EDUCATION?

The purpose of education can only be to develop, at the same time as the uniqueness, the social consciousness or reciprocity of the individual. As a result of the infinite permutations of heredity, the individual will inevitably be unique, and this uniqueness, because it is something not possessed by anyone else, will be of value to the community. It may be only a

Education Through Art, by Sir Herbert Read (London: Faber & Faber Ltd., 1943 and New York: Pantheon Books, 1945), pp. 5–7, 202–3. Reprinted by permission of Faber & Faber Ltd. and Random House, Inc.

unique way of speaking or of smiling—but that contributes to
life's variety. But it may be a unique way of seeing, of thinking, of inventing, of expressing mind or emotion—and in that
case, one man's individuality may be of incalculable benefit
to the whole of humanity. But uniqueness has no practical
value in isolation. One of the most certain lessons of modern
psychology and of recent historical experiences, is that education must be a process, not only of individuation, but also of
integration, which is the reconciliation of individual uniqueness with social unity. . . .

But, many people will hasten to point out, this conception
of organic wholeness implies potentialities of success or failure which differ in nothing but name from the old potentialities for good and evil. If an individual achieves social integration you will call him a good citizen; if he does not,
you will call him bad. In this sense, if in no other, education must discriminate between good and evil inclinations,
and therefore, in addition to its creative function, it must
have a destructive or repressive function.

If the objection is in this manner posed abstractly, then it
must be admitted. But it is really a question of social dynamics. To talk of encouraging in one direction and of repressing in another direction implies an exercise of power
from a centre, and that is precisely the false authoritarian
concept I am anxious to avoid. Evolution, history in the making, does not proceed from a fixed point. To describe the real
nature of its activity some philosophers have used the word
'emergent' (Bergson used 'creative' with the same intention).
But the point I wish to make is not quite covered by these
terms. Freedom should not be conceived in a negative sense,
as freedom *from* certain wants or restrictions. It is a state of
being with positive characteristics, characteristics to be developed in all their self-sufficiency. My contention will be,
that the development of these positive qualities inevitably
eliminates their opposites. We avoid hate by loving: we avoid
sadism and masochism by community of feeling and action.
We shall not need to repress because we shall have made education a process which, in the old and literal sense of the
word, *prevents* us in the ways of evil. The impulses which
education will release precede and preclude the formation of
those egoistic and antisocial impulses which are the present
product of the social process. . . .

Though it seems obvious that in a democratic society the
purpose of education should be to foster individual growth,

many problems arise when we begin to consider what methods we should adopt to this end. . . . It will be my purpose to show that the most important function of education is concerned with this psychological 'orientation', and that for this reason the education of the aesthetic sensibility is of fundamental importance. . . . The theory to be put forward embraces all modes of self-expression, literary and poetic (verbal) no less than musical or aural, and forms an integral approach to reality which should be called *aesthetic* education—the education of those senses upon which consciousness, and ultimately the intelligence and judgment of the human individual, are based. It is only in so far as these senses are brought into harmonious and habitual relationship with the external world that an integrated personality is built up. Without such integration we get, not only the psychologically unbalanced types familiar to the psychiatrist, but what is even more disastrous from the point of view of the general good, those arbitrary systems of thought, dogmatic or rationalistic in origin, which seek in despite of the natural facts to impose a logical or intellectual pattern on the world of organic life. . . .

The secret of our collective ills is to be traced to the suppression of spontaneous creative ability in the individual. The lack of spontaneity, in education and in social organization, is due to that disintegration of the personality which has been the fatal result of economic, industrial, and cultural developments since the Renaissance. The personality has become disintegrated because the growth natural to it has been thwarted—thwarted by coercive discipline and authoritarian morality, by social convention and mechanical toil—until instead of the wholeness of the expansive tree we have only the twisted and stunted bush. But man is more complex than a tree, and the effects of repression are far more disastrous. Man not only turns against himself, but against his fellows. The forces of his destructiveness are social as well as individual: when the individual is not bent on destroying himself, he attempts to destroy the weight of oppression, which he will identify with some specific group or nation. 'It would seem,' writes [Erich Fromm], 'that the amount of destructiveness to be found in individuals is proportionate to the amount to which expansiveness of life is curtailed. By this we do not refer to individual frustrations of this or that instinctive desire, but to the thwarting of the whole of life, the blockage of spontaneity of the growth and expression of man's sensuous, emotional, and intellectual capacities. Life has an inner dynamism of its own; it tends to grow, to be expressed, to be lived. It seems that if this tendency is thwarted the energy directed towards life undergoes a process of decomposition and changes into energies directed towards destruction. In other words: the drive for life and the drive for destruction are not mutually independent factors but are in a reversed interdependence. The more the drive toward life is thwarted, the stronger is the drive toward destructiveness. *Destructiveness is the outcome of unlived life.*' Support for my thesis could not be more apposite, more forceful. It is only education in its widest sense, as guided growth, encouraged expansion, tender upbringing, that can secure that life is lived in all its natural creative spontaneity, in all its sensuous, emotional and intellectual fullness.

THE SPONTANEOUS EMERGENCE OF MORALITY AND DISCIPLINE

The good teacher is one who is able to . . . establish a wholly personal relationship with his pupil, one which is based on love and understanding for the unique personality which has been entrusted to his care. Such a teacher will not attempt to impose on his pupil arbitrary conceptions of "good" and "bad," which the child is unable to feel or understand (and which therefore lead to a state of tension or disunity which is one origin of neurosis). He will ignore the whole system of "make-believe" with its rewards and punishments, its constraints and inhibitions. He will try instead to establish a relationship of reciprocity and trust between himself and his pupil, and one of co-operation and mutual aid between all the individuals within his care. The teacher should identify himself with the pupil in the same degree that the pupil identifies himself with the teacher, and he should probably endeavor to make this process, on the pupil's part, more conscious than it would normally be. What is required is the give and take of a mutual relationship. . . .

If this right relationship is developed between the teacher and his pupil, and the teacher thus becomes the focus of a

Education for Peace, by Sir Herbert Read (New York: Charles Scribner's Sons, 1949 and London: Routledge & Kegan Paul Ltd., 1949), pp. 139–52. Copyright 1949 Charles Scribner's Sons. Reprinted by permission of Charles Scribner's Sons and Routledge & Kegan Paul Ltd. Subheads provided by the editors.

group of pupils who love him and trust him, it is then easy to establish the precepts of mutual aid within that group. This means that within the group—the class, the house, the school —a relationship of reciprocity has been formed which can take the place of those relationships of constraint that are normal in traditional methods of education.

If this feeling of trust in the teacher were the only psychological motive active within such a group, it is possible that complications due to envy and rivalry would ensue. But actually the group develops spontaneously a social life and cohesion which is independent of the teacher. The spontaneous emergence of groups among children has been studied by educationalists like Jean Piaget and Susan Isaacs, and a social experiment on a large scale which covers the whole development of the individual is being conducted at the Peckham Health Centre, with results which fully support this thesis. The importance of this development, in the life of the child, is that it leads the child *by natural stages* from a self-centred state of egotism to an attitude of social co-operation. There is then no question of forcing the child to recognize and accept a moral code whose justice it cannot appreciate. That abstract "sense of duty" is wholly outside the child's mental range: the child can only be coerced into its observance. But that sense of "playing the game" which emerges when children evolve their own activities is a real thing: it is a felt relationship between little human beings who must co-operate to achieve their common aim. And to achieve this aim they must create a pattern—the rules of the game which give coherence and form to their activities. In such spontaneously evolved patterns, giving pleasures and satisfaction to the growing animal instincts and desires, lies hidden the pattern of a society in which all persons are free, but freely consenting to a common purpose.

It is impossible to exaggerate the fundamental nature of this aspect of education, which I have called *initiation*. At this stage of life a choice must be made which inevitably dictates the form which our society will take. In one direction we can institute objective codes of conduct and morality to which our children are introduced before the age of understanding and to which they are compelled to conform by a system of rewards and punishments. That way conducts us to an authoritarian society, governed by laws and sanctioned by military power. It is the kind of society in which most of the world now lives, ridden by neuroses, full of envy and avarice, ravaged by war and disease.

In the other direction we can avoid all coercive codes of morality, all formal conceptions of "right" and "wrong." For a morality of obedience we can substitute a morality of attachment or reciprocity, that living together in perfect charity which was once the ideal of Christianity. Believing that the spontaneous life developed by children among themselves gives rise to a discipline infinitely nearer to that inner accord or harmony which is the mark of the virtuous man, we can aim at making our teachers the friends rather than the masters of their pupils; as teachers they will not lay down readymade rules, but will encourage their children to carry out their own co-operative activities, and thus spontaneously to elaborate their own rules. Discipline will not be imposed, but discovered—discovered as the right, economical and harmonious way of action. We can avoid the competitive evils of the examination system, which merely serves to re-enforce the egocentrism inherent in the child: we can eliminate all ideas of rewards and punishments, substituting a sense of the collective good of the community, to which reparation for shortcomings and selfishness will be obviously due and freely given. In all things, moral and intellectual, we should act on the belief that we really possess only what we have conquered ourselves—that we are made perfect by natural habits, but slaves by social conventions. . . .

I hope I may now expect from my reader a clearer understanding of what is meant by "freedom in education." We can now see that it is more exact to speak of "education for freedom" or "education for peace." But this is a misleading slogan unless we remember the means, which is the discipline of art, the only discipline to which the senses naturally submit. Art, as we have seen, is a discipline which the senses seek in their intuitive perception of form, of harmony, of proportion, of the integrity or wholeness of any experience. It is also the discipline of the tool and the material—the discipline imposed by pencil or pen, by the loom or the potter's wheel, by the physical nature of paint, textiles, wood, stone or clay.

But the point about such discipline is that it is innate: it is part of our physiological constitution, and is there to be encouraged and matured. It does not have to be imposed by the schoolmaster or the drill sergeant: it is not a kind of physical torture. It is a faculty within the child which responds to sympathy and love, to the intelligent anticipation of impulses and trends in the individuality of the child. For this reason the teacher must be primarily a person and not a pedagogue, a friend rather than a master or mistress, an infinitely patient collaborator. . . .

The art of children is supremely important for this very reason: it is the earliest and most exact index to the child's individual psychology. Once the psychological tendency or trend of a child is known, its own individuality can be developed by the discipline of art, till it has its own form and beauty, which is its unique contribution to the beauties of human nature.

Though a half century has dulled his renown, in 1910 Francisco
Ferrer was the center of international excitement. He was known
as the man who had founded a number of libertarian schools in
Spain, edited and published the review *L'École Renovée*, and established a radical publishing house at Barcelona. His International
League for the Rational Education of Children was supported by
such figures as Jack London, Upton Sinclair, and Anatole France.
But his educational work would probably have been less celebrated
had not a conspiracy of clerics and politicians subjected him to an
outrageously unjust trial for being "the chief of a military rebellion."
Ferrer was condemned to death on the basis of half truths against
which he was permitted no defense.

Seldom has the anarchist cause found a more genuine and effective martyr. Ferrer became the hero both of scrupulous investigations
released by British weeklies and of blazing manifestoes in Emma
Goldman's *Mother Earth*. More important, Ferrer's work and death
inspired a host of libertarian experiments in education from Rio de
Janeiro to Denver—all bearing his name and the distinctive mark of
his concept of "rational education."

Basic to Ferrer's view is the principle that education should develop men who are in all ways independent of the devices of political
and ecclesiastical authority and who are equipped to build and maintain an anarchist society. This principle, however, may conflict with
the anarchist insight that education is the paradigm of ideal human
relations, as well as a training ground for revolutionary activity.

The word "education" should not be accompanied by any
qualification. It means simply the need and duty of the generation which is in the full development of its powers to prepare the rising generation and admit it to the patrimony of
human knowledge. This is an entirely rational ideal, and it

The Origins and Ideals of the Modern School, by Francisco Ferrer
(New York and London: Putnam, 1913), pp. 85–89.

will be fully realized in some future age, when men are wholly freed from their prejudices and superstitions.

In our efforts to realize this ideal we find ourselves confronted with religious education and political education: to these we must oppose rational and scientific instruction. The type of religious education is that given in the clerical and convent schools of all countries; it consists of the smallest possible quantity of useful knowledge and a good deal of Christian doctrine and sacred history. Political education is the kind established some time ago in France, after the fall of the Empire, the object of which is to exalt patriotism and represent the actual public administration as the instrument of the common welfare.

Sometimes the qualification "free" or "secular" is applied abusively and maliciously to education, in order to distract or alienate public opinion. Orthodox people, for instance, call "free schools" certain schools which they establish in opposition to the really free tendency of modern pedagogy; and many are called "secular schools" which are really political, patriotic, and anti-humanitarian.

Rational education is lifted above these illiberal forms. It has, in the first place, no regard to religious education, because science has shown that the story of creation is a myth and the gods legendary; and therefore religious education takes advantage of the credulity of the parents and the ignorance of the children, maintaining the belief in a supernatural being to whom people may address all kinds of prayers. This ancient belief, still unfortunately widespread, has done a great deal of harm, and will continue to do so as long as it persists. The mission of education is to show the child, by purely scientific methods, that the more knowledge we have of natural products, their qualities, and the way to use them, the more industrial, scientific, and artistic commodities we shall have for the support and comfort of life, and men and women will issue in larger numbers from our schools with a determination to cultivate every branch of knowledge and action, under the guidance of reason and the inspiration of science and art, which will adorn life and reform society.

We will not, therefore, lose our time praying to our imaginary God for things which our own exertions alone can procure.

On the other hand, our teaching has nothing to do with politics. It is our work to form individuals in the full possession of all their faculties, while politics would subject their faculties to other men. While religion has, with its divine power, created a positively abusive power and retarded the development of humanity, political systems also retard it by encouraging men to depend for everything on the will of others, on what are supposed to be men of a superior character—on those, in a word, who from tradition or choice exercise the profession of politics. It must be the aim of the rational schools to show the children that there will be tyranny and slavery as long as one man depends upon another, to study the causes of the prevailing ignorance, to learn the origin of all the traditional practices which give life to the existing social system, and to direct the attention of the pupils to these matters.

We will not, therefore, lose our time seeking from others what we can get for ourselves.

In a word, our business is to imprint on the minds of the children the idea that their condition in the social order will improve in proportion to their knowledge and to the strength they are able to develop; and that the era of general happiness will be the more sure to dawn when they have discarded all religious and other superstitions, which have up to the present done so much harm. On that account there are no rewards or punishments in our schools; no alms, no medals or badges in imitation of the religious and patriotic schools, which might encourage the children to believe in talismans instead of in the individual and collective power of beings who are conscious of their ability and knowledge.

Rational and scientific knowledge must persuade the men and women of the future that they have to expect nothing from any privileged being (fictitious or real); and that they may expect all that is reasonable from themselves and from a freely organized and accepted social order. . . .

I would like to call the attention of my readers to this idea: All the value of education rests in respect for the physical, intellectual, and moral will of the child. Just as in science no demonstration is possible save by facts, just so there is no real education save that which is exempt from all dogmatism, which leaves to the child itself the direction of its effort, and confines itself to the seconding of that effort. Now there is nothing easier than to alter this purpose, and nothing harder than to respect it. Education is always imposing, violating, constraining; the real educator is he who can best protect the child against his (the teacher's) own ideas, his peculiar

whims; he who can best appeal to the child's own energies. . . .

Let us not fear to say that we want men capable of evolving
without stopping, capable of destroying and renewing their
environments without cessation, of renewing themselves also;
men whose intellectual independence will be their greatest
force, who will attach themselves to nothing, always ready
to accept what is best, happy in the triumph of new ideas,
aspiring to live multiple lives in one life. Society fears such
men; we therefore must not hope that it will ever want an
education able to give them to us.

What, then, is our own mission? What method are we
going to choose to contribute to the renovation of the school?

We shall follow the labors of the scientists who study the
child with the greatest attention, and we shall eagerly seek
for means of applying their experience to the education we
wish to build up, in the direction of an ever fuller liberation
of the individual. But how can we attain our end? Shall it
not be by putting ourselves directly to the work favoring
the foundation of new schools, which shall be ruled as much
as possible by this spirit of liberty, which we foresee will
dominate the entire work of education in the future?

As the preceding selection shows, Francisco Ferrer strongly insisted that education must restrict itself to the "seconding" of the child's own aptitudes and energies. In the essay that follows, Bayard Boyeson, who helped to organize the Ferrer Day School in New York City, deepens this and other insights fundamental to Ferrer's position. That education must take the child for its "center of gravity" is a point developed throughout this section, and it must surely be counted as a distinctively libertarian contribution to educational theory and practice.

There seems to be a popular notion that Ferrer's ideas concerning education were born full-fledged out of nothing and put precipitately into practice. In reality, they are but one manifestation of the many efforts of the revolutionary spirit to bring perhaps the most important sphere of human endeavor into some sort of logical connection with the radical thought and feeling of the world. . . . The Modern School of New York (founded by the Francisco Ferrer Association) purposes to achieve in the United States an end similar to that which Ferrer achieved in Spain.

It bases itself, above all, upon the idea that the child has as much right to itself as has the adult and that the personality of the child, during the sensitive and hazardous years of early youth, must be kept free from the intrusive hands of those who would mould and fashion it according to preconceived models, who would thwart this quality and divert that, in order to fit the child into the ideals of the teacher. We take the center of gravity, which has lain hitherto in the teacher, and put it firmly in the child itself, for it is our aim not to lead, but to follow, the activities of the child; using its natural interests as points upon which it can be allowed to fasten knowledge and aiding the child always to draw out and

---

"The Modern School," by Bayard Boyeson (New York: Ferrer Association, n.d.).

develop its native qualities. Facts and environment, we supply: such facts and such an environment as will enable the children to work out *for themselves*, with only the spur of tutorial enthusiasm and sympathy and understanding the significance of their thoughts and deeds as they act and react upon themselves and their fellows. . . .

Furthermore, we let the children choose (so far as our means allow) what subjects they wish to study. When some boys and girls have shown a desire to follow up a particular branch of knowledge, we form a class and present to them the necessary facts. The pupils may interrupt and ask questions whenever they wish to; and when the facts have been apprehended, indeed while the facts are being apprehended, they will be encouraged to discuss them, to interpret and to relate them to their own interests. It is our purpose to have all study develop directly out of the lives of the pupils, instead of being imposed from without. Thus, for instance, nearly all the major parts of anthropology may be taught to very young children through the desire that so many of them have to make things, to construct. In place of the purposeless manual training of the Public Schools, we have here a class which combines training of the senses and of the mind, skill of hand and skill of brain. The children, of course, are not required to learn lessons outside of class, since the aim of the class is not to quiz them. They will, however, be taught how to use books as works of reference, and they will know that the teachers are glad to discuss at any time the subjects which interest the pupils.

The main point, I repeat, is that all the work should be developed out of the lives and living interests of the children. That point is basic, and that is the very point which, though recognized by some teachers, is never held to consistently in the Public Schools. . . .

And this brings me to the question of discipline. The only discipline which is of any educative value is self-discipline; and that is obtained by any child or man who undertakes to make anything or to study anything. Authoritative discipline, imposed from without, is invariably immoral in its results because it sets up in the child's mind a double standard of conduct, the one public, the other private; and because it teaches him that punishment is the result not of his actions, but of detection. Discipline of this kind either confuses the child utterly or leads him to the natural conclusion that punishment and immorality are the same thing, that the deed for which he is punished is immoral and the deed for which he is not punished (though it be essentially the same as the other) is moral.

Furthermore, discipline breeds the habit of secrecy and distrust in the person disciplined, and this destroys the possibility of successful education, which requires confidence and openness of motive and action between teacher and pupil. If the teacher has once punished the child for an act which the teacher deemed wrong, the child will henceforth try to conceal all similar acts; and from this first concealment he will go on to other concealments, and finally—not before long —he will attempt to hide all thoughts and acts which have not been definitely approved of in advance. Thus, what budding harmonies his nature held will be made discordant; something (who knows how precious in its potentialities?) will be driven inward for unwholesome brooding or be utterly destroyed, and the teacher will be, from that time forward, merely a stranger wielding harsh authority over an alien child.

We do away, therefore, with all coercive discipline and all the rules and paraphernalia of such discipline: the raised desk of the teacher, the rigid rows of seats for the children, and the idea that every class should be conducted according to particular, preconceived codes of order. We prefer the "free order" which is developed by the class itself, since (as I have already said) we desire to place the center of gravity in the children; and we do not bother about dignity, since we know that in proportion as the teacher thinks about external dignity for himself he prevents the growth of inward dignity in the pupils.

Having done away, then, with the old notions of discipline in the school and, consequently, with fear and overtimidity in the pupils, we find ourselves able to have a class which is distinctive in our school and which is of the very greatest aid in developing the children as separate thinking individuals and as members of a social unit—a class of free discussion of problems suggested by the children. These classes invariably provoke much stimulating argument and, during the year, they touch upon and delve into an astonishingly large number of subjects. To give an example: a strike of some schoolboys took place last winter and immediately all of the children wished to discuss the question of the advantages and merits of this particular occurrence. This led us on to the subject of strikes in general and of organization, and this again, since it happened that the newspapers were featuring a foreign strike at the time, carried us to a consideration and comparative study of the methods of the different industrial bodies: the American Federation, the Industrial Workers of the World, the Confederation Generale du Travail, etc., etc. Some weeks later, the same class came with a story of a boy in a public school who had been punished because he refused to tell on a friend and who had therefore, when next asked to do the same thing, lied to save both himself and his comrade. One can readily imagine the nice moral problems which were thrown out by this single incident. It afforded food for many days of valuable discussion.

In these classes, the teacher's chief duty is simply to keep the ideas from dancing too far afield, to hold them coherent to a central point, and to restrain himself from supplying the conclusions which the children are working out for themselves. If he does these things, the classes become, in a sense, classes in reasoning; and the ability to reason, to interpret facts in such a way as will allow one to arrive at a conclusion, is basic in education. Anyone who has not been present while work of this kind was going on would be, I think, greatly surprised at the speed with which the children learn to use their minds—though they use concrete, instead of abstract terms, the process is that of pure reasoning—and at the delight which they have in discovering in themselves powers before unsuspected and at the new attitude of the children towards themselves, their new pride, their new poise, their new dignity as human beings.

William Godwin had an abiding interest in education. In 1783 he published a pamphlet containing the prospectus and philosophy of a school that he was to supervise. In this pamphlet, Godwin assigned to education the task of combatting the noxious effects of political authority which he was to examine and criticize more thoroughly in *Political Justice*. And in 1798, Godwin dealt with the theory and practice of education in a work entitled *The Enquirer: Reflections on Education, Manners, and Literature*. It is from this work, and more specifically from the essay "Of the Communication of Knowledge," that the following selection is taken.

Godwin is *not* concerned with the empirical issue of which measures will most effectively train the student to restate what his teachers lay down as fact. On the contrary, his inquiry relates to the ultimate goals of education, and his aim is to determine how the great moral and libertarian principles proclaimed in selection 17 would have us impart skills, theories, insights, and experiences. As Godwin himself admonished: "Let us not, in the eagerness of our haste to educate, forget all the ends of education."

We should note that selections 42 and 43 form a self-contained unit with the present essay. Godwin there employs his conception of the permanent norms of education to analyze specific educational abuses.

In what manner would reason, independently of the received modes and practices of the world, teach us to communicate knowledge?

Liberty is one of the most desirable of all sublunary advantages. I would willingly therefore communicate knowledge without infringing, or with as little as possible violence to, the volition and individual judgment of the person to be instructed.

"Of the Communication of Knowledge," by William Godwin in *The Enquirer: Reflections on Education, Manners, and Literature* (Dublin: J. Moore, 1797), pp. 76–83.

Again; I desire to excite a given individual to the acquisition of knowledge. The only possible method in which I can excite a sensitive being to the performance of a voluntary action is by the exhibition of motive.

Motives are of two sorts, intrinsic and extrinsic. Intrinsic motives are those which arise from the inherent nature of the thing recommended. Extrinsic motives are those which have no constant and unalterable connection with the thing recommended, but are combined with it by accident or at the pleasure of some individual.

Thus I may recommend some species of knowledge by a display of the advantages which will necessarily attend upon its acquisition or flow from its possession. Or, on the other hand, I may recommend it despotically, by allurements or menaces, by showing that the pursuit of it will be attended with my approbation, and that the neglect of it will be regarded by me with displeasure.

The first of these classes of motives is unquestionably the best. To be governed by such motives is the pure and genuine condition of a rational being. By exercise it strengthens the judgment. It elevates us with a sense of independence. It causes a man to stand alone and is the only method by which he can be rendered truly an individual, the creature not of implicit faith but of his own understanding.

If a thing be really good, it can be shown to be such. If you cannot demonstrate its excellence, it may well be suspected that you are no proper judge of it. Why should not I be admitted to decide upon that which is to be acquired by the application of my labor?

Is it necessary that a child should learn a thing before it can have any idea of its value? It is probable that there is no one thing that it is of eminent importance for a child to learn. The true object of juvenile education is to provide against the age of five-and-twenty a mind well regulated, active and prepared to learn. Whatever will inspire habits of industry and observation will sufficiently answer this purpose. Is it not possible to find something that will fulfill these conditions, the benefit of which a child shall understand, and the acquisition of which he may be taught to desire? Study with desire is real activity; without desire it is but the semblance and mockery of activity. Let us not, in the eagerness of our haste to educate, forget all the ends of education.

The most desirable mode of education therefore, in all instances where it shall be found sufficiently practicable, is that which is careful that all the acquisitions of the pupil shall be preceded and accompanied by desire. The best motive to learn is a perception of the value of the thing learned. The worst motive, without deciding whether or not it be necessary to have recourse to it, may well be affirmed to be constraint and fear. There is a motive between these, less pure than the first but not so displeasing as the last, which is desire, not springing from the intrinsic excellence of the object, but from the accidental attractions which the teacher may have annexed to it.

According to the received modes of education, the matter goes first and the pupil follows. According to the method here recommended, it is probable that the pupil should go first, and the matter follow.* If I learn nothing but what I desire to learn, what should hinder me from being my own preceptor? . . .

Nothing can be more happily adapted to remove the difficulties of instruction, than that the pupil should first be excited to desire knowledge, and next that his difficulties should be solved for him, and his path cleared, as often and as soon as he thinks proper to desire it.

This plan is calculated entirely to change the face of education. The whole formidable apparatus which has hitherto attended it is swept away. Strictly speaking, no such characters are left upon the scene as either preceptor or pupil. The boy, like the man, studies because he desires it. He proceeds upon a plan of his own invention, or which, by adopting, he has made his own. Everything bespeaks independence and equality. The man, as well as the boy, would be glad in cases of difficulty to consult a person more informed than himself. That the boy is accustomed almost always to consult the man, and not the man the boy, is to be regarded rather as an accident than anything essential. Much even of this would be removed if we remembered that the most inferior judge may

---

* To some persons this expression may be ambiguous. The sort of "going first" and "following" here censured may be compared to one person's treading over a portion of ground and another's coming immediately after, treading in his footsteps. The adult must undoubtedly be supposed to have acquired their information before the young; and they may at proper intervals incite and conduct their diligence, but not so as to supersede in them the exercise of their own discretion.

often, by the varieties of his apprehension, give valuable information to the most enlightened. The boy, however, should be consulted by the man unaffectedly, not according to any preconcerted scheme, or for the purpose of persuading him that he is what he is not.

There are three considerable advantages which would attend upon this species of education.

First, liberty. Three fourths of the slavery and restraint that are now imposed upon young persons would be annihilated at a stroke.

Secondly, the judgment would be strengthened by continual exercise. Boys would no longer learn their lessons after the manner of parrots. No one would learn without a reason, satisfactory to himself, why he learned; and it would perhaps be well, if he were frequently prompted to assign his reasons. Boys would then consider for themselves whether they understood what they read. To know when and how to ask a question is no contemptible part of learning. Sometimes they would pass over difficulties and neglect essential preliminaries, but then the nature of the thing would speedily recall them and induce them to return to examine the tracts which before had been overlooked. For this purpose it would be well that the subjects of their juvenile studies should often be discussed, and that one boy should compare his progress and his competence to decide in certain points with those of another. There is nothing that more strongly excites our inquiries than this mode of detecting our ignorance.

Thirdly, to study for ourselves is the true method of acquiring habits of activity. The horse that goes round in a mill, and the boy that is anticipated and led by the hand in all his acquirements, are not active. I do not call a wheel that turns round fifty times in a minute active. Activity is a mental quality. If therefore you would generate habits of activity, turn the boy loose in the fields of science. Let him explore the path for himself. Without increasing his difficulties, you may venture to leave him for a moment and suffer him to ask himself the question before he asks you, or in other words, to ask the question before he receives the information. Far be it from the system here laid down to increase the difficulties of youth. No, it diminishes them a hundredfold. Its office is to produce inclination, and a willing temper makes every burden light.

Lastly, it is the tendency of this system to produce in the young, when they are grown up to the stature of men, a love of literature. The established modes of education produce the opposite effect, unless in a fortunate few, who, by the celerity of their progress, and the distinctions they obtain, perhaps escape from the general influence. But, in the majority of cases, the memory of our slavery becomes associated with the studies we pursued, and it is not till after repeated struggles, that those things can be rendered the objects of our choice, which were for so long a time the themes of compulsion.

42 Censorship: Obligation or Abomination?

The first of the two following selections was published in *The Enquirer*, while the second is taken from Volume II of Godwin's *Political Justice*. In both, Godwin raises objections to educational practices which, despite the cogency of his attack over one hundred and fifty years ago, are obviously not dead today.

In the two pieces which follow, there is a reciprocal relation between axiom and theorem. On one hand, the principles of justice and obligation are indispensable for an understanding of these two critical essays. On the other, Godwin's arguments against censorship at any stage in the education of a human being and his analysis of the defects of centralizing education serve to reveal, or even create, the full meaning of those fundamental principles. And this reciprocal relation between ultimate standards and educational values is ultimately tied to Godwin's insistence, in selection 41, that we appeal to intrinsic motives in order to communicate knowledge.

A difficulty which frequently presents itself in the private and domestic intercourse of parent and child is that of determining what books it is proper that children should read, and what books they should not read. . . . Is it our duty to digest for our offspring, as the church of Rome has been accustomed to digest for her weaker members, an *Index Expurgatorius*, a catalogue of those books in the reading of which they may be permitted to indulge themselves?

Various are the mischiefs that inevitably flow out of such a precaution.

First, a wall of separation is thus erected between children and adults. They are made prisoners and subjected to certain arbitrary regulations, and we are constituted their jailors. All generous reciprocity is destroyed between the two parties. I cannot ardently love a person who is continually warning

---

"Of Choice in Reading," by William Godwin in *The Enquirer: Reflections on Education, Manners, and Literature* (Dublin: J. Moore, 1797), pp. 129–44.

me not to enter his premises, who plants a hedge about my
path and thwarts me in the impulses of my heart. I cannot
understand the reasons that dictate his judgments; it is well
if he understand them himself. . . . What I do not understand cannot excite my affections. The man who shuts against
me the secrets of his heart cannot be unreservedly beloved
by me. Friendship requires that the hearts of persons should,
as it were, be amalgamated into one substance, that their
thoughts should be transparent to each other and their communications entire. This perhaps can never be effected in its
utmost extent. But it is of the most unfavorable effect,
where the division and reserve pertinaciously force themselves upon observation.

Secondly, the despotism which is thus exercised is peculiarly grating to a mind of generosity and spirit. Curiosity is
one of the strongest impulses of the human heart. To curiosity it is peculiarly incident to grow and expand itself under
difficulties and opposition. The greater are the obstacles to
its being gratified, the more it seems to swell and labor to
burst the mounds that confine it. Many an object is passed
by with indifference till it is rendered a subject of prohibition, and then it starts up into a source of inextinguishable
passion. It may be alleged that "this uneasiness and impatience
in a young person are capable of being corrected." But is
this anything more than saying in other words that the finest
springs of the human mind may be broken, and the whole
reduced to a chaos of dishonorable lumber? As long as the
fiery grandeur of the soul remains, that will not be controlled, and cannot be moulded by the frigid dictates of
another's will, the kind of prohibitions here spoken of will be
felt with exquisite indignation and, though involuntarily,
will be registered as examples of a galling injustice.

Thirdly, the trial of skill thus instituted between the parent and child is of the most pernicious tendency. The child
is employed in doing that in which it is his endeavor not to
be detected. He must listen with anxious attention, lest he
should be burst in upon before he is aware. He must break
off his reading and hide his book a thousand times upon a
false alarm. At length, when the interruption really occurs,
he must rouse his attention and compose his features. He
imposes imperious silence upon the flutterings of his heart;
he pitches to the true key of falsehood the tone of his voice;
the object of his most anxious effort is to appear the thing

that he is not. It is not possible to imagine a school of more refined hypocrisy.

The great argument in favor of this project of an *Index Expurgatorius* is derived from the various degrees of moral or immoral tendency that is to be found in literary compositions.

One of the most obvious remarks that offer themselves under this head is that authors themselves are continually falling into the grossest mistakes in this respect, and show themselves superlatively ignorant of the tendency of their own writings. Nothing is more futile than the formal and regular moral frequently annexed to Esop's fables of animals. Examine the fable impartially, and you will find that the lesson set down at the foot of it is one of the last inferences that would have occurred to you. . . . To ascertain the moral of a story, or the genuine tendency of a book, is a science peculiarly abstruse. As many controversies might be raised upon some questions of this sort as about the number six hundred and sixty-six in the book of Revelations. . . .

Thus far we have considered moral and tendency as if they were two names for the same thing. This is however by no means the case.

The moral of any work may be defined to be that ethical sentence to the illustration of which the work may most aptly be applied. The tendency is the actual effect it is calculated to produce upon the reader, and cannot be completely ascertained but by the experiment. The selection of the one, and the character of the other, will in a great degree depend upon the previous state of mind of the reader.

Let the example be the tragedy of the Fair Penitent. The moral deduced from this admirable poem by one set of readers will be the mischievous tendency of unlawful love, and the duty incumbent upon the softer sex to devote themselves in all things to the will of their fathers and husbands. Other readers may perhaps regard it as a powerful satire upon the institutions at present existing in society relative to the female sex, and the wretched consequences of that mode of thinking by means of which, in a woman "one false step entirely damns her fame." They will regard Calista as a sublime example of a woman of the most glorious qualities, struggling against the injustice of mankind. . . . It is of no consequence whether the moral contemplated by the author were different from both of these. The tendency again may be distinct from them all, and will be various according to the various tempers and habits of the persons by whom the work is considered.

From the distinctions here laid down it seems to follow that the moral of a work is a point of very subordinate consideration, and that the only thing worthy of much attention is the tendency. It appears not unlikely that, in some cases, a work may be fairly susceptible of no moral inference, or none but a bad one, and yet may have a tendency in a high degree salutary and advantageous. The principal tendency of a work, to make use of a well-known distinction, may be either intellectual or moral, to increase the powers of the understanding or to mend the disposition of the heart. These considerations are probably calculated to moderate our censures against many of the authors whose morality we are accustomed to arraign. A bad moral to a work is a very equivocal proof of a bad tendency. To ascertain the tendency of any work is a point of great difficulty. The most that the most perfect wisdom can do is to secure the benefit of the majority of readers. It is by no means impossible that the books most pernicious in their effects that ever were produced were written with intentions uncommonly elevated and pure. . . .

Books will perhaps be found, in a less degree than is commonly imagined, the corruptors of the morals of mankind. They form an effective subsidiary to events and the contagion of vicious society; but, taken by themselves, they rarely produce vice and profligacy where virtue existed before. Everything depends upon the spirit in which they are read. He that would extract poison from them must for the most part come to them with a mind already debauched. The power of books in generating virtue is probably much greater than in generating vice. Virtue is an object that we contemplate with a mind at peace with itself. The more we contemplate it, the more we find our fortitude increase, enabling us to contend with obstacles, and even to encounter contempt. But vice is an object of a peculiarly unfavorable sort. The thought of entering into a vicious course is attended with uneasiness, timidity and shame; it disarms still more strongly than it excites us; and our reluctance to a life of profligacy can scarcely be overcome but by the stimulus of bold and impudent society.

Another observation of considerable importance in deciding on the subject we are here examining relates to an error that too often pervades the whole course of an attentive and affectionate education. The regard of a parent to his child will frequently rise to the most extravagant height. He considers him as a prodigy. He thinks no labor too great to be expended on him. He scarcely suffers the idea of him at any time to escape from his recollection. He regards him with the fondness of an enthusiastic lover for his mistress; and treats him as the child himself would treat some precious toy, which he will not suffer to be put out of his sight. He protects him with as much anxiety as if a rude shock would dash him to pieces or a rough blast wither the very essence of his frame.

This is essentially wrong. The true end of human existence is not to serve as a toy and amusement to another. Man can never appear in his genuine dignity but so far as he is capable of standing alone. A child is not to be reared as that precious thing that no wind may blow and no sun may scorch. Let us never forget that our child is a being of the same nature with ourselves; born to have passions and thoughts and sentiments of his own; born to fill a station and act a part; with difficulties that he ought to surmount and duties that he is bound to discharge.

Such is the genuine vocation of man. In the remembrance of this vocation he ought to be bred. The man ought to descend upon the child by insensible degrees till his whole bosom swells with the generous freight. He should begin to stand by himself and respect his own dignity as soon as he is able to utter an articulate sound.

For this purpose there is always a portion of confidence which it is our duty to repose in him. He should neither be bred apart from the world nor in ignorance of what passes in the world. He should be accustomed to behold the faces of his species. He should know something of the story of their passions, their singularities and even of their vices. He should be suffered to stand where their inclinations may sometimes interfere and jostle with his. It is much to be feared, if we breed him in indolent effeminacy to a certain age, that his whole life will bear the marks of it. The human mind is never so ductile and pliant as in early youth. Whatever therefore we would wish to find it at years of maturity, we should endeavor to begin in it at the tenderest years.

These remarks are obviously applicable to the subject of choice in reading. As, relative to the question of social intercourse, the child should early begin in some degree to live in the world, that is, with his species, so should he do as to the books he is to read. It is not good that he should be shut up forever in imaginary scenes and that, familiar with the apothegms of philosophers and the maxims of scientifical and elevated morality, he should be wholly ignorant of the perverseness of the human heart and the springs that regulate the conduct of mankind. Trust him in a certain degree with himself. Suffer him in some instances to select his own course of reading. There is danger that there should be something too studied and monotonous in the selection we should make for him. Suffer him to wander in the wilds of literature. There is a principle in the human mind by which a man seems to know his own time, and it will sometimes be much better that he should engage in the perusal of books at the period of his own choice than at the time that you may recollect to put them in his hands. Man is a creature that loves to act from himself, and actions performed in this way have infinitely more of sound health and vigor in them than the actions to which he is prompted by a will foreign to his own.

The injuries that result from a system of national education
are, in the first place, that all public establishments include
in them the idea of permanence. They endeavor, it may be,
to secure and to diffuse whatever of advantageous to society
is already known, but they forget that more remains to be
known. If they realized the most substantial benefits at the
time of their introduction, they must inevitably become less
and less useful as they increased in duration. But to describe
them as useless is a very feeble expression of their demer-
its. They actively restrain the flights of mind and fix it in the
belief of exploded errors. It has frequently been observed of
universities and extensive establishments for the purpose of
education that the knowledge taught there is a century behind the knowledge which exists among the unshackled and
unprejudiced members of the same political community. The
moment any scheme of proceeding gains a permanent establishment, it becomes impressed, as one of its characteristic
features, with an aversion to change. Some violent concussion
may oblige its conductors to change an old system of philosophy for a system less obsolete, and they are then as pertinaciously attached to this second doctrine as they were to the
first. Real intellectual improvement demands that mind
should, as speedily as possible, be advanced to the height of
knowledge already existing among the enlightened members
of the community, and start from thence in the pursuit of
further acquisitions. But public education has always expended its energies in the support of prejudice; it teaches its
pupils, not the fortitude that shall bring every proposition to
the test of examination, but the art of vindicating such tenets
as may chance to be established. We study Aristotle, or
Thomas Aquinas, or Bellarmine, or chief justice Coke, not
that we may detect their errors, but that our minds may be

*An Enquiry Concerning Political Justice and Its Influence on Morals
and Happiness*, by William Godwin (London, 1798). Facsimile of
3rd ed., with Notes and Introduction by F. E. L. Priestly (Toronto:
The University of Toronto Press, 1946), Vol. II, pp. 298–303.

fully impregnated with their absurdities. This feature runs through every species of public establishment; and even in the petty institution of Sunday schools, the chief lessons that are taught are a superstitious veneration for the church of England, and to bow to every man in a handsome coat. All this is directly contrary to the true interests of mankind. All this must be unlearned before we can begin to be wise.

It is the characteristic of mind to be capable of improvement. An individual surrenders the best attribute of man the moment he resolves to adhere to certain fixed principles for reasons not now present to his mind, but which formerly were. The instant in which he shuts upon himself the career of inquiry is the instant of his intellectual decease. He is no longer a man; he is the ghost of departed man. There can be no scheme more egregiously stamped with folly than that of separating a tenet from the evidence upon which its validity depends. If I cease from the habit of being able to recall this evidence, my belief is no longer a perception but a prejudice: it may influence me like a prejudice but cannot animate me like a real apprehension of truth. The difference between the man thus guided and the man that keeps his mind perpetually alive is the difference between cowardice and fortitude. The man who is, in the best sense, an intellectual being delights to recollect the reasons that have convinced him, to repeat them to others, that they may produce conviction in them, and stand more distinct and explicit in his own mind; and he adds to this a willingness to examine objections because he takes no pride in consistent error. The man who is not capable of this salutary exercise, to what valuable purpose can he be employed? Hence it appears that no vice can be more destructive than that which teaches us to regard any judgment as final and not open to review. The same principle that applies to individuals applies to communities. There is no proposition at present apprehended to be true so valuable as to justify the introduction of an establishment for the purpose of inculcating it on mankind. Refer them to reading, to conversation, to meditation; but teach them neither creeds nor catechisms, either moral or political.

Secondly, the idea of national education is founded in an inattention to the nature of mind. Whatever each man does for himself is done well; whatever his neighbors or his country undertake to do for him is done ill. It is our wisdom to incite men to act for themselves, not to retain them in a state of perpetual pupillage. He that learns because he desires to learn will listen to the instructions he receives and apprehend their meaning. He that teaches because he desires to teach will discharge his occupation with enthusiasm and energy. But the moment political institution undertakes to assign to every man his place, the functions of all will be discharged with supineness and indifference. Universities and expensive establishments have long been remarked for formal dullness. Civil policy has given me the power to appropriate my estate to certain theoretical purposes, but it is an idle presumption to think I can entail my views as I can entail my fortune. Remove those obstacles which prevent men from seeing, and which restrain them from pursuing, their real advantage; but do not absurdly undertake to relieve them from the activity which this pursuit requires. What I earn, what I acquire only because I desire to acquire it, I estimate at its true value; but what is thrust upon me may make me indolent, but cannot make me respectable. It is an extreme folly to endeavor to secure to others, independently of exertion on their part, the means of being happy. —This whole proposition of a national education is founded upon a supposition which has been repeatedly refuted in this work, but which has recurred upon us in a thousand forms, that unpatronized truth is inadequate to the purpose of enlightening mankind.

Thirdly, the project of a national education ought uniformly to be discouraged on account of its obvious alliance with national government. This is an alliance of a more formidable nature than the old and much contested alliance of church and state. Before we put so powerful a machine under the direction of so ambiguous an agent, it behooves us to consider well what it is that we do. Government will not fail to employ it to strengthen its hands and perpetuate its institutions. If we could even suppose the agents of government not to propose to themselves an object which will be apt to appear in their eyes not merely innocent but meritorious, the evil would not the less happen. Their views as institutors of a system of education will not fail to be analogous to their views in their political capacity: the data upon which their conduct as statesmen is vindicated, will be the data upon which their instructions are founded. It is not true that our youth ought to be instructed to venerate the constitution, however excellent; they should be led to venerate truth, and the constitution only so far as it corresponds with their uninfluenced deductions of truth. Had the scheme of a national education been adopted when despotism was most triumphant, it is not to be believed that it could have forever stifled the voice of truth. But it would have been the most formidable and profound contrivance for that purpose that imagination can suggest. Still, in the countries where liberty chiefly prevails, it is reasonably to be assumed that there are important errors, and a national education has the most direct tendency to perpetuate those errors and to form all minds upon one model.

44 A Psychological Basis of Freedom for Youth

Tony Gibson is a contemporary English anarchist who has written a host of essays applying the principles of anarchism to topics ranging from the population crisis ("Food Production and Population") to the division of labor ("Who Will Do the Dirty Work?"). His pamphlet "Youth for Freedom" begins with an acute study of the achievements and deficiencies of progressive education in Great Britain. Then, in the passages reprinted below, he turns to a question which anarchist thinkers have often neglected: What are the primary goals, instincts, and capacities of children and adolescents? In answering it, he provokes us with a sometimes bizarre, sometimes terrifying, rarely implausible foundation for a libertarian approach to youth.

THE CHILD REBEL

A mass of adult prejudice has grown up against the real passions and aspirations of childhood, and, the adults having all the developed and coherent means of propaganda in their hands, recognition of the real nature of childhood is suppressed as an improper subject, and a fictitious model is held up as the Normal Child. Most children realize that there is some sort of humbug about the Normal Child standard, but in their inexperience they are much influenced by it. Practically all the books they read or have read to them reinforce the humbug; it is rare that any author will write of children as they really are—such books as *Poil de Carotte* and *High Wind in Jamaica*, which deal frankly with the reality of childhood, are so unusual that few people take them seriously.

Although the child has not the ability to formulate its ideas into any coherent ideology of revolt, revolt it certainly does against the whole adult imposture. This revolt may not be apparent to adults, for the child, with good reason, con-

"Youth for Freedom," by Tony Gibson (London: Freedom Press, 1951), pp. 33–48. Subheads provided in part by the editors.

ceals it by many artifices; but I would stress that never was a revolt more justified than the spiritual revolt of children against adults.

In our society the adults *as a class* own everything both natural and manufactured, and children *as a class* have access to anything only on sufferance. Adults blatantly and selfishly reserve many pleasures to themselves: they smoke yet deny this to children; adults copulate, yet suppress all the sexual pleasures of children; adults indulge huge orgies of violence in war, yet suppress hooliganism in children; adults rob and cheat one another in their everyday dealings, yet sternly suppress minor pilfering among children; adults lie as a matter of course whenever convenient, yet demand that children shall tell the truth. All this may be argued away, but adult sophistry passes over the heads of children, and so these facts in their crude form are more or less plain to children; they *know* beyond all intellectual reasoning, that adults as a class are gross hypocrites and enemies of their freedom. . . . The child-revolutionist knows pretty well that it has no chance of overthrowing the tyranny of the adult class; it can only seek some degree of freedom by preserving within itself an independence of spirit. To the adult world it may present an outward front of truculence, of docility, of pretty coquetry, of timid respect, of open frankness—all these guises are means of concealing its innermost self from the invading inquisitiveness of the adult class. The child's greatest protection is its slyness, its superb ability at acting a character part. Max Stirner saw the slyness of children in its true light. He writes:

. . . In childhood liberation takes the direction of trying to get to the bottom of things, to get at what is "back of" things; therefore we spy out the weak points of everybody, for which, it is well known, children have a sure instinct . . . Back of everything we find our *courage*, our superiority; back of the sharp command of parents and authorities stands, after all, our courageous choice of our outwitting shrewdness. And the more we feel ourselves, the smaller appears that which before seemed invincible. And what is our trickery, shrewdness, courage, obduracy? What else but—Mind! . . .

Adults tend to think of children as beings of their own species with mental and physical powers in a merely *immature* state. The process of "bringing them up" is therefore interpreted as conditioning them to accept adult social values so that they will become adult beings well fitted to play their part in society. This is, I maintain, a colossal misunderstanding, and so drastically wrong that it largely accounts for the high percentage of basically normal children who grow up into neurotic adults—or perhaps I should say, the neurotic character of adult society today. . . .

Consider now an entirely different species, the Dragonfly. We can think of it in two different ways; first, as a winged creature living with a crowd of its fellows a short and brilliant life devoted almost entirely to lovemaking; second, as a solitary, slow-moving, creature living for a year or more under water with no other interest in life than to hunt and eat. Which of these totally dissimilar creatures is to be considered as the essential Dragonfly—the long-lived crawling *larva*, or the ephemeral winged *imago*?

I could give a thousand instances of animals in which the individual differs in form and essential instinctual make-up during the earlier and latter parts of its life, but I mention this merely as an analogy to stress the fact that it is stupid to think of the species Man entirely as the adult animal: it would be equally correct to regard the species as properly represented by the child—the adult being dismissed as degenerate modification in the latter part of life to reproduce and do necessary work.

Unlike the Dragonfly, the physical form of man is pretty much the same all his life outside the womb—the change is chiefly in size. What we are by no means certain about, however, is in what way the basic instincts of the Man-child differ from those of the Man-adult. We spend all our energies on training the child so that when it has acquired adult instincts it will be a passable member of adult society, and thereby we make it impossible to study just what are the natural instincts of the child. . . . The more scientific approach would be to study the instinctual make-up of children without any bias as to what it *ought to* be.

My own experience with children, coordinated with that of other observers, has led me to form the following rough hypothesis. The child is a gregarious but not a truly social animal; when in mental and physical health, it is aggressive to the point of ferocity and capable of a ruthlessness which normal adults do not possess. It is entirely self-centered, and its love for other persons is of an essentially different nature from the affection which an adult may feel for another person. Richard Hughes has likened the psyche of a child to that of an insane person; within certain well-defined limits this must be admitted as true—in that an adult with the psyche of a child would be not only "simple" but *insane* by adult standards.

All these instinctual endowments of the child would seem to have been necessary for the survival of the animal in its physically weak state, as an adjunct to parental care. Another instinctual endowment which makes it difficult to study the normal make-up of the child is its supreme power of adaptation to environment (again a quality which makes for survival of the weak). The child will easily become, to outward appearances, whatever its adult guardians expect it to be. It may have one personality in the home, another in the school, another when visiting grandparents—these various masks being effortlessly assumed and discarded as the environment demands in order to protect the integrity of its own real personality from the onslaughts of the adult world with its unnatural (to the child) values. . . .

What we humans have to consider is what degree of interference with the natural instincts of our young is wise. I maintain that we have gone too far with interfering in the natural instinctive life of children—gone so far, in fact, that we now no longer recognize how basically different they are from our adult selves. The danger is that if we try to make the child live in a manner too much at variance with its natural instincts, it will never live a proper instinctive life in childhood and therefore it will retain in its adult life a certain amount of the asocial and ferocious instincts of childhood. The world is full of beings adult by age but partly child by instincts. The nice young men who lightheartedly fly bombers and devastate towns are simply neurotic beings who have had to wait until their twenties to give proper expression to the instincts of infancy. The well-meaning social moralists who bring up children according to an idealized adult code of behavior have to bear their full share of the blame for the supreme immorality of adult behavior.

Much surprise has been aroused by the fact that children from the so-called "progressive" schools generally join the armed forces like kids from more conventional schools. Anyone who knows something of the progressive schools will realize that there is no lack of earnest social moralists on their staffs who would be only too pleased if their pupils would become war-resisters. But propaganda by deed and example has little effect on children when it is directed against their own innate instincts. Pacifist propaganda directed against the war games and the self-glorification of the child can only succeed in making it somewhat shamefaced and may delay and warp its natural expression. If adults are revolted by the spectacle of children behaving as children, they should avoid contact with the young animal; true, they can interfere with and suppress the manifestation of childhood instincts, but they cannot *eradicate* them. The children who grow up with a satisfactory gratification of their instinctual life in the various phases of their development are more likely to have sound adult instincts at a comparatively early age and therefore resist the fantastic demands of the State in the matter of military service.

I am not suggesting that there is any easy solution to the problem of education. Whatever we do, there is no possibility of breaking the vicious circle of environment in one generation. What I am chiefly concerned to demonstrate is that the moral training of children has direct results quite other than is intended because the child must live out its life as a natural animal, and too great an interference with its natural propensities leads to its never undergoing the mental and emotional metamorphosis into a natural adult. . . .

The individual achieves maturity. All the abuses of power, the unfair privilege, the humbug, the senseless repression of joy, that he experienced from adults *as a class*, he now sees going on round him in adult society in exactly the same manner. The Many are being repressed, cheated, humbugged and emotionally starved by the action of the Few—just as if the masses were children and their rulers adults. The parallel is strikingly exact. The State in its drive towards totalitarian dominion assumes more and more the aspect of a hypocritical and repressive adult controlling a lot of children. In all the aspects of State interference with individual liberty we see the nasty schoolmarm, the pompous father.

If the individual has retained something of his childhood independence of spirit, it will serve him in good stead in adult life. He will not become the stooge of the exploiters; he will react *childishly*, that is, he will revolt as and when he can. . . . There is nothing derogatory to the revolutionary urge in the fact that it has its roots in childhood. Experience teaches us that those people whose anarchism is entirely a matter of intellectual conviction often do not stay the course. If they have been beaten down by the adult counter-revolution in childhood—beaten down so that they no longer own themselves, but submit to the "rightness" of being owned by some person, institution or abstract idea, they will fear freedom in adult life. The prospect of freedom means giving them back the ownership of themselves. Such people, however convinced they may be in their conscious minds by the hard logic of anarchism, will reject freedom in their innermost being and dread the advent of social revolution.

LIBERATING THE ADOLESCENT

Adolescence is the time of metamorphosis from child to adult, a time when loyalties fluctuate between the two classes. In our society the period of adolescence is artificially lengthened by a number of factors. The adult counter-revolution has made a great deal of use of this latter period of the child's life; older children are made the upholders of adult morality by the same means by which the oppressed classes of every country are made to produce the manpower for the police force to uphold the privileges of the oppressors. The prefect or monitor in school, the patrol leader in the Boy Scouts, the bossy elder child who gladly enforces parental authority in the home—all are recruited from the ranks of childhood and moved by the same motives as the policeman who is recruited from the laboring classes to enforce their servitude.

Younger children are far more clear-sighted and independent than adolescents, for the latter are rendered unstable by the shock of the new emotional drives that they can neither understand nor control. Sexual potency comes in the early teens, and the frustration which adult society imposes on it upsets the personality of the child. The adolescent hates its own youngness; it desperately strives to be mature; maturity (it thinks) will bring relief to the awful problems of sex and power. So the adolescent despises childhood, despises its own nature, and worships the adult way of life. . . .

"At this stage [adolescence] in the biological development of youth, the sex impulses are new and strong; and control of them, *essential in a civilized society*, is only attained by 'letting it out' in another direction."

I have italicized the words which give the key to the whole problem. The sort of civilization which is maintained depends on the authoritarian repression of childhood and the defeat of adolescence by denying the facilities by which ripening sexual instincts may achieve maturity. I will agree with Thistle T. Harris that this control is essential—*if we want to perpetuate the kind of society we now have.* If, however, we want to alter our social pattern and achieve a libertarian society, there is no valid reason for this repression. On the contrary, the revolutionary will see in the sexual impulse a valuable source of energy in the struggle for emancipation. . . .

Those people who just cannot tolerate the idea of adolescents enjoying a full sex life will do anything to oppose the idea. Their arguments range from sheer mudslinging abuse to harping on the fact that birth control is not yet utterly perfect. Of course birth control is not perfect; neither is road transport, food canning, household electricity or a host of other artificial processes by which our society lives and occasionally dies. But few would suggest that social habits based on artificial processes should be prohibited because of the casualties which occasionally occur through imperfections. No, we seek to make our road transport, our canning industry, our electrical apparatus more and more foolproof: this provides the whole answer to the problem of birth control and unwanted children in adolescence. Birth control is still in its crude infancy, and the forces of law and order seem determined that adolescents shall have the maximum difficulty in obtaining protection through even the cruder forms of it.

The question then is not one of whether adolescent sexual satisfaction is practicable or impracticable, but what would be the result on society if boys and girls entered on full sexual relationships as soon as they were ready for it. Many revolutionaries would say that it would make little difference, that the sex life of the individual is a private matter which hardly concerns his relations with society. On this matter the reactionaries are unquestionably wiser; those who comprise the ruling class, who have inherited the traditional science of how to hold down the masses and exploit them—they know what makes for docility. They do not fall into the error of thinking that sexual questions are unimportant, nor do they mince words in pointing out that the *status quo* is dependent on the moral training of the young and the preservation of the present family pattern. It is the revolutionaries who deceive themselves when they look on Colonel Blimp as a fool when he pontificates on "purity" and "decent standards." Colonel Blimp is no fool when it comes to the science of government —within this narrow context he is cleverer than most revolutionaries, and he can afford to look on them with contempt, and to disdain to notice their puny efforts to raise the masses by political propaganda alone. . . .

Generally speaking the mass of people lack the proper human guts to be revolutionaries largely because of the warping effect of their defeat in adolescence. They may get a "baptism" of repression in infancy, but this is doubly effective when followed by a repressive "confirmation" in adolescence.

It is difficult for us to have much influence over the conditions of infancy in the mass of the people, but it is less difficult to reach the adolescent. Here I suggest that it would be better to concern ourselves with his real basic needs and with what type of individual he will grow up into than with improving his mind with such tracts as Kropotkin's *Appeal to the Young*. There is nothing wrong with directly agitational and educational material of this kind, but young people are often unable to take it in, not from their lack of mental equipment, but because of their unbalanced emotional disposition. . . .

Anarchism is too difficult a path to appeal very seriously to those who are muddled and self-hating like the average adolescent. Some of the most valuable work that needs to be done is against the stifling of the natural aspirations of adolescence. This work may not directly produce anarchists like sausages out of a machine, but it is directed to furthering the development of people temperamentally fit to stand in responsible opposition to authority. Only when people have achieved a reasonable balance in their own lives are they fit to work for a properly integrated society. Balance cannot be achieved by the stifling of natural impulses. The individual who has suppressed his sensual and emotional life in order to work for "the cause" is a most dangerous person: he is merciless and intolerant of the humanity of other people. Even though he embraces the cause of individual freedom, he is oppressive in the means he chooses to achieve the end. The discipline fostered in the ranks of the Young Communists is truly successful in producing the narrow, life-hating men and women who become the executive officials of the Party.

What is the alternative? . . . The grimness of the social reality today, and the terrible future which may be its outcome, gives all our propaganda a very somber note. This is not to be avoided if we are to adhere to an honest policy; we do not underestimate the problems which confront us, nor have we any interest in painting a rosy picture of the future. . . . But anarchism is not a dreary messianic cult; it is a thing of life and vigor, a rising against the life-denying forces of our time. The positive aspect of anarchism has much to appeal to the adolescent; it emphasizes the need of realizing all his potentialities to the full, *now* in the present. We do not seek to fob him off with pie in the sky, with present toil and careful restraint in the interests of well-being in the problematical future. We point out that the only sane road to healthy living, both personal and social, is through present happiness.

The entertainment provided by the cinema, dance-halls, fun-fairs, and football matches leaves a staleness in the mouth of the young. They crave for more but feel cheated of real fulfilment. We must emphasize that this depression is not due to anything basically unhealthy in these pursuits but to the fact that the amount of pleasure that they can give is *simply not enough* to satisfy the avid appetites of adolescents. They instinctively seek excitement, love, mental stimulus, creative expression and sensual intoxication—and they find only tepid and shoddy substitutes which the old grudgingly allow them. As emphasized previously, the sexual question is without doubt central to the problems of adolescence, but it is certainly not exclusive. The healthy young person should have such an appetite for life that he should seek to devour the whole world of experience; that he should be prepared to admit no barriers to the development of his humanity.

Young people sense that there is a conspiracy of age against youth, and they are right. Too much is preached about the responsibilities which adolescents must learn to accept, responsibilities which involve going like cattle into the military corral, sweating as underpaid apprentices, grinding at studies to make themselves more efficient units of production, denying their lusty sexuality when it is at its height, dutifully fulfilling the vicarious ambitions of their parents. We are not going to preach social revolution as another *duty* which the young generation have got to shoulder. Our message to the young is entirely one of encouragement, of realizing the value of their own aspirations, of spurning the burdens that authority would place upon them and the shoddy rewards cynically offered in return for the sacrifice of their own natures. . . . Youth, disturbed in its natural harmony, is too willing to sacrifice, to *give*; we must show it how to *take*.

Surprisingly, the individualist anarchists have said very little on education. Of them all, only Josiah Warren seems to have developed even a cursory account of educational methods and ideals. Whatever the reason for this, it needs to be stressed at the outset that, on Warren's view, contacts between parent and child, or between teacher and pupil, fall under the same principles that hold for adult relationships; and for him these are the principles of disconnection of interests and cost the limit of price (see selections 18 and 28). Plainly, this view is another reflection of the libertarian doctrine that there is an essential identity between the ideal aims of the educator and what is desirable within *any* social context.

Our brief selection separates Warren's position from other libertarian concepts of education. For it seems clear that Warren is *not* prepared to trust to the child for a spontaneous recognition of the tenets of equitable commerce. Nor would he assent without qualification to Ferrer's doctrine that education should restrict itself to seconding the child's own efforts. Indeed, Warren's entire program of educating the young in his own moral principles seems to rest on the view, just criticized by Gibson, that children are merely immature instances of the human species whose education should involve nothing save that which prepares them for adult life.

The perplexing problem as to which of these alternatives is more tenable—or which fits more harmoniously with what is central to anarchism—still awaits resolution. Moreover, this point has another side, which shapes it into something of a paradox, for Warren's control of the child has a recognized libertarian purpose: that of severing every vestige of dependence and developing the child's individual sovereignty.

My little daughter was between seven and eight years old when I commenced the application of these principles to her education, thus:

Equitable Commerce, by Josiah Warren (New Harmony, Ind.: 1846), pp. 110–13.

"You know that you eat and drink every day, that you have clothes, that you live in a house, that you sit by the fire, have books, playthings, attendance when you are sick, etc.; and yet, you cannot make any kind of food, you cannot make any part of your clothing—no part of the house you live in, nor the fire-wood; these must be made for you by others, and how do you get them? Do you know how you get them?" "I get them from you and mother," said she. . . .

"Now, here is the great question: How much should you properly do for us for what you receive? Should we require all your time night and day? Would this be too much, or not enough? Is there any limit, any bounds that we can set, so that you may understand when your obligations to us are discharged, and you can feel yourself free to pursue your own objects without being interrupted by our unlimited claims and calls, and that we may feel free to require, knowing that you see and acknowledge its necessity? Can you suggest any way to do this?" "No, sir," said she, "I cannot, but I should like it very much." "Well, then, I will tell you what I have thought; that I would as soon buy and sell goods an hour as to wash dishes an hour; so if you will wash as many dishes as I or your mother would wash in an hour, I should consider that you had paid us for an hour of our labor; this would take you more than an hour, but no matter. Each of us, in our family, consume, under our present circumstances, about three hours of men's labor per day. You consume about so much of mine and your mother's labor or time. Now, how much of your time do you think you ought to work for us, to do as much for us as we should do for ourselves in three hours?" "I do not know," she replied, "but I am willing to do whatever you think I ought." "But," said I, "I want your own understanding and feelings to act in this; I want the decision to come from yourself, from the clear perception that you are governed by the necessity of things, and not by me or your mother personally, and then all will go smoothly. But, as it is impossible for you to judge, suppose we say that six hours of your labor at present shall be considered an equivalent for what you receive of us ('yes, sir'), and then, you know, we can change from time to time, and in order to show you that I take no advantage of your dependence on us, or your confidence in me, if you can do better for yourself at any time, you have a right to do it; I lay no claim to your person or time, but the return for labor, which you see we must all have in order to live. And whenever you do not do your part of this necessary labor, it is but reasonable to conclude that you cannot have the benefit of it, and your income or supplies must necessarily stop. And, remember, that this would not be done in anger, or for punishment, but, because if no labor was performed, there would be nothing to live upon, and they who do not do their share, must not expect to live on the labor of others."

Even at this age she comprehended me, and seemed to feel the justice of her position. It then only remained to disconnect that portion of her time from the remainder, so that both parties might be free to act up to just limits, and not overstep them. We agreed that from between seven and nine, from twelve to two, and from five till seven, should be the six hours of each day to be devoted to our work, and that all the rest of her time was to be entirely her own; and if we required her services during any of this time, we would make a contract with her as with any stranger, and pay her by the time employed, and the pay was to be absolutely her own, of which she was to be supreme sovereign disposer. If she chose to ask our advice, of course we would give it; but we should exercise no authority, nor even give advice unasked, and if she spent it inconsiderately, the consequences would show her the necessity of asking the advice of older friends. . . .

Under these circumstances, if we call children in the morning, it is for them, and not for us, we do it, as their supplies would stop if the contract was not fulfilled. If we advise them not to spend their money or time foolishly, it is for them, and not for us; it is not our money or time they spend, and they can see that our advice is DISINTERESTED. Then they listen and thank us for that which otherwise they would have considered an interested, selfish exercise of authority. If there is ever to be undisturbed harmony between parents and children, it will be found where their interests and responsibilities are entirely *individualized, disconnected* from each other, where one exercises no power or authority over the persons, property, time, or responsibilities of the other. I speak from seventeen years' experiments, of which more will be said in the proper place, but will add here, that these principles can be only partially applied under the present mixture of the interests and responsibilities of parents and children—that where parents are obliged to bear the consequences of the child's acts, the parents must have the deciding power; but in things in which the child can alone assume the *cost of its acts,* he may safely be intrusted to the natural government of consequences.

In *The Community of Scholars* Paul Goodman deplores the present state of university education in America: nowhere else, he asserts, are such grand possibilities so perpetually frustrated by "extraneous regulation and taxation, by management and the goals of management." Higher education, affirms Goodman, is ideally based upon a long and laudable tradition of autonomous, "anarchically self-regulating" communities; these communities were guided by the same cooperative principles that attracted Kropotkin in scholarly societies and educational libraries. But it is just this tradition which today is jeopardized by the growth of a huge class of administrators whose relations with both faculty and students are always "official" and never personal.

What can be done? Goodman's answer, set forth below, unfolds in two stages. He first introduces a number of principles which in his view characterized the first universities that rose in the West and have inspired good universities ever since. Then, drawing upon these principles, he advances an exciting and detailed proposal that would return the task of education to the teacher and his pupils and resurrect the libertarian tradition of "the community of scholars."

The university was a small, face-to-face community of scholars—in effect a tiny city, invisibly walled away from the larger city of, say, Padua or Prague. With few exceptions it hovered in size between five hundred and a thousand, and there were celebrated universities that numbered no more than a hundred people. Such communities required no more than a handful of administrators—rectors and chancellors often elevated unwillingly from the faculty, and a few functionaries.

Condensed from the *Harper's Magazine* article "A Reactionary Experiment in Education" (November, 1962), which appears in expanded form in *The Community of Scholars*, by Paul Goodman (New York: Random House, Inc., 1962). © Copyright 1962 by Paul Goodman. Reprinted by permission of Random House, Inc. Subhead supplied by the editors.

Why the invisible wall between this community of scholars and the outer world? First, because it was a completely international community whose scholars often came from all over Europe; they shared not simply a common Latin, but a common concern for truth and common standards of evidence and discourse which could not be disregarded merely because of expediency. They did not easily abide the local and national prejudices.

Secondly, because it was a self-governing community where the masters alone decided who was fit to teach and graduate. (The universities have never ceased to regard themselves as such.) In differing degrees, the student guilds were also self-governing, taking responsibility for their social and physical behavior.

In this community of scholars, teaching and learning could only be a personal relation. The student worked with and often lived close by his masters. It was his principal master himself—not a chancellor or dean—who gave the student the kiss or handshake which signified the act of Commencement: the recognition by his chosen adults that he had become their peer and could proceed on his own initiative in the adult world. This culmination came only after years of assessment, and a convincing demonstration by the student to his masters that he could do an adult job of work. (Compare this with our June ritual as it survives today.) . . . Then as now, the student on leaving his family desperately needed older adults to whom he could transfer his affection—men whom he could identify with and imitate; who could show him ways to order his confusion by principled thought, and help him prepare for a meaningful career in the adult world. This is what teachers did. It cannot be done if they are cut off from students. . . .

Finally, and crucially, in the traditional community of scholars, the college teacher was a veteran. By this I mean that he had demonstrated his way of learning in the outer world, and he taught the subject not as an isolated exercise, but as something which had authority and relevance outside the walled city of scholars. *"For centuries,"* the Columbia historian Richard Hofstader tells us, the *faculties* of the great universities *"were consulted again and again on vital questions of doctrine and law, and were expected to state their findings and intervene in ecclesiastical and social affairs."*

This is in melancholy contrast to our colleges today. In

America, individual professors are free to speak out in public, and they often hire their services to government and private business. But departments and colleges never commit themselves *as scholarly communities*, asserting their own principles to the outer world. No wonder that their authority is frequently blurred and unreal to their students.

Conceive of a faculty with a permanent staff of full-time tenured teachers—people who have a special calling for teaching and veterans who have returned to it. To these we should add many practicing veterans teaching temporarily or part-time—but with the authority of professors. And through these, the faculties can extend out among the artists and professionals of the region. I have little doubt that many of our best writers, politicians, diplomats, journalists, engineers, bankers, business people, editors, etc., would be glad to join the scholarly guild if they were given some freedom and some power. (But now they cannot join—they have no Ph.D.s!) If the faculties were composed in this way, they could not be so easily controlled by the administration. There would be too many distinguished independents; their combined voice would be too authoritative. More important, this voice could become a force to be reckoned with, exercising the ancient function of the universities as the loyal opposition and watchdog of society. The physics department could notify the government when unnecessary official secrecy was hindering research. The school of architecture could speak up about public housing and the absence of decent social planning in the civil engineering in cities like New York. The departments of English and journalism could cooperate in criticizing the disgraceful inadequacy of our weekly book reviewing, or the press associations, or the tone of advertising. (Isn't it odd that the Federal Communications Commissioner can call TV a wasteland but the Harvard English Department, speaking as a department, cannot?)

My point is not that the faculties should take day-to-day political positions. That would be too transient. But they must affirm intransigently their disinterested ideals and principles to the outer world when they are relevant. If they could do this, young people would be proud of their elders and their school. The embarrassed distance between teachers and students would lessen. And I think that teaching and learning would be more for keeps.

THE CASE FOR SECESSION

In fairness, the constantly reiterated defense of the administrators should be mentioned. Their factorylike and businesslike ways are said to be inevitable under modern conditions. Harold Taylor, the former President of Sarah Lawrence, explains, "The most important reason [for the lack of educational responsibility] is the drastic increase in the number of students and the consequent growth of mass-educational needs . . . to be met in a hurry. The major forces are all in the direction of submerging the individual teacher in a mass of rules, formulae, administrative authority . . ."

Maybe. The fact remains that the administrators of the various schools engage in tooth-and-nail competition to aggrandize their institutions, and *they* are among the major forces. They hardly ever co-operate to effect a judicious sharing of resources among them, or to diversify the colleges, or to experiment. And furthermore, the number of administrators is growing. With all our centralization and "efficiency," my judgment is that the ratio of students to teacher may fall, but the ratio of administrators to population will rise far more than proportionately. In the New York State school system there are already more administrators than in all of Western Europe. And this does not count the auxiliary armies of College Board and scholarship testers. There is, in short, no sign that the grip of the administrators will relax.

So let us propose to go outside the present collegiate framework. The simplest remedy is the historical one—for bands of students and teachers to secede and set up small shops where they can teach and learn under their own simple conditions. Such a movement would be difficult but not impractical. If it could succeed in a dozen cases, I think the entire system might experience a profound and salutary shock.

Secession is inevitably occurring in any case, but it is occurring in the wrong way. As [Professor Oscar] Handlin notes, many dissatisfied young people—some of our most sensitive and intelligent among them—will not or cannot conform, and they leave the schools. Some form into little groups to find a culture or create it out of nothing—the vicissitudes of the Beat youngsters are by now familiar. What is wrong is that they have cut themselves off from both the senior scholars who know something, and the veterans who can teach them professions. They can hardly believe now that professional work might ever be possible for them. In a tiny community of scholars they might find both the cultural traditions and the veterans who could help them operate confidently in society, whether they succeed or fail.

There are strong precedents for secession as the remedy of disaffected communities of scholars, starting with the great revolts in the medieval universities against Church control. The most effective secession was, of course, that of the Protestant rectors and vicars who refused in the seventeenth century to sign the Anglican articles of Faith, left Oxford and Cambridge and set up their own dissenting academies. In our own century, the founding of the New School of Social Research in 1919 in New York was in effect a secession of teachers, since its leading spirits—e.g., Charles A. Beard and Thorstein Veblen—could not conform to the Stanfords and Columbias of their day, and they were joined by scholars who were restive at such places.

The most recent and suggestive secession was the founding of Black Mountain College in North Carolina during the 'thirties by teachers fired from Rollins College in Florida when they protested the denial of "academic freedom" to John Rice. Significantly, Rice espoused no particular heresy—it was his general nonconformity and nuisance value that was condemned. He and his friends formed, really, the first Beat School—and its graduates have been leaders in this kind of art and culture. The teachers often went unpaid, but they continued because the school was theirs; it had no trustees and no administration. When I taught at Black Mountain, I found it very feeble in traditional culture, but nobody hindered me from teaching more scholastically. It was a justified boast that students who dropped out of the Ivy League could still get some kind of education at Black Mountain College. The school lasted nearly twenty-five years and then, like a little magazine, folded. But its spirit survives.

A small secession from a dozen colleges and universities would now be immensely profitable for American education.

I propose that a core faculty of about five professors secede from a school, taking some of their students with them; that they attach themselves to an equal number of like-minded professionals in the region; collect a few more students; and set up a small unchartered university that would be nothing but an association. Ten teachers would constitute a sufficient faculty for such a community of scholars. (Jefferson's University of Virginia had eight teachers.) With individual classes of about fifteen, there would be 150 students. (I choose this class-size simply from my own experience. When the number falls to seven or eight, I begin to feel I am conducting group therapy; when it rises to twenty I begin to feel I am lecturing too formally. But the right number depends on the subject and the style of the teacher.)

A strong group of professionals would be particularly important in a small school composed entirely of teachers in close relation, with no administrative rules; without them it could become too clubby, like some excellent progressive schools or like Black Mountain. It is evident, I hope, that I am not thinking here of any particular educational experiment like Antioch, Goddard, or Sarah Lawrence, aiming at communal living, community service, individual creativity and so on. These are fine things; but I am proposing simply that the students and teachers create a small university where they can associate in the traditional way, *but entirely dispensing with the external control, administration, bureaucratic machinery and other excrescences that have swamped our communities of scholars.*

Three immediate problems arise—financing, equipment, accreditation.

(1) This is not a social experiment, but an attempt to prepare working professionals, taking society as it is. Even though the teachers and professionals would no doubt be willing to work at a sacrifice, an attempt should be made to pitch the prices of the current inflated national standard of living. If we adopt the national median salary of $10,000 for a full professor, the expenses for the school are:

Salaries	$100,000
Rent for ten classrooms in an urban middle-class district	4,000
Total	$104,000

Dividing the cost among 150 students, we arrive at a tuition of $693. This is nearly $500 less than a good liberal-arts college and less than half of the Ivy League. It includes no extras, no medical service, and of course no endowed library, laboratories, or athletic facilities. But these are "extras" at universities as well.

(2) With regard to equipment, this scholarly community would have immediately available to it some 10,000 to 20,000 carefully selected books and apparatus. It is simplest to

think of it located in a large city with a municipal library, YMCA, and many available part-time professionals.

But another possibility for providing books and plant would be for the small university to be a kind of unofficial adjunct of a great university which extends it friendly services because it is a worthwhile experiment and a source of good graduate students. The secession of a small faculty from a large administration need *not* mean a rupture of friendly relations.

(3) Finally, a major difficulty of any uncharted *ad hoc* association of scholars is that it cannot grant degrees leading to licenses. It is not expected, and is *not desirable*, that young people spend their years and money in study that does not lead to careers in society.

One obvious solution would be a European plan—the graduates would matriculate for a period at an accredited school having a system of broad comprehensive examinations for the A.B. degree. (The University of Chicago used to accept candidates for its comprehensive after three months of residence.) The drawbacks here are obvious—examinations following a prescribed curriculum would contradict the idea of a community of scholars where teaching and learning are freed from imposed standards. I believe—perhaps I am sanguine—that after several years of good schooling, a graduate could make up the usual college requirements with a semester's cramming. But a far more attractive solution would be a friendly arrangement whereby graduate and professional schools, competing for good students, would accept these students on their merits as set forth in the recommendations of their teachers. Then their first accredited degree would be a master's or a doctor's.

H O W complicated this simple proposal may seem! We must get together 150 persons, subject the young to considerable expense, anticipate problems irrelevant to learning. And yet I have no doubt that many such faculties—both dissatisfied academics and professionals who would like to teach—are already in potential existence, willing to risk privileges and tenure if a good and willing group could be formed. Certainly there would be no dearth of students, though such academic and professional faculties would choose the students very strictly, probably too strictly.

There is no doubt at all about the authenticity of such a plan. In medieval Paris, [the historian Hastings] Rashdall tells us, "*the intellectual ferment was most vigorous, the teaching most brilliant . . . almost before a university existed at all."*

This spontaneous quest by the anarchic early community of scholars to understand their culture and take responsibility for changing it should be ours as well. Our children not only grow up in a civilization immeasurably more confused and various than any before, but they are now prevented from undertaking the quest itself by foolish rules, meaningless tasks, and an absence of responsible veterans to guide them. We must restore to them the chance to discover their culture and make it their own. And if we cannot do this within the universities, it would be good for the universities themselves if we tried to do it from without.

The two following selections provide an ideal way of completing
the anarchists' presentation of their case. They disclose essential but
forgotten portions of the work of their respective authors. (Tolstoy's educational writings are omitted from a major edition of his
collected works, and *Parents Day* is one of few books by Paul Goodman that is out of print.) Further, they convey aspects of anarchism, some minute, others crucial, that defy the discursive categories of philosophical argument. Indeed, there would be little
exaggeration in the claim that these selections exhibit with literary
precision exactly what the principles, blueprints, and arguments of
anarchist thinkers are all about. Finally, they point out a first step
for those committed to a libertarian reconstruction of society: the
task of replacing the need for centralized and imposed standards of
judgment and conduct by the free association and creative resources
of autonomous personalities can begin in educational communities
like those depicted below.

Here, then, are descriptions of two schools. The first is taken from
Paul Goodman's novel, whose characters, drawn from life, probably
include a portrait of Goodman himself. The second school is even
less fictitious, for in the early 1860s it was educating the children
of Yásnaya Polyána, the manor on which Tolstoy was reared.
These accounts, both excerpted from literary works of art, should
serve to establish that anarchist philosophy has not been the only
loss in the general neglect of libertarian writing.

1

The question was often asked amongst us: How did he come
here?—that is, from what kind of difficult or broken home
the child was sent to our school.

The question also: And how did *you* come to come here?
—from Frankfort or Baden, or perhaps sent as an ambulatory

Parents Day, by Paul Goodman (Saugatuck, Conn.: The 5 × 8
Press, 1951), passim. Subsection numbers provided by the editors.
Reprinted by permission of the author.

patient from the State institution nearby, or being a war-widow, or that it was convenient for a person having a child and no home to come to a school to teach. . . . In principle it was an ideal arrangement for parents and children, far better than a private home. We were a community. Our children had the presence of a parent, to love and console them and be individually concerned for them; but the authority over them was shared by many, by all the teachers. The authority was less tyrannical, more avoidable, and did not have to be faced alone, for all the children were brothers and sisters. No parent would intervene directly for his or her child; yet the child would come freely to our rooms. The voices of love and of authority were not the same voice.

The misfortune was that we did not adopt this better arrangement as free choosers, but we brought into it our old disasters.

How did *he* come to come here? And how did *you* come to come here? To this question there were not many gentle or happy answers.

I came there, I think, because of my unfinished childhood. It is said, "Those who cannot do it, teach it"—and what if the subject is the art of being happy? The teacher will come where the children, the other children, are even now repeating the disaster for him.

2

At the Staff Meeting, the principal discussion turned on whether or not Donald Torgesson should be permitted to go home during the weekend to visit his mother. He was in the Second Group, and their teacher was Caroline Brandywine, a plain colorless young woman.

In meticulous detail Caroline explained the situation in the Second Group. When somebody went home, the little clique, the two Jimmies and Steve, began masturbating, and they tortured the children in Group I. . . . Donald had a good relationship with his mother, but then he himself was thrown off when he returned, and boasted, this hurt; but if she would put it up to him not to boast because it hurt the others' feelings, he would be sensitive and intelligent enough to cooperate. This would have the effect of deepening his understanding of the social group. But it was too much to ask of him to sacrifice the trip altogether. On the other hand, some, especially Shirley, brightened up when Donny came back and boasted. . . .

Caroline's explanations were interminable not because anything was petty or irrelevant, but because taken as a whole they did not add up to a conclusion nor even to a dilemma. They had the ring of primary experience, either the infinity of creative possibility or the impassable morass of the facts of life (one could not tell which). . . .

I sat on the edge of my chair, enthralled by the concern of so many, more or less wise and expert, for an individual child, an individual act of an individual child. Being new, I had resolved to say nothing. I was sensitive of my importance and sensitive of my immodesty. The result of deciding to hold my peace in any eventuality was that the room buzzed about me and, sitting on the edge of the chair, I had a painful crick in the neck. . . .

Lawrence Dixon rubbed his palms wildly and sprang up and began to prowl. I looked at him in disgust. "In such a case," he giggled, "we cannot penalize happiness! Young Torgesson has a good relationship with his mother. That's his good luck. We must support the positive side. We cannot afford to quench radiance. It shines far. Shirley Thomas is made happy by it in turn. Do you want to reduce excellence to the level of misery? Hm. Hm.

"Furthermore, this happens after every Parents Day." He unaccountably giggled. "It takes a week before they settle down. I say, Good! excellent! We do not want the troubles kept under. Let them out! It is an invaluable opportunity. What's more trouble for us in the short run is better for them in the long run. We have to live in the world we make, we and our children's children."

This astonishing speech, full of the creator spirit, raised me to a glow of glory. "Yes! yes!" I wheezed. The others were more accustomed to Dixon's high style.

To me it was an infallible sign if a person said one true thing, for nothing comes from nothing, and the proposition, "we must not penalize happiness," was true. I gave my allegiance to Dixon. But what the devil was he giggling about?

"It's very well," said Caroline dissatisfied. "But I have only two hands, even if I weigh 130 pounds."

"You take out your aggressions on the children," said Dixon.

"Lawrence!" cried some one, shocked.

"That's the meanest remark you ever made to me, Lawrence Dixon," said Caroline. "You could have said it in private."

"I'm sorry," said Dixon, confused.

Bernardine brought cups and a pitcher of tea and at once everything became sociable. I was bewildered.

"What was the decision about Donny?" I asked Dolly Homers. "Is there no vote?"

"Vote? If there's a difference of opinion, it's permissive."

"Permissive to whom?"

"To Donny, of course."

"Ah. Does Dixon always carry?"

"No. But he's usually right. You'll see."

—I was not so sure. He spoke too close to my own sentiments, and my sentiments were suspect to me. Nevertheless, I was suffused with joy and pride at what seemed to me to be the big fact: that there was no vote! because all of us wanted, in a well-intentioned way, to reach unanimity. The aim of the discussion was to conjure up the good idea that all would spontaneously assent to. That there was this aim proved that there was a basis of mutual love.

"It is a beautiful meeting," I said, moved, to Mark Anders. "I never sat at a more beautiful meeting."

3

The Assembly started to collect in numbers and they switched on the lights. The tempera and crayon drawings spoke from the walls—deeper than their markers knew, as Harrison had said; in fact, near to free violence.

At the Assembly the lower groups sat in front on the floor, and the greater ones and the Staff on benches behind and on the sides. But I sat on the floor with Tony and Dolly Homers' boy on my knees. The chorus and the recorders massed behind the piano. . . .

The chorus and the instruments sang *Absalom*.

I was becoming very gloomy. The two small bodies heavy on my knees were not alien but very close. . . . In an infantile voice Annie was reading the Group I creative-writing; but these pieces were always disappointing—"I am a Jack-rabbit;" "We took a walk across the bridge and saw the leaves falling off the trees"—because in everything the voice of Annie, who took down the dictation, sounded very loud. . . .

But the tales of the Second Group were excellent! one looked up and bared one's teeth.

Caroline had the knack of inspiring them, she had a "method." It was to discuss some simple and shocking fact of life, as that boys and girls often try to kill their baby sisters and brothers, and then to get them to write something. (It began to be clear to me that, with her blundering literalism, Caroline was a great teacher.) This week of "sibling rivalry," as Caroline entitled it, Katerina Jamison, aged ten, fair-haired and blue-eyed, had written as follows: Beverly became angry with her brother and she chopped him up into a hundred pieces with an axe. She buried the pieces under a tree. Then she was frightened and sorry and tried to put the pieces together again, but she couldn't. They wouldn't fit, some were lost. But a frog jumped out of the brook and hopping from one piece to another, showed her how to put the pieces together. And when she put them all together at last, it was not her little brother but Prince Charming.

We did not like to applaud the efforts of the children, but
    "this pleasant tale was like a little copse,"
and we flushed and clapped our hands.

Davy Drood clapped and cried out with pleasure. Who was it cried out? It was Davy Drood. —There was no use in fooling myself. The fact was that here, whatever else he was to me, was a youth who needed help, and he could be helped, he accepted help; and I could help him, and did offer the help, and was going to offer it; and *therefore* (whatever else) it was impossible for me not to love Davy Drood; because this is what love is. I understood it and stopped holding my breath and at once the tears flowed down my cheeks.

4

The boy was lying in wait for me. He appeared from the sere-leaved bushes that had once been thick with forsythia.

I was pleased to see him. It was exciting to touch him in the night; but the air was cold.

"It's you again. You'd better be getting back before they start looking for you. I'll walk you down the road."

We walked hand in hand. On the left the black brook meandered away from the white road.

He withdrew his hand and came to it directly: I was to get him a contraceptive at the village drug-store, if he needed it.

"Why, yes—" I said spontaneously enough. "That's the kind of thing that a friend does for a friend."

"When? tomorrow?"

"Oh? . . . Why tomorrow? I'll have to discuss it with Lawrence Dixon, but I'll do that as soon as I can."

He cried in alarm, "Don't do that."

"Why don't do that? He might not say No. But even if he

does say No I'll do it anyway, since I've given my word. He'd be wrong."

"No no!" cried Davy. "Don't mention it at all. Don't do it at all, then."

"Why, I must mention it. It's important, don't you see?"

"I'm sorry I asked you," said Davy bitterly. "What the hell's it his business—after all these years?"

"Davy! it's for your own good. You ought to have a decent place; it's not pleasant outside in this cold weather. It's not so simple."

"It is simple," said Davy. "You yourself said so, and you were right. Now you keep saying 'why, why?' You know damned well why. No, don't!" he cried. "Don't mention it to anybody, and don't do it. Anyway, she won't, so what's the use?"

I took his hand, dumbly, to show that he had support. He had trapped me saying "Why, why?"—which I said because I did not know. I was puzzled—but I could not find the answer without initiating new complications—whether his request expressed a physical urgency or was an idea in his mind. If he failed (which was probable, the first time, in such circumstances) it would be unfortunate if his desire was not immediate and strong. The thing was to slow down. But now he had no time. And my guilty involvement made me too weak to talk plainly and take the upper hand.

"You hardly know this girl. Can't you wait a couple of days?"

"I've had nothing but an erection ever since!" he cried,—"ever since you mentioned it before. You were right about that too. No! Don't mention it to anybody, because she won't anyway, she's afraid. Forget it. Forget I ever asked you for anything. I should have known I couldn't rely on you. Don't you mention it again or I'll never be your friend again."

I seized him by the shoulders and squared to him in the darkness. "See here. This is enough of this hocus-pocus. Listen carefully to what I say. I'll discuss it with Lawrence Dixon no matter what you think, because it's more important than you think; it's a matter of policy. I'll discuss it with him tonight, at eleven o'clock sharp. Whether he says Yes or No, I'll do what I can for you. What you want is perfectly sensible and, you're right, it's simple. Furthermore, she's not afraid. You're the one who's afraid. Don't be. I'm your friend and you can rely on me. I'm not such a good friend as I should be or as you deserve, because you're remarkable; but just now I'm saying the best I know how. Good-night, boy."

He called after me, but I would not look back. I was animated by my forthright speech—you could see the breath in the night—and I was ashamed of the falsehood distorting it in the past and in the future.

5

"Lawrence, I am glad to have this opportunity," I said. "I want to talk to you about Davy Drood."

I was glad to be able to broach the subject not with Dixon alone, but with the others there, with just these others there; they put us both on the spot. Publicity was the end of hocus-pocus.

"We just now," I said, "have a chance to do something worthwhile for Davy. The main thing he needs, of course, is to accept and affirm his sexuality—with our approval, because he is afraid. Well! He has found a girl he wants to have sexual relations with, and she too wants to. We ought to encourage them by furnishing contraceptives and also by giving them a convenient occasion together. What do you think?"

Dixon's face was frozen.

"It needn't even be a general policy," I said, "but only the special case of Davy Drood. Remember he's seventeen years old. The girl is fifteen."

"No," said Dixon.

"I'm sorry you say that. Remember, you can't stop them from doing what they want anyway. Don't you think we have a duty to provide decent circumstances?"

No one said anything.

"I never heard anything so fantastic in my life!" cried Seraphia. "What kind of school does he think we are running?"

"Hush, Seraph," said Dixon, "it's not fantastic at all. If—if it were only Davy, I might say Yes. How can I say Yes for the girl? I ask you that. Who is the girl?"

"I'm damned if I'll tell you who the girl is!" I cried. "Aren't you ashamed to sit there? Afraid of the parents. You know that everywhere they carry on anyway. What's the good of your school if it doesn't provide better circumstances than the average? Where else is a boy supposed to learn to use his powers?"

Dixon began to rub his hands and wring his fingers, with a grin of delight.

"You had him for twelve years!" I shouted angrily. "And now look. Nobody cared for him, till I came." This I ought not have said. . . .

"The reason you're so excited," said Lawrence Dixon, with the peculiar vibrancy in his voice that sounded during his flyers in interpretation, "is your homosexual attachment to Davy. This is just why you have homosexual tendencies, in order to have sexual relations with women by proxy, thru other men. Exactly. Now you want to use Davy Drood."

I was pleased; I was only too eager to air my guilty secrets, and I exclaimed, "Right! this time you hit the nail on the head. Why do you think I have been forced into this stupid way? Not thru my doing—but just because when I was at the age of the boys in Lawrence Dixon's group, instead of their encouraging me to love my girls honestly and honorably and gladly, they frightened me, and shamed me, and thwarted me, and made me guilty. It happens that I can remember the exact incidents that did the work! Very banal! But that was not at a so-called progressive school." . . .

I said in a low voice, "The kids are right, I thought they were wrong. Do you know what they say? They say that it's really worse for them here than at a strict place. We encourage them to unblock their feelings; we let them know that sexual pleasure is beautiful and fundamental to everything else. We raise the tension. Then we say No. At another place they would not have expectations, they would not be tormented."

"Who says it?" cried Dixon. "You're putting it in their mouths."

"Oh no I'm not. Let me finish. What we have devised is a trap. If they were at some other place, they'd manage all right. They'd make the adjustment to concealment and subterfuge; they wouldn't give their feelings away—then the smart adults could imagine there were no such things. Meantime they'd perfect tricks for sneaking out; they'd have places to go to; and they'd protect each other with sadistic punishments for stool-pigeons. Am I making any of it up? But at our school—nothing. Freedom!"

"If that's how you feel, why don't you get out?" said Seraphia. But Lawrence Dixon said, "No, Seraph, it's his school too."

He looked groggy, as if I had fished up beatings of his childhood. He said, "Is that how it is? Is that what they say?"

I became frightened that he was going to break down and

give in, and leave me with Victory on my hands. I did not want Victory. I was unable to wield it.

He said, "I don't deny it! If a fire broke out and burnt our school to the ground, they might be better off.

"Probably we are trying to prevent their pleasures simply out of resentment. Maybe all of it is a rationalization."

I did not press my plea further. "I am sorry we got so heated," I said.

6

But it was Sophie's day. In the afternoon her group would give its play, prepared for months. In the morning her parents, the grandparents of the two children, were going to be married. . . .

When Sophie's parents—she was nearly thirty and they looked to be in their early sixties—first came to America, they were socialists of that period, with anarchistic wisdom, no friends of the State, Religion, Private Property. They had great hopes in the innate dignity of individuals and in their natural social groups. Such persons did not submit to legal marrying—any more than the man submitted to military conscription, so long as there was a corner of the world to escape to; he came to America. But alas! in the land of freedom Jake Landsberger helped organize the electricians, he rose to a position of respect and respectability in trade-union politics, which is not dissociated from governmental politics; and now there was a little private property and the problem of inheritance.

The couple were delightful; they had courtly manners that seemed to be showing off for company but were usually an habitual overestimation of the company. Jake had assiduously perfected his English in 1908, and he still spoke the slang of that period. Minnie still did not speak English well and was fearful that by not catching the nuances she was likely to cause offense. It was impossible not to show them that they were with friends by making fun of them.

"You see, Jake," I said, "now you are in the trap, like all the other fools. First you begin to compromise by sitting down with Federal mediators—"

"On our terms!" protested Jake. "They came to us; we didn't go to them. In 1912–1923—the Norris-LaGuardia act! Why shouldn't there be orderly process, due process?"

"Naturally. Look what happens. Next—wait, let me talk, I'll

soon be finished, then you can say your say—next, as if by
magic, you own a little property. An accident—it's not!"

"A fortune it's not!"

"And now you have to protect the inheritance and you get
married! Really, no fake, did you foresee it?"

Minna cried out in alarm. "I told you, Jake. They think it's
wicked. We should think it thru again." She lapsed into Yid-
dish. The matter was too important to be treated as a mere
convenience. It set a bad example.

"I'm joking, Minna, I'm joking," I protested.

"He's joking, mama," said Sophie.

"With her you mustn't joke," warned Jake. "Everything is
earnest."

"I'm very sorry."

"With me you can joke!" cried Jake. "Please, go on, I'm interested. You say one thing leads to another. Minnie, you go
with Sophie and meet people."

Corny's father, the judge who was to marry them, came to
be introduced.

"You see, Jake?" I nudged him, "a Judge."

"What kind of judge is he?" said Jake thoughtfully.

"He's in the Appellate Division."

He puffed out his cheeks and blew. "The Appellate Division is not so bad! We went to the Appellate Division in
Jaspers vs. Tin and Tube. We won, didn't we?" He spread
out his hands.

"*Adelman!*" I called. My algebrist was flying by, shirt-tails
out. "Come here, Adelman. This is worthwhile. I want you to
meet Sophie's father, Jake Landsberger. He's vice-president of
the Electricians. He says that the Appellate Division is not so
bad as the rest of the system. It's a nice distinction, let *him*
explain it."

"Adelman? Ephraim Adelman's boy? —I am pleased to
meet you. I used to know your father. Sophie mentions you."

It was passionately moving. Again I saw—what had to be
brought home to me again and again, and *was* brought home
to me again and again—that we were the salt of the earth, the
"lunatic fringe," as we would say (but let no one else dare to
say it!); and that the target-center of us was just in our
school, in such schools, so that here all gathered together and
proved to be acquainted. Acquainted? Lovers.

But Adelman, judicially, more judicially than the judges of
the Appellate Division, was interested only in the line of
argument. He asked a few probing questions that showed he

knew all about it, more than any one else could possibly know. Not to show off, just to establish himself.

The old man was on his mettle. With marvellous grace he did the impossible: he simplified the technicalities to the understanding of a smart boy and at the same time sharpened the distinctions in the shadings and subtleties of an intra-party faction fight. I had expected the boy to run rings around the old man; instead I was rocked by the fact that both of them began to fish up arguments that cast light on matters of fact. It seemed grim that Jake Landsberger should be wasting his time with Electricians (of course I do not mean the electricians) instead of teaching at our school. And the *whole* truth was that we were all teaching at our school.

Adelman got heated and began to shout: "That's what you *say!* that's what *you* say, Landsberger! 'Win here—hold 'em there!' And Bang! tomorrow! tomorrow they drop a bomb on my *head—my* head—" he pounded his head as if the chief concern of his hot idealism was his head. "*Your* fault!"

"*My* fault? *I* drop the bomb?" said Jake, sadly.

"I'm sorry," said Ephraim Adelman's son. "It's a manner of speaking."

"Now I have to go and get married!" said Jake merrily.

7

Lawrence Dixon's appeal for funds for the New Building before the Group III play was his supreme effort during the period that I had the pleasure and pain of hearing him.

This time we were all there, the whole school, both the school and the parents, in the old gymnasium our theatre.

He began with reminiscences of the burned building dear to them all. . . . He went on to describe the idea of a New Building, a model of function and beauty, repeating the things he had said prematurely at the Staff-meeting. He drove home the educational value for every one, of planning and constructing, and paying for, such a New Building.

So far he was excellent. There required only to give some rough figures of the cost, and to sit down.

But once on his feet, it was impossible for him to sit down. Not that he was long-winded; on the contrary, Dixon was usually rather elliptical and rarely boring. But therefore the only way for him to continue, if he could not expatiate, was to tackle ever new subject-matter.

"When I think of what we stand for," he said, "I realize proudly that we are pioneers." There was a changed ring in his voice and I turned pale; it meant that he had left his notes behind and from here out was sailing on his own. "I have become obsessed, obsessed with the thought that we do not go far enough; we do not dare. All right! we are to have a New Building!"

—He had said the fatal words, "All right!"

"Modern society," said Lawrence Dixon, "is sick in three basic functions: Community, Economics, and Sex. At our school we have community." He giggled. "We teach community because we have a community. Our people communicate; we are sensate. Our assemblies are beautiful; the unknown conflicts rise to the surface, and we reproach them against one another. But what's the good of it if, because we fail in the other two functions, we ourselves *create* the conflicts with which we reproach one another? As I am reproaching us here, now!" He rubbed his hands and giggled.

"So what are the *two* most important issues in modern life, in modern evaluation and reform? the goals of modern education! Remember, I am looking forward to the future, but the future is upon us. *Sex and Economics.* In these aspects is our school a preparation for life? are we doing the job?

"Remember, in progressive education we hold that only life is a preparation for life. Childhood is not a previous, preparatory, inferior condition. It is a life in itself, with its own demands, its own laws."

And he proceeded, with perfect directness and continually mounting hysteria, before the curiously assorted audience, to argue that the children could not live because their parents did not make them economically independent and our school did not grant them sexual autonomy. . . .

The play, Race Problems, did not deceive one's expectations. . . . it was a composition and collaboration and execution by a sampling of the best intellects and the freest expression in the United States. I am writing soberly. Of Adelman, and Leila, and Harvey with his grotesque I. Q., and Netty Fieldston, and Schuman; and teachers who could not, in the end, suppress the secret longing for paradise; and others who fled from the tyrant. In our school, the heart-center of the "lunatic fringe," as we would call it, but let not the others dare to!—we at-sea and demented ones, we poised ones who at least suspected how it was with us, not like the others; refusing to resign our creative natures that would, in the end, draw on the energy of the heavens and the earth, first the earth then the heavens, lonely, yet surprisingly we found ourselves acquainted thru a hundred connections. Here was the proof of it! that we were the salt of the earth.

8

The devil with it! Let me describe again the excellences of our school. There were, to repeat it, four groups, and each had its own style. In Group I the following occurred:

Group I (ages 6–8)

The butcher came at an unusual time, to slaughter and dress a calf. The teacher of the youngest group was unwarned, and the kids were roaming in the field. They hastened in fascination to the spot. They did not see the killing but they watched the flaying, they could not be torn away. They were sick with fright and feasted their eyes.

Their teacher came and saw that they could not be removed without commands and threats. Tho she was herself a squeamish little woman, she put up a brave front and said, "How interesting! and isn't it interesting what he's doing now!" She pointed out which was the heart and which the lungs, and where the round steak came from and where the rib roast, while the poor dead beast hung with its hide dangling over its ears.

At meal time the children were nauseous. There was meat on the platter. They were not encouraged to eat; but their teacher thought—she herself, to her surprise, ate voraciously —that they should experience enough of the dining-room to make them vomit, and not hold back their vomiting. For several weeks they would not touch the meat.

She watched for some spontaneous motion from them. They began to indulge in an apparently pointless horseplay of tearing off each other's overcoats and jackets. They were mutely reliving the flaying.

She heightened it to a game, a dance, a ceremonial. One of the number would be the calf, dressed in two, three, or four coats: it was comic if under the brown coat suddenly appeared a white coat. But the red sweater was the underflesh. The butchers wailed in woe, but the victim was dead and supposed to be silent; often he laughed boisterously.

In this totemic sacrifice, different children preferred different roles: the Victim, the One who Holds, the One who Cuts the throat, the One who Flays. The little teacher screwed up her courage and said, "How interesting! and isn't *this* interesting?"

After a time, they were all beasts of the field, going on all fours and bellowing. And the game turned into the more amiable play of animal-masks.

Group II (9–11)

When the language of her group became stupidly dirty, obsessively returning to a few words, as if they were soldiers or sailors, Caroline could not hope to teach them articulate composition. They did not learn new words.

She stood at the blackboard and carefully printed the words most frequently heard:

FUCK   BASTARD   COCKSUCKER   SHIT

She asked them for contributions; their vocabulary in this kind was somewhat greater than her own. The words were accurately defined.

Suddenly it struck her that the classroom itself was in a mess; papers and crushed chalk underfoot, the blackboard dusty gray; the condition of the books was shameful.

"Shoot!" she cried. "I can't stand it any more. Let's clean it up here."

—We had recently been mentioning an amusing passage in Fourier, where he says that since children have a passion for filth, the garbage-collecting of society should be given into their hands.

They brought pails, rags, and soap and went to work on hands and knees with much slopping, and much thoroness. With continuing enthusiasm (I saw it so I believe it), they proceeded thru every classroom in the school, driving us others out of the way. This took all day and recurred sporadically for months.

Group III (12–14)

From the city they sent us a desperate and "probably hopeless" case. We were the last resort; if we could not manage with him, Norman would have no social schooling whatever. Norman was large and fat, intelligent, malcoordinated; he was a complete baby, given to wailing and full-dress tantrums.

We warned Sophie's gang, since by age and knowledge he would go in with them. They set themselves to cooperate, with their beautiful tact and fraternity.

But so far as we could help, Norman was hopeless. Taken in by his brightness, a teacher would encourage him to speak up in class. But whether one agreed with him or disagreed, or kept silent, he would at once go on to reproaches, anger, tears of selfpity, rage in which he would tear up books; whether one restrained him or not, it ended with a tantrum. Every class hour was spoiled. If one of the kids threw Nor-

man's soap into the brook, Norman, bawling with self-vindi-
cation, would throw the other's camera into the brook. This
was his idea of justice. A week of this experiment was enough
for the staff.

The boys were exasperated with the fat boy and pitied him;
away from him they burst into fits of ridicule and endless
discussions. (He was not dangerous except to property.) But
when we tried to call it off and admit failure, they became
indignant with us for not really trying. We relented for a few
more days.

"We try to be brotherly!" they said. "We are brotherly!
This doesn't work. *What do we do wrong?*"

—Once they had admitted it to themselves, that there was
such a thing as a brute fact, unamenable to discussion, our
algebrists were remarkably transformed. They became moth-
erly. Their feminine feelings rose to the surface, accompanied
by a softening, and deepening, of their hitherto metallic
voices. Their affection for one another rapidly changed. Too
rapidly and strongly: we did not dare allow it, allow these
alert conformists to grow independently into the condition of
being willing to confront brute facts.

The Staff was not ready for it. We were willing to admit
the fact of failure: the disproportion between our general task
and aims and this particular burden; but we were not willing
to go so far as to make our school a true sampling of the nature of the entire world. It was we, not Sophie's gang, who
violently brought the situation to an end and sent Norman
back home.

None too soon. In a few more days Group III would have
fought us, for their fact, with fists and claws.

"All very well!" said Schuman bitterly, "but what will become of him now? No other school will take him, we were
the last resort. No one takes the responsibility? Is this supposed to make *us* feel secure and happy, the way you boast?"

Group IV (15–17)

For a couple of months the big ones had a new counsellor,
a tall homely fellow, the son of a country pastor, but himself
not religious. (He was a pacifist and our local conscription
judged that the interests of the people were best served by
putting him in a prison.)

As best he could by reasoning and cajolery, he tried to get
the girls and boys to be more prompt and orderly in cleaning
the rooms and making the beds.

Finally he resorted to satyagraha; he took it upon himself

to make the unmade beds and to do the sweeping; he ostenta-
tiously spent several hours a day at this work. He hoped to
shame them.

He did not understand them at all. With a few jests, but
no twinges of either guilt or compassion, they let him do their
duties for them. Indeed, one or two who had used to make
their own beds, now left it for the counsellor. All were glad
to slip into this new convenient convention. "If he thinks it's
so important," said Seraphia's daughter, "he has the mental
set to do it. I don't and I haven't."

Not like a good satyagrahi, he became angry and said, "You
all think you're making a fool of me"—indeed nobody thought
this—"but in the long run I'll win out. The same thing happened to me. My father said, 'The important thing is to get
used to its being clean and neat, no matter how it gets that
way. After a while one will make the effort himself, because
it's too disgusting when it's dirty.' You'll see. After I'm gone
and it goes back to filth you won't be able to stand it and I'll
have my revenge!"

"Ho!" cried Michael. "You have a father, a conscience!
That's what's wrong with you. Long as your father did it you
didn't notice; but after he was gone he began to talk out inside of you. That's called the Super-ego. Now we don't have
any consciences. It won't work!"

—It worked. His conscience, or father's voice, or common
reason, or whatever it was, led him to being dragged off to
prison. And now he was gone. And the girls and boys could
not bear to see the place disorderly, too disorderly; for they
loved him, and they were not unwilling to have him win the
victory.

These were four episodes of our school, one from each
group.

We have four teachers. Two old ones, who have been teaching
in the school for two years, and have become accustomed to
the pupils, their work, the freedom and the external disorder
of the school. The two new teachers—both themselves fresh
from school—are lovers of external precision, programmes,
bells, and so forth, and have not yet adapted themselves to
the school so well as the first. . . . The order of instruction
is as follows: At about eight o'clock, the teacher living in the
school, a lover of external order and the administrator of the
school, sends one of the boys who nearly always stay over-
night with him to ring the bell.

In the village, people rise with the fires. From the school
the fires have long been observed in the windows, and half
an hour after the ringing of the bell there appear, in the
mist, in the rain, or in the oblique rays of the autumnal sun,
dark figures, by twos, by threes, or singly, on the mound (the
village is separated from the school by a ravine). The herding
feeling has long disappeared in the pupils. A pupil no longer
has the need of waiting and shouting: "O boys, let's to
school! She has begun." He knows by this time that "school"
is neuter, and he knows a few other things, and, strange to
say, for that very reason has no longer any need of a crowd.
When the time comes to go, he goes.

It seems to me that the personalities are becoming more
independent, their characters more sharply defined, with
every day. I have never noticed the pupils playing on their
way, unless it be a very young child, or a new pupil, who had
begun his instruction in some other school. The children
bring nothing with them,—neither books, nor copy-books. No
lessons are given for home.

Not only do they carry nothing in their hands, but they

"The School at Yásnaya Polyána" and "Are the Peasant Children to
Learn to Write from Us?" by Leo Tolstoy in Vol. II of the Collected Works of Leo Tolstoy (A Landed Proprietor), edited by Leo
Weiner (New York: L. C. Page, 1904), passim. Subheads provided by the editors.

have nothing to carry even in their heads. They are not obliged to remember any lesson,—nothing that they were doing the day before. They are not vexed by the thought of the impending lesson. They bring with them nothing but their impressionable natures and their convictions that to-day it will be as jolly in school as it was yesterday. They do not think of their classes until they have begun.

No one is ever rebuked for tardiness, and they never are tardy, except some of the older ones whose fathers now and then keep them back to do some work. In such cases they come running to school at full speed, and all out of breath. . . .

The teacher comes to the room, where on the floor lie screaming children, shouting, "The heap is not large enough!" or, "You are choking me, boys!" or, "That will do! Don't pull my hair!" and so forth.

"Peter Mikháylovich!" a voice at the bottom of the heap calls out to the teacher as he enters, "tell them to stop!"

"Good morning, Peter Mikháylovich!" shout the others, continuing their game.

The teacher takes the books and gives them to those who have gone with him up to the bookcase; those who are lying on top of the heap, without getting up, also ask for books. The heap becomes smaller by degrees. The moment the majority have books, the rest run to the bookcase and cry: "Me too, me too. Give me yesterday's book; and me the *Koltsóvian* book," and so forth. If there are two left who, excited from the struggle, still keep rolling on the floor, those who have the books cry out to them:

"Don't bother us! We can't hear a word! Stop now!"

The excited boys submit and, out of breath, take hold of their books, and only at first, while sitting at their books, keep swinging their legs from unallayed excitement. The martial spirit takes flight, and the reading spirit reigns in the room.

With the same enthusiasm with which he was pulling Mítka's hair, he is now reading the *Koltsóvian* book (so they call Koltsov's works with us), almost clenching his teeth, his eyes aflame, and seeing nothing about him but his book. It will take as much effort to tear him away from the book as it took before to get him away from fighting.

They sit down wherever they please: on the benches, the tables, the window-sill, the floor, and in the arm-chair. . . . I have never noticed any one whispering, or pinching his neighbour, or giggling, or snorting into his hand, or com-

plaining against another. When a pupil who has been studying with a sexton or in a county school comes to us with
such a complaint, we say to him: "Why don't you pinch
back?" . . .

According to the programme, there are to be four lessons
before noon, but there sometimes are only three or two, and
sometimes there are entirely different subjects. The teacher
may begin with arithmetic and pass over to geometry, or he
may start on sacred history, and end up with grammar. At
times the teacher and pupils are so carried away, that, instead of one hour, the class lasts three hours. Sometimes the
pupils themselves cry: "More, more!" and scold those who
are tired of the subject. "If you are tired, go to the babies,"
they will call out contemptuously.

All the pupils meet together for the class of religion; . . .
they also meet together for the drawing class. Before these
classes there is animation, fighting, shouting, and the most
pronounced external disorder: some drag the benches from
one room into another; some fight; some of the children of
the manorial servants run home for some bread, which they
roast in the stove; one is taking something away from a boy;
another is doing some gymnastics, and, just as in the disorder
of the morning, it is much easier to allow them to quiet
themselves and resume their natural order than forcibly to
settle them. . . .

In my opinion, this external disorder is useful and not
to be replaced by anything else, however strange and inconvenient it may seem for the teacher. I shall often have occasion to speak of the advantages of this system, and now I
will say only this much about the reputed inconveniences:
First, this disorder, or free order, is terrible to us only because we are accustomed to something quite different, in
which we have been educated. Secondly, in this case, as in
many similar cases, force is used only through haste and
through insufficient respect for human nature. We think that
the disorder is growing greater and greater, and that there are
no limits to it,—we think that there is no other means of
stopping it but by the use of force,—whereas we only need to
wait a little, and the disorder (or animation) calms down
naturally by itself, growing into a much better and more
permanent order than what we have created.

School children, small men though they be, have the
same needs as we, and they reason in the same manner; they
all want to learn, coming to school for this only, and so they

will naturally arrive at the conclusion that they must submit
to certain conditions in order to acquire knowledge.

They are more than merely men, they are a company of
men, united by one idea. And where three are gathered in
My name, there will I be with them! When they submit only
to natural laws, such as arise from their natures, they do not
feel provoked and do not murmur; but when they submit
to your predetermined interference, they do not believe in
the legality of your bells, programmes, and regulations.

How often have I seen children fighting, when the teacher
would rush up to take them apart, which would only make
the separated enemies look awry at each other, and would
not keep them, even in the presence of a stern teacher, from
rushing later against each other in order to inflict a more
painful kick! How often do I see every day some Kiryúshka,
with set teeth, fly at Taráska, pull his hair, knock him down,
and, if it costs him his life, try to maim his enemy,—and not
a minute passes before Taráska laughs underneath Kiryúshka,
—it is so much easier personally to square up accounts; in less
than five minutes both become friends and sit down near
each other. . . .

How often such matters are settled no one knows on the
basis of what law, and yet satisfactorily to both sides. How
arbitrary and unjust in comparison with it are all educational
methods employed in such cases!

"You are both guilty, get down on your knees!" says the
educator, and the educator is wrong, because only one of
them is guilty, and that guilty one is now triumphant, as he is
kneeling and ruminating his unspent rage, while the innocent
boy is doubly punished.

Or, "You are guilty of having done this or that, and you
will be punished," says the educator, and the punished boy
hates his enemy so much the more, because the despotic
power, the legality of which he does not acknowledge, is on
his enemy's side.

Or, "Forgive him, as God orders you to, and be better
than he," says the educator. You tell him to be better than
he, and he only wants to be stronger, and does not, and cannot, understand anything better.

Or, "Both of you are wrong: ask each other's forgiveness
and kiss each other, children!" That is worst of all, on account of the lie and the flimsiness of that kiss, and because the feeling which was being allayed only flames out
anew. . . .

Leave them alone and see how simply and naturally the whole matter will settle itself, and at the same time in what a complicated and varied manner, like all unconscious vital relations. . . .

I am convinced that . . . the school has no right and ought not to reward and punish; that the best police and administration of a school consist in giving full liberty to the pupils to study and settle their disputes as they know best. I am convinced of it, and yet, in spite of it, the old habits of the educational schools are so strong in us that we frequently depart from that rule in the Yásnaya Polyána school. Last semester, namely in November, there happened two such cases of punishment. . . .

In the summer, while the building was being repaired, a Leyden jar had disappeared from the physical cabinet; later, when there were no longer any carpenters or calciminers in the house, there disappeared on various occasions pencils and books. . . .

A few days later the thief was found: he was a manorial boy from a distant village. He had influenced a peasant boy who came with him from the same village, and both together had hidden the stolen objects in a small chest. This discovery produced a strange effect on his schoolmates: something like relief, and even joy, and at the same time contempt and compassion for the thief.

We proposed to them to mete out a punishment to the thief: some demanded that he be flogged, but that they themselves should do the flogging; others said that a label with the inscription "thief" ought to be sewn on his coat. This punishment, to our shame be it said, had been used by us before, and the very boy who the year before had worn such a label, with the inscription "liar," was the most persistent in demanding that label for the thief. We agreed on the label, and while a girl was sewing it on, all the pupils, with malicious joy, looked at the punished boys, and made fun of them. They demanded that the punishment be increased: "Take them through the village! Let them keep on the labels until the holidays," said they.

The punished boys wept. The peasant child, who had been influenced by the manorial boy, a talented story-teller and joker, a white-skinned, plump little fellow, was crying his heart away at the top of his boyish voice. The other, the chief criminal, a hump-nosed boy, with fine features and an intelligent face, was pale; his lips quivered; his eyes looked wildly and angrily at the triumphant boys, and now and then his face twitched unnaturally as though getting ready to cry. His cap, with torn visor, was poised on the back of his head, his hair was dishevelled, and his clothes soiled with chalk.

All that struck me and everybody else forcibly, as though we saw it all for the first time. The hostile attention of all was directed upon him. And this he was painfully conscious of. When he, without looking around and with bent head, and with a peculiar criminal gait, as I thought, walked home, and the children, running after him in a crowd, teased him in a peculiarly unnatural and strangely cruel manner, as though an evil spirit were guiding them against their will, something told me that it was not good. But the matter stood as it was, and the thief went with the label for a whole day. From that time on I thought he was studying with less zeal, and he no longer took part in the games and conversations of the boys outside the school.

Once I came to the classroom, when all the pupils with a certain terror informed me that the boy had again stolen. He had taken away twenty kopeks in copper from the teacher's room, and he had been caught hiding the money under the staircase. We again attached the label to him,—and the old monstrous scene was repeated. I began to admonish him, just as all educators admonish; a grown up boy, a good talker, who was present, began to admonish him, too, repeating the words which he, no doubt, had heard from his father, an inn-keeper.

"You steal once, and you steal a second time," he spoke, solemnly declaiming his words, "and it becomes a habit, and leads to no good."

I began to feel vexed. I was almost enraged against the thief. I looked at the face of the punished boy, which now was even paler, more suffering, and more cruel than before; I for some reason thought of prisoners in jail, and I suddenly felt so ashamed and felt such loathing for myself that I tore off the stupid label, told him to go wherever he pleased, and suddenly convinced myself, not through reasoning, but with my whole being, that I had no right to torment the unfortunate boy, and that I would not make of him what I and the innkeeper's son would like to make of him. I convinced myself that there were secrets of the soul, hidden from us, upon which only life can act, and not moral precepts and punishments.

What nonsense! The boy has stolen a book. By a whole, complicated road of feelings, thoughts, faulty ratiocinations, he was led to take a book belonging to somebody else, which he for some reason locked up in a chest,—and I paste on him a piece of paper with the word "thief," which means something entirely different! What for? To punish him by shaming him, I shall be told. To punish him by shaming him? What for? What is shame? How do we know that shame destroys the inclination toward thieving? Maybe it only encourages it. Maybe that which was expressed in his face was not at all shame. . . . Let people, who themselves have been punished, invent rights and duties to punish. Our world of children—of simple, independent men—must remain pure from self-deception and the criminal faith in the legality of punishment, free from that self-deception and belief that the feeling of revenge becomes just the moment you call it punishment. . . .

At times, when the classes are uninteresting, and there have been many of them (we often have seven long hours a day), and the children are tired, or before the holidays, when the ovens at home are prepared for a hot bath, two or three boys will suddenly rush into the room during the second or third afternoon class-hour, and will hurriedly pick out their caps.

"What's up?"

"Going home."

"And studies? There is to be singing yet!"

"The boys say they are going home," says one, slipping away with his cap.

"Who says so?"

"The boys are gone!"

"How is that?" asks the perplexed teacher who has prepared his lesson. "Stay!"

But another boy runs into the room, with an excited and perplexed face.

"What are you staying here for?" he angrily attacks the one held back, who, in indecision, pushes the cotton batting back into his cap. "The boys are way down there,—I guess as far as the smithy."

"Have they gone?"

"They have."

And both run away, calling from behind the door: "Goodbye, Iván Ivánovich!"

Who are the boys that decided to go home, and how did

they decide it? God knows. You will never find out who decided it. They did not take counsel, did not conspire, but simply, some boys wanted to go home, "The boys are going!" —and their feet rattle down-stairs, and one rolls down the steps in catlike form, and, leaping and tumbling in the snow, running a race with each other along the narrow path, the children bolt for home.

Such occurrences take place once or twice a week. It is aggravating and disagreeable for the teacher,—who will not admit that? But who will not admit, at the same time, that, on account of one such an occurrence, the five, six, and even seven lessons a day for each class, which are, of their own accord and with pleasure, attended by the pupils, receive a so much greater significance? Only by the recurrence of such cases could one gain the certainty that the instruction, though insufficient and onesided, was not entirely bad and not detrimental.

If the question were put like this: Which would be better, that not one such occurrence should take place during the whole year, or that this should happen for more than half the lessons,—we should choose the latter. At least, I was always glad to see these things happen several times a month in the Yásnaya Polyána school. In spite of the frequently repeated statements to the boys that they may leave any time they wish, the influence of the teacher is so strong that, of late, I have been afraid that the discipline of the classes, programmes, and grades might, imperceptibly to them, so restrict their liberty that they would submit to the cunning of the nets of order set by us and that they would lose the possibility of choice and protest. Their continued willingness to come to school, in spite of the liberty granted them, does not, I think, by any means prove the especial qualities of the Yásnaya Polyána school,—I believe that the same would be repeated in the majority of schools, and that the desire to study is so strong in children that, in order to satisfy their desire, they will submit to many hard conditions and will forgive many defects. The possibility of such escapades is useful and necessary only as a means of securing the teacher against the most detrimental and coarsest errors and abuses.

In an account that confirms Sir Herbert Read's principle of spontaneous initiation (see selection 39 above), Tolstoy now describes what was done by his pupils at Yásnaya Polyána school after an

attempt to impose mechanical reading (and later, mechanical penmanship) broke down.

"OF THEIR OWN ACCORD"

We abandoned the reading from the booklets, and racked
our brains to discover a means of mechanical reading. The
simple idea that the time had not yet come for good mechanical reading, that there was no urgent need for it at the present time, and that the pupils themselves would find the best
method, when that need should arise, burst upon us only
within a short time. During that search the following processes established themselves of their own accord:

During the reading lessons, now divided in name only
into graded and mechanical, the worst readers come in twos
and take some book (sometimes fairy-tales, or the Gospel,
and at times a song collection or a number of the *Popular
Reading*) and read by twos for the process of reading only,
and when that book is an intelligible fairy-tale, they read it
with comprehension, after which they demand of the teacher
that he should ask them questions, although the class is called
mechanical. At times the pupils, generally the poorest, take
the same book several times in succession, open it at the
same page, read one and the same tale, and memorize it, not
only without the teacher's order, but even in spite of his explicit prohibition; sometimes these poor pupils come to the
teacher, or to an older boy, and ask him to read with them.
Those who can read better, pupils of the second class, are
not so fond of reading in company, less often read for the
process of reading, and if they memorize anything, it is some
poem, but not a prose tale.

With the oldest boys the same phenomenon is repeated,
with this one difference which has struck me during the last
month. In their class of graded reading they get some one
book, which they read in turn, and then all together tell its
contents. They were joined this fall by a very talented boy,
Ch——, who had studied for two years with a sexton and who
therefore is ahead of them all in reading. . . . Last month
one of these declared that, cost what it might, he would
read as well as Ch—— within a week; others made the same
declaration, and suddenly mechanical reading became the
favourite subject. They would sit an hour or an hour and a
half at a time, without tearing themselves away from the
book, which they did not understand; they began to take

their books home, and really made in three weeks such progress as could hardly have been expected. . . .

We have now abandoned mechanical reading entirely, and matters are carried on as described above; each pupil is permitted to use whatever method is most convenient for him. . . .

With penmanship there happened this summer the same that had happened with the mechanical reading. The pupils wrote very wretchedly, and the new teacher introduced writing from copy (again a comfortable and easy method for the teacher). The pupils lost interest, and we were compelled to abandon penmanship and were unable to discover a means for improving the handwriting. The oldest class found that means by itself. Having finished the writing of sacred history, the pupils began to ask to be allowed to take their copy-books home. These copy-books were soiled, torn, and horribly scribbled over. The precise mathematician R—— asked for some scraps of paper, and began to rewrite his history. They all took a liking for that. "Let me have paper! Let me have the copy-book!" and there was started the fashion of penmanship which has continued up to the present in the higher class.

They took their copy-books, placed before them the model alphabet, copied each letter, and contended with each other. In two weeks they made great progress.

Nearly all of us were as children made to eat bread with our other food, though we did not like it, and yet now we do not eat otherwise than with bread. Nearly all of us were compelled to hold the pen with outstretched fingers, but we held it with bent fingers because they were short,—and now we stretch our fingers. The question then is: Why did they torment us so when what is necessary comes later quite naturally? Will not the desire and the necessity of knowledge . . . come in the same way? . . .

ARE EXAMINATIONS DESIRABLE?

The new teacher introduced the sitting on benches and single answers. The one called out was silent and embarrassed, and the teacher, looking aside, with a *sweet* expression of submission to fate, or with a meek smile, said, "Well, and then? Well, very well!" and so forth,—in that teacher's manner which we all know so well.

Moreover, I have convinced myself in practice that there is nothing more injurious to the development of the child than that kind of single questioning and the authoritative relation of teacher to pupils, arising from it, and for me there is nothing more provoking than such a spectacle. . . .

Why one should be taught to speak singly, nobody knows. Perhaps in order to make the child read a fable in the presence of his or her Excellency. I shall probably be told that without it it is impossible to determine the degree of his knowledge. To which I shall answer that it is indeed impossible for an outsider to determine the knowledge of a pupil in an hour, while the teacher always feels the measure of that knowledge without the pupil's answer and without examinations. . . .

The visitors, who were so detrimental to the instruction in the Yásnaya Polyána school, in one way were very useful to me. They completely convinced me that the recitation of lessons and the examinations were a remnant of the superstitions of the mediaeval school, and that with the present order of things they were positively impossible and only injurious. Frequently I was carried away by a childish vanity, wishing in an hour's time to show to an honoured visitor the knowledge of the pupils, and it turned out either that the visitor convinced himself that the pupils knew that which they did not know (I entertained him by some hocus-pocus) or that the visitor supposed that they did not know that which they knew very well. Such a tangle of misunderstandings took place between me and the visitor—a clever, talented man and a specialist in his business—during a perfect freedom of relations! What, then, must take place during the inspections of directors, and so forth,—even if we leave out of consideration that disturbance in the progress of teaching and the indefiniteness of ideas produced in the pupils by such examinations?

At the present time I am convinced of this: to make a résumé of all the pupil's knowledge is as impossible for the teacher as it is for an outsider, just as it is impossible to make a résumé of my own knowledge and yours in respect to any science whatsoever. If a forty-year-old man were to be taken to an examination in geography, it would be as stupid and strange as when a ten-year-old child is led to the examination. Both of them have to answer by rote, and in an hour of time it is impossible to find out their actual knowledge. In order to find out the knowledge of either, it is necessary to live for months with them.

Where examinations are introduced (by examination I understand every demand for an answer to a question), there only arises a new subject, demanding special labour, special ability: that subject is called "preparation for examinations or lessons." A pupil in the gymnasium studies history, mathematics, and, the main subject, the art of answering questions at the examinations. I do not regard this art as a useful subject of instruction. I, the teacher, judge of the degree of my pupils' knowledge as correctly as I judge of the degree of my own knowledge, although neither the pupils nor I myself recite any lessons. If an outsider wants to judge of the degree of that knowledge, let him live awhile with us and let him study the results of our knowledge and their applications to life. There is no other means, and all attempts at examination are only a deception, a lie, and an obstacle to instruction. In matters of instruction there is but one independent judge, the teacher, and only the pupils can control him.

EDUCATION: THE PROCESS OF CREATION

The reading of the collection of Snegirév's proverbs has long formed one of my favourite occupations,—nay, enjoyments. To every proverb I imagine individuals from among the people and their conflicts in the sense of the proverb. Among the number of unrealizable dreams, I always imagine a series of pictures, or stories, written to fit the proverbs. Once, last winter, I forgot everything after dinner in the reading of Snegirév's book, and even returned to the school with the book. It was the lesson in the Russian language.

"Well, write something on a proverb!" I said.

The best pupils, Fédka, Sémka, and others, pricked up their ears.

"What do you mean by 'on a proverb'? What is it? Tell us!" the questions ran.

I happened to open to the proverb: "He feeds with the spoon, and pricks the eye with the handle."

"Now, imagine," I said, "that a peasant has taken a beggar to his house, and then begins to rebuke him for the good he has done him, and you will get that 'he feeds with the spoon, and pricks the eye with the handle.'"

"But how are you going to write it up?" said Fédka and all the rest who had pricked up their ears. They retreated, having convinced themselves that this matter was above their strength, and betook themselves to the work which they had begun.

"Write it yourself," one of them said to me.

Everybody was busy with his work; I took a pen and ink-stand, and began to write.

"Well," said I, "who will write it best? I am with you." . . .

Fédka kept looking up from his copy-book to me, and upon meeting my eyes, smiled, winked, and repeated: "Write, write, or I'll give it to you!" He was evidently amused to see a grown person write a theme.

Having finished his theme worse and faster than usual, he climbed on the back of my chair and began to read over my shoulders. I could not proceed; others came up to us, and I read to them what I had written.

They did not like it, and nobody praised it. I felt ashamed, and, to soothe my literary ambition, I began to tell them the plan of what was to follow. In the proportion as I advanced in my story, I became enthusiastic, corrected myself, and they kept helping me out. One would say that the old man should be a magician; another would remark: "No, that won't do,—he will be just a soldier; the best thing will be if he steals from him; no, that won't go with the proverb," and so forth.

All were exceedingly interested. It was evidently a new and exciting sensation for them to be present at the process of creation, and to take part in it. Their judgments were all, for the most part, of the same kind, and they were just, both as to the very structure of the story and as to the details and characterizations of the persons. Nearly all of them took part in the composition; but, from the start, there distinguished themselves positive Sémka, by his clearly defined artistic quality of description, and Fédka, by the correctness of his poetical conceptions, and especially by the glow and rapidity of his imagination.

Their demands had so little of the accidental in them and were so definite, that more than once I debated with them, only to give way to them. I was strongly possessed by the demands of a regular structure and of an exact correspondence of the idea of the proverb to the story; while they, on the contrary, were only concerned about the demands of artistic truth. I, for example, wanted that the peasant, who had taken the old man to his house, should himself repent of his good deed,—while they regarded this as impossible and created a cross old woman.

I said: "The peasant was at first sorry for the old man, and later he hated to give away the bread."

Fédka replied that that would be improbable: "He did

not obey the old woman from the start and would not submit later."

"What kind of man is he, according to you?" I asked.

"He is like Uncle Timoféy," said Fédka, smiling. "He has a scanty beard, goes to church, and he has bees."

"Is he good; but stubborn?" I asked.

"Yes," said Fédka, "he will not obey the old woman." . . .

Sémka seemed to see and describe that which was before his eyes: the still, frozen bast shoes, and the dirt oozing from them, as they melted out, and the toast into which they were changed when the old woman threw them into the oven.

Fédka, on the contrary, saw only such details as evoked in him the particular feeling with which he looked upon a certain person. Fédka saw the snow drifting behind the peasant's leg-rags, and the feeling of compassion with which the peasant said: "Lord, how it snows!" (Fédka's face even showed how the peasant said it, and he swung his hands and shook his head.) He saw the overcoat, a mass of rags and patches, and the torn shirt, behind which could be seen the haggard body of the old man, wet from the thawing snow. He created the old woman, who growled as, at the command of her husband, she took off his bast shoes, and the pitiful groan of the old man as he muttered through his teeth: "Softly, motherkin, I have sores here." . . .

I beg the reader to read the first chapter of the story and to notice that wealth of features of true creative talent scattered through it; for example, the feature when the woman in anger complains about her husband to the gossip, and yet weeps, although the author has an apparent dislike for her, when the gossip reminds her of the ruin of her house. For the author, who writes by reasoning out and from memory, the cross woman represents only the opposite of the peasant,— she had to invite the gossip for no other reason than the desire to annoy her husband; but with Fédka the artistic feeling extends also to the woman, and she, too, weeps, fears, and suffers,—she is not guilty, to his manner of thinking. Then the accessory feature when the gossip puts on a woman's fur coat. I remember how struck I was by this and how I asked: "Why a woman's fur coat?" None of us had led Fédka up to the idea that the gossip had put on a fur coat.

He said: "It is more like it!"

When I asked him whether it would do to say that he put on a man's fur coat, he said:

"No, a woman's fur coat is better."

Indeed, this feature is extraordinary. At first it does not occur to one why it should be a woman's fur coat, and yet one feels that it is excellent and cannot be otherwise.

Every artistic word, whether it belongs to Göthe or to Fédka, differs from the inartistic in that it evokes an endless mass of thoughts, images, and explanations.

The gossip in a woman's fur coat involuntarily presents himself to us as a sickly, narrow-chested peasant, just such as he apparently ought to be. The woman's fur coat, carelessly thrown on the bench and the first to fall into his hands, in addition, present to us a winter evening scene in the life of the peasant. The fur coat leads you to imagine the late evening, during which the peasant is sitting without his wraps near a torch, and the women, coming in and out to fetch water and attend to the cattle, and all that external disorder of the peasant life, where not a person has his clearly defined clothes, and no one thing a definite place. With this one sentence, "He put on a woman's fur coat," the whole character of the surroundings, in which the action takes place, is clearly outlined, and this phrase is not used by accident, but consciously. . . .

To my proposition to describe what the peasant was thinking while his wife had run over to the gossip, there immediately rose before him the very form of the thought: "If you got in the way of Savóska the corpse, he would pull all your locks out!" He said this in such a fatigued and calmly serious and habitual and, at the same time, good-natured voice, leaning his head on his hand, that the boys rolled in laughter. . . .

We worked from seven to eleven o'clock; they felt neither hunger nor fatigue, and even got angry with me when I stopped writing, but they soon gave that up as matters would not go well.

It was then for the first time that Fédka asked my name. We laughed because he did not know.

"I know," he said, "how to call you; but how do they call you in the manor? We have such names as Fokanýchev, Zyábrey, Ermílin."

I told him.

"Are we going to print it?" he asked.

"Yes."

"Then we shall have to print: Work by Makárov, Morózov, and Tolstóy."

He was agitated for a long time and could not fall asleep,

and I cannot express that feeling of agitation, joy, fear, and almost regret, which I experienced during that evening. I felt that with that day a new world of enjoyment and suffering was opened up to him,—the world of art; I thought that I had received an insight into what no one has a right to see, —the germination of the mysterious flower of poetry. . . . I was happy, as must be happy the man who beholds that which no one beheld before.

SECTION VII

How Sound Is Anarchism?

Not very long ago a political philosophy class at LSU in New Orleans set about to assemble and appraise the arguments against the anarchist position. They found an extremely heterogeneous corpus of objections, ranging from the bombasts of retired police captains to fair-minded critiques by Bertrand Russell. But on the whole, their experience with this corpus was disappointing. Only rarely did they encounter an author who separated the principles from the tactics of anarchism or who was aware of important distinctions among (and within) the various forms of anarchism. Moreover, the class was unable to locate anything approaching comprehensive critical works on such front-rank libertarian thinkers as Berdyaev, Bakunin, and the individualist anarchists.

In consequence, the selections that follow constitute far more than a sample of the serious efforts to evaluate the anarchist position; with little exaggeration, we could offer them as the only efforts of this sort. Some, like Estey's work on syndicalism, can stake a claim to being definitive. But for the most part they are suggestive pieces that do no more than initiate inquiries, the conclusions of which are not yet in sight.

Bertrand Russell is probably the most renowned and undoubtedly
the most prolific philosopher of our time. Beginning with a series of
lectures, published in 1896, on the fate of Marxism in Germany, he
has made a number of important contributions to political theory.
Nowhere in his works does he have much to say for the modern
centralized state. Nonetheless, he found anarchist arguments defec-
tive and in the following selection presents some of the most common objections to anarchism with uncommon clarity and force, although the notion of freedom that Russell's case explicitly assumes
would hardly have been acceptable to Berdyaev, Stirner, or Godwin.

Government and Law, in their very essence, consist of restrictions on freedom, and freedom is the greatest of political
goods.* A hasty reasoner might conclude without further ado
that Law and government are evils which must be abolished
if freedom is our goal. But this consequence, true or false,
cannot be proved so simply. In this chapter we shall examine
the arguments of Anarchists against law and the State. We
shall proceed on the assumption that freedom is the supreme
aim of a good social system; but on this very basis we shall
find the Anarchist contentions very questionable.

Respect for the liberty of others is not a natural impulse
with most men: envy and love of power lead ordinary human
nature to find pleasure in interferences with the lives of
others. If all men's actions were wholly unchecked by external authority, we should not obtain a world in which all
men would be free. The strong would oppress the weak, or

*Proposed Roads to Freedom: Socialism, Anarchism, and Syndical-
ism*, by Bertrand Russell (London: George Allen & Unwin Ltd.,
1919), pp. 111–37. Reprinted by permission of the publisher.

* I do not say freedom is the greatest of *all* goods: the best things
come from within—they are such things as creative art, and love, and
thought. Such things can be helped or hindered by political conditions, but not actually produced by them; and freedom is, both in
itself and in its relation to these other goods, the best thing that
political and economic conditions can secure.

the majority would oppress the minority, or the lovers of violence would oppress the more peaceable people. I fear it cannot be said that these bad impulses are *wholly* due to a bad social system. . . . In a world where none could acquire much power, the desire to tyrannize would be much less strong than it is at present. Nevertheless, I cannot think that it would be wholly absent, and those in whom it would exist would often be men of unusual energy and executive capacity. Such men, if they are not restrained by the organized will of the community, may either succeed in establishing a despotism, or, at any rate, make such a vigorous attempt as can only be defeated through a period of prolonged disturbance. And apart from the love of political power, there is the love of power over individuals. If threats and terrorism were not prevented by law, it can hardly be doubted that cruelty would be rife in the relations of men and women, and of parents and children. It is true that the habits of a community can make such cruelty rare, but these habits, I fear, are only to be produced through the prolonged reign of law. Experience of backwoods communities, mining camps and other such places seems to show that under new conditions men easily revert to a more barbarous attitude and practice. It would seem, therefore, that, while human nature remains as it is, there will be more liberty for all in a community where some acts of tyranny by individuals are forbidden, than in a community where the law leaves each individual free to follow his every impulse. . . .

The conclusion, which appears to be forced upon us, is that the Anarchist ideal of a community in which no acts are forbidden by law is not, at any rate for the present, compatible with the stability of such a world as the Anarchists desire. In order to obtain and preserve a world resembling as closely as possible that at which they aim, it will still be necessary that some acts should be forbidden by law. We may put the chief of these under three heads:

1   Theft.

2   Crimes of violence.

3   The creation of organizations intended to subvert the Anarchist *régime* by force. . . .

1   *Theft.*   It is true that in an Anarchist world there will be no destitution, and therefore no thefts motived by starvation. But such thefts are at present by no means the most considerable or the most harmful. The system of rationing, which is to be applied to luxuries, will leave many men with

fewer luxuries than they might desire. It will give opportunities for peculation by those who are in control of the public
stores, and it will leave the possibility of appropriating such
valuable objects of art as would naturally be preserved in
public museums. It may be contended that such forms of
theft would be prevented by public opinion. But public
opinion is not greatly operative upon an individual unless it
is the opinion of his own group. A group of men combined
for purposes of theft might readily defy the public opinion
of the majority unless that public opinion made itself effective by the use of force against them. Probably, in fact, such
force would be applied through popular indignation, but in
that case we should revive the evils of the criminal law with
the added evils of uncertainty, haste and passion, which are
inseparable from the practice of lynching. If, as we have suggested, it were found necessary to provide an economic stimulus to work by allowing fewer luxuries to idlers, this would
afford a new motive for theft on their part and a new necessity for some form of criminal law.

2 *Crimes of Violence.* Cruelty to children, crimes of
jealousy, rape, and so forth, are almost certain to occur in any
society to some extent. The prevention of such acts is essential to the existence of freedom for the weak. If nothing were
done to hinder them, it is to be feared that the customs of a
society would gradually become rougher, and that acts which
are now rare would cease to be so. If Anarchists are right in
maintaining that the existence of such an economic system
as they desire would prevent the commission of crimes of this
kind, the laws forbidding them would do no harm to liberty.
If, on the other hand, the impulse to such actions persisted,
it would be necessary that steps should be taken to restrain
men from indulging it.

3 The third class of difficulties is much the most serious
and involves much the most drastic interference with liberty.
I do not see how a private army could be tolerated within an
Anarchist community, and I do not see how it could be prevented except by a general prohibition of carrying arms. If
there were no such prohibition, rival parties would organize
rival forces, and civil war would result. Yet, if there is such a
prohibition, it cannot well be carried out without a very considerable interference with individual liberty. No doubt, after a time, the idea of using violence to achieve a political
object might die down, as the practice of duelling has done.
But such changes of habit and outlook are facilitated by legal

prohibition, and would hardly come about without it. . . .
At present a very large part of the criminal law is concerned
in safeguarding the rights of property, that is to say—as things
are now—the unjust privileges of the rich. Those whose principles lead them into conflict with government, like Anarchists, bring a most formidable indictment against the law
and the authorities for the unjust manner in which they support the *status quo*. Many of the actions by which men have
become rich are far more harmful to the community than the
obscure crimes of poor men, yet they go unpunished because
they do not interfere with the existing order. If the power
of the community is to be brought to bear to prevent certain
classes of actions through the agency of the criminal law, it is
as necessary that these actions should really be those which
are harmful to the community, as it is that the treatment of
"criminals" should be freed from the conception of guilt and
inspired by the same spirit as is shown in the treatment of
disease. But, if these two conditions were fulfilled, I cannot
help thinking that a society which preserved the existence of
law would be preferable to one conducted on the unadulter-
ated principles of Anarchism. . . .

We may now sum up our discussion of the powers of Government.

The State, in spite of what Anarchists urge, seems a necessary institution for certain purposes. Peace and war, tariffs,
regulation of sanitary conditions and of the sale of noxious
drugs, the preservation of a just system of distribution: these,
among others, are functions which could hardly be performed
in a community in which there was no central government.
Take, for example, the liquor traffic, or the opium traffic in
China. If alcohol could be obtained at cost price without
taxation, still more of it could be obtained for nothing, as
Anarchists presumably desire, can we believe that there
would not be a great and disastrous increase of drunkenness?
China was brought to the verge of ruin by opium, and every
patriotic Chinaman desired to see the traffic in opium restricted. In such matters freedom is not a panacea, and some
degree of legal restriction seems imperative for the national
health.

50 Anarchist Tactics: A Pageant of Futility, Obstruction, and Decadence?

George Plekhanov was a major Marxist theorist in the decades immediately following Marx's death. As such, he regarded political reform as a key weapon in the workers' struggle against economic injustice. And, like the author of the subsequent selection, Plekhanov viewed the democratic state as a necessary condition for proletarian well-being.

Anarchists have of course disdained political activity, holding that it is ineffectual and serves only to create new forms of alienation and servitude. This despisal reached a zenith in the theories and tactics of Bakunin, who rejected all attempts to alter society through legislation and the extension of suffrage in favor of what he termed the social revolution. For the most part, Plekhanov aims his sarcastic and (at times) penetrating attack against the strategies devised by Bakunin and his followers. But no libertarian program, whatever its inspiration, can afford to look away from the challenge presented by this attack.

Bakounine cannot understand that the working class in its political action can completely separate itself from all the exploiting parties. According to him, there is no other *rôle* in the political movement for the workers than that of satellite of the Radical bourgeoisie. He glorifies the "essentially economic" tactics of the old English Trade Unions, and has not the faintest idea that it was these very tactics that made the English workers the tail of the Liberal Party.

Bakounine objects to the working class lending a hand in any movement whose object is the obtaining or the extension of political rights. In condemning such movements as "bourgeois," he fancies himself a tremendous revolutionist. As a matter of fact he thus proves himself essentially Conserva-

Anarchism and Socialism, by G. Plekhanov, translated by Eleanor Marx Aveling (London: Twentieth-Century Press, 1895), pp. 96–100, 128–41.

tive, and if the working class were ever to follow this line of inaction the Governments could only rejoice.*

The true revolutionists of our days have a very different idea of Socialist tactics. They "everywhere support every revolutionary movement against the existing social and political order of things;" which does not prevent them (but quite the contrary) from forming the proletariat into a party separate from all the exploiter parties, opposed to the whole "reactionary mass. . . ."

Bakounine would not have politics at any price. . . . Those who speak of working-class candidates are but mocking the proletariat. "Working-class candidates, transferred to bourgeois conditions of life, and into an atmosphere of completely bourgeois political ideas, ceasing to be actually workers in order to become statesmen, will become bourgeois, and possibly will become even more bourgeois than the bourgeois themselves. For it is not the men who make positions, but, on the contrary, positions which make the men."

This last argument is about all Bakounine was able to assimilate of the materialist conception of history. . . . He does not understand that the environment which makes man may change, thus changing man its own product. The environment he has in his mind's eye when speaking of the political action of the proletariat, is the bourgeois parliamentary environment, that environment which must necessarily fatally corrupt labour representatives. But the environment of the *electors*, the environment of a working-class party, conscious of its aim and well organised, would this have no influence upon the elected of the proletariat? No! Economically enslaved, the working class must always remain in political servitude; in this domain it will always be the weakest; to free itself it must begin by an economic revolution. Bakounine does not see that by this process of reasoning he inevitably arrives at the conclusion that a victory of the proletariat is absolutely impossible, unless the owners of the means of production voluntarily relinquish their possessions to them. In effect the subjection of the worker to capital is the source not only of political but of moral servitude. And how can the workers, morally enslaved, rise against the bourgeoisie? For the working-class movement to become possible,

* The anathemas pronounced by Bakounine against political liberty for a time had a very deplorable influence upon the revolutionary movement in Russia.

according to Bakounine, it must therefore first make an economic revolution. But the economic revolution is only possible as the work of the workers themselves. So we find ourselves in a vicious circle, out of which modern Socialism can easily break, but in which Bakounine and the Bakounists are for ever turning with no other hope of deliverance than a logical *salto mortale*. . . .

In repudiating all "politics" Bakounine was forced to adopt the tactics of the old English Trade Unions. But even he felt that these tactics were not very revolutionary. He tried to get out of the difficulty by the help of his "Alliance," a kind of international secret society, organised on a basis of frenetic centralisation and grotesque fancifulness. Subjected to the dictatorial rule of the sovereign pontiff of Anarchy, the "international" and the "national" brethren were bound to accelerate and direct the "essentially economic" revolutionary movement. At the same time Bakounine approved of "riots," of isolated risings of workers and peasants which, although they must inevitably be crushed out, would, he declared, always have a good influence upon the development of the revolutionary spirit among the oppressed. It goes without saying that with such a "programme" he was able to do much harm to the working-class movement, but he was not able to draw nearer, even by a single step, to that "immediate" economic revolution of which he "dreamed." . . .

Error has its logic as well as truth. Once you reject the political action of the working class, you are fatally driven—provided you do not wish to serve the bourgeois politicians—to accept the tactics of the Vaillants and the Henrys. . . . Kropotkine advises the Russian revolutionists to give up their political struggle against Tzarism. They must follow an "immediately economic" end. "The emancipation of the Russian peasants from the yoke of serfdom that has until now weighed upon them, is therefore the first task of the Russian revolutionist. In working along these lines he directly and immediately works for the good of the people . . . and he moreover prepares for the weakening of the centralised power of the State and for its limitation."

Thus the emancipation of the peasants will have prepared the way for the weakening of Russian Tzarism. But how to emancipate the peasants before overthrowing Tzarism? Absolute mystery! . . . Old Liscow was right when he said, "It is easier and more natural to write with the fingers than with the head." . . .

All this would be very ridiculous, if it were not too sad, as the Russian poet Lermontoff says. And it is sad indeed. Whenever the proletariat makes an attempt to somewhat ameliorate its economic position, "large-hearted people," vowing they love the proletariat most tenderly, rush in from all points of the compass, and depending on their halting syllogisms, put spokes into the wheel of the movement, do their utmost to prove that the movement is useless. We have had an example of this with regard to the eight hours day, which the Anarchists combated, whenever they could, with a zeal worthy of a better cause. When the proletariat takes no notice of this, and pursues its "immediately economic" aims undisturbed—as it has the fortunate habit of doing—the same "large-hearted people" re-appear upon the scene armed with bombs, and provide the government with the desired and sought for pretext for attacking the proletariat. . . . An Anarchist will have nothing to do with "parliamentarism," since it only lulls the proletariat to sleep. He will [have] none of "reforms," since reforms are but so many compromises with the possessing classes. He wants the revolution, a "full, complete, immediate, and immediately economic" revolution. To attain this end he arms himself with a saucepan full of explosive materials, and throws it amongst the public in a theatre or a café. He declares this is the "revolution." For our own part it seems to us nothing but "immediate" madness.

Plekhanov concludes by slightly shifting the target of his objections from anarchist tactics to the anarchist concept of right and wrong. In doing so, he raises an interesting and neglected point: that the moral principles of anarchism tacitly sanction forms of injustice and brutality which the anarchists themselves uniformly repudiated. If Plekhanov is correct here, it would seem to follow that anarchist theory is involved in a fundamental contradiction.

Kropotkine would have us believe that Anarchist morality, a morality free from all obligations or sanction, opposed to all utilitarian calculations, is the same as the natural morality of the people, "the morality from the habit of well doing." The morality of the Anarchists is that of persons who look upon all human action from the abstract point of view of the unlimited rights of the individual, and who, in the name of these rights, pass a verdict of "Not guilty" on the most atrocious deeds, the most revolting arbitrary acts. "What matter the victims," exclaimed the Anarchist poet Laurent Tailhade . . . "provided the gesture is beautiful?" . . . In fact the Anarchists combat democracy because democracy, according to them, is nothing but the tyranny of the majority as against the minority. The majority has no right to impose its wishes upon the minority. But if this is so, in the name of what moral principle do the Anarchists revolt against the bourgeoisie? Because the bourgeoisie are not a minority? Or because they do not do what they "will" to do?

"Do as thou would'st," proclaim the Anarchists. The bourgeoisie "want" to exploit the proletariat, and do it remarkably well. They thus follow the Anarchist precept, and the "companions" are very wrong to complain of their conduct. They become altogether ridiculous when they combat the bourgeoisie in the name of their victims. "What matters the death of vague human beings"—continues the Anarchist logician Tailhade—"if thereby the individual affirms himself?" Here we have the true morality of the Anarchists; it is also that of the crowned heads. *Sic volo, sic jubeo!*

Thus, in the name of the revolution, the Anarchists serve the cause of reaction; in the name of morality they approve the most immoral acts; in the name of individual liberty they trample under foot all the rights of their fellows.

51 Neither Communist Nor Individualist
Anarchism

In March of 1885, George Bernard Shaw, though a member of the
Fabian Society, wrote an article that he entitled "The Anarchist"—
a straightforward and unapologetic defense of anarchism. Eight years
later, when the Fabian creed of gradual and bureaucratic socialism
had ossified, Shaw recanted his earlier position. The fortunate result
was the following essay, which advances the strongest and most comprehensive case ever constructed against anarchism.

Unlike other critics of anarchism, Shaw recognized the dangers in
speaking loosely of *"the* anarchist position." Thus he carefully separates two major libertarian views and proceeds to shape a different
set of arguments to fit their distinctive features. The tacit assumption here, of course, is that these two views exhaust the possible
forms of anarchism.

[T]he following criticism of Anarchism . . . is confined to the
practical measures proposed by Anarchists, and raises no discussion as to aims or principles. As to these we are all agreed.
Justice, Virtue, Truth, Brotherhood, the highest interests of
the people, moral as well as physical: these are dear not only
to Social-Democrats and Anarchists, but also to Tories,
Whigs, Radicals, and probably also to Moonlighters and
Dynamitards. It is with the methods by which it is proposed
to give effect to them that I am concerned here; and to them
I shall now address myself. INDIVIDUALIST ANARCHISM. The
full economic detail of Individualist Anarchism may be in-
ferred with sufficient completeness from an article entitled
"State Socialism and Anarchism: how far they agree, and
wherein they differ," which appeared in March, 1888, in
Liberty, an Anarchist journal, then published in Boston,
Mass., and still issued and edited by the author of the article,
Mr. Benjamin R. Tucker. . . .

"The Impossibilities of Anarchism," by George Bernard Shaw (London: Fabian Society, 1893), passim (published as Fabian Tract 45).
Reprinted by permission of the Fabian Society.

"The economic principles of Modern Socialism," says Mr. Tucker, "are a logical deduction from the principle laid down by Adam Smith in the early chapters of his *Wealth of Nations:* namely, that labor is the true measure of price. From this principle, these three men [Josiah Warren, Proudhon, and Marx] deduced 'that the natural wage of labor is its product.'"

Now the Socialist who is unwary enough to accept this economic position will presently find himself logically committed to the Whig doctrine of *laissez-faire.* To this Mr. Tucker will not object. He may say, "Why not? *Laisser-faire* is exactly what we want. Destroy the money monopoly, the tariff monopoly, and the patent monopoly. Enforce then only those land titles which rest on personal occupancy or cultivation; and the social problem of how to secure to each worker the product of his own labor will be solved simply by everyone minding his own business." . . .

Let us see. Suppose we decree that henceforth no more rent shall be paid in England, and that each man shall privately own his house, and hold his shop, factory, or place of business jointly with those who work with him in it. Let every one be free to issue money from his own mint without tax or stamp. Let all taxes on commodities be abolished, and patents and copyrights be things of the past. Try to imagine yourself under these promising conditions with life before you. You may start in business as a crossing sweeper, shopkeeper, collier, farmer, miller, banker, or what not. Whatever your choice may be, the first thing you find is that the reward of your labor depends far more on the situation in which you exercise it than on yourself. If you sweep the crossing between St. James's and Albemarle Streets you prosper greatly. But if you are forestalled not only there, but at every point more central than, say, the corner of Holford Square, Islington, you may sweep twice as hard as your rival in Piccadilly, and not take a fifth of his toll. At such a pass you may well curse Adam Smith and his principle that labor is the measure of price, and either advocate a democratically constituted State Socialist municipality, paying all its crossing sweepers equally, or else pitch your broom into the Thames and turn shopkeeper. Yet here again the same difficulty crops up. Your takings depend not on yourself, but on the number of people who pass your window per hour. At Charing Cross or Cheapside fortunes are to be made: in the main street at Putney one can do enough to hold up one's head: further out, a thousand yards right or left of the Portsmouth Road, the most industrious man in the world may go whistle for a customer. Evidently retail shopkeeping is not the thing for a man of spirit after Charing Cross and Cheapside have been appropriated by occupying owners on the principle of first come first served. . . .

[T]here will be farming, milling, and mining, conducted by human agents, under Anarchism. Now the farmer will not find in his perfect Anarchist market two prices at one time for two bushels of wheat of the same quality; yet the labor cost of each bushel will vary according to the fertility of the farm on which it was raised, and the proximity of that farm to the market. A good soil will often yield the strongest and richest grain to less labor per acre or per bushel than must be spent on land that returns a crop less valuable by five shillings a quarter. When all the best land is held by occupying owners, those who have to content themselves with poorer soils will hail the principle that labor is the measure of price with the thumb to the nose.

Among the millers, too, there must needs be grievous mistrust of Proudhon and Josiah Warren. For of two men with equally good heart to work and machinery to work with, one may be on a stream that will easily turn six millstones; whilst the other, by natural default of water, or being cut off by his fellow higher up stream, may barely be able to keep two pairs of stones in gear, and may in a dry season be ready to tie these two about his neck and lie down under the scum of his pond. Certainly he can defy drought by setting to work with a steam or electro motor, steel rollers, and all the latest contrivances; yet, after all his outlay, he will not be able to get a penny a sack more for his stuff than his competitor, to whose water-wheel Nature is gratuitously putting her shoulder. . . .

And how would occupying ownership of mines work, when it is an easier matter to get prime Wallsend and Silkstone out of one mine than to get slates and steam fuel out of another, even after twenty years preliminary shaftsinking? Would Mr. Tucker, if he had on sale from a rich mine some Silkstone that had only cost half as much labor as steam coal from a relatively poor one, boldly announce: "Prices this day: Primer Silkstone, per ton, 25s.; best steam ditto, 50s. Terms, cash. Principles, those of Adam Smith: see *Wealth of Nations, passim*"? Certainly not with "competition everywhere and always," unless custom was no object to him in comparison with principle.

It is useless to multiply instances. There is only one country in which every square foot of land is as favorably situated for conducting exchanges, and as richly endowed by nature for production, as any other square foot; and the name of that country is Utopia. In Utopia alone, therefore, would occupying ownership be just. In England, America, and other places rashly created without consulting the Anarchists, Nature is all caprice and injustice in dealing with Labor. Here you scratch her with a spade; and earth's increase and foison plenty are added to you. On the other side of the hedge twenty steam-diggers will not extort a turnip from her. Still less adapted to Anarchism than the fields and mines is the crowded city. The distributor flourishes where men love to congregate: his work is to bring commodities to men; but here the men bring themselves to the commodities. Remove your distributor a mile, and his carts and travellers must scour the country for customers. . . .

Now Mr. Tucker's remedy for idle landlordism is to make the occupier—the actual worker—the owner. Obviously the effect would be, not to abolish his advantage over his less favorably circumstanced competitors, but simply to authorize him to put it into his own pocket instead of handing it over to a landlord. He would then, it is true, be (as far as his place of business was concerned) a worker instead of an idler; but he would get more product as a manufacturer and more custom as a distributor than other equally industrious workers in worse situations. He could thus save faster than they, and retire from active service at an age when they would still have many years more work before them. . . .

Again, his retirement from his place of business would leave him still in possession, as occupying owner, of his private residence; and this might be of exceptional or even unique desirability in point of situation. It might, for instance, be built on Richmond Hill, and command from its windows a beautiful view of the Thames valley. Now Richmond Hill will not hold all the people who would rather live there than in the Essex marshes. It is easy to say, Let the occupier be the owner; but the question is, Who is to be the occupier? Suppose it were settled by drawing lots, what would prevent the winner from selling his privilege for its full (unearned) value under free exchange and omnipresent competition? To such problems as these, Individualist Anarchism offers no solution. It theorizes throughout on the assumption that one place in a country is as good as another.

Under a system of occupying ownership, rent would exist in its primary form of an excess of the prices of articles over the expenses of producing them, thus enabling owners of superior land to get more for their products than cost price, and to sell their occupancy for the capital value of the rent. If, for example, the worst land worth using were only one-third as productive as the best land, then the owner-occupiers of that best land would get in the market the labor cost of their wares three times over. This 200 per cent premium would be just as truly ground rent as if it were paid openly as such to the Duke of Bedford or the Astors; and the occupancy could be sold as easily as any stock yielding the same dividend.

It may be asked why prices must go up to the expenses of production on the very worst land. Why not ascertain and charge the average cost of production, taking good and bad land together? Simply because nothing but Socialism can put the good and bad lands into the same ownership, and their accounts into the same ledger. Under Anarchism, with the good and bad lands in separate competing hands, nothing short of the maximum labor cost would repay the owners of the worst land. In fact, the worst land would not be cultivated until the price had risen. The process would be as follows. Suppose the need of the population for wheat were more than satisfied by crops raised from the best available land only. Free competition in wheat-producing would then bring the price down to the labor cost or expenses of production; and no inferior land would be cultivated. Now suppose an increase of population sufficient to overtax the wheat-supplying capacity of the best land. The supply falling short of the demand, the price of wheat would rise. When it had risen to the labor cost of production from land one degree inferior to the best, it would be worth while to cultivate that inferior land. When that new source came to be overtaxed by the still growing population, the price would rise again, until it would repay the cost of raising wheat from land yet lower in fertility than the second grade. But these descents would in nowise diminish the fertility of the best land, from which wheat could be raised as cheaply as before, in spite of the rise in the price, which would apply to all the wheat in the market, no matter where raised. That is, the holders of the best land would gain a premium, rising steadily with the increase of population, exactly as the landlord now enjoys a steadily rising rent. . . .

As the agricultural industry is typical of all industries, it will be seen now that price does not rise because worse land is brought into cultivation, but that worse land is brought into cultivation by the rise of price. Or, to put it in another way, the price of the commodity does not rise because more labor has been devoted to its production, but more labor is devoted to its production because the price has risen. Commodities, in fact, have a price before they are produced: we produce them expressly to obtain that price; and we cannot alter it by merely spending more or less labor on them. It is natural for the laborer to insist that labor *ought to be* the measure of price, and that the *just* wage of labor is its average product; but the first lesson he has to learn in economics is that labor is not and never can be the measure of price under a competitive system. Not until the progress of Socialism replaces competitive production and distribution, with individual greed for its incentive, by Collectivist production and distribution, with fair play all round for its incentive, will the prices either of labor or commodities represent their just value.

Thus we see that "competition everywhere and always" fails to circumvent rent whilst the land is held by competing occupiers, who are protected in the individual ownership of what they can raise from their several holdings. And "the great principle laid down by Adam Smith," formulated by Josiah Warren as "Cost is the proper limit of price," turns out—since in fact price is the limit of cost—to be in practice merely a preposterous way of expressing the fact that under Anarchism that small fraction of the general wealth which was produced under the least favorable circumstances would fetch at least its cost, whilst all the rest would fetch a premium which would be nothing but privately appropriated rent with an Anarchist mask on.

We see also that such a phrase as "the natural wage of labor is its product" is a misleading one, since labor cannot produce subsistence except when exercised upon natural materials and aided by natural forces external to man; nor can any human lawgiver ever settle the question of how much of the crop of a farm has been produced by the horses, how much by the ploughman, how much by the farmer, and how much by the agricultural chemist in his laboratory. And in any case the value in exchange of the product depends in nowise on the share taken by labor in its production, but solely on the demand for it in society. The economic problem of Socialism is the just distribution of the premium given to certain portions of the general product by the action of demand. As Individualist Anarchism not only fails to distribute these, but deliberately permits their private appropriation, Individualist Anarchism is the negation of Socialism, and is, in fact, Unsocialism carried as near to its logical completeness as any sane man dare carry it.

COMMUNIST ANARCHISM

[A]s we have seen, when the Individualist Anarchist proceeds to reduce his principle to practice, he is inevitably led to Mr. Tucker's program of "competition everywhere and always" among occupying owners, subject only to the moral law of minding their own business.

No sooner is this formulated than its effect on the distribution of wealth is examined by the economist, who finds no trouble in convicting it of privilege, monopoly, inequality, unjust indirect taxation, and everything that is most repugnant to Anarchism. But this startling reverse, however it may put the Anarchist out of conceit with his economic program, does not in the least reconcile him to State Socialism. It only changes his mind on one point. Whilst his economic program satisfied him, he was content to admit that State Socialism was the only possible alternative to Individualist Anarchism: nay, he rather insisted on it, because his dislike of the State Socialism alternative was a strong incentive to the acceptance of the other. But the moment it becomes apparent that neither of them can abolish rent, the disillusioned Individualist Anarchist seeks a *tertium quid,* or third system which shall collect and justly distribute the rent of the country, and yet prevent the collecting and distributing organ from acquiring the tyrannous powers of governments as we know them. There are two such systems at present before the world: Communism and Social-Democracy. Now there is no such thing as Anarchist Social-Democracy; but there is such a thing as Anarchist Communism or Communist Anarchism. . . . Most people will tell you that Communism is known in this country only as a visionary project advocated by a handful of amiable cranks. Then they will stroll off across the common bridge, along the common embankment, by the light of the common street lamp shining alike on the just and the unjust, up the common street, and into the common Trafalgar Square, where, on the smallest hint on their part that Communism is to be tolerated for an instant in a civilized country, they will be handily bludgeoned by the common policemen, and haled off to the common gaol. When you suggest to these people that the application of Communism to the bread supply is only an extension, involving no new principle, of its application to street lighting, they are bewildered. Instead of picturing the Communist man answering the knock of the Communal baker, and taking what bread he needs (the rate collector presenting the bill at the end of the half year), they imagine him bursting obstreperously into his neighbor's house and snatching the bread off his table on the "as much mine as yours" principle—which, however, has an equally sharp edge for the thief's throat in the form "as much yours as mine." In fact, the average Englishman is capable of understanding Communism only when it is explained as a state of things under which everything is paid for out of the taxes, and taxes are paid in labor. . . .

Now a Communist Anarchist may demur to such a definition of Communism as I have just given; for it is evident that if there must be rates and taxes, there must also be some authority to collect them. I submit, however, that if any article—bread, for instance—be communized, by which I mean that there shall be public daily house-to-house distributions of bread, sufficient to satisfy everybody, which all may share without question or payment, wheat must be grown, mills must grind, and bakers must sweat daily in order to keep up the supply. There is no more difficulty about such a distribution than about the present house-to-house collection of dust; but the first condition of solvency for the enterprise is that every consumer of the bread shall contribute to its support as much as the bread he consumes costs to produce. Communism or no Communism, he must pay, or else leave somebody else to pay for him. Communism will cheapen bread—will save the cost of scales and weights, coin, bookkeepers, counter-hands, policemen, paupers, and other expenses of private property; but it will not do away with the cost of the bread and its storage and distribution. Now supposing voluntary co-operation and public spirit prove equal to the task of elaborately organizing the farming, milling, and baking industries for the production of bread, how will the voluntary co-operators recover the cost of their operations from the consumers? If they are given powers to collect the cost from the public, and to enforce their demands by punishing or distraining non-payers, then they at once become a

State department levying a tax for public purposes; and the Communism of the bread supply becomes no more Anarchistic than our present Communistic supply of street lighting is Anarchistic. Unless the taxation is voluntary—unless the bread consumer is free to refuse payment without incurring any penalty save the reproaches of his conscience and his neighbors, the Anarchist ideal will remain unattained. Now the pressure of conscience and public opinion is by no means to be slighted. Millions of men and women, without any legal compulsion whatever, pay for the support of institutions of all sorts, from churches to tall hats, simply out of their need for standing well with their neighbors. But observe, this compulsion of public opinion derives most of its force from the difficulty of getting the wherewithal to buy bread without a reputation for respectability. Under Communism a man could snap his fingers at public opinion without starving for it. Besides, public opinion cannot for a moment be relied upon as a force which operates uniformly as a compulsion upon men to act righteously. Its operation is for all practical purposes quite arbitrary, and is as often unrighteous as righteous. It is just as hostile to the reformer as to the criminal. It hangs Anarchists and worships Nitrate Kings. It insists on a man wearing a tall hat and going to church, on his marrying the woman he lives with, and on his pretending to believe whatever the rest pretend to believe; and it enforces these ordinances in a sufficient majority of cases without help from the law: its tyranny, in fact, being so crushing that its little finger is often thicker than the law's loins. But there is no sincere public opinion that a man should work for his daily bread if he can get it for nothing. Indeed, it is just the other way: public opinion has been educated to regard the performance of daily manual labor as the lot of the despised classes. . . .

Kropotkin, too optimistically as I think, disposes of the average man by attributing his unsocialism to the pressure of the corrupt system under which he groans. Remove that pressure, and he will think rightly, says Kropotkin. But if the natural man be indeed social as well as gregarious, how did the corruption and oppression under which he groans ever arise? Could the institution of property as we know it ever have come into existence unless nearly every man had been, not merely willing, but openly and shamelessly eager to quarter himself idly on the labor of his fellows, and to domineer over them whenever the law enabled him to do so? Granted that he is not morally responsible for the iniquity of our present distribution of wealth; granted that if he had understood and foreseen the phenomenon of economic rent, he would never have allowed land and industrial capital to be privately appropriated; granted that the Socialist movement is a proof that now he sees the mischief he is seeking the remedy; granted that he voluntarily pays a good deal of Income Tax that he could evade if he chose; granted that if four-fifths of the population were habitually to do the utter worst in the way of selfishness that the present system invites them to do, society would not stand the strain for six weeks. So far we can claim to be better than our institutions. But the fact that we are too good for complete Unsocialism by no means proves that we are good enough for complete voluntary Communism. The practical question remains, How many men trained under our present system could be trusted to pay for their food scrupulously if they could take it for nothing with impunity? Clearly, if a very large proportion did not so pay, Anarchist Communism would go bankrupt.

The answer is that all the evils against which Anarchism is directed are caused by men already taking advantage of the institution of property to commit this very sin—consume their subsistence without working for it. What reason is there for doubting that many of them would attempt to take exactly the same advantage of Anarchist Communism? And what reason is there to doubt that the community, finding its bread store bankrupt, would instantly pitch its Anarchism to the four winds, and come down on the defaulters with the strong hand of a law to make them pay, just as they are now compelled to pay their Income Tax? I submit, then, to our Communist Anarchist friends that Communism requires either external compulsion to labor, or else a social morality which the evils of existing society shew that we have failed as yet to attain. I do not deny the possibility of the final attainment of that or any other degree of public conscience; but I contend that the path to it lies through a transition system which, instead of offering fresh opportunities to men of getting their living idly, will destroy those opportunities altogether, and wean us from the habit of regarding such an anomaly as possible, much less honorable.

It must not be supposed that the economic difficulties which I pointed out as fatal to Individualist Anarchism are entirely removed by Communism. . . . It would take an extraordinary course of demolition, reconstruction, and landscape gardening to make every dwelling house in London as desirable as a house in Park Lane, or facing Regent's Park, or overlooking the Embankment Gardens. And since everybody cannot be accommodated there, the exceptionally favored persons who occupy those sites will certainly be expected to render an equivalent for their privilege to those whom they exclude. Without this there would evidently be no true socialization of the habitation of London. This means, in practice, that a public department must let the houses out to the highest bidders, and collect the rents for public purposes. Such a department can hardly be called Anarchistic, however democratic it may be. I might go on to enlarge considerably on the limits to the practicability of direct Communism, which varies from commodity to commodity, but one difficulty, if insurmountable, is as conclusive as twenty.

It is sufficient for our present purpose to have shewn that Communism cannot be ideally Anarchistic, because it does not in the least do away with the necessity for *compelling* people to pay for what they consume; and even when the growth of social conscience removes that difficulty there will still remain the question of those commodities to which the simple Communist method of so-called "free distribution" is inapplicable.

One practical point more. Consider the difficulty of communizing any branch of distribution without first collectivizing it. For instance, we might easily communize the postal service by simply announcing that in future letters would be carried without stamps just as they now are with them, the cost being thrown entirely upon imperial taxation. But if the postal service were, like most of our distributive business, in the hands of thousands of competing private traders, no such change would be directly possible. Communism must grow out of Collectivism, not out of anarchic private enterprise. That is to say, it cannot grow directly out of the present system.

SOCIAL-DEMOCRACY VS. ANARCHY

If the majority believed in an angry and jealous god, then, State or no State, they would not permit an individual to offend that god and bring down his wrath upon them: they would rather stone and burn the individual in propitiation. They would not suffer the individual to go naked among them; and if he clothed himself in an unusual way, which struck them as being ridiculous or scandalous, they would laugh at him, refuse him admission to their feasts, object to be seen talking with him in the streets, and perhaps lock him up as a lunatic. They would not allow him to neglect sanitary precautions which they believed essential to their own immunity from zymotic disease. If the family were established among them as it is established among us, they would not suffer him to intermarry within certain degrees of kinship. Their demand would so rule the market that in most places he would find no commodities in the shops except those preferred by a majority of the customers; no schools except those conducted in accordance with the ideas of the majority of parents; no experienced doctors except those whose qualifications inspired confidence in a whole circle of patients. This is not "the coming slavery" of Social-Democracy: it is the slavery already come. What is more, there is nothing in the most elaborately negative practical program yet put forward by Anarchism that offers the slightest mitigation of it. That in comparison with ideal irresponsible absolute freedom it is slavery, cannot be denied. But in comparison with the slavery of Robinson Crusoe, which is the most Anarchistic alternative Nature, our task-mistress, allows us, it is pardonably described as liberty. Robinson Crusoe, in fact, is always willing to exchange his unlimited license and puny powers for the curtailed license and relatively immense powers of the "slave" of majorities. . . .

The majority cannot help its tyranny even if it would. The giant Winkelmeier must have found our doorways inconvenient, just as men of five feet or less find the slope of the floor in a theatre not sufficiently steep to enable them to see over the heads of those in front. But whilst the average height of a man is 5ft. 8in. there is no redress for such grievances. Builders will accommodate doors and floors to the majority, and not to the minority. For since either the majority or the minority must be incommoded, evidently the more powerful must have its way. There may be no indisputable reason why it ought, and any clever Tory can give excellent reasons why it ought not; but the fact remains that it will, whether it ought or not.

And this is what really settles the question as between democratic majorities and minorities. Where their interests conflict, the weaker side must go to the wall, because, as the evil involved is no greater than that of the stronger going to the wall, the majority is not restrained by any scruple from compelling the weaker to give way. . . .

In practice this does not involve either the absolute power of majorities or "the infallibility of the odd man." There are some matters in which the course preferred by the minority in no way obstructs that preferred by the majority. There are many more in which the obstruction is easier to bear than the cost of suppressing it. For it costs something to suppress even a minority of one. The commonest example of that minority is the lunatic with a delusion; yet it is found quite safe to entertain dozens of delusions, and be generally an extremely selfish and troublesome idiot, in spite of the power of majorities; for until you go so far that it clearly costs less to lock you up than to leave you at large, the majority will not take the trouble to set itself in action against you. Thus a minimum of individual liberty is secured, under any system, to the smallest minority.

It is true that as minorities grow, they sometimes, in forfeiting the protection of insignificance, lose more in immunity than they gain in numbers; so that probably the weakest minority is not the smallest, but rather that which is too large to be disregarded and too weak to be feared; but before and after that dangerous point is weathered, minorities wield considerable power. The notion that they are ciphers because the majority could vanquish them in a trial of strength leaves out of account the damage they could inflict on the victors during the struggle. Ordinarily an unarmed man weighing thirteen stone can beat one weighing only eleven; but there are very few emergencies in which it is worth his while to do it, because if the weaker man resists to the best of his ability (which is always possible) the victor will be considerably worse off after the fight than before it. In 1861 the Northern and Southern States of America fought, as prize-fighters say, "to a finish"; and the North carried its point, yet at such a heavy cost to itself that the Southern States have by no means been reduced to ciphers; for the victorious majority has ever since felt that it would be better to give way on any but the most vital issues than to provoke such another struggle. But it is not often that a peremptory question arises between a majority and minority of a whole nation. In most matters only a fragment of the nation has any interest one way or the other; and the same man who is in a majority on one question is in a minority on another, and so learns by experience that minorities have rights which must be attended to. Minorities, too, as in the case of the Irish Party in the English Parliament, occasionally hold the balance of power between majorities which recognize their rights and majorities which deny them. Further, much can be done by decentralization to limit the power of the majority of the whole nation to questions upon which a divided policy is impracticable.

In short, then, Democracy does not give majorities absolute power, nor does it enable them to reduce minorities to ciphers. Such limited power of coercing minorities as majorities must possess, is not given to them by Democracy any more than it can be taken away from them by Anarchism. A couple of men are stronger than one: that is all. There are only two ways of neutralizing this natural fact. One is to convince men of the wickedness of abusing the majority power, and then to make them virtuous enough to refrain from doing it on that account. The other is to realize Lytton's fancy of *vril* by inventing a means by which each individual will be able to destroy all his fellows with a flash of his own electricity, so that the majority may have as much reason to fear the individual as he to fear the majority. No method of doing either is to be found in Individualist or Communist Anarchism; consequently these systems, as far as the evils of majority tyranny are concerned, are no better than the Social-Democratic program of adult suffrage with maintenance of representatives, payment of polling expenses from public funds, &c. Faulty devices enough, no doubt, but capable of accomplishing all that is humanly possible at present to make the State representative of the nation; to make the administration trustworthy; and to secure the utmost power to each individual and consequently to minorities. What better can we have whilst collective action is inevitable? Indeed, in the mouths of the really able Anarchists, Anarchism means simply the utmost attainable thoroughness of Democracy. Kropotkin, for example, speaks of free development from the simple to the composite by "the free union of free groups"; and his illustrations are "the societies for study, for commerce, for pleasure and recreation," which have sprung up to meet the varied requirements of the individual of our age. But in every one of these societies there is government by a council elected annually by a majority of voters; so that Kropotkin is not at all afraid of the democratic machinery and the majority of power. Mr. Tucker speaks of "voluntary association," but gives no illustrations, and in-

deed avows that "Anarchists are simply unterrified Jeffersonian Democrats." . . .

Fortunately there is . . . a fine impartiality about the
policeman and the soldier, who are the cutting edge of the
State power. They take their wages and obey their orders
without asking questions. If those orders are to demolish the
homestead of every peasant who refuses to take the bread out
of his children's mouths in order that his landlord may have
money to spend as an idle gentleman in London, the soldier
obeys. But if his orders were to help the police to collect an
Income Tax (of not more than twenty shillings in the pound)
on unearned incomes, the soldier would do that with equal
devotion to duty, and perhaps with a certain private zest that
might be lacking in the other case. Now orders of this kind
come ultimately from the State: meaning, in this country,
the House of Commons. A House of Commons consisting of
660 gentlemen and 10 workers will order the soldier to take
money from the people for the landlords. A House of Commons consisting of 660 workers and 10 gentlemen, will probably, unless the 660 are fools, order the soldier to take money
from the landlords to buy the land for the people. With that
hint I leave the matter, in the full conviction that the State,
in spite of the Anarchists, will continue to be used against
the people by the classes until it is used by the people against
the classes with equal ability and equal resolution.

52   Equity and Interest

Frédéric Bastiat, a Frenchman, and Hugo Bilgram, an American, were nineteenth-century economists who were both certain that the financial programs proposed by Proudhon and his American disciples should not be adopted. But they reached this conclusion in very different ways. Bastiat was primarily concerned with establishing a *moral justification* for the very interest- and rent-practices that individualist anarchists wished to expunge from the economy. And to do so, he appealed to Proudhon's own principle of reciprocity.

Bilgram's major work was *Involuntary Idleness*, a book that was warmly praised by Benjamin Tucker for its treatment of problems that still plague economists. His was an entirely empirical approach, from which he argued that a Proudhonian bank could not realize its aims of equalizing income and shattering the sources of unearned wealth. Only a state-controlled financial system could be expected to attain goals of such magnitude. Bilgram's remarks are taken from two letters to Tucker's journal *Liberty*, where they were printed in February and April of 1890 along with detailed rejoinders by the editor.

I conceive that there is in a loan an actual exchange, an actual service rendered by the lender, and which makes the borrower liable to an equivalent service. . . . Now, if it is so, the perfect lawfulness of what is called house-rent, farm-rent, interest, will be explained and justified. Let us consider the case of *loan*.

Suppose two men exchange two services or two objects, whose equal value is beyond all dispute. Suppose, for example, Peter says to Paul, "Give me ten sixpieces, I will give you a five-shilling piece." We cannot imagine an equal value more unquestionable. . . . Thus it follows, that if one of the parties wishes to introduce into the bargain an additional clause, advantageous to himself, but unfavourable to the

---

Essays in Political Economy, by Frédéric Bastiat (New York: Putnam, 1874), pp. 15–18.

other party, he must agree to a second clause, which shall re-establish the equilibrium, and the law of justice. . . . This granted, we will suppose that Peter, after having said to Paul, "Give me ten sixpieces, I will give you a crown," adds, "You shall give me the ten sixpieces *now*, and I will give you the crown-piece *in a year;*" it is very evident that this new proposition alters the claims and advantages of the bargain; that it alters the proportion of the two services. Does it not appear plainly enough, in fact, that Peter asks of Paul a new and an additional service; one of a different kind? Is it not as if he had said, "Render me the service of allowing me to use for my profit, for a year, five shillings which belong to you, and which you might have used for yourself?" And what good reason have you to maintain that Paul is bound to render this especial service gratuitously; that he has no right to de-mand anything more in consequence of this requisition. . . . Is it not incomprehensible that the economist, who preaches such a doctrine to the people, can reconcile it with this prin-ciple of *the reciprocity of services?* . . .

Suppose, for example, a house and a vessel of a value so perfectly equal that their proprietors are disposed to ex-change them even-handed, without excess or abatement. . . . At the moment of each taking possession, the shipowner says to the citizen, "Very well; the transaction is completed, and nothing can prove its perfect equity better than our free and voluntary consent. Our conditions thus fixed, I shall propose to you a little practical modification. You shall let me have your house to-day, but I shall not put you in possession of my ship for a year; and the reason I make this demand of you is, that, during this year of *delay*, I wish to use the vessel." . . . I ask of every candid man, I ask of M. Proudhon himself, if the citizen has not a right to answer, "The new clause which you propose entirely alters the proportion or the equal value of the exchanged services. By it, I shall be deprived, for the space of a year, both at once of my house and of your vessel. By it, you will make use of both. If, in the absence of this clause, the bargain was just, for the same reason the clause is injurious to me. It stipulates for a loss to me, and a gain to you. You are requiring of me a new service; I have a right to refuse, or to require of you, as a compensation, an equivalent service." If the parties are agreed upon this compensation, the principle of which is incontestable, we can easily distin-guish two transactions in one, two exchanges of service in one. First, there is the exchange of the house for the vessel;

after this, there is the delay granted by one of the parties, and the compensation correspondent to this delay yielded by the other. These two new services take the generic and abstract names of *credit* and *interest*. But names do not change the nature of things; and I defy any one to dare to maintain that there exists here, when all is done, a service for a service, or a reciprocity of services. To say that one of these services does not challenge the other, to say that the first ought to be rendered gratuitously, without injustice, is to say that justice consists in one of the parties giving and not receiving, which is a contradiction in terms.

My studies have led me to the conviction that mutual banking cannot deprive capital of its power to bring unearned returns to its owner. . . .

The members of such banks must no doubt be in some way assessed to defray the expenses and losses incurred by the banking associations, and these assessments are virtually interest payable for the loan of mutual money. . . .

We must now assume that the assessments of the mutual banks are in substance equitably distributed among their members; otherwise, such banks cannot compete against others who have adopted the more equitable rules. . . . But other outlays, such as the making of the notes, together with all the attending expenses, must also be paid by the members of the mutual banks, and this increases the interest virtually payable by the borrowers beyond the rate of risk. Consequently competition will be incompetent to lower the current rate of interest to this desirable point. Money-lenders will therefore still be able to obtain an income from the mere loan of money, and capital will continue to return interest to the wealthy. The germ of the inequitable congestion of wealth will still linger after the introduction of mutual banking.

At this point the question arises as to who should pay for that part of the expenses of the financial system that relates to the production of the money tokens. The answer is not difficult when it is considered that the benefit of the medium of exchange accrues to those who use it. They should contribute, as near as possible, in the proportion in which their handling wears the tokens, for in the long run the cost of production will virtually resolve itself into the cost of replacement. Not the borrowers, then, who as members of the mutual banks would be obliged to do so, but the people at large, in whose hands the money circulates, are in equity un-

From two letters by Hugo Bilgram, printed in Benjamin R. Tucker, *Instead of a Book* (New York: Benjamin R. Tucker, 1893), pp. 265–68.

der the obligation of this expense. And to accomplish this I see no other way than for the people to instruct their representatives to make the notes at public expense, distribute them according to the demand, and charge no cost to the borrowers exceeding the rate of risk attached to the securities offered by them. . . .

The expenses of mutual banks may be divided into three categories,—i.e., risks, cost of making loans, and cost of making the tokens. These three items are represented in the interest payable by the patrons of such banks, and, while they determine the current rate of interest, those who lend money which they have acquired have to bear only two of these items, and will obtain interest composed of the three, and consequently receive pay for work they have not performed. And capital having the power of bringing an unearned income as long as money is thus blessed, I still hold that justice is not attained until the gross interest is reduced to the rate of risk and cost of making loans, the cost of making the tokens being defrayed by public contributions.

Should the question of free banking become a political issue, I should heartily cooperate with you in furthering the object. But this does not prevent me from advocating a government issue, provided the borrowers are charged no more than risk and cost of making the loans, as a preferable measure.

54　The Impossibilities of a Syndicalist Society

In section I, James A. Estey argued that syndicalism could not be considered a form of anarchism. Here we reprint his critique of the syndicalist movement, an impressive collection of historical fact, prediction, and analysis.

Estey devoted two extensive chapters of his *Revolutionary Syndicalism* to the evaluation of syndicalist methods and aims. In the first of these, he contended that the program of syndicalism had no chance of success. This contention he based upon a thorough examination of the *Confédération Générale du Travail*, an examination which revealed (a) that a majority of capitalists were moving toward "conciliation between Capital and Labor" by means of "legislation to remove the evils of the wage-system" and (b) that "at least one-half of the wage-earners are, in the normal course of events, passive if not active advocates of the methods of reform rather than revolution." And if this be true of France, Estey continued, then "surely it is also true of any other industrial country."

In his second critical chapter, almost all of which appears below, Estey focused on the projected syndicalist society. (*Anarchy* magazine should be consulted for discussions of the possibilities of syndicalism.)

A discussion of Syndicalism would not be complete without some critical consideration of the organisation of industrial society which would characterise any Syndicalist state. . . . To state the question in concrete terms, Revolutionary Syndicalism sets forth these two basic propositions: (1) that the syndicats or trade unions, when they have reached a certain stage of development, must take over and carry on, without any alien interference, all the process of production; (2) that the organisation of production must follow the federalistic lines exhibited in the French labour unions of today, suppressing the centralisation which crushes all initiative, and

Revolutionary Syndicalism, by J. A. Estey (London: P. S. King, 1913), pp. 181–98. Reprinted by permission of Marten S. Estey.

giving full play to that principle of autonomy whereby is ensured a system which is at once free, harmonious and efficient. These are the underlying principles of Syndicalism as an economic philosophy of the future. Upon them all discussion must take place. Will the trade unions actually be capable of carrying on the processes of production? Will harmony be assured and chaos averted by a system of economic federalism?

In the first place, can a trade unionism guarantee efficient production? Can it furnish to the members of a society, which it dominates, the goods necessary to a well-ordered and comfortable existence, and this at a reasonable cost? . . . Now, bodies of workers, whether organised as syndicats or not, have frequently, since the industrial revolution, undertaken to carry on without the interference of an employer some form of industry, organising themselves for this purpose into producers' co-operative associations. As independent societies, controlling in their own interests the whole of their product, completely free from the domination of "nonproducers," they have, more or less unconsciously, and in a limited fashion, put into practice what might be called constructive Syndicalism. For upon just such associations, elaborated and extended throughout the industry of a whole nation, Syndicalism builds all its constructive proposals. It is, then, both interesting and instructive, though of course not conclusive, to note the result of Syndicalist experience.

What has been the outcome of producers' co-operation? As is well known, while consumers' co-operation has met with a considerable degree of success, producers' co-operation seems to have succeeded only in exceptional cases. While here and there individual associations have carried on industry with moderate, sometimes with almost brilliant success, the disasters have been so frequent as to occasion wonder whether an industrial society could ever be founded upon the extension of such a system. The reasons for this failure have frequently been set forth, and are attested by students of every shade of economic opinion, Socialists and Syndicalists included. Undoubtedly the principal causes are to be found in (1) the lack of capital and equipment and (2) bad business management. . . . An even more vital cause of the failure of producers' co-operation lies in the incapacity, in certain matters, of the labourers themselves. Of the order and administration which are necessary for the success of an enterprise the working classes seem to have little conception.

Qualities of managership they constantly underestimate. Refusing in many cases to pay a wage sufficient to attract competent managers or to draw out latent directive abilities from among their own ranks, they have subjected their operations to a shiftless, incompetent direction which makes failure almost certain. If they do get a good manager, the more competent he is, the less do they seem willing to submit to his authority. Jealous of any inequality, chafing under the yoke of discipline, they have made the position of the foreman precarious and undesirable, not unfrequently censuring, after hours, when he ceases to exercise any authority, the acts he has committed in the workshop in his official capacity as director. Under such circumstances the man who does not hasten to resign can only sink into inefficiency. No enterprise can be carried to success under a manager subject to the will —the arbitrary, capricious will—of those whom he is supposed to manage.

The question now arises, will Syndicalism proper improve on these Syndicalist experiments? Has one a right to deduce the failure of Syndicalism from the failure of producers' co-operation? Evidently, between such enterprises and the proposed productive operations of Syndicalism there are certain notable differences. For one thing, constructive Syndicalism is not likely to fail for lack of capital, or of sufficient technical equipment. . . . At the same time, equipment is not everything, it is not even the essential thing. . . . In organising and directive power, in the brains necessary to carry on a business, not in the merely material aids to production, lies the only hope of workmen's co-operation; and if such abilities are lacking to-morrow as they seem to be lacking to-day, Syndicalism is doomed to failure. . . . In short, it is directive capacity which counts, and if Syndicalism succeeds, it will be because it is able, not only to call forth that capacity, but to give it the scope which it requires.

But both in calling forth capacity and in giving it scope, there is every reason to believe that Syndicalism is singularly deficient. There is nothing about trade union organisations which is peculiarly fitted to educate the labourers in handling modern industries. Trade unions may inculcate the principles of solidarity, they may be useful in gaining material reforms from the bourgeoisie, they may succeed in promoting workmen's insurance or technical education; but with all this they do not supply the quality which can make their members capable of carrying on independently the industries in which they are engaged. The direction of an industry involves an administrative mechanism and powers of controlling it, of which the labourers are ignorant, and with which they could only become familiar by actual experience. And that experience the syndicats cannot give them, and will not be able to give them, until industry is taken over through the social revolution. . . . If such be the case, it will go ill with a society accustomed to efficient productive management, compelled, suddenly, to submit to the awkward and destructive attempts of a labouring class, assuming for the first time, in many cases, the direction of industry. Before the somewhat tardy education could be completed, the productive mechanism of the country would be so disjointed as to endanger the very existence of the new social order.

Even if this difficulty were overcome, even if, in the stress of necessity, directive capacity were engendered where it had not existed before, there is the still graver danger lest in a Syndicalist state there should not be given to directive abilities that scope which, alone, would make them effective. The supreme defect of the labouring classes is their tendency to distrust directive ability. When productive co-operation fails, it is much more frequently because the manager has been mistrusted than that no manager of ability has been forthcoming. This defect, if anything, Syndicalism accentuates. In theory, Syndicalists love to dwell on the superior virtues of the minority as compared with the sheep-like stupidity of the majority. They have declared that in the syndicats there are comrades who, by their very competence, unconsciously assume command over the others, and whose authority, though moral only, is nevertheless very real. . . . This theory, unfortunately, is actually vitiated by another doctrine most vigorously preached wherever Syndicalism finds a hearing. The notion which has been most incessantly drummed into the minds of the wage-earners, which completely permeates their organisations, is, not that the masses should subordinate themselves to the capable few, but that all authority is to disappear, that in the syndicat every man is free and equal, as in the Federations each syndicat, and in the C.G.T. each Federation. Growing up in an atmosphere in which complete autonomy is a byword, the wage-earning classes inherit a spirit of insubordination which concerts ill with the attempts to enforce minority rule. . . . If the labourer does not distrust ability, he has learned to distrust authority; and when authority and ability are combined, as they must be in any efficient system of production, ability must suffer the consequences of the hatred of authority. . . .

Technical education may give a mechanical efficiency, freedom from restraint may give a vigor of productiveness, that will surpass anything the present system can show, but an insubordination which must discourage the appearance of directive abilities would have a destructive effect which no advantages could counterbalance. Nor if the mass of wage-earners determine to put in practice the libertarian principles preached by their leaders, if they insist on equality in the workshop, and some kind of control over their managers to express that equality, would there be, according to Syndicalist theory itself, any power capable of compelling them to be otherwise. They would be as free to accept or reject propositions made by their own or fellow organisations, as they are free now to accept or reject the recommendations of the C.G.T. It is one of the ironies of the history of Socialism that Syndicalism, by the propagation of one of its fundamental principles, should seriously endanger its own ultimate success. In the contempt of directive functions which their anarchistic doctrines engenders, Syndicalists tend to perpetuate the errors which have been so largely responsible for the failure of producers' co-operation.

The dangers arising from such a state of things seem particularly grave, when one comes to consider the large industries so typical of modern industrialism. It may happen that, just as the only successes of producers' co-operation have been, with few exceptions, in small industries, so Syndicalism may escape failure when practiced in small shops with a few dozen workmen, where the differentiation of function is not minute, where the absence of complicated details and the security of the market makes the question of management of comparatively slight importance. . . . But this fails to touch large-scale production. Industry may not be concentrating so rapidly as Marx predicted, but one must admit that combinations, trusts, large-scale industries in general, constitute the most characteristic feature of modern industrialism, and this in France as in other countries. It is in the management of railways, mines, steel works, textile industries, etc., that Syndicalism is put to the real test, the test from which it must emerge triumphant, if the future is to be within its power.

Now it is obvious that the difficulty of maintaining equality in a workshop or factory is enhanced according as the business grows larger, and that at a certain stage equality becomes absolutely incompatible with the growing necessity for efficient and more or less autocratic management. At that stage, in fact, either equality breaks down or the industry ceases to grow, or, what is more likely, begins to decay. To which of these alternatives industry in a Syndicalist State would tend, is patent. So long as industry remained characteristically Syndicalist, with no central authority to enforce obedience, but relying entirely either on the harmonious self-interest or the altruistic solidarity of the working class, there can be no question that such industries as were nascent would cease to grow, and that with the large-sized industries of modern society the labourers would be utterly unable to cope. . . . The complicated processes involved in the handling of a steel industry, a mine, or any large industrial concern—the purchase of raw material, the marketing of the product, the problems of capitalisation and accounting, the rewards to be apportioned to the thousand operations resulting from differentiation of process—call for a degree of authority on the one hand and of subordination on the other, which only some form of centralisation can secure. But with centralisation Syndicalism has nothing in common, and either Syndicalism will break down or progress will cease.

Once again it is instructive to turn to the experience of producers' co-operation, brought face to face with the problems of development. In the case of such enterprises as meet with success, particularly if they become of more than moderate size, it is of frequent occurrence that equality breaks down, and the direction is assumed by an authoritative body consisting very largely of the workers who originally began the business. As trade expands, and it becomes expedient to take into the firm more workers, the charter members only too readily form a close association, constituting themselves a body of employers and paying the newcomers wages only. A well-known example in France is that of the association of spectacle-makers (*lunetiers*), which in 1900 consisted of 65 associates, 60 adherents, and 1,300 wage-earning *employés*. Thus is the struggle of equality *versus* efficiency settled in favour of efficiency by a return to a modified form of capitalism, and a reintroduction of the very wage-system which such associations were formed to abolish. To this same tendency, Syndicalism would undoubtedly be exposed. Face to face with the necessity of carrying on industries in every stage of development and complication, the labourers would be compelled to work out some form of centralised direction. In every considerable factory authority would be assumed by the few. In every growing industry the original workers would tend to form a society excluding the newcomers. Not only capital but capitalism would reappear. The very lack of central authority would serve to facilitate the growth of an employing class, whose interests would be in opposition to those of their former fellow-labourers. In the autonomy afforded to every factory and every local body of wage-earners would be engendered the atmosphere favourable to the growth of petty economic despotisms. If the minority of the working-men, "the capable, the best, the élite," should assume the direction of industry, it would be by becoming employers, not by remaining workmen anxious to do well by their fellows. In the welter of modern industrialism, the republic of free and equal producers would be little more than the fiction which it is to-day. Equality could not long exist, and from its ruins would rise a modified form of capitalistic industry.

To such an unsocialistic outcome, considering the present and future development of industry, is doomed any form of Socialism which neglects the coercive and authoritative function; and it is just because it does not err in this respect that State Socialism offers a more reasonable guarantee of success. That authority and coercion could be carried by State Socialism to a degree not far removed from tyranny, and that such a development would be not only obnoxious in the extreme, but subversive of individual initiative and responsibility, it would be idle to deny. But State Socialism, despite the abuse which Syndicalists heap upon it, has this advantage over its rival, that it is compatible with some kind of central direction of industry, and permits the exaltation of the powers of direction, not to the exaggerated heights which they have reached to-day, but to an independent position safely above the paralysing interference of a mass of labourers, jealous of authority and discipline, and anxious to assert in practice the impossible dogma that all men are free and equal. Only by such means will Socialism be prevented from falling back into Capitalism. Only a Socialism which depends on some more reliable bond of union than the sentiment of solidarity among labourers, can evoke a regular, harmonious and efficient production, and ensure the disappearance of the wage-system, as it is now understood, beyond all recall.

The question of competition offers a similar difficulty. It is the hope of Syndicalists not only to produce efficiently, but to replace competition and avoid its attendant evils by the harmonious co-operation of bodies of workers, the prime aim of whose labour would be, not to acquire profits, but to satisfy in the most economic fashion the material needs of society. Instead of the unorganised squabble of competition there will be a careful and scientific division of product, to each syndicat or to each federation being assigned that proportion of production which is its share. Now it is a serious question whether the federalism by which this harmony is to be achieved does not run the greatest risk of degenerating into chaos. If the optimism of Syndicalists leads them to see in the spirit of solidarity and altruism every guarantee for the smooth and harmonious working of their industrial system, the most ordinary recognition of human weaknesses discovers that such guarantees are of all the most unstable, and apt completely to break down before the force of aroused self-interest. . . . Far from displaying an edifying spirit of solidarity, the workers of France, in the professedly Syndicalist congresses and organisations in general, have revealed dissensions as bitter as those to which the French Socialist parties have been subjected. Nor is there any reason to believe that a different state of affairs would exist in the Syndicalist State. The community of interest would be as lacking then as now. If the labouring-class to-day displays some solidarity, it is because it unites all its members against a common oppressor. But when the common oppressor has disappeared, when the capitalistic system no longer exists, and the labouring classes become a society of free and equal producers, one of the strongest motives towards union is withdrawn. When once the labourers have been released from the bonds which defence against Capital necessitates, they will tend, under the sway of self-interest, to form communities which, among themselves, will reproduce the rivalry of the capitalistic system.

It is, in short, a question whether competition would not rather be perpetuated than abolished. It is the experience of producers' co-operation that the rivalry between different associations of labourers in the same trade is frequently more intense, more bitter than that which dominates Capitalism. When the product of industry falls back into the hands of those who produce, when the return to labour depends not upon the will of an employer, but upon the volume of sales, it is almost inevitable that associations of labourers, far from being willing to limit their own production and thus their share in material wealth, should rather try to extend their business at the expense of other associations. . . . [C]ompetition is by no means a monopoly of capitalistic industry. It exists among wage-earners as well as among the bourgeoisie, and if it is perpetuated in producers' co-operation, it has an equal chance of life in the Syndicalist State.

In any case, however anxious the workers may be, as a result of their experience of its evils, to get rid of competition, the federalism which pervades their organisations is not equal to the task. If there is any lesson to be drawn from the experience of capitalistic industry, it is that competition can only be permanently averted by a union based on something more solid than the bonds of voluntary agreement. Nothing is more characteristic of modern industrial development than the movement whereby competition has given place to agreement, and rival businesses have to a greater or less degree sunk their individuality in some form of combination. Moreover in this essentially self-defensive process, one can notice a progression from merely voluntary agreements, such as pools, to associations in which the bond is material enough to afford some sort of control over constituent members, such associations as kartells, which are held together by a legally incorporated agency, or trusts, in which, as far as outside relations are concerned, the individual companies form a single corporative unity. For it seems that despite the advantages in escaping industrial rivalry, agreements depending on the voluntary consent of the parties concerned have so constantly been wrecked upon the rocks of self-interest, that producers, rather than fall back into the anarchy of competition, have been compelled to subject themselves to central control, with authority and coercion in its power. It has been seen that so soon as a producer finds more profit in breaking than in keeping the rules which have been laid down voluntary combinations fall to pieces. Such action may be short-sighted, but it is so constantly exhibited as to make it doubtful whether the mere desire to escape competition is sufficient to bring about its disappearance.

It is surely probable that what is true of producers to-day will be true of producers to-morrow. The voluntary association to which Syndicalism has committed itself, the federalism in economic matters which asserts the privilege of each body of workers to act as seems to it advisable, will make it well nigh impossible to prevent the competitive instinct from finding expression. If syndicats in the same industry discover that it is more to their taste to vie with each other in producing and selling their commodities, than to take their part in the harmony which their Federation is supposed to assure, there is absolutely no arrangement which can prevent them from doing so. That they are perfectly free to accept or reject the recommendations of any larger organisation to which they may belong, is the very essence of Syndicalist ideas on association. Under such circumstances it is extremely probable, if the experience, not only of capitalistic industry but of workmen's co-operation, be taken as a guide, that self-interest will prevail, and that competition will spasmodically arise to replace the harmony of federation. If the proletariat is to inherit the organised industry of the capitalist, it will be called upon to operate many industries where, especially between the larger establishments, competition is both brisk and bitter, and where among the labourers, no longer bound together in opposition to a common enemy, there would be a tendency to revert to those particularist sentiments which make most men ardent defenders of their own place of work. It will have to face also the problem of controlling the amalgamations, whereby rival concerns have contrived to avoid the evils of competition, and whose success depends peculiarly upon a management that is authoritative and centralised, and in every part opposed to the principles of Syndicalism. And in these situations, it is incumbent upon the proletariat to effect or maintain the disappearance of competition, and the establishment of a federalistic régime. The task is impossible. The inherited competition of the former class of industry would with difficulty be subdued by a system depending on the solidarity of the labourers, and the introduction of federalism as the organising principle of amalgamations would result only in weakening the bonds which hold them together, and in hurling them back into the competitive anarchy from which they had arisen. However keenly the labourers may recognise the evils of competition, there will arise so many opportunities for the satisfaction of local or particular interests, that only the voluntary submission of producers to a control which will forcibly keep them from yielding to otherwise irresistible temptations, can prevent Syndicalism from being swallowed up in a return of the individualism of to-day. Society might solve its difficulties by evolving some form of adequate control, it might prevent the recurrence of competition by suppressing the freedom and autonomy of local units, but in so doing it would have destroyed all that is characteristic of Syndicalism.

It is not only in the matter of competition that the federalistic arrangements of Syndicalism would be liable to break down. It is an assumption too little founded on probability that the system of exchange will be any more satisfactory. What will be the basis for the determination of price? . . . There must be prices for transportation as for any other service, prices which will be fixed by those who do the transporting; and it is at least equally probable that the prices so determined will be unsatisfactory to the users of railways as that they will be satisfactory. Particularly in an industry which tends to become a monopoly and is at the same time indispensable to the public, prices are liable to become too elevated for general acceptance. To-day there is a remedy at hand for consumers feeling themselves unduly exploited. More than one modern industrial nation has been compelled to recognise its duty to supervise the rates imposed by railways, and other forms of monopolised public utilities, and to limit the arbitrary power which such producers may assume of fixing prices where they will bring in the highest net profits. But Syndicalism is barred from the application of this remedy. If the Federations controlling transport chose to set up a scale of prices unsatisfactory to others, there is absolutely no machinery competent to restrain their self-interest, and hold them to a policy more in harmony with the needs of the general public. A refusal to follow the recommendations, say of the Committees of the C.G.T., would be quite in accordance with the most cherished principles of Syndicalist writers. If they object that the relations among the workers would be so harmonious that such examples of revolt would never arise, one can only reply that the assumption is too bold, and that the dissensions among the labouring classes to which every industrial nation can testify, would lead one to believe that the solidarity of labour is unequal to the task Syndicalists would impose upon it. For if solidarity is insufficient to-day, what would it be in the Syndicalist state, when the labourers are deprived of their most powerful bond of union—the common hatred of Capitalism?

That any future society, whatever the model on which it was built, could long allow the interests of the mass of consumers to be set at naught by the selfish action of particular bodies of workers seems hardly probable. But it is absolutely certain that the only steps which society could take to prevent this evil, would, like any action to prevent the recurrence of competition, be at the expense of the fundamental principles of Syndicalism. It is no paradox to declare that harmony can be achieved only through some measure of compulsion. But if a Syndicalist society allows, say, the Federal Committees of the C.G.T., or in local matters a *Bourse du travail*, to supplement their recommendations by compulsory measures to have them put into execution, it is well on the road towards a centralisation foreign to Syndicalism. To save society from chaos, the central body, intended originally only for purposes of administration, would rapidly usurp functions of authority and coercion, and though a certain leaven of federalism might be retained, and the powers of the central body be delegated much more than at present to local units, the anarchism of groups, which is so characteristic of a Syndicalism of which Proudhon is the forerunner, would inevitably disappear. In its place would be erected a central organisation, which, with its external will, would reproduce many of the features of the present-day State, and would in fact be, what in many ways is the very opposite of Syndicalism—State Socialism. If trade unions or any other purely labour organisations, excluding all non-producers, succeeded in accomplishing the work of production, it might be on a basis which would retain the semblance of Syndicalism, but it would be a Syndicalism which its exponents to-day would be the first to disown.

55 Law and Stability: The Unfeasibility of Pacifist Anarchism

Aylmer Maude was a close friend of Leo Tolstoy's, and perhaps his foremost translator and biographer. A Christian pacifist, he lived for three years in a Tolstoyan colony in Essex, England, and conducted the migration of the persecuted antimilitarist Doukhobors from the Caucasus to Canada in 1899. Unlike other critics of Tolstoy (see V. I. Lenin's *Tolstoy and His Time*), Maude presupposes neither the necessity of the class struggle nor the precept that ideas and principles are relative to their historical circumstances. The basis for his critique of Tolstoy lies in no continental ideology but in what we may term British common sense. He assumes that there are a number of diverse goods and obligations that all reasonable men would accept. Drawing on his experience with the "Tolstoy Colonies," he then argues that Tolstoy's teachings are both practically and theoretically incompatible with this set of values shared by reasonable men. (For some anarchist replies to this criticism, see selections 13, 14, 17, 19, 26, and 27.)

1

It was when the Colonies got to work that the real defects of Tolstóyism as a constructive policy became obvious. . . . To them civil and criminal law was an abomination. They had stepped out of the customary ruts of life to guide their lives solely by the dictates of reason and conscience. There was no longer any trade-custom or accepted routine to guide them, and when they turned to Tolstóy for help it appeared that his teaching did not supply what was needed. Such general indications as it contains furnish no sufficient guidance for the life of a community; and 'reason and conscience' are so differently developed in different people that, where there is neither fixed law and accepted custom nor a Moses wield-

"The Life of Tolstoy: Later Years," by Aylmer Maude in *The Works of Leo Tolstoy*, Vol. II, translated by Aylmer Maude (London: Oxford University Press, 1928), pp. 221–24. Reprinted by permission of the publisher.

ing a theocratic power, discussion and friction absorb much of the time and energy that should go into work. Misunderstandings arise, co-operation becomes more and more impossible, and people learn by sad experience how essential law and government are if any man is to know what he may expect of his fellows and what others may reasonably demand of him. The chief lesson taught by the failure of the Tolstóy Colonies is, that definiteness in our relations with our fellow men is essential to harmonious intercourse, and that the ultimate and chief reason for the existence and persistence of legal tribunals is not (as Tolstóy supposed) to enable the rich to exploit the poor, the cunning to prey on the simple, and lawyer-sharks to live on the community at large—but to supply men with the nearest approach we can get to impartial arbitration for the settlement of their disputes. If two men quarrel about the ownership of a field, the essential thing is, not that A should have it or that B should have it, but that the quarrel should be settled, and the field again become the undisputed possession of somebody, in order that use may be made of it and that both A and B may be free to get on with their business, without having to discuss points they are unable to agree upon. Remove the law, and induce men to believe that no fixed code or seat of judgement should exist, and the only people who will be able to get on at all decently will be those who, like the Russian pre-revolutionary peasantry, follow a traditional way of life, doing their work as their fathers and grandfathers did before them and always travelling in custom's deep-worn ruts. . . .

A great stumbling-block in the Tolstóy Colonies proved to be the law of Non-Resistance, which condemns all physical force used to prevent any one from doing what he likes. . . . Non-Resistance occasioned harm when a man or a community adopted it as a rigid rule and thereby deprived himself, or itself, of the power to check obvious wrongs in what was sometimes the only way they could be checked.

Without attempting a history of the Tolstóy Colonies, I may mention a few typical instances of the way in which they broke down.

The first occurred in the Schavéevski Colony in the Province of Smolénsk. The colonists adopted a neglected youngster and took him to live with them. He listened to their discussions, readings, and conversations, and learnt that no physical force should be used to any one, that it is wrong to possess property, and that no colonist should have anything to do with the police or the Law Courts. One morning the colonist who had special charge of the lad awoke and began to dress, but could not find his waistcoat until at last he discovered that the boy was wearing it. The colonist asked for the waistcoat, but the boy refused to give it up. The man explained how wrong it is to steal, but the boy could not see the point of the argument. If property is wrong, why was it any more wrong for a boy to have it than a man? The other colonists were gradually drawn into the dispute, and as it developed it became more and more apparent that the whole battery of Tolstóy's arguments concerning property and judging, as well as his insistence on condoning all offences, claiming no rights, and acknowledging only duties, were on the boy's side in the controversy. He was accusing no one: and was therefore able to assume a tone of moral superiority. He wanted the waistcoat as much as the man did. He was quite willing to discuss the subject; but it was impossible to alter his opinion that he was going to keep the waistcoat and that it was very wrong of any one to want to take it from him. That particular waistcoat might not have mattered, but the question at stake was, Whether any one might rely on retaining anything: a pen, a tool, or even a book he had begun to write? It was a question of principle going to the root of the possibility of efficiency and co-operation. The incident showed that the colonists did not know what they really approved or disapproved of. It further showed that in undermining the bases of Church and State, Tolstóy had unwittingly tunnelled much further, and endangered the very bases of any possible code or of any fixed agreement between man and man. If we accept all he has said as valid, any lunatic, drunkard, wayward child, or angry man, may block the traffic in Cheapside indefinitely, and it would not need many such people to plunge a whole community into chaos.

2

Tolstoy always meant to be entirely honest, but so strong was his bias that, as George Moore once said, he 'sacrifices truth to theory.' He values morality, but sacrifices morality for the sake of his theory. Stead once asked Tolstoy whether he would use force to prevent a drunken man kicking a child to death. Tolstoy, after reflection, wrote a reply saying that

Leo Tolstoy, by Aylmer Maude (New York: Dodd, Mead & Co., 1918), pp. 207–17. Reprinted by permission of the publisher.

not even in such a case should evil be resisted by force. But this decision outrages one's conscience. George Moore puts the case excellently as follows: 'If you were to say to Tolstoy, "I am willing to live in obedience to a moral standard; but which moral standard, for there are so many?" he would answer, "There is but one, and that one you will find in the Gospels." "But how do I know that the Gospels are true? You yourself are forced to make a selection of Christ's teaching." "My interpretation of Christ's teaching is a true one, for it is in agreement with the voice of conscience which you hear speaking within you." But no man's conscience tells him that he should not use force to prevent a drunkard from kicking a child to death!'

Tolstoy condemns all civil and criminal courts of justice; and their defects, in England as well as in Russia, are obvious enough to make the condemnation plausible. But experience shows wherein the great value of law lies. It may often fail to render justice, but at least it obliges men to face the light of publicity, and by the decision of an impartial third party it settles many a dispute which would otherwise continue indefinitely. Neither side can refuse to have its case examined; and even if the decision arrived at be sometimes unjust, it is still a decision. In reality an enormous number of cases are settled every day (without going to law at all) by simply ascertaining what the law is. Many agreements are concluded voluntarily, because the more cantankerous of the disputants is aware that by refusing a fair arrangement he cannot prevent some impartial settlement from being arrived at. In a word, the healthy root which enables juridical institutions to survive in spite of their many defects, is the fact that without them quarrels would be more frequent and harmony more difficult to attain than is now the case.

Someone has said of Sir Henry Maine that he 'never sacrificed the *complexity* of organic evolution to unity of conception and clearness of exposition. Whatever his failings, he undoubtedly possesses the merits of an Englishman in his search for *the meaning of life as it really is.*' Much of Tolstoy's work is on the contrary marked by an apparent obliviousness of the complexity of social problems. . . .

The question, 'Is war right or wrong?' evades the fact that the problems of real life are not simple, but complex. The choice is seldom between what is right and what is wrong; it is usually between a number of possible roads—a choice of evils, or of courses made up of good and evil intertwined. Would it, for instance, have been better for America to acquiesce in the disruption of the Union? Would it have been better to leave 4,000,000 slaves in captivity, whom Lincoln was afterwards able to release? Would it have been better for him to refuse the difficult and dangerous duty of steering the ship of State, when he alone commanded the confidence of his fellows sufficiently to save the country from still greater disasters?

My contention is that one has to weigh *the special circumstances of each case*, and cannot safely guide one's conduct by hard-and-fast rules which know nothing of the *circumstances or character of the people concerned*.

Surely the duty of man is not to do what he can't, but to do the best he can; and I believe that, by adopting abstract rules never to do this or that, never to use force, or money, or support a Government, or go to war, and by encumbering our consciences with line upon line and precept upon precept, we become less likely to behave reasonably and rightly than if we attended more to those *next steps*, the wisdom of which can be tested in daily life. . . .

The justification for using force to one's neighbour lies in the fact that there are circumstances under which (judging the matter with one's faculties at their best) one would oneself wish to be restrained by force. All that Tolstoy says holds good as against malevolent and vindictive force; but it breaks down as soon as we come to consider cases in which a man's motive for using force (or for using the law, or going to war) is a well-considered belief that it is, on the whole, the best course to pursue in the ultimate interest of the various people concerned. . . .

A firm of forgers of bank-notes or of bills of exchange should, on the Tolstoyan theory, neither be prosecuted, nor arrested, nor have their implements seized. He regards the problem as limited to the forger and the prosecutor, and as being decided by the prosecutor's willingness to forgive the man who asks to be let off. In reality such matters relate to the whole community; and if men followed Tolstoy's advice and refused to be policemen, judges, jurymen, witnesses, etc., human affairs would be thrown into inextricable confusion.

Sidney Hook, Professor of Philosophy at New York University, has
for three decades unrelentingly joined issue with the problems and
preceptors of political philosophy. In what follows, he lucidly ex-
pounds Karl Marx's critique of Max Stirner's libertarian egoism, a
critique which originally appeared in Part II of *The German Ideology*.
In Stirner's defense, let us note that Marx's appeal to class loyalty
would surely have been ridiculed by Stirner as a "wheel in the head."

THE EGO AS AN ABSTRACTION

Marx begins his criticism of Stirner by going to the roots of
Stirner's philosophy. That philosophy, he claims, is as idealistic as the philosophy of the "ghostly dualists" whom Stirner
had attacked. Stirner had merely rejected their specific ideals
such as the quest for God, freedom, immortality and humanity. But he had retained their method—a method which disregarded the temporal and social locus of ideals and which
sought to find one absolute ideal as the outcome of abstract
logical or psychological analysis. What had Stirner actually
done? He had replaced the abstractions of religion and speculative philosophy—God and Man—with an even more monstrous abstraction, the ego. After all, why were the ideals of
patriotism, church, family, rejected by Stirner as empty abstractions? Because they were an inverted and disguised expression of certain objective social relations. They pretended
to be something they were not. Men could not literally live
for God or country. But is it any different, Marx asks, with
the ego? Is a life in the interests of the ego any more valid?
What is the self? Is it not an abstraction from a whole complex of social relationships, of selves in relation? Strip a man
of his social dependencies. Do we find his ego to be a fleshy
cushion into which his friendships, his vocation, his love, his

From Hegel to Marx, by Sidney Hook (Ann Arbor: University of
Michigan Press, 1962), pp. 176–85. Reprinted by permission of the
author.

political relationships are stuck like so many pins? Or is it not truer to say that if a man is so stripped, he is destroyed—at least his uniqueness is destroyed. . . . Different social systems will give us different personalities and a different ideal of personality. The very attempt to understand personality involves, if not a reduction of the peculiar and unique to the general social framework of tradition, at least an attempt to discover its significance in the light of such reference. To worship the "pure ego" is to worship something which never was or can be.

STIRNER'S SUBJECTIVISM

Stirner was not content with asserting an ethical subjectivism. His abstract conception of the self as a condition of social life, instead of as a result of social life, leads him to epistemological subjectivism as well. From the proposition: 'nothing is good or bad, but thinking makes it so' he goes on to derive the proposition that 'nothing exists but thinking makes it so.' Having proved that the ideas of state, emperor, country, etc., do not correspond to what they claim to represent, that they are devoid of all supernatural sanctions, that they involve a slave-conception of the self—having proved all this —Stirner stops short. As if he had thereby deprived the institutional equivalents of these ideas of their power! The state does not cease being an enemy—a force to be reckoned with —after it has been pointed out that if there were no subjects there would be no state. . . . I am not through with the state when I understand that state piety has been artificially induced in me by education. It still remains a power which recognises me even if I do not recognise it.

Marx's point here can be driven home by citing an amusing incident from the life of Edgar Bauer who shared Stirner's subjectivism but not his egoism. Edgar Bauer had been brought before the Prussian courts for denouncing the Prussian State. After sentence had been pronounced, he was asked if he had anything to say. He calmly replied that the decision was logically null and void. The existence of the state implied the existence of subjects. The state had no jurisdiction on any but its own subjects. But he, Edgar Bauer, refused to recognise the state. It had no validity for him. It therefore did not exist for him. The dialectic was perfect but what it did not prove was that the state had no power over him. The iron bars and stone walls of his cells were proof of that power. It was rumoured, however, that Bauer convinced himself on the basis of his solipsism that this was a mistake, and that the prison—cells, bars, and all—had been posited by his deeper Self-consciousness.

Stirner's philosophical weakness, Marx claimed, derived from the fact that he, too, thought that a dialectical sentence of coventry upon the state would conjure its power away. To refuse to admit the sovereignty of the state as Stirner and his anarchistic followers did, is futile unless this is the beginning of a concrete struggle against the state institutions. But Stirner and those who share his ideas cannot effectively struggle against the state because they do not realise what the real source of its corporate abstractions is. "Stirner forgets that he has only destroyed the fantastic and ghostly form which the notion of 'fatherland,' etc., assumes in the skull of 'the adolescent' (*Junglings*) but that he has not even touched upon these ideas in so far as they express real relations" (*Gesamtausgabe*, I, 5, 107). Those real relations are to be found in the economic, socio-historical foundations of the age.

EGOISTIC ANARCHISM AS SELF-DEFEATING

Marx never lost an opportunity to attack the fundamental premise of all varieties of anarchism, viz., the abstract conception of the self and human freedom which made it impossible for the consistent anarchist to accept the principles of organisation and authority. The trouble with Stirner, the most noteworthy of them all, was that he drew an easy but oversharp dichotomy between the I and the external world. . . . His *I* corresponds to nothing empirically real in social intercourse but is a pure conceptual product of two philosophical categories—disembodied idealism and naïve, gross materialism. As a matter of fact no individual begins his career by feeling himself in opposition to his environment. He only distinguished himself from it comparatively late in life. Self-consciousness is the last mental trait to be acquired. The opposition therefore between the claims of the self and the claims of others is always specific, conditioned by certain historical and psychological factors. Although it is the source of all moral rules, it is not itself a morality. Neither love your neighbour nor love yourself can serve as an intelligent maxim. For it is clear that sometimes we do not love our neighbours for the sake of our neighbour's neighbours, and sometimes in loving oneself we may be serving others, to wit, our family or class.

"The Communists," says Marx, "do not preach morality. That is what Stirner is doing. They do not desire to
turn the 'private individual' into a professional 'for-love-
sacrificing creature.' . . . But they alone have discovered
that what have been called 'general interests' in the
whole course of history have really been the extension
of the 'private interests' of particular men. . . . The opposition between these two forms of interest is only apparent, for the general is continually being produced
from the other, the private interest. General interests do
not represent an independent power with an independent history. The apparent opposition between them is
always being produced and destroyed. We are not here
confronted with an Hegelian 'negative unity' of the two
sides of an opposition but by a materially conditioned
destruction of a previously existing form of the individual."
(*Gesamtausgabe*, I, 5, 227–8).

Marx's position may be clarified by an illustration familiar
to all trade union organisers and a commonplace problem already in Marx's time. Suppose an individual refuses to join a
trade union organisation on the ground that his freedom to
produce, to take advantage of his monopoly of skill, would
be lost. The general interest of the group of workers conflicts
with the private interest of the individual in question. The
individual as he finds himself at any definite moment can
choose to throw in his lot with his fellow-workers at an immediate material loss or run the risk of even a greater loss
and restriction of freedom which comes from the absence of
union organisation. The question, however, is not only one
of material interests. It is that, and something more. Every
individual regards certain values of loyalty, sympathy, co-
operation, as goods, too. They are part of that structure of values which defines the self. By throwing in his lot with his fellow-workers his whole personality is fulfilled in a way which
would be impossible if he were to stand aside and alone.
The general interest of the group demands a temporary sacrifice of the pecuniary interests of the individual to the end
that the very character of the individual be so transformed
that this pecuniary sacrifice appear as natural and uncom-
pelled. When he identifies himself with the group, then the
group will more naturally regard and effectively protect his
individual differences than he himself can. The absence of

group support, in time, deprives the individual of an opportunity to capitalise his specific abilities, since in an open competitive market their value tends to sink. His private interest, which includes the non-economic as well as the economic, lies with the group, unless he is prepared to play a lone hand against all. The conflict of interests, here, is real and whatever harmony is achieved involves genuine sacrifice. But the common activity which harmony between fellow-workers makes possible tends to create the institutional guarantees and mechanisms by which the advantages of the specific capacities of all may be made available for all.

THE PETTY-BOURGEOIS ROOTS OF ANARCHISM

The hidden strength of Stirner's argument lay in its peculiar natural law doctrine. The Hobbesian morality is an instrument to enable the individual to get and keep what is his own. Giving each man his own is, in a way, Stirner's definition of justice. But what is a man's own? A man's own is his *Eigenthum*—his property, any object of his desire. In preaching a moral philosophy upon the basis of egoism, Stirner is really coming to the defence of the petty-bourgeois proprietor who sees what he produces, interprets the whole process of production on the basis of its local character, and regards both the development of large industry and the organisation of workmen as a conspiracy to deprive him of the legitimate fruits of his labour. Despite its Bohemian flavour, Stirner's thought reveals that painstaking and touchy sensitiveness to what belongs solely and exclusively to the individual which is generally associated with the peasant proprietor or shopkeeper. Says Marx, "He offers us an additional proof of how the most trivial sentiments of the petty-bourgeois can borrow the wings of a high flown ideology," (*Gesamtausgabe*, I, 5, 236).

The two key concepts of Stirner's which Marx selects for analysis are the allied terms—"one's own" and "one's interest." Marx has no difficulty in showing that one's own is a highly artificial abstraction from communal effort and production. No man working together with others, dependent upon the funded store of social knowledge and material can make a claim for what is exclusively his own. Even when working alone he finds that much more than his own "unaided" efforts have gone into the production of the specific goods he creates, e.g., the techniques, traditions, language, and science without which he could do nothing. Marx is not interested in denying that there are certain principles of individual desert which should be applied in certain historical periods to the varying capacities and achievements of individual men. But his primary purpose is to show that the nature of the social productive process is such that it makes the absolute slogan "each is to receive the full product of his toil" inapplicable. Whatever is produced is a collective product. It is only the collectivity of labour, as Marx later showed in *Capital*, which can claim exclusive right to what is produced.

Marx's criticism of Stirner's concept of self-interest, even though it is left undeveloped, is even more profound. He quite properly traces Stirner's use of the term to an uncritical acceptance of Bentham's psychology. For Bentham, interests are psychologically invariable. The motives to human conduct can be sought in these fixed and inflexible interests. They are part of the psycho-physical organism. In appealing to them, Stirner seems to be preserving the appearance of naturalism and yet applying unchangeable criteria of the good and bad. Marx denies that interests are the primary subjects of psychological study. They are socially conditioned, not psychologically primitive. They cannot be discovered merely by studying minds or bodies, immediate desires or thought. These are all mediated by a highly complex social environment which gives a definite cast to man's psychological drives. . . .

Stirner can no longer argue from the universality of the interest of self-preservation to any specific mode of selfish social behaviour. The interests of self-preservation determine, perhaps, the great susceptibility of the human being to the social stimuli and habits which he naturally acquires. But in any case the explanation of the specific interests for which men struggle must be sought not in their minds and hearts but in the society and classes in which they live.

D. H. Monro's *Godwin's Moral Philosophy* is a model of philosophical interpretation and criticism. In the selections from this book reprinted here, Monro, a contemporary Australian philosopher, has three aims: first, "to show that the usual criticism of Godwin is much too facile"; second, to reconstruct Godwin's views in a way that reveals their clear relevance to such problems in moral philosophy as whether there is a rational basis for moral judgments; and last, to indicate the real difficulties in Godwin's position, as reconstructed.

Monro's discussion has implications for anarchism that are not limited to Godwin's doctrines. One of these concerns the common complaint that anarchists operate with an overly optimistic model of human nature. Monro sets forth an ingenious and perceptive interpretation of Godwin's belief in man's natural goodness and rationality. From this interpretation it emerges that libertarian views of man cannot be written off as simple-minded empirical falsehoods and that anarchist philosophers have presented ways of analyzing and guiding moral thought that still repay close scrutiny.

Put in its briefest form, the most common objection is that Godwin was absurdly optimistic about human nature. When we consider the way in which human beings actually behave, it seems absurd to suggest that they are 'naturally good'. . . . It is fashionable at the present moment to reject the whole concept of natural goodness and to revert to the earlier doctrine of original sin. The reason usually given is that Godwin and his contemporaries have been refuted by history. In the eighteenth and nineteenth centuries, it is said, men could easily believe in the inevitable march of progress. The growth of science, of industry, and of education had opened up new possibilities of material comfort and mental enlightenment:

Godwin's Moral Philosophy, by D. H. Monro (Oxford: The Clarendon Press, 1953), pp. 172–202. Reprinted by permission of the publisher.

it was natural to suppose that these would be accompanied by a moral revolution as well. But we can no longer believe this. For men do today live in tolerable comfort, and they do know a good deal about their physical environment; but they do not treat each other better. On the contrary, the twentieth century has shown us new abysses of cruelty and evil.

Now nothing in all this really touches Godwin. No doubt he was influenced, in a general way, by the prevailing belief that man was on the march; he does put his proposals for human betterment in the form of a prophecy. And he did think that machinery could, if wisely used, help to make a golden age possible. But he certainly did not think that it was being wisely used in his own time, nor would he think that it has been wisely used since. . . . If Godwin were restored to life today, he might well regard the history of the twentieth century as confirming his central thesis, not as refuting it. The causes of prejudice were, he insisted, the complexity of civilization and the power of centralized authority. Civilization has become more complex and authority more powerful; it is not at all surprising that there have been new forms of evil. . . .

It is surely odd to regard *Political Justice* as the work of a man who looks upon the world and finds it good. 'The history of mankind', he wrote in that book, 'is little else than a record of crimes. . . . Though the evils that arise to us from the structure of the material universe are neither trivial nor few, yet the history of political society sufficiently shows that man is of all other beings the most formidable enemy to man.' . . .

Godwin had a very real, and possibly morbid, sense of the extent of man's inhumanity to man. His theory of natural goodness cannot be refuted by pointing to any number of instances of human cruelty, however bestial. Godwin had considered them all, only too thoroughly: and in saying that man is naturally good, he does not mean that man does not act evilly.

But perhaps this only opens the way to a more profound criticism. If the theory of natural goodness cannot be refuted by any appeal to the facts, by looking at man and seeing how he does actually behave, isn't it unverifiable and therefore meaningless? I have much more sympathy with this objection. But we must notice that it applies also to the opposing theory, about original sin. For this will not be refuted, either, by pointing to any number of instances of benevolence and heroism. To call man 'naturally' good or 'naturally' evil is indeed to say very little. The truth is that he sometimes behaves well and sometimes badly. The history of our own century, or of any other, will not really take us very far beyond that conclusion.

But of course this is not all that can be said. For Godwin's belief in natural goodness has nothing to do with the extent or the frequency of evil: it is a hypothesis about its causes. More accurately, it is the hypothesis that it has causes, and that we ought to look for them. To talk about original sin is to give up the search for the causes of sin. It is as if we were to say: 'Disease is a natural phenomenon', and turn our backs on medicine. Of course disease is a natural phenomenon; but that does not alter the fact that any given disease has an assignable cause, and that if we can find the cause we may be able to cure it. You do not in the least refute that assertion by pointing to the vast extent of disease, or even by showing that the modern advances that have enabled us to cure some diseases have caused others to multiply. Godwin is making the same assertion about human wickedness. In general, no doubt, it is always with us, like disease; but any particular piece of wickedness, like any particular disease, has specific causes, usually social ones; and it may be possible to remove them. That the causes are far-reaching and difficult to remove, Godwin did not deny.

Of course natural goodness, as a hypothesis, is quite unverifiable. You cannot refute it by pointing to an evil whose cause cannot be discovered and removed, any more than you can refute the more general hypothesis, of which this is little more than an application, that every event has a cause. But, though unverifiable, neither is meaningless, for both point the way to a method of procedure. It cannot be said that that method of procedure, as applied to evil, is a fruitless one, or that it has been tried and found wanting. Godwin has every right to retort, like the defenders of Christianity, that it has not been tried at all. . . .

One obstacle in the way of assessing Godwin fairly today is that he uses concepts and categories that we have discarded. His moral philosophy is put in terms of a faculty psychology which leads him to hypostatize 'Reason' and to ask whether men are motivated by 'Universal Benevolence'. We do not feel that we can either agree or disagree. Our first question is: what does this really mean? We cannot begin to discuss his philosophy until we have translated it into our own idiom.

I am going to begin, then, by summarizing what I take to be Godwin's basic beliefs. The danger in this procedure is that it gives us not so much Godwin as a twentieth-century gloss on Godwin. With this reservation I think we can say that Godwin's basic beliefs are three: one about ethics, one about logic, and one about social psychology. They are:

1   To be virtuous is to feel the right emotions. The right emotions are those that men do feel when they see all the facts clearly. When we analyse these emotions, we find that they are all consistent with the greatest happiness principle and the principle of impartiality.

2   True knowledge is of particulars, and all generalizations are, if not false, at least seriously misleading.

3   The generalizations men believe depend on the political institutions they live under. . . .

The conclusions that follow from these three basic beliefs are:

1   If we want to improve human beings, we must help them to see things, and particularly each other, as they are.

2   This can be done: (a) by simplifying society, (b) by sweeping away social categories, like rank, and the legal categories that depend on punishment, (c) by encouraging individual judgement, so that men will no longer trust to rules of thumb.

Now let us see what can be said about these beliefs.

1   I have condensed Godwin's ethics to three propositions; and each of these is, to say the least, highly doubtful.

We have already seen that Godwin is in doubt whether to say that virtue consists in feeling the right emotions or in seeing which emotions are the right ones. Is virtue, that is to say, 'the desire to promote the happiness of all intelligent beings' or the conviction that the happiness of all intelligent beings is desirable? It is because Godwin does not make this distinction that he is able to say that men's voluntary actions originate in their opinions (i.e. their opinions about what is desirable); whereas all he is entitled to say is that they originate in their desires. To say 'X is good' no doubt is to say 'X is desirable'; but that is not to say 'X is desired'.

Now this strikes at the heart of Godwin's system. For, if it is possible to be convinced that X is desirable without desiring X, it follows that more may be needed to reform men's conduct than an appeal to reason. And this is of course what Godwin's critics have always said.

Godwin's reply is that no one is fully convinced that X is

desirable unless he is fully seized of the facts on which that conclusion is based. This is the way that the spectator, in Hume's illustration, becomes convinced that the rescue of the shipwrecked sailors is desirable. To grasp all that is involved in their suffering is both to think that their rescue is desirable and to desire it. The two are hardly separable. The only reason we commonly suppose that it is possible to think X desirable without desiring X is that by 'thinking X desirable' we usually mean something less than a full conviction, based on an intimate knowledge of all the facts: we mean a rule of thumb.

Godwin, in short, escapes from the objections we have raised to the first of these three propositions by falling back on the second. To be virtuous is to feel the emotions that men do feel when they know all the facts. But even if we grant that thinking (or feeling) X desirable is not, under these circumstances, really different from desiring X, there is still a clear distinction between our knowledge of the facts and the emotions that arise from that knowledge. Because the knowledge is true knowledge it does not follow that the emotions are 'right'. To suppose that they are is a pure hypothesis. It may be a reasonable hypothesis; but it needs to be verified.

The truth is, however, that it cannot be verified. For if anyone produces an instance of a man who is fully seized of all the relevant facts and still does not feel the right emotions, the reply will simply be: 'But in that case he cannot really understand all the relevant facts.' If the ship in our illustration is sunk by an enemy aeroplane, and the pilot watches all the scenes that Hume describes with callous delight, Godwin will certainly say: 'Ah, but he is blinded by prejudice; he does not really understand what he sees.' Now there are good reasons for saying this: we know, as a matter of experience, that people who do behave in this way in wartime view the same scenes quite differently in times of peace. Nevertheless, it may be said that there is no sure way of knowing whether anyone 'knows the full facts' or not. Feeling 'the right emotions' is taken as proof of knowing them; and, conversely, not feeling them is taken as proof of prejudice.

Much the same may be said of our third proposition, about the greatest happiness principle. I do not think that Godwin seriously attempts to prove this: he simply assumes it. Later the opponents of utilitarianism attempted to disprove it by finding negative instances: actions which we agree to call right, but which do not make for the greatest happiness of the greatest number. The favourite ones are promise-keeping, and family obligations. The utilitarian usually denies that these are negative instances; and he can make out a fair case. But if this defence fails, it is always open to him to say that these actions are not right after all, and that we are mistaken in supposing that they are. Godwin does actually take this line both about family obligations ('the famous fire cause') and about promise-keeping. And this means of course that the greatest happiness principle can never be disproved.

It is, then, not unfair to say that the whole of Godwin's moral philosophy is a mere tissue of assumptions. His basic hypotheses are not merely unverified, but intrinsically unverifiable. What he is really saying is that, if we could see things as they are, we would not only feel convinced that universal benevolence is desirable, but would also all feel benevolent to all men. This is the dogma of natural goodness. Since he also admits that it is ultimately impossible to see things as they are, this hypothesis must remain untested. Those who say that it has been disproved by the facts are quite wrong. The truth is that it could not be disproved by any facts. But that may well be a much more damning criticism.

At the same time, there is something to be said in Godwin's defence. Modern writers on ethics have been puzzled to explain in what sense ethical propositions can be supported by reasons. It is indeed demonstrable that they cannot be. You cannot argue from what is to what ought to be. At least these basic assumptions, then cannot be supported by any reasons. Nevertheless, we do find ourselves adducing facts in support of our moral convictions, and we do find that we can sometimes change the convictions of our friends by advancing these reasons.

The conclusion is sometimes drawn that the connexion between X *is* and Y *ought to be* is not a logical but a psychological one. That is to say, it is a fact that you can make human beings think Y *ought to be* by convincing them that X *is*; but the truth of X *is* does not guarantee the truth of Y *ought to be*. Either ethical propositions are not capable of being true or false, or, if they are, we can never have good reasons for supposing that they are.

Now one way of avoiding these conclusions is to take it for granted that Y *ought to be* is true if we do find ourselves believing it when we believe that X *is*, and if X *is* is true.

But this may take us further than we want to go. For sometimes we want to say that men are wrong in the moral inferences they draw. For example, Godwin thought that men were wrong in supposing that, if anyone has committed a crime, then he ought to be punished. But he would hardly deny that men do think in this way. We want, in short, to say that the reasons brought in support of moral propositions may be good or bad reasons. What is the criterion of a bad reason? I think Godwin would say that the proof that 'If A has committed a crime, he ought to be punished' is false is that we do not continue to hold it if we know further facts about the committing of crimes, the facts which the determinist alleges, and which Godwin accepted. A bad reason, then, is one that does not continue to be effective when we know all the facts; and a good one is one that does.

Now this means that we must assume two things. We must assume that, if men knew all the facts, they would draw the same moral conclusions from them. If, as Godwin believed, to know all is to pardon all, then A's not pardoning all is proof that he does not know all. We must dismiss the possibility that A can know all and pardon all and B know all and not pardon all. Secondly, if it is true that to know all is to pardon all, we must assume that it is right to pardon all. We must not say that this merely proves that human beings are at bottom sentimental.

These two assumptions are the doctrines that human beings are reasonable and that they are 'naturally good'. There are grave difficulties in the way of accepting either of them. But at least it can be said that, if we do accept them, we can go on supposing that there are good reasons for believing moral propositions. At any rate this seems to be as tenable as any of the alternative explanations of how this is possible.

2 True knowledge is of particulars, and generalizations are, if not false, at least misleading.

Godwin was not a logician or an epistemologist, and it is perhaps misleading to put the second of his basic beliefs in this form. He applies it chiefly to human beings; and it might be fairer to say that he believed in the uniqueness of every human being, and every human action. That is the basis of his objection to law. No one action is quite like another: no two murders, for example, are committed from quite the same motives; human motives, indeed, are almost infinitely complex. . . . And the result is, he suggests, that the law loses its one advantage, certainty. . . .

Now whatever may be thought about this criticism of law,

there is a good deal to be said in support of the principle that human beings are unique. It is certainly easier to defend than the generalization about generalizations. And, it may be asked, if this was what Godwin chiefly meant, why saddle him with the much more vulnerable opinion?

The answer is that for Godwin there is a general problem of error. 'Man, considered in himself, is merely a being capable of impression, a recipient of sensations.' But how, then, does he come to make mistakes? The camera cannot lie. Godwin does not raise this question specifically, but I think his answer is implicit in what he says about abstraction. . . . 'the human mind is perhaps incapable of entertaining any but general ideas. Take, for example, a wine-glass. If, after this glass is withdrawn, I present to you another from the same set, you will probably be unable to determine whether it is another or the same. . . . It is impossible to individualize our remarks as to cause our ideas to be truly particular, and not special.' And, significantly, he concludes from this that there are no 'perfect ideas'. . . . Generalization, then, is at once the source of knowledge and of error. Without it we could not organize our perceptions; but without it, we could not commit the follies that we do commit. . . .

It would take us too far afield to criticize this position in detail; and in any case we would be treading well-worn ground. But it may be noticed that this position is not quite consistent with what Godwin says about the power of reason. The classic rationalist position is that reason enables us to penetrate beyond the deceitful appearances of things, as revealed in sensation, to their hidden essences. It is because reason deals with this underlying reality that it cannot lead us astray. It is hard to maintain this conclusion if you say that reason deals with general ideas which are necessarily imperfect approximations to the particulars which are alone real. . . .

3   The generalizations men believe depend on the political institutions they live under.

I have interpreted this as an anticipation of the modern anthropologist's belief in the all-pervading influence of 'the culture pattern'. . . . Something must, however, be said about Godwin's application of the theory and the conclusions he draws from it. For there are two important differences between Godwin and the modern anthropologists. He says that 'Government' is the cause of our beliefs: they say 'the culture', or society. Further, he thinks of these beliefs as distorting glasses, which we can and should discard; without government we will see things as they are. They would say that 'culture' can never be discarded.

The two differences are connected. For Godwin wants to discard government, but not society. He is inclined to say that the choice is between seeing the facts in all their naked individuality, and seeing them through the distorting medium of political ideologies. But, just as 'the human mind is incapable of entertaining any but general ideas', so it is impossible to look at the facts except in the light of some ideology. Godwin's ideal society engenders a very definite set of beliefs: in equality, in the iniquity of property, in the injustice of punishment, and so on. These beliefs colour our judgement of men's actions and characters just as the beliefs in honour or in virtue colour them. But the beliefs of his ideal society, Godwin would say, are true. The opposition is not really between beliefs engendered by social institutions, which are necessarily false, and the beliefs that arise without social institutions which are necessarily true; it is between true beliefs and false beliefs, each of which may be engendered by social institutions. And this means that we cannot simply assume that the beliefs that arise in the anarchic society are true: we must prove this independently.

This criticism is, in one way, not very damaging to Godwin. For he is not really a primitivist; and of course he does not deny that it is possible to arrive at true beliefs in spite of the effect of social prejudice. It is indeed an essential part of his position that men are bound to glimpse at least some part of the truth in spite of prejudice. But this means, of course, that men's beliefs do not depend entirely on the political institutions they live under. In this he differs from at least some modern anthropologists, who are inclined to say that value judgements (in Godwin's language, 'opinions about what is desirable') are entirely 'a function of the culture', and that the question is not whether they are true or false, but whether they are appropriate to a given society; so that it is impossible to judge between the beliefs of two different societies. There are grave objections to this position, and it is hardly a fault in Godwin that he did not hold it.

It may be argued, however, that he ought to have held it; for it does follow from some of his basic assumptions. If opinions about what is desirable arise, as Hartley had suggested, from associations with self-interest, and if the associations we form depend on the society we live in, then this conclusion is unavoidable. Godwin could only avoid it by asserting that it is possible for reason either to confirm or reject our opinion; and, as we have seen, it is not clear how he reconciles this assertion with his associationism.

The point may be put in terms of Godwin's determinism. Men are not to be blamed for their actions, because their actions are determined by their opinions, and their opinions are themselves determined. Determined by what? Partly, it seems, by the associations they happen to have formed, and partly by reason; and there is a conflict between these two. But what determines the issue of the conflict? Temperament, upbringing, the social and intellectual climate? But, if it is any of these, then this is what determines our opinions. For to talk of truth vanquishing prejudice is merely to say that a true opinion replaces a false one, and to say that an opinion has conquered is to say that we believe it to be true. If the case is put in the way Godwin puts it, there seems no escape from the conclusion that our opinion about what is true is determined by some quite irrelevant factor, in the way that the anti-determinists want 'free will' to come in; and he is faced with exactly the same dilemma as they. . . .

It seems sensible to say that, while education, or background, or peculiarities of temperament may lead us into false beliefs, we have also a capacity for seeing facts that enables us to correct these beliefs. Nevertheless, we can hardly talk about 'truth' as one determinant of opinion among others; we must rather say that, of the determinants of opinion, some lead us to form false beliefs and others to form true beliefs. It might be thought that, if Godwin cares to dramatize this as 'the struggle between truth and prejudice', no great harm has been done. But a difficulty still remains. We seem to be assuming that there are tests for truth which are quite distinct from the determinants of opinion; whereas what determines an opinion does so by determining what tests of truth we will accept.

The difficulty faces all who have entertained theories about what is currently called 'the sociology of knowledge', or 'cultural determinism'. If all opinions are socially determined, this applies to theories about the sociology of knowledge. And this means that we cannot say of such theories: 'this is true', but only 'this is what my social background determines me to believe'. Obviously the sociologist of knowledge wants to say more than this: he wants to break out of the charmed circle altogether. One way of avoiding this difficulty is to say that our theories apply only to certain kinds of opinion: for example, value judgements or 'opinions about what is desirable'. And this involves us in saying that such judgements can never be known to be true or false, and are perhaps not capable of being true or false. . . . But Godwin is emphatically not prepared to say this; he is quite sure that some things really are desirable, and can be known to be desirable.

I think this problem is a real one, and I do not pretend to know the answer. But it looks as if we cannot consistently regard our capacity for reasoning as one determinant of opinion of the same type as our social background or the inhibitions we acquired in infancy. The point may perhaps be put by saying that Godwin does not sufficiently distinguish between causal necessity and entailment or 'logical necessity.' But this is rather glib; for, while it is true that the conclusion of a syllogism follows from the premisses in quite a different sense from that in which a knee-jerk follows from the doctor's tap, it seems reasonable to say that, just as I cannot help jerking my knee, once I have been tapped, so I cannot help assenting to the conclusion once I have grasped the premisses. That is the point that Godwin insists on; but insisting on it does seem to raise some very difficult problems.

Anarchism: The Method of Individualization

In a brief essay we cannot expect to conclude every train of thought that this anthology has set in motion. Nor can we attempt to confront every objection to anarchism presented in the last section. Instead, our purpose is to map out terrain that is central to anarchism, to chart the main features of the conceptual landscape without much close attention to empirical details or peculiarities that lie on its periphery. It may be true that some anarchists would dissociate themselves from the arguments we offer, but this possibility will put us on the track of instructive distinctions among libertarians. At any rate, the conceptual analysis that is here advanced will indicate how many familiar objections to anarchism arise, not from disagreements concerning human nature and society, but from misrepresentation or misconception of the basic contentions of anarchism.

Our anthology has shown that anarchism cannot be filed away as an outburst of the romantic mood in politics, as a rough category of deviant violent behavior, as an end product of atheism or socialism, as a nervous version of philosophical liberalism, as an incoherent voice of protest. Such stabs at definition are at best occasionally appropriate in thinking of special instances in the history of anarchism. A more tenable definition might be found by concentrating on anarchism's fundamental standard of human conduct. Negatively, anarchism is the teaching that the habit men have of governing one another, as well as those institutions that conduct government, must be effaced. And positively, the anarchists declare that all social activity must reflect the ability of individual men to initiate, or genuinely consent to, the human events that influence their desires and possibilities. These two formulations imply one another: when government, in all its guises, is no longer tolerated, what will then prevent men from achieving individual sovereignty and developing their full store of human powers? But so long as the principle of authority persists, these positive aims will be stultified.

Even this brief account shows the necessity of distinguishing anarchism from the traditional commendation of liberty as security against infringements and impositions. The anarchist does not regard such negative liberty as wholly undesirable. He insists, however, that attempts to protect it should never take precedence over the aims of rooting out authority and developing personality. Negative liberty is much like charity. It is necessary only because a crucial source of social evil has not yet been destroyed. And to extol such liberty is likely to intensify this evil. The major task is always to eliminate the habit of governing, that is, the habit of infringing and imposing.

Having thus identified the ultimate principle of anarchist thought, we must admit that several conflicts among anarchists complicate our attempt at definition. These conflicts cannot be reduced to any pat formula. George Woodcock's simple categories, for example, do not reveal them: "The differences between the various anarchist schools, though at first sight they seem considerable, actually lie in two fairly limited regions: revolutionary methods (especially the use of violence) and economic organization." Since most anarchists contend that means and ends are indivisible, any dispute over "revolutionary methods" will probably engender a more basic controversy over the ends to be sought. Accordingly, we must attempt to illuminate the issues in these deeper controversies.

We must differentiate, for example, derivative from non-derivative anarchists. Especially for religious anarchists like Tolstoy, Ballou, Hennacy, and Day, the notion that government and authority are evils which men should efface is a deduction from more fundamental truths, such as the supreme ethical ideal of non-resisting love. In contrast, Warren and Andrews regard their principle of individual sovereignty as an ultimate truth nearly indistinguishable from anarchism itself. Here are two incompatible attitudes toward the status of libertarian values, for the non-derivative anarchist would deny that there are any social or moral truths which, being superior to anarchism, must be brought to its justification. It may be asked, of course, what practical difference this disagreement makes as long as the libertarian values in question are the same. But we shall see that the non-derivative anarchist exhibits an approach to ethics which is presumably not available to those who derive anarchism as a corollary from more highly-ranked ethical precepts.

A sharper cleavage exists between those anarchists who hold that what is fundamental to anarchism can be realized immediately and those who feel that stages of preparation must precede any significant fulfillment of their principles. In *Drawing The Line*, Paul Goodman speaks clearly for the immediatists.

> The free spirit is rather millenarian than utopian. A man does not look forward to a future state of things . . . but he draws now, as far as he can, on the natural force in him that is no different from what it will be in the new society. . . . *Merely by continuing to exist and act in nature and freedom, a free man wins the victory, establishes the society.* . . .

This view underlies Hennacy's "One-Man Revolution" as well as Emma Goldman's abhorrence of the Bolshevik separation of means from ends. The opposite position was held by the editors of *Vanguard*, who chided Emma Goldman for forgetting that anti-electionism is only a tactic in the achievement of anarchy. Geoffrey Ostergaard has used the example of Indian anarchists, followers of Gandhi like Vinoba Bhave, who "see the anarchist goal in much the same way as Godwin did, as something to be reached only after men have grown more perfect than they now are." Their divergences from what Ostergaard calls the "mainstream of Western anarchism" can be seen in their willingness to support good democratic government for the time being. The dispute here may seem merely factual: Are men now ready for complete anarchy or not? But to act on the assumption that one can decide for another which goals he is qualified to seek, is *to govern*; consequently, the gradualist position lends itself to the perpetuation of authority. In any case, it forfeits anarchist alternatives in the present.

Less easily analyzed is the disagreement between those who sanction no form of coercion in their presentation of anarchist principles and those, like Paul Goodman, who draw a line between natural and unnatural authority. Goodman is only the most explicit on this point: we have seen how Josiah Warren's determination to run his household on the cost principle imposed on his daughter's unlimited freedom. If some anarchists hold that aspects of social life—such as child rearing for Warren or shop management for some syndicalists —naturally manifest authority in ways immune to the criticisms leveled against government, then the differences among anarchists have arisen over matters more important than violence as a recourse or styles of economic organization. And the hard issue of whether men can only be moved toward the positive goals of anarchism by subjecting them to one form or another of coercion must be faced.

The importance of these disputes must not be exaggerated. In all three cases, both sides share the anarchist aims of abolishing government and enabling men to realize the positive ideal well described by Kropotkin:

> If, it is contended, society were organized on these principles, man would not be limited in the free exercise of his powers in productive work by a capitalist monopoly, maintained by the state; nor would he be limited in the exercise of his will by a fear of punishment, or by obedience towards individuals or metaphysical entities, which both lead to depression of initiative and servility of mind. He would be guided in his actions by his own understanding, which necessarily would bear the impression of a free action and reaction between his own self and the ethical conception of his surroundings. Man would thus be enabled to obtain the full development of all his faculties, intellectual, artistic and moral, without being hampered by overwork for the monopolists, or by the servility and inertia of mind of the great number. He would thus be able to reach full *individualization*, which is not possible either under the present system of *individualism*, or under any system of state-socialism in the so-called *Volkstaat* (popular state).

It will be noticed that Kropotkin recasts the positive ethical ideal we have already placed at the core of anarchism: he proposes that ethics be completely individualized. This view, that true ethics is the product of an individual's unshackled analysis of his surroundings, affords the anarchist a notion of moral influence that is free of coercion. Instead of defining morality as a set of obligatory imperatives, it stresses the state of character underlying and expressed by any moral decision. In addition, ethical behavior of this sort, uncoerced and uncoercing, is the dynamic of human improvement. Kropotkin's meaning is not so dark: it is a common observation that children in friendly surroundings develop abilities for their own creative fulfillment as long as their parents do not take upon themselves the burden of filling their children's hours. Free of interference, the child begins to own himself, to become individualized, to create his own identity. Without implying total agreement between Kropotkin and such other anarchists as Stirner, it is safe to say that we are on the track of a general anarchist attitude toward ethics. This individualization of morality, in which influence replaces coercion, helps to explain the importance anarchists have attached to education: the end of teaching is not to drill in particular doctrines and standards but to develop the child's autonomy in facing any intellectual problem. The anarchists insist that each individual follow his own judgment without being enslaved to previously decided systems. With the possible exception of the derivative anarchist, they reject the governance of moral rules that determine one's conduct by imposing commitments impervious to the demands of specific situations. Such rules we follow predictably, and they indeed become wheels in the head, *idées fixes*. Each time we obey a moral maxim there must be a separate act of judgment, a separate decision to consent to what it prescribes. Otherwise, whatever is done becomes unethical, impersonal, inappropriate.

The emphasis on a method for arriving at ethical decisions, as opposed to a set of categorical obligations, is not unique to anarchism. It is also central to the pragmatist's insistence that there are no ultimate moral standards, only the transitory values that emerge out of a scientific testing of the needs and interests present in particular situations. But though pragmatism espouses a situational ethics, it often fails to take the anarchist's next step. It refuses to recognize what Godwin termed the right of private judgment, and hesitates to make judgments of value relative to the views and objectives of each particular agent as well as to specific external circumstances. This failure to individualize ethics leaves pragmatism open to two criticisms, neither of which has force against anarchism: First, that what tends to be operative in the pragmatist's conduct and recommendations are certain traditional moral ideals like equality and benevolence and *not* his allegedly scientific method of testing values. (This renders that method pragmatically meaningless.) Second, that in group situations, where interests diverge, scientific neutrality can sanction tyrannical consequences for the minority to whom the pragmatic method tenders no guarantee. For the anarchist, these are but different forms of a single objection: pragmatism that is not individualized retains a governing form of morality. Moral prescriptions and collective ethics must go the way of government.

The positive goal of anarchism, then, can be regarded as

a consistently individualized pragmatism. But is this goal achievable? Perhaps to pursue it actively involves infringing upon others and thus reinstates the habit of governing. Our account of non-coercive moral influence provides one answer to this line of criticism. Another is Emma Goldman's contention that it begs the question of human nature by assuming that what men have been like under authority indicates what they will be like under all circumstances. But for a complete reply, we must amplify the notion of anarchism as a method of individualization.

"Methodological individualism" is a phrase used by J. W. N. Watkins, Karl Popper, and other philosophers of social science to describe their view that social events must always be explained by the dispositions, beliefs, capacities, and activities of the individuals involved and not by inevitable social laws or fixed cultural patterns. To see how anarchists extend this view into what we can call "methodological individualization," consider this avowal by the German anarchist Gustave Landauer: "The state is a condition, a certain relationship between people, a way of behavior; and we destroy it when we contract different relationships and behave in a different way." Consider, too, the immediatist or millenarian anarchist's belief that man can draw at once on the resources of a remade society. Anarchists not only agree with the methodological individualists that men in consort, with the necessary information, can prevent the fulfillment of any social prediction. They go further: any man can free himself from the bonds of social causality. All behavior can be self-governing and individualized. To the objection that individualization self-deceptively ignores the statistical control of social laws, the anarchist replies that a generalization about behavior is not necessarily an explanatory law. What statistical laws there may be only further count against social institutions that presently coerce mankind. In any event, statistical laws are not unbreakable. Men as individuals can assert freedom now and influence their fellows without employing coercion any more than does the parent who forebears to arrange his child's personality. Governing is no more than a habit. It is neither ethically necessary nor socially inevitable. Like all habits, it cannot be *totally* erased. But at the same time, habits are a matter of degree: any man can continually enlarge the area in which he will not govern and will not tolerate the government of others. Tolstoy's career well illustrates methodological individualization, moving from the dismissal of "over-all" explanation in *War and Peace* to the attacks on economic laws in *The Slavery of Our Times*. In general, the rejection of social laws braces the anarchist against such criticisms as Shaw's appeal to supply-and-demand and speculations about intractable human nature.

Methodological individualization, in short, saves the anarchist from being hobbled by any necessity to put off positive action until society has completely abandoned government. He stresses instead that one man always has a chance to upset the applecart of government and that the least he can gain by the effort is his own freedom. This stress is ultimately linked to our original definition of anarchism. For social norms or laws, like political authority and coercive moral codes, are forms of government. For the anarchist, they too must be abolished to allow for the individualization of ethics.

An important extension of methodological individualization is the anarchist analysis of crime. First, it is argued that government, basing its legitimacy on fear of crime, enjoys the same moral status as a protection racket. Second, that those crimes worth taking steps to remove are almost fully eradicable through the methods of individualization. Let us trace these converging trains of analysis.

Anarchists favor the metaphor of slavery to characterize the way in which government pre-empts from the individual the competence to make, or consent to, decisions that affect him. Now early capitalism was often described as wage-slavery, on the grounds that the worker was intimidated by the threat of starvation into unjust contracts that surrendered his rights and output. Analogously, anarchists might call government protection-slavery. Horrendous predictions of criminality and chaos, plus warnings of punishments to be dealt out to offenders, are the two main ways governments ensure apparent consent. These same predictions and warnings were presented to reinforce chattel-slavery and wage-slavery. For the anarchist, they are only a bogus element of social control. In the face of such threats, the "choice" of government is coerced and unethical. This alone casts substantial doubt on the common philosophical view that there is an obligation to submit to and preserve government. A system of institutions, more easily than a single villain, can so manipulate the range of seemingly plausible options as to infect a whole society with indefensible servility. The anarchist does not rely on any model of deliberate conspiracy to make his case that the threat of crime is fabricated by government to perpetuate governmental control.

Furthermore, anarchism will not concede that the fear of crime provides any warrant for relinquishing individual sovereignty. Rather, it asserts that there is no natural criminal threat, that crime is cultural. This does not mean that man is instinctively altruistic. What is meant by calling crime cultural is that no one, save possibly the insane, commits crime for its own sake. Crime is not performed except as a means to some further end; it is not intrinsically satisfying except under the most restrictive of imaginable circumstances. Most humane men are prepared to concede that prisons create criminals. But this admission may substantiate the anarchist case against government. Prisons are the most invasive form of the principle of authority, they are the apex of government coercion. If they must be characterized as "colleges of crime," it seems to follow that the habit of governing is the cardinal source of criminal behavior. Other institutions—armies, factories, unions, parties—add to the graduating class in crime in proportion as they are saturated with the habit of governing. Thus the method of eliminating this habit assumes increased importance.

At this stage in the argument, the dogma of government as a necessary evil appears a cruel hoax. It becomes clear why anarchists have seen the crime rate as a direct function of the depravity of institutions and why they hold that criminal behavior in an anarchist society will be so slight as to require no permanent institution to control it. But how to deal with today's criminal? The only moral influence necessary for the anarchist, as we have seen, is to own himself and allow others to own themselves. Those society marks as criminals must be treated like growing children: society must stop arranging everything for them. In this way, individualized ethics can begin to strike down fear-based penal arrangements which, like all forms of government, promote the evils they pretend to check.

Here then is a sketch of a consistent anarchist theory of crime and its dependence on government. Crime, viewed as an injury to personality and not as a mere violation of statute, is normal to a pathological, or governed, society. It is motivated by repressive institutions. The same applies to war: War is a form of crime, is culturally motivated, varies with institutional depravity, and can be ended by the pervasion of the anarchist method of living. It cannot be ended by government. According to Shaw,

> there is a fine impartiality about the policeman and the soldier, who are the cutting edge of the State's power. They take their wages and obey their orders without asking questions. . . .

It seemed to follow that:

> A House of Commons consisting of 660 gentlemen and 10 workers will order the soldier to take money from the people for the landlords. A House of Commons consisting of 660 workers and 10 gentlemen will probably, unless the 660 are fools, order the soldier to take money from the landlords to buy land for the people.

This is a standard socialist inference, which methodological individualization rejects. The state is not bound by its economic matrix; its dominant aims are to secure and extend the domain over which it can command obedience. A House of Commons, therefore, will try, regardless of its makeup, to maintain the British Empire, to ensure its own re-election. It will keep from its electorate facts about its development of nuclear weapons and will restrain local groups from working out their own solutions to vital problems. Though it may conduct peace conferences, it will perpetuate the stuff of dispossession and war. This is why Paul Goodman thinks any peace movement is potentially anarchistic, why he tells today's peace movements they must face up to anarchism.

What, in conclusion, does anarchism recommend to other present-day movements? It has nothing to offer the "liberal" who extends liberty by dropping bombs to protect dictatorial regimes, to the "conservative" who conserves freedom by frustrating pleas for minority rights, to the "socialist" who protects collective ownership by Party discipline and secret police. Anarchism is a comprehensive position whose recommendations cannot be adopted piecemeal. To Benjamin R. Tucker, it was the only consistent system, developing insights from Adam Smith in a way neither Marxist nor Manchesterite dared.

Nonetheless, the anarchist can speak to some modern movements. Its message is to reduce the operating room of government by laying claim to functions the movement can better perform by its own devices. What would it mean for the civil rights movement if its endowments of money and human energy were devoted to anarchist reconstruction? Instead of begrudged and sporadic protection by the federal government of the right to equal participation in second-class educational facilities offered by the state governments, suppose the Negroes sought to develop new facilities of their own. With the finances and talent now depleted by demonstrations against the government, campaigns for its offices, appeals to its courts, a network of economically autonomous communities might be established which would have no place for government, prejudice, or oppression. Some will say that they would still need the protection of government against racist thugs. But for one thing the thugs are governors. For another, what protection there is now seems activated only by Northern guilt at the martyrdom of civil rights workers, and this source of protection will not dry up if the martyrs initiate their own programs rather than plead for admission to those of the states. Again, the price of protection may resemble that paid in the labor movement, whose unwieldiness, unresponsiveness, unimaginativeness, and corruptness are today disenchantingly familiar.

The anarchist might inspire different kinds of wars on poverty too. If shrewd and dedicated college students can rally slum dwellers to withhold their rents and force the law to keep its distance, what obstacle is there to groups of tenants collecting their own rent and making their own improvements? (And if this can be accomplished, the return of other vital community functions, like education and policing, to local control might become a live option.) Such action seems likely to lead to better results than a new law saying that government may again, if it chooses and is properly staffed, protect tenants from irate slumlords who want withheld rents but refuse to make directed improvements. A similar argument could be made for "depressed areas": unless local initiative is allowed to free itself the government will pollute their water, bulldoze their hillsides, subsidize roads and motels, and promote eyesores as resorts. On the other hand, anarchists from Kropotkin to Senex have argued that decentralized modern technology could make every man in these same areas autonomous and part of a self-sufficient locality.

These examples suggest only the tenor of anarchist alternatives. The promise of many more is held out by the method of individualization. For when men treat their fellows as resources in uncoercive circumstances, they can chip away at the habit of governing, and enable each other to draw "on the natural force . . . that is no different from what it will be in the new society."

SELECTED BIBLIOGRAPHY

Limitations of space preclude a complete list of writings on anarchism. We have therefore included only English-language publications and, further, have excluded works that have been used and cited in the body of the anthology. The list emphasizes writings in which may be found further discussion of topics raised in this book. We have tried to represent different kinds of source materials in the hope that one item may lead the reader to another. In this last connection it should also be noted that most works listed under the first heading possess bibliographies of their own.

A. GENERAL STUDIES, HISTORIES, BIOGRAPHIES

ALLEN, MARY B. "P. J. Proudhon in the Revolution of 1848." *Journal of Modern History*, XXIV:1 (March, 1952), 1–14.

BROGAN, D. W. *Proudhon*. London: Hamish Hamilton, 1934.

CARR, E. H. *Michael Bakunin*. London: Macmillan, 1937.

CARR, E. H. *The Romantic Exiles*. Hammondsworth: Penguin, 1949.

COLE, G. D. H. *Socialist Thought: Marxism and Anarchism, 1850–1890*. London: Macmillan, 1957.

DE LUBAC, HENRI. *The Un-Marxian Socialist: A Study of Proudhon*. R. E. Scantlebury, trans. New York: Sheed & Ward, 1948.

DOCTOR, A. H. *Anarchist Thought in India*. Bombay: Asia Publishing House, 1964.

DRINNON, RICHARD. *Rebel in Paradise: A Biography of Emma Goldman*. Chicago: Univ. of Chicago, 1961.

FLEISHER, D. *William Godwin: A Study in Liberalism*. London: Allen & Unwin, 1951.

HOLGATE, P. *Malatesta*. London: Freedom Press, 1956.

HOROWITZ, IRVING LOUIS, ed. *The Anarchists*. New York: Dell, 1964.

KORNBLUTH, JOYCE, ed. *Rebel Voices: An I.W.W. Anthology*. Ann Arbor: Univ. of Michigan, 1964.

LEVINE, LOUIS. *The Labor Movement in France: A Study in Revolutionary Syndicalism*. New York: Columbia University, 1912.

LORWIN, VAL. *The French Labor Movement*. Cambridge: Harvard Univ., 1954.

MADISON, CHARLES A. *Critics and Crusaders: A Century of American Protest*. New York: Ungar, 1959.

MARTIN, JAMES J. *Men Against the State*. De Kalb, Ill.: Adrien Allen Associates, 1953.

NOMAD, MAX. *Dreamers, Dynamiters and Demagogues*. New York: Waldon Press, 1964.

NOMAD, MAX. "Johann Most" (six articles). *Modern Monthly*, IX–X (1936–38).

PYZIUR, E. *The Doctrine of Anarchism of M. A. Bakunin.* Milwaukee: Marquette University, 1955.

REICHERT, WILLIAM O. "The Philosophical Anarchism of Adin Ballou." *Huntington Library Quarterly*, XXVII:4 (Aug., 1964), 357–74.

SCALAPINO, ROBERT, and GEORGE T. YU. *The Chinese Anarchist Movement.* Berkeley: Univ. of Cal., 1961.

SCHUSTER, EUNICE MINETTE. *Native American Anarchism.* Northampton, Mass.: Dept. of History, Smith Coll., 1932.

SIMMONS, ERNEST J. *Leo Tolstoy.* New York: Vintage, 1960.

SIMON, S. FANNY. "Anarchism and Anarcho-Syndicalism in South America." *Hispanic American Historical Review*, XXVI (Feb., 1946), 38–59.

SPITZER, ALAN B. "Anarchy and Culture: Fernand Pelloutier and the Dilemma of Revolutionary Syndicalism." *International Review of Social History*, III (1963), Part 3, 379–88.

STERN, MADELEINE B. "Stephen Pearl Andrews and Modern Times, Long Island." *Journal of Long Island History*, IV:4 (Summer, 1964).

WOODCOCK, GEORGE. *Anarchism.* Cleveland: Meridian, 1961.

WOODCOCK, GEORGE, and IVAN AVAKUMOVIC. *The Anarchist Prince.* London: Boardman, 1950. (Kropotkin)

VIZETELLY, ERNEST ALFRED. *The Anarchists: Their Faith and Their Record.* New York: John Lane, 1911.

YARMOLINSKY, A. *Road to Revolution: A Century of Russian Radicalism.* London: Cassell, 1957.

B. DEFINITIONS, GENERAL PRESENTATIONS

ELTZBACHER, PAUL. *Anarchism: Exponents of the Anarchist Philosophy.* New York: Libertarian Book Club, 1960.

GOLDMAN, EMMA. *Anarchism and Other Essays.* New York: Mother Earth, 1911.

GOODMAN, PAUL, ed. *Seeds of Liberation.* New York: Braziller, 1965.

GREENE, W. *Socialistic, Communistic, Mutualistic and Financial Fragments.* Boston: Lea & Shepard, 1873.

JASZI, OSCAR. "Anarchism." *Encyclopaedia of the Social Sciences.* New York: Macmillan, 1930. Vol. II, 46–53.

KROPOTKIN, PETER. *Memoirs of a Revolutionist.* Boston: Houghton-Mifflin, 1930.

LABADIE, JOSEPH A. *Anarchism: What It Is and What It Is Not.* Detroit: Liberty Club of Michigan, n.d.

LUM, DYER. *Economics of Anarchy: A Study of the Industrial Type.* New York: Twentieth Century Library, 1890.

MALATESTA, ERRICO. *Anarchy.* London: Freedom Press, 1942.

MALATO, CHARLES. "Some Anarchist Portraits." *Fortnightly Review,* LXII, N.S. (Sept. 1, 1894), 315–33.

MORRIS, WILLIAM. *Selected Works.* Asa Briggs, ed. Baltimore: Penguin, 1963.

The Works of Leo Tolstoy. London: Oxford, 1928–37. Vols. 1, 2, 11, 12, 14, 20, 21.

TUCKER, BENJAMIN R. *Individual Liberty.* New York: Vanguard Press, 1926.

C. ANARCHISM AND SOCIALISM

BERKMAN, ALEXANDER. *The "Anti-Climax": The Concluding Chapter of My Russian Diary.* Berlin: Maurer & Demmick, 1925.

BERKMAN, ALEXANDER. *The Bolshevik Myth (Diary, 1920–1922).* New York: Boni & Liveright, 1925.

BERKMAN, ALEXANDER. *The Russian Tragedy (A Review and an Outlook).* Berlin: Der Syndikalist, 1922.

BERNIERI, M. L. *Workers in Stalin's Russia.* London: Freedom Press, n.d.

BRENAN, GERALD. *The Spanish Labyrinth.* New York: Macmillan, 1943.

DURANT, WILL. *Socialism and Anarchism.* New York: Albert and Charles Boni, 1914.

ELY, RICHARD T. *French and German Socialism.* New York: Harper, 1883.

FOOTMAN, DAVID. *Civil War in Russia.* London: Faber, 1961.

GERTH, HANS H. *The First International: Minutes of the Hague Congress of 1872.* Madison: Univ. of Wisconsin, 1958.

GOLDMAN, EMMA. *My Disillusionment in Russia.* Garden City: Doubleday, Page, 1923.

JACKSON, JAMES H. *Marx, Proudhon, and European Socialism.* London: English Univ. Press, 1957.

KENAFICK, K. J. *Michael Bakunin and Karl Marx.* Melbourne: 1958.

LICHTHEIM, GEORGE. *Marxism: An Historical and Critical Study.* New York: Praeger, 1961.

OSGOOD, HERBERT LEVI. *Socialism and Anarchism.* Boston: Ginn, 1889. Columbia Ph.D. Dissertation.

STEKLOFF, G. M. *History of the First International.* London: M. Lawrence, 1928.

TANDY, F. D. *Voluntary Socialism.* Denver: The Author, 1896.

VOLINE (V. M. EICHENBAUM). *Nineteen Seventeen: The Russian Revolution Betrayed.* New York: Libertarian Book Club, 1954.

VOLINE. *The Unknown Revolution.* London: Freedom Press, 1955.

D. PHILOSOPHICAL FOUNDATIONS

BERDYAEV, N. *The Meaning of the Creative Act.* New York: Harper, 1955.

DE LIGT, BART. *The Conquest of Violence.* London: Routledge, 1937.

GOODMAN, P. *Drawing the Line.* New York: Random House, 1962.

GUYAU, J. M. *A Sketch of Morality Independent of Obligation or Sanction.* London: Watts, 1898.

KROPOTKIN, P. *Ethics: Origin and Development.* New York: Dial, 1924.

MAXIMOFF, G. P., ed. *The Political Philosophy of Bakunin.* Glencoe, Ill.: Free Press, 1953.

PROUDHON, P. J. *General Idea of the Revolution in the Nineteenth Century.* New York: Vanguard Press, 1923.

PROUDHON, P. J. *What Is Property?* trans. by B. Tucker. New York: Humboldt, 1890(?).

READ, H. *Anarchy and Order.* London: Faber, 1954.

WOODCOCK, G. *Anarchism and Morality.* London: Freedom Press, 1945.

E. ANARCHISM ON THE ATTACK

BERDYAEV, N. *The Bourgeois Mind and Other Essays.* London: Sheed & Ward, 1934.

BERKMAN, A. *Prison Memoirs of an Anarchist.* New York: Mother Earth, 1912.

BROWN, T. *What's Wrong with the Unions?* London: Syndicalist Workers' Pamphlet, n.d.

GRAVE, J. *Moribund Society and Anarchy.* San Francisco: A. Isaak, 1899.

HERBERT, AUBERON. "The Ethics of Dynamite." *Contemporary Review,* May, 1894.

RICHARDS, V. *Lessons of the Spanish Revolution.* London: Freedom Press, 1953.

F. CONSTRUCTIVE ANARCHISM

BAILIE, W. *Josiah Warren: The First American Anarchist.* Boston: Twentieth-Century Library, 1906.

The Bomb, Direct Action, and the State. London: Syndicalist Workers' Federation. Pamphlet no. 7.

BUBER, M. *Paths in Utopia.* Boston: Beacon Press, 1958.

GIDE, C. *Communist and Co-operative Colonies,* trans. by E. Row. New York: Crowell, 1930, chap. VII.

GILLESPIE, JAMES. *Free Expression in Industry.* London: Pilot Press, 1948.

GOODMAN, PAUL and PERCIVAL. *Communitas*. New York: Vintage, 1960.

GREGG, R. *The Power of Non-Violence*, 2nd ed. Nyack, N. Y.: Fellowship Pub., 1959.

KROPOTKIN, P. *Fields, Factories and Workshops*. London: Nelson, 1912.

MAXIMOFF, G. *Constructive Anarchism*. Chicago: Maximoff Memorial Pub. Comm., 1952.

MIDDLETON, J. and TAIT, D., eds. *Tribes Without Rulers*. London: Routledge & Kegan Paul, 1958.

PATAUD, E. and POUGET, E. *Syndicalism and the Cooperative Commonwealth*. Oxford: The New International Pub., 1913.

RITTER, P. *Planning for Man and Motor*. New York: Macmillan, 1964.

SAMSOM, P. *Syndicalism: The Worker's Next Step*. London: Freedom Press, 1951.

TURNER, M. *Safe Lodging*. London: Hutchinson, 1961.

WARREN, J. *True Civilization*. Boston, 1863.

WARREN, J. *Practical Applications of the Principles of "True Civilization."* Princeton, Mass., 1872.

WOODCOCK, G. *New Life to the Land*. London: Freedom Press, 1942.

WRIGHT, A. T. *Islandia*. New York: Farrar & Rinehart, 1942.

G. ANARCHY IN EDUCATION

BURN, M. *Mr. Lyward's Answer*. London: Hamish Hamilton, 1956.

COHEN, J. T. and A. C. FERM. *The Modern School of Stelton, A Sketch*. Stelton, N. J.: The Modern School, 1925.

HEWETSON, J. *Sexual Freedom for the Young*. London: Freedom Press, 1962.

LANE, HOMER. *Talks to Parents and Teachers*. New York: Hermitage Press, 1949.

MCCABE, J. *The Martyrdom of Ferrer, Being a True Account of His Life and Works*. London: Watts & Co., 1909.

NEILL, A. S. *The Free Child*. London: Jenkins, 1953.

NEILL, A. S. *Summerhill: A Radical Approach to Child Rearing*. New York: Hart, 1960.

RITTER, JEAN, and PAUL RITTER. *The Free Family*. London: V. Gollancz, 1959.

WARREN, JOSIAH. *Modern Education*. Long Island, N. Y., 1861.

WEAVER, A. *They Steal for Love*. New York: International Universities Press, 1959.

WILLS, W. DAVID. *Common Sense about Young Offenders*. Toronto: Doubleday, 1962.

WILLS, W. DAVID. *Homer Lane: A Biography*. London: Allen & Unwin, 1964.

WILLS, W. DAVID. *The Hawkspur Experiment*. London: G. Allen, 1941.

WILLS, W. DAVID. *Throw Away Thy Rod*. London: V. Gollancz, 1960.

H. HOW SOUND IS ANARCHISM?

CHAMBERLAIN, JOHN. "Blueprints for a New Society; II: The Dream of Anarchism." *New Republic*, C:1283 (Sept. 13, 1939), 155–58.

ENGELS, F. "The Bakunists at Work." *The Communist . . . Published Monthly by the Communist Party of the U.S.A.*, XVII:2 (Feb., 1938), 143–57.

MACDONALD, J. RAMSEY. *Syndicalism: A Critical Examination*. London: Constable, 1912.

MARX, K. *The Poverty of Philosophy*. New York: International Publishers, 1963.

OAKESHOTT, M. "The Anarchist." [Review of Herbert Read] *The Spectator*, May 14, 1954. (Reply by P. E. Winch, May 21, 1954.)

SCHAPIRO, J. S. "Pierre-Joseph Proudhon, Harbinger of Fascism." *American Historical Review*, L:4 (July, 1945), 714–37.

WEBB, S. *The Difficulties of Individualism* in *Fabian Socialist: Series 3, Socialism and Individualism*. London: Fifield, 1908.

WILLIAMS, DONALD D. "Is This a Phantom Freedom?" [Review of Berdyaev] *The Christian Century*. Sept. 6, 1944, 1024–25.

I. LIBERTARIAN PERIODICALS

Direct Action (New York: 1945–)

Direct Action: World Labor News. (London: Syndicalist Workers' Federation, 1960s to present)

The Indian Libertarian (Bombay: 1952–)

Liberation (New York: 1956–)

Man (San Francisco: 1933–37)

Mother Earth (New York: 1906–17). Emma Goldman, ed.

Radical Review (New Bedford, Mass.: 1877–78). Benjamin Tucker, ed.

Strike (Cleveland: 1964–)

Why? An Anarchist Bulletin (New York: c. 1942–47)

University Libertarian (Manchester: 1955–)

Views and Comments (New York: 1950s to present)

The Word (Princeton and Cambridge, Mass.: 1872–90, 1892–93)

ANCHOR BOOKS

GOVERNMENT AND POLITICAL SCIENCE

ANCHOR BOOKS

HISTORY

History (continued)

ANCHOR BOOKS

ECONOMICS